Integrating and Extending BIRT

Third Edition

Integrating and Extending BIRT

Third Edition

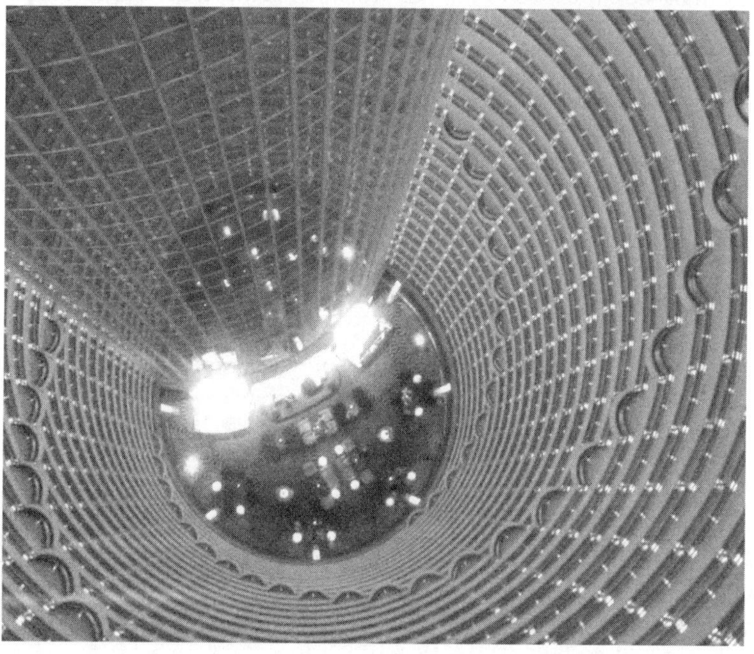

Jason Weathersby • Tom Bondur • Iana Chatalbasheva

Addison-Wesley

Upper Saddle River, NJ • Boston • Indianapolis • San Francisco
New York • Toronto • Montreal • London • Munich • Paris • Madrid
Capetown • Sydney • Tokyo • Singapore • Mexico City

The publisher offers excellent discounts on this book when ordered in quantity for bulk purchases or special sales, which may include electronic versions and/or custom covers and content particular to your business, training goals, marketing focus, and branding interests. For more information, please contact:

U.S. Corporate and Government Sales
(800) 382-3419
corpsales@pearsontechgroup.com

For sales outside the United States please contact:

International Sales
international@pearsoned.com

Visit us on the Web: informit.com/aw

Library of Congress Control Number: 2011932838

ISBN-13: 978-0-321-77282-4
ISBN-10: 0-321-77282-2

Text printed on recycled paper in the United States at Courier in Westford, Massachusetts.
First printing, August 2011

Contents

Foreword

It is a common misconception that Eclipse projects are focused on simply providing great tools for developers. Actually, the expectations are far greater. Each Eclipse project is expected to provide both frameworks and extensible, exemplary tools. As anyone who has ever tried to write software with reuse and extensibility in mind knows, that is far more difficult than simply writing a tool.

"Exemplary" is one of those handy English words with two meanings. Both are intended in its use above. Eclipse projects are expected to provide tools that are exemplary in the sense that they provide an example of the use of the underlying frameworks. Eclipse tools are also intended to be exemplary in the sense that they are good and provide immediate utility to the developers who use them.

Since its inception, the BIRT project has worked hard to create both reusable frameworks and extensible tools. This book focuses primarily on how to extend BIRT and how to use BIRT in your own applications and products. As such, it illustrates BIRT's increasing maturity and value as an embedded reporting solution.

As Executive Director of the Eclipse Foundation, I'm pleased with the tremendous progress the BIRT team has made since the project's inception in September of 2004, and I'm equally pleased with the vibrant community that has already grown up around it. As you work with BIRT and the capabilities that are described in this book, I'd encourage you to communicate your successes back to the community, and perhaps consider contributing any interesting extensions you develop. The BIRT web site can be found here:

`http://www.eclipse.org/birt`

It includes pointers to the BIRT newsgroup, where you can communicate and share your results with other BIRT developers, and pointers to the Eclipse installation of Bugzilla, where you can contribute your extensions. If you like BIRT—and I am sure this book will help you learn to love it—please participate and contribute. After all, it is the strength of its community that is the true measure of any open source project's success.

Mike Milinkovich
Executive Director, Eclipse Foundation

About this book

The second of a two-book series on business intelligence and reporting technology, *Integrating and Extending BIRT*, introduces programmers to BIRT architecture and the reporting framework. Its companion book, *BIRT: A Field Guide*, shows report developers how to create reports using the graphical tools of BIRT Report Designer. Built on the open-source Eclipse platform, BIRT is a powerful reporting system that provides an end-to-end solution, from creating and deploying reports to integrating report capabilities in enterprise applications.

BIRT technology makes it possible for a programmer to build a customized report using scripting and BIRT APIs. This book informs report developers about how to write scripts that:

- Customize the report-generation process
- Incorporate complex business logic in reports

This book also informs application developers about how to:

- Debug and deploy reports
- Integrate reporting capabilities into other applications
- Extend BIRT functionality

A programmer can extend the BIRT framework by creating a new plug-in using the Eclipse Plug-in Development Environment (PDE). This book provides extensive examples that show how to build plug-ins to extend the features of the BIRT framework. The source code for these examples is available for download at http://www.actuate.com/birt/contributions.

The topics discussed in this book include:

- Installing and deploying BIRT
- Deploying a BIRT report to an application server
- Understanding BIRT architecture

- Scripting in a BIRT report design
- Integrating BIRT functionality into applications
- Working with the BIRT extension framework

This revised BIRT 2.6 edition adds the following new content:

- Updated architectural diagrams
- Expanded scripting examples
- Debugging Event Handlers
- Developing an advanced report item with data binding
- Developing a Data Extraction Extension
- Developing a Charting Extension

Who should read this book

This book is intended for people who have a programming background. These readers can be categorized as:

- Embedders and integrators

  These individuals work with the software to integrate it into their current application infrastructure.

- Extenders

  These individuals leverage APIs and other extension points to add capability or to establish new interoperability between currently disparate components or services.

To write scripts in report design, you need knowledge of JavaScript or Java. More advanced tasks, such as extending BIRT's functionality, require Java development experience and familiarity with the Eclipse platform.

Contents of this book

This book is divided into several parts. The following sections describe the contents of each of the parts and chapters.

Part 1, Installing and Deploying BIRT

Part 1 introduces the currently available BIRT reporting packages, the prerequisites for installation, and the steps to install and update the packages. Part 1 includes the following chapters:

- *Chapter 1. Introducing BIRT Report Designers.* BIRT provides a number of separate packages as downloadable archive (.zip) files on the Eclipse web site. Some of the packages are stand-alone modules, others require an existing Eclipse environment, and still others provide additional functionality to report developers and application developers. This chapter describes the prerequisites for each of the available packages.

- *Chapter 2. Installing a BIRT Report Designer.* BIRT provides two report designers as separate packages, which are downloadable archive (.zip) files on the Eclipse web site. This chapter describes the steps required to install each of the available report designers.
- *Chapter 3. Installing Other BIRT Packages.* This chapter describes the steps required to install and update each of the available packages.
- *Chapter 4. Deploying a BIRT Report to an Application Server.* This chapter introduces the distribution of reports through an application server such as Apache Tomcat, IBM WebSphere, or BEA WebLogic. The instructions in the chapter provide detailed guidance about deploying a BIRT report to Apache Tomcat version 6.0. From those instructions, a developer can infer how to deploy to other versions.

Part 2, Understanding the BIRT Framework

Part 2 introduces the BIRT architecture and the Report Object Model (ROM) and provides background information that helps programmers design or modify reports programmatically, instead of using the graphical tools in BIRT Report Designer. Part 2 includes the following chapters:

- *Chapter 5. Understanding the BIRT Architecture.* This chapter provides an architectural overview of BIRT and its components, including the relationships among the BIRT components and BIRT's relationship to Eclipse and Eclipse frameworks. Architectural diagrams illustrate and clarify the relationships and workflow of the components. The chapter also provides brief overviews of all the major BIRT components.
- *Chapter 6. Understanding the Report Object Model.* This chapter provides an overview of the BIRT ROM. ROM is a specification for a set of XML elements that define both the visual and non-visual elements that comprise a report design. The ROM specification includes the properties and methods of those elements, and the relationships among the elements.

Part 3, Scripting in a Report Design

Part 3 describes how a report developer can customize and enhance a BIRT report by writing event handler scripts in either Java or JavaScript. Part 3 includes the following chapters:

- *Chapter 7. Using Scripting in a Report Design.* This chapter introduces the writing of a BIRT event handler script in either Java or JavaScript, including the advantages and disadvantages of using one language over the other. BIRT event handlers are associated with data sets, data sources, and report items. BIRT fires specific events at specific times in the processing of a report. This chapter identifies the events that BIRT fires and describes the event firing sequence.

- *Chapter 8. Using JavaScript to Write an Event Handler.* This chapter discusses the coding environment and coding considerations for writing a BIRT event handler in JavaScript. This chapter describes several BIRT JavaScript objects that a developer can use to get and set properties that affect the final report. The BIRT JavaScript coding environment offers a pop-up list of properties and functions available in an event handler. A JavaScript event handler can also use Java classes. This chapter includes a tutorial that describes the process of creating a JavaScript event handler.
- *Chapter 9. Using Java to Write an Event Handler.* This chapter discusses how to write a BIRT event handler in Java. BIRT provides Java adapter classes that assist the developer in the creation of Java event handlers. The report developer uses the property editor of the BIRT Report Designer to associate a Java event handler class with the appropriate report element. This chapter contains a tutorial that steps through the Java event handler development and deployment process. This chapter also describes the event handler methods and their parameters.
- *Chapter 10. Working with Chart Event Handlers.* This chapter describes the BIRT event handler model for the Chart Engine. The model is similar to the model for standard BIRT report elements and supports both the Java and JavaScript environments. This chapter provides details on both environments. The Chart Engine also supports this event model when used outside of BIRT.
- *Chapter 11. Using Scripting to Access Data.* This chapter describes how to access a data source using JavaScript code. A data source that you access using JavaScript is called a scripted data source. With a scripted data source, you can access objects other than an SQL, XML, or text file data source. A scripted data source can be an EJB, an XML stream, a Hibernate object, or any other Java object that retrieves data.
- *Chapter 12. Debugging Event Handlers.* This chapter describes how to use the BIRT report debugger to debug BIRT reports and event handlers written in JavaScript and Java. The BIRT report debugger enables users to run reports step by step, set breakpoints, inspect instance properties, and watch and evaluate variable values in certain contexts. The debugger supports advanced report developers in spotting the errors in report designs quickly, and makes it easy to understand and identify exceptions during run time. The chapter provides a tutorial with step-by-step instructions about debugging Java and JavaScript report event handlers.

Part 4, Integrating BIRT into Applications

Part 4 describes the public APIs that are available to Java developers, except the extension APIs. Part 4 includes the following chapters:

- *Chapter 13. Understanding the BIRT APIs.* This chapter introduces BIRT's public API, which are the classes and interfaces in three package hierarchies:
  - The report engine API, in the org.eclipse.birt.report.engine.api hierarchy, supports developers of custom report generators.
  - The design engine API, in the org.eclipse.birt.report.engine.api hierarchy, supports the development of custom report designs.
  - The chart engine API, in the org.eclipse.birt.chart hierarchy, is used to develop a custom chart generator.
- *Chapter 14. Programming Using the BIRT Reporting APIs.* This chapter describes the fundamental requirements of a reporting application and lists the BIRT API classes and interfaces that are used to create a reporting application. This chapter describes the tasks that are required of a reporting application and provides an overview of how to build a reporting application. The org.eclipse.birt.report.engine.api package supports the process of generating a report from a report design. The org.eclipse.birt.report.model.api package supports creating new report designs and modifying existing report designs.
- *Chapter 15. Programming Using the BIRT Charting API.* This chapter describes the requirements of a charting application, either in a stand-alone environment or as part of a reporting application. The org.eclipse.birt.chart hierarchy of packages provides the charting functionality in BIRT. By describing the fundamental tasks required of charting applications, this chapter introduces the API classes and interfaces that are used to create a chart. This chapter also describes the chart programming examples in the chart examples plug-in.

Part 5, Working with the Extension Framework

Part 5 shows Java programmers how to add new functionality to the BIRT framework. By building on the Eclipse platform, BIRT provides an extension mechanism that is familiar to developers of Eclipse plug-ins. This part also provides information about how to build the BIRT project for developers who need access to the complete BIRT open source code base. Part 5 includes the following chapters:

- *Chapter 16. Building the BIRT Project.* This chapter explains how to download BIRT 2.6 source code and build the BIRT project for development. This chapter describes how to configure an Eclipse workspace, download BIRT source code, and build the BIRT report and web viewers.
- *Chapter 17. Extending BIRT.* This chapter provides an overview of the BIRT extension framework and describes how to use the Eclipse Plug-in Development Environment (PDE) and the BIRT extension points to create, build, and deploy a BIRT extension.

- *Chapter 18. Developing a Report Item Extension.* This chapter describes how to develop a report item extension. The rotated text extension example is a plug-in that renders the text of a report item as an image. The extension rotates the image in the report design to display the text at a specified angle. This chapter describes how to build the rotated text report item plug-in and add the report item to the BIRT Report Designer using the defined extension points.
- *Chapter 19. Developing a Report Rendering Extension.* This chapter describes how to develop a report rendering extension using the Eclipse PDE with sample CSV and XML report rendering extensions as the examples. The chapter describes how to extend the emitter interfaces using the defined extension points to build and deploy a customized report rendering plug-in that runs in the BIRT Report Engine environment.
- *Chapter 20. Developing an ODA Extension.* This chapter describes how to develop several types of DTP ODA extensions. The CSV ODA driver example is a plug-in that reads data from a CSV file. The Hibernate ODA driver example uses Hibernate Query Language (HQL) to provide a SQL-transparent extension that makes the ODA extension portable to all relational databases. This chapter shows how to develop an ODA extension to the BIRT Report Designer 2.6.0 user interface that allows a report designer to select an extended ODA driver.
- *Chapter 21. Developing a Data Extraction Extension.* This chapter describes how to develop a report data extraction extension using the Eclipse PDE. The data extraction example exports report data to XML format. The Eclipse PDE provides the basis for the extension.
- *Chapter 22. Developing a Fragment.* This chapter describes how to build a fragment. The BIRT Report Engine environment supports plug-in fragments. A plug-in fragment is a separately loaded package that adds functionality to an existing plug-in, such as a specific language feature in a National Language Support (NLS) localization application. The example in this chapter creates a Java resource bundle that adds translations to the messages defined in the messages.properties files for the org.eclipse.birt.report.viewer plug-in.
- *Chapter 23. Developing a Charting Extension.* This chapter discusses the process of adding a new chart type to the BIRT chart engine. BIRT provides a radar chart type with the chart engine as an example of how to build new chart types. This chapter describes how to create this radar chart example.

The *Glossary* contains a glossary of terms that are useful to understanding all parts of the book.

Typographical conventions

Table P-1 describes the typographical conventions that are used in this book.

Table P-1 Typographical conventions

Item	Convention	Example
Code examples	Monospace font	`StringName = "M. Barajas";`
File names	Initial capital letter, except where file names are case-sensitive	SimpleReport.rptdesign
Key combination	A + sign between keys means to press both keys at the same time	Ctrl+Shift
Menu items	Capitalized, no bold	File
Submenu items	Separated from the main menu item with a small arrow	File➤New
User input	Monospace font	`2008`
User input in Java code	Monospace font italics	`chkjava.exe` *`cab_name`*`.cab`

Syntax conventions

Table 3-1 describes the symbols that are used to present syntax.

Table 3-1 Syntax conventions

<table>
<tr><th>Symbol</th><th>Description</th><th>Example</th></tr>
<tr><td>[ ]</td><td>Optional item</td><td>int count [= <value>];</td></tr>
<tr><td></td><td>Array subscript</td><td>matrix[ ]</td></tr>
<tr><td>< ></td><td>Argument that you must supply</td><td><expression to format></td></tr>
<tr><td></td><td>Delimiter in XML</td><td><xsd:sequence></td></tr>
<tr><td>{ }</td><td>Groups two or more mutually exclusive options or arguments when used with a pipe</td><td>{TEXT_ALIGN_LEFT | TEXT_ALIGN_RIGHT}</td></tr>
<tr><td></td><td>Defines array contents</td><td>{0, 1, 2, 3}</td></tr>
</table>

(continues)

Table 3-1 Syntax conventions (continued)

<table>
<tr><th>Symbol</th><th>Description</th><th>Example</th></tr>
<tr><td>{ }</td><td>Delimiter of code block</td><td>if (itemHandle == null)
{
  // create a new handle
}</td></tr>
<tr><td>|</td><td>Separates mutually exclusive options or arguments in a group</td><td>[public | protected | private] <data type> <variable name>;</td></tr>
<tr><td></td><td>Java bitwise OR operator</td><td>int newflags = flags |4</td></tr>
</table>

Acknowledgments

John Arthorne and Chris Laffra observed, "It takes a village to write a book on Eclipse." In the case of the BIRT books, it continues to take a virtual village in four countries to create these two books. Our contributors, reviewers, Addison-Wesley editorial, marketing, and production staff, printers, and proofreaders are collaborating by every electronic means currently available to produce the major revisions to these two books. In addition, we want to acknowledge the worldwide community of over one million Java programmers who have completed over ten million downloads of the multiple versions of the software. Their enthusiastic reception to the software creates an opportunity for us to write about it.

We want to thank Greg Doench, our acquisitions editor, who asked us to write a book about BIRT and has been supportive and enthusiastic about our success. Of course, we want to acknowledge the staff at Addison-Wesley who worked on the first and second editions and this third revision. In particular, we would like to acknowledge John Fuller, Michelle Housley, Anne Jones, Mary Kate Murray, Julie Nahil, Stephane Nakib, Elizabeth Ryan, Sandra Schroeder, Beth Wickenhiser, and Lara Wysong. We also want to thank Mike Milinkovich at the Eclipse Foundation and Mark Coggins at Actuate Corporation for providing the forewords for the books.

We particularly want to acknowledge the many, many managers, designers, and programmers too numerous to name who have worked diligently to produce, milestone by milestone, the significant upgrades to BIRT, giving us a reason for these two books. You know who you are and know how much we value your efforts. The following engineers have been of particular assistance to the authors: Linda Chan, Xiaoying Gu, Wenbin He, Petter Ivmark, Rima Kanguri, Nina Li, Wenfeng Li, Yu Li, Jianqiang Luo, Kai Shen, Aniruddha Shevade, Pierre Tessier, Yulin Wang, Mingxia Wu, Gary Xue, Jun Zhai, and Lin Zhu. We want to recognize the important contribution of David Michonneau in the area of charting. We wish to acknowledge Zhiqiang Qian who created a data bound report item extension used to develop the report item extension chapter. Yasuo Doshiro worked closely with the authors on "Developing a Fragment," which provides suggestions for the practical application of BIRT technology to the challenges of translation and localization. Doshiro manages BIRT translation and develops and executes test plans. In addition, we want to acknowledge the support and significant contribution that was provided by Paul Rogers. Dan Melcher's and Daniel O'Connell's insights into the techniques for building reusable components that can be applied to building internationalized reports. Working examples are to be found at

`http://reusablereporting.blogspot.com/`

Creating this book would not have been possible without the constant support of the members of the Developer Communications team at Actuate Corporation. Many of them and their families sacrificed long personal hours to take on additional tasks so that members of the team of authors could create this material. In particular, we wish to express our appreciation to Terry Ryan for his work on the glossary that accompanies each of the books. In addition, Mary Adler, Minali Balaram, Frances Buran, Bruce Gardner, Shawn Giese, Mike Hovermale, Melia Kenny, James Monaghan, Lois Olson, James Turner, Jeff Wachhorst, C. J. Walter-Hague, and Forest White all contributed to the success of the books.

Actuate's active student intern program under the Executive Sponsorship of Dan Gaudreau, Chief Financial Officer, made it possible for Maziar Jamalian and Rodd Naderzad to support the project in Developer Communications while actively engaged in pursuing undergraduate and graduate degrees in accounting, business, and information science at several different universities.

Part

I

Installing and Deploying BIRT

Chapter

1

Introducing BIRT Report Designers

There are two designer applications that you can use to create BIRT reports:

- BIRT Report Designer

  A tool that a report developer uses to build a BIRT report design and preview a report. BIRT Report Designer is a set of Eclipse plug-ins that includes BIRT Report Engine, BIRT Chart Engine, and BIRT Demo Database. This tool supports Java and JavaScript customization. BIRT Report Designer requires multiple Eclipse platform components and a Java Development Kit (JDK).

- BIRT RCP Report Designer

  A simplified tool that a novice report developer uses to build a BIRT report design and preview a report. BIRT RCP (Rich Client Platform) Report Designer includes BIRT Report Engine, BIRT Chart Engine, and BIRT Demo Database without the additional overhead of the full Eclipse platform. This tool supports JavaScript customization, but does not support Java customization or debugging.

Understanding BIRT components

BIRT Report Designer 2.6 consists of the following components:

- Eclipse Software Development Kit (SDK) 3.6

  The SDK is a framework that supports the development of plug-ins and extensions to the Eclipse platform. The SDK includes the core platform, the Java Development Tools (JDT), and the Plug-in Developer Environment (PDE).

- Data Tools Platform (DTP) 1.8.0

  The DTP is a set of development tools used to develop plug-ins that access data sources and retrieve data.

- Eclipse Modeling Framework (EMF) 2.6.0

  The EMF supports the development of BIRT charts. The EMF includes the Service Data Objects (SDO), which is a graph-structured data object that supports applying changes to a graph back to the data source.

- Graphical Editing Framework (GEF) 3.6.0

  The GEF is an Eclipse plug-in that the BIRT Report Designer user interface requires. This framework provides a rich, consistent, graphical editing environment for an application running on the Eclipse Platform.

- Eclipse Web Tools Platform (WTP) 3.2

  The WTP is a set of Eclipse plug-ins that support deploying the BIRT report viewer to an application server. The package includes source and graphical editors, tools, wizards, and APIs that support deploying, running, and testing.

Understanding Eclipse BIRT packages

Eclipse BIRT provides the following packages. These packages do not include the required Java 1.5 JDK.

- Report Designer Full Eclipse Install (All-in-One)

  Contains BIRT and the Eclipse Integrated Development Environment (IDE). This all-in-one installation is the easiest way to install BIRT.

- Report Designer

  Contains only BIRT for installing in an existing Eclipse Integrated Development Environment (IDE).

- RCP Report Designer

  Contains a simplified version of BIRT without the Eclipse IDE.

- Software Development Kit (SDK)

  Contains the source code for the BIRT plug-ins, documents, and examples.

- Report Engine

  Contains the run-time version of BIRT for installing in a J2EE application server.

- Chart Engine

  Contains the stand-alone library that supports embedding a chart in a Java application.

- BIRT Web Tools Integration

Contains the plug-ins required to use the BIRT Web Project Wizard in a Web Tools Project, including the source code.

- BIRT Source Code

  Contains the BIRT source code for a specific build. All source code is in a plug-in format ready to import into a workspace to build BIRT. These plug-ins are the required libraries for a standard BIRT installation. Additional libraries may be necessary. For example, this package does not include the Data Tools Platform (DTP) source code.

- BIRT Samples

  Contains sample reports and charts, plus application examples that use the Chart, Report Engine, and Design Engine APIs.

- BIRT Demo Database

  Contains the package for defining and loading the demonstration database into Apache Derby and MySQL, including SQL and data files. The demonstration database package is a convenient way to install the Classic Models database schema and data in the Apache Derby and MySQL systems. The package does not include any BIRT software. The Report Designer and the RCP Report Designer packages include the demonstration database for Apache Derby.

  The demonstration database supports the following Apache and MySQL versions:

  - Apache Derby version 5.1 or higher
  - MySQL Connector/J version 3.1 or MySQL client version 4.x

About types of BIRT builds

The Eclipse BIRT download site makes several types of builds available for BIRT. The following list describes these builds:

- Release build

  A production build that passes the complete test suite for all components and features. Use the release build to develop applications.

- Milestone build

  A development build that provides access to newly completed features. The build is stable, but it is not production quality. Use this type of build to preview new features and develop future reporting applications that depend on those features.

- Stable build

  A development build that is stable, but passes a reduced test suite. New features are in an intermediate stage of development. Use a stable build to preview new features.

- Nightly build

  The Eclipse BIRT development team builds BIRT every night. As BIRT is an open-source project, these builds are available to anyone. These builds are unlikely to be useful to a report developer.

  If a certain feature that you require does not work in a nightly build, you can provide feedback to the development team by filing a bug report. Later, you can download a new build to confirm that the fix solves the problem that you reported.

Chapter

2

Installing a BIRT Report Designer

Installing BIRT Report Designer adds a report design perspective to the Eclipse Integrated Development Environment (IDE). To install BIRT Report Designer, download an archive file from the Eclipse web site and extract it in your existing Eclipse environment. BIRT Report Designer is available for various Linux and Microsoft Windows platforms. The following sections describe how to install BIRT Release 2.6.

Installing BIRT Report Designer Full Eclipse Install

If you are new to Eclipse and BIRT, download and install BIRT Report Designer Full Eclipse Install (All-in-One) package to start developing and designing BIRT reports immediately. This package includes the Eclipse Integrated Development Environment (IDE), BIRT Report Designer, and all other required Eclipse components. You must also download and install Java JDK 1.5.

Complete the following procedure to download this installation package on a Windows or Linux system.

How to install BIRT Report Designer All-in-One

1 Using your browser, navigate to the main BIRT web page at:

   `http://www.eclipse.org/birt/phoenix`

2 From BIRT Project, choose Download BIRT 2.6.

3 From BIRT Report Downloads, choose All-in-One.

4 On BIRT Report Downloads, select the Download Link that meets your requirements, for example, Windows 64-bit.

   Eclipse downloads - mirror selection appears. This page shows all the sites that provide this download file.

5 Choose the download site that is closest to your location.

   The BIRT Report Designer all-in-one archive file downloads to your system.

6 Extract the archive file to a hard drive location that you specify.

   The extraction creates a directory named eclipse at the location that you specify.

To test the BIRT Report Designer installation, start Eclipse, then start BIRT Report Designer as described in the following procedure. BIRT Report Designer is a perspective within Eclipse.

How to test the BIRT Report Designer installation

1 Start Eclipse.

2 Close the welcome window. In the Eclipse Window menu, choose Open Perspective➛Report Design. If Report Design does not appear in the Open Perspective window, choose Other. A list of perspectives appears. Choose Report Design.

   Eclipse displays the BIRT Report Designer perspective.

Installing BIRT RCP Report Designer

BIRT RCP Report Designer is a stand-alone report design application that enables report developers to produce reports in both web and PDF formats. This application uses the Eclipse Rich Client Platform (RCP) to provide a report design environment that is less complex than the full Eclipse platform. If you need the project-based environment that the full Eclipse platform provides, return to the section on installing BIRT Report Designer. BIRT RCP Report Designer runs on Windows only.

To install BIRT RCP Report Designer, download and extract an archive file. The following examples use Release 2.6.

Complete the following procedure to download and install BIRT RCP Report Designer on a Windows system.

How to install BIRT RCP Report Designer

1 Using your browser, navigate to the main BIRT web page at:

   `http://www.eclipse.org/birt/phoenix`

2 From BIRT Home, choose Download 2.6.

3 From BIRT Report Downloads, choose RCP Designer.

   Eclipse downloads - mirror selection appears. This page shows all the sites that provide this download file.

4 Choose the download site that is closest to your location.

   The BIRT RCP Report Designer archive downloads to your system.

5 Extract the archive file to a hard drive location that you specify.

   The extraction creates a directory named birt-rcp-report-designer-2_6_0 at the location that you specify.

To test the installation, start BIRT RCP Report Designer as described in the following procedure.

How to test the BIRT RCP Report Designer installation

1 Navigate to the birt-rcp-report-designer-2_6_0 directory.

2 To run BIRT RCP Report Designer, double-click BIRT.exe. BIRT RCP Report Designer appears.

Troubleshooting installation problems

Installing a BIRT report designer is a straightforward task. If you extract the archive file to the appropriate location and the required supporting files are also available in the expected location, your BIRT report designer will work. One of the first steps in troubleshooting an installation problem is confirming that all files are in the correct location.

Verify that the /eclipse/plugins directory contains JAR files whose names begin with org.eclipse.birt, org.eclipse.emf, and org.eclipse.gef. The following sections describe troubleshooting steps that resolve two common installation errors.

Avoiding cache conflicts after you install a BIRT report designer

Eclipse caches information about plug-ins for faster start-up. After you install or upgrade BIRT Report Designer or BIRT RCP Report Designer, using a cached copy of certain pages can lead to errors or missing functionality. The symptoms of this problem include the following conditions:

- The Report Design perspective does not appear in Eclipse.
- You receive a message that an error occurred when you open a report or use the Report Design perspective.
- JDBC drivers that you installed do not appear in the driver manager.

The solution is to remove the cached information. The recommended practice is to start either Eclipse or BIRT RCP Report Designer from the command line with the -clean option.

To start Eclipse, use the following command:

```
eclipse.exe -clean
```

To start BIRT RCP Report Designer, use the following command:

```
BIRT.exe -clean
```

Specifying a Java Virtual Machine when starting BIRT report designer

You can specify which Java Virtual Machine (JVM) to use when you start a BIRT report designer. This specification is important, particularly for users on Linux, when path and permission problems prevent the report designer from locating an appropriate JVM to use. A quick way to overcome such problems is by specifying explicitly which JVM to use when you start the BIRT report designer.

On Windows and Linux systems, you can either start a BIRT report designer from the command line or create a command file or shell script that calls the appropriate executable file with the JVM path. The example in this section uses BIRT Report Designer on a Windows system.

How to specify which JVM to use when you start a BIRT report designer

On the command line, type a command similar to:

```
eclipse.exe -vm $JAVA_HOME/jdk1.5/bin/java.exe
```

Installing a language pack

All BIRT user interface components and messages are internationalized through the use of properties files. BIRT uses English as the default language, but supports other languages by installing a language pack that contains the required properties files. BIRT 2.6 provides one language pack, NLpack1, which supports the following languages:

- French
- German
- Spanish
- Japanese
- Korean
- Simplified Chinese

The following instructions explain how to download and install the language pack for BIRT 2.6 on Windows.

How to download and install a language pack

To download and install a language pack, perform the following steps:

1 Using your browser, navigate to the BIRT language pack web page at:

   `http://www.eclipse.org/babel/downloads.php`

2 From Babel Language Packs for Galileo, download the language pack for the product that you need.

3 Extract the language pack archive file into the directory above the Eclipse directory.

   For example, if C:/eclipse is your Eclipse directory, extract the language pack into C:/.

4 Start Eclipse and choose Window➛Preferences➛Report Design➛Preview.

5 Select the language of choice from the drop-down list in Choose your locale.

6 Restart Eclipse.

If Windows is not running under the locale you need for BIRT, start Eclipse using the -nl <locale> command line option, where <locale> is a standard Java locale code, such as es_ES for Spanish as spoken in Spain. A list of locale codes is available at the following URL:

```
http://www.oracle.com/technetwork/java/javase/locales-
   137662.html
```

Eclipse remembers the locale you specify on the command line. On subsequent launches of Eclipse, the locale is set to the most recent locale setting. To revert to a previous locale, launch Eclipse using the -nl command line option for the locale to which you want to revert.

Updating a BIRT Report Designer installation

Because BIRT Report Designer is a Java-based application, updating an installation typically requires replacing the relevant files. Eclipse supports the update process for BIRT Report Designer by providing the Update Manager. BIRT RCP Report Designer is a stand-alone product, so you must replace the existing version with a newer version.

This section describes the steps required to update the following BIRT packages:

- Report Designer
- RCP Report Designer

You can use the Eclipse Update Manager to find and install newer major releases of BIRT Report Designer.

How to update a BIRT Report Designer installation using the Update Manager

1 In Eclipse, choose Help→Check for Updates.

2 In Available Updates, choose Select All then choose Next.

3 In Update Details, choose Next.

4 In Review Licenses, accept the license agreement terms and choose Finish.

5 When the update completes, restart your computer.

How to update BIRT Report Designer manually

1 Back up the workspace directory if it is in the eclipse directory structure.

2 To remove the BIRT files, use one of the following techniques:

- To prepare for a new all-in-one installation, remove the entire eclipse directory.
- To prepare for only a BIRT Report Designer installation, remove only the BIRT components.
  1 Navigate to the eclipse\features directory.
  2 Delete all JAR files and subdirectories with birt in their names.
  3 Navigate to the eclipse\plugins directory.
  4 Delete all JAR files and subdirectories with birt in their names.

3 Download and install BIRT Report Designer as described earlier in this book.

4 Restore the workspace directory, if necessary.

5 Restart BIRT Report Designer with the -clean option:

```
eclipse.exe -clean
```

Updating BIRT RCP Report Designer installation

Unlike BIRT Report Designer, BIRT RCP Report Designer is a stand-alone application. To update this application, you delete the entire application and reinstall a newer version. If you created your report designs and resources in the birt-rcp-report-designer-<version> directory structure, you must back up your workspace directory and any resources that you want to keep before you delete BIRT RCP Report Designer. After you install a newer version of the application, you can copy your files back to the application directory structure.

As a best practice, do not keep your workspace in the birt-rcp-report-designer-<version> directory structure. Keeping your workspace in a different location enables you to update your installation more easily in the future.

How to update BIRT RCP Report Designer

1. Back up the workspace directory and any other directories that contain report designs, libraries, and other resources, if they are in the birt-rcp-report-designer-<version> directory structure.
2. Delete the birt-rcp-report-designer-<version> directory.
3. Download and install BIRT RCP Report Designer as described earlier in this book.
4. Restore the directories that you backed up in step 1, if necessary.
5. Restart BIRT RCP Report Designer with the -clean option:

   ```
   BIRT.exe -clean
   ```

Chapter

3

Installing Other BIRT Packages

Beyond the BIRT Report Designer packages, BIRT provides a number of other separate packages as downloadable archive files on the Eclipse web site. Some of these packages are stand-alone modules, others require an existing Eclipse or BIRT environment, and still others provide additional functionality to report developers and application developers. This chapter describes the steps required to install the BIRT packages shown in the following list:

- Chart Engine
- Data Tools Platform (DTP) Integration
- Demo Database
- Report Engine
- Samples
- Source Code
- Web Tools Integration

Installing Chart Engine

Chart Engine supports adding charting capabilities to a Java application. An application can use Chart Engine without using the BIRT reporting functionality or Report Engine. Chart Engine integrates into an existing Eclipse platform on Microsoft Windows, UNIX, or Linux. You can also install Chart Engine on an existing J2EE application server. To use Chart Engine, you use its public API, org.eclipse.birt.chart.

Both BIRT Report Designer and BIRT RCP Report Designer include all the components of Chart Engine. If you are using a BIRT report designer, you do not need to install BIRT Chart Engine separately.

How to install BIRT Chart Engine

On the BIRT web site, perform the following operations:

1. Navigate to BIRT Downloads for build 2.6.0.

   For more information about how to navigate to the BIRT web site and BIRT Downloads for build 2.6.0, see Chapter 2, "Installing a BIRT Report Designer."

2. In the Chart Engine section, choose the Chart Engine archive file:

   ```
   birt-charts-2_6_0.zip
   ```

3. In File Downloads, choose Open.
4. Extract the archive file to a location of your choice.
5. Start Eclipse from the command line with the -clean option to remove cached information.

The archive extraction process creates the following subdirectories in the extraction directory:

- ChartRuntime

  This directory contains the plug-ins and libraries that an Eclipse platform requires to run, render, and edit charts.

- ChartSDK

  This directory contains the plug-ins and libraries from the ChartRuntime directory plus the SDK that you need to create your own charting applications. It also includes examples, source code, and a Web Tools Platform (WTP) extension to support charts in web applications.

- DeploymentRuntime

  This directory contains the libraries that you need to run your charting application in a non-Eclipse environment such as on an application server.

The Chart Engine download file also includes extensive Frequently Asked Questions (FAQ) and examples illustrating how to use Chart Engine. After extracting the archive, you can find the FAQ at the following location:

```
<CHART_ENGINE>/DeploymentRuntime/ChartEngine/docs/Charts_FAQ.doc
```

The examples are in a JAR file located at:

```
<CHART_ENGINE>/ChartSDK/eclipse/plugins
   /org.eclipse.birt.chart.examples_<version>.jar
```

Installing BIRT Data Tools Platform Integration

This package includes the minimal set of Data Tools Platform (DTP) plug-ins that BIRT Report Designer requires. If you install the BIRT Report Designer package in an existing Eclipse installation, you can install this BIRT DTP Integration package instead of the full DTP platform.

How to install BIRT DTP Integration

On the BIRT web site, perform the following operations:

1. Navigate to BIRT Downloads for build 2.6.0.
2. In the BIRT DTP Integration section, choose the BIRT DTP Integration archive file:

   ```
   birt-dtp-integration-2_6_0.zip
   ```
3. On Eclipse downloads, choose your closest download site.
4. Extract the archive file to the directory that contains your Eclipse directory.

   Extracting creates the DTP features and plug-ins in the eclipse\features and eclipse\plugins directories.
5. Start Eclipse from the command line with the -clean option.

To test the BIRT DTP Integration package, open the Report Design perspective in Eclipse, as described in the following procedure.

How to test the BIRT DTP Integration installation

1. Start Eclipse.
2. From the Eclipse main menu, choose Open Perspective➛Report Design. If Report Design does not appear in the Open Perspective window, choose Other. From the list of perspectives, choose Report Design.

   Eclipse displays the BIRT Report Designer perspective.

Installing BIRT Demo Database

The BIRT Demo Database package provides the Classic Models database that this book uses for example procedures. The database is provided in the following formats:

- Apache Derby
- MySQL

BIRT Report Designer and BIRT RCP Report Designer include this database in Apache Derby format, as the Classic Models Inc. sample database data source. Install BIRT Demo Database if you want to use the native drivers to access this data source.

How to install BIRT Demo Database

On the BIRT web site, perform the following operations:

1. Navigate to BIRT Downloads for build 2.6.0.
2. In the Demo Database section, choose the Demo Database archive file:

   `birt-database-2_6_0.zip`
3. In File Download, choose Open.
4. Extract the archive file to a location of your choice.

   Extracting creates a directory, ClassicModels, that contains the BIRT Demo Database in Apache Derby and MySQL formats.

To test the BIRT Demo Database, first connect to the database with the native database client tool or a Java application.

How to access BIRT Demo Database using a database client tool

Perform one of the following sets of tasks, based on your preferred database:

- Apache Derby database

  Connect to the database in the derby subdirectory of ClassicModels.
- MySQL
  1. Navigate to the mysql subdirectory of ClassicModels.
  2. Create a database to use or edit create_classicmodels.sql to uncomment the lines that create and select the classicmodels database.
  3. Use the mysql command line interface to run create_classicmodels.sql.
  4. Review load_classicmodels.sql to determine if you can use the script on your platform without editing. Use the mysql command line interface to run load_classicmodels.sql.

Next, connect to the database from BIRT Report Designer or BIRT RCP Report Designer.

How to access BIRT Demo Database from a BIRT report designer

Connect to the database using BIRT Report Designer or BIRT RCP Report Designer.

1. To access the Classic Models database in Apache Derby or MySQL format, first add the driver JAR files to a BIRT report designer installation.
2. In any report design, create a data source on the database. In the same report design, create a data set on the data source.

Installing Report Engine

Report Engine supports adding reporting capabilities to a Java application. BIRT Report Engine integrates into an existing Eclipse platform on Microsoft Windows, UNIX, or Linux. You can also install report engine components on an existing J2EE application server. To support quick deployment of reporting functionality to an application server, Report Engine includes a web archive (.war) file.

How to install BIRT Report Engine

On the BIRT web site, perform the following operations:

1 Navigate to BIRT Downloads for build 2.6.0.

2 In the Report Engine section, choose the Report Engine archive file:

```
birt-runtime-2_6_0.zip
```

3 In File Download, choose Open.

4 Extract the archive file to a suitable directory.

5 Create a system variable, BIRT_HOME.
Set the value of BIRT_HOME to the BIRT Report Engine installation directory. For example, if you extracted the BIRT Report Engine to C:\, the value of BIRT_HOME is:

```
C:\birt-runtime-2_6_0
```

To test the installation, run the Report Engine report generation command line example. This example uses a batch (.bat) file on a Windows system and a shell script (.sh) file on a UNIX or Linux system. This file takes the parameters shown in Table 3-1.

Table 3-1 Parameters for the genReport script

Parameter	Valid for mode	Values
Execution mode -m		Valid values are run, render, and runrender. The default is runrender.
Target encoding -e	render, runrender	A valid encoding. The default is utf-8.
Output format -f	render, runrender	Valid values are HTML and PDF. The default value is HTML.
Report parameters file -F	run, runrender	Path to the parameter file. This file contains lines with the format: <parameter name>=<value>

(continues)

Table 3-1 Parameters for the genReport script (continued)

Parameter	Valid for mode	Values
Locale -l locale	run, runrender	A valid locale string. The default locale is en.
Output file name -o	render, runrender	The full path of the output file. The default value is the name of the report design with an extension based on the output format, .html for an HTML file and .pdf for a PDF file.
Report parameter -p "parameter name=value"	run, runrender	If you provide parameter values with the -p parameter, these values override the values in the report parameters file specified by -F.
HTML format -t	run, runrender	Valid values are HTML and ReportletNoCSS. HTML is the default. This format wraps the HTML output in an <HTML> tag. ReportletNoCSS does not wrap the HTML output in an <HTML> tag.
Report design file	All modes	The full path of the report design file. This parameter must be the last parameter on the command line.

How to test the BIRT Report Engine installation

1. From the command line, navigate to the directory where you installed BIRT Report Engine.
2. Navigate to the ReportEngine subdirectory.
3. To run the genReport script, run the appropriate file for your operating system:
   - On a Windows platform, run genReport.bat.
   - On a UNIX or Linux platform, run genReport.sh.

   Enclose the value for a command line parameter in quotes. For example, the following Windows platform command uses the value, Hello, for the parameter, sample, to generate an HTML file from the report design, test.rptdesign:

   ```
   genReport -p "sample=Hello"
      "C:\birt-runtime-2_6_0\WebViewerExample\test.rptdesign"
   ```

   genReport generates the required output file.
4. Open the output file. In this example, the file is C:\birt-runtime-2_6_0 \WebViewerExample\test.html.

For more information about setting up the BIRT Report Engine, see Chapter 4, "Deploying a BIRT Report to an Application Server."

Installing BIRT Samples

BIRT Samples provides examples of a BIRT report item extension and of charting applications. The report item extension integrates into BIRT Report Designer and BIRT Report Engine.

How to install BIRT Samples

On the BIRT web site, perform the following operations:

1. Navigate to BIRT Downloads for build 2.6.0.
2. In the Samples section, choose the Samples archive file:

   `birt-samples-plugins-2_6_0.zip`
3. In File Download, choose Open.
4. Extract the archive file to the directory that contains your Eclipse directory.

Installing BIRT Source Code

This package includes the source code for all BIRT plug-ins. You can examine this code to see how BIRT generates reports from designs. You can also import this source code into a workspace to build a custom BIRT installation.

How to install BIRT Source Code

1. Navigate to BIRT Downloads for build 2.6.0.
2. In the BIRT Source Code section, choose the BIRT Source Code archive file:

   `birt-source-2_6_0.zip`
3. In File Download, choose Open.
4. Extract the archive file to a new workspace directory.

   Extracting creates the build files and BIRT features and plugins directories in that workspace directory.

To test the BIRT Source Code package, import the source code projects into your workspace.

How to test the BIRT Source Code installation

1. Start Eclipse.
2. Set the Java preferences for BIRT.

1 From the Eclipse window menu, choose Window➛Preferences.

2 Expand Java, select Compiler. Make the following selections:

- Set Compiler Compliance Level to 1.6.
- Deselect Use default compliance settings.
- Set Generated .class files compatibility to 1.6.
- Set Source compatibility to 1.6.

3 Choose OK.

3 From the Eclipse window menu, choose File➛Import.

4 In Import—Select, expand General and select Existing Projects into Workspace. Choose Next.

5 In Import—Import Projects, select Select root directory, then type or browse to your workspace directory.

The BIRT features and plug-ins appear in Projects.

6 Choose Finish.

Eclipse builds the BIRT projects.

If the projects do not build correctly, check that you installed the prerequisites for BIRT Report Designer, as described in Chapter 1, "Introducing BIRT Report Designers." If you have not installed the BIRT Report Designer Full Eclipse Install, download this package and extract any JAR files that the build requires. Add any libraries that Eclipse does not find to the build paths of specific projects to resolve other build errors.

Installing BIRT Web Tools Integration

This package includes the minimal set of BIRT plug-ins that the Eclipse Web Tools Platform (WTP) requires to build a BIRT web project using the BIRT Web Project Wizard. This package also includes the source code for these plug-ins.

How to install BIRT Web Tools Integration

On the BIRT web site, perform the following operations:

1 Navigate to BIRT Downloads for build 2.6.0.

2 In the BIRT Web Tools Integration section, choose the BIRT Web Tools Integration archive file:

```
birt-wtp-integration-sdk-2_6_0.zip
```

3 In File Download, choose Open.

4 Extract the archive file to the directory that contains your Eclipse directory.

Extracting creates the BIRT features and plug-ins in the eclipse\features and eclipse\plugins directories.

To test the BIRT Web Tools Integration package, create a BIRT web project in Eclipse.

How to test the BIRT Web Tools Integration installation

1 Start Eclipse.

2 From the Eclipse window menu, choose File➛New➛Project.

3 In New Project—Select a wizard, expand Web, select Dynamic Web Project. Choose Next.

4 In New Project—Dynamic Web Project, make the choices that you need for your BIRT web project, then choose Finish.

 If you do not have the Java EE perspective open, Eclipse displays the following message:

 > This kind of project is associated with the Java EE perspective. Do you want to open this perspective now?

 Choose Yes.

Chapter

4

Deploying a BIRT Report to an Application Server

One way to view a BIRT report on the web is to deploy the BIRT report viewer to an application server, such as Apache Tomcat, IBM WebSphere, JBoss, or BEA WebLogic. The BIRT Report Engine includes the BIRT report viewer as a web archive (.war) file and as a set of files and folders. Deploying the BIRT report viewer requires copying files from the BIRT Report Engine, which you must install separately from the BIRT Report Designer. This chapter provides information about deploying the BIRT report viewer using the WAR file or the set of files and folders.

About application servers

The instructions in this chapter specifically address deploying a BIRT report to Apache Tomcat version 6.0. Although the information in this chapter is specific to this version of Tomcat, a BIRT report can also be deployed to other versions of Tomcat and to other application servers.

About deploying to Tomcat

There are only minor differences between the requirements for deploying to Tomcat version 6.0 and deploying to other versions of Apache Tomcat. Apache Tomcat 6.0 runs Java 5 by default, which is also one of the recommended versions to use for BIRT 2.6. If you use an earlier version of Java, you need to install a compatibility package and configure Apache Tomcat to use the Java 1.4 run-time environment. For information about configuring Apache Tomcat to use Java 1.4 run-time, see the Apache Tomcat help pages.

About deploying to other application servers

Most application servers require a WAR file that contains everything that the application requires, including a web.xml file describing the application and various deployment preferences. The BIRT Report Engine includes a WAR file appropriate to Tomcat. Typically, the WAR file does not require modification. In some cases, developers who have experience with other application servers can modify the web.xml file to reflect the requirements of their environments. The section on mapping the report viewer folders, later in this chapter, discusses setting the web.xml parameters.

Deployment to JBoss may require copying axis.jar and axis-ant.jar from WEB-INF/lib to the following directory:

```
jboss/server/default/lib
```

This step is not necessary for all versions of JBoss, but if there are difficulties with a JBoss deployment, copying these files can resolve the problem.

Placing the BIRT report viewer on an application server

You must place the BIRT report viewer in a location where Apache Tomcat can access it. Typically, this location is the $TOMCAT_INSTALL/webapps directory. On restarting Apache Tomcat, the application server automatically recognizes and starts the BIRT report viewer application if the BIRT report viewer is in this folder.

Installing the BIRT report viewer as a web application

The BIRT report viewer files provide core functionality to run, render, and view BIRT reports. To use additional JDBC drivers that are not part of the standard BIRT packages, you must install these drivers as well as the BIRT report viewer itself. If you install the BIRT report viewer as a WAR file, you must include the JDBC drivers in the WAR file.

The following instructions assume that you have installed the BIRT Report Engine from the BIRT web site, that your web application directory is $TOMCAT_INSTALL/webapps, and that your BIRT run-time installation directory is $BIRT_RUNTIME.

How to install the BIRT report viewer from the BIRT Report Engine WAR file

The steps to install the BIRT report viewer from the WAR file differ depending upon whether you need to include additional JDBC drivers for your reports. If there are no additional drivers, install the WAR file from the BIRT Report Engine installation. If you use additional JDBC drivers, you must pack them into the WAR file before you deploy it.

- To install the BIRT report viewer from the BIRT Report Engine WAR file, copy the BIRT Report Engine WAR file, birt.war to the Tomcat applications folder, $TOMCAT_INSTALL/webapps, as illustrated by the following DOS command:

  ```
  copy $BIRT_RUNTIME/birt.war $TOMCAT_INSTALL/webapps
  ```

  Then, restart Apache Tomcat.

- To install the BIRT report viewer with additional JDBC drivers, perform the following steps:

  1 Create a temporary directory and navigate to that directory.

  2 Unpack the BIRT Report Engine WAR file into the temporary directory, using a command similar to the following one:

  ```
  jar -xf $BIRT_RUNTIME/birt.war
  ```

  The BIRT Report Engine application unpacks into the temporary directory.

  3 Copy the JAR files for your JDBC drivers to the following folder in the temporary directory:

  ```
  WEB-INF/platform/plugins/
     org.eclipse.birt.report.data.oda.jdbc_<version>/drivers
  ```

  4 Repack the BIRT Report Engine WAR file from the temporary directory into a new birt.war file, using a command similar to the following one:

  ```
  jar -cf birt.war *
  ```

  This command creates birt.war in the temporary directory.

  5 Copy the new birt.war file to the Tomcat applications folder, $TOMCAT_INSTALL/webapps, as illustrated in the following DOS command:

  ```
  copy birt.war $TOMCAT_INSTALL/webapps
  ```

  6 Restart Apache Tomcat.

How to install the BIRT report viewer from the BIRT Report Engine viewer folder

To install the BIRT report viewer as an application in a file system folder, use the WebViewerExample folder in the BIRT Report Engine installation.

1 Navigate to $TOMCAT_INSTALL/webapps.

2 Create a subdirectory named birt.

3 Copy the web viewer example directory and all its subdirectories to this new folder, as illustrated by the following DOS command:

```
xcopy /E "$BIRT_RUNTIME/WebViewerExample"
   $TOMCAT_INSTALL/webapps/birt
```

4 If the BIRT reports need additional JDBC drivers, add the JAR files for the JDBC drivers to the following directory:

```
$TOMCAT_INSTALL/birt/WEB-INF/platform/plugins/
   org.eclipse.birt.report.data.oda.jdbc_<version>/drivers
```

5 Restart Apache Tomcat.

Testing the BIRT report viewer installation

To test the installation of the BIRT report viewer described in earlier sections, type the following URL in a web browser address field:

```
<server_name>:<port>
```

<server_name> is the name of the application server and <port> is the port that the application server uses.

Tomcat opens the JavaServer Page (JSP), index.jsp. This file exists in both the WAR file and in the BIRT report viewer root directory. A link on this page runs the simple BIRT report design file, test.rptdesign. If the BIRT report viewer is installed correctly, Tomcat uses index.jsp to process the report design and generate and render the report that it describes. The first time you run the report, Tomcat compiles the JSP files that comprise the viewer, so there is a delay before the report appears in the web browser.

Changing the BIRT report viewer context root

By default, the context root of the URL for a web application is the path to the application directory or the WAR file. The default WAR file for the BIRT report viewer is birt.war, so the default URL to access a BIRT report from Apache Tomcat is similar to the following one:

```
http://localhost:8080/birt/run?__report=myReport.rptdesign
```

To change the BIRT context root, change the name of the /birt directory or the WAR file in $TOMCAT_INSTALL/webapps. Next, restart Apache Tomcat. In the URL to access your BIRT report, specify the name that you chose. For example, if you chose reports, the URL to access a BIRT report becomes:

```
http://localhost:8080/reports/run?__report=myReport.rptdesign
```

The URL examples in this section use a relative path to access the report design. The BIRT_VIEWER_WORKING_FOLDER parameter sets the path to access a report design as a relative path.

Changing the BIRT report viewer location

To place the BIRT report viewer in a location other than $TOMCAT_INSTALL/webapps, add a context mapping entry to the server.xml file in $TOMCAT_INSTALL/conf.

To add a context mapping entry, add the following line to server.xml just above the </host> tag near the end of the file:

```
<Context path="/birt_context" docBase="BIRT_Path"/>
```

where *birt_context* is the context root for the BIRT report viewer application and *BIRT_Path* is the absolute path to the directory containing the BIRT report viewer.

Save the changes to server.xml and restart Apache Tomcat to make the changes active.

Understanding the BIRT report viewer context parameters

To determine the locations for report designs, images in reports, and log files, the BIRT report viewer uses context parameters defined in the web.xml file. The path provided as the value for any of these parameters can be relative or absolute. A relative path is relative to the root folder of the BIRT report viewer application. A path to a writable location for a BIRT report viewer that is deployed as a WAR file must be an absolute path.

By default, the relative path for report designs is relative to the BIRT report viewer's root folder. Place all report designs in this folder or use the full path to the report design in the URL. Using a relative path is not convenient for deployment of the BIRT report viewer in a WAR file as changes to report designs would require repackaging the WAR file. To set a different location for report designs, change the BIRT_VIEWER_WORKING_FOLDER parameter in the BIRT report viewer application's web.xml file.

Other context parameters determine other aspects of the behavior of the BIRT report viewer, such as the default locale and the level of detail in the viewer's log files.

How to set the location for report designs

1. Navigate to $TOMCAT_INSTALL/webapps.
2. Open web.xml in a code editor by performing one of the following steps, based on your deployment configuration:
   - If you use a WAR file to deploy the BIRT report viewer, extract WEB-INF/web.xml from birt.war into a temporary location.
   - If you use a folder to deploy the BIRT report viewer, navigate to <context root>/WEB-INF.
3. Locate the following element:

   ```
   <context-param>
      <param-name>BIRT_VIEWER_WORKING_FOLDER</param-name>
      <param-value></param-value>
   </context-param>
   ```

4. Change the param-value element, so that it includes the absolute path to the folder for the report designs, similar to the following code where *Report_Folder* is the absolute path to the folder for the report designs:

```
<context-param>
   <param-name>BIRT_VIEWER_WORKING_FOLDER</param-name>
   <param-value>Report_Folder</param-value>
</context-param>
```

5 Save web.xml and close the editor.

6 If you use a WAR file to deploy the BIRT report viewer, replace WEB-INF/web.xml in birt.war with the file just modified.

7 Copy the report designs into the folder specified in the param-value element for BIRT_VIEWER_WORKING_FOLDER.

8 Restart Apache Tomcat.

Verifying that Apache Tomcat is running BIRT report viewer

If there are problems accessing the BIRT report viewer, use the Tomcat manager to verify that the BIRT report viewer is running on Apache Tomcat. Running the Tomcat manager requires a manager's account. If a Tomcat manager account does not exist, create one by adding the following line to $TOMCAT_INSTALL/conf/tomcat-users.xml:

```
<user name="admin" password="tomcat" roles="manager" />
```

Having a manager's account available, first open the Tomcat main page, which for a typical Apache Tomcat installation is http://localhost:8080, as shown in Figure 4-1.

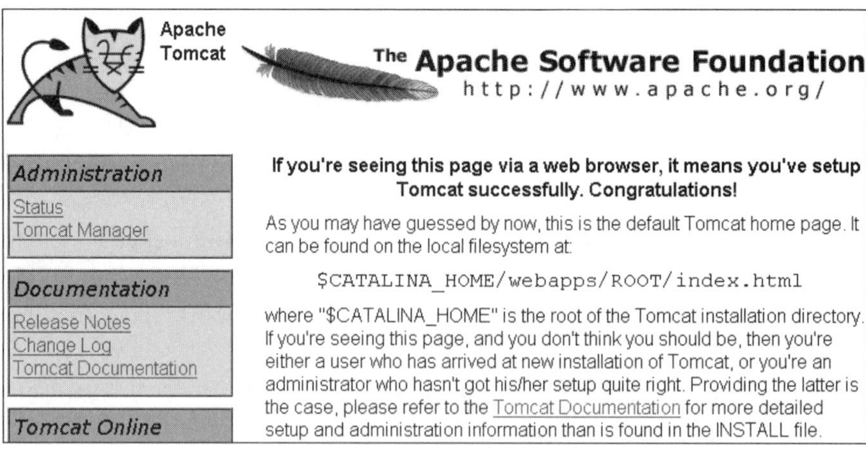

Figure 4-1 Apache Tomcat home page

On the Tomcat main page, in the Administration panel, choose Tomcat Manager. In the manager login window, type the user name and password of the manager account defined in the tomcat-users.xml file. When the BIRT report viewer application is running, the Running status for Eclipse BIRT Report Viewer is true, as shown in Figure 4-2.

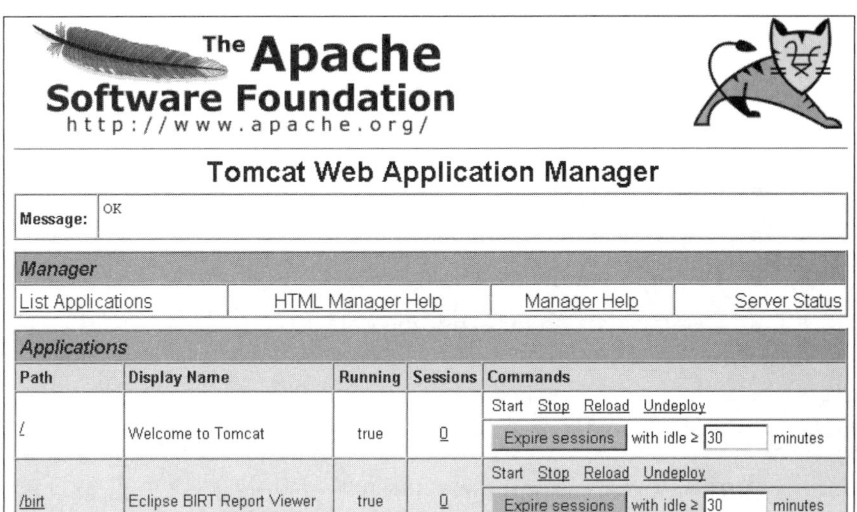

Figure 4-2 Running status for the BIRT report viewer

Placing fonts on the application server

BIRT Report Engine requires certain TrueType fonts to display a PDF report. BIRT searches for fonts in the common font directories for Windows and Linux. The directories that BIRT searches on a Windows system include:

- /windows/fonts for drives A through G
- /WINNT/fonts for drives A through G

and on a Linux system include:

- /usr/share/fonts/default/TrueType
- /usr/share/fonts/truetype

If PDF reports appear to be missing content, place the necessary fonts in any of the directories in the preceding list. Alternatively, specify your own font search path in the environment variable BIRT_FONT_PATH.

Viewing a report using a browser

After deploying the BIRT report viewer to your J2EE container, you can use the two available BIRT report viewer servlets to access your BIRT reports using a web browser. To view a BIRT report using a browser, use a URL of one of the following formats, where *parameter_list* is a list of URL parameters:

```
http://localhost:8080/birt/run?parameter_list
http://localhost:8080/birt/frameset?parameter_list
```

The run and frameset servlets display reports in two different ways. The run servlet displays the report as a stand-alone web page or a PDF file. If the report requires parameters, specify them in the URL. The frameset servlet displays a page in the browser with a toolbar containing four buttons to do the following tasks:

- Print the report.
- Display a table of contents.
- Display a parameters dialog.
- Display a dialog for exporting data.

Using connection pooling on Tomcat

BIRT provides support for connection pooling. For a Tomcat application server with a connection pool configured, BIRT reports can be set up to use a connection from the connection pool when connecting to a JDBC database. A BIRT JDBC data source uses the JNDI URL property to access the connection pool service on the web application server to get a connection from the pool.

Setting up a report to use connection pooling

Use BIRT Report Designer to configure reports to use connection pooling. The BIRT JDBC data source wizard requires configuring a direct-access connection as well as the JNDI URL. The reason for this requirement is that some JNDI service providers do not support client-side access. During design time, such JDBC drivers use the direct-access JDBC connection. The JDBC data-set query builder uses the direct JDBC connection to obtain its metadata.

In BIRT Report Designer, only the design functions directly related to a data-source design, such as Test Connection and Preview Results of a data set, attempt to use a JNDI name path. If the JNDI connection fails for any reason, the data source reverts to using the JDBC driver direct-access URL.

Similarly, at report run time, such as during report preview, the JDBC run-time driver attempts to look up its JNDI data source name service to get a pooled JDBC connection. If such look-up is not successful for any reason, the JDBC driver uses the direct-access URL to create a JDBC connection.

Using a jndi.properties file

Each individual JNDI application on the web application server uses its own environment settings stored in the JVM system properties.

The JNDI reads the following standard JNDI properties from the system properties:

```
java.naming.factory.initial
java.naming.factory.object
java.naming.factory.state
java.naming.factory.control
java.naming.factory.url.pkgs
java.naming.provider.url
java.naming.dns.url
```

To simplify the task of setting up the JNDI initial context environment for an individual JNDI application, the JNDI feature supports the use of a jndi.properties resource file. Install this file in the drivers subfolder of the oda.jdbc plugin located at the following path:

```
WEB-INF\platform\plugins\
   org.eclipse.birt.report.data.oda.jdbc_<version>\drivers
```

This file contains a list of key-value pairs in the properties file format, key=value. The key is the name of the property, and the value is a string, for example, java.naming.factory.object=jnp://localhost:1099.

Here is an example of a JNDI resource file used with JBoss application server:

```
java.naming.factory.initial=
   org.jnp.interfaces.NamingContextFactory
java.naming.provider.url=jnp://localhost:1099
java.naming.factory.url.pkgs=org.jboss.naming:org.jnp.interfaces
```

The JDBC run-time driver looks for the jndi.properties file in the web application's folder tree. If the driver does not find the file or has a problem reading from it, the initial context uses the default behavior, as defined by javax.naming.Context, to locate any JNDI resource files. Configuring the classpath for classes referenced by the environment properties is necessary.

Configuring a JNDI connection object on Tomcat

The JNDI URL property for the JDBC data source supports retrieving a JDBC connection from a pool when BIRT reports are deployed to a web application server. More information about configuring connection pooling on Tomcat is available at:

```
http://tomcat.apache.org/tomcat-6.0-doc/jndi-resources-howto.html
```

How to configure a JNDI connection object on Tomcat

The following example assumes you already have deployed the BIRT report viewer to a Tomcat 6.0 application server in the folder, $TOMCAT_INSTALL /webapps/birt, as described earlier in this chapter.

1 Install the JDBC Driver. Make an appropriate JDBC driver available to both Tomcat internal classes and the web application, for example, by

installing the driver's JAR files into the following library directory in the Tomcat application server home folder:

```
$CATALINA_HOME/common/lib
```

2 Declare the resource requirements in the BIRT report viewer's WEB-INF/web.xml file. For example, add the following entry to set up a JNDI service for a MySQL format database with the name, MySqlDB:

```
<resource-ref>
   <description>Resource reference to a factory for
      java.sql.Connection</description>
   <res-ref-name>jdbc/MySqlDB</res-ref-name>
   <res-type>javax.sql.DataSource</res-type>
   <res-auth>Container</res-auth>
</resource-ref>
```

3 Configure Tomcat's resource factory as a Resource element in the BIRT report viewer's META-INF/context.xml file, similar to the following lines:

```
<Context>
   <Resource name="jdbc/MySqlDB" auth="Container"
      type="javax.sql.DataSource" maxActive="5" maxIdle="-1"
      maxWait="10000" username="root" password=""
      driverClassName="com.mysql.jdbc.Driver"
      url="jdbc:mysql://localhost:3306/classicmodels"
      description="MySQL DB"/>
</Context>
```

4 Make the JNDI URL in your report design match Tomcat's resource factory, similar to the following line:

```
java:comp/env/jdbc/MySqlDB
```

5 Open the report design using BIRT Report Designer. Edit the data source. In Edit Data Source, in JNDI URL, type the URL, as shown in Figure 4-3.

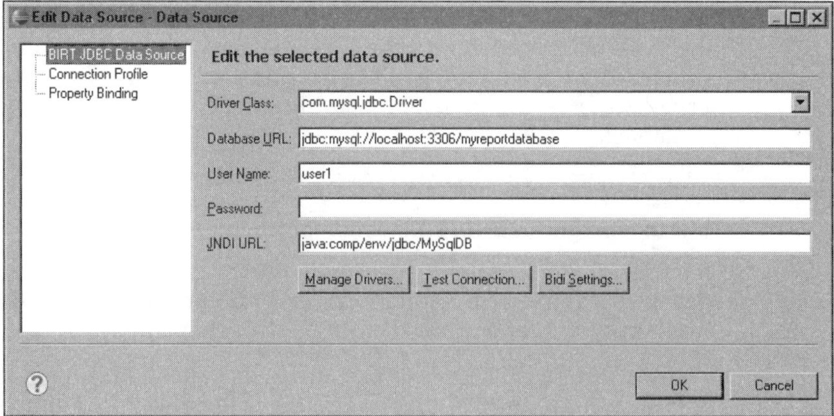

Figure 4-3 Setting the JNDI URL for a JDBC data source

6 Copy the report design to the BIRT report viewer root folder.

7 Restart the Tomcat service.

8 Run the report using a URL similar to the following one:

```
http://localhost:8080/birt/run?__report=myJNDIReport.rptdesign
```

The report uses a connection from the connection pool to connect to the database on a MySQL server.

Part

Understanding the BIRT Framework

Chapter

5

Understanding the BIRT Architecture

BIRT consists of many related components. This chapter provides an overview of the BIRT architecture, the BIRT components, the Eclipse components upon which BIRT relies, and the relationships that tie them all together.

Understanding the BIRT integration

As an Eclipse project, BIRT is tightly integrated with Eclipse frameworks and platforms. Like all Eclipse projects, BIRT is implemented as a set of Eclipse plug-ins. The BIRT plug-ins provide the functionality for all BIRT components, including BIRT applications, the engines that drive the applications, and supporting application programming interfaces (APIs). The BIRT plug-ins also provide the interface mechanism for communicating with several Eclipse frameworks and platforms.

The relationships between BIRT and the Eclipse components are most easily viewed as a stack. Each tier in the stack depends upon, uses, and integrates with the tier below it, as shown in Figure 5-1.

Figure 5-2 presents the various BIRT components and how they relate to one another. In this diagram, a component in a solid box is a standard BIRT component. A component in a dashed box is a custom component that a Java developer can provide. Some custom components are extensions of BIRT and others are applications that use the BIRT APIs. A component in a dotted box is a standard BIRT component that the containing component uses. For example, because BIRT Report Designer uses the design engine, the design engine appears in a dotted box within the box for BIRT Report Designer.

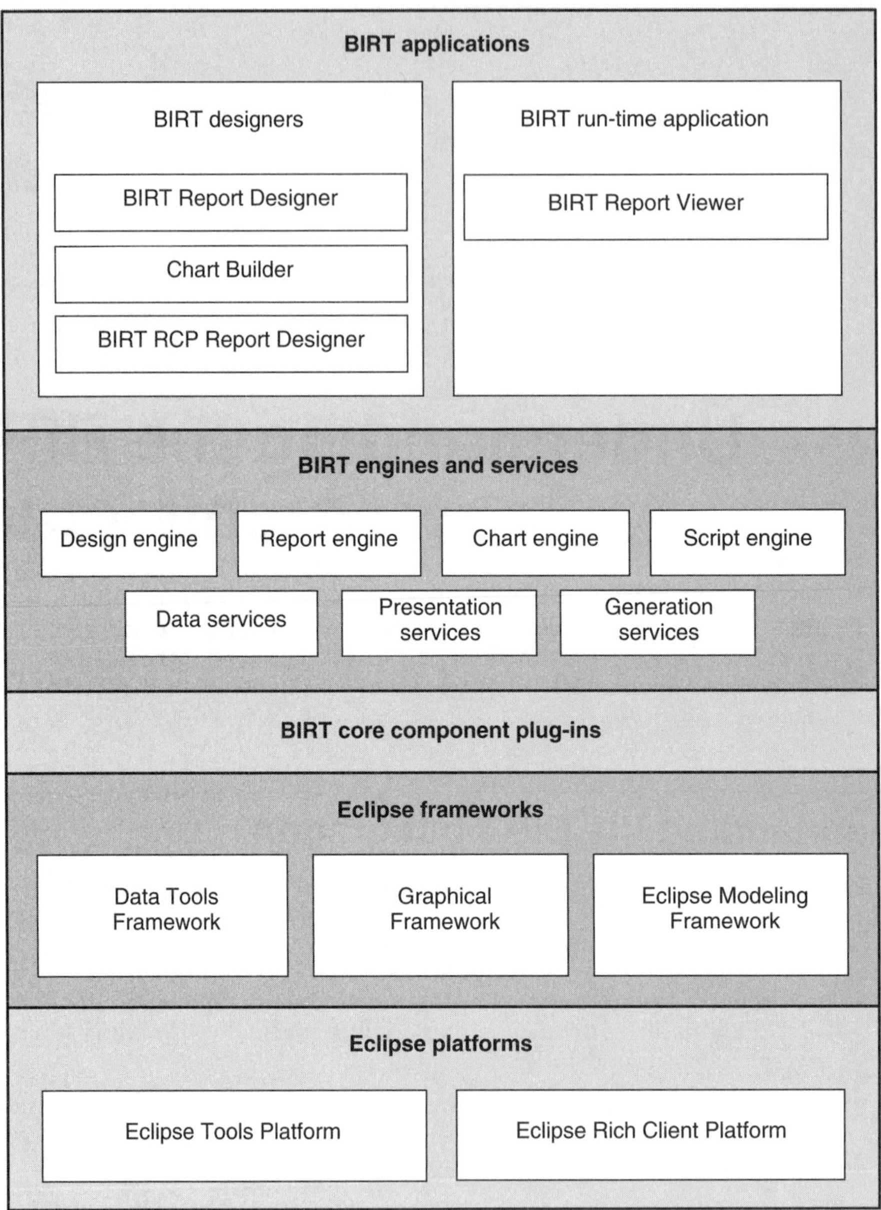

Figure 5-1 BIRT components as plug-ins to the Eclipse platform

Figure 5-3 shows the relationships among BIRT components as they generate a formatted report from a design.

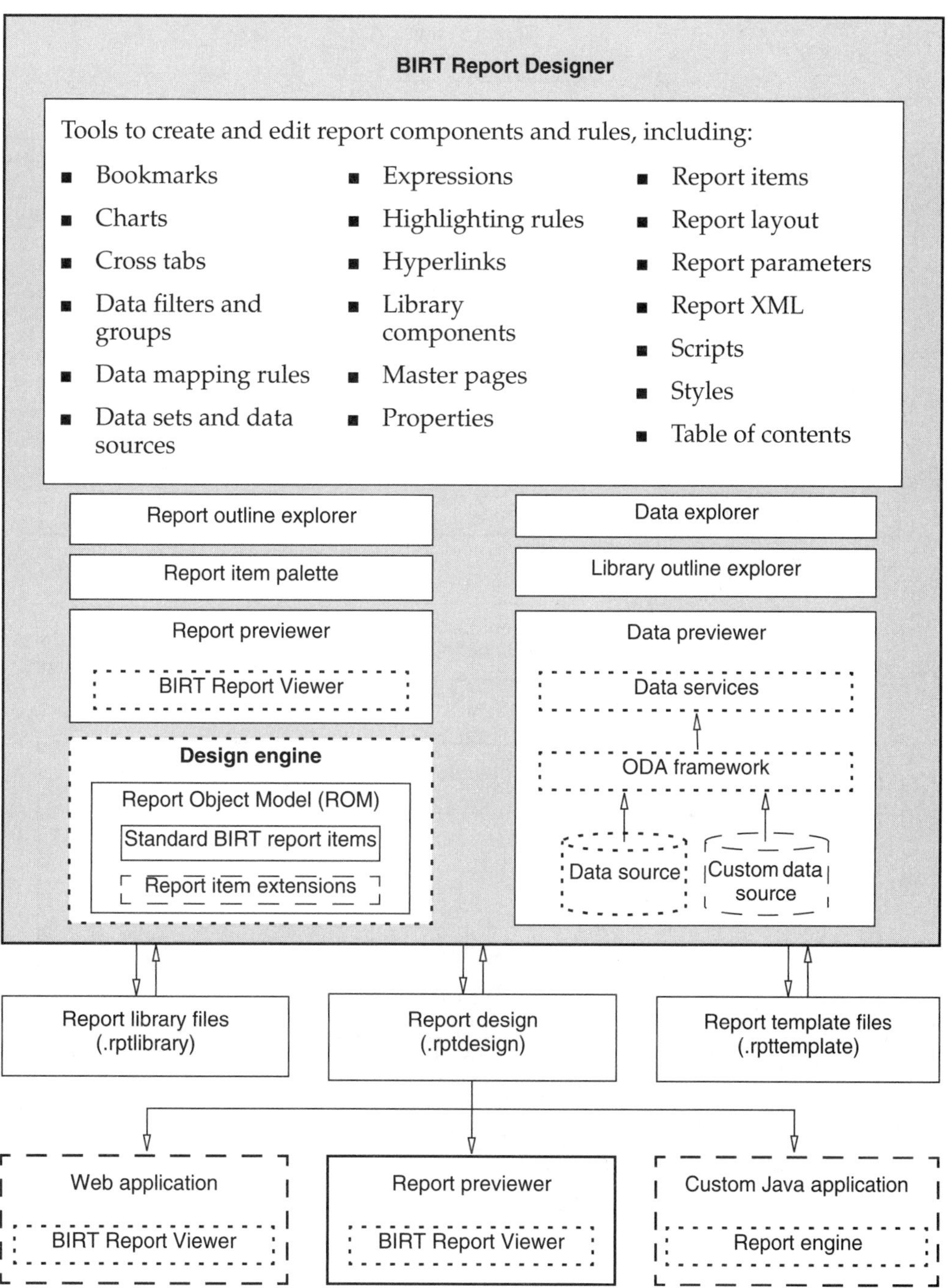

Figure 5-2 Task flow among standard BIRT components and custom components

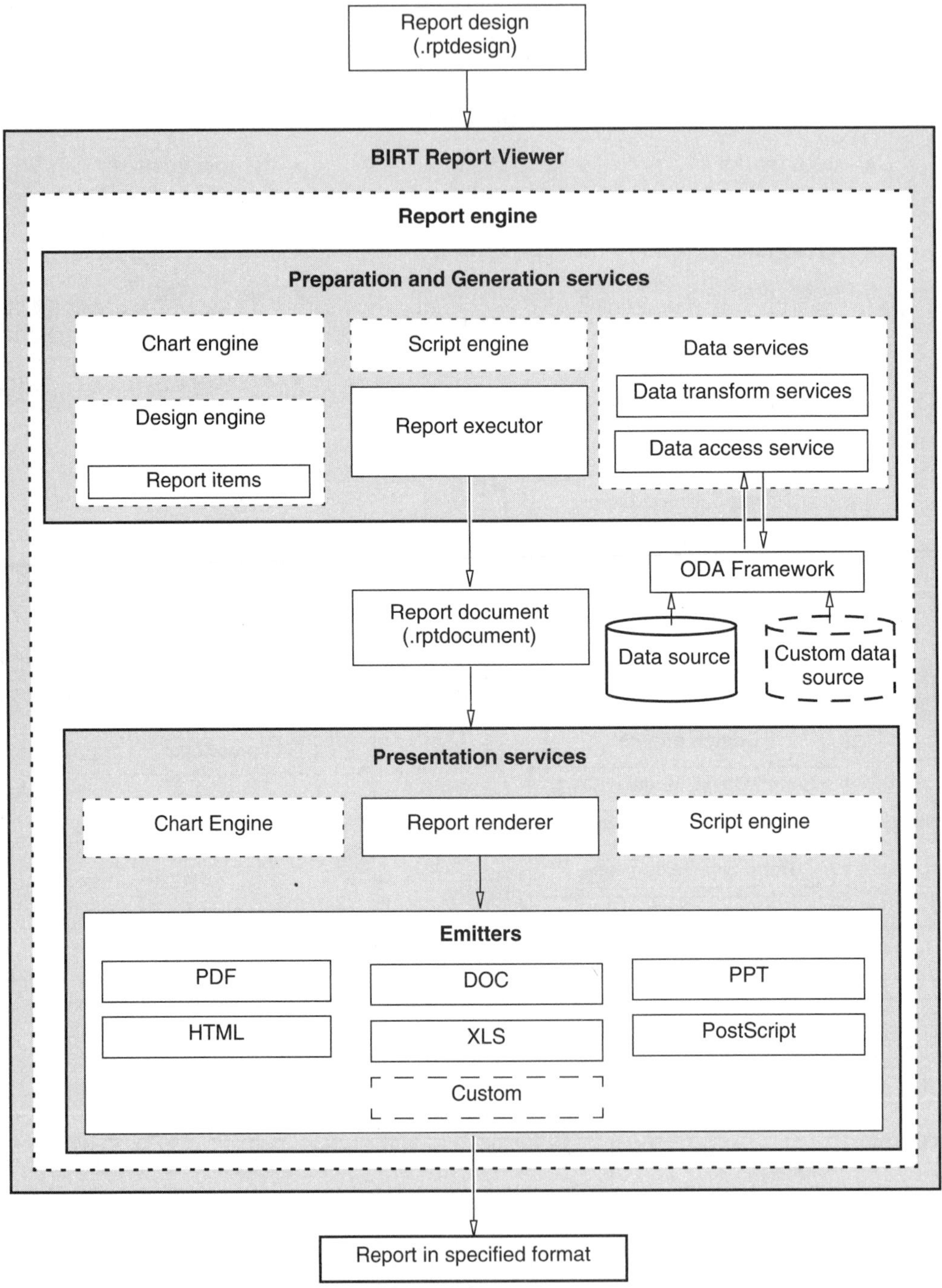

Figure 5-3 Task flow among BIRT and custom components to generate a report

BIRT Report Designer provides drag-and-drop capabilities to design reports quickly. The report designer uses the design engine to produce XML report design files. The BIRT Report Engine consumes these report design files, then, at run-time, fetches the appropriate data using queries defined at design-time. A BIRT report for immediate viewing is generated in memory and emitted in the desired output format, which can be a Microsoft Excel, non-paginated HTML, paginated HTML, PDF, PostScript, Microsoft PowerPoint, or Word file. To create a persistent report, the report engine transforms and summarizes the data and caches the generated report in an intermediate binary file, the report document file. This caching mechanism enables BIRT to scale to handle large quantities of data. BIRT also provides a tightly integrated charting component, which supports including a variety of chart types in reports. The charts are rendered at runtime using the charting engine. This charting engine also supports creating chart output separate from a report. Figure 5-4 illustrates this architecture and process flow.

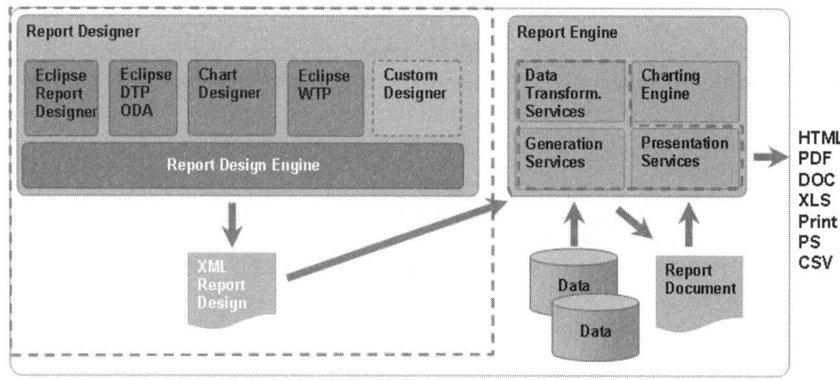

Figure 5-4 BIRT architecture and process flow

About the BIRT applications

There are three BIRT applications: BIRT Report Designer, BIRT RCP Report Designer, and BIRT Report Viewer. The two report designers are very similar. BIRT Report Designer runs as a set of Eclipse plug-ins and lets you build reports within the Eclipse workbench. BIRT RCP Report Designer has a simplified report design interface based on Eclipse Rich Client Platform.

About BIRT Report Designer and BIRT RCP Report Designer

BIRT Report Designer is a graphical report design tool. BIRT Report Designer uses the design engine to generate a report design file based on the report object model (ROM). ROM supports the standard set of BIRT report items and custom report items. BIRT Report Designer also supports the reuse of a report design by saving it as a template. You can also save individual report components in a component library, making those components accessible to other report designs.

The primary functional differences between the BIRT RCP Report Designer and BIRT Report Designer are:

- BIRT RCP Report Designer has no integrated debugger.
- BIRT RCP Report Designer does not support Java event handlers.

Other than these differences, the functionality of the two report designers is identical and all further mentions of BIRT Report Designer in this chapter apply equally to BIRT RCP Report Designer.

About the BIRT Viewer

BIRT provides the BIRT Viewer web application that includes all the necessary files to deploy to most J2EE application servers. This web application supports running reports and viewing paginated HTML, with a table of contents and bookmarks, and extracting data to a values file. URLs provide this level of integration. The host application forwards the reporting request to the BIRT Viewer and allows the user to interact directly with the report.

The BIRT Viewer is also available as an Eclipse plug-in. This plug-in is used within the report designer to preview and display a report while it is being developed. Within BIRT Report Designer, it is deployed to and works with the Eclipse Tomcat application server plug-in. As report requests are made, the Eclipse workbench starts the Tomcat application and launches the BIRT Viewer.

About the BIRT engines and services

An engine is a set of Java APIs that provide basic functionality in a specific domain. BIRT contains several engines, for example, the report engine, design engine, and chart engine. These engines provide several different types of services. A service is a set of Java classes that provide functionality using the API provided from different engines. For example, the generation services use the design engine API and report engine API to generate reports and produce report documents respectively.

About the design engine

The design engine contains the APIs used to validate and generate a report design file. BIRT Report Designer and any custom Java application that generates a BIRT report design use the design engine. The generation services also use the design engine when building the report document. The design engine contains APIs that validate the elements and structure of the design file against the ROM specification.

About the report engine

The BIRT report engine enables XML report designs created by the BIRT Report Designer to be used by a J2EE/Java application. To support this functionality, the report engine provides two core services, generation and presentation.

The report engine provides extensions to support custom report items and custom output formats. The report engine also supports Java application developers who want to integrate powerful report generation and viewing capabilities into their applications without having to build the infrastructure from lower-level Java components.

The BIRT report engine API supports integrating the run-time part of BIRT into Java applications. The report engine provides the ability to specify parameters for a report, run a report to produce HTML, PDF, DOC, PS, or PPT output and fetch an image or chart.

About the generation services

The generation service within the report engine connects to the data sources specified in a report design, uses the data engine to retrieve and process the data, creates the report layout, and generates the report document. Report content can be either viewed immediately using the presentation services, or saved for later use. The saved report documents containing snapshot views of data can be retained for use and comparison over time.

About the presentation services

The presentation services process the report document created by the generation services and render the report to the requested format and the layout specified in the design. The presentation services use the data engine to retrieve and process data from the report document. The presentation services use whichever report emitter they require to generate a report in the requested format. BIRT has several standard emitters, HTML PDF, DOC, PPT, PS, and XLS. BIRT also supports custom emitters that modify these default formats or deliver new formats.

Extensions to the presentation engine and services provide display capability for chart report items and custom report items.

About the chart engine

The chart engine contains APIs to generate charts and associate them with data from a data source. The BIRT Report Viewer interprets any chart information in a report design and uses the chart engine to generate the chart specified by the design. Use of the chart engine is not restricted to a BIRT application. Any Java application can use chart engine APIs to create and display a chart.

About the data engine and services

The data engine contains the APIs and provides services to retrieve and transform data. The data services retrieve data from its source and process the data as specified by the report design. When used by the generation engine, the data services retrieve data from the data source specified in the design. When used by the presentation engine, the data services retrieve data from the report document. The data engine extension of ODA provides the connection method and the drivers for data sources.

About data services

The data engine provides two key service types: data access services and data transformation services. The data access services communicate with the ODA framework to retrieve data. The data transformation services perform such operations as sorting, grouping, aggregating, and filtering the data returned by the data access services.

About the ODA framework

BIRT uses the ODA framework provided by the Eclipse Data Tools Platform project to manage ODA and native drivers, load drivers, open connections, and manage data requests. The ODA framework contains extension points that support adding a custom ODA driver. Write a custom ODA driver if you have a data source that BIRT does not support and a scripted data source is not desired. Use of a custom ODA driver may require extending not only the data engine but also BIRT Report Designer. A BIRT Report Designer extension is necessary if the data source requires a user interface component to specify the data set and data source properties.

About the types of BIRT report items

A report item is a visual component of a report, such as a label, a list, or a chart. There are three categories of report items in BIRT: standard report items, custom report items, and the chart report item.

About standard report items

A report item is a visual component of a report. A report item can be as simple as a label or as complex as a cross tab. Every report item has an icon on the Palette view in BIRT Report Designer.

About custom report items

Custom report items are either new report items or extensions of existing report items. An example of an extension to a report item is adding a property, such as color. An example of a new report item is the rotated text report item, which is a reference implementation of a report item extension.

Creating a new report item and extending an existing report item both involve extending BIRT through the Eclipse plug-in mechanism. Custom items require an extension to one or more of the following components to support the new item:

- BIRT Report Designer

  Extending BIRT Report Designer provides user interface components for a report developer to specify properties and other settings for the report item.

- The design engine

  Extending the design engine validates the report item settings provided by a report developer.

- The report engine

  Extending the report engine supports generating and presenting report output for the report item.

About the chart report item

A chart report item is a standard BIRT component implemented as a BIRT extension. The user interface for creating a chart report item is a chart builder that steps the report developer through the process of designing the chart and associating it with the appropriate data columns.

About the Report Object Model (ROM)

ROM is the model upon which BIRT is based. ROM is a specification for the structure, syntax, and semantics of the report design. The formal expression of ROM is through an XML schema and a semantic definition file. The ROM specification appears in the following plug-in JAR file:

```
$INSTALL_DIR\eclipse\plugins\
   org.eclipse.birt.report.model_<version>.jar
```

About the types of BIRT files

BIRT Report Designer uses four types of files:

- Report design files

- Report document files
- Report library files
- Report template files

The following sections provide a brief overview of each of these file types.

About report design files

A report design file is an XML file that contains the report design, the complete description of a BIRT report. The report design describes every aspect of a report, including its structure, format, data sources, data sets, JavaScript event handler code, and the names of Java event handlers. BIRT Report Designer creates the report design file and BIRT report engine processes it.

The file extension of a report design file is rptdesign.

About report document files

A report document file is a binary file that encapsulates the report design, incorporates the data, and contains additional information, such as data rows, pagination information, and table of contents information.

The file extension of a report document file is rptdocument.

About report library files

A report library file is an XML file that contains reusable and shareable BIRT report components. A report developer uses Resource Explorer in BIRT Report Designer to provide shared access to a library, update a library, and use report elements from a library.

A BIRT report library can contain any report element, such as:

- Data sets and data sources
- Embedded images
- Event handler code
- Styles
- Visual report items

The file extension of a report library file is rptlibrary.

About report template files

A report template is an XML file that contains a reusable design. A report developer can use a template as a basis for developing a new report. A report developer uses a report template to maintain a consistent style across a set of report designs and for streamlining the report design process. A report template can specify many different elements of a report, including:

- One or more data sources
- One or more data sets
- Part or all of the layout of a report design, including grids, tables, lists, and other report items
- Grouping, filtering, and data binding definitions
- Styles
- Library components
- Master pages
- Cheat sheets

Report templates act as a starting point for report development. They speed up report development by capturing the layout of common types of reports. They also make it easy to create reports with a consistent look. Building BIRT templates is similar to building BIRT reports. The difference lies in converting report items into template report items which act as placeholders.

The file extension of a report template file is rpttemplate.

About custom Java applications

Java developers can use the BIRT APIs to create a custom report designer or a custom report generator.

About a custom report designer

A custom report designer is a Java application that a Java developer creates to generate a well-formed report design file based on specific requirements. A custom report designer does not necessarily include a user interface. A typical example of a custom report designer is a Java application that dynamically determines the content, structure, or data source for a report, based on business logic. A custom report designer uses the same design engine API as BIRT Report Designer.

About a custom Java report generator

A custom Java report generator performs the same function as the BIRT report generator and is typically integrated into either a web application or a stand-alone Java application. A custom Java report generator uses the report engine API to read a report design file and generate a report. A custom Java report generator can use business logic to implement security requirements, control content, and determine the output format.

About extensions to BIRT

Through its public APIs and the BIRT extension framework, BIRT enables a Java developer to expand the capabilities of BIRT. BIRT uses Eclipse extensions to enable extending the functionally of the framework. The extension points provided by BIRT support the creation of new graph types, additional data sources, report controls, and emitters for rendering to additional outputs. These extension points appeal to users who have specialized data access and formatting needs. The following list shows some of the possible custom extensions:

- A custom report item

  A custom report item is a report item extension. This report item can be an extension, an existing BIRT report item, or a new report item.

- A custom ODA data source driver

  A custom ODA data source driver is a custom ODA extension that connects to a data source type other than those that BIRT directly supports.

- A custom report emitter

  A custom report emitter generates a report in a format other than HTML or PDF.

Later chapters in this book provide fully worked examples of all these types of extensions.

Chapter

6

Understanding the Report Object Model

This chapter provides an overview of the BIRT Report Object Model (ROM) and the primary elements that comprise the model. ROM defines the rules for constructing a valid report design file in much the same way that HTML defines the rules for constructing a valid web page. ROM, therefore, is the model for the BIRT report design, template, or library file in the same way that HTML is the model for the web page. For information about every component of ROM, see the online help entry Report Object Model (ROM) Definitions Reference in BIRT Programmer Reference.

About the ROM specification

The ROM specification defines a set of XML elements that describe the visual and non-visual components of a report. The XML file that BIRT Report Designer generates to describe a report design, library, or template consists entirely of ROM elements. Visual components, known as report items, include data items, labels, and tables. ROM also provides the framework for extended report items such as charts and cross tabs. Non-visual components, for example, data cubes, data sets, data sources, report parameters, and styles, support report items, but do not appear in a report. The ROM specification defines elements, their properties, and an element's relationship to other elements. The ROM specification describes elements by their methods, properties, slots, and styles. ROM elements describe:

- The data source and query with which to populate a report
- The placement, size, style, and structure of report items
- The report page layout

The report design, template, or library file contains XML elements that describe the ROM elements in the file. The BIRT design engine interprets the ROM elements using the ROM specification and the ROM schema. The ROM specification describes the content of each report element type. The ROM schema describes the supported structure of the XML in a file. Each BIRT file type appears in the ROM schema. Examining the XML in a BIRT file and the ROM schema shows that a template's structure is identical to a report design.

BIRT Report Designer displays the elements that the design engine interprets. Visual report items appear in the layout window. Data-related items such as cubes, data sets, and report parameters appear in the data explorer. All elements in the report design appear in the Outline view.

ROM methods

A ROM element can have one or more methods, called event handlers. BIRT fires many different events during the course of executing a report. When BIRT fires an event, the appropriate event handler executes to handle the event. By default, event handlers are empty methods that do nothing. By supplying code for an event handler, a report developer customizes and extends the functionality of BIRT. Supplying code for an event handler is called scripting. An event handler can be scripted in either JavaScript or Java.

Report items can have four events: onPrepare, onCreate, onPageBreak, and onRender. Each event fires in a specific phase of report creation. onPrepare fires in the preparation phase. onCreate fires during the generation phase. onRender and onPageBreak fire during the presentation phase.

ROM properties

ROM element properties are typed. Property types are similar to variable types in programming or data types in database terminology. Like variables and data types, ROM property types can be simple or complex. Design.xsd defines these types. Simple types include color, dimension, number, and string. Complex types include lists and structures. A complex type contains more than one component. For example, a text type contains both the text and a resource key used to internationalize the text.

ROM slots

A ROM slot is a container for elements of defined types. For example, a report element has a Body slot that contains any number of any type of report item. The Styles slot in the report element contains only Style items, which are the styles available to the report.

ROM styles

The ROM style system is based on cascading style sheets (CSS), where a style set in a container cascades to its contents. The Report element contains all other elements, so the style property of the Report element defines the default style for the entire report. An element within the report can override the default style. A report developer can either choose a style from a defined set of styles or create a new style. Typical style attributes include alignment, background image, color, and text size.

About the ROM schema

The ROM schema, written in the XML Schema language, encapsulates the ROM specification. XML Schema provides a standard way of defining the structure, content, and semantics of an XML file. XML Schema is similar to Document Type Definition (DTD). The ROM schema, therefore, contains the formal expression of the content, structure, and semantics of the ROM report design. The ROM schema, design.xsd, is located at:

```
http://www.eclipse.org/birt/2005/design
```

Design.xsd is also in the plug-in, org.eclipse.birt.report.model.

A statement similar to the following one appears at the top of every report design, library, or template file:

```
<report xmlns="http://www.eclipse.org/birt/2005/design"
   version="3.2.21" id="1">
```

BIRT uses this statement, which identifies the version of the schema, to interpret the file structure. A file is not valid if it contains elements that are not defined in the schema or that violate the rules in the schema.

Opening a file using a schema-aware tool such as XMLSpy supports verifying the file against the schema. Using a schema-aware tool also enables a developer of a custom report designer to verify the output of the custom report designer.

The ROM schema defines syntax that supports extensions to BIRT without making changes to the actual schema. For example, an extended item uses the following tag:

```
<extended-item name="extension">
```

The ROM schema defines properties using the following syntax:

```
<property name="propertyName">value</property>
```

The ROM schema does not define any actual properties. ROM element properties are defined in another file, rom.def.

About the rom.def file

The rom.def file contains metadata defining the specific ROM elements, their properties, their slots, and their methods. You can find rom.def in:

```
$INSTALL_DIR\eclipse\plugins
   \org.eclipse.birt.report.model_<version>.jar
```

The rom.def file is an internal file that the design engine uses to present a property sheet for a ROM element. The property sheet for an element contains the element's properties and their types, the element's methods, and valid choice selections for each of the element's properties. When the BIRT development team changes the structure of a ROM element, the changed item includes an attribute that shows the BIRT version in which that change occurred, for example:

```
<Structure displayNameID="Structure.FormatValue"
   name="FormatValue" since="2.6">
```

The rom.def file specifies the following kinds of metadata:

- Choice

  A choice definition specifies all the allowable values that an attribute can have. Most choice definitions relate to style attributes. The following example from rom.def defines all the allowable font families available to a fontFamily style specification:

  ```
  <ChoiceType name="fontFamily">
     <Choice displayNameID="Choices.fontFamily.serif"
        name="serif" />
     <Choice displayNameID="Choices.fontFamily.sans-serif"
        name="sans-serif" />
     <Choice displayNameID="Choices.fontFamily.cursive"
        name="cursive" />
     <Choice displayNameID="Choices.fontFamily.fantasy"
        name="fantasy" />
     <Choice displayNameID="Choices.fontFamily.monospace"
        name="monospace" />
  </ChoiceType>
  ```

- Class

  A class definition defines a Java class that a report designer application can access using the BIRT model API. Class definitions describe the following component types:

  - Data types, such as Array, Number, and String
  - Functional classes, such as Global, Math, and RegExp

  A class definition defines attributes, constructors, localization, members, and methods identifiers. The following example from rom.def shows part of the definition of the Number class:

  ```
  <Class displayNameID="Class.Number" name="Number"
     native="true" toolTipID="Class.Number.toolTip">
     <Constructor displayNameID="Class.Number.Number"
        name="Number" returnType="Number"
        toolTipID="Class.Number.Number.toolTip">
  ```

```
    <Argument name="value" tagID="Class.Number.Number.value"
    type="Object"/>
  </Constructor>
  <Member dataType="number"
    displayNameID="Class.Number.MAX_VALUE" isStatic="true"
    name="MAX_VALUE"
    toolTipID="Class.Number.MAX_VALUE.toolTip"/>
  <Member dataType="number"
    displayNameID="Class.Number.MIN_VALUE" isStatic="true"
    name="MIN_VALUE"
    toolTipID="Class.Number.MIN_VALUE.toolTip"/>
  ...
  <Method displayNameID="Class.Number.toExponential"
    name="toExponential" returnType="String"
    toolTipID="Class.Number.toExponential.toolTip" >
    <Argument name="digits"
      tagID="Class.Number.toExpoential.digits" type="number"
    />
  </Method>
  <Method displayNameID="Class.Number.toFixed" name="toFixed"
    returnType="String"
    toolTipID="Class.Number.toFixed.toolTip">
    <Argument name="digits"
      tagID="Class.Number.toFixed.digits" type="number"/>
    </Method>
  ...
</Class>
```

- Element

  The rom.def file contains an element definition for every ROM element. Every element definition includes attributes, such as the element's name, display name, and the element type that it extends. ROM supports methods, properties, property visibility, slot, and style properties in an element definition. The following example from the rom.def file illustrates an element definition:

  ```
  <Element allowsUserProperties="true" canExtend="true"
    displayNameID="Element.Parameter" extends="ReportElement"
    hasStyle="false" isAbstract="true" isNameRequired="true"
    name="Parameter" nameSpace="parameter" since="1.0">
    <Property displayNameID="Element.Parameter.helpText"
      name="helpText" runtimeSettable="false" since="1.0"
      type="string"/>
    <Property displayNameID="Element.Parameter.helpTextID"
      name="helpTextID" type="resourceKey"/>
    <Property displayNameID="Element.Parameter.promptText"
      name="promptText" runtimeSettable="false" since="2.0"
      type="string"/>
    <Property displayNameID="Element.Parameter.promptTextID"
      name="promptTextID" since="2.1" type="resourceKey"/>
  ```

```
    <Property displayNameID="Element.Parameter.hidden"
        name="hidden" runtimeSettable="false" since="1.0"
        type="boolean">
        <Default>false</Default>
    </Property>
    <Method context="factory"
        displayNameID="Element.Parameter.validate"
        name="validate" returnType="boolean" since="2.5"
        toolTipID="Element.Parameter.validate.toolTip">
        <Argument name="reportContext"
            tagID="Element.Parameter.validate.reportContext"
            type="org.eclipse.birt.report.engine.api.script
            .IReportContext"/>
    </Method>
</Element>
```

The property visibility property specifies whether BIRT exposes an inherited property to the user interface. For example, the label element extends ReportItem, which has dataSet and dataBindingRef properties. Because a label does not bind data, a property inherited by a label element must not appear visible to a user. The following example shows the use of property visibility to hide these properties:

```
<Element canExtend="true" displayNameID="Element.Label"
    extends="ReportItem" isAbstract="false"
    javaClass="org.eclipse.birt.report.model.elements.Label"
    name="Label" selector="label" since="1.0" xmlName="label">
    ...
    <PropertyVisibility name="dataSet" visibility="hide"/>
    <PropertyVisibility name="dataBindingRef" visibility="hide"
    />
    ...
</Element>
```

A Slot property defines the element as a container and specifies the types of items that the slot contains. Slots appear in the user interface in BIRT views such as Outline. The following example illustrates a slot definition:

```
<Element allowsUserProperties="true" canExtend="true"
    displayNameID="Element.CascadingParameterGroup"
    extends="ParameterGroup" hasStyle="false" isAbstract="false"
    isNameRequired="true" javaClass="org.eclipse.birt.report
    .model.elements.CascadingParameterGroup"
    name="CascadingParameterGroup" since="2.0"
    xmlName="cascading-parameter-group">
    ...
    <Slot displayNameID="Element.CascadingParameterGroup.slot
    .parameters" multipleCardinality="true" name="parameters"
    since="2.0" xmlName="parameters">
        <Type name="ScalarParameter"/>
        <Trigger validator="CascadingParameterTypeValidator"/>
    </Slot>
</Element>
```

A style property defines the style components supported by the ROM element. The following example illustrates style property definitions for the data element. The label element definition does not have these style properties because it contains only string values, not numbers.

```
<Element allowsUserProperties="true" canExtend="true"
   displayNameID="Element.Data" extends="ReportItem"
   hasStyle="true" isAbstract="false" isNameRequired="false"
   javaClass="org.eclipse.birt.report.model.elements.DataItem"
   name="Data" selector="data" since="1.0" xmlName="data">
   ...
   <StyleProperty name="numberFormat"/>
   <StyleProperty name="numberAlign"/>
   ...
</Element>
```

- Structure

  A structure is a complex data type that typically consists of two or more members. A few structures that are candidates for future expansion have only a single member. The following example from the rom.def file illustrates the definition of a structure.

```
<Structure displayNameID="Structure.TimeInterval"
   name="TimeInterval" since="2.5.2">
   <Member displayNameID="Structure.TimeInterval.measure"
      isIntrinsic="true" name="measure" since="2.5.2"
      type="integer"/>
   <Member detailType="interval"
      displayNameID="Structure.TimeInterval.unit"
      isIntrinsic="true" name="unit" since="2.5.2"
      type="choice">
      <Allowed>hour,minute,second</Allowed>
   </Member>
</Structure>
```

- Style

  A style definition contains the least information of any type of metadata described in rom.def. A style definition defines the name of the style, its display name, and a reference value, as shown in the following example.

```
<Style displayNameID="Style.Report" name="report"
   reference="Overall default" />
```

- Validator

  A validator definition specifies a Java class with which to do validation. Two of the validator classes are for validating values. The rest are semantic validators. The following example from rom.def illustrates a semantic validator definition.

```
<SemanticValidator
   class="org.eclipse.birt.report.model.api.validators
   .CascadingParameterTypeValidator" modules="design, library"
   name="CascadingParameterTypeValidator" />
```

Understanding ROM elements

ROM elements are defined in a set of hierarchies. Abstract elements, which cannot be used directly in a BIRT file, are at the top of each hierarchy. These elements define key characteristics of concrete elements in the same way that abstract classes in Java define methods and variables that a concrete class implements. Report designs are made of concrete elements that derive from the abstract elements.

About the primary ROM elements

The primary ROM elements consist of abstract elements from which other elements derive and concrete elements that provide the overall file definition.

The following elements are the abstract components that form the basis for understanding ROM:

- DataSet

  DataSet defines the fundamental properties of a data set relating to columns and parameters.

- DataSource

  DataSource defines the methods that a concrete data source element must support.

- DesignElement

  DesignElement defines basic features of ROM elements. DesignElement represents any component of a report design that has properties.

- Listing

  Listing is the abstract base element for list and table items. Both items support a data set, filtering, sorting, and methods.

- MasterPage

  MasterPage defines the basic properties of a page.

- ReportElement

  ReportElement represents any item that can be named and customized. Most components in ROM derive from ReportElement, including the elements that are visible in the user interface, such as data sets, styles, master pages, and report items.

- ReportItem

  ReportItem is the base element for the visual elements. A report item includes a style. The style provides visual characteristics for any element that appears in a report, such as a section or report item.

The following concrete elements describe the root element of a BIRT file:

- ReportDesign

  ReportDesign contains information about a report design, defining properties that describe the design as a whole. Report design properties do not support inheritance because a design cannot extend another design. ReportDesign is the root element of a report design or a template.

- Library

  Library is similar to ReportDesign, extending LayoutModule, but has a different set of slots and does not have methods.

About report item elements

BIRT provides many types of visual report components. Every type of visual report component has a corresponding ROM element that derives from the ReportItem element. Visual report components are called report items. Every report item has an entry in the palette, the view in BIRT Report Designer that the report developer uses to build a report layout.

About report items

BIRT provides container and simple report items. Container items are structural components that provide slot elements to hold one or more other report items. The slots in container items support both container and simple report items, so a grid can contain tables that contain other tables and grids, and so on. Simple report items are not structural and do not contain other items. These report items have properties that describe their behavior and appearance and do not provide slots. For example, the Image element is a simple report item.

Examples of container report items include:

- Grid

  A grid contains a set of report items arranged into a matrix having a fixed set of columns and rows. Each cell in the grid can contain one or more simple or container report items.

- List

  A list contains a set of arbitrary content based on data retrieved from a data set. A list is appropriate when some report items require a sophisticated layout and repeat that layout for each row in a query.

- Table

  A table contains a set of report items arranged into a matrix. A table has a fixed set of columns and an arbitrary number of rows. A table produces a detail row for every row of data retrieved from a data set.

Understanding report item element properties

Each type of report item has its own set of properties in addition to the properties it inherits from ReportItem. Types of inherited properties include:

- Method, which defines executable code.
- Property, which includes such values as names and dimensions.
- Slot, which contains Type elements that define its contents, as shown in the following element definition.

```
<Slot name="reportItems"
   displayNameID="Element.FreeForm.slot.reportItems"
   multipleCardinality="true">
      <Type name="Label" />
      <Type name="Data" />
      <Type name="Text" />
</Slot>
```

- StyleProperty, which defines style-related characteristics, such as color and font size.

About data report elements

Several elements in the ROM specification apply to data rather than visual report items. These data report elements describe data sources and data sets. The following elements are data report elements:

- OdaDataSource

  The OdaDataSource element represents a connection to an external data system, such as an RDBMS, text file, or XML file.

- ScriptedDataSource

  The ScriptedDataSource element represents a connection to an external data system that is not an ODA data source. The developer must provide scripts for opening and closing a scripted data source. ScriptedDataSource inherits from DataSource.

- OdaDataSet

  The OdaDataSet element represents a tabular result set retrieved from a data source. An OdaDataSet element defines a data source, query, filters, parameters, and result set columns.

- JointDataSet

  The JointDataSet element represents a data set that results from a join of several data sets.

- ScriptedDataSet

  The ScriptedDataSet element represents a data set that is associated with a scripted data source. The developer must provide scripts for opening, closing, and fetching a row from a scripted data source.

Part

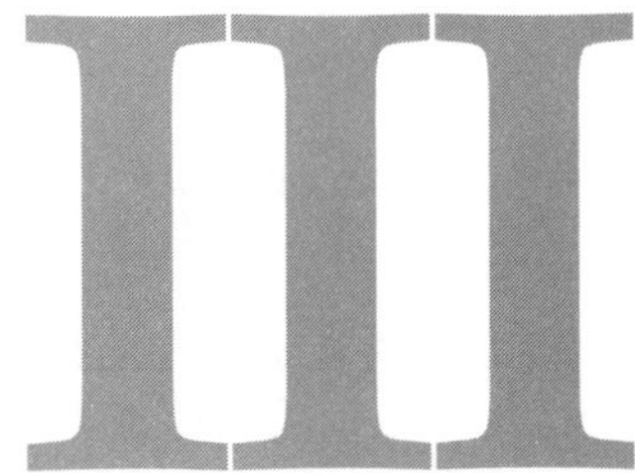

Scripting in a Report Design

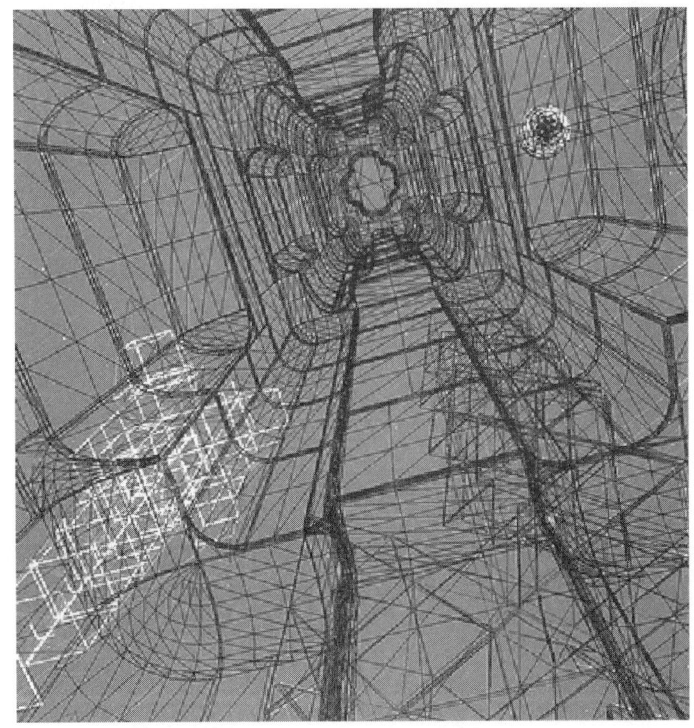

Chapter

7

Using Scripting in a Report Design

BIRT provides a powerful scripting capability that enables a report developer to create custom code to control various aspects of report creation. This chapter provides an overview of scripting in BIRT. Subsequent chapters focus on implementing script event handlers in JavaScript and Java, writing event handlers for charts, and accessing data using scripted data sources.

Overview of BIRT scripting

BIRT Report Designer supports writing custom event handlers in both Java and JavaScript. BIRT RCP Report Designer supports writing custom event handlers only in JavaScript.

Choosing between JavaScript and Java

Both JavaScript and Java have advantages and disadvantages when writing an event handler. For a developer who is familiar with only one of the two languages, the advantage of using the familiar language is obvious, but for others the decision depends on the report requirements.

The advantages of using JavaScript to write an event handler include:

- Ease of adding a simple script for a particular event handler
  Adding a JavaScript event handler to a report is less complicated than adding an event handler written in Java. To write a JavaScript event handler, there is no need to create a Java environment in Eclipse or to learn the Eclipse Java development process. There is no requirement to

specify a package, implement an interface, or know the parameters of the event handler you write.

To add a JavaScript event handler, first select the name of the event handler from a drop-down list on the Script tab. Then, type the code.

- Simpler language constructs, looser typing, and less strict language rules

  JavaScript is less demanding to code than Java due to its more relaxed requirements.

The advantages of using Java to write an event handler include:

- Availability of the Eclipse Java development environment

  The Eclipse Java development environment is very powerful and includes such features as autocompletion, context sensitive help, keyboard shortcuts, and parameter hints.

- Ease of finding and viewing event handlers

  All the Java event handlers for a report exist in readily viewable Java files. By contrast, the JavaScript event handlers are embedded in the design and you can view only one handler at a time.

Using both JavaScript and Java

There is no requirement to write all event handlers in one language. You can write some in JavaScript and others in Java. If both a JavaScript and a Java event handler for the same event are available, BIRT uses the JavaScript handler.

Events overview

When writing event handlers, understanding the event order is imperative. The order in which events fire depends on several factors. These factors include which BIRT processing phase is executing, the engine task executing the process, and what event type is processing.

Engine task processes

The scripting chapters make continuous reference to engine task processes. This section provides an overview of what these processes are and how they affect scripting.

The Report Engine that executes reports is task-oriented and provides three tasks related to the execution and rendering of reports. These tasks are RunAndRenderTask, RunTask, and RenderTask.

The RunAndRenderTask uses one process to open the report design and produce a specific output, such as PDF. The RunTask opens a report design and executes the report producing a report document file with a

.rptdocument extension. This report document is an intermediate binary file that can then be used by a RenderTask to produce a report output type, such as HTML, PDF, PPT, PS, Word, or XLS. The RenderTask opens a report document (.rptdocument) and renders the appropriate output format. This task can be executed any time after a RunTask. This task can even occur on a separate system.

BIRT Report Designer uses the report engine to show a preview of a report. Selecting Preview in the Editor launches a RunAndRenderTask to produce the report. Selecting any other previewing option in BIRT Report Designer toolbar launches a RunAndRenderTask to produce the output, with the exception of the Run report in BIRT Web Viewer, which produces the report using a RunTask followed by a RenderTask.

The tasks RunTask and RenderTask can be used when the tasks need to occur at separate times or on separate systems. Using separate run and render tasks therefore requires two processes to run and render a report to a particular output format.

When RunAndRenderTask processes a report, the event firing order is different from the RunTask and RenderTask are used as two separate processes. The differences in processing are discussed throughout these chapters.

The following sections describe how the report engine processes reports in the BIRT Report Designer environment.

BIRT Web Viewer

The example BIRT Web Viewer application is a J2EE application that encapsulates the report engine to produce reports. This viewer contains three Servlet mappings used to generate reports. These are the frameset, run, and preview mappings.

In the example web viewer, two processes, RunTask and RenderTask, generate and render to the output format to create a report document. Selecting the Export report icon in the Web Viewer toolbar initiates a RenderTask to execute on the current report document.

BIRT processing phases

The BIRT services for generating and presenting report data create a report during the following processing phases:

- Preparation

  RunTask or RunAndRender Task prepare the report items for execution.

- Generation

  RunTask or RunAndRender Task create an instance of each report item, connect to the data source, execute the data sets, and process the data to produce the report.

- Presentation

  RenderTask or RunAndRender Task select the correct emitters to produce the output specified for the report.

The RunTask handles the preparation and generation phases and the Render Task handles the presentation phase. RunAndRenderTask handles all phases of report processing. The types of events and the order in which these events fire depends on the processing phase currently executing in an engine task.

BIRT event types

BIRT supports the following types of events:

- Parameter
- Report design
- Data source and data set
- Report item

Each event type has a series of events that fire during report processing.

Parameter events

BIRT currently supports two parameter level events that can be used to customize the parameter selection choices and default values before the parameter entry box is displayed. In addition, BIRT supports one parameter level event that is called after the parameters have been selected. These events are summarized in Table 7-1. These events are currently available only in JavaScript. Parameter events fire only if the report contains parameters.

Table 7-1 Parameter events

Event	Description
getDefaultValueList	Sets the parameter's default value. If the parameter is set to allow multiple values, this script should return an array of values that will then be pre-selected in the parameter entry box. This event fires first.
getSelectionValue List	Returns a single value or an array of values. This event fires before the parameter entry box displays for parameters presenting a list of values. Simple text parameters do not call this event.
validate	This event fires after the user selects the report parameters and before the initialize event. This event fires for each parameter and returns a value of true or false. Returning false throws an exception that states which parameter failed validation. Returning true processes the report normally.

Listing 7-1 provides an example of getDefaultValueList and getSelectionValueList event handlers for a parameter formatted as a list box. The array dSLArray contains four values that a report user can select. The array dVLArray contains two values that are the default values of the parameter. These values are selected in the list of available values when the user runs the report.

Listing 7-1 Example event handlers for a parameter formatted as a list box

```
//getDefaultValueList
var dVLArray = [];
dVLArray[0]= "10104";
dVLArray[1] = "10108";
dVLArray;

//getSelectionValueList
var dSLArray = [];
dSLArray[0]= "10101";
dSLArray[1]= "10104";
dSLArray[2]= "10105";
dSLArray[3] = "10108";
dSLArray;
```

The getDefaultValueList can be useful to provide date parameters as well.

If changes to the parameter are necessary after a user enters a parameter or if extra parameter validation is required, write an event handler for the validate event. The following example shows a validate script for a string parameter:

```
params["MyParameter"].value = "Something Else";
true;
```

Report design events

Report design events fire for all reports. Table 7-2 describes these events. The events support event handlers to provide additional processing of the report.

Table 7-2 Report design events

Event	Description
initialize	Fires every time a task accesses the report design (.rptdesign) or the report document (.rptdocument). This event occurs once when using RunAndRenderTask. When the processing phases run separately, RunTask triggers once for the generation phase and RenderTask triggers once for every render operation. Displaying the first page of a report in the presentation phase and using the page navigation control to access a new page also triggers this event handler.

(continues)

Table 7-2 Report design events (continued)

Event	Description
beforeFactory	Fires just prior to the generation phase after the elements in the report have been prepared in the preparation phase. This event handler fires only once. Use beforeFactory( ) when modifications to the report design are required before execution.
beforeRender	Fires just prior to the presentation phase and is called for every render operation. In the RunAndRender task, this event occurs once just after the beforeFactory event.
afterFactory	Fires at the conclusion of the generation phase and fires only once. If using a RunTask or RunAndRenderTask, this event is the last one fired. If using a RenderTask, this event does not execute.
afterRender	Fires at the conclusion of the presentation phase for a specific render operation. If using a single RunAndRenderTask process, this event is called only once. If using separate RunTask and RenderTask processes, this event fires for every render operation.
onPageStart	Fires prior to placing content on a specific page and supports the use of page-level variables to modify the page. This event fires only when processing phases run separately, for example, a RunTask followed by a RenderTask. This event fires prior to the onPageBreak events for the individual elements to be placed on the page. This event is also available on the master page.
onPageEnd	Fires after all the onPageBreak events have fired for the content to be placed on a page and prior to evaluating the autotext items for the page. This event is also available on the master page.

Types of data source and data set events

There are several kinds of data sources and data sets. A data source can be a flat file, a JDBC data source, a scripted data source, a web services data source, or an XML data source. All data sources have a common set of event handlers. A scripted data source has two additional event handlers.

Data set events can be called multiple times to support multipass aggregation and data set sharing. It is not advisable to write event handlers that rely on the data set event firing order. An additional issue is that data set event handlers may only be called once because of data set caching.

Table 7-3 describes the data source events.

Table 7-3 Data source events

Event	Description
beforeOpen	This event is most often used to modify public properties of the data source, including database URL, username, password, driver class and JNDI URL. This event fires only once, before the connection to the data source opens event, when the connection uses multiple data sets. Fires prior to opening a connection to a data source.
afterOpen	Fires after the connection to the data source opens.
beforeClose	Fires at the conclusion of the generation phase, just prior to closing the data source connection.
afterClose	Fires after the data source connection closes.
open	Fires only for a scripted data source, providing a location for the developer to set up a connection to an external source.
close	Fires only for a scripted data source, providing a location for the developer to close a connection to an external source.

Data source and data set events fire in the generation phase prior to the onCreate event of the report item that uses them. Data set events can fire several times. The event order is covered in more detail later in this chapter. Table 7-4 describes the data set events.

Table 7-4 Data set events

Event	Description
beforeOpen	Fires prior to opening a data set and used most often to modify public properties of the data set. For example, when using a JDBC data set, the query text can be altered using this event. This event fires for every report item bound to the data set. If two tables use the same data set, the data set is called twice, resulting in this event firing twice. BIRT 2.6 allows report items to be bound to other report items, in which case the data set is called only once, resulting in the event triggering only once. Data set caching options continue to be added which affect how often data source and data set events fire.
afterOpen	Fires after the data set opens.

(continues)

Table 7-4 Data set events (continued)

Event	Description
onFetch	Fires as the data set retrieves each row of data. This event fires for all rows of data before the onCreate event for the particular report item that uses the data set.
beforeClose	Fires before closing the data set after creating the report item that uses the data set.
afterClose	Fires after the data set closes.
open	Fires for a scripted data set, providing a location for the developer to set up a data set.
fetch	Fires for a scripted data set, providing a location for the developer to populate rows from the scripted data set.
close	Fires for a scripted data set, providing a location for the developer to close the set.

Data source and data set events fire prior to being used on a data bound item. If the data set is never used in the report, the data source and data set are never called. A scripted data set is a data set that accesses a scripted data source. A non-scripted data set is one that accesses a standard data source. Use the scripted data source and data set to write custom code to retrieve data values.

Scripted data source events

A scripted data source contains the afterOpen, afterClose, beforeOpen, and beforeClose events common to all data sources, and open and close events. Use the event handlers for the open and close events to perform the actions of opening and closing the data source.

Scripted data set events

A scripted data set contains the afterOpen, afterClose, OnFetch, beforeOpen, beforeClose, open, close, and fetch events. Use the event handlers for the open and close events to perform the actions of opening and closing the data set. Use the fetch method to fetch a row from the data source. Using a scripted data set requires an event handler to be written for the fetch event.

ReportItem events

ReportItem events trigger for report items that are placed in the report. Most items support writing event handlers for the events listed in Table 7-5.

Table 7-5 Report item events

Event	Description
onPrepare	Fires at the beginning of the preparation phase before data binding or expression evaluation occurs. This event is useful for changing the design of the item prior to generating the item instance.
onCreate	Fires at the time the generation phase creates the element. This event is useful when a particular instance of a report item needs alteration.
onRender	Fires in the presentation phase. This event is useful for operations that depend on the type or format of the output document.
onPageBreak	Fires for all report items currently on the page when the page break occurs. Not all report items support the onPageBreak event.

Event order sequence

Table 7-6 summarizes which engine task is responsible for a particular phase. The following sections describe the order of event firing for each phase in more detail.

Table 7-6 Engine task by phase

Report engine task	Preparation phase	Generation phase	Presentation phase
RunTask	Yes	Yes	No
RenderTask	No	No	Yes
RunAndRenderTask	Yes	Yes	Yes

Preparation phase operation

The preparation phase includes parameter validation as well as initialization and report element preparation for every element in the report. The preparation phase is identical for all reports. Table 7-7 lists the event types for RunTask and RunAndRenderTask in the order in which the events execute.

The RenderTask does not have a preparation phase. In a RunAndRenderTask, the preparation phase triggers a beforeRender event.

Table 7-7 Preparation phase events

Element type and event	RunTask	RunAnd RenderTask
Parameter getDefaultValueList	Yes	Yes
Parameter getSelectionValueList	Yes	Yes
Parameter validate	Yes	Yes
ReportDesign Initialize	Yes	Yes
ReportItem onPrepare (iterative)	Yes	Yes
ReportDesign beforeFactory	Yes	Yes
ReportDesign beforeRender	No	Yes

The parameter events fire first for each parameter. Before the parameter entry box is displayed, the getDefaultValueList is called for each parameter. This script returns either a single value or a list of values, depending on the parameter type.

Next, each parameter that provides a list of choices to the user calls the getSelectionValueList. If running reports using the API for RunTask or RunAndRenderTask, the getDefaultValueList script event fires for only parameters that have no value passed. The getSelectionValueList is not called. If using createGetParameterDefinitionTask to build your own parameter entry screen, these events fire much like the example Viewer.

After a user enters values for the parameters, the next event is the validate event, which fires for each parameter. The ReportDesign event, initialize, follows. The initialize event fires once when using only one engine task. Using a separate engine task triggers the initialize event at least two times, one time for the preparation phase, and a second time for the render phase. Additional render tasks or phases also trigger the initialize method.

After the initialize event, the preparation phase triggers the onPrepare event for every element in the report. This process starts with the master page content and proceeds from left to right and top to bottom in the report body. All nested elements process before proceeding to the next element.

The beforeFactory event fires next. This event signals that report creation is about to occur and provides a location for altering a running report.

The beforeRender event fires when using a RunAndRenderTask. When using two tasks, this event does not fire until a render operation occurs.

Generation phase operation

The generation phase includes connecting to data sources, executing data sets and data cubes, evaluating data bindings, and creating all the report items in the report. The data source and data set events fire before the creation of data-bound items, but this processing may not occur before the creation of other report items. For example, if a table is bound to a data set and the report uses a master page with only a label in the footer, the master page content onCreate event fires before the data source and data set events for the data set bound to the table.

This phase triggers the onCreate event for every report item. BIRT processes the report body after processing content on the master page. The report body contains all the report items to be created and rendered. BIRT processes all items at all levels in an iterative fashion, following the same process at each level as it does for the top-level items. A report item that is not contained in another report item is called a top-level report item. BIRT processes the top-level items, going from left to right and proceeding a row at a time toward the bottom right. Every report has at least one top-level report item, usually a grid, list, or table. All nested elements complete OnCreate processing before the next element's onCreate fires.

For each top-level item, BIRT processes all the second-level items before proceeding to the next top-level item. A second-level report item is a report item that is contained within a top-level item. For example, a table contained in a grid is a second-level report item.

There can be any number of levels of report items. To see the level of a particular report item, examine the structure of the report design in Outline, in the BIRT Report Designer, as shown in Figure 7-1.

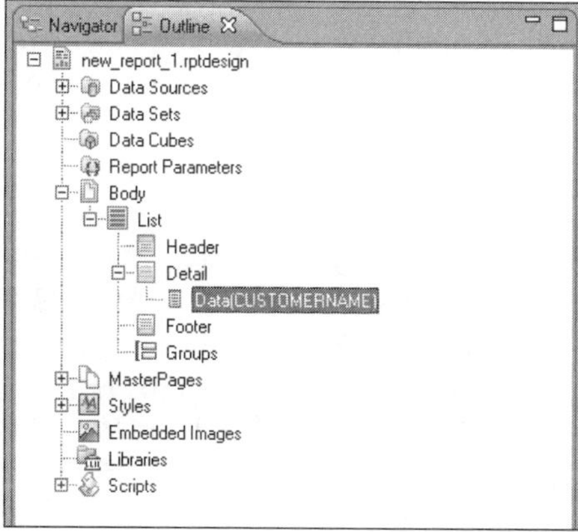

Figure 7-1 Outline showing the level of a report item

If a RunAndRenderTask process executes the generation phase, each element is created and immediately rendered, which fires the onRender event before proceeding to the next element. If a RunTask process executes the generation phase, the onRender events do not fire.

Table 7-8 lists the events triggered in the generation phase for each major report component in the order in which these events execute. The data source, data set, and onPageBreak events are optional.

Table 7-8 Generation phase events

Report component	RunTask	RunAndRenderTask
Master Page content	Data source and data set events (optional) onCreate onPageBreak (optional)	Data source and data set events (optional) onCreate onRender onPageBreak (optional)
Body (iterative)	Data source and data set events (optional) onCreate onPageBreak (optional)	Data source and data set events (optional) onCreate onRender onPageBreak (optional)

Data source and data set events do not fire if a report item is not data bound or if the report item is bound to another report item that executed previously. The onPageBreak event fires only when an actual page break occurs.

The next three sections describe the data source, data set, data binding, and page break events in more detail.

About data source and data set events

Events for data source and data set elements fire just prior to creating the report item bound to the data set. This sequence occurs for every report item bound to a data set with the exception of the data source beforeOpen and afterOpen events. These events do not fire if a data source has already been used. When a report item is bound to another report item, none of these events fire for the bound report item, supporting two data-bound items sharing one data set without re-executing the data set.

The data source beforeClose and afterClose events fire at the end of the generation phase just before the afterFactory event fires. In the generation phase, there is no difference in data source or data set processing in RunTask and RunAndRenderTask.

BIRT supports data set caching, by which data sets execute only once and are used multiple times. In this case, the data set events fire on only the first use. If a data set is parameterized and the actual parameter value is changed within a report item, the query executes again using the new parameter value. This query execution causes the data set events to fire again. Table 7-9 lists the data source and data set types and events in the order in which these events execute.

Table 7-9 Data source and data set events

Event type and event	RunTask	RunAnd RenderTask
Data source beforeOpen	Yes	Yes
Data source afterOpen	Yes	Yes
Data set beforeOpen	Yes	Yes
DataSet afterOpen	Yes	Yes
DataSet onFetch for all rows of data	Yes	Yes
Process the data-bound Report Item	Yes	Yes
DataSet beforeClose	Yes	Yes
DataSet afterClose	Yes	Yes

About data binding

Data binding in BIRT makes a logical separation between BIRT data sets and data-bound elements, such as tables and lists. Selecting a table or list and then the Binding tab in the Property Editor displays the current bindings for the item. A report developer can create bound columns that use external objects to calculate a specific column value. The bound data set continues to determine the number of rows that are processed for a given table or list.

In a table or list, evaluation of the data bindings for the detail rows occurs before the onCreate event on the current row. This approach supports the onCreate event handler retrieving the appropriate values for the row.

The bindings are evaluated for each detail row in a bound data set. Table footers containing data elements that use a binding are evaluated before the last onCreate event for the final detail row.

Trying to alter a bound column using the onCreate script is discouraged. For example, it is possible to concatenate a column value for a row with all previous rows for the given column using the onCreate script with a JavaScript variable. If this value is in the expression of a bound column, the last value is excluded from the bound column. To display the last value, use a computed column, an aggregation report item, or the dynamic text <VALUE-OF> tag in a text element to display the JavaScript value.

A report developer must not assume any particular evaluation order of binding expressions relative to the various table item events, except that a binding evaluates before the onCreate event of an item that uses it. Best practice is to perform any required manipulation of the data in a data set script or the binding expression.

Data binding evaluation for a group evaluates the bound column many times before creating the table or list item. BIRT performs multiple passes over the data to support grouping. Any script in a group-bound column expression is called every time the data binding evaluates, affecting report performance.

All bindings of a table are always calculated, whether or not these bindings are used by the table. For performance reasons, check the binding list and remove any unused items from the report design.

Report items can share data bindings. For example, two tables can share the same set of bindings. The second table does not re-evaluate the data bindings. To use this feature in the BIRT Report Designer, select the second table, choose Binding in Property Editor, select Report Item, and select the appropriate report item from the list. The list supports only named data-bound report items.

The above scenarios affect any BIRT expression that uses the Available Column Bindings category.

About page break events

Many report items support page breaks. Setting a page break interval on a table instructs the table to process a certain number of rows and then apply a page break. Setting a page break on a group section applies a page break both before and after or only after the group processes. A page break can be applied before many other report items. For example, applying a page break before a row in a table instructs the engine to apply a page break before every row of data that a table processes.

Page events are based on the paginated HTML emitter. If a report generates 5 HTML pages but has 20 PDF pages, the page events fire only 5 times.

The general order of the events is as follows.

- The engine creates the page.
- The onPageStart event fires for the report.
- The onPageStart event fires for the selected master page.
- For items that are to appear on the page, the onPageBreak event fires.
- The onPageEnd event fires for the selected master page.
- The onPageEnd event for the report fires.
- The engine evaluates the Master Page Auto Text fields.

The onCreate events for all items that are to appear on a page fire before the report's onStart event. Some items have their onCreate triggered but do not appear on a page because of the keep together flag. Such items appear on the following page.

The page-level scripts are used when the Run and Render tasks are separated.

About chart event order

Chart events are handled by the chart engine and execute within the presentation phase. These events are covered in a later chapter.

About table and list event order

The BIRT engine fires the onCreate event for report items iteratively. When processing report items that iterate over data rows, such as a table or list, the event order changes to add additional events for each row of data. Row containers process data rows.

Row execution sequence

Tables, lists, and groups have rows. BIRT processes all rows identically. There are three kinds of rows:

- Header
- Detail
- Footer

Figure 7-2 illustrates the execution sequence for a row. A list or table can contain multiple elements, such as detail rows or table header rows.

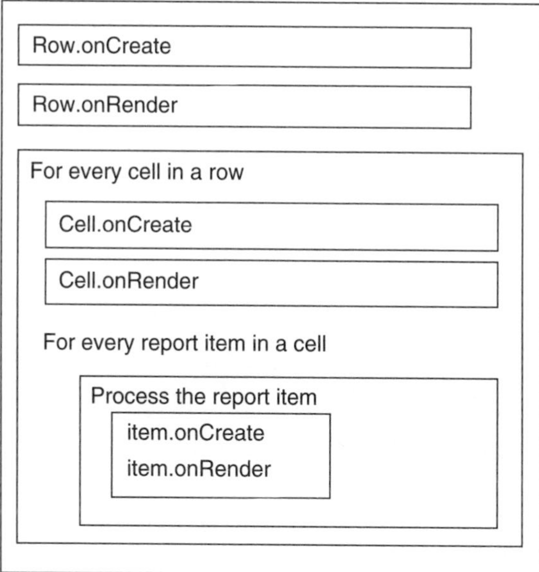

Figure 7-2 Row execution sequence

Table and list method execution sequence

A list is equivalent to a table that has only a single cell in every row. BIRT processes tables and lists identically, except that for a list, BIRT does not iterate through multiple cells. BIRT processes tables in three steps, the setup, detail, and wrap-up processing steps.

The following sections describe the table and list execution sequence steps.

Table and list setup step

The pre-table processing step is the same for all tables, both grouped and ungrouped.

Figure 7-3 illustrates the execution sequence for the pre-table processing step. This illustration shows the event order when using a RunAndRenderTask in the generation phase.

A RunTask does not fire onRender events. A RenderTask does not fire onCreate, data source, and data set events. The data source and data set events are optional.

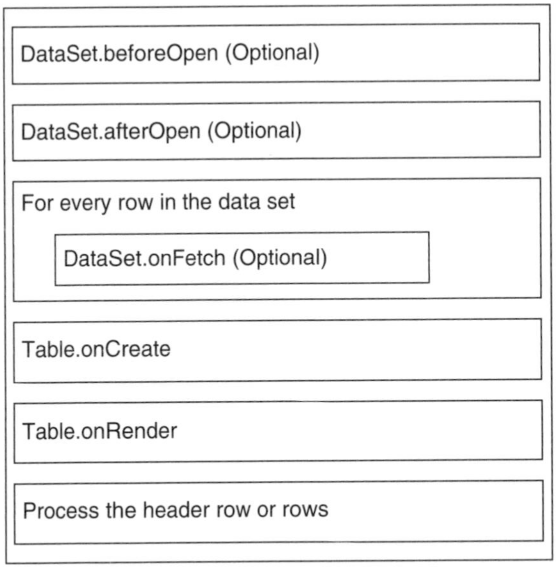

DataSet.beforeOpen (Optional)

DataSet.afterOpen (Optional)

For every row in the data set

DataSet.onFetch (Optional)

Table.onCreate

Table.onRender

Process the header row or rows

Figure 7-3 Table and list setup execution sequence

Table and list processing step

The sequence for the table and list processing step depends on whether the table or list is grouped. A table or list having no grouping has a different sequence from one that has grouping.

Figure 7-4 illustrates the execution sequence for a table or list without grouping.

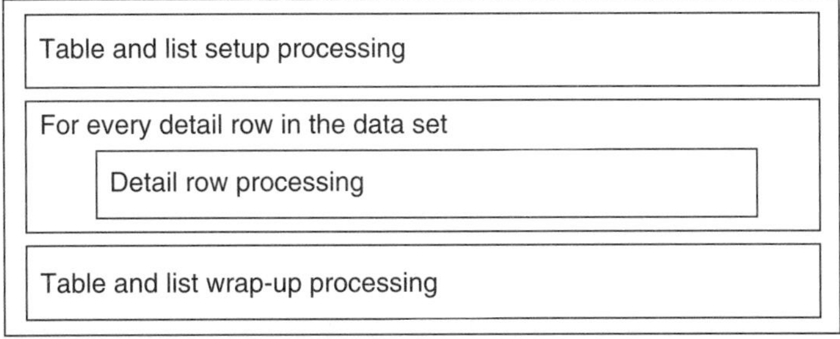

Figure 7-4 Ungrouped table or list detail execution sequence

For a table having grouping, BIRT creates one ListingGroup item per group.

A ListingGroup is similar to a table in that it has one or more header rows and one or more footer rows. BIRT processes grouped rows in the same way that it processes a table row.

In addition to the standard onPrepare, onCreate, and onRender events for these rows, the ListingGroup fires the onPageBreak and onPrepare events for the group. To access the script location for these event handlers, locate the group in the outline view and select the script tab. Use code in the onPrepare event handler to modify grouping behavior, such as changing the sort order.

Figure 7-5 illustrates the method execution sequence for a table that has groups.

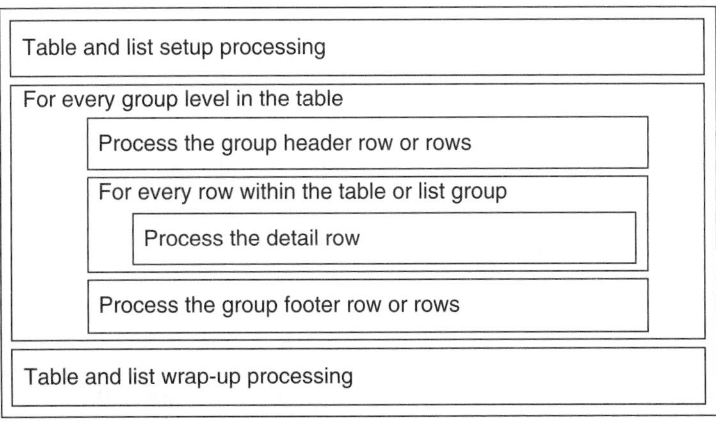

Figure 7-5 Grouped table execution sequence

To verify the execution sequence of event handlers for a specific report, add logging code to the event handlers.

Table and list wrap-up step

The post-table processing step is the same for all tables, both grouped and ungrouped.

Completion of the generation phase

On completion of the generation phase, all data sources, beforeClose and afterClose events fire, followed by the afterFactory event. If using the RunAndRenderTask, the afterRender event fires before closing the data sources. Table 7-10 describes the events available at completion of the generation phase.

Table 7-10 Completing the generation phase

Element type and event	RunTask	RunAndRenderTask
afterRender	No	Yes
Data Source(s) beforeClose	Yes	Yes
Data Source(s) afterClose	Yes	Yes
afterFactory	Yes	No

Presentation phase operation

The presentation phase launches the appropriate emitter and produces report output based on the generated report. This phase fires the onRender events for all items as they are created. If using the RenderTask to render an existing report document, the initialize event triggers first and then each rendered report item's onRender event fires.

If the RenderTask renders pages individually, the onRender event fires only for items that are rendered. For example, BIRT Web Viewer uses a RunTask to create a report document. The web viewer uses a RenderTask to render the first page. This action fires the initialize event first and the onRender event for each item that appears on the page. Selecting a new page and using the pagination controls results in a new RenderTask that calls the initialize event again and triggers the onRender event for each item on the new page.

Event order summary

Table 7-11 summarizes the report design and report item events triggered in each processing phase. The events are listed in the order they are fired for a particular task. Page break, getDefaultValueList, getSelectionValueList, data source, and data set events are not shown for brevity.

Table 7-11 Event order summary

Element type and event	RunTask	RunAnd Render Task	Render Task	Notes
Parameter validate	Yes	Yes	n/a	Only available in JavaScript.

Table 7-11 Event order summary

Element type and event	RunTask	RunAnd Render Task	Render Task	Notes
Report initialize	Yes	Yes	Yes	Called multiple times using the RenderTask.
MasterPage Content onPrepare	Yes	Yes	n/a	
Body Iterate onPrepare	Yes	Yes	n/a	
Report beforeFactory	Yes	Yes	n/a	
Data source and data set beforeOpen and afterOpen	Yes	Yes	n/a	
Report beforeRender	n/a	Yes	Yes	
MasterPage Content onCreate	Yes	Yes	n/a	
Body Iterate onCreate	Yes	Yes	n/a	
Page Events	Yes	Yes	n/a	
Body Iterate onRender	n/a	Yes	Yes	RunAndRenderTask triggers this event immediately after onCreate for a report item.
Report afterRender	n/a	Yes	Yes	
Data source and data set beforeClose and afterClose	Yes	Yes	n/a	
Report afterFactory	Yes	Yes	n/a	

Chapter

8

Using JavaScript to Write an Event Handler

BIRT scripting is based on the Mozilla Rhino implementation of JavaScript, also called ECMAScript. Rhino implements ECMAScript version 1.5 as described in the ECMA standard ECMA-262 version 3. The complete specification for Rhino is located at:

```
http://www.ecma-international.org/publications/standards
   /Ecma-262.htm
```

Using BIRT Report Designer to enter a JavaScript event handler

You can use BIRT Report Designer to enter a JavaScript event handler and associate it with a specific event for a particular element.

How to use BIRT Report Designer to enter a JavaScript event handler

1 In Outline, select the report element, data source, or data set for which to write an event handler.

2 Choose the Script tab.

3 Select an event handler from the drop-down list of methods.

4 Type the event handler code in the script editor.

Figure 8-1 shows a line of code in the onPrepare( ) method of a List element.

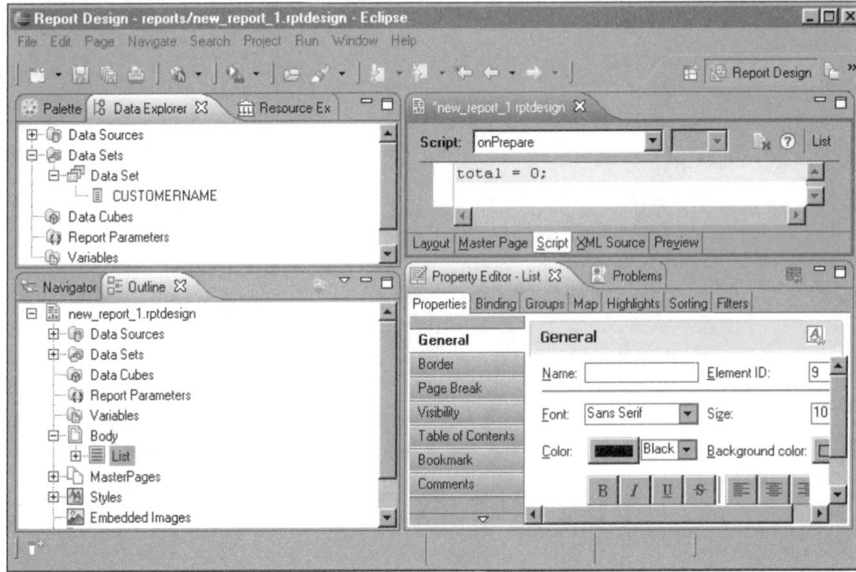

Figure 8-1 Code entry for the onPrepare( ) method

Creating and using a global variable

JavaScript has global variables and local variables. A local variable can only be accessed in the scope of the method in which it is created. You use the var identifier to create a local variable in JavaScript, as shown in the following line of code:

```
var localCounter = 0;
```

To create a global variable, omit the var identifier and replace local with global, as shown in the following line of code:

```
globalCounter = 0;
```

A global variable in JavaScript is visible to all other JavaScript code that executes in the same process. For example, use a global variable to count the detail rows in a table by first creating a global variable in the onCreate( ) method of the table, as shown in the following line of code:

```
rowCount = 0;
```

Because rowCount is global, the onCreate( ) method of the detail row can access and increment it, as shown in the following line of code:

```
rowCount++;
```

To store global variables, use the reportContext.setGlobalVariable( ) method. This approach supports passing the global variable to a Java event handler.

If a report is being executed using two separate processes, such as RunTask and RenderTask, a global variable is only available to both processes if set using the reportContext.setPersistentGlobalVariable( ) method. This method writes the value of the variable to the report document before rendering. If you are setting a global variable in the initialize method, remember that this event fires many times when using two processes.

Creating and using page variables and scripts

On the master page, BIRT supports using autotext report items to add page-specific values. Some examples include page number, filename, date created, and total page count. The specific autotext item, variable, can be used in conjunction with page scripts to customize page presentation. This autotext element can use either a page variable or a report variable. Page and report variables are created in the data explorer view. Page variables are evaluated for every page of a report and report variables are evaluated for the entire report. As an analogy think of the page n of m autotext item. The n represents the current page number and the m represents the total number of pages. The n variable is analogous to a page level variable and the m variable is analogous to the report variable. To support modifying these variables, BIRT provides onPageStart and onPageEnd scripts for the report and any master pages that exist in the report. Using these scripts and variables, a report developer can create reports that have customized headers and footers such as showing sub-pagination based on groups or phone book style headers that show first and last page entry information.

Use page variables and scripts when using separate run and render tasks, for example when using the BIRT Viewer. For example, assume a report is needed that lists customers and the header needs to contain the first and last customer numbers for the specific page. To implement this report, the developer creates two page variables, FIRST_CUSTOMER and LAST_CUSTOMER, using the data explorer view. Next, the developer adds an OnPageStart event script for the report that sets these variables to null.

Listing 8-1 onPageStart event script

```
reportContext.setPageVariable("FIRST_CUSTOMER", null);
reportContext.setPageVariable("LAST_CUSTOMER", null);
```

These values are set to null for every new page. Finally, the developer selects the customer number data item and types the following onPageBreak script:

Listing 8-2 onPageBreak event script

```
var customer = this.getValue( );
var first = reportContext.getPageVariable("FIRST_CUSTOMER");
var last = reportContext.getPageVariable("LAST_CUSTOMER");

if (first == null)
{
   reportContext.setPageVariable("FIRST_CUSTOMER", value );
}
reportContext.setPageVariable("LAST_CUSTOMER", value);
```

The specific customer number and the two page variables are retrieved and then stored in a local JavaScript variable.

This onPageBreak event fires for every instance of this data item that is to appear on the page. Set the FIRST_CUSTOMER only once per page. If the first variable is null, the page variable FIRST_CUSTOMER is set to the current customer number. This condition is true only once per page. Next, the LAST_CUSTOMER page variable is set to the current customer number. This setting ensures that the LAST_CUSTOMER page variable is set to the last customer number on the page. The developer then adds two variable autotext report items to the master page header and assigns them the values FIRST_CUSTOMER and LAST_CUSTOMER.

Understanding execution phases and processes

There are three BIRT execution phases: preparation, generation, and presentation. There can be one or two execution processes. When a report runs in the BIRT Report Designer previewer, there is only one execution process, which executes a RunAndRenderTask.

There are two execution processes when the report runs in the viewer. The first process, called the factory process, contains the preparation and generation phases. The second execution process, called the render process, contains only the presentation phase. The render process can occur at a much later time than the factory process and possibly on a different machine.

Because variables are visible only in the process in which they are created, it is important to know which event handlers run in which process. If the render process uses a variable created in the factory process, the code works in the previewer but not at run-time if using two processes.

Using the reportContext object

Almost every event handler has access to an object called the reportContext object. Table 8-1 lists commonly used reportContext object methods.

Table 8-1 Methods of the reportContext class

Method	Task
deleteGlobalVariable( )	Deletes a global variable created using setGlobalVariable( ).
deletePersistentGlobalVariable( )	Deletes a persistent global variable created using setPersistentGlobalVariable( ).
evaluate( )	Evaluates a JavaScript expression.

Table 8-1 Methods of the reportContext class (continued)

Method	Task
getAppContext( )	Returns the application context that stores many variables that the engine uses to process the reports.
getDesignHandle( )	Retrieves the design handle for the currently running report. Use the design handle to manipulate the report design before processing starts. For example, to add, modify or drop report items programmatically. Modify a design in the beforeFactory event.
getGlobalVariable( )	Returns a global variable created using setGlobalVariable( ). This type of global variable is not stored in a report document.
getHttpServletRequest( )	Returns the HTTP servlet request object.
getLocale( )	Returns the current java.util.Locale object.
getMessage( )	Returns a localized message from the localization resource file.
getOutputFormat( )	Returns the format of the emitted report.
getPageVariable( )	Gets a page variable. Do not use this method in report level events such as the beforeFactory as the page variables have not yet initialized.
getParameterDisplayText( )	Returns the display text of the parameter name passed to the method.
getParameterValue( )	Returns a parameter value.
getPersistentGlobalVariable( )	Returns a persistent global variable created using setPersistentGlobalVariable( ). This type of global variable is stored in the report document.
getReportRunnable( )	Returns the runnable report design handle to retrieve report properties and engine configuration information.
getResource( )	Returns the URL to the resource passed to the method, such as the URL of an image stored in the resource folder.

(continues)

Table 8-1 Methods of the reportContext class (continued)

Method	Task
getTimeZone( )	Retrieves the com.ibm.icu.util .TimeZone instance for the currently running report.
setGlobalVariable( )	Creates a global variable accessible using getGlobalVariable( ).
setPageVariable( )	Sets a page variable. Do not use this method in report level events such as the beforeFactory as the page variables have not yet initialized.
setParameterValue( )	Sets the value of a named parameter.
setPersistentGlobalVariable( )	Creates a persistent global variable accessible using getPersistentGlobalVariable( ).

Using getOutputFormat

To change styling for an element at render time depending on the output format, use the reportContext object to add the code to the onRender event handler, as shown in Listing 8-3.

Listing 8-3 onRender event script

```
if (reportContext.getOutputFormat( ) == "pdf"){
   this.getStyle( ).backgroundColor = "red";
}else{
   this.getStyle( ).backgroundColor = "blue";
}
```

To create two different master pages in the design and swap pages based on the output format, set the beforeFactory event handler, as shown in Listing 8-4.

Listing 8-4 beforeFactoring event script

```
rptDesignHandle = reportContext.getDesignHandle( );
tbl = rptDesignHandle.findElement("mytable");
var myoutputformat = reportContext.getOutputFormat( );
if( myoutputformat == "html" ){
   tbl.setProperty("masterPage","MasterPageTwo");
}else{
   tbl.setProperty("masterPage","MasterPageOne");
}
```

This example uses the reportContext object to retrieve a handle to the report design. The design handle locates a table element named mytable and, depending on the output format, sets the masterPage property to the first or second master page. It important to understand that master page creation occurs during report generation and can not change at render time. The example works in the following two cases:

- Recreating the entire report document
- Running and rendering the report using one task

Using reportContext to retrieve the report design handle

You can use the reportContext object to retrieve the report design handle in the beforeFactory event handler. You can modify the currently running design before the design executes.

Place the following event handler examples in the beforeFactory method, which executes only during the generation phase of report creation. The examples use the Design Engine API, which is described in a later chapter.

The example in Listing 8-5 uses the design handle to add a filter based on report parameters to a table:

Listing 8-5 Using a parameter to filter a table

```
importPackage(Packages.org.eclipse.birt.report.model.api.elements)
   ;
importPackage(Packages.org.eclipse.birt.report.model.api);

tableHandle =
   reportContext.getDesignHandle( ).findElement("mytable");
if( params["FilterCol"].value.length > 0 ){
   fc = StructureFactory.createFilterCond( );
   fc.setExpr("row['" + params["FilterCol"] + "']");
   fc.setOperator(params["FilterEq"]);
   fc.setValue1("\"" + unescape(params["FilterVal"]) + "\"");
   ph = tableHandle.getPropertyHandle(TableHandle.FILTER_PROP);
   ph.addItem(fc);
}
```

The example in Listing 8-6 is similar to the filter example. It adds a sort condition to a table, as shown in the following code:

Listing 8-6 Sorting a table

```
importPackage(Packages.org.eclipse.birt.report.model.api);
importPackage(Packages.org.eclipse.birt.report.model.api.elements)
   ;
tbl= reportContext.getDesignHandle( ).findElement("mytable");
sc = StructureFactory.createSortKey( );
sc.setKey("row[\"PRODUCTCODE\"]");
sc.setDirection("desc");
ph = tbl.getPropertyHandle(TableHandle.SORT_PROP);
ph.addItem(sc);
```

A report developer may decide to hide a portion of report content using the visibility property. Hidden content can perform an unrendered calculation or customize the display of data based on report parameters. A report item hidden by its visibility property is still processed, which may or may not be desirable.

As an alternative to hiding report content using the visibility property, use the report design handle to drop elements from a running design, as shown in the following code:

```
reportContext.getDesignHandle( ).findElement("table1").drop( );
```

You can alter additional properties of report items. Listing 8-7 shows how to resize the width of a column within a table and change the bound data set. If the bound data set for a report item changes, the new data set must contain the same columns as the previous data set.

Listing 8-7 Changing table properties

```
table = reportContext.getDesignHandle( ).findElement("table1");
ch = table.getColumns( ).get(0);
ch.setProperty("width", "10%");
table.setProperty( "dataSet", "My Alternate Data Set" );
```

You can change the styles property in the beforeFactory event. Listing 8-8 uses one style for PDF generation and another style for all others. This example requires the report document be recreated to effect the change. Alternatively, use the RunAndRender task.

Listing 8-8 Changing a table style

```
tableHandle = reportContext
   .getDesignHandle( ).findElement("mytable");
rowHandle = tableHandle.getDetail( ).get(0);
if( reportContext.getOutputFormat( ) == "pdf" ){
   rowHandle.setStyleName("style2");
}else{
   rowHandle.setStyleName("style1");
}
```

Passing a variable between processes

Although a global JavaScript variable cannot pass between processes, BIRT provides a way to pass a variable from the factory process to the render process. The setPersistentGlobalVariable( ) method of the report context object creates a variable that is accessible using the getPersistentGlobalVariable( ) method. The only restriction is that the variable must be a serializable Java object.

For example, generate two strings at run time and display one string when rendering in PDF and a different string in other format contexts. Use the setPersistentGlobalVariable( ) method at generation time to store the variables in the report document. At render time, retrieve the variables in a render event handler using the getPersistentGlobalVariable( ) method.

Listing 8-9 calls the setPeristentGlobalVariable( ) method in the onCreate event handler of a label element to initialize two strings then calls the getPersistentGlobalVariable( ) method in the onRender event handler to specify the format context.

Listing 8-9 Using persistent global variables

```
//Label onCreate
reportContext.setPersistentGlobalVariable("mypdfstr",
   "My PDF String");
reportContext.setPersistentGlobalVariable("myhtmlstr",
   "My HTML String");

//Label onRender
if( reportContext.getOutputFormat( ) == "pdf" ){
   this.text =
   reportContext.getPersistentGlobalVariable("mypdfstr");
}else{
   this.text =
   reportContext.getPersistentGlobalVariable("myhtmlstr");
}
```

Using getAppContext

BIRT uses an application context map to store values and objects for use in all phases of report generation and presentation. To add an object to the application context, use the Report Engine API or the setAttribute( ) method of the request object.

The following JSP example adds an object to the application context. AppContextKey is the name that references the object and AppContextValue contains the value of the object.

Listing 8-10 Adding an object to the application context

```
<%
java.lang.String teststr = "MyTest";
session.setAttribute( "AppContextKey", teststr  );
java.lang.String stringObj = "This test my Application Context
   From the Viewer";
session.setAttribute( "AppContextValue", stringObj );
String redirectURL = "http://localhost:8080/2.5.0/
   frameset?__report=AppContext.rptdesign";
response.sendRedirect(redirectURL);
%>
```

Reference an object in the application context. Listing 8-11 uses a try-catch block to detect whether the object is not found and returns an appropriate error message.

Listing 8-11 Checking for the presence of an object

```
try {
   MyTest.toString( );
} catch (e) {
  "My Object Was Not Found";
}
```

Use the EngineConfig class or the EngineTask class in Report Engine API to add an object, as shown in Listing 8-12.

Listing 8-12 Adding an object to the application context

```
config = new EngineConfig( );
HashMap hm = config.getAppContext( );
hm.put( "MyTest", stringObj);
config.setAppContext(hm);
```

The application context object contains many useful settings. For example, set the driver location for JDBC drivers using code similar to the following lines:

```
config.getAppContext( ).put("OdaJDBCDriverClassPath",
   "C:/apps/apache-tomcat-5.5.20/webapps/2.5.0/WEB-INF/lib");
```

Setting a location for JDBC drivers precludes putting the driver jar in the jdbc plug-in, eliminating the possible deployment of multiple copies of a JDBC driver to the application server. Additionally, the connection object can be passed in to the BIRT engine using the OdaJDBCDriverPassInConnection setting of the application context. The value of the object must be an instance of a java.sql.Connection object. By passing in a connection, you can control whether the engine closes the external connection object by using the OdaJDBCDriverPassInConnectionCloseAfterUse setting. The value for this setting is a boolean value.

Setting application context objects from script is also possible. Properties must be set before use. Many settings apply to all tasks that the engine spawns. Changed settings affect all subsequent report runs.

Use the reportContext.getAppContext method to iterate through all the objects in the application context, as shown in Listing 8-13.

Listing 8-13 Examining all objects in the application context

```
iter = reportContext.getAppContext( ).entrySet( ).iterator( );
siz = reportContext.getAppContext( ).size( );
kys = "";
vls = "";
while (iter.hasNext( )){
   innerObject = iter.next( );
   kys = kys + innerObject.getKey( ) + "\n";
   val = innerObject.getValue( );
   if( val != null ){
      vls = vls + innerObject.getValue( ).toString( ) + "\n";
```

```
    }else{
        vls = vls + "NULL" + "\n";
    }
}
```

This code makes the variables, kys and vls, available for display in a data element or text element. Use kys and vls in an expression for a data element or <VALUE-OF>kys</VALUE-OF> and <VALUE-OF>vls</VALUE-OF> in a text element.

Getting information from an HTTP request object

The HTTP servlet request object contains various methods to retrieve information about the request to run the report. One useful method of the HTTP request object gets the query string that follows the path in the request URL. The query string contains all the parameters for the request. By parsing the query string, the code can extract the parameters in the request URL conditionally to determine the report output. For example, use this feature to pass in a user ID or to set or override a report parameter.

Listing 8-14 gets the query string.

Listing 8-14 Getting the query string from a request URL

```
importPackage( Packages.javax.servlet.http );
httpServletReq = reportContext.getHttpServletRequest( );
formatStr=httpServletReq.getQueryString( );
```

You can retrieve the Session object using reportContext, as shown in the following code:

```
var request = reportContext.getHttpServletRequest( );
var session = request.getSession( );
session.setAttribute("ReportAttribute", myAttribute);
```

Using the this object

Every JavaScript event handler is specific to a particular report element, such as a report item, a data source, a data set, or the report itself. Most report elements have properties that an event handler can access and, in some cases, change. Many report elements also have callable functions. A JavaScript event handler accesses these properties and functions through a special object called the this object.

Using this object methods

The this object represents the element for which the event handler is handling events. To use the this object, type the keyword, this, followed by a period in the script window for the event handler. When you type the period, a scrollable list of all the properties and functions for the element appears, as shown in Figure 8-2.

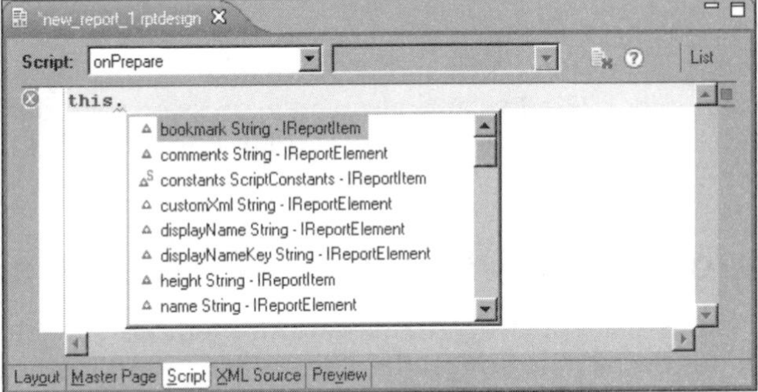

Figure 8-2 Using the this object to display a list of functions and properties

Scroll down the list and press Enter or double-click when the property or function you want is highlighted.

Using the this object to set a report item property

This list of properties and functions is available for other objects as well as this object. The following procedure sets the background color of a label to yellow. The general process explained in this procedure is not specific to the label report item. All report item event handlers support this functionality.

How to set a property of a report item using JavaScript

1 Select a label by navigating in the Outline view, as shown in Figure 8-3.

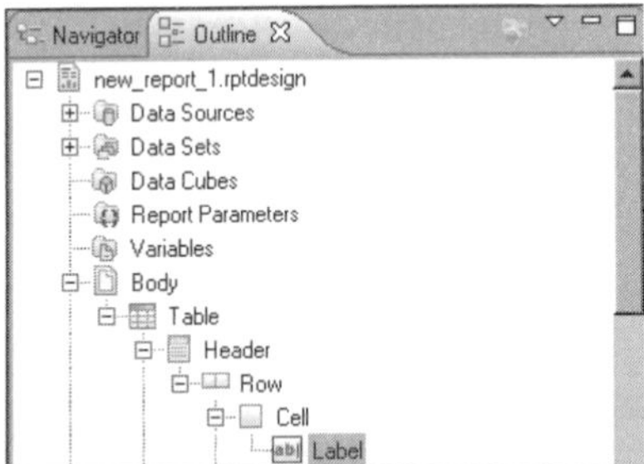

Figure 8-3 Selecting a report item to modify

2 Select onPrepare in the Script editor, as shown in Figure 8-4.

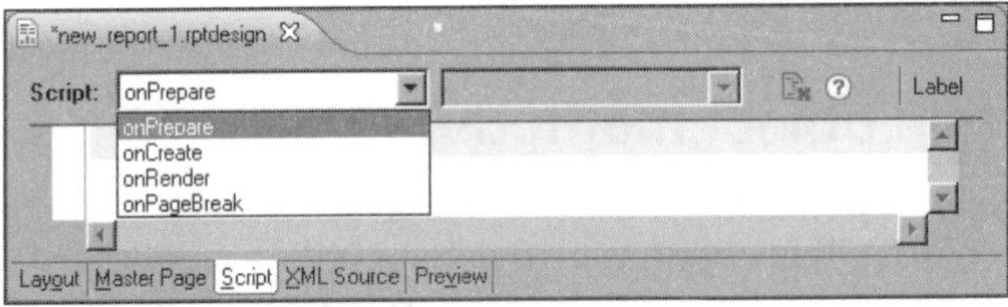

Figure 8-4 Selecting onPrepare( )

3 In the onPrepare script editor, type the keyword this, followed by a period to open the scrollable list of properties and functions, as shown in Figure 8-5.

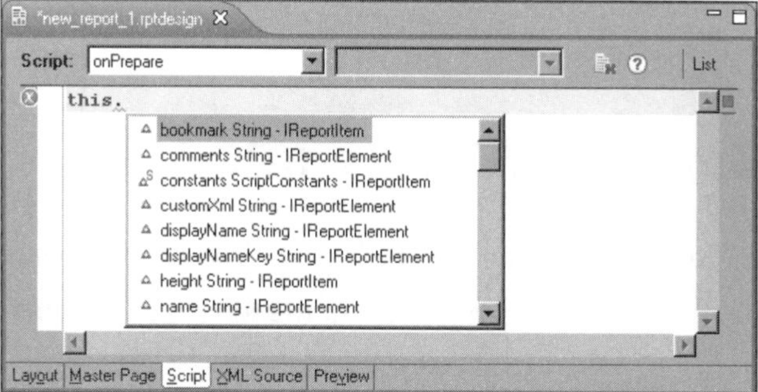

Figure 8-5 Using the this object

4 Select the getStyle( ) method from the list. The onPrepare script editor appears, as shown in Figure 8-6.

Figure 8-6 The onPrepare script window

5 Move the cursor to the end of the line in the onPrepare script window and type a period. The scrollable list of properties and functions of the Style element appears, as shown in Figure 8-7.

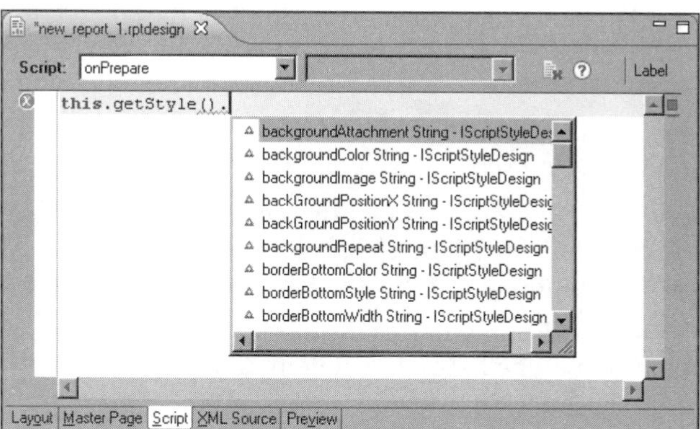

Figure 8-7 Properties and functions of the Style element

6 Select backgroundColor from the list of Style properties and functions.

7 Complete the line of JavaScript in the onPrepare script window by typing ="yellow" as shown in Figure 8-8.

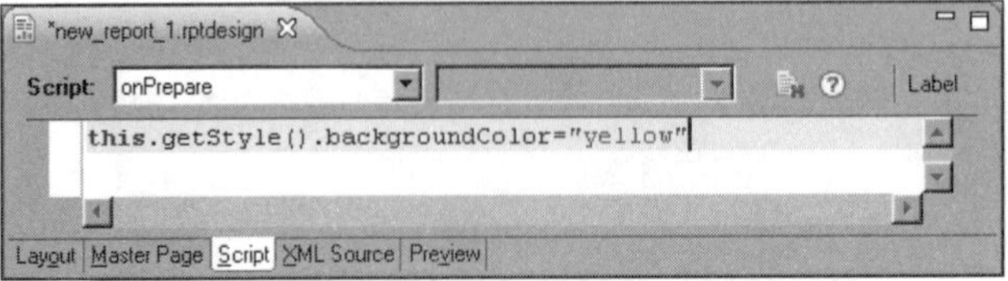

Figure 8-8 Changing the color of an element

8 Choose Preview to see the effect of the onPrepare event handler script.

The label has a yellow background in the report, as shown in Figure 8-9.

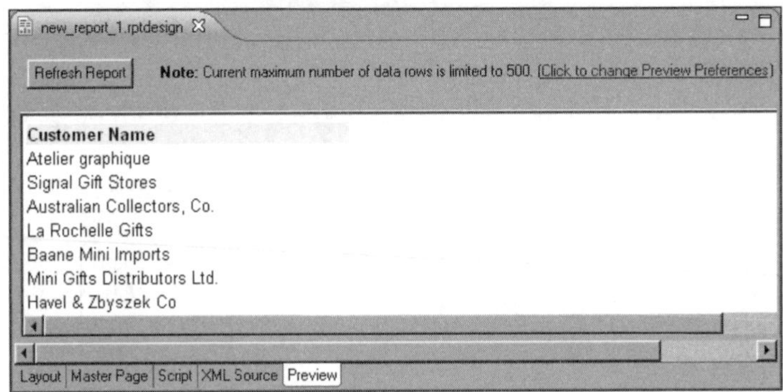

Figure 8-9 Preview of the color change

Using the row object

The row object provides access to the columns of the current row from within the DataSet.onFetch( ) method. You can retrieve the value of any column, using the column name in a statement similar to the following examples:

```
col1Value = row["custNum"];
col1Value = row.custNum;
```

You can only index the column position with the column name if the name is a valid JavaScript name with no spaces or special characters. Alternatively, you can use the column alias if the alias is a valid JavaScript name.

You can also get a column value by numerically indexing the column position, as shown in the following statement:

```
col1Value = row[1];
```

When you index the column position numerically, the number inside the brackets is the position of the column, beginning with 1. You can retrieve the row number with row[0].

Although you use array syntax to access the row object in JavaScript, this object is not a JavaScript array. For this reason, you cannot use JavaScript array properties, such as length, with the row object.

Getting column information

The DataSet object has a getColumnMetaData( ) method, which returns an IColumnMetaData object. The IColumnMetaData interface has methods that provide information about the columns in a data set, as shown in Table 8-2.

Table 8-2 Methods of the IColumnMetaData interface

Method	Returns
getColumnAlias( )	Alias of the specified column.
getColumnCount( )	Number of columns in a row of the result set.
getColumnLabel( )	Column label.
getColumnName( )	Column name at the specified index.
getColumnNativeTypeName( )	Returns the native data type. The data type is null if the column is a computed field or if the type is not known.
getColumnType( )	BIRT data type of the column at the specified index.
getColumnTypeName( )	BIRT data type name of the column at the specified index.
isComputedColumn( )	True or false depending on whether the column is a computed field.

Get the IColumnMetaData object from the dataSet object, as shown in the following statement:

```
columnMetaData = this.getColumnMetaData( );
```

This call is not supported in the beforeOpen or the afterClose events as the instance has not been constructed or has been removed respectively at the time these two events fire.

You can use the count of columns to iterate through all the columns in the data set, as shown in Listing 8-15.

Listing 8-15 Iterating through columns in afterOpen

```
importClass(org.eclipse.birt.report.engine.script.internal
   .instance.DataSetInstance);
//Do not execute when dataset is previewed
if( this instanceof DataSetInstance ){
```

```
cmd = this.getColumnMetaData( );
colCount = cmd.getColumnCount( );
importPackage( Packages.java.io );
out = new PrintWriter( new FileWriter( "c:/temp/columndata.txt",
   true ) );
for ( i = 1; i <= colCount; i++ )
{
   out.println( "Column Details for Column " + i );
   out.println( "Alias: " + cmd.getColumnAlias(i));
   out.println( "Label: " +cmd.getColumnLabel(i));
   out.println( "Name: " +cmd.getColumnName(i));
   out.println( "Native Type: " +cmd.getColumnNativeTypeName(i));
   out.println( "Computed?: " +cmd.isComputedColumn(i));
   out.println( "Type: " +cmd.getColumnType(i));
   out.println( "Type Name: " +cmd.getColumnTypeName(i));
}
out.close( );
}
```

Getting and altering the query string

Get the text of a JDBC query in any DataSet event handler as shown in the following example:

```
query = this.queryText;
```

You can modify a query in the DataSet beforeOpen( ) event handler by setting the value of the queryText string. To change the query, set the queryText string to a valid SQL query, as shown in the following example:

```
queryText = "select * from CLASSICMODELS.CUSTOMERS
   WHERE CLASSICMODELS.CUSTOMERS.CUSTOMERNUMBER
   BETWEEN + params[lownumber].value + AND
   + params[highnumber].value;
```

One advantage of dynamically altering the query is that you can use business logic to determine the query to run. This approach can be more flexible than using parameters. Use this technique to alter other properties of the data source. BIRT also supports modifying data set properties using the property binding feature in the data source and data set editors. One difference between these methods is that property binding applies only to a running report. Scripts also function when previewing the data set.

Use a similar technique to change the query text field for a flat file data source. In the flat file data source, the query stores the name of the flat file from which to read as well as column information. Listing 8-16 shows an example XML snippet for a flat file query.

Listing 8-16 A query on a flat file data source

```
[CDATA[
```

```
select "Age", "Male", "Female"
from CSV1.csv :
{"Age","Age",STRING;"Male","Male",STRING;"Female","Female",STRING}
]]
```

In this example, CSV1 is the file to read. A beforeOpen dataset script can modify the file to read using a simple string replace method, as shown in the following code:

```
qry = this.queryText
this.queryText = qry.replace( "CSV1.csv", "CSV2.csv");
```

Some data sources do not use a queryText field. To change the query for those data sources, modify other data source properties.

Changing data source connection properties

Change the connection properties of a data source by accessing the extensionProperties array of the DataSource object. The ODA extension defines the list of connection properties that can be set at run time.

Table 8-3 describes the JDBC data source properties that affect the connection.

Table 8-3 JDBC data source run-time connection properties

Property	Description
odaUser	Login user name
odaPassword	Login password
odaURL	URL that identifies the data source
odaDriverClass	Driver class for accessing the data source

To change these properties, add code similar to the statements in the data source beforeOpen script in Listing 8-17.

Listing 8-17 Changing data source connection properties in beforeOpen

```
extensionProperties.odaUser = "JoeUser";
extensionProperties.odaPassword = "openSesame";
extensionProperties.odaURL = "jdbc:my_data_source:xxx";
extensionProperties.odaDriverClass = "com.companyb.jdbc.Driver";
extensionProperties.odaJndiName = "java:/MySQLDs";
extensionProperties.OdaConnProfileName = "myprofile";
extensionProperties.OdaConnProfileStorePath = "c:/conprof";
```

Alternatively, set these properties using the following syntax:

```
this.setExtensionProperty("odaURL",
   "jdbc:mysql://localhost/mysql");
```

The beforeFactory event also supports changing connection properties as shown in Listing 8-18.

Listing 8-18 Changing data source connection properties in beforeFactory

```
report = reportContext.getDesignHandle( );
dsHandle = report.findDataSource("Data Source");
dsHandle.setProperty("odaDriverClass", "myDriver");
dsHandle.setProperty("odaURL", "myUrl");
```

You can also set data source and data set properties using the property binding feature in the data source editor.

Getting a parameter value

A script gets the value of a report parameter by passing the name of the parameter to the getParameterValue( ) method of the reportContext object. The following statement gets the value of the UserID parameter:

```
userID = reportContext.getParameterValue( "UserID" );
```

You can also retrieve parameter values using the BIRT global variable, params, in a statement that has the following syntax:

```
userID = params["UserID"].value;
```

BIRT also supports dynamic parameters that allow selecting multiple values. Access these parameters using the following syntaxes:

```
reportContext.getParameterValue( "MultiParm" )[0];
```

```
params["MultiParm"].value[0];
```

The previous statements retrieve the first value of a multivalued parameter. Determine the number of selected values by using the following syntaxes:

```
reportContext.getParameterValue( "MultiParm" ).length;
```

```
params["MultiParm"].value.length;
```

You can use these features when implementing a beforeOpen event handler to apply an IN clause to a query, as shown in Listing 8-19.

Listing 8-19 Accessing multiple parameter values in beforeOpen

```
var parmcount = params["parmorders"].value.length
var whereclause = "";
if( parmcount > 0 ){
   whereclause = " where customernumber in ( ";
}
for( i=0; i < parmcount; i++ ){
   if( i == 0 ){
      whereclause = whereclause + params["parmorders"].value[i];
```

```
   }else{
      whereclause = whereclause + " , " +
   params["parmorders"].value[i];
   }
}
if( parmcount > 0 ){
   this.queryText = this.queryText + whereclause + " ) ";
}
```

Data sets also have parameters. These parameters affect the specific data set. Typically, data set parameters are linked to a report parameter or bound to an outer table column value when the data set is bound to a nested table. Data set scripts support getting and setting values for parameters. Set the value of the parameter before the data set runs in the beforeOpen of the data set, as shown in Listing 8-20.

Listing 8-20 Setting a data set parameter value in beforeOpen

```
//set input parameter
inputParams["alpha"] = 5;
//or
this.setInputParameterValue("alpha", 5);
You can get the value by referencing the inputParams array or
   using the this.getInputParameterValue method.
```

Determining script execution sequence

You can determine the script execution sequence by writing code that generates a file containing a line for every script that you want to track.

To create an output file containing the script execution sequence, include initialization code in the ReportDesign.initialize script and finalization code in the ReportDesign.afterFactory script. In each script that you want to track, add code to write a line of text to the output file. It is easier to write the code in JavaScript than Java, but it is possible to write analogous code in Java.

The following sections show how to use JavaScript to determine script execution sequence.

Providing the ReportDesign.initialize code

The following code in the ReportDesign.initialize method creates a file on your hard drive and adds one line to the file.

```
importPackage( Packages.java.io );
fos = new java.io.FileOutputStream( "c:\\logFile.txt" );
printWriter = new java.io.PrintWriter( fos );
printWriter.println( "ReportDesign.initialize" );
```

The preceding code performs the following tasks:

- Imports the Java package, java.io
- Creates a file output stream for the file you want to create
- Creates a PrintWriter object that every script can use to track script execution sequence

How to provide code for the ReportDesign.initialize script

1 Choose the Script tab.

2 In Outline, select the top line, as shown in Figure 8-10.

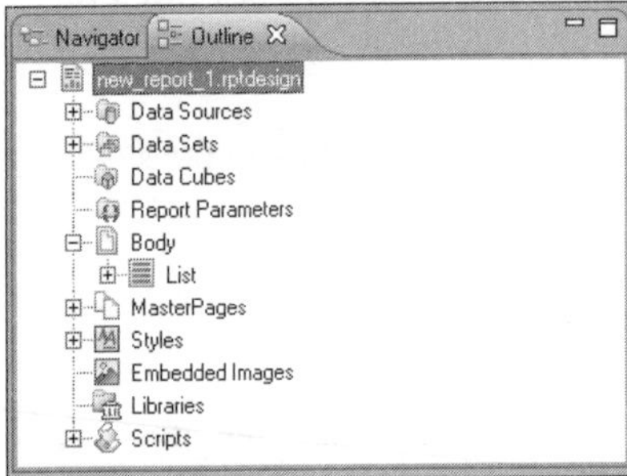

Figure 8-10 Selecting the report design

3 In Script, select initialize.

4 Type the code into the script editor, as shown in Figure 8-11.

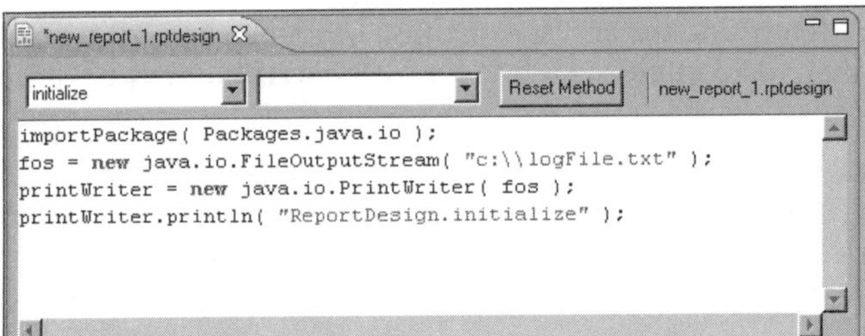

Figure 8-11 Providing ReportDesign.initialize code

Providing code for the scripts you want to track

In every script that you want to track, type a single statement generating a line of output to your log file, as shown in the following statement:

```
printWriter.println( "Table.onRow" );
```

First, select the appropriate report element in Outline. Then, select the appropriate script from the script selection list. Use the same steps to type code into the script as shown in the preceding section.

Providing the ReportDesign.afterFactory code

To close the log file, add the following statement to ReportDesign.afterFactory:

```
printWriter.close( );
```

Using this method flushes all the buffers and ensures that all script output appears in the file.

To provide the ReportDesign.afterFactory code, select the top line of the outline and select the afterFactory script on the script page.

Tutorial 1: Writing an event handler in JavaScript

This tutorial provides instructions for writing a set of event handlers. The tutorial shows a basic report design that accesses the Classic Models, Inc. sample database. The design contains a table of customers with a column for the customer name. In this tutorial, you count customer names containing the string, Mini, then display the result in a pop-up window. These event handlers provide functionality equivalent to using an aggregate report item without the use of script.

In this tutorial, you perform the following tasks:

- Create the report design
- Create a counter in Table.onCreate
- Conditionally increment the counter
- Display the result

Task 1: Create the report design

Create a report design that uses the Classic Models, Inc. sample database to display a list of customer names.

The design appears in the layout editor, as shown in Figure 8-12.

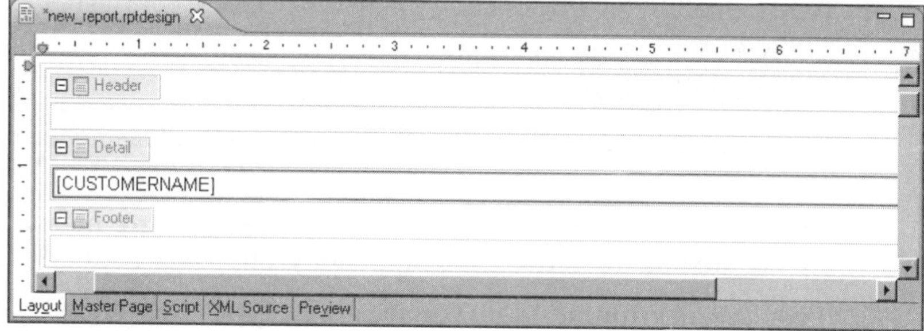

Figure 8-12 Report design in the layout editor

Task 2: Create a counter in Table.onCreate

To count the number of customers whose names contain the string Mini, first declare a global counter and set its value to zero. The Table.onCreate method is the most appropriate place to perform this task because Table.onCreate executes before retrieving any rows. In the next task, you conditionally increment this counter in the Row.onCreate( ) method.

1 In Layout, select the list by placing the cursor near the bottom left corner of the list. The list icon appears, as shown in Figure 8-13.

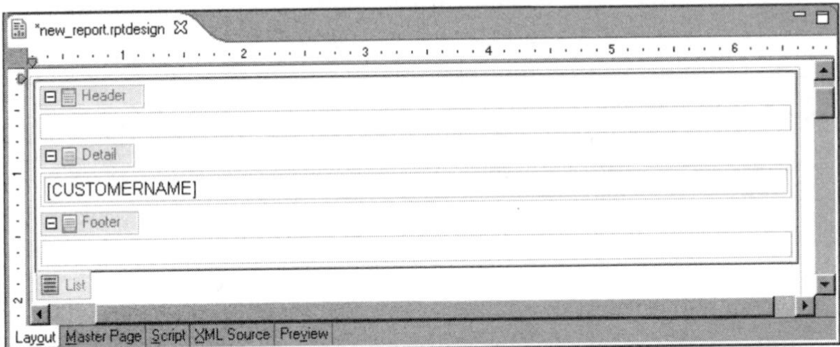

Figure 8-13 List icon in the layout editor

2 Choose the Script tab. The script editor appears, as shown in Figure 8-14.

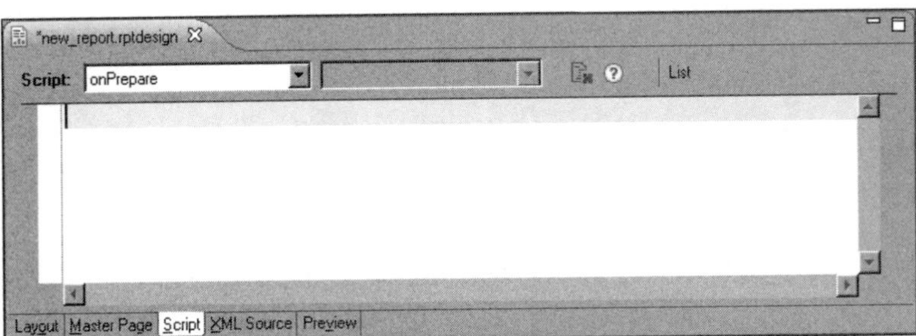

Figure 8-14 Script window

3 Select onCreate from the list of available scripts.

4 Type the following line of code in the script editor for the onCreate method:

```
countOfMinis = 0;
```

5 To run the report and verify that the code did not create any errors, choose Preview.

6 Scroll to the bottom of the report, where JavaScript error messages appear. If there are no errors, the report appears as shown in Figure 8-15.

If you see an error message, you may have typed the statement incorrectly. If so, go back to the script window, select the method you just modified, correct the error, and choose Preview again.

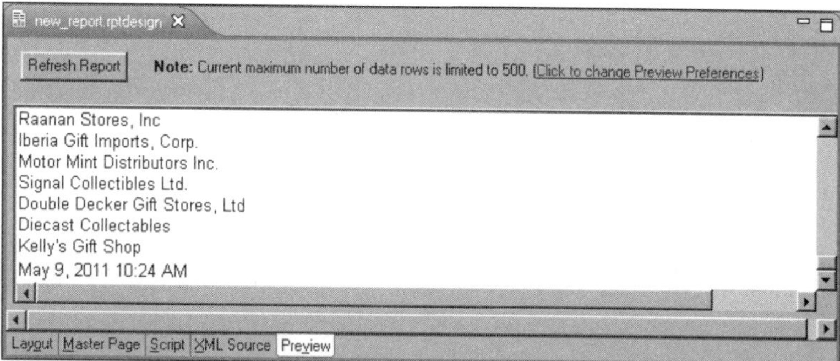

Figure 8-15 Report preview

Task 3: Conditionally increment the counter

To count the number of customers with the string Mini in their names, examine each customer's name and add one to the counter for every occurrence. A logical place to perform this task is in the Row.onCreate method, which executes for every retrieval of a row of data from the data source.

1 In Layout, select the Row. Then, choose Script.

2 From the list of available scripts at the top of the script window and select onCreate, as shown in Figure 8-16.

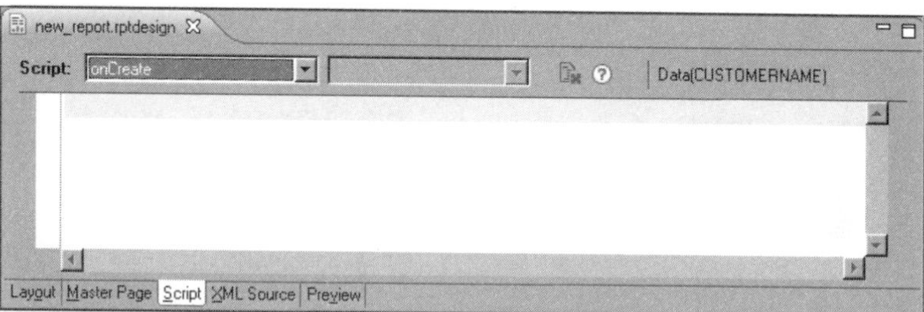

Figure 8-16 onCreate( ) in the script window

3 Type the following line of JavaScript code in the Script window:

```
row=this.getRowData( );
```

Notice that when you enter the period after this, a pop-up containing all the available methods and properties, including getRowData appears. This line of code gets an instance of IRowData, which has a method, getExpressionValue( ), to get the contents of a column of the row.

4 Type the following line of JavaScript below the line you typed in step 3:

```
CustName=row.getExpressionValue( "row[CUSTOMERNAME]" );
```

This line of code returns the contents of the table column that comes from the CUSTOMERNAME column in the data set.

5 Type the following line of code to increment conditionally the counter you created in Task 2:

```
if( CustName.indexOf( "Mini" ) != -1 ) countOfMinis += 1;
```

You can use the JavaScript palette to insert each of the following elements in the preceding line:

- indexOf( )
  Select Native (JavaScript) Objects➛String Functions➛indexOf( )
- !=
  Select Operators➛Comparison➛!=
- +=
  Select Operators➛Assignment➛+=

6 Choose Preview to run the report again to verify that the code you entered did not create any errors.

Task 4: Display the result

To display the count of customers with the string Mini in their names, insert code in a method that runs after the processing of all the rows in the list. One logical place for this code is in the ReportDesign.afterFactorymethod.

1 In Outline, select the report design, as shown in Figure 8-17.

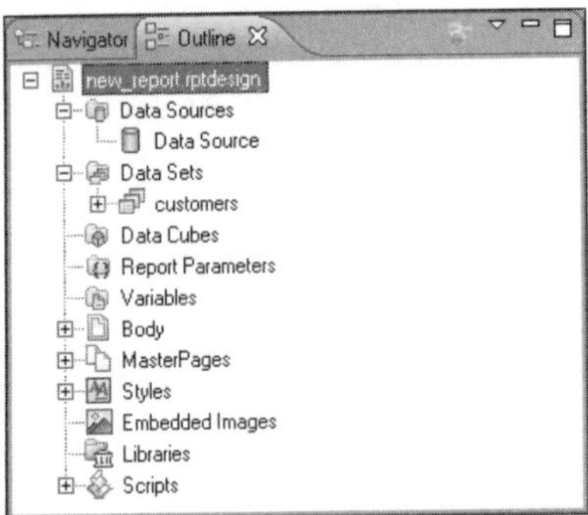

Figure 8-17 Selecting the report design in Outline

2 Select the afterFactory method from the list of available scripts in the script editor.

3 Type the following code into the afterFactory method:

```
importPackage( Packages.javax.swing );
frame = new JFrame( "Count of Minis = " + countOfMinis );
frame.setBounds( 310, 220, 300, 20 );
frame.show( );
```

4 Select Preview to see the results. If there are no errors in the code, you see a report similar to the one in Figure 8-18.

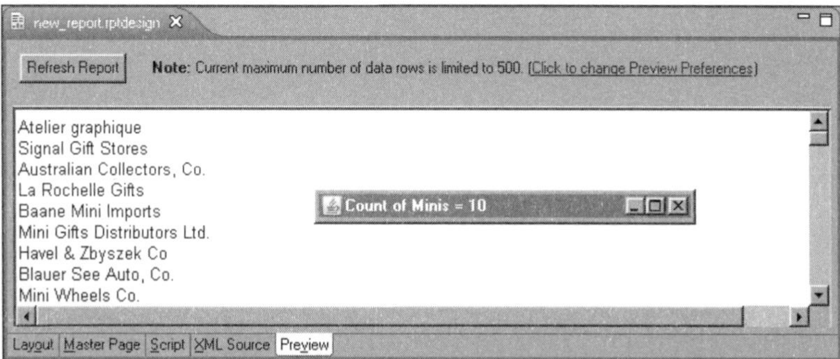

Figure 8-18 Result of changing the afterFactory( ) method

If you do not see the Count of Minis window, look for it behind the Eclipse window. If the Count of Minis window does not appear, the most likely reason is a scripting error caused by an error in one of your code entries.

If you suspect that a scripting error occurred, scroll to the bottom of the report where all scripting error messages appear. In most situations, there is a brief error message next to a plus sign (+). The plus sign indicates that there is a more detailed error message that is only visible after you expand the brief error message. To expand the brief error message, choose the plus sign. Scroll down to see the more detailed error message.

JavaScript event handler examples

The following examples illustrate some of the common functions that you can use JavaScript event handlers to perform.

JavaScript onPrepare example

The onPrepare event fires for all report elements during the preparation phase of the generation process. This location is ideal for changing the design of a particular report element before generating the individual report item instances.

For example, BIRT supports grouping in tables and lists. To permit the user to group the data, you can implement this feature by performing the following developer tasks:

- Add a group to a table
- Select the group in the outline view of the report
- Create an onPrepare script that changes the group definition for the table

Listing 8-21 groups a table by country or city using a Boolean parameter to determine the grouping column to use:

Listing 8-21 Setting a table grouping key

```
if( params[ "grp_p" ].value == true ){
   this.keyExpr = "row[ 'CITY' ];";
   grpname = "City";
}else{
   this.keyExpr = "row[ 'COUNTRY' ];";
   grpname = "Country";
}
```

JavaScript onCreate examples

The onCreate event fires when the generation process creates an instance of the report element. Writing an event handler for an onCreate event is useful when changing an instance of a report item. The following examples illustrate this concept.

Image elements can source image data from a URL, an embedded image in a report, an image file in the resource folder, or a blob type from a database. To retrieve the data for the image at run time, use an onCreate event handler. Listing 8-22 illustrates how to use Java to read the data from an image stored on the local file system.

Listing 8-22 Accessing an image from a file

```
importPackage( Packages.java.io );
importPackage( Packages.java.lang );

var file = new File( "c:/temp/test.png" );
var ist = new FileInputStream( file );
var lengthi = file.length( );

bytesa = new ByteArrayOutputStream( lengthi );
var c;
while( ( c=ist.read( ) ) != -1 ){
      bytesa.write( c );
}
ist.close( );
this.data = bytesa.toByteArray( );
```

If the image element is in a table, you can choose the selected file based on the data retrieved from the dataset. For example, the onCreate script in Listing 8-23 selects an image from the resource folder based on calculations made on the table bound columns.

Listing 8-23 Conditionally selecting an image file

```
if ( ( ( this.getRowData( ).getColumnValue( "total2005" ) / 5 ) /
   ( this.getRowData( ).getColumnValue( "total2004" ) / 12)) >=
```

```
        .96 ) {
    this.file ="up.gif";
}
else if( ( ( this.getRowData( ).getColumnValue( "total2005" ) /
            5 ) / ( this.getRowData( ).getColumnValue( "total2004" )
    /
            12 ) ) <= .85 ) {
                this.file ="down.gif";
        }
    else {
        this.file ="even.gif";
}
```

BIRT supports conditional element formatting, using the highlight editor. You can also use the onCreate event handler to do conditional formatting, as shown in Listing 8-24. This example is an onCreate event handler for a table row. If the table column QUANTITYORDERED is greater than 40, the row height increases to 2 centimeters, is highlighted in yellow, and the content appears in the middle of the row.

Listing 8-24 Conditionally formatting a report item

```
if( this.getRowData( ).getColumnValue( "QUANTITYORDERED" ) > 40 ){
    this.getStyle( ).backgroundColor = "yellow";
    this.getStyle( ).verticalAlign = "Middle";
    this.height = "2cm";
}
```

JavaScript onRender examples

Rendering content may occur anytime after generation. Often users run a report and re-render it many times in different formats. The onRender events support some customization at render time. For example, a user may want a label in the page footer to show the render time of the report or the day of the month the report rendered. You can achieve this effect by using the onRender method of a label element, as shown in the following the following script:

```
importPackage( Packages.java.util );
cl = new GregorianCalendar( );
this.text = cl.get( Calendar.DAY_OF_MONTH );
```

Cross-tab script examples

Cross tabs support writing event scripts. As with other report items the cross tab supports an onPrepare, onCreate, and onRender event. Each of these events supports writing a handler for the cross tab or the cross-tab cell. When implementing an onCreate event for the cross-tab cell, the handler is passed a cellInst object. This object is an instance of a cell object that provides methods to determine the cell properties. For example, the developer can call cellInst.getCellType( ). This method returns either aggregation or header, representing a cross tab. Use the cellInst.getCellID( ) to determine what specific design-time cell is being processed. This method returns the Element ID defined in the general properties for a cell. The cellInst object also provides a method, getDataValue, which returns the specific value of a cross-tab binding at the time the cell is created. The method getStyle( ) supports customizing the appearance of a specific cell. The following script illustrates the mechanics of using these methods.

The script in Listing 8-25 is executed for the header cells that are either in the row header cells or column header cells. The script then checks to see if the dimension value for the specific cell is equal to Planes. If it is the background is set to red and the font size is set to 12. All other header cells are set to yellow.

Next the cell id is checked and if the element ID is 24, the cell background color is set to Orange.

Listing 8-25 Setting cross-tab header cell properties

```
function onCreateCell( cellInst, reportContext )
{
   //Can reference cells by type or id - valid types "header" or
   "aggregation"
   if( cellInst.getCellType( ) == "header" ) {
      //Get data values see binding tab on crosstab
      if( cellInst.getDataValue("PRODUCTLINE") == "Planes" ){
            cellInst.getStyle( ).setBackgroundColor("#FF0000");
         cellInst.getStyle( ).setFontSize("12");
      }else{
         //Set the rest to yellow
         cellInst.getStyle( ).setBackgroundColor("#FFFF00");
         cellInst.getStyle( ).setFontSize("12");
      }
   }
   //refer to crosstab header
   if( cellInst.getCellID( ) == 24){
      cellInst.getStyle( ).setBackgroundColor("Orange");
   }
```

The script in Listing 8-26 continues the onCreateCell script in Listing 8-25, handling setting colors for the aggregation elements which make up the bulk of the cross tab. First, if the product line is Planes the cell background color is set to blue-gray. This setting ensures all the cells in the particular row or column that correspond to the Planes value of the product line appear blue-gray. So, if the product line dimension is on the column level the specific column appears blue-gray or if the product dimension is on the row level, the specific row appears blue-gray. Finally, if the measure amount is greater than 50000, the cell background color is set to green and the font color is set to white. In this example, you can use getDataValue to retrieve data binding values that are defined in the bindings tab for the cross tab.

Listing 8-26 Setting aggregation cell properties

```
if( cellInst.getCellType( ) == "aggregation"){
   //Can reference value using getDataValue or
   if( cellInst.getDataValue("PRODUCTLINE") == "Planes" ){
      //set color to blue-gray

cellInst.getStyle( ).setBackgroundColor("RGB(169,170,226)");
   }
   //by using reportContext.evaluate
   //if( reportContext.evaluate("measure['amount']") > 50000 ){
   if( cellInst.getDataValue("amount_DateGroup/
quarter_ProductGroup/PRODUCTLINE") > 50000 ){
      cellInst.getStyle( ).setBackgroundColor("Green");
      cellInst.getStyle( ).setColor("White");
   }
}
}
```

Alternatively, you can use the reportContext.evaluate( ) method to evaluate a specific expression. In the example:

```
if( reportContext.evaluate("measure['amount']") > 50000 ){
```

and

```
if( cellInst.getDataValue("amount_DateGroup/
   quarter_ProductGroup/PRODUCTLINE") > 50000 ){
```

are equivalent if the expression for the amount_DateGroup /quarter_ProductGroup/PRODUCTLINE binding is measure['amount']. The value for this binding is the value for row-column intersection point.

Calling external JavaScript functions

In addition to executing JavaScript within a report, BIRT provides the option to use external JavaScript files located in the resource folder. Use the resources View and the property editor to associate these files with the selected report. For example, an external JavaScript file has the following content:

```
function getMyValue( ){
   return "This is a test of the add js button";
}
```

If this file is located in the resource folder, a report developer can select the resources tab of the property editor and add the JavaScript file to the report. The JavaScript file is not imported, but is referenced in the report. After making this association, the developer can call getMyValue( ) in any BIRT expression or any of the event handler scripts.

Calling Java from JavaScript

Rhino provides excellent integration with Java classes, supporting a BIRT script working seamlessly with business logic written in Java. Using a JavaScript wrapping means the developer can leverage both internal and external libraries of existing Java code. You can use static methods, non-static methods, and static constants of a Java class.

Understanding the Packages object

The Packages object is the JavaScript gateway to the Java classes. It is a top-level Rhino object that contains properties for every top-level Java package, such as java and com. The Packages object contains a property for every package that it finds in its classpath. Use the Packages object to access a Java class for which Packages has a property by preceding the class name with Packages, as shown in the following statement:

```
var nc = new Packages.javax.swing.JFrame( "MyFrame );
```

You can also use the Packages object to reference a Java class that is not a part of a package, as shown in the following statement:

```
var nc = new Packages.NumberConversion( );
```

For BIRT to find a custom Java class or package, the file must be in the classpath, as discussed later in this chapter.

Understanding the importPackage method

You can avoid writing a fully qualified reference to a Java class by using the top-level Rhino method importPackage( ). The importPackage( ) method functions like a Java import statement. Use the importPackage( ) method to specify one or more Java packages that contain the Java classes that you need to access, as shown in the following statement:

```
importPackage( Packages.java.io, Packages.javax.swing );
```

You must prefix the name of each package with Packages. After the first time BIRT executes a method containing the importPackage( ) method, the specified packages are available to all succeeding scripts. For this reason, include the importPackage( ) in the ReportDesign.initialize script, which is always the first script that BIRT executes.

Java imports java.lang.* implicitly. Rhino, on the other hand, does not import java.lang.* implicitly because JavaScript has several top-level objects of the same names as some classes defined in the java.lang package. These classes include Boolean, Math, Number, Object, and String. Importing java.lang causes a name collision with the JavaScript objects of the same name. For this reason, avoid using importPackage( ) to import java.lang.

Using a Java class

To use a Java class in a BIRT script, set a JavaScript object equal to the Java object. Then, call the Java class methods on the JavaScript object. Listing 8-27 creates a Java Swing frame and sets the JavaScript object named frame to the Java JFrame object. Then, the code calls the setBounds( ) and show( ) methods directly on the JavaScript object.

Listing 8-27 Calling Java methods on a JavaScript object

```
importPackage( Packages.javax.swing );
frame = new JFrame( "My Frame" );
frame.setBounds( 300, 300, 300, 20 );
frame.show( );
```

The effect of this code example is to display a Java window containing the title, My Frame, on your desktop. This code example works only in the BIRT Report Designer.

Placing Java classes

For BIRT report viewer to find Java classes, the classes must be under the following folder:

```
$ECLIPSE_INSTALL\plugins org.eclipse.birt.report
   .viewer_*\birt\WEB-INF\classes
```

Alternatively, package the classes as a JAR file put in into:

```
$ECLIPSE_INSTALL\plugins org.eclipse.birt.report
   .viewer_*\birt\scriptlib
```

BIRT Report Designer also finds classes in a Java project within the same workspace as the report project. Attach additional JAR files in the resource folder to a specific report by using the resource properties tab for the report.

If you deploy the example Viewer to an application server, you must also deploy these classes or JAR files to the run-time environment., unless the JAR files already exist in the classpath of the application.

Place event handlers and Java classes in the SCRIPTLIB directory defined in the web.xml of the web viewer application. If using the SCRIPTLIB directory, the classes must be in JAR format.

If you are using the report engine API, the classes must be in the classpath. Alternatively, use a system variable that the report engine adds to the classpath as follows:

```
System.setProperty( EngineConstants.WEBAPP_CLASSPATH_KEY,
              "c:/myjars/class.jar" );
```

If you are using the report engine API, you can set the parent class loader for the engine by setting the APPCONTEXT_CLASSLOADER_KEY in the application context, as shown in Listing 8-28:

Listing 8-28 Setting the parent class loader for the report engine

```
config = new EngineConfig( );
HashMap hm = config.getAppContext( );
hm.put( EngineConstants.APPCONTEXT_CLASSLOADER_KEY,
     YourClass.class.getClassLoader( ) );
config.setAppContext( hm );
```

Setting the application context class loader supports report script accessing objects in the parent class loader.

Issues with using Java in JavaScript code

There are many nuances to writing Java code, such as how to handle overloaded methods and how to use interfaces. For more information on these topics, refer to the Rhino page on scripting Java at http://www.mozilla.org/rhino/ScriptingJava.html.

Calling the method of a class in a plug-in

Both Java and JavaScript event handlers have access to all the public methods of any class that resides in an Eclipse plug-in. The plug-in can be one of the core Eclipse plug-ins, a plug-in supplied by a third party, or one of your own creations. As long as the plug-in is available to the BIRT report at run time, a BIRT script has access to all the public methods of all the classes within that plug-in.

Listing 8-29 shows how to call a method of a Java class that resides in an Eclipse plug-in:

Listing 8-29 Using JavaScript to access a method of a Java class in an Eclipse plug-in

```
importPackage( Packages.org.eclipse.core.runtime );
mybundle = Platform.getBundle( "org.eclipse.myCorp.security" );
validateClass = mybundle.loadClass(
   "org.eclipse.myCorp.security.Validate" );
validateInstance = validateClass.newInstance( );
var password = validateInstance.getPass( loginID );
```

In the example, the first statement makes the Eclipse core package, org.eclipse.core.runtime, available to the JavaScript code. This package contains two classes, Platform and Bundle, which the rest of the script requires.

The Platform class contains a static method, getBundle( ), that returns a Bundle object. The sole argument to getBundle( ) is the name of the plug-in that contains the target class.

The Bundle class contains a loadClass( ) method that returns a java.lang.Class object. The only argument to loadClass( ) is a fully qualified class name, which in this case is org.eclipse.myCorp.security.Validate.

The java.lang.Class class represents the target class and contains a newInstance( ) method that returns an instance of the class. newInstance( ) creates the instance using the default constructor, which has no arguments. The final statement in the example calls the target method of the newly instantiated object of the target class.

Listing 8-30 shows the Java equivalent of Listing 8-29:

Listing 8-30 Using Java to access a method of a Java class in an Eclipse plug-in

```
#import org.eclipse.core.runtime.Bundle;
#import org.eclipse.core.runtime.Platform;
#import org.eclipse.myCorp.security.Validate;

Bundle mybundle = Platform.getBundle(
   "org.eclipse.myCorp.security" );
java.lang.Class validateClass = mybundle.loadClass(
   "org.eclipse.myCorp.security.Validate" );
Validate validateInstance = validateClass.newInstance( );
String password = validateInstance.getPass( loginID );
```

Chapter

9

Using Java to Write an Event Handler

Creating a Java event handler is more complex than creating a JavaScript event handler. You cannot type Java code directly in BIRT Report Designer.

To create a Java event handler class, compile the source for the Java class and make the class visible to BIRT. Creating a Java event handler for BIRT is simplified, however, by the fact that Eclipse is a robust Java development environment and supports integrating a Java project with a BIRT project.

Writing a Java event handler class

To provide one or more Java event handlers for a scriptable BIRT element, create one class that contains all the Java event handlers for that element. Creating a class that contains event handler methods for more than one element is not advisable.

BIRT provides a set of Java interfaces and Java adapter classes to simplify the process of writing a Java event handler class. There is one interface and one adapter class for every scriptable BIRT element. An element's event handler interface defines all the event handler methods for that element. A handler class must implement every method defined in the interface, even if some of the methods are empty. You provide code for only the event handlers that you want to implement.

Locating the JAR files for a BIRT event handler

Each of two JAR files contains all the classes and interfaces that an event handler requires. One of the JAR files is a part of BIRT Report Designer and

SDK and the other one is a part of BIRT Report Engine. Use either JAR file to develop a custom event handler.

The first JAR file that you can use for developing a Java event handler is org.eclipse.birt.report.engine_<version>.jar, which is located in the Eclipse plugins directory for BIRT Report Designer and SDK. The second JAR file that you use when you develop and deploy your report is scriptapi.jar, which is located in the \WebViewerExample\WEB-INF\lib directory of BIRT Report Engine.

All JAR files in the \WebViewerExample\WEB-INF\lib directory are in the deployed report classpath, so scriptapi.jar is accessible at run time. To use the scriptapi.jar file in the development phase, download the Report Engine and reference scriptapi.jar from within the build path.

The required JAR files are also in the ReportEngine\lib directory of BIRT Report Engine. If you are using the Report Engine API to run reports, add the JAR files in this directory to the classpath and build path. If you are using the report engine plug-in in an Eclipse application, this step is not required, because the plug-in already contains the dependency and classpath entries.

Extending an adapter class

An element adapter class implements the element interface and provides empty stubs for every method. To use the adapter class, extend the adapter class and override the methods for which you are providing handler code. Eclipse recommends extending an adapter class rather than implementing an interface directly.

BIRT naming conventions for the event handler interfaces and adapter classes are discussed later in this chapter.

How to create an event handler class and add it to the Java project

This section describes the process for using the Eclipse Java development environment to create an event handler class for a scriptable BIRT element. The steps assume that the Java perspective is open and that a Java project exists in the workspace.

1 Add org.eclipse.birt.report.engine_<version>.jar to a Java project, as described in the following steps:

   1 In Navigator, select a Java project and choose File→Properties. In Properties, select Java Build Path→Libraries. In Java Build Path, choose Add External JARs.

   2 In JAR Selection, navigate to the Eclipse /plugins directory. In a default Eclipse installation, this directory is in the following location:

   ```
   <ECLIPSE_INSTALL>\eclipse\plugins
   ```

   3 Select org.eclipse.birt.core_<version>.jar. Use control-click to select org.eclipse.birt.report.engine_<version>.jar. Choose Open. Java Build Path appears, as shown in Figure 9-1. Choose OK.

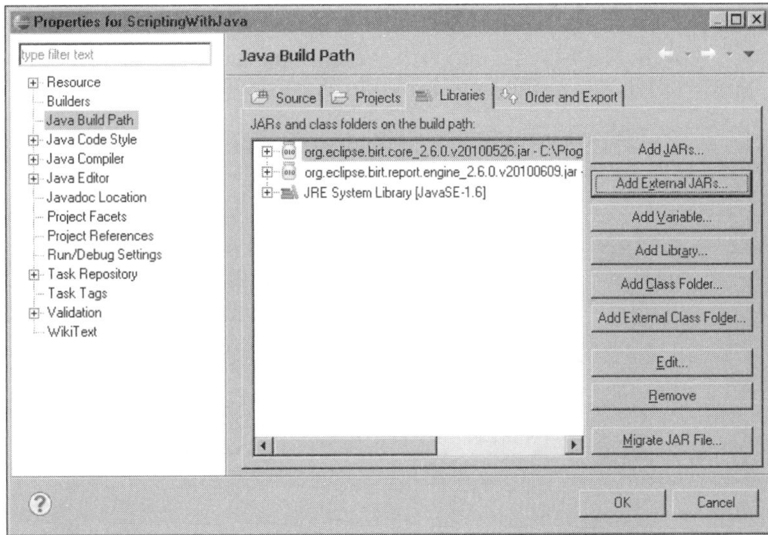

Figure 9-1 The report engine JAR file in the build path

2 Select the Java project and choose File➛New➛Class.

3 To set up the Java class properties, perform the following steps in New Java Class:

1 Navigate to the folder where you want the Java source file to reside by choosing the Browse button beside Source Folder.

2 If the new Java class is a part of a package, type the fully qualified package name in Package.

3 In Name, type a name for the class.

4 In Modifiers, select Public.

5 Select the ROM element event adapter class to extend:

- Choose the Browse button beside Superclass.
- In Superclass Selection, in Choose a type, type the name of the event adapter class for the ROM element. For example, for a label element, type LabelEventAdapter, as shown in Figure 9-2.

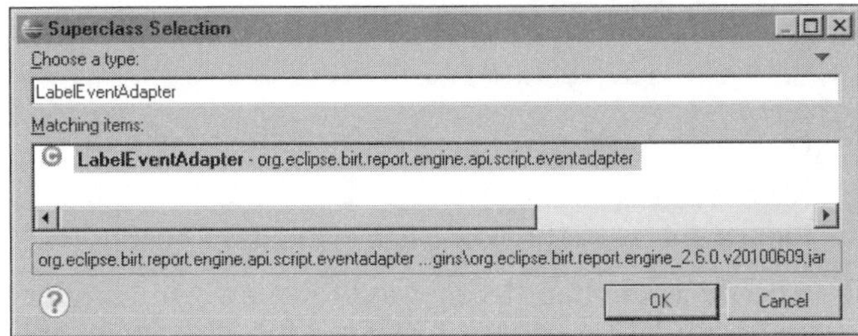

Figure 9-2 Selecting a Superclass

- Choose OK.

4 In New Java Class, select Generate comments. New Java Class appears similar to the one shown in Figure 9-3.

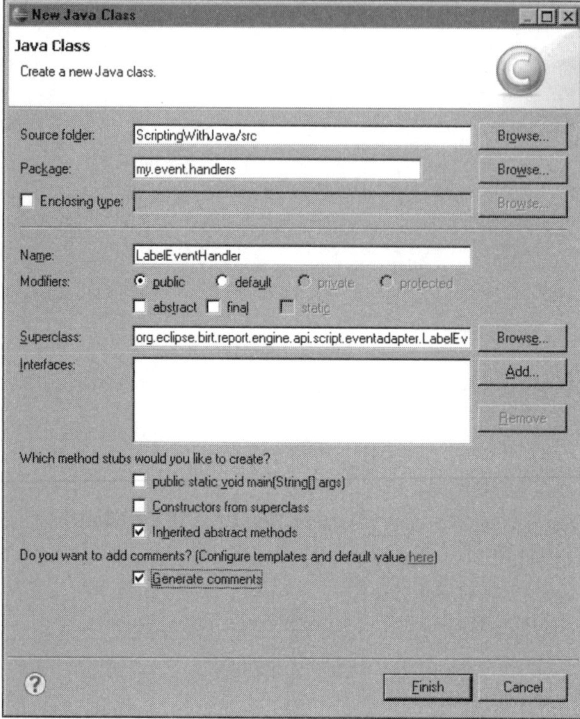

Figure 9-3 New Java Class final properties

5 Choose Finish. The Java editor appears, similar to the one shown in Figure 9-4.

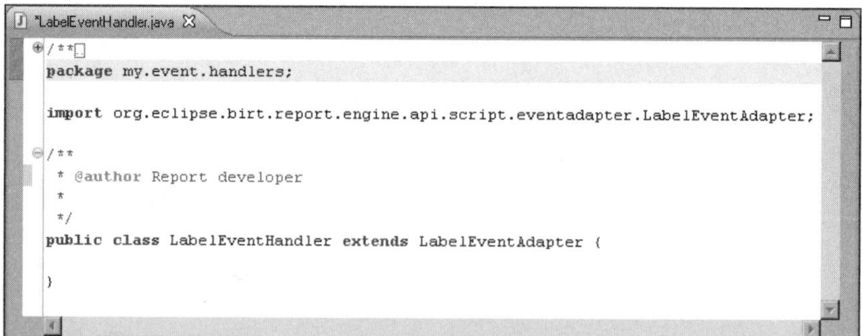

Figure 9-4 The new class in the Java editor

6 Add the event handler method for the event handler class. Import all required classes. Figure 9-5 shows the addition of an onPrepare( ) method that sets the background color of a label to red.

```
/**
package my.event.handlers;

import org.eclipse.birt.report.engine.api.script.IReportContext;
import org.eclipse.birt.report.engine.api.script.ScriptException;
import org.eclipse.birt.report.engine.api.script.element.ILabel;
import org.eclipse.birt.report.engine.api.script.eventadapter.LabelEventAdapter;

/**
 * @author Report developer
 *
 */
public class LabelEventHandler extends LabelEventAdapter {
    public void onPrepare( ILabel arg0, IReportContext arg1 ){
        try {
            arg0.getStyle().setBackgroundColor( "red" );
        } catch (ScriptException e) {
            e.printStackTrace();
        }
    }
}
```

Figure 9-5 The onPrepare( ) method in the Java editor

7 Choose File➛Save.

Making the Java class visible to BIRT

One way to make a Java event handler class visible to the BIRT report designer is to create a Java development project to compile the class in the same workspace as the BIRT report project. The other option is to place the class in a directory or JAR file specified in the BIRT classpath. To deploy the report to an application server, copy the Java class to the appropriate location on the server.

Associating a Java event handler class with a report element

After creating the Java event handler class and coding the appropriate handler methods, associate the class with a report element.

How to associate a Java class with a report element

The steps in this procedure make the following assumptions:

- A report design is open in the Report Design perspective.
- The report design includes a scriptable report item, such as a label.
- A Java class containing event handler methods for the scriptable report item is visible to BIRT.

1 In Outline, select the report element for which an event handler class is visible to BIRT, as shown in Figure 9-6.

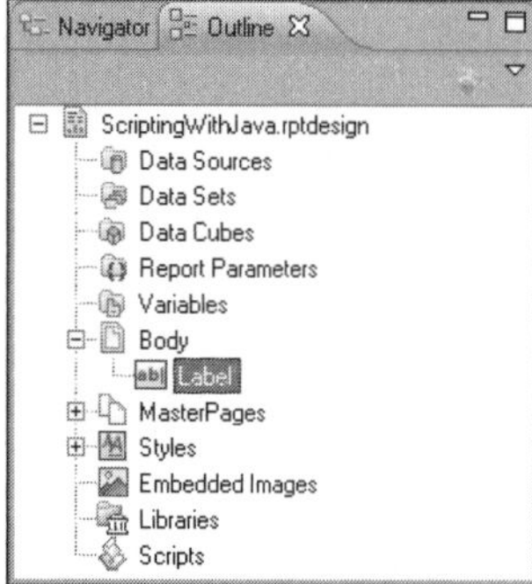

Figure 9-6 Selecting a report element

2 In Property Editor, choose Event Handler, as shown in Figure 9-7.

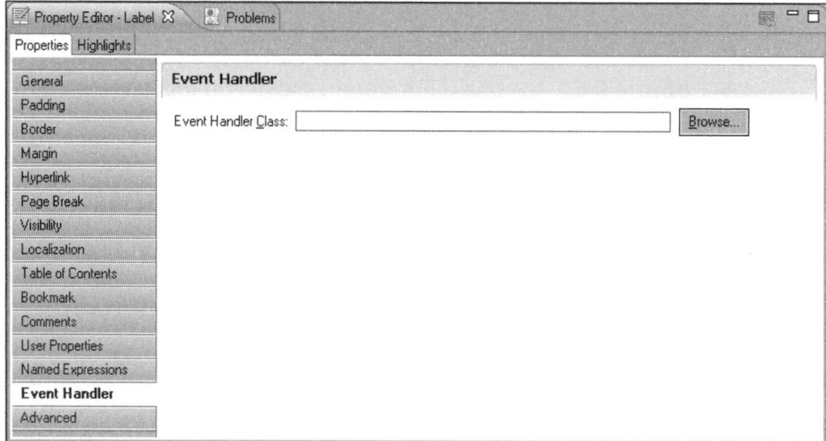

Figure 9-7 Event handler properties

3 Choose Browse. Class Selection shows available event handler classes.

4 Select the event handler class that extends the BIRT ROM event adapter class, as shown in Figure 9-8. Then, choose OK.

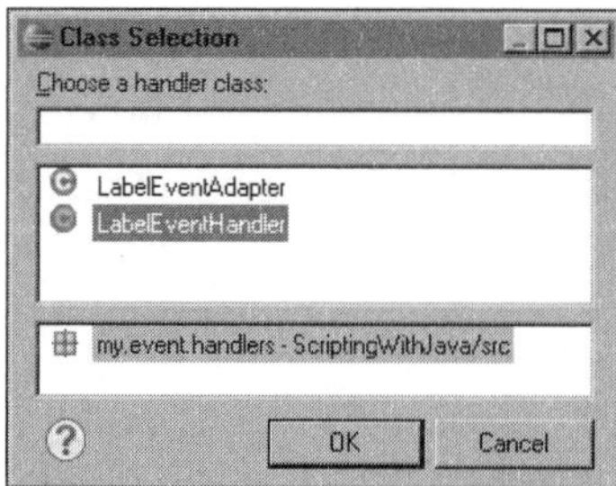

Figure 9-8 Selecting the event handler class

The fully qualified name of the event handler class appears in Property Editor, as shown in Figure 9-9.

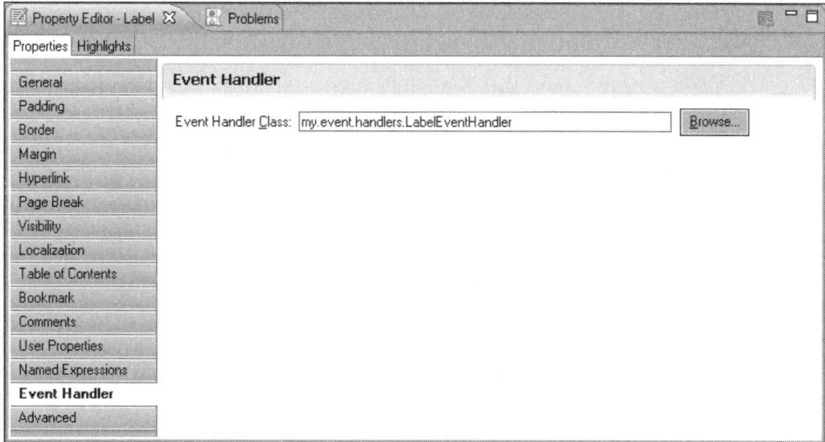

Figure 9-9 The event handler class name

5 Preview the report. The label's background color is red.

BIRT Java interface and class naming conventions

BIRT event handler class and interface names use the following conventions:

- Event handler interfaces
  All BIRT ROM element interface names begin with the letter I, which is followed by the name of the ROM element and then EventHandler. For example, the interface for the Label element is ILabelEventHandler.
- Event handler adapter classes
  All BIRT ROM element adapter class names begin with the name of the element, followed by EventAdapter. For example, the name of the adapter class for a Label element is LabelEventAdapter.
- ROM element instance interfaces
  All BIRT ROM element instance interface names begin with the letter I, followed by the name of the element and then Instance. For example, the ROM element instance interface for a Label element is ILabelInstance.
- ROM element design interfaces
  All BIRT ROM element instance design interface names begin with the letter I, followed by the name of the element. For example, the design interface for a Label element is ILabel.

Writing a Java event handler

Most scriptable elements have more than one event for which you can write a handler. If you write an event handler for any event of an element, the event handler class must include methods for all the events for that element. You can leave empty those methods that do not require handler code.

You can give an event handler class any name you choose. Associate the class with a report element in BIRT Report Designer in the Properties view, as explained earlier in this chapter. The Java event handler class can either extend an adapter class or implement an event handler interface. The following sections explain adapter classes and handler interfaces.

Using event handler adapter classes

BIRT provides event handler adapter classes for every scriptable report element. An event handler adapter class contains empty methods for every event handler method for the element. If your class extends an adapter class, override only the methods for the events for which you want to provide handler code.

One advantage of using an adapter class instead of implementing an interface is that the class compiles even if methods are added to the interface in a future release. If the signature of an event handler method changes in a future release, however, you must change your implementation of that method to reflect the signature change. The class compiles even if you do not change the method with the changed signature, but the method with the wrong signature is never called.

Using event handler interfaces

BIRT provides event handler interfaces for every scriptable report element. If your event handler class extends an adapter class, the adapter class implements the correct interface. If your class does not extend an adapter class, then your class must implement the appropriate interface for the report element.

There are some advantages of specifying an interface instead of extending an adapter class. Eclipse generates stubs for every method the interface specifies. The stubs show the method arguments, so you can see the argument types of the methods to implement. If your class extends an adapter class, there are no generated stubs for you to examine. You also have more freedom in the design of your class structure if you avoid using an adapter class.

For example, you might want two or more event handler classes to extend a single base class. Because Java does not support multiple inheritance, the event handler class cannot extend both the adapter class and the base class. If, however, the event handler class implements an interface instead of extending an adapter class, Java does not prevent the event handler class from extending the base class.

The disadvantage of using an interface over an adapter class is that if additional methods are added to an interface in a future release, a class that implements the interface fails to compile.

About the Java event handlers for report items

You can write an event handler for any or all of the events that BIRT fires for a report item. Table 9-1 describes the events BIRT fires for each report item.

Table 9-1 Report item event handler methods

Method	Description
onPrepare( )	The onPrepare( ) method for every report element uses the following two arguments: ■ Element design interface ■ Report context interface
onCreate( )	The arguments to the onCreate( ) method depend on the particular element. Every onCreate( ) method uses at least the following two arguments: ■ Element instance interface ■ Report context interface
onPageBreak( )	The onPageBreak( ) method for every report element uses the following two arguments: ■ Element instance interface ■ Report context interface
onRender( )	The onRender( ) method for every report element uses the following two arguments: ■ Element instance interface ■ Report context interface

Using Java event handlers for a data source element

The DataSource event handler interface has four methods that you can use to respond to events. A Java class to handle these events must implement the IDataSourceEventHandler interface or extend the DataSourceAdapter class. All the event methods receive an IReportContext object. All the methods except the afterClose( ) method also receive an IDataSourceInstance object. These interfaces are discussed later in this chapter. Table 9-2 lists the methods that you can implement for a DataSource element.

Table 9-2 Data source event handler methods

Method	Description
beforeOpen(IDataSourceInstance dataSource, IReportContext reportContext)	Called immediately before opening the data source. This handler is often used to change the connection properties, such as user name and password.

(continues)

Table 9-2 Data source event handler methods (continued)

Method	Description
afterOpen(IDataSourceInstance dataSource, IReportContext reportContext)	Called immediately after opening the data source.
beforeClose(IDataSourceInstance dataSource, IReportContext reportContext)	Called immediately before closing the data source.
afterClose(IReportContext reportContext)	Called immediately after closing the data source.

Using Java event handlers for a data set element

BIRT fires five events for the DataSet element. A Java class to handle these events must implement the IDataSetEventHandler interface or extend the DataSetAdapter class. All DataSet event handler methods receive an IReportContext object. Additionally, all DataSet event handler methods except the afterClose( ) method receive an IDataSetInstance object. The onFetch( ) method receives a third object, an IDataSetRow object. Table 9-3 lists the methods that you can implement for a DataSet element.

Table 9-3 Data set event handler methods

Method	Description
beforeOpen(IDataSetInstance dataSet, IReportContext reportContext)	Called immediately before opening the data set. This event handler is often used to change the query text for a data set.
afterOpen(IDataSetInstance dataSet, IReportContext reportContext)	Called immediately after opening the data set.
onFetch(IDataSetInstance dataSet, IDataSetRow row, IReportContext reportContext)	Called upon fetching each row from the data source.
beforeClose(IDataSetInstance dataSet, IReportContext reportContext)	Called immediately before closing the data set.
afterClose(IReportContext reportContext)	Called immediately after closing the data set.

Using Java event handlers for a scripted data source element

The scripted data source interface extends the IDataSourceEventHandler interface, which has four methods. The ScriptedDataSource interface adds two new methods to the four methods of the IDataSourceEventHandler interface. A Java class that provides the ScriptedDataSource event handlers must implement IScriptedDataSourceEventHandler interface or extend the ScriptedDataSourceAdapter class. A Java class that provides the ScriptedDataSource event handlers must implement the two methods of the IScriptedDataSourceEventHandler interface plus the four methods of the IDataSourceEventHandler interface, which it extends.

Both of the two event handler methods of IScriptedDataSourceEventHandler receive an IDataSourceInstance object. Table 9-4 lists the two additional methods that you must implement for a ScriptedDataSource element.

Table 9-4 Scripted data source event handler methods

Method	Description
open(IDataSourceInstance dataSource)	Use this method to open the data source.
close(IDataSourceInstance dataSource)	Use this method to close the data source and perform clean-up tasks.

Using Java event handlers for a scripted data set element

The scripted data set interface extends the IDataSetEventHandler interface, which has four methods. The scripted data set interface adds four new methods to the four of the IDataSourceEventHandler interface. Of the four new methods, three must be fully implemented and the fourth may be empty. A Java class that provides scripted data set event handlers must implement the IScriptedDataSetEventHandler interface or extend the ScriptedDataSetAdapter class. A Java class that provides scripted data set event handlers must implement the four methods of the IScriptedDataSetEventHandler interface plus the four methods of the IDataSourceEventHandler interface, which it extends. Table 9-5 lists the four additional methods that you must implement for a scripted data set element.

Table 9-5 Scripted data set event handler methods

Method	Description
open(IDataSetInstance dataSet)	Called when the data set is opened. Use this method to initialize variables and to prepare for fetching rows.
fetch(IDataSetInstance dataSet, IUpdatableDataSetRow dataSetRow)	Called at row processing time. Use this method to fetch data with which to populate the row object. This method must return true if the fetch is successful and false if it is not.

(continues)

Table 9-5 Scripted data set event handler methods (continued)

Method	Description
close(IDataSetInstance dataSet)	Called upon completion of processing a data set. Use this method to perform cleanup operations.

Using Java event handlers for a report design

BIRT fires several events that the report design element handles. A Java class to handle these events must implement the IReportEventHandler interface or extend the ReportEventAdapter class. All of the event handler methods receive an IReportContext object. The beforeFactory( ) method also receives an IReportDesign object. Table 9-6 lists the methods that you can implement for a ReportDesign element in the order in which they run.

Table 9-6 ReportDesign event handler methods

Method	Description
initialize(IReportContext reportContext)	Called twice, once before the generation phase begins and once before the render phase begins.
beforeFactory(IReportDesign report, IReportContext reportContext)	Called before the generation phase begins.
afterFactory(IReportContext reportContext)	Called after the generation phase ends.
beforeRender(IReportContext reportContext)	Called before the presentation phase begins.
afterRender(IReportContext reportContext)	Called after the presentation phase ends.

Understanding the BIRT interfaces

A developer of Java event handlers needs to be familiar with several Java interfaces. Most of the handler method parameters and return values are Java interfaces rather than classes. The most important Java interfaces for developing Java event handlers are:

- Element design
- IReportElement
- Element instance
- Report context
- IColumnMetaData
- IDataSetInstance
- IDataSourceInstance
- IDataSetRow
- IRowData

About the element design interfaces

Every element has a unique element design interface. The Java interface specifies methods for accessing and setting specific features of the element design. Every element design interface inherits methods from IReportElement.

About the methods for each report element

As well as the methods defined in IDesignElement, each report element has methods that are relevant only for that report element. For example, ICell, the design interface for a Cell object, includes the following methods in addition to those defined in IDesignElement:

- getColumn( )
- getColumnSpan( )
- getDrop( )
- getHeight( )
- getRowSpan( )
- getWidth( )
- setColumn(int column)
- setColumnSpan(int span)
- setDrop(java.lang.String drop)

In contrast, the methods for ITextItem, the design interface for a text element, includes these additional methods:

- getContent( )
- getContentKey( )
- getContentType( )
- getDisplayContent( )
- setContent(java.lang.String value)
- setContentKey(java.lang.String resourceKey)
- setContentType(java.lang.String contentType)

About the IReportElement interface

The IReportElement interface is the base interface for all the report element interfaces. IReportElement has the following methods:

- getComments( )
- getCustomXml( )
- getDisplayName( )

- getDisplayNameKey( )
- getName( )
- getNamedExpression(java.lang.String name)
- getParent( )
- getQualifiedName( )
- getStyle( )
- getUserProperty(java.lang.String name)
- setComments(java.lang.String theComments)
- setCustomXml(java.lang.String customXml)
- setDisplayName(java.lang.String displayName)
- setDisplayNameKey(java.lang.String displayNameKey)
- setName(java.lang.String name)
- setNamedExpression(java.lang.String name, java.lang.String exp)
- setUserProperty(java.lang.String name, java.lang.Object value)

About the element instance interfaces

The element instance interfaces are available at run time, but not at design time. These interfaces provide access to the run-time instance of the element. Both onCreate( ), the generation phase event handler, and onRender( ), the presentation phase event handler, receive the element instance interface as an argument. Through instance interfaces, you have access to a different set of properties than you do at design time. There is no superinterface from which all element instance interfaces inherit. Like the element design interface, the set of methods in the instance interfaces vary from element type to element type. For example, ICellInstance, the Cell instance interface, contains the following methods:

- getColSpan( )
- getColumn( )
- getRowSpan( )
- setColSpan(int colSpan)
- setRowSpan(int rowSpan)

By comparison, IRowInstance, the Row instance interface, contains these methods:

- getBookmarkValue( )
- getHeight( )
- getStyle( )
- setBookmark( )
- setHeight( )

Using the IReportContext interface

All event handlers except those for ScriptedDataSource and ScriptedDataSet objects use an object of type IReportContext. The IReportContext interface includes the methods shown in Table 9-7.

Table 9-7 IReportContext interface methods

Method	Task
deleteGlobalVariable(java.lang .String name)	Removes a global variable created using the setGlobalVariable( ) method.
deletePersistentGlobalVariable (java.lang.String name)	Removes a persistent global variable created using the setPersistentGlobalVariable( ) method.
getAppContext( )	Retrieves the application context object as a java.util.Map object. The report application can use the application context object to pass any information that is application-specific.
getGlobalVariable(java.lang .String name)	Returns the object saved with the setGlobalVariable( ) method. The string argument is the key used when saving the object.
getHttpServletRequest( )	Returns the HttpServletRequest object associated with the URL requesting the report. The HttpServletRequest object provides access to the HTTP session object, the request URL, and any parameters appended to the request.
getLocale( )	Returns the locale associated with the report execution or rendering task. This locale can be different from the local machine's system or user locale.
getMessage(java.lang.String key)	Returns a message from the default properties file.
getMessage(java.lang.String key, java.util.Locale locale, java .lang.Object [ ] params)	Returns a message from the properties file for a specified locale, using a parameters array.
getMessage(java.lang.String key, java.lang.Object[ ] params)	Returns a message from the default properties file, using a parameters array.

(continues)

Table 9-7 IReportContext interface methods (continued)

Method	Task
getOutputFormat( )	Returns a string containing html, pdf, postscript, ppt, xls, or doc, depending on the format specified in the __format parameter of the request URL.
getParameterValue(java.lang .String name)	Returns the value of the parameter named in the name argument. The value returned is a java.lang.Object.
getPersistentGlobalVariable(java .lang.String name)	Returns the serializable object saved using setPersistentGlobalVariable( ) method. The string argument is the key used when saving the serializable object.
getRenderOption( )	Gets the render options used to render the report.
getReportRunnable( )	Gets the report runnable instance used to create or render this report.
getTaskType()	Gets the type of the current task.
setGlobalVariable(java.lang .String name,java.lang.Object obj)	Saves an object that can be retrieved in the same execution phase as it is saved. The setGlobalVariable( ) method takes a string argument and an Object argument. Use the string argument as a key with which to retrieve the saved object.
setParameterDisplayText(java .lang.String name, java.lang.Object value)	Sets the display text for a parameter.
setParameterValue(java.lang .String name, java.lang.Object value)	Sets the value of a named parameter with the value contained in the value argument.
setPersistentGlobalVariable(java .lang.String name, java.io.Serializable obj)	Saves an object that can be retrieved in a different execution phase from the phase that saves the object. The setPersistentGlobalVariable( ) method takes a string argument and a serializable object argument. Use the string argument as a key with which to retrieve the serializable object. The serializable object is saved in the report document. The object is serializable to persist it between

Table 9-7 IReportContext interface methods (continued)

Method	Task
setPersistentGlobalVariable(java .lang.String name, java.io.Serializable obj)	phases supporting executing the two phases at different times and possibly on different machines.

Using the IColumnMetaData interface

The IColumnMetaData interface provides information about the columns of the data set. Table 9-8 lists the methods in the IColumnMetaData interface.

Table 9-8 IColumnMetaData interface methods

Method	Returns
getColumnAlias(int index)	Alias assigned to the column at the position indicated by index
getColumnCount( )	Count of columns in the data set
getColumnLabel(int index)	Label assigned to the column at the position indicated by index
getColumnName(int index)	String containing the name of the column at the position indicated by index
getColumnNativeTypeName (int index)	Name of the type of data in the column at the position indicated by index
getColumnType(int index)	Data type of the column at the position indicated by index
getColumnTypeName (int index)	Name of the type of data in the column at the position indicated by index
isComputedColumn (int index)	True or false, depending on whether the column at the position indicated by index is a computed field

Using the IDataSetInstance interface

The IDataSetInstance interface provides access to many aspects of the data set and associated elements. Every DataSet event handler method receives an IDataSetInstance object as an argument. Table 9-9 describes the methods in the interface IDataSetInstance.

Table 9-9 IDataSetInstance interface methods

Method	Returns
getAllExtensionProperties( )	The data set extension properties in the form of a java.util.Map object. The map object maps data extension names to their values.
getColumnMetaData( )	An IColumnMetaData object that provides the data set's metadata.
getDataSource( )	A DataSource object associated with the data set.
getExtensionID( )	The unique ID that identifies the type of the data set, assigned by the extension that implements this data set.
getExtensionProperty(java.lang .String name)	The value of a data set extension property.
getName( )	The name of this data set.
getQueryText( )	The query text of the data set.
setExtensionProperty(java.lang .String name, java.lang.String value)	The value of an extension property.
setQueryText(java.lang.String queryText)	The query text of the data set.

Using the IDataSetRow interface

An object of the IDataSetRow type passes to the DataSet.onfetch( ) event handler method. IDataSetRow has two getColumnValue( ) methods. The two methods differ only in the argument that specifies the column containing the value. They both return a java.lang.Object object, which you must cast to the appropriate type for the column. Table 9-10 lists the methods in the IDataSetRow interface.

Table 9-10 IDataSetRow interface methods

Method	Returns
getColumnValue(int index)	The column data by index. This index is 1-based.
getColumnValue(java.lang.String name)	The column data by column name.
getDataSet( )	An IDataSetInstance object representing the data set that contains this row.

Using the IRowData interface

The getRowData( ) method of IReportElementInstance, which every report element instance interface extends, returns an object of the IRowData type. IRowData provides access to the bound values that appear in the table or list. The IRowData interface has two getExpressionValue( ) methods. Both methods return the display value for a specific column in the table. The two methods differ in the argument that specifies the required column. Table 9-11 lists the methods in the IRowData interface.

Table 9-11 RowData interface methods

Method	Returns
getColumnCount( )	The count of the binding expressions.
getColumnName(int index)	The name of the binding expression by index.
getColumnValue(int index)	The value of the binding expression by index. This index is 1-based.
getColumnValue(String name)	The value of the binding expression by name.

Java event handler example

The following list provide some common examples that illustrate event handlers written in Java. The examples illustrated in Chapter 8, "Using JavaScript to Write an Event Handler," can be used as reference as well.

Report level events

Report level events include initialize, beforeFactory, afterFactory, beforeRender, and afterRender. When these events are called depends on the type of report execution occurring.

The beforeFactory( ) method is often overridden, because changes to the report design can occur in this event handler. Listing 9-1 checks a boolean parameter. If this value is true, the report design drops a table named Mytable.

Listing 9-1 Using the Report Engine API in beforeFactory

```
package my.event.handlers;

import org.eclipse.birt.report.engine.api.script.IReportContext;
import org.eclipse.birt.report.engine.api.script.element
   .IReportDesign;
import org.eclipse.birt.report.engine.api.script.eventadapter
   .ReportEventAdapter;
import org.eclipse.birt.report.model.api.*;
```

```
import org.eclipse.birt.report.model.api.activity
   .SemanticException;

public class MyReportEvents extends ReportEventAdapter {
   @Override
   public void beforeFactory(IReportDesign report,
      IReportContext reportContext) {
      if((Boolean)reportContext.getParameterValue( "DropTable" )){
         ReportDesignHandle rdh = ( ReportDesignHandle )
            reportContext.getReportRunnable( ).getDesignHandle( );
         try{
            rdh.findElement( "Mytable" ).drop( );
         }catch( SemanticException e ){
            e.printStackTrace( );
         }
      }
   }
```

This example, using the Design Engine API, requires adding modelapi.jar and coreapi.jar to the buildpath and classpath. This example also uses the Design Engine API to add a data source, data set, and table to a report using the beforeFactory event.

In Listing 9-2, the library mylibrary.rptlibrary, located in the resource folder, opens. The data source named mydatasource, the data set named mydataset, and the table named mytable are all added to the current report design.

Listing 9-2 Using the Design Engine API in beforeFactory

```
package my.event.handlers;

import org.eclipse.birt.report.engine.api.script.IReportContext;
import org.eclipse.birt.report.engine.api.script.element
   .IReportDesign;
import org.eclipse.birt.report.engine.api.script.eventadapter
   .ReportEventAdapter;
import org.eclipse.birt.report.model.api.ReportDesignHandle;
import org.eclipse.birt.report.model.api.LibraryHandle;
import org.eclipse.birt.report.model.api.DesignElementHandle;
import org.eclipse.birt.report.model.core.DesignSession;

public class MyReportAddTableEvent extends ReportEventAdapter {
   @Override
   public void beforeFactory( IReportDesign report,
      IReportContext reportContext ) {
      ReportDesignHandle rdh = ( ReportDesignHandle )reportContext
           .getReportRunnable( ).getDesignHandle( );
      DesignSession ds =rdh.getModule( ).getSession( );
      try{
         String rsf = ds.getResourceFolder( );
         LibraryHandle libhan = ds.openLibrary(
            rsf + "/mylibrary.rptlibrary" ).handle( );
```

```
      DesignElementHandle deh1 =
         libhan.findDataSource( "mydatasource" );
      DesignElementHandle deh2 =
         libhan.findDataSet( "mydataset" );
      DesignElementHandle deh3 =
         libhan.findElement( "mytable" );
      rdh.getDataSources( ).add( deh1 );
      rdh.getDataSets( ).add( deh2 );
      rdh.getBody( ).add( deh3 );
      libhan.close( );
   }catch(Exception e){
      e.printStackTrace( );
   }
  }
}
```

Report item events

Report item events support changing the default behavior of an item. Changes made in the onPrepare event can change the design of the item, changes made in the onCreate event can change the particular instance of an item at generation time, and the onRender event can change properties of an instance of the item at render time. Consider the image item example in Listing 9-3.

This example illustrates changing image sources for different types of image items. If the image type is a URL image, the output format is checked and the URL for the image changes. If the image type is a file from the resource folder, the filename is searched for the string, up. If this string is found the image is replaced with an image with the name, down. If the image type is an embedded image, the report parameter, SwapImage, is checked. If the value is true, the image is swapped to another embedded image. If the image is a BLOB type image from a database, the bytes for the image are swapped to the bytes read from the local file system.

Listing 9-3 Changing report item properties in onRender

```
package my.event.handlers;

import org.eclipse.birt.report.engine.api.script.IReportContext;
import org.eclipse.birt.report.engine.api.script.eventadapter
   .ImageEventAdapter;
import org.eclipse.birt.report.engine.api.script.instance
   .IImageInstance;
import org.eclipse.birt.report.engine.content.IImageContent;
import java.io.*;

public class myImageHandler extends ImageEventAdapter {

   public void onRender( IImageInstance image,
      IReportContext reportContext ) {
      if( image.getImageSource( ) == IImageContent.IMAGE_URL ){
```

```
            if( reportContext.getOutputFormat( )
               .equalsIgnoreCase( "html" )){
               image.setURL(
               "http://us.i1.yimg.com/us.yimg.com/i/ww/beta/y3.gif" );
            } else {
               image.setURL(
               "http://www.google.com/intl/en_ALL/images/logo.gif" );
            }
         }
         if( image.getImageSource( ) == IImageContent.IMAGE_FILE ){
            String rpl = image.getFile( );
            if( rpl.contains( "up" ) ){
               String newstr = rpl.replaceAll( "up", "down" );
               image.setFile( newstr );
            }
         }
         if( image.getImageSource( ) == IImageContent.IMAGE_NAME ){
            if( ( Boolean )reportContext
               .getParameterValue( "SwapImage" ) ){
               if( image.getImageName( ).compareToIgnoreCase(
                  "tocico.png" ) == 0 ){
                  image.setImageName( "clientprintico.PNG" );
               }
            }
         }
         if( image.getImageSource( ) ==
            IImageContent.IMAGE_EXPRESSION){
            try{
               File myfile = new File( "c:/temp/test.png" );
               FileInputStream ist = new FileInputStream( myfile );
               long lengthi = myfile.length( );
               byte[ ] imageData = new byte[ ( int )lengthi ];
               ist.read( imageData );
               ist.close( );
               image.setData( imageData );
            }catch( Exception e ){
               e.printStackTrace( );
            }
         }
      }
```

As stated earlier, onPrepare event handlers can affect the design of a particular report item. In the example shown in Listing 9-4, an onPrepare event handler adds a hyperlink and a table of contents entry to a data element design. The onCreate event is overridden to modify the hyperlink based on the value of the data item instance.

Listing 9-4 Changing report item properties in onCreate and onPrepare

```
package my.event.handlers;
import org.eclipse.birt.report.engine.api.script.IReportContext;
import org.eclipse.birt.report.engine.api.script.element.IAction;
import org.eclipse.birt.report.engine.api.script.element
   .IDataItem;
import org.eclipse.birt.report.engine.api.script.eventadapter
   .DataItemEventAdapter;
import org.eclipse.birt.report.engine.api.script.instance
   .IActionInstance;
import org.eclipse.birt.report.engine.api.script.instance
   .IDataItemInstance;
import org.eclipse.birt.report.model.api.elements
   .DesignChoiceConstants;

public class MyDataElementEvent extends DataItemEventAdapter {
   @Override
   public void onCreate( IDataItemInstance data,
      IReportContext reportContext ) {
      IActionInstance ai =data.getAction( );
      if( ( Integer )data.getValue( ) == 10101 ){
         ai.setHyperlink( "http://www.yahoo.com","_blank" );
      }
   }

   @Override
   public void onPrepare(IDataItem dataItemHandle,
      IReportContext reportContext) {
      IAction act =dataItemHandle.getAction( );
      try{
         act.setTargetWindow( "_blank" );
         act.setURI( "'http://www.google.com'" );
         act.setLinkType(
            DesignChoiceConstants.ACTION_LINK_TYPE_HYPERLINK );
         dataItemHandle.setTocExpression("row[\"ORDERNUMBER\"]");
      }catch( Exception e ){
         e.printStackTrace( );
      }
   }
}
```

Using an onCreate event handler for a row provides access to the bound columns. For example, the code in Listing 9-5 retrieves the QUANTITYORDERED column for each row of data in a table element. If the value is greater than 40, the background for the row is set to green.

Listing 9-5 Accessing bound data values in onCreate

```
package my.event.handlers;

import org.eclipse.birt.report.engine.api.script.IReportContext;
import org.eclipse.birt.report.engine.api.script.eventadapter
   .RowEventAdapter;
import org.eclipse.birt.report.engine.api.script.instance
   .IRowInstance;

public class MyRowEvents extends RowEventAdapter {
   @Override
   public void onCreate( IRowInstance rowInstance,
      IReportContext reportContext ) {
      try{
      Integer qty =
         ( Integer )rowInstance.getRowData( ).getColumnValue(
            "QUANTITYORDERED" );
      if( qty > 40 ){
         rowInstance.getStyle( ).setBackgroundColor( "green" );
      }
      }catch( Exception e ){
         e.printStackTrace( );
      }
   }
}
```

Event handlers can share data by using the setPersistentGlobalVariable( ) method on reportContext. This method writes the variable to the report document if generating a report with two processes. Consider an order listing report that requires the last order number to appear in the page header. The report items described and LISTING NEXT shows how to perform this operation when using two processes to generate and render the report.

The master page header contains first, a dynamic text element with the following expression:

```
"placeholder"+pageNumber;
```

The generated report produces placeholder1, placeholder2, and so on for all pages in the report. The master page header also contains a data item. An event handler for the onPageBreak event for the data item contains the code in Listing 9-6.

This code adds an array list item for each page. When the onPageBreak event fires, the data item contains the last value for the page. The array list is saved to the report document using the setPersistentGlobalVariable method.

Listing 9-6 Preparing a persistent global variable in the generation phase

```
package my.event.handlers;

import org.eclipse.birt.report.engine.api.script.IReportContext;
```

```
import org.eclipse.birt.report.engine.api.script.eventadapter
   .DataItemEventAdapter;
import org.eclipse.birt.report.engine.api.script.instance
   .IDataItemInstance;
import java.util.*;

public class MyCustomHeaderDataItem extends DataItemEventAdapter {
   @Override
   public void onPageBreak( IDataItemInstance data,
      IReportContext reportContext) {
      ArrayList ar =
         (ArrayList)reportContext.getPersistentGlobalVariable(
            "MyArrayList" );
      if( ar == null ){
         ar = new ArrayList( );
      }
      ar.add( "Page Ends with: " + data.getValue( ) );
      reportContext.setPersistentGlobalVariable(
         "MyArrayList", ar);
   }
}
```

An onRender event handler for the dynamic text element in the master page header contains the code in Listing 9-7.

This code first verifies that the dynamic text element is correct by checking for the placeholder text in the value of the dynamic text item. The array list produced by the data item is retrieved from the report document using the getPersistentGlobalVariable method. The specific page string is retrieved from the array list by getting the page number from the current value of the dynamic text item.

Listing 9-7 Using a persistent global variable in the presentation phase

```
package my.event.handlers;

import org.eclipse.birt.report.engine.api.script.IReportContext;
import org.eclipse.birt.report.engine.api.script.eventadapter
   .DynamicTextEventAdapter;
import org.eclipse.birt.report.engine.api.script.instance
   .IDynamicTextInstance;
import java.util.*;
public class MyCustomHeaderDynamicTextItem extends
   DynamicTextEventAdapter {
   @Override
   public void onRender( IDynamicTextInstance text,
      IReportContext reportContext) {
      String cmp = "nomatch";
      if( text.getText( ).length( ) > 10 ){
         cmp = text.getText( ).substring( 0,10 );
      }
      if( cmp.compareToIgnoreCase("placeholde" ) == 0 ){
```

```
            ArrayList ar =
               ( ArrayList )reportContext
                  .getPersistentGlobalVariable( "MyArrayList" );
            if( ar == null ){
               return;
            }
         Integer ccount =
            Integer.parseInt( text.getText( ).substring( 11 ) )-1;
         text.setText( ( String )ar.get( ccount ) );
         }
      }
   }
```

This technique works only when generation and presentation occur in two separate processes. The reason is that the onRender event for the dynamic text item in the master page fires after the onCreate and onPageBreak events for all report items when using two processes. When using one process, the onRender event fires immediately after the onCreate event for the dynamic text item in the master page header.

Debugging a Java event handler

One of the main advantages of writing an event handler in Java is the ability to debug the code using Eclipse. To assist this process, BIRT supplies a BIRT Report launch configuration to the debugger. Debug the event handler by opening the event handler class in the Java Perspective, setting appropriate break points, and selecting Run→Open Debug Dialog.

Select BIRT Report from the available configurations and choose Launch Configuration. Select the projects that contain reports using the event handler from the list of available projects and choose Debug to launch a separate instance of Eclipse.

In the new instance, navigate to a report that contains a reference to the event handler and choose Preview. Any breakpoints in the event handler fire.

Chapter

10

Working with Chart Event Handlers

BIRT supports an event handler model specific to the Chart Engine. The model is similar to the model for standard BIRT report elements and supports both the Java and JavaScript environments. This chapter provides details on both environments. The Chart Engine also supports this event model when used independently from the BIRT Engine or a report design.

Chart events overview

A chart is a graphical representation of data. A chart event occurs before, during, or after the drawing of a chart. Table 10-1 lists the chart event handler methods and identifies when these methods are called.

Table 10-1 Chart event handler methods

Method	Called
afterDataSetFilled(Series series, DataSet dataSet, IChartScriptContext icsc)	After populating the series data set
afterDrawAxisLabel(Axis axis, Label label, IChartScriptContext icsc)	After rendering each label on a given axis
afterDrawAxisTitle(Axis axis, Label label, IChartScriptContext icsc)	After rendering the title of an axis
afterDrawBlock(Block block, IChartScriptContext icsc)	After drawing each block

(continues)

Table 10-1 Chart event handler methods (continued)

Method	Called
afterDrawDataPoint(DataPointHints dph, Fill fill, IChartScriptContext icsc)	After drawing the graphical representation or marker for each data point
afterDrawDataPointLabel(DataPointHints dph, Label label, IChartScriptContext icsc)	After rendering the label for each data point
afterDrawFittingCurve(CurveFitting cf, IChartScriptContext icsc)	After rendering a point-fitting curve
afterDrawLegendItem(LegendEntryRenderingHints lerh, Bounds bounds, IChartScriptContext icsc)	After drawing each entry in the legend
afterDrawMarkerLine(Axis axis, MarkerLine mLine, IChartScriptContext icsc)	After drawing each marker line in an axis
afterDrawMarkerRange(Axis axis, MarkerRange mRange, IChartScriptContext icsc)	After drawing each marker range in an axis
afterDrawSeries(Series series, ISeriesRenderer isr, IChartScriptContext icsc)	After rendering the series
afterDrawSeriesTitle(Series series, Label label, IChartScriptContext icsc)	After rendering the title of a series
afterGeneration(GeneratedChartState gcs, IChartScriptContext icsc)	After generating a chart model to GeneratedChartState
afterRendering(GeneratedChartState gcs, IChartScriptContext icsc)	After the chart renders
beforeDataSetFilled(Series series, IDataSetProcessor idsp, IChartScriptContext icsc)	Before populating the series data set using the DataSetProcessor
beforeDrawAxisLabel(Axis axis, Label label, IChartScriptContext icsc)	Before rendering each label on a given axis
beforeDrawAxisTitle(Axis axis, Label label, IChartScriptContext icsc)	Before rendering the title of an axis
beforeDrawBlock(Block block, IChartScriptContext icsc)	Before drawing each block
beforeDrawDataPoint(DataPointHints dph, Fill fill, IChartScriptContext icsc)	Before drawing each data point graphical representation or marker
beforeDrawDataPointLabel(DataPointHints dph, Label label, IChartScriptContext icsc)	Before rendering the label for each data point
beforeDrawFittingCurve(CurveFitting cf, IChartScriptContext icsc)	Before rendering a point-fitting curve

Table 10-1 Chart event handler methods (continued)

Method	Called
beforeDrawLegendItem(LegendEntryRenderingHints lerh, Bounds bounds, IChartScriptContext icsc)	Before drawing each entry in the legend
beforeDrawMarkerLine(Axis axis, MarkerLine mLine, IChartScriptContext icsc)	Before drawing each marker line in an axis
beforeDrawMarkerRange(Axis axis, MarkerRange mRange, IChartScriptContext icsc)	Before drawing each marker range in an axis
beforeDrawSeries(Series series, ISeriesRenderer isr, IChartScriptContext icsc)	Before rendering the series
beforeDrawSeriesTitle(Series series, Label label, IChartScriptContext icsc)	Before rendering the title of a series
beforeGeneration(Chart cm, IChartScriptContext icsc)	Before generating a chart model to GeneratedChartState
beforeRendering(GeneratedChartState gcs, IChartScriptContext icsc)	Before the chart renders

The following sections describe how to implement the chart events based on the event handler model for the BIRT Chart Engine.

Understanding the Chart script context

All chart event handler methods for both Java and JavaScript receive a Chart script context, which is a ChartScriptContext object, as a parameter. The Chart script context object provides access to the following objects:

- Chart instance
- Locale
- ULocale
- Logging
- External context

Table 10-2 lists the methods of the chart script context object and their actions.

Table 10-2 Chart script context methods

Method	Action
getChartInstance( )	Returns the chart instance object.

(continues)

Table 10-2 Chart script context methods (continued)

Method	Action
getExternalContext( )	Returns the IExternalContext object that provides access to an external scriptable object. The user application defines the external scriptable object.
getLocale( )	Returns the Locale object for the current locale.
getLogger( )	Returns the Logger object for use in logging messages and errors.
getULocale( )	Returns the ULocale object for the current locale.
setChartInstance(Chart)	Sets the Chart instance.
setExternalContext (IExternalContext)	Sets the external context.
setLogger(ILogger)	Sets the logger.
setULocale(ULocale)	Sets the ULocale.

Using the Chart instance

The chart script context object provides access to a Chart instance object. Use methods on the chart instance contains methods to access chart properties. These methods support getting, changing, and testing chart properties.

Chart instance getter methods

The chart instance getter methods provide the current values of a chart's properties. Table 10-3 lists the Chart instance getter methods and returned property values.

Table 10-3 Chart instance getter methods

Method	Property value returned
getBlock( )	The Block containment reference
getDescription( )	The Description containment reference
getDimension( )	The Dimension attribute
getExtendedProperties( )	The Extended Properties containment reference list
getGridColumnCount( )	The Grid Column Count attribute
getInteractivity( )	The Interactivity containment reference
getLegend( )	Legend block
getPlot( )	Plot block
getSampleData( )	The Sample Data containment reference

Table 10-3 Chart instance getter methods

Method	Property value returned
getScript( )	The Script attribute
getSeriesForLegend( )	Array of series containing captions or markers that render in the Legend
getSeriesThickness( )	The Series Thickness attribute
getStyles( )	The Styles containment reference list
getSubType( )	The Sub Type attribute
getTitle( )	Title block for the chart
getType( )	The Type attribute
getUnits( )	The Units attribute
getVersion( )	The Version attribute

Chart instance setter methods

The chart instance setter methods support settiing the values of various chart properties. Table 10-4 lists the chart instance setter methods and the values set by these methods.

Table 10-4 Chart instance setter methods

Method	Property value set
setBlock(Block value)	The Block containment reference
setDescription(Text value)	The Description containment reference
setDimension (Chart Dimension value)	The Dimension attribute
setGridColumnCount (int value)	The Grid Column Count attribute
setInteractivity (Interactivity value)	The Interactivity containment reference
setSampleData( )	The Sample Data containment reference
setScript( )	The Script attribute
setSeriesThickness( )	The Series Thickness attribute
setSubType( )	The Sub Type attribute
setType( )	The Type attribute
setUnits( )	The Units attribute
setVersion( )	The Version attribute

Chart instance methods

Use Chart instance methods if the simple charting API is not sufficient for your requirements. Table 10-5 provides examples of Chart instance methods and describes the action performed by each method.

Table 10-5 Miscellaneous chart instance methods

Method	Action
clearSections(int iSectionType)	Walks through the model and clears sections of the specified type
createSampleRuntime Series( )	Builds run-time series instances for each design-time series based on the sample data contained in the model
setDimension(Chart Dimension value)	Sets the value of the Dimension attribute
unsetDimension( )	Unsets the value of the Dimension attribute
unsetGridColumn( )	Unsets the value of the Grid_Column_Count attribute
unsetSeriesThickness( )	Unsets the value of the Series_Thickness attribute
unsetVersion( )	Unsets the value of the Version attribute

Accessing the Chart instance in an event handler

Most event handlers use the chart script context to access the Chart instance. The beforeGeneration event, which occurs after the data set events and just before creating the chart, provides direct access to the Chart instance.

The JavaScript example in Listing 10-1 contains a beforeGeneration event handler that sets the unit spacing for the entire chart. The beforeDrawSeries event handler uses the chart context to retrieve the Chart instance and set the unit spacing for one series, having a title, series one. Running this script for a chart containing a two-bar series makes one bar series wider than the other. afterDrawSeries resets the unit spacing for the series. Only a ChartWithAxes instance, which extends the Chart object, supports setUnitSpacing.

Listing 10-1 Setting unit spacing in the beforeGeneration event handler

```
function beforeGeneration( chart, context )
{
   chart.setUnitSpacing( 20 );
}

var oldSpacing;

function beforeDrawSeries( series, seriesRenderer, context )
{
   oldSpacing = context.getChartInstance().getUnitSpacing( );
```

```
    if ( series.getSeriesIdentifier( ) == "series one" ) {
        context.getChartInstance( ).setUnitSpacing( 70 );
    }
}
function afterDrawSeries( series, seriesRenderer, context )
{
    context.getChartInstance( ).setUnitSpacing( oldSpacing );
}
```

Understanding the external context

When running from a report, the Chart Engine uses the report's reportContext object to access its external context. Retrieving the external context from JavaScript uses a different method from Java. To get the external context in a chart event handler written in JavaScript, use the context.getExternalContext( ).getScriptable( ) method. In a Java-based chart event handler, use context.getExternalContext( ).getObject( ).

An event handler can access the variables and methods of the external context object. For example, set the chart axis title to a report parameter using a JavaScript event handler, as shown in Listing 10-2, or a Java event handler, as shown in Listing 10-3.

Listing 10-2 Setting the chart axis title using a JavaScript event handler

```
function beforeDrawAxisTitle ( axis, title, context )
{
    importPackage(
        Packages.org.eclipse.birt.chart.model.attribute );
    if ( axis.getType( ) == AxisType.LINEAR_LITERAL ) {
        title.getCaption( ).setValue
            ( context.getExternalContext( ).getScriptable( )
                .getParameterValue( "chartTitle" ) );
    }
}
```

Listing 10-3 Setting the chart axis title using a Java event handler

```
public void beforeDrawAxisTitle( Axis axis, Label label,
        IChartScriptContext icsc )
{
    IReportContext rc = ( IReportContext )
        icsc.getExternalContext( ).getObject( );
    String mytitle =
        ( String )rc.getParameterValue( "chartTitle" );
    if ( axis.getType( ) == AxisType.TEXT_LITERAL ) {
        label.getCaption().setValue(mytitle);
    }
}
```

Understanding when chart events fire

The Chart Engine generator processes charts in the following four phases in the BIRT reporting environment:

- Prepare
- Data binding
- Build
- Render

These phases correspond to the following methods called when the BIRT Chart Engine generates a chart:

- Generator.prepare( )
- Generator.bindData( )
- Generator.build( )
- Generator.render( )

The following sections describe these phases and provide more information about the context in which chart events fire.

Prepare phase

The prepare phase sets up the chart script context. All chart event handlers use this script context object. This phase sets the class loader for the scripting environment to the same class loader that the BIRT scripting environment uses. This phase does not trigger any event handlers.

Data binding phase

The data binding phase prepares all data sets associated with a series, which is a set of values plotted in a chart. This preparation performs the following two tasks:

- Retrieving the data values provided by a dynamic data set
- Creating one or more run-time series from a series definition object

The Chart Engine supports both static and dynamic data. Static data does not need a data binding phase because the data is already prepared in the necessary format. The Chart Engine also provides extension points to support custom data set types.

An object implementing the org.eclipse.birt.chart.model.data.DataSet interface provides static data. For each data type, an implementation class having a static create method initializes the run-time series data values. For example, the following code creates a static NumberDataSet for a series:

```
NumberDataSet seriesOneValues =
   NumberDataSetImpl.create( new double[ ]{ 15, 23, 55, 76 }
   );
```

Sources of dynamic data include BIRT data sets and java.sqlResultSet objects. BIRT uses a series definition object to define the dynamic data a series contains. For example, row["month"] populates a series with the month column from a BIRT data set. The data binding phase uses the series definition object to create a run-time series bound to a static, typed chart data set. BIRT supports defining groups and sorting in a series definition using dynamic data. When using these features, BIRT creates additional run-time series as necessary, each with its own chart data set.

To get the run-time series for a series, call the getRunTimeSeries( ) method for the series definition object. Listing 10-4 gets a run-time series and sets the first bar series to have a riser type of triangle.

Listing 10-4 Getting a run-time series

```
function beforeGeneration( chart, icsc )
{
   importPackage(
      Packages.org.eclipse.birt.chart.model.attribute );

   var xAxis = chart.getBaseAxes( )[0];
   var yAxis = chart.getOrthogonalAxes( xAxis, true )[0]
   var seriesDef = yAxis.getSeriesDefinitions( ).get( 0 )
   var runSeries = seriesDef.getRunTimeSeries( );
   var firstRunSeries = runSeries.get( 0 );
   firstRunSeries.setRiser( RiserType.TRIANGLE_LITERAL );
}
```

The binding phase triggers the following event types:

- beforeDataSetFilled
- afterDataSetFilled

About the beforeDataSetFilled event

The Chart Engine calls the beforeDataSetFilled event handler before creating and populating the run-time series chart data set. This event handler receives two parameters: an IDataSetProcessor implementation and the Chart script context.

The IDataSetProcessor implementation must contain a populate method that creates one of the static chart data set types. The populate method is called just after this event fires. The DataSetProcessorImpl class, which contains empty methods, is the default implementation of IDataSetProcessor. Extend this interface using the chart extension points to provide your own data set processor to add calls to the beforeDataSet event.

About the afterDataSetFilled event

The Chart Engine calls the afterDataSetFilled event handler after creating and populating the run-time series chart data set. This event handler receives three parameters: the Chart script context, the run-time series, and the populated static, typed chart data set.

The series object is an implementation of the run-time series type being created. This object is a SeriesImpl object for the category series and a chart-specific type for other series. For example, in a bar chart, the series instance is a BarSeriesImpl object. Get the class type to determine the current series type, as shown in Listing 10-5. In a JavaScript event handler, casting to a specific type is not necessary. In a Java event handler, cast to a specific type if the method to call in the series object is not defined by the Series interface.

This event fires for each run-time series. To identify the triggering series, use the series identifier, as shown in the following code:

```
if ( series.getSeriesIdentifier( ) == "series one" ) {
   ...
}
```

By default, the series identifier value is undefined. Set the identifier in the Chart Builder Wizard under series title. If a series definition creates more than one run-time series, this identifier is the same for all these generated run-time series.

Listing 10-5 Checking the class type to determine the type of series

```
function afterDataSetFilled( series, dataSet, icsc )
{
   importPackage( Packages.java.io );
   importPackage(
      Packages.org.eclipse.birt.chart.model.type.impl );

   if ( series.getClass( ) == LineSeriesImpl ) {
      series.getLineAttributes( ).setThickness( 5 );
   }

   if ( series.getClass( ) == BarSeriesImpl ) {
      ...
   }
}
```

The chart data set passed to the method is the chart data set object for the current series. The chart data set values are available for manipulation at this point. For example, Listing 10-6 replaces null values and values below 24,000 in the data set with 0.

Listing 10-6 Replacing null values in a data set

```
function afterDataSetFilled( series, dataSet, icsc )
{
   var list = dataSet.getValues( );
```

```
   for ( i=0; i<list.length; i=i+1 ) {
      if ( ( list[i] == null ) || ( list[i] < 24000 ) ) {
         list[i]= 0;
      }
   }
}
```

Building phase

Do not confuse the chart building phase with the BIRT report generation phase, which occurs during rendering. The chart building phase starts when a chart model binds to a data set to produce a GeneratedChartState object. This object contains most of the information required to render the chart. A chart consists of blocks, which are the rectangular sub-regions of the chart that act as containers for specific chart information. The chart model contains the following blocks:

- Outermost block that contains all other blocks
- Title block for the chart title
- Plot block to render the series and any axes
- Legend block to display the legend

The building phase calculates the following values:

- Bounds for all blocks
- Minimum, maximum, and scale values for any axes

The building phase performs the following tasks:

- Initializes all series renderers
- Creates rendering hints for the legend, each run-time series, and the data points in each series
- Stores all calculations in the chart model in a GeneratedChartState object

The building phase triggers the following script events:

- beforeGeneration
- afterGeneration

About the beforeGeneration event

The Chart Engine calls the beforeGeneration event handler after completing the data binding phase. This event handler receives two parameters: the chart model bound to data from the binding phase and the Chart script context.

The chart model is an instance of a subclass of either ChartWithAxesImpl or ChartWithoutAxesImpl. To implement a Java event handler, it may be necessary to cast to the specific implementation of the chart interface. You can get the chart's class to determine the chart type. For example, to write a beforeGeneration event handler for a pie chart to explode slices that contain large values, use script similar to the example in Listing 10-7. The example shows the values series for a pie chart nesting under a second-level series definition. The category series nests below the top-level series definition.

Listing 10-7 Modifying pie slice properties

```
function beforeGeneration( chart, icsc )
{
   importPackage( Packages.org.eclipse.birt.chart.model.impl );
   importPackage(
      Packages.org.eclipse.birt.chart.model.type.impl );
   if ( chart.getClass( ) == ChartWithAxesImpl ) {
      //Do something if a line chart...
   }

   if ( chart.getClass( ) == ChartWithoutAxesImpl ) {
      seriesDef = chart.getSeriesDefinitions( ).get( 0 );
      catRunSeries = seriesDef.getRunTimeSeries( );
      // Pie Charts use nested series definitions for value series
      valSeriesDef = seriesDef.getSeriesDefinitions( ).get( 0 );
      valRunSeries = valSeriesDef.getRunTimeSeries( ).get( 0 );
      if ( valRunSeries.getClass( ) == PieSeriesImpl ) {
         valRunSeries.setExplosion( 10 );
         valRunSeries.setExplosionExpression("valueData > 15000");
      }
   }
}
```

About the afterGeneration event

The Chart Engine calls the afterGeneration event handler after processing all calculations, just prior to entering the rendering phase. This event handler receives two parameters: the GeneratedChartState object and the Chart script context. Modifications to the chart can be made by using the GeneratedChartState object to retrieve the chart model. For example, Listing 10-8 adds a blue border around the plot area.

Listing 10-8 Setting plot area properties

```
function afterGeneration( gcs, icsc )
{
   importPackage(
      Packages.org.eclipse.birt.chart.model.attribute );
   importPackage(
      Packages.org.eclipse.birt.chart.model.attribute.impl );
   var outline = gcs.getChartModel( ).getPlot( ).getOutline( );
   outline.setColor( ColorDefinitionImpl.BLUE( ) );
   outline.setStyle( LineStyle.SOLID_LITERAL );
   outline.setVisible( true );
}
```

Rendering phase

The rendering phase takes the GeneratedChartState object and renders the chart. This phase also sets up chart interactivity. The rendering phase uses the following main object types to render a chart:

- Device renderer
- Display server
- Model renderers

The device renderer object implements the IDeviceRenderer interface, which provides methods for drawing primitives such as drawPolygon, drawRectangle, drawText, and fillArc. The Chart Engine provides device renderers for Standard Widget Toolkit (SWT) and Swing. The device renderers for BMP, JPEG, PDF, PNG, and SVG formats extend the Swing renderer. The Chart Engine provides an extension point to extend this list.

The display server provides generic services to the device renderer for such operations as getting the dots-per-inch (DPI) resolution and providing text metrics. A display server implements the IDisplayServer interface. The Chart Engine provides implementations for SWT and Swing.

The display server links to a specific device renderer based on an Eclipse extension point entry for the renderer. Currently, all Swing-related renderers use the Swing display server and the SWT device renderer uses the SWT display server. The Chart Engine provides an extension point to extend the list of display servers.

Model renderers render a specific series and use the device renderer to render the actual graphic primitives that make up the chart series data points. All chart series renderers extend from the BaseRenderer or AxesRenderer abstract classes and implement the ISeriesRenderer interface, which provides the methods listed in Table 10-6.

Table 10-6 ISeriesRenderer methods

Name	Called	Performs
compute( )	Before the end of the building phase	Prerendering calculations
renderLegendGraphic ( )	During the render phase	Drawing the graphic markers in the legend
renderSeries( )	During the render phase	Drawing the series using the provided device renderer and series rendering hints

Table 10-7 lists the series-specific renderers. The Chart Engine provides an extension point to extend this list.

Table 10-7 Series-specific renderers

AxesRenderer	BaseRenderer
Bar	Dial
Bubble	Pie
Scatter	
Line	
Difference	
Gantt	
Stock	

The rendering phase loops through and renders all the run-time series for a chart. In Listing 10-9, pseudo-code shows the order of the rendering events. The axis rendering code applies only to chart types containing axes.

Listing 10-9 Pseudo-code illustrating the order of the rendering operations

```
Loop for all renderers
   Render Main block - Only on first series
   Render Title block - Only on first series
   Render Plot block
      Render Background - Only on first series
      Render Axis structure - Only on first series
         Render Series (Series-specific, such as Line or Bar)
      Render Axis labels - Only on last series
   Render Legend block (call to specific series renderer for
   graphic) - Only on last series
End Loop
```

Rendering phase script events

The bulk of the chart events fire during the rendering phase. Some events are specific to a particular chart type and are not called for all series renderers. In Listing 10-10, pseudo-code expands the code in Listing 10-9 to show the triggering order of most events. The order varies slightly depending on the specific series renderer. This chapter does not attempt to describe every event in detail. The common objects used in each script are presented in the following sections.

Listing 10-10 Pseudo-code showing the triggering order of rendering events

```
beforeRendering
   Loop all run-time series
      If first series
         beforeDrawBlock - Main block
         afterDrawBlock - Main block
         beforeDrawBlock - Title block
         afterDrawBlock - Title block
```

```
      beforeDrawBlock - Plot block

      Loop all marker ranges
         beforeDrawMarkerRange
         afterDrawMarkerRange
      End Loop

      Loop all marker lines
         beforeDrawMarkerLine
         afterDrawMarkerLine
      End Loop

      beforeDrawSeries - Category series
      afterDrawSeries - Category series
      afterDrawBlock - Plot Block
   End If

   beforeDrawBlock - Plot Block
   beforeDrawSeries - For specific series

   Loop all data points - For specific series
      beforeDrawDataPoint
      afterDrawDataPoint
   End Loop
   Loop all data point labels - For specific series
      beforeDrawDataPointLabel
      afterDrawDataPointLabel
   End Loop
   beforeDrawFittingCurve
   afterDrawFittingCurve
   afterDrawSeries

   If last series and chart contains axes
      Loop for each axis
         beforeDrawAxisLabel
         afterDrawAxisLabel
      End Loop
      beforeDrawAxisTitle
      afterDrawAxisTitle
   End If

   afterDrawBlock - Plot Block

   If last series
      beforeDrawBlock - Legend
         Loop all legend entries
            beforeDrawLegendItem
            afterDrawLegendItem
         End Loop
      afterDrawBlock - Legend
   End If
 End Loop
afterRender
```

Rendering blocks

Charts are composed of blocks. These blocks are rectangular sub-regions that contain sub-components of the chart. For example, the plot block contains the rendering of data points and the title block contains the chart title. The beforeDrawBlock event fires before rendering each block. Use this event handler to modify a block's properties before the chart renders.

The beforeDrawBlock and afterDrawBlock events fire once for the Main, Title, and Legend blocks and multiple times for the Plot block. These two events both receive two parameters: a BlockImpl object and the Chart script context.

The block class provides methods for determining which block triggered the event. Both event handlers support manipulating the block, for example setting the anchor points, background fill, or outline, by using the block's methods and properties. Listing 10-11 shows how to set the anchor point for the legend in a legend block.

Listing 10-11 Setting the anchor point for the legend in a legend block

```
function beforeDrawBlock( block, icsc )
{
   importPackage(
      Packages.org.eclipse.birt.chart.model.attribute.impl );
   importPackage(
      Packages.org.eclipse.birt.chart.model.attribute );

   if ( block.isLegend( ) ) {
      block.getOutline( ).setVisible( true );
      block.getOutline( ).getColor( ).set( 21,244,231 );
      block.setBackground( ColorDefinitionImpl.YELLOW( ) );
      block.setAnchor( Anchor.NORTH_LITERAL );
   }
   else if ( block.isPlot( ) ) {
      ...
   }
   else if ( block.isTitle( ) ) {
      ...
   }
   else if ( block.isCustom( ) ) {
      // Main Block
      ...
   }
}
```

Rendering series

The beforeDrawSeries and afterDrawSeries events fire prior once for every run-time series in a chart. The event handlers for these events receive a Series object, an ISeriesRenderer object, and the Chart script context as parameters.

To modify a series, use an event handler for the beforeDrawSeries event. In Listing 10-12, the event handler sets the visibility for the series identifier, SalesBalance, to false, so the series does not render in the chart.

Listing 10-12 Using the beforeDrawSeries event to set visibility in a chart

```
function beforeDrawSeries( series, seriesRenderer, context )
{
   if ( series.getSeriesIdentifier() == "SalesBalance" )
   {
      series.setVisible( false );
   }
}
```

Rendering data points and data point labels

The beforeDrawDataPoint, afterDrawDataPoint, beforeDrawDataPointLabel, and afterDrawDataPointLabel events each fire once for every run-time series value.

The event handlers for all of these events receive a DataPointHints object and the Chart script context as parameters. The building phase creates a DataPointHints object for every run-time series value. The series renderer renders this object using the object's data. All these event handlers support accessing and, for some properties, manipulating the DataPointHints object using the object's methods. Use DataPointHints property values to examine or modify the chart before rendering a data point. For example, the script in Listing 10-13 prints the *x*- and *y*-locations of a data point in the plot bounds, the category and series values, and the size of the bar for each value in a run-time series of a two-dimensional bar chart.

Listing 10-13 Displaying *x*- and *y*-locations in a two-dimensional bar chart

```
function beforeDrawDataPoint( dph, fill, icsc )
{
   importPackage( Packages.java.io );

   out = new PrintWriter( new FileWriter(
      "C:/data/datapoints.txt", true ) );
   out.println(
      "BaseValue X-Axis Value " + dph.getBaseValue( ) );
   out.println(
      "Orthogonal Y-Axis Value " + dph.getOrthogonalValue( ) );
   out.println( " X location " + dph.getLocation( ).getX( ) );
   out.println( " Y Location "  + dph.getLocation( ).getY( ) );
   out.println( " Size " + dph.getSize( ) );
   out.close( );
}
```

The beforeDrawDatapoint and afterDrawDatapoint event handlers receive two further parameters: a Fill object and the Chart script context. Subclasses of Fill provide support for a solid color, a gradient color, a pattern, or an image to display for the data point. For example, using an instance of the ColorDefinitionImpl class, which implements the Fill interface, supports setting a solid color for a data point.

These events fire before and after rendering a data point in a chart. Use these events to modify how the data point is rendered. In Listing 10-14, the event handler renders a bar chart with positive and negative bars and colors the negative bars red. The beforeDrawDataPoint event handler retrieves the value and determines if the bar is negative. If the bar is negative, the event handler saves the current fill color. The afterDrawDataPoint uses these settings to restore the color, setting the bar color back to red.

Listing 10-14 Rendering a bar chart with positive and negative bars

```
previousFill = null;
function beforeDrawDataPoint( dph, fill, icsc )
{
   val = dph.getOrthogonalValue( );
   if ( val < 0 ){
      previousFill = new Object( );
      previousFill.r = fill.getRed( );
      previousFill.g = fill.getGreen( );
      previousFill.b = fill.getBlue( );
      fill.set( 255, 0, 0 );
   }
   else{
      previousFill = null;
   }
}
function afterDrawDataPoint( dph, fill, icsc )
{
   if ( previousFill != null ){
      fill.set( previousFill.r, previousFill.g, previousFill.b);
   }
}
```

The beforeDrawDataPointLabel and afterDrawDataPointLabel event handlers receive the DataPointHints object and the Chart script context and one further parameter: a Label object.

The Label object is an instance of the LabelImpl class and provides many methods for altering the label. For example, modify the label caption or color based on DataPointHints property values. Listing 10-15 shows how to change the appearance and text of a data point label.

Listing 10-15 Changing the values for a label on a data point

```
function beforeDrawDataPointLabel(dph, label, icsc)
{
   value = dph.getOrthogonalValue( ) .doubleValue( );
   if ( ( value >= 0 ) && ( value < 500 ) ) {
```

```
      label.getCaption( ).getColor( ).set( 32, 168, 255 );
      label.getCaption( ).getFont( ).setItalic( true );
      label.getCaption( ).getFont( ).setRotation( 5 );
      label.getCaption( ).getFont( ).setStrikethrough( true );
      label.getCaption( ).getFont( ).setSize( 22 );
      label.getCaption( ).getFont( ).setName( "Arial" );
      label.getOutline( ).setVisible( true );
      label.getOutline( ).setThickness( 3 );
   }
   else if (  value >= 500  ) {
      label.getCaption( ).getFont( ).setRotation( 5 );
      label.getOutline( ).setVisible( true );
   }
   else if ( value < 0 ) {
      label.getCaption( ).getColor( ).set( 0, 208, 32 );
   }
}
```

Rendering axes

The beforeDrawAxisLabel, afterDrawAxisLabel, beforeDrawAxisTitle, afterDrawAxisTitle, beforeDrawMarkerLine, afterDrawMarkerLine, beforeDrawMarkerRange, and afterDrawMarkerRange events each fire at least once for every axis in a chart with axes.

The event handlers for all of these events receive two parameters: an axis object and the Chart script context. The axis object is an instance of the AxisImpl class and provides many methods and properties for use in the scripting environment. These features support functionality such as retrieving the run-time series associated with the axis and setting min, max, and scale values.

To work with an axis object, first determine which axis it is by getting the axis type or the axis title caption, as shown in Listing 10-16. The getType( ) method used in this example returns one of the following values:

- DATE_TIME_LITERAL
- LINEAR_LITERAL
- LOGARITHMIC_LITERAL
- TEXT_LITERAL

If a chart has multiple *y*-axes all of a specific type such as LINEAR_LITERAL, use the axis title to determine the current axis. The title need not be visible, but the value must exist.

Use the beforeDrawAxisTitle and beforeDrawAxisLabel events to modify the axis title and label elements respectively. Listing 10-16 shows how to check the axis title caption and the axis type to modify the title colors.

Listing 10-16 Checking the axis type to modify the title colors

```
function beforeDrawAxisTitle( axis, label, icsc )
{
   importPackage(
      Packages.org.eclipse.birt.chart.model.attribute.impl );
   importPackage(
      Packages.org.eclipse.birt.chart.model.attribute );

   if ( axis.getTitle( ).getCaption( ).getValue( ) ==
      "myYaxisTitle" ) {
      label.getCaption( ).setColor( ColorDefinitionImpl.BLUE( ) );
   }

   if ( axis.getType( ) == AxisType.DATE_TIME_LITERAL ) {
      label.getCaption( ).setColor( ColorDefinitionImpl.RED( ) );
   }
}
```

The beforeDrawAxisLabel event fires for each label rendered on a chart axis. Provide an event handler for this event to modify the labels. In Listing 10-17, the modified labels provide an abbreviated number format, making the chart more readable.

Listing 10-17 Modifying labels in a beforeDrawAxisLabel event

```
function beforeDrawAxisLabel( axis, label, context )
{
   value = label.getCaption( ).getValue( );
   if ( value >= 1000 && value < 1000000 )
      value = value/1000 + "k";
   else if ( value >= 1000000 )
      value = value/1000000 + "M";

   label.getCaption( ).setValue( value );
}
```

When the beforeDrawAxisXXX events fire, the axis lines and grids are already rendered, so, to modify the basic properties of an axis, make these changes in an earlier event. Listing 10-18 shows how to modify an axis using this approach. The code retrieves all the axes and checks that the *x*-axis is a date-and-time axis. After the verification, the code specifies the format for the axis labels.

Listing 10-18 Retrieving the axis to modify axis properties

```
function beforeGeneration( chart, icsc )
{
   importPackage(
      Packages.org.eclipse.birt.chart.model.attribute.impl );
   importPackage(
      Packages.org.eclipse.birt.chart.model.attribute );
```

```
    // The chart model supports only one base axis
    xAxis = chart.getBaseAxes( )[ 0 ];
    yAxis = chart.getOrthogonalAxes( xAxis, true )[ 0 ];
    yAxisNumber2 = chart.getOrthogonalAxes( xAxis, true )[ 1 ];

    if ( yAxis.getType( ) == AxisType.DATE_TIME_LITERAL ) {
       xAxis.setFormatSpecifier(
          JavaDateFormatSpecifierImpl.create( "MM/dd/yyyy" ) );
    }
}
```

Rendering legend items

The beforeDrawLegendItem and afterDrawLegendItem events fire once for each legend entry while the legend is rendering. The event handlers receive three parameters: an instance of the LegendEntryRenderingHints class, an instance of the BoundsImpl class, and the Chart script context.

The LegendEntryRenderingHints object contains the following items:

- A data index, the index for the entry being rendered
- A Fill object, defining the color, image, or pattern filling the legend entry graphic
- A Label object, an instance of the LabelImpl class, representing the label for the legend entry
- A value label, an instance of the LabelImpl class, used when coloring the legend by values and the show values check box is selected

The BoundsImpl object contains the top, left, width, and height values for the legend entry graphic. If you change these values, be careful to avoid making the legend entry bounds wider or taller than the legend block. Listing 10-19 shows how to make modifications to the legend entry label and the graphic size. Making these changes in the afterDrawLegendItem function has no effect, as the entry is already rendered.

Listing 10-19 Make modifications to the legend entry label

```
function beforeDrawLegendItem( lerh, bounds, icsc )
{
   importPackage(
      Packages.org.eclipse.birt.chart.model.attribute.impl );

   label = lerh.getLabel( );
   labelString = label.getCaption( ).getValue( );

   if ( labelString == "true" ) {
      label.getCaption( ).getColor( ).set( 32, 168, 255 );
      label.getCaption( ).getFont( ).setItalic( true );
      label.getCaption( ).getFont( ).setRotation( 5 );
      label.getCaption( ).getFont( ).setStrikethrough( true );
      label.getCaption( ).getFont( ).setSize( 12 );
```

```
        label.getCaption( ).getFont( ).setName( "Arial" );
        label.getOutline( ).setVisible( true );
        label.getOutline( ).setThickness( 3 );

        var mycolor = ColorDefinitionImpl.BLUE( );
        r = mycolor.getRed( );
        g = mycolor.getGreen( );
        b = mycolor.getBlue( );
        lerh.getFill( ).set( r, g, b );

        var graphicwidth = bounds.getWidth( );
        var graphicheight = bounds.getHeight( );
        var chartModel = icsc.getChartInstance( );
        var legendBounds = chartModel.getLegend( ).getBounds( );
        var legendInsets = chartModel.getLegend( ).getInsets( );

        // This test does not account for the label text
        var availablewidth = legendBounds.getWidth( ) -
           legendInsets.getLeft( ) - legendInsets.getRight( );
        if ( availablewidth > ( graphicwidth + 15 ) ) {
           bounds.setWidth( graphicwidth + 15 );
           bounds.setHeight( graphicheight + 15 );
        }
    }
}
```

Writing a Java chart event handler

Write a Java chart event handler in the same way as a Java event handler for any other kind of report item. The only difference is that the chart event handler must contain all the implemented event handlers in a single Java class. The Java chart event handler also requires additional Java archive (.jar) files in the build path.

Setting up the chart event handler project

To create a new Java chart event handler project requires the following JAR files in the build path and classpath:

- chartengineapi.jar
- org.eclipse.emf.ecore_<version>.jar
- org.eclipse.emf.common_<version>.jar
- Optionally, scriptapi.jar, to access the reportContext
- Optionally, com.ibm.icu_<version>.jar, to use the ULocale methods

To write a Java event handler for a chart, implement the IChartEventHandler interface or extend the ChartEventHandlerAdapter. The examples in this chapter extend the adapter.

To apply a Java chart event handler to the chart, select the chart in the report design. In Properties, select the event handler property and type the fully qualified class name or choose Browse to locate the class. The browser displays only classes in your workspace or classpath that implement IChartEventHandler or extend ChartEventHandlerAdapter.

Debug chart event handlers written in Java in the same way as other Java event handlers.

Java chart event handler examples

This section provides some examples of common uses of Java chart event handlers.

The code in Listing 10-20 uses the beforeDrawBlock event handler to outline the legend block in red and the plot block in green, and set the background color of the title block to cream and its outline to blue.

Listing 10-20 Setting outline and background colors in a chart

```
package my.chart.events;

import org.eclipse.birt.chart.script.ChartEventHandlerAdapter;
import org.eclipse.birt.chart.model.layout.Block;
import org.eclipse.birt.chart.script.IChartScriptContext;
import org.eclipse.birt.chart.model.attribute.impl
   .ColorDefinitionImpl;

public class BlockScript extends ChartEventHandlerAdapter
{
   public void beforeDrawBlock( Block block,
      IChartScriptContext icsc )
   {
      if ( block.isLegend( ) ) {
         block.getOutline( ).setVisible( true );
         block.getOutline( ).getColor( ).set( 255, 0, 0 );
      }
      else if ( block.isPlot( ) ) {
         block.getOutline( ).setVisible( true );
         block.getOutline( ).getColor( ).set( 0, 255, 0 );
      }
      else if ( block.isTitle( ) ) {
         block.getOutline( ).setVisible( true );
         block.setBackground( ColorDefinitionImpl.CREAM( ) );
         block.getOutline( ).getColor( ).set( 0, 0, 255 );
      }
   }
```

Listing 10-21 uses the beforeDrawSeries event handler to set the series labels to red and apply a curve fitting line to the series. If the series is a line series, the code changes the marker type to a triangle.

Listing 10-21 Setting a series label color and applying a curve fitting line

```
package my.chart.events;

import org.eclipse.birt.chart.script.ChartEventHandlerAdapter;
import org.eclipse.birt.chart.model.component.Series;
import org.eclipse.birt.chart.script.IChartScriptContext;
import org.eclipse.birt.chart.render.ISeriesRenderer;
import org.eclipse.birt.chart.model.type.LineSeries;
import org.eclipse.birt.chart.model.attribute.Marker;
import org.eclipse.birt.chart.model.attribute.MarkerType;
import org.eclipse.birt.chart.model.component.impl
   .CurveFittingImpl;

public class SeriesScript extends ChartEventHandlerAdapter
{
   public void beforeDrawSeries( Series series,
   ISeriesRenderer isr, IChartScriptContext icsc )
   {
      if( series instanceof LineSeries ) {
         Marker mk = ( ( Marker )( ( LineSeries )series )
               .getMarkers( ).get( 0 ) );
         mk.setType( MarkerType.TRIANGLE_LITERAL );
      }
      series.setCurveFitting( CurveFittingImpl.create( ) );
      series.getLabel().getCaption().getColor().set( 255, 0, 0 );
   }
}
```

In Listing 10-22, the code creates event handlers for the beforeGeneration event and for the beforeDrawSeries event. The beforeGeneration event handler sets the plot background color to gray. If the chart has axes, the event handler sets the *x*-axis labels to an angle of 45 degrees and places the labels below the axis. This event handler also makes the major grid lines for the *y*-axis visible. The beforeDrawSeries event handler adds a mouse-over event to the series to show the value of the current data point.

Listing 10-22 beforeGeneration and beforeDrawSeries event handlers

```
package my.chart.events;

import org.eclipse.birt.chart.script.ChartEventHandlerAdapter;
import org.eclipse.birt.chart.model.Chart;
import org.eclipse.birt.chart.script.IChartScriptContext;
import org.eclipse.birt.chart.model.attribute.impl
   .ColorDefinitionImpl;
import org.eclipse.birt.chart.model.impl.ChartWithAxesImpl;
import org.eclipse.birt.chart.model.component.Axis;
```

```
import org.eclipse.birt.chart.model.attribute.Position;
import org.eclipse.birt.chart.model.component.Series;
import org.eclipse.birt.chart.model.attribute.TooltipValue;
import org.eclipse.birt.chart.model.attribute.impl
   .TooltipValueImpl;
import org.eclipse.birt.chart.model.data.Action;
import org.eclipse.birt.chart.model.data.impl.ActionImpl;
import org.eclipse.birt.chart.model.attribute.ActionType;
import org.eclipse.birt.chart.model.data.impl.TriggerImpl;
import org.eclipse.birt.chart.model.attribute.TriggerCondition;

public class ChartModScript extends ChartEventHandlerAdapter
{
   public void beforeGeneration( Chart cm,
      IChartScriptContext icsc)
   {
      cm.getPlot( ).getClientArea( ).setBackground(
         ColorDefinitionImpl.GREY( ) );
      if ( cm instanceof ChartWithAxesImpl ) {
         // x axis
         Axis xaxis = ( ( ChartWithAxesImpl ) cm)
            .getPrimaryBaseAxes( )[ 0 ];
         xaxis.setLabelPosition( Position.BELOW_LITERAL );
         xaxis.getLabel( ).getCaption( ).getFont( )
            .setRotation( 45 );
         Axis yaxis = ( ( ChartWithAxesImpl ) cm )
            .getPrimaryOrthogonalAxis( xaxis );
         yaxis.getMajorGrid( ).getLineAttributes( )
            .setVisible( true );
      }
   }

   public void beforeDrawSeries( Series series,
   ISeriesRenderer isr, IChartScriptContext icsc )
   {
      TooltipValue tt = TooltipValueImpl.create( 500, null );
      Action ac = ActionImpl.create(
         ActionType.SHOW_TOOLTIP_LITERAL, tt );
      series.getTriggers( ).add( TriggerImpl.create(
            TriggerCondition.ONMOUSEOVER_LITERAL, ac ) );
   }
}
```

Writing a JavaScript chart event handler

The process of writing a JavaScript chart event handler differs from the process of writing a JavaScript event handler for other report items. In BIRT Report Designer, Script displays only the onRender event in the list of

JavaScript events for a chart report item. The list next to the JavaScript events list contains a list of the all the chart events, as shown in Figure 10-1.

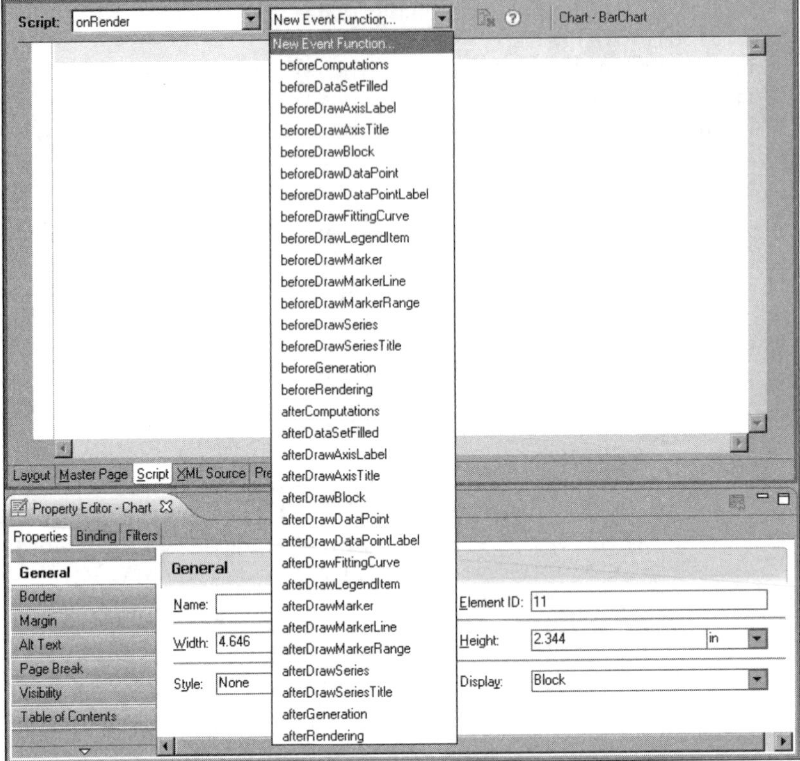

Figure 10-1 Script event functions for a chart in BIRT Report Designer

When you select one of the events from the list, BIRT adds a stub for that event in the onRender script window, as shown in Figure 10-2.

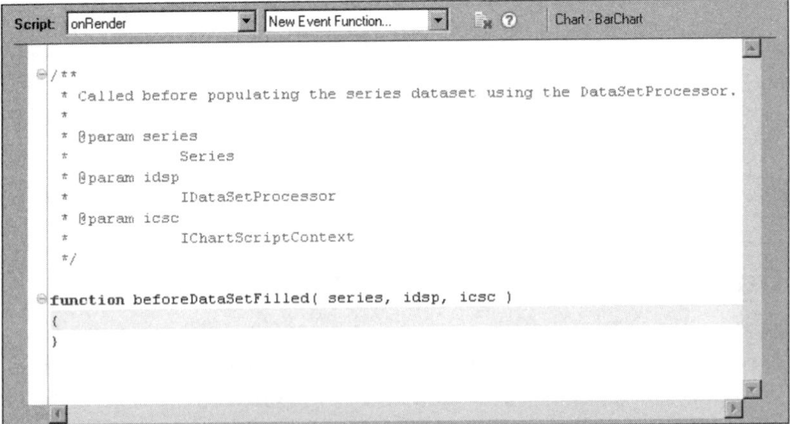


```
/**
 * Called before populating the series dataset using the DataSetProcessor.
 *
 * @param series
 *          Series
 * @param idsp
 *          IDataSetProcessor
 * @param icsc
 *          IChartScriptContext
 */
function beforeDataSetFilled( series, idsp, icsc )
{
}
```

Figure 10-2 Chart script stub

To write handler code for an event, type the handler code between the parentheses, as shown in Figure 10-3.

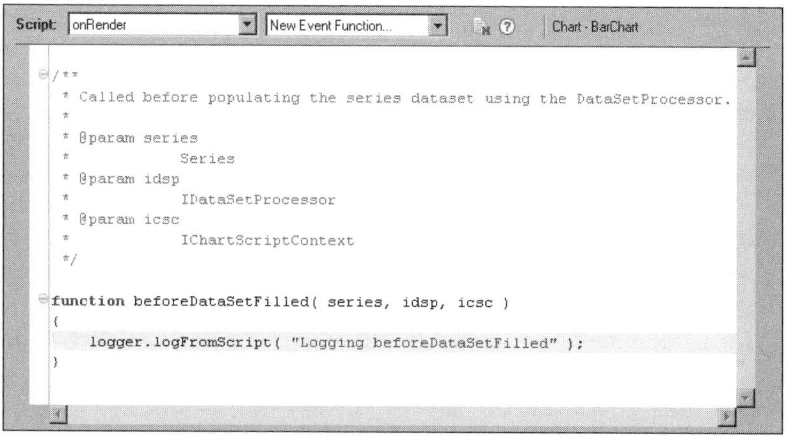

```
Script: onRender    New Event Function...    Chart - BarChart

/**
 * Called before populating the series dataset using the DataSetProcessor.
 *
 * @param series
 *            Series
 * @param idsp
 *            IDataSetProcessor
 * @param icsc
 *            IChartScriptContext
 */

function beforeDataSetFilled( series, idsp, icsc )
{
    logger.logFromScript( "Logging beforeDataSetFilled" );
}
```

Figure 10-3 Chart event handler stub

To code more chart event handlers, select the event from the list. Stub code for the event appears at the end of the script editor page. This page contains the JavaScript code for every event handler for the chart.

Using the simplified charting API

BIRT provides a simplified API for manipulating chart properties. In earlier versions, accessing the chart model was less straightforward and the differences between the chart model and the report model often led to confusion. The simplified charting API integrates the chart model with the report model script API, and uses an interface that is more like the API for other report items.

Listing 10-23 shows how earlier versions of BIRT set color by category.

Listing 10-23 Setting color by category in earlier versions of BIRT

```
public void beforeGeneration( Chart cm, IChartScriptContext icsc )
{
   cm.getLegend( ).setItemType(LegendItemType.CATEGORIES_LITERAL);
}
```

Listing 10-24 shows how to implement the same functionality using the simplified charting API in the beforeFactory event handler for a report that contains a chart named Chart1.

Listing 10-24 Setting color by category using the simplified charting API

```
var chart1 = this.getReportElement( "Chart1" )
chart1.setColorByCategory( true );
```

A typical use for the simplified charting API is to modify an existing chart in a report design. In addition, a Java application uses the simplified charting API to modify the chart's content.

Getting an instance of a chart item

The key component of the simplified charting API is the IChart interface. Like the other report item interfaces, IChart extends IReportItem. Because of the more complex nature of the Chart item, the IChart interface is in a different package and has a more extensive set of methods than the other report item interfaces. To obtain an IChart instance, use the name of the chart element as the argument to the getReportElement( ) method.

Use the following code to get an IChart object in a Java application using the Design Engine API or when developing a Java event handler:

```
IChart chart = (IChart)rptdesign.getReportElement( "Chart name" );
```

In a JavaScript event handler, use the following code to get the IChart object:

```
var chart1 = this.getReportElement( "Chart1" )
```

Understanding the sub-interfaces of IChart

There are two sub-interfaces of IChart:

- IChartWithAxes
- IChartWithoutAxes

IChartWithoutAxes adds only one method to IChart. IChartWithAxes adds several methods. Typically, in a Java application, cast the chart element to an appropriate sub-interface, as shown in the following code:

```
IChartWithAxes chart = ( IChartWithAxes )
   rptdesign.getReportElement("Name of an Axis-containing Chart");
```

Table 10-8 lists the methods of the IChart interface.

Table 10-8 IChart methods

Method	Action
getCategory( )	Returns an ICategory instance containing the category. This object supports changing settings, such as grouping and sorting for a chart category.
getDescription( )	Returns an IText instance containing the chart description. Supports changing the description.
getDimension( )	Gets the current dimension setting.
getFactory( )	Returns an IComponentFactory instance used to create chart elements.

Table 10-8 IChart methods

Method	Action
getLegend( )	Returns an ILegend instance containing the chart legend.
getOutputType( )	Returns a String containing the output type.
getTitle( )	Returns an IText instance containing the chart title. Supports changing the title.
isColorByCategory( )	Returns the color-by-category setting.
setColorByCategory (boolean flag)	Indicates whether to set the color by category.
setDimension(String type)	Set the dimension for the chart: ▪ TwoDimensional ▪ TwoDimensionalWithDepth ▪ ThreeDimensional
setOutputType(String type)	Sets the output type of the chart to one of the following formats: ▪ PNG ▪ SVG ▪ JPG ▪ BMP

Table 10-9 lists the methods of the IChartWithAxes interfaces.

Table 10-9 IChartWithAxes methods

Method	Action
getCategoryAxis( )	Returns an IAxis instance containing the category axis.
getValueAxes( )	Returns an array of IAxis instances containing the set of value axes.
getValueSeries( )	Returns a two dimensional array of IValueSeries instances containing the value series.
isHorizontal( )	Returns a boolean value indicating whether the chart orientation is horizontal.
setHorizontal(boolean flag)	Sets the orientation of the chart to horizontal when true or vertical when false.

Table 10-10 describes the method of the IChartWithoutAxes interfaces.

Table 10-10 IChartWithout Axes method

Method	Action
getValueSeries( )	Returns a one-dimensional array of IValueSeries instance containing the value series.

The most typical use of the API is in a beforeFactory event handler, which the Report Engine calls prior to generating the report. This event handler also supports modifying the design of the report. Listing 10-25 uses script in the report's beforeFactory event handler to locate a chart named Chart1, set the chart title to the string, My New Title, and render the title in red.

Listing 10-25 Using the beforeFactory event handler

```
var chart1 = this.getReportElement( "Chart1" );
var color1 = chart1.getTitle().getCaption().getColor();

chart1.setColorByCategory( true );
chart1.getTitle().getCaption().setValue( "My New Title" );

color1.setRed( 255 );
color1.setGreen( 0 );
color1.setBlue( 0 );
chart1.getTitle( ).getCaption( ).setColor( color1 );
```

Adding the following line to the script changes the chart to a three-dimensional chart:

```
chart1.setDimension( "ThreeDimensional" );
```

The following line of script sets the output type of the chart to PNG:

```
chart1.setOutputType( "PNG" );
```

Because IChart extends ReportItem, you can set chart dimensions by using the setWidth( ) and setHeight( ) methods. For example, to set the width and height to six inches, use the following script:

```
chart1.setWidth( "6in" );
chart1.setHeight("6in");
```

Chapter

11

Using Scripting to Access Data

BIRT supports accessing data using JavaScript code. This type of data source is called a scripted data source. Using a scripted data source, you can access objects other than the built-in data source types.

Because the JavaScript code for accessing and managing a scripted data source can wrap Java objects, a scripted data source can access an EJB, an XML stream, a Hibernate object, or any other Java object that retrieves data. A scripted data source must return data in tabular format, so that BIRT can perform sorting, aggregation, and grouping.

Using a Scripted Data Source

Creating a scripted data source and a non-scripted data source are similar tasks. The differences between creating a scripted data source and a non-scripted data source are:

- The scripted data source must be selected from the list of data source types when creating a scripted data source.
- Two event handler methods, open( ) and close( ), are available only for a scripted data source.

Every scripted data source must have at least one scripted data set. The differences between creating a scripted data set and a non-scripted data set are:

- The scripted data set must be associated with a scripted data source.

- The code for the scripted data set fetch( ) event handler method must be provided.
- There is a different dialog for identifying the columns of a scripted data set.

When using BIRT Report Designer to create a scripted data source, the following tasks must be performed:

- Create a scripted data source.

  Right-click on Data Sources in Data Explorer and select Scripted Data Source in the list of data source types.
- Create a scripted data set.

  Right-click on Data Sets in Data Explorer and select a scripted data source from the list of available data sources.
- Define output columns.

  Define the names and types of output columns, using the scripted data set editor.
- Supply code for the data source open( ) and close( ) methods.

  There are two scripted data source event handler methods, open( ) and close( ). It is not mandatory to implement either method, but most applications require the use of the open( ) method to initialize a data source. Typically, you create a Java object for accessing the data source in the open( ) method.

  Use the close( ) method to clean up any loose ends, including setting object references to null to ensure that the objects are deleted during garbage collection.
- Supply code for the data set methods.

  There are three scripted data set event handler methods, open( ), fetch( ), and close( ). Implementing the fetch( ) method is mandatory to initialize variables and to prepare the data source for fetching data.

  Use the fetch( ) method to get a row of data from the data source and to populate the columns of the row object. The fetch( ) method must return either true or false. A true value tells BIRT that there is another row to process. A false return value signifies that there are no more rows to process.

  Use the close( ) method to perform cleanup operations.
- Place the columns on the report layout.

  Place a data set column on a report layout the same way you place a column for a non-scripted data set.

The following tutorial guides you through the procedure required to perform each task in this process.

Tutorial 2: Creating a scripted data source

This tutorial provides instructions for the process of creating and scripting a simulated scripted data source.

In this tutorial, you perform the following tasks:

- Create a new report design.
- Create a scripted data source.
- Create a scripted data set.
- Write the open( ) and close( ) methods of the data source.
- Write the open( ) method of the data set.
- Write the fetch( ) method of the data set.
- Place the columns on the report layout.

Task 1: Create a new report design

In this task, you create a new report in BIRT Report Designer and name it ScriptedDataSrc.rptdesign.

1 Choose File➛New➛Report.

2 In File Name in New Report, type:

```
ScriptedDataSrc.rptdesign
```

3 In Enter or Select the Parent Folder, accept the default folder. Choose Next.

4 In Report Templates, select My First Report. Choose Finish. The BIRT report design screen appears. If a Cheat Sheet tab appears, close it.

Task 2: Create a scripted data source

In this task you create the new data source.

1 In Data Explorer, right-click Data Sources and choose New Data Source. Select a Data Source type appears.

2 In New Data Source, select Scripted Data Source.

3 In Data Source Name, type:

```
ScriptedDataSource
```

4 Choose Finish.

Data Explorer and the code window for ScriptedDataSource appear, as shown in Figure 11-1.

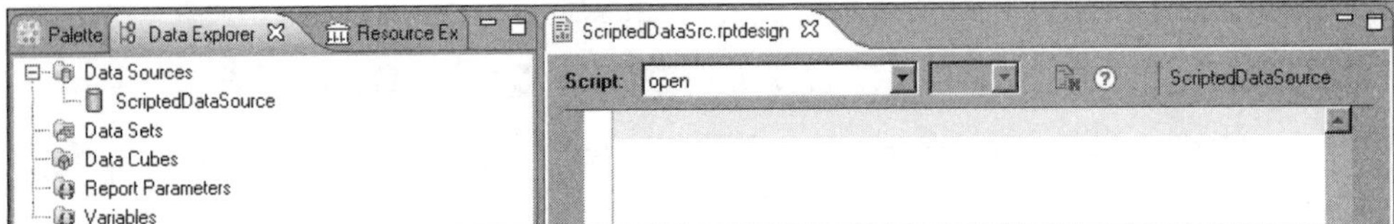

Figure 11-1 Data Explorer and ScriptedDataSource code window

Task 3: Create a scripted data set

In this task, you create the new data set.

1 In Data Explorer, right-click Data Sets. Choose New Data Set. New Data Set appears, as shown in Figure 11-2.

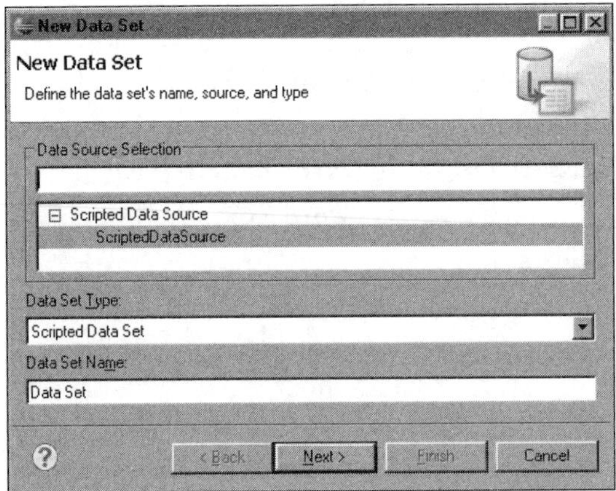

Figure 11-2 New data set for a scripted data source

2 In Data Set Name, replace the default name by typing:

`ScriptedDataSet`

3 Choose Next. Output columns appears, as shown in Figure 11-3.

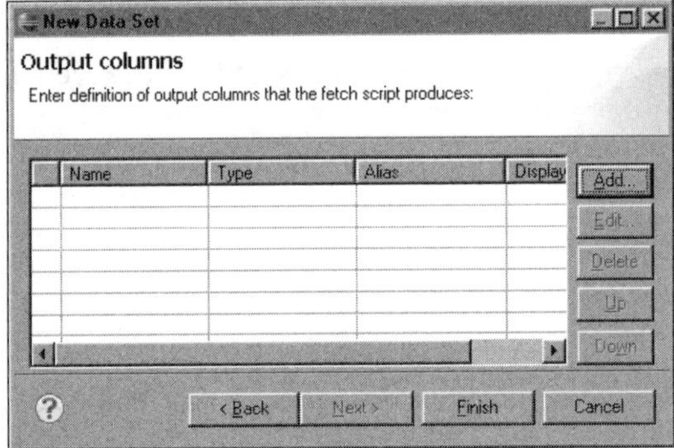

Figure 11-3 Preparing to define the output columns

4 In Output columns choose Add to define the first column for the data set. New Script Data Set Column appears.

5 In the Column Name, type:

```
col1
```

6 In Data Type select Integer from the drop-down list. New Script Data Set Column now contains the definition of one output column, as shown in Figure 11-4.

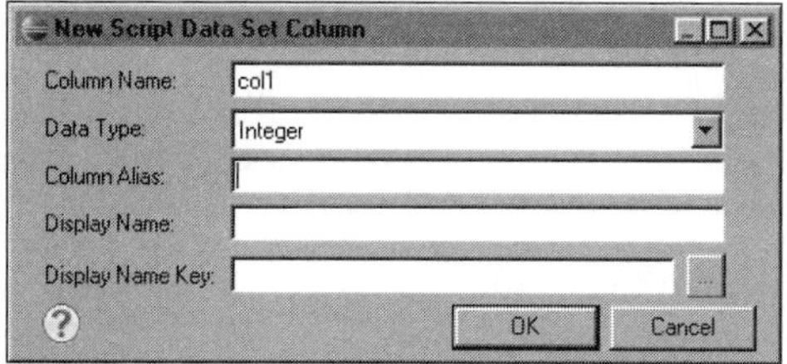

Figure 11-4 Defining the first output column

7 Choose OK. The col1 column definition appears in the Output columns list.

8 Using the same procedure create the definitions for col2 and col3. These data types are respectively String and Float. When you finish, the column definitions should look the ones shown in Figure 11-5.

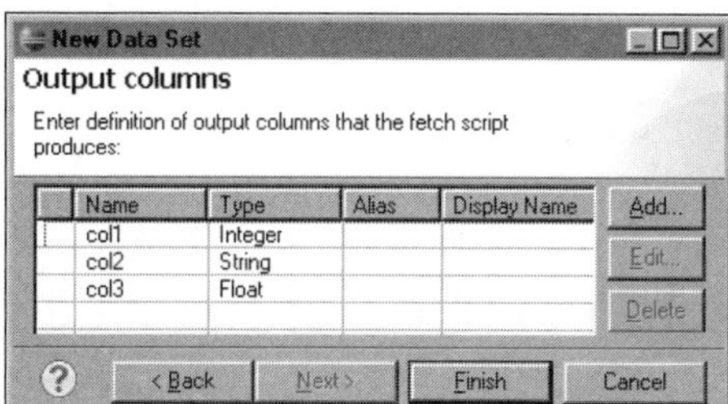

Figure 11-5 Completed column definitions

9 In Data Explorer, select ScriptedDataSet. The script window for the data set appears, including the column definitions, as shown in Figure 11-6.

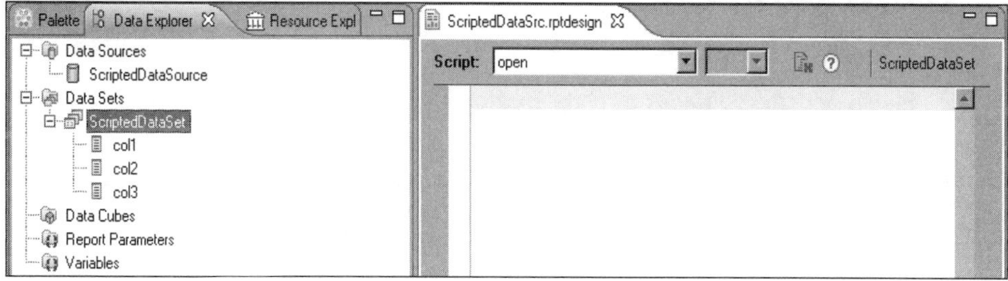

Figure 11-6 Code window for ScriptedDataSet

Task 4: Write the open( ) and close( ) methods of the data source

Use the open( ) method to open the data source. Use the close( ) method to do cleanup tasks. Typically, you need to place some code in these methods. The open( ) method is the default selected method upon creating a data set.

1 Select open from the pull-down list of methods.

2 Type the following code into the code window for the open( ) method:

```
dummyObject = new Object( );
```

The previous example code is placeholder code for this simplified example. In a typical application, you use this method to initialize a Java object that provides access to the data for the report.

3 Select close from the pull-down list of methods.

4 Type the following code into the code window for the close method:

```
dummyObject = null;
```

Task 5: Write the open( ) method of the data set

When you create the data set, the open( ) method is selected by default. Use the open( ) method of the data set to do initialization, such as defining a counter and setting it to zero.

1 Select open from the pull-down list of methods.

2 Type the following code into the code window:

```
recordCount = 0;
```

Task 6: Write the fetch( ) method of the data set

Use the fetch( ) method to process row data. The fetch( ) method must return either true or false. Fetch( ) returns true to indicate that there is a row to process. Fetch( ) returns false to indicate that there are no more rows to process. The fetch( ) method also calculates the values of computed fields. The report only has column headings at this point. To include data, you must add code to the fetch( ) method.

1 Choose the Script tab.

2 Select ScriptedDataSet in Data Explorer. Select fetch in the drop-down list of methods.

3 Type the following code into the code window. This code limits the number of rows that appear in the report to 19.

```
if(recordCount < 20) {
   recordCount++;
   row.col1 = recordCount;
```

```
        row["col2"] = "Count = " + recordCount;
        row[3] = recordCount * 0.5;
        return true;
    }
else return false;
```

Task 7: Place the columns on the report layout

You place columns for a scripted data set in the same way as for a non-scripted data set.

1 On ScriptedDataSrc.rptdesign, select Layout.

2 In Data Explorer, select ScriptedDataSet and drag the data set into the report layout.

Figure 11-7 shows the three columns of the data set in the layout editor.

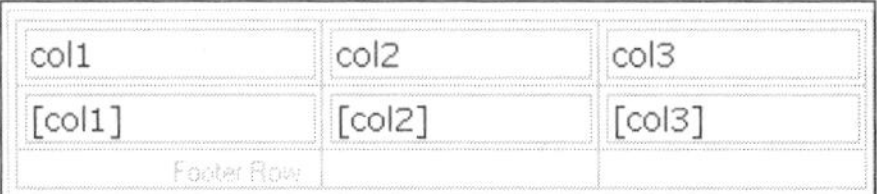

Figure 11-7 New columns in the report design

3 Choose Preview.

The preview of the report appears, as shown in Figure 11-8.

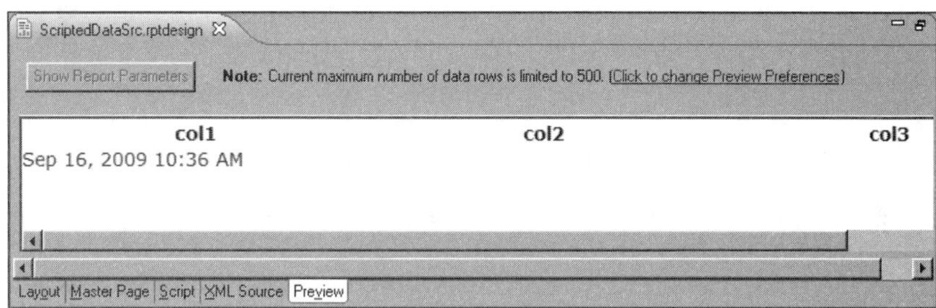

Figure 11-8 Report preview, showing the new columns

4 Choose Preview. The report now contains 20 rows and 3 columns of data. Rows 1-6 of the report preview are shown in Figure 11-9.

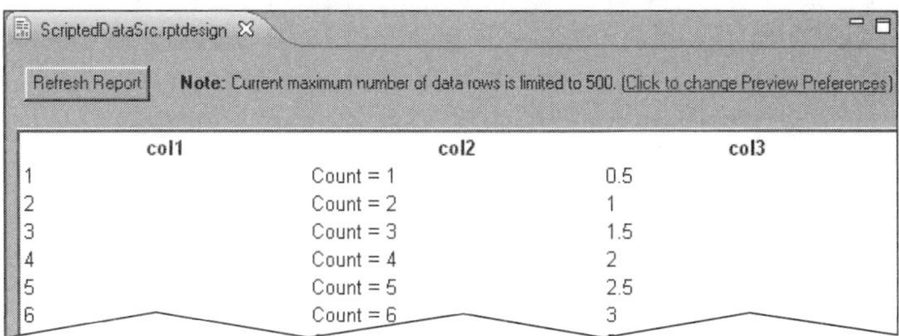

Figure 11-9 Report preview, rows 1 through 6

5 Rows 7 through 20 of the report preview are shown in Figure 11-10.

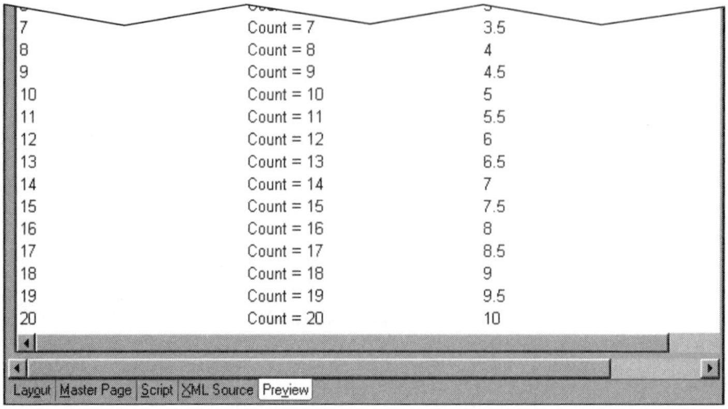

7	Count = 7	3.5
8	Count = 8	4
9	Count = 9	4.5
10	Count = 10	5
11	Count = 11	5.5
12	Count = 12	6
13	Count = 13	6.5
14	Count = 14	7
15	Count = 15	7.5
16	Count = 16	8
17	Count = 17	8.5
18	Count = 18	9
19	Count = 19	9.5
20	Count = 20	10

Layout | Master Page | Script | XML Source | Preview

Figure 11-10 Report preview, rows 7 through 20

Writing the scripted data set in Java

You can also implement this example in Java. Setup the Java project in the same workspace as the BIRT report project. In the report project, repeat the previous tasks, omitting tasks 4, 5, and 7.

In the Java project, add the Java class file in Listing 11-1. Finally, in the report project, select the scripted data set and set the event handler class property to the class in Listing 11-1.

Listing 11-1 MyScriptedDataSet.java

```
import org.eclipse.birt.report.engine.api.script
   .IScriptedDataSetMetaData;
import org.eclipse.birt.report.engine.api.script
   .IUpdatableDataSetRow;
import org.eclipse.birt.report.engine.api.script.eventadapter
   .ScriptedDataSetEventAdapter;
import org.eclipse.birt.report.engine.api.script.instance
   .IDataSetInstance;

public class MyScriptedDataSet extends ScriptedDataSetEventAdapter
   {
   public int recordCount = 0;
   @Override
   public boolean fetch( IDataSetInstance dataSet,
      IUpdatableDataSetRow row ) {
      try{
         if( recordCount < 20) {
            recordCount++;
            row.setColumnValue( "col1", recordCount );
            row.setColumnValue( "col2", "Count =
               " + recordCount );
```

```
            row.setColumnValue( "col3", recordCount*.05 );
            return true;
         }else{
            return false;
         }
      }catch( Exception e ){
         e.printStackTrace( );
         return false;
      }
   }
   @Override
   public void open( IDataSetInstance dataSet ) {
      recordCount = 0;
   }
}
```

Selecting Browse for the event handler property displays the scripted data set class. This example shows how to implement the scripted data set in Java. You can implement a scripted data source in a similar way.

In this example, the recordCount is stored as a global variable of the MyScriptedDataSet object. Using the global variable in this way is only valid for the data source or data set event handlers and should not be used when extending other event adapters. All other event adapters create a new instance of the event handler class for each instance of a report item. For example, when extending the RowEventAdapter, a new instance of the extending class is created for each row that uses the extended adapter.

Using a Java object to access a data source

A common use of a scripted data set is to access a Java object that accesses or generates the data for a report. This section shows how to access a Java class in the JavaScript code for a scripted data set.

Performing initialization in the data set open( ) method

Use the data set open( ) method to perform initialization tasks. A typical initialization task is to get an instance of the Java object that provides the data for the report.

When referring to a Java object, first import its package into the JavaScript environment. For example, the following code imports the package com.yourCompany.yourApplication:

```
importPackage( Packages.com.yourCompany.yourApplication );
```

This statement is like the import statement in Java and allows you to omit the package name when referencing a class. This statement is normally the first line in the open( ) method. You typically follow the importPackage statement with code to create the Java object instance, as shown in the following code:

```
var myList = MyListFactory.getList( );
```

A typical way of getting rows of data from a Java object is to use an iterator object. The open( ) method is the proper place to create an iterator object. For example, the following statement gets an iterator from myList:

```
var iterator = myList.getIterator( );
```

Getting a new row of data in the data set fetch( ) method

Once you have a way to get rows of data from your Java object, use the fetch( ) method to call the Java method that returns the rows. The fetch( ) method determines if there are any more rows of data and returns false if there are none, as shown in the following code:

```
if( iterator.hasNext( ) == false ){
   return false;
}
```

At this point, the fetch( ) method can populate a row with the data that it gets from the iterator, as shown in the following code:

```
var node = iterator.next( );
row[1] = node.getFirstCol( );
row[2] = node.getSecondCol( );
row[3] = node.getThirdCol( );
```

You must return true to signal BIRT that there is a valid row of data to process, as shown in the following code:

```
return true;
```

Cleaning up in the data set close( ) method

You can perform any cleanup in the close( ) method. This method is a good place to set to null any objects that you created. For example, the following code sets three object references to null:

```
myList = null;
iterator = null;
node = null;
```

Deciding where to place your Java class

If a scripted data source uses a custom Java class, that class must reside in a location where BIRT can find it. BIRT can find the Java class if its location meets any of the following requirements:

- The Java class is in the classpath of the Java Runtime Environment (JRE) under which Eclipse runs.

  Consider using this option if your Java class is in this location for other reasons.

- The Java class is in <ECLIPSE_INSTALL>\plugins\org.eclipse.birt.report.viewer\birt\WEB-INF\lib.

Consider using this option if your Java class is built, tested, and ready to deploy.

- The Java class is a part of an Eclipse Java project that is in the same workspace as the BIRT report project.

  Consider using this option if you are developing your Java class simultaneously with developing your BIRT report.

Deploying your Java class

Before you deploy your BIRT report to an application server, you must place your Java class in a JAR file. You must then deploy that JAR file to the proper location on the application server, so that the BIRT report viewer can find it at run time.

Using input and output parameters with a scripted data set

The scripted data set JavaScript event handler methods have two arrays you can use to access parameters, inputParams and outputParams. The inputParams array contains one string for every parameter defined as input. The outputParams array contains one string for every parameter whose direction is defined as output.

For example, assume that you have a scripted data set with an input and an output parameter, as shown in Figure 11-11.

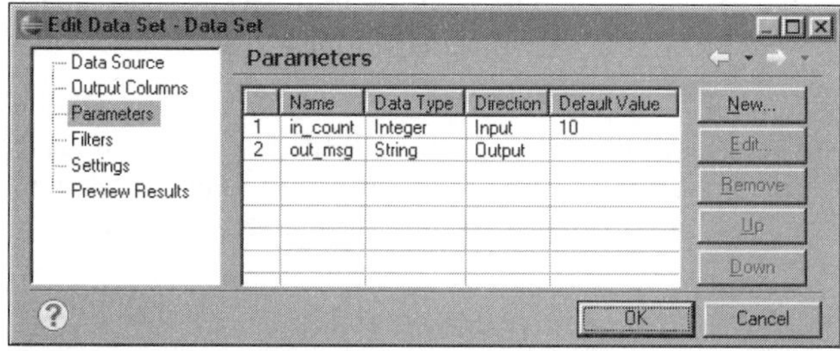

Figure 11-11 A scripted data set, with input and output parameters

You can get and set the values of the out_msg and in_count parameters by using the inputParams and outputParams arrays as in the following example:

```
outputParams[ "out_msg" ] = "Total rows: " +
   inputParams[ "in_count"];
```

You can access a parameter in the array either by the name of the parameter or by a 1-based index value. The inputParams and outputParams arrays are not accessible to Java event handlers.

Creating a web services data source using a custom connection class

As stated earlier, you can use a custom connection class to create a web services data source. The custom connection class is responsible for returning an Input Stream that contains a SOAP XML response. This class must implement a connect( ) method. This method has to return an Object, implementing a executeQuery( ) and disconnect( ) method.

The connect( ) method accepts two parameters, which contain the connection properties and application context.

BIRT uses an application context map to store values and objects for use in all phases of report generation and presentation. You can reference objects in the application context from Script, the Expression Builder, in the ODA layer, and so forth. The application context map contains specific name value pairs that are passed to all generation and rendering processes.

You can use the application context to pass a security identifier that can be validated in the connection class and passed in as part of the SOAP request. In many cases the web services require such identifiers.

The Connection Class

If the connectionClass public property of the data source is set to a non-empty string, the run-time driver uses a custom connection class to create connections to the web service. The custom connection class is also responsible for executing the web services queries for web services data sets associated with this data source.

The connection class property is the fully qualified name of a Java class, which must implement the following class method to establish a web services connection. The Java class must be in the application classpath.

```
public static Object connect(
      java.util.Map connectionProperties,
      java.util.Map appContext );
```

The connectionProperties parameter specifies the run-time values of all public connection properties available to the driver as a (String, String) map keyed by the connection property name. The map may contain any or all of the following map keys: soapEndPoint, connectionTimeOut, connectionClass, OdaConnProfileName, and OdaConnProfileStorePath.

The appContext parameter provides all the application context values as (String, Object) pairs. Its value is never null, but its collection may be empty.

The connection Instance

The connect(...) method of the custom driver class, after establishing a successful connection, returns a non-null object which implements the following two methods.

```
public Object executeQuery(
     java.lang.String queryText,
     java.util.Map parameterValues,
     java.util.Map queryProperties
);

public void disconnect( );
```

The executeQuery( ) Method

The queryText parameter specifies the query text. It can be null if the connection class does not require the report design to provide a query text.

The parameterValues parameter specifies values of all the data set parameters as a (String, Object) map keyed by parameter name. It can be null if the data set does not define any parameters.

The queryProperties parameter specifies values of all the data set public properties as a (String, String) map keyed by property name. The map can contain the queryTimeOut map key.

The query method must return a value of either of the following data types:

- java.lang.String

  The returned String is the complete SOAP response.

- java.io.InputStream

  The returned stream is SOAP response stream.

The disconnect( ) method

This method closes the connection. The driver implementation of the disconnect method is optional. If it is implemented, BIRT calls this method when the associated data source closes.

Method calling and error handling

The driver calls the custom driver class using Java reflection. The class and connection object do not need to implement any predefined interface. Any exception thrown by any of the defined methods is treated as an error and results in a failure and a thrown ODA Exception.

Custom connection class example

Listing 11-2 is an example of a custom class that accesses a set of connection properties, then instantiates a query object.

Listing 11-2 Custom Connection class

```
import java.util.Iterator;
import java.util.Map;
public class MyConnectionClass {
   public static Object connect( Map connProperties,
      Map appContext )
   {
      Iterator it = connProperties.keySet( ).iterator( );
       while ( it.hasNext( ) ) {
           Object key = it.next( );
       }
      it = connProperties.values( ).iterator( );
       while ( it.hasNext( ) ) {
           // Get value
           Object value = it.next( );
       }
      MyWSQuery msg = new MyWSQuery( );
      return msg;
   }
}
```

Listing 11-3 is an example of a query class implementation that executes a query by opening a file input stream and disconnects, closing the file.

Listing 11-3 Query class implementation

```
import java.io.FileInputStream;
import java.util.Map;
   public class MyWSQuery {
      public Object executeQuery( String queryText,
         Map parameterValues, Map queryProperties )
      {
         FileInputStream fis = null;
         try {
            fis = new FileInputStream( "c:/ExchangeRates.xml" );
         } catch ( Exception e ) {

         }
         return fis;
      }
      public void disconnect( )
      {
         If( fis != null )
         {
            fis.close( );
            fis = null;
         }
      }
   }
```

Chapter

12

Debugging Event Handlers

The report debugger tool in BIRT provides functionality similar to other debugger frameworks, such as those in Java and C++ IDEs. The BIRT report debugger enables users to run reports step by step, set breakpoints, inspect instance properties, and watch and evaluate variable values in certain contexts. Using the debugger supports advanced report developers in spotting the errors in report designs quickly and making it easy to understand and identify exceptions during run time.

Unlike the standard Java debugger, the report debugger is based on the report object model tree. The report debugger provides the following functionality:

- Syntax checking of JavaScript expressions
- Debugging JavaScript event handlers
- Debugging Java event handlers
- Debugging report execution exceptions
- Inspecting report iteminstance and variable values

Based on the standard Eclipse debugging framework, the report debugger framework enhances the Eclipse built-in debugging features.

BIRT report debugger consists of the following parts:

- Report JavaScript debugger
- Report Java EventHandler debugger

In earlier versions of BIRT, the Java EventHandler debugger required setting an Eclipse workbench start-up parameter. In the current release, the new mechanism allows direct debugging of the report engine in the JVM.

The JavaScript debugger is implemented as a BIRT Report Script Virtual Machine (VM). The VM extends the standard Eclipse debug extension point and communicates directly with the Eclipse Debugging Framework. This VM handles all script debugging tasks, such as managing breakpoints, communicating with the engine task thread, and reporting to eclipse listeners. Figure 12-1 presents the BIRT Debugger architecture.

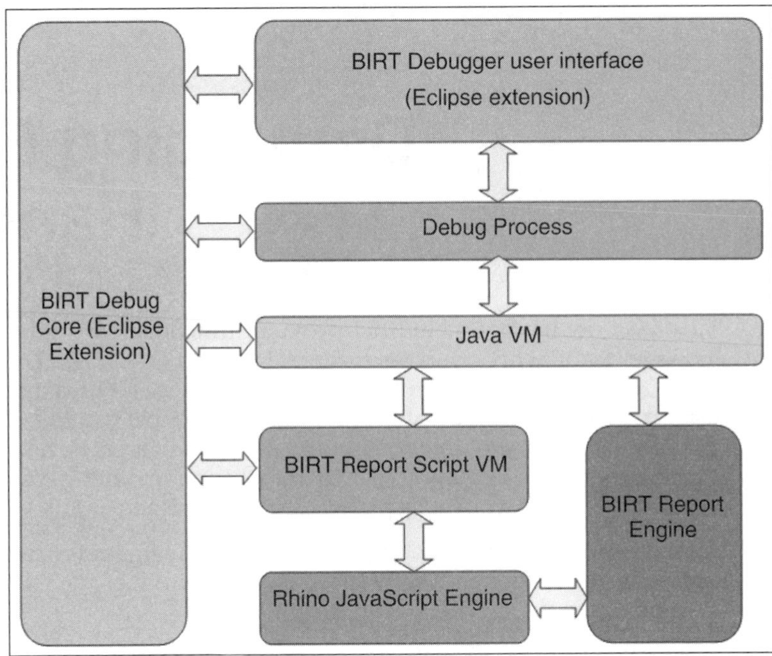

Figure 12-1 BIRT Debugger architecture

Checking the syntax of JavaScript expressions

BIRT Report Designer's expression builder and script editor support writing JavaScript. Both editors validate the code by checking for syntax errors. The checking validates only JavaScript grammar not the semantics of the scripts.

The expression builder supports checking the code for syntax errors, as shown in Figure 12-2, in the following two ways:

- Selecting the Validate button. Information about the syntax error appears below the expression builder title bar.

- Choosing OK. A warning message appears if the script editor detects a syntax error. Choosing OK on the message saves the code. Choosing Cancel closes the message and returns focus to the expression builder.

The script editor validates code dynamically. As the developer types JavaScript code, the editor validates the syntax and uses a red cross mark on the left border to indicate any line containing an error.

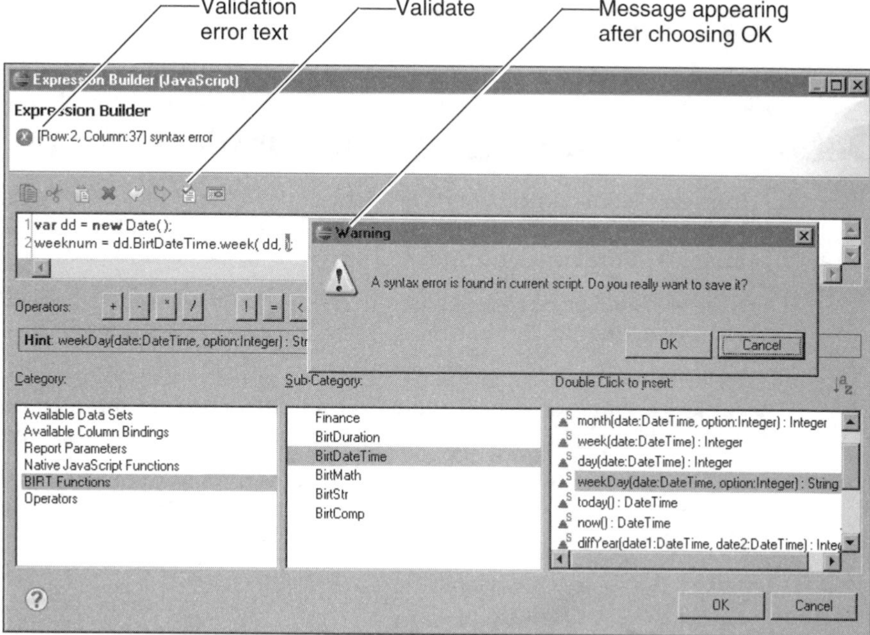

Figure 12-2 Checking for JavaScript syntax errors in the expression builder

The line containing the error is marked and the exact location of the syntax error is highlighted, as shown in Figure 12-3.

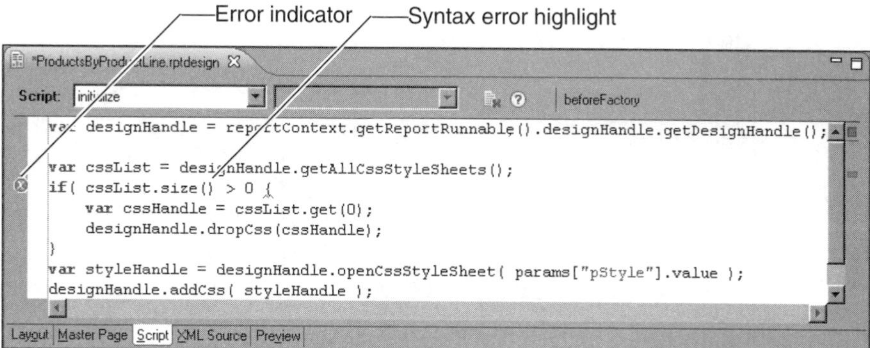

Figure 12-3 Checking for JavaScript syntax errors in the script editor

A description of the error appears in a text box when the developer moves the mouse pointer over the error indicator on the left border, as shown in Figure 12-4.

```
var cssList = designHandle.getAllCssStyleSheets();
missing ) after condition e() > 0 {
    var cssHandle = cssList.get(0);
    designHandle.dropCss(cssHandle);
}
```

Figure 12-4 Displaying a syntax error message in the script editor

Debugging JavaScript event handlers code

Users can set breakpoints on JavaScript code at specific execution points. During debugging, execution stops at a breakpoint and the user can inspect variables in the current context.

To debug JavaScript code, switch to the script editor and set a breakpoint by double clicking the left border at a specific line.

The BIRT report debugger uses the standard Eclipse debugging feature. This chapter provides only basic details about the debugger main components. Refer to the Eclipse documentation for more information about the debugger.

You manage the debugging or running of reports in the Debug perspective. To open the Debug perspective, choose Window➛Open Perspective➛Other ➛Debug, as shown in Figure 12-5.

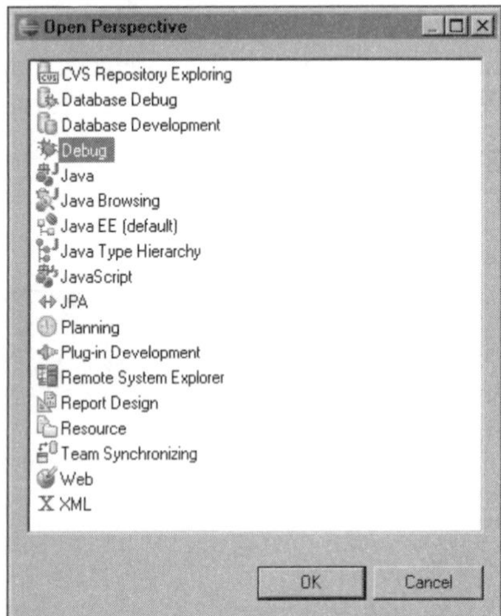

Figure 12-5 Selecting the Debug perspective

The Debug perspective and its views are shown in Figure 12-6.

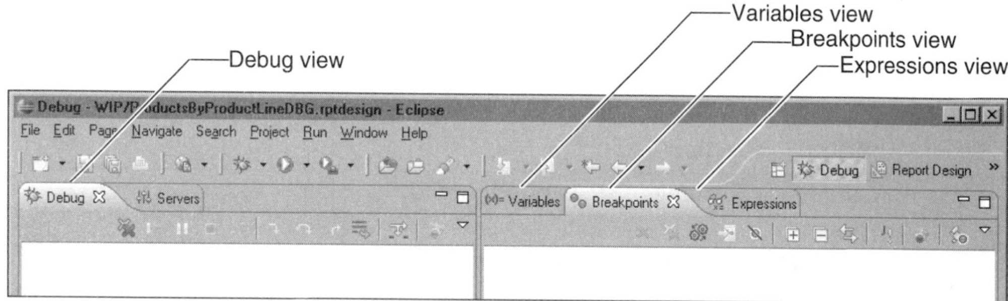

Figure 12-6 The upper portion of the Debug perspective

The Debug perspective contains the following views:

- Debug view

  The Debug view shows reports you are currently debugging as well as any others you were debugging before you terminated them. This view includes processes and threads associated with the reports. An example of a debug view is shown in Figure 12-7.

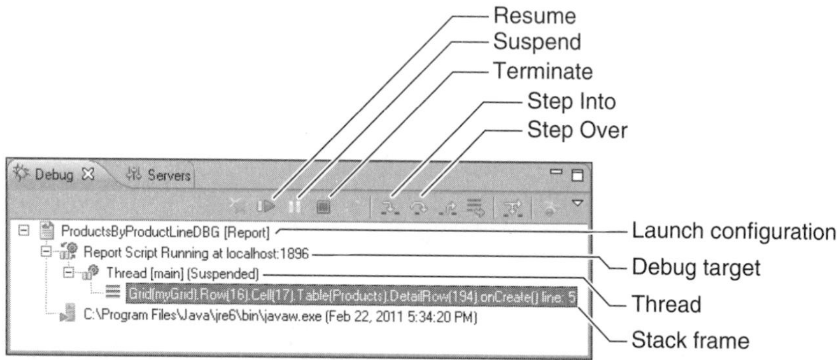

Figure 12-7 Debug view

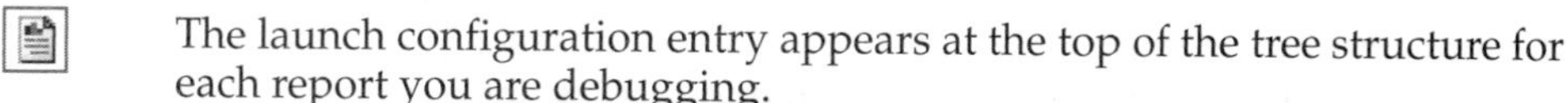

The launch configuration entry appears at the top of the tree structure for each report you are debugging.

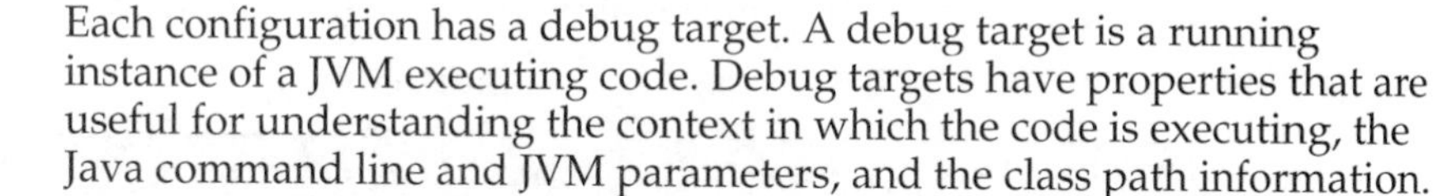

Each configuration has a debug target. A debug target is a running instance of a JVM executing code. Debug targets have properties that are useful for understanding the context in which the code is executing, the Java command line and JVM parameters, and the class path information.

The debug view displays suspended threads for each report you are debugging. Each thread in your program appears as a node in the tree under the debug target.

You can think of a stack frame as a method invocation. When one method invokes another, a stack frame is added to the top of the stack. When the method returns, that stack frame is removed from the top of the stack. An example of a stack frame appears as selected in Figure 12-7.

The Debug view provides the main buttons in Table 12-1 to control the debugging process, as shown in Figure 12-7.

Table 12-1 Debugger user interface buttons

Icon	Button	Action
	Resume	Resumes a suspended thread.
	Step Into	Steps into the highlighted statement.
	Step Over	Steps over the current statement. Execution continues at the next line in the same method or, if at the end of a method, in the method calling the current method. The cursor jumps to the declaration of the method. The line to execute is highlighted.
	Suspend	Suspends the selected thread of a target so that you can browse or modify code, inspect data.
	Terminate	Terminates the selected debug target.

- Variables view
  Displays information about the variables associated with the stack frame selected in the Debug view, as shown in Figure 12-8.

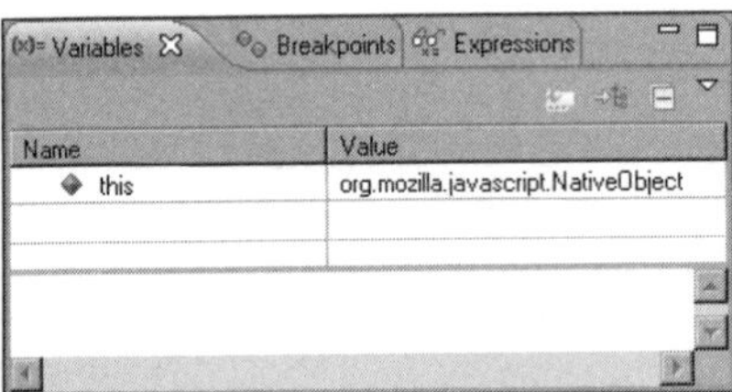

Figure 12-8 Variables view

- Breakpoints view
  Lists all the breakpoints you currently have set in your workspace. Figure 12-9 shows a single breakpoint in the Breakpoints view.

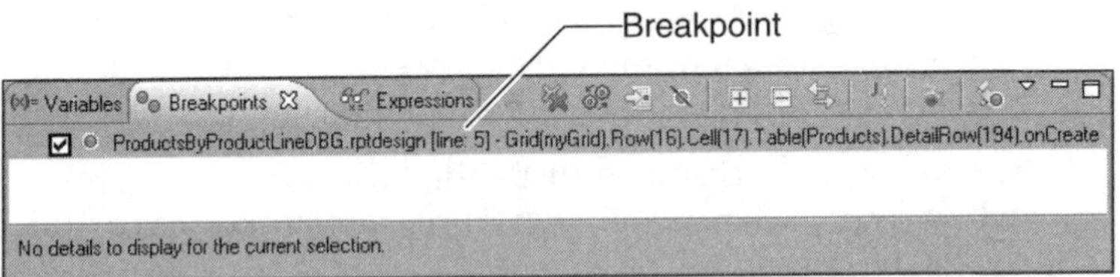

Figure 12-9 List of breakpoints containing one breakpoint

Double-click a breakpoint to display its location in the script editor. You can delete, add, enable, or disable breakpoints. You can group breakpoints by working set or set hit counts.

- Expressions view

  Displays selected variables defined and manipulated in the script code, as shown in Figure 12-10.

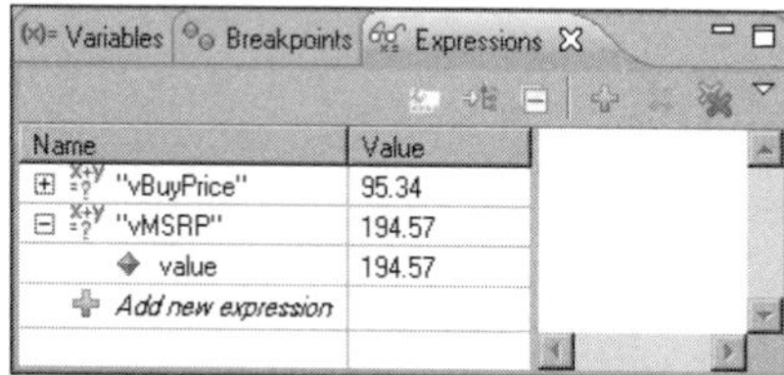

Figure 12-10 Expressions view

The script editor and other views used by the Debug perspective appear in the lower portion of the Eclipse workbench, as shown in Figure 12-11.

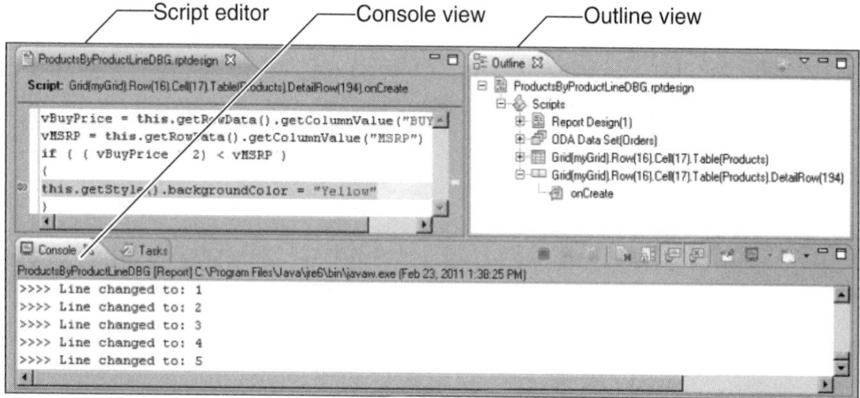

Figure 12-11 Script, Console, and Outline views

- Script editor

  Shows the script you are debugging in the debug and report design perspectives.

  In Script, to set a breakpoint, double-click the vertical border on the left side at a specific line, as shown in Figure 12-12. The breakpoint appears in the border as a blue circle. The breakpoint is also added in the breakpoints view, as shown in Figure 12-9.

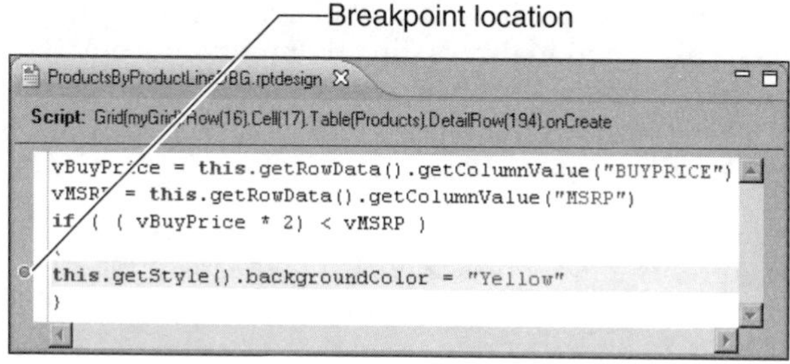

Figure 12-12 Setting a breakpoint

- Outline view

  Shows the report structure in the Debug and Report Design perspectives. In the Debug perspective, this view shows only the scripts defined in the report design, as shown in Figure 12-11.

- Console view

  Displays a variety of consoles depending on the type development and the current user settings.

  The Process Console in the Debug perspective, as shown in Figure 12-11, displays the output of a process and accepts keyboard input to a process. The Process Console displays the following three kinds of text:

  - Standard error
  - Standard input
  - Standard output

  To specify different colors for these kinds of text, choose Window➛Preferences. Then, in Preferences, expand Run/Debug and select Console.

Debugging Java event handler code

To set breakpoints on Java event handler code, use the standard Eclipse Java Development Tools (JDT) user interface. The JDT UI (org.eclipse.jdt.ui) plug-in implements the Java-specific user interface classes that manipulate Java elements. Packages in the JDT UI implement the Java-specific extensions to the workbench. During report execution, the report engine stops at each specific breakpoint. Developers can then inspect report item instances and variable values in the current context.

Debugging report execution exceptions

Exceptions are one of the most evident symptoms of execution errors. You can set breakpoints on certain exception classes when an exception occurs. Exception breakpoints stop execution whenever an exception of a selected type is thrown. This functionality is directly inherited from the JDT debugger and has the same capabilities. When a selected exception occurs, the report engine stops execution, and the report item instance and variable values can be examined in the current context.

Exception breakpoints can be viewed, enabled, or disabled using the standard Breakpoints view. Choosing Add Java Exception Breakpoint from the Breakpoints view activates these breakpoints, as shown in Figure 12-13. Alternatively, add a Java exception breakpoint by choosing Run➛Add Java Exception Breakpoint.

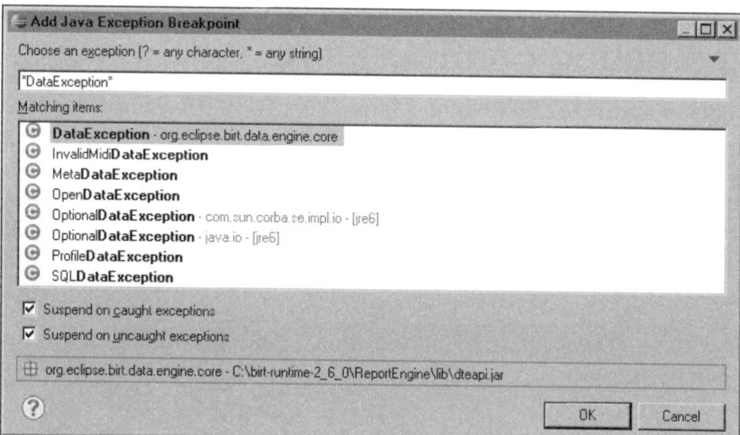

Figure 12-13 Selecting an exception breakpoint

Execution can be stopped when the exception is either caught or uncaught, or both. The breakpoint appears in the Breakpoints view as shown in Figure 12-14. Enable or disable these breakpoints using the context menus in the Breakpoints view, the Java Editor ruler, and the script editor ruler.

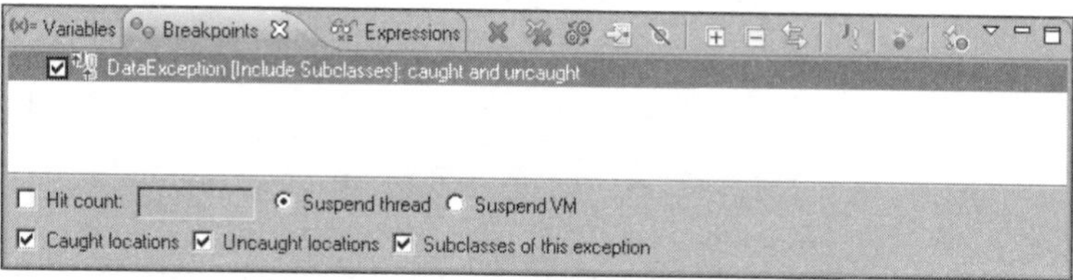

Figure 12-14 Viewing a breakpoint in Breakpoint view

Using exception breakpoint debugging can be very helpful when you work on complex reports. For example, if a column in a report has an invalid data type, every time the report is run, the report engine throws a DataException. If the report uses multiple data sets or libraries, the exact column definition is not easy to find. In that situation, add a breakpoint exception for DataException and debug the report. When the DataException occurs again, the debugger stops the execution at the specific breakpoint. Inspect the current report context in the Variables view to identify the data set and the library names. The reportContext and rowInstance variables are shown in Figure 12-15. Knowing the data set makes locating and correcting the column definition to fix the error into a straightforward task.

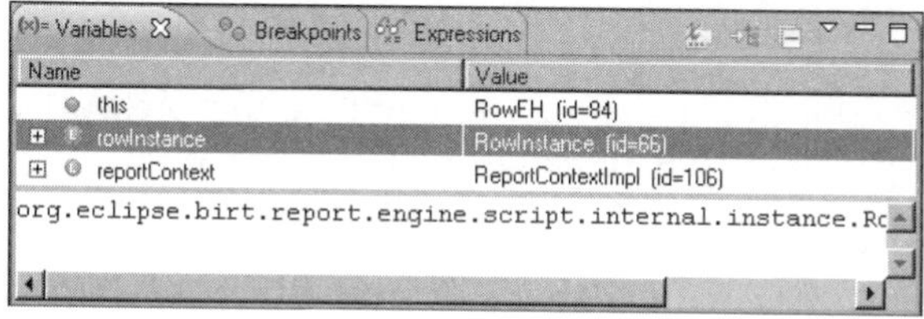

Figure 12-15 Inspecting variables

Creating a debug configuration

Use the standard Eclipse debug launch configuration interface to start the report debugger. Set specific report debugger options on the configuration page. Ideally, use only one launch configuration type for both report and code debugging. To run a report in the Debug perspective, create a Report debug configuration by choosing Run➛Debug Configurations. Figure 12-16 shows the Main page, which contains the key configuration settings for the Report debug configuration type.

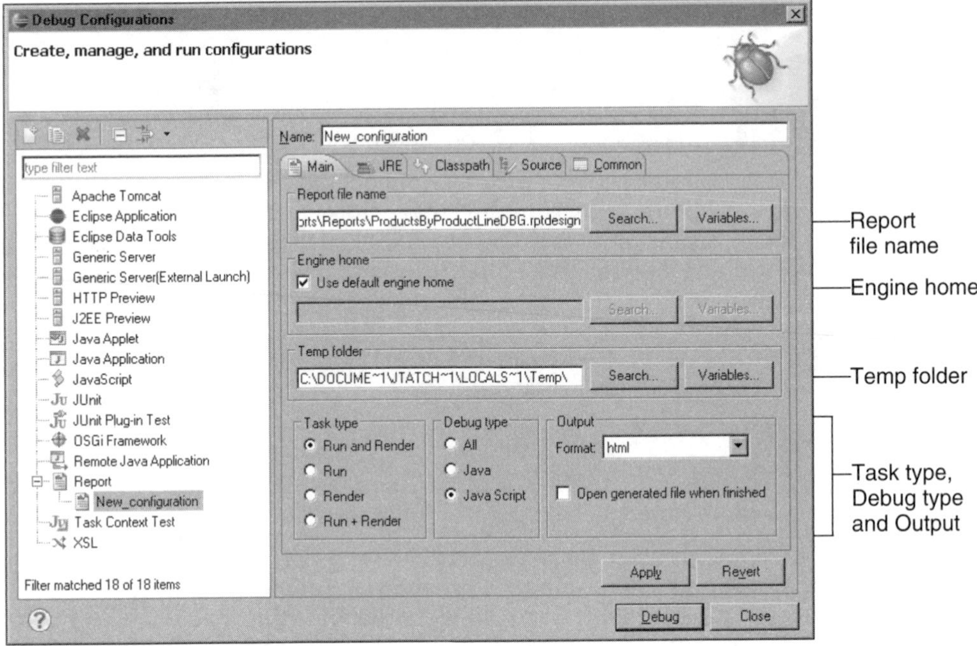

Figure 12-16 Settings for a Report debug configuration

In Main, configure the following settings:

- Name

  The name of the debug configuration. Good practice is to use the report name as the configuration name to aid in distinguishing among multiple configurations.

- Report file name

  The path to the report file to debug. Debugging either a report design or a report document is available, depending on the task type.

- Engine home

  The BIRT report engine home path. By default, BIRT uses the same engine that starts the debugger. Specify an external engine home to test the report using a different version of BIRT runtime libraries. The external report engine home typically points to a BIRT run-time folder, for example, C:\birt-runtime-2_6_0\ReportEngine.

- Temp folder

  The temporary working folder for the report debugging process. By default, this folder is the system temp folder.

- Task type

  The engine task type to use for the debug process. Table 12-2 lists and describes the available types:

  Table 12-2 Engine task types for debugging a report

Task type	Report engine action
Run and Render	Processes the report. The engine does not generate a report document file. The engine renders the design file directly to a target output format.
Run	Generates only a report document. The engine does not render the document to a target output format.
Render	Renders a report document file to a target output.
Run + Render	First, generates a report document using a Run task. Then, the engine renders the document to a target output format using a Render task.

- Debug Type

  The available types of debugging: All, Java, or JavaScript.

- Output

  The available output format types for the debug process: DOC, HTML, PDF, PostScript, PPT, or XLS.

  To open the generated output file when the debug process completes, select Open generated file when finished.

Launching the debug configuration establishes a connection between the debugger and the running report. You can then use breakpoints, stepping, or expression evaluation to debug your program.

How to create a debug configuration

The following section shows how to create a launch configuration to debug a BIRT report. The report name is ProductsByProductLineDBG.rptdesign.

1 Open a BIRT report in BIRT Report Designer.

2 Choose Run➛Debug Configurations. Debug Configuration appears.

3 From the list of launch types, select Report. Then, choose New launch configuration, as shown in Figure 12-17.

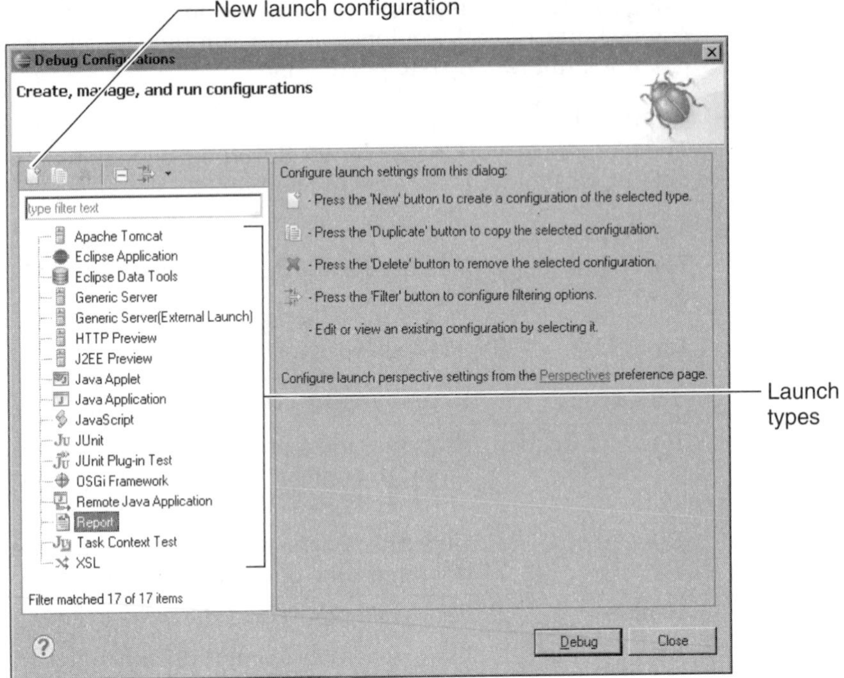

Figure 12-17 Selecting New launch configuration

Debug Configuration creates a default report launch configuration named New_configuration, as shown in Figure 12-16.

4 In Name, type the name of the report to debug. By default, a new configuration uses the currently opened report as the file to debug. Change the name and other debug settings as required. For example, in Output, select the output format for the report.

5 If you are debugging a Java event handler, set the Java Classpath to ensure the report engine can find the event handler class. Choose Classpath, as shown in Figure 12-18. In Classpath, choose Add Project, Add JARs, or Add External JARs, according to the location of the eventhandlers.jar file.

6 Choose Apply to create the report debug configuration.

Tutorial 3: Debugging a report that contains Java and JavaScript code

This tutorial provides step by step instructions about how to debug a report that contains Java and JavaScript event handlers. The report example in this tutorial uses the Classic Models sample database and displays the car sales, grouping the data by country and customer. Additional analysis in the report highlights the orders having prices above the median price in fuschia and the orders having prices below the median price in yellow. The orders for the product line selected by the user appear in bold font. The report uses a JavaScript event handler to implement the highlighting and a Java event handler to set the bold font for certain rows.

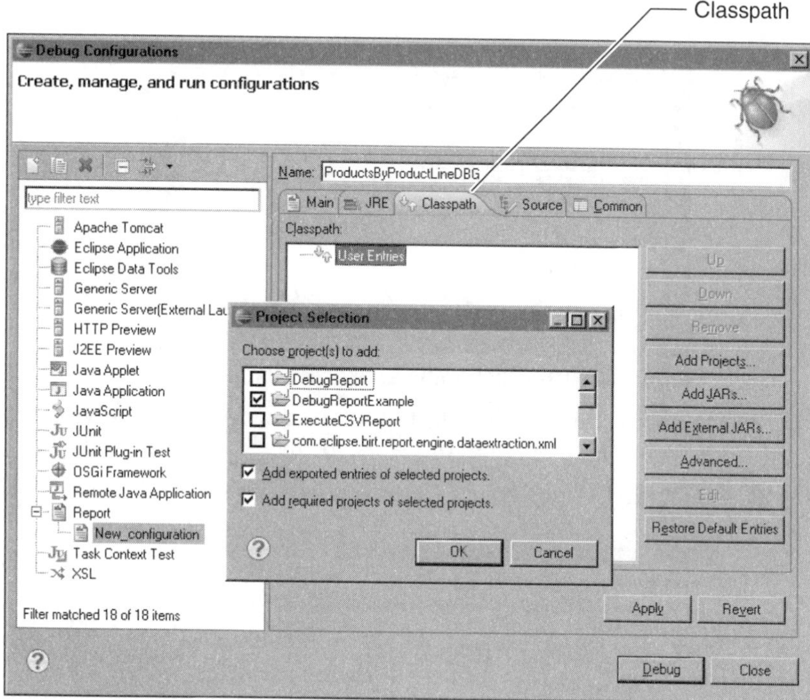

Figure 12-18 Setting the classpath to Java event handlers in a project

Compiling the Java event handler class requires the coreapi.jar and scriptapi.jar files to be in the build classpath. These libraries are provided in the BIRT runtime package. Download the BIRT report engine runtime archive (.zip) file, birt-runtime-2_6_0.zip, from the Eclipse BIRT web site. Unzip the file in your environment.

To prepare to perform this tutorial, download the example project, DebugReportExample.zip containing SalesByCountry.rptdesign, from http://www.actuate.com/birt/contributions. This tutorial provides instructions about how to import the project into your workspace and how to debug the report.

Task 1: Preparing the report for debugging

This task assumes you have already uncompressed the example project into your workspace and opened BIRT Report Designer.

1 Import the project to the workspace.

  1 Choose File➛Import.

2 In Import, choose General➛Existing Projects into Workspace as shown in Figure 12-19.

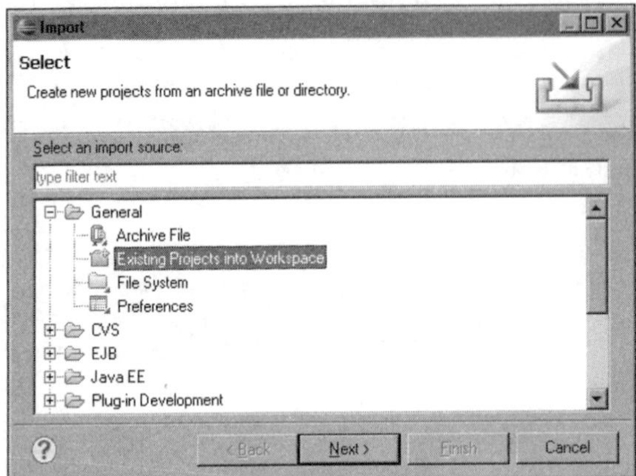

Figure 12-19 Importing an existing project

2 On Import Projects, in Select root directory, type the path to the workspace folder in the file system or choose Browse to find the folder.

3 Select the DebugReportExample project, as shown in Figure 12-20.

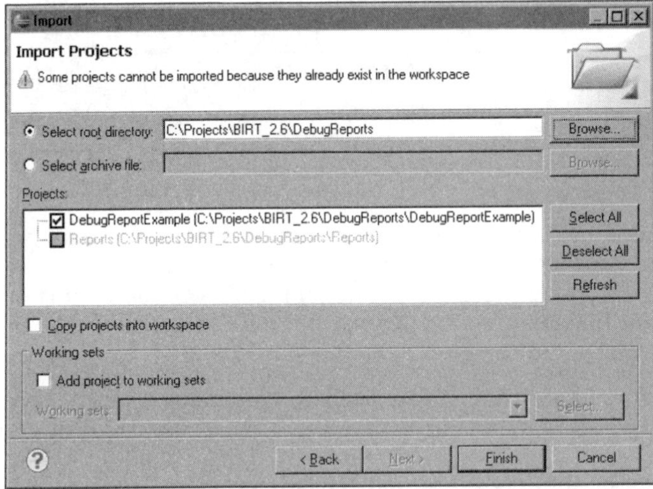

Figure 12-20 Selecting the project to import

Choose Finish. Navigator displays the imported project.

4 Expand the project to review its contents, as shown in Figure 12-21. The project contains the report design and supporting files, such as the Java event handler class DataItemProductNameEH.java and the logo image ClassicMogels.jpg.

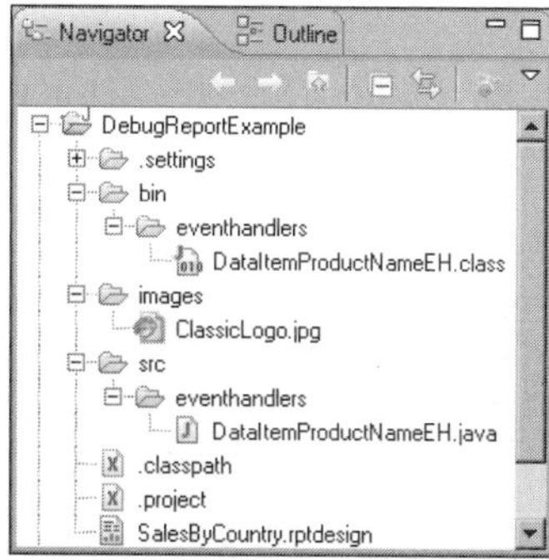

Figure 12-21 Reviewing the project in Navigator

5 Choose the Problems view to confirm that the project compiled properly. If you see errors similar to those in Figure 12-22, update your Java build path to correct the paths to the scriptapi.jar and coreapi.jar libraries. If you do not see errors, proceed to step 7.

Property Editor | Problems

8 errors, 0 warnings, 0 others

Description	Resource	Path	Location	Type
Errors (8 items)				
DataItemEventAdapter cannot be resolved to a type	DataItemProductNameEH.java	/DebugReportEx...	line 8	Java Problem
IDataItemInstance cannot be resolved to a type	DataItemProductNameEH.java	/DebugReportEx...	line 13	Java Problem
IReportContext cannot be resolved to a type	DataItemProductNameEH.java	/DebugReportEx...	line 13	Java Problem
ScriptException cannot be resolved to a type	DataItemProductNameEH.java	/DebugReportEx...	line 21	Java Problem

Figure 12-22 Reviewing errors in Problems view

6 Update the Java Build Path.

1 In Navigator, right-click the DebugReportExample project and choose Properties from the context menu.

2 In Properties, select Java Build Path. Errors indicate the missing libraries. In JARs and class folders on the buildpath, select coreapi.jar and scriptapi.jar, as shown in Figure 12-23, and choose Remove.

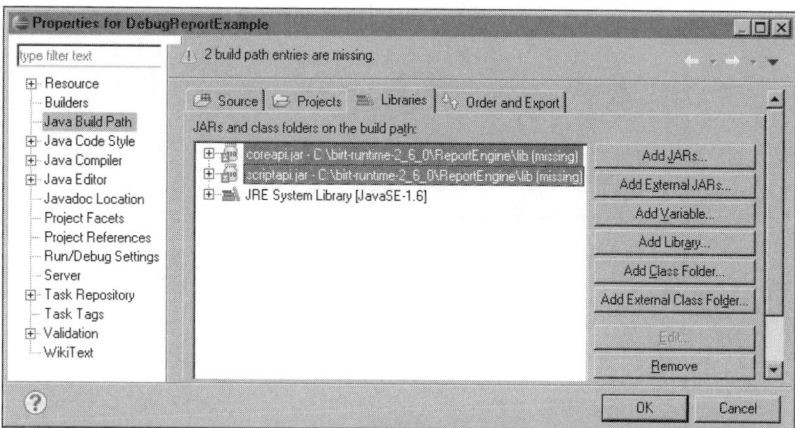

Figure 12-23 Removing JARs from the build path

3 Choose Add External Jars. JAR Selection appears.

4 Navigate to the folder containing the libraries. Press the Ctrl key and select coreapi.jar and scriptapi.jar. Choose Open.

   The JARs are added to the build path as shown in Figure 12-24.

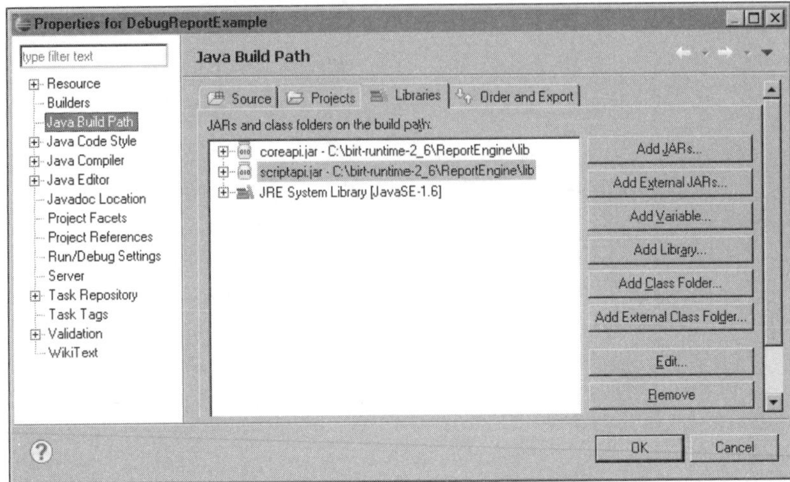

Figure 12-24 Adding external JARs to the build path

5 In Properties, choose OK. The errors in Problems disappear. If errors remain, right-click the DebugReportExample project. Choose Validate.

7 In Navigator, double-click SalesByCountry.rptdesign to open the report design. The report layout looks like the one shown in Figure 12-25.

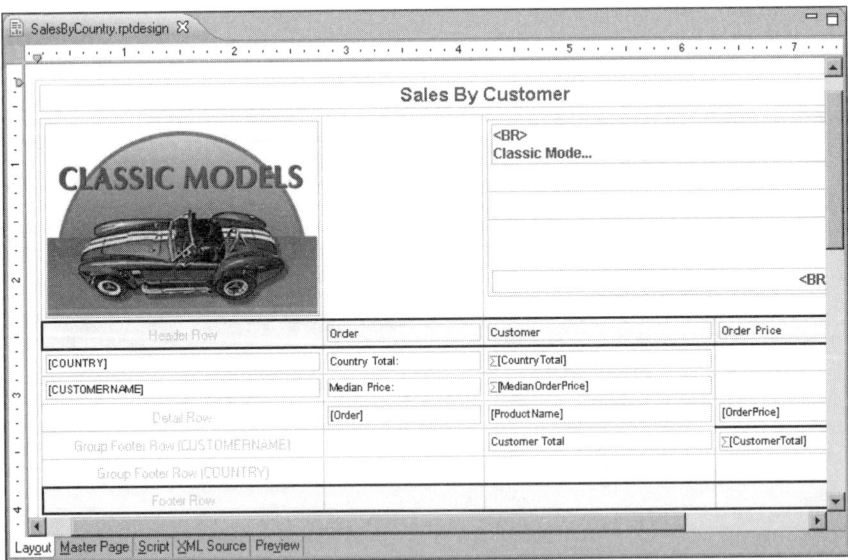

Figure 12-25 Viewing the layout of the report design

8 Choose Preview to run the report. Enter Parameters appears.

9 In pProductLine, choose Planes from the drop-down list, as shown in Figure 12-26. Choose OK.

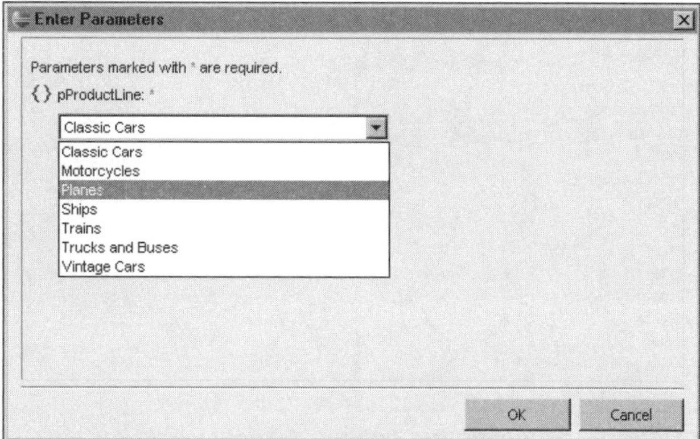

Figure 12-26 Selecting a parameter

The report preview looks like the one in Figure 12-27. The orders displaying in dark gray on the image and in fuchsia on your screen have a price greater than the median price of $1814.40. The orders having a price less than the median price are displayed in a light gray color, which displays silver on your screen. Orders for planes appear in a Bold font.

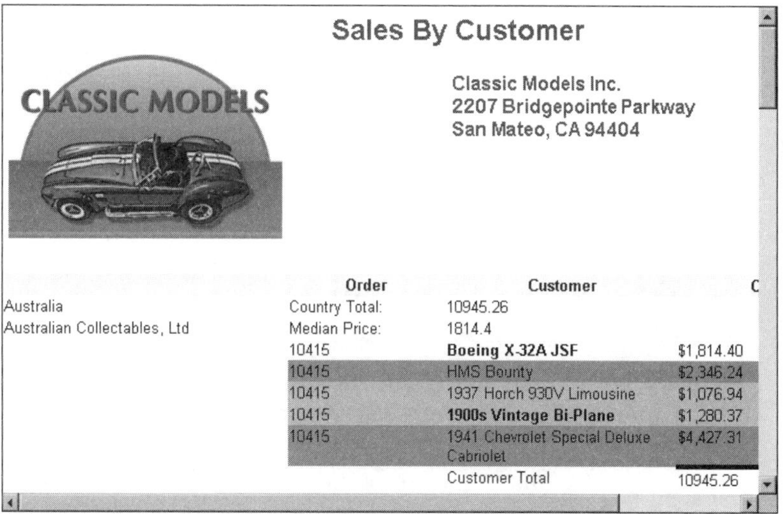

Figure 12-27 Previewing the SalesByCustomer report

Task 2: Setting a JavaScript breakpoint

In this task, you set breakpoints in JavaScript code. During debugging, you stop at a specific execution point and inspect variables.

1 Choose Layout to return to the layout editor.

2 In Outline, expand Scripts and Table. Select the onCreate method, as shown in Figure 12-28. In the editor, choose Script. The code appears in the script editor.

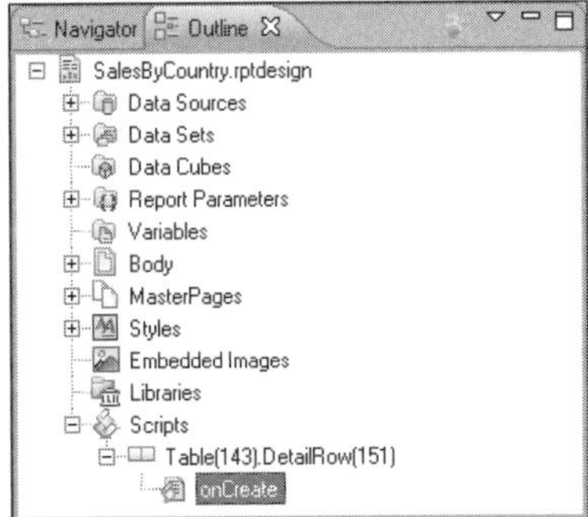

Figure 12-28 Selecting the onCreate script

3 In Script, to set a breakpoint, double-click the gray border at the left side of the following line:

```
if (  vOrderPrice   > vMedianPrice );
```

The breakpoint appears in the gray border as a blue circle, as shown in Figure 12-29.

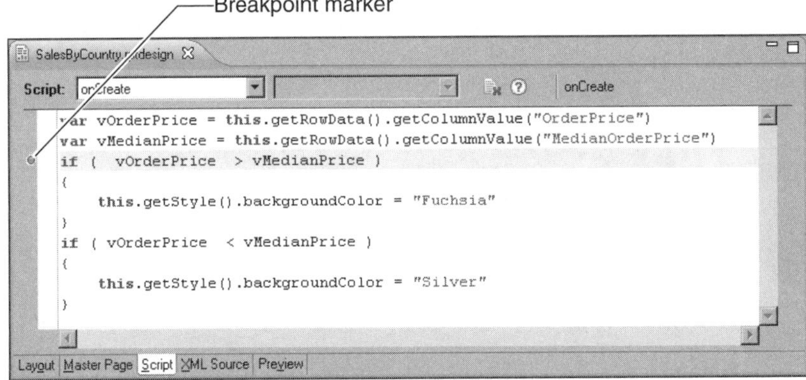

Figure 12-29 Setting a JavaScript breakpoint

Another way to add a breakpoint, as Figure 12-30 shows, is to right-click the gray border to the left of the line on which to add the breakpoint and from the context menu, choose Toggle Breakpoint.

Task 3: Setting a Java breakpoint

To debug a Java event handler, open the Java source file in the Java editor and set breakpoints. Use the same technique to create a breakpoint as for a JavaScript event handler.

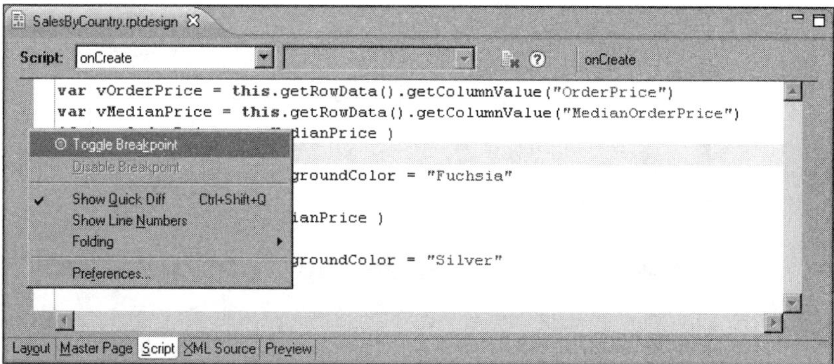

Figure 12-30 Using Toggle Breakpoint

1 In Navigator, right-click DataItemProductNameEH.java. From the context menu, choose Open. The file opens in the Java editor.

2 Choose Window➛Open Perspective➛Other➛Debug to open the Debug perspective.

3 To set a breakpoint, double-click the gray border to the left of the following line, as shown in Figure 12-31. Alternatively, place the cursor in the line of code and choose Run➛Toggle Breakpoint.

```
String ProductLine = ( String )data.getRowData( )
   .getColumnValue( "dsProductLine" );
```

```
package eventhandlers;

import org.eclipse.birt.report.engine.api.script.IReportContext;

public class DataItemProductNameEH extends DataItemEventAdapter {
    /* (non-Javadoc)
     * @see org.eclipse.birt.report.engine.api.script.eventadapter.DataItemEve
     */
    @Override
    public void onCreate(IDataItemInstance data, IReportContext reportContext)
        try{
            String ProductLine = ( String )data.getRowData( ).getColumnValue(
            System.out.println( ProductLine );
            String productline = ( String )reportContext.getParameterValue( "p
            if( productline.equals( ProductLine ) ) {
                data.getStyle().setFontWeight("bold");
            }
        }catch(ScriptException e){
            e.printStackTrace();
        }catch(Exception e){
            e.printStackTrace();
        }
    }
}
```

Figure 12-31 Setting a Java breakpoint

4 Choose the Breakpoint view to review the list of the breakpoints, as shown in Figure 12-32.

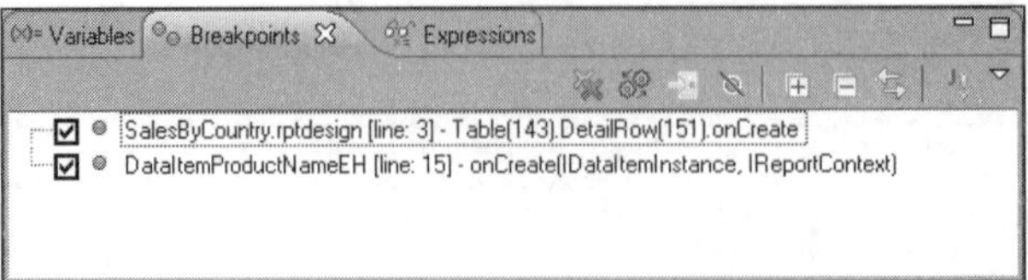

Figure 12-32 Reviewing breakpoints

Task 4: Create the debug configuration

In this task, you set up the debug configuration. The default configuration uses the current opened report design as the default report file to debug. Change this file name and other debug settings as required. Then, debug the report on your workstation by running the debug configuration.

1 Choose Run➛Debug Configurations. Debug Configuration appears.

2 From the list of launch types, select Report. From the toolbar, choose New launch configuration. A new configuration appears, as shown in Figure 12-33.

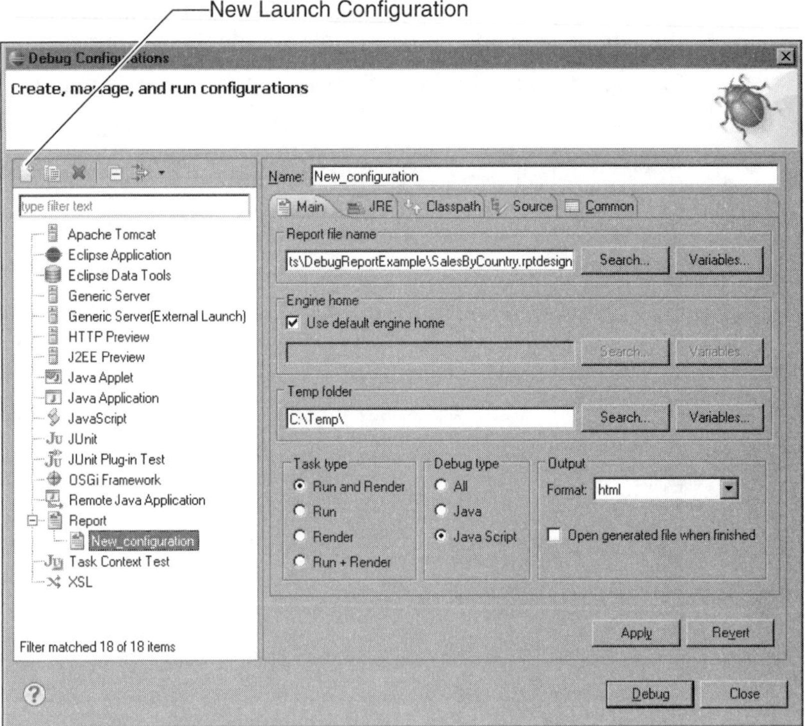

Figure 12-33 Setting up a debug configuration

3 In Name, type:

```
SalesByCustomer
```

4 In Debug type, select All.

5 In Output, select:

```
Open generated file when finished
```

Leave the suggested default values for the rest of the settings.

6 Set the Java Classpath. Add the path to the event handler class to ensure the report engine can find the class.

   1 In Debug Configurations, choose Classpath.

   2 In Classpath, select User Entries and then choose Add Project. Project Selection appears.

   3 Select the DebugReportExample project as shown in Figure 12-34. The list of available projects includes projects in your workspace, which is likely to be different from the list shown in Figure 12-34.

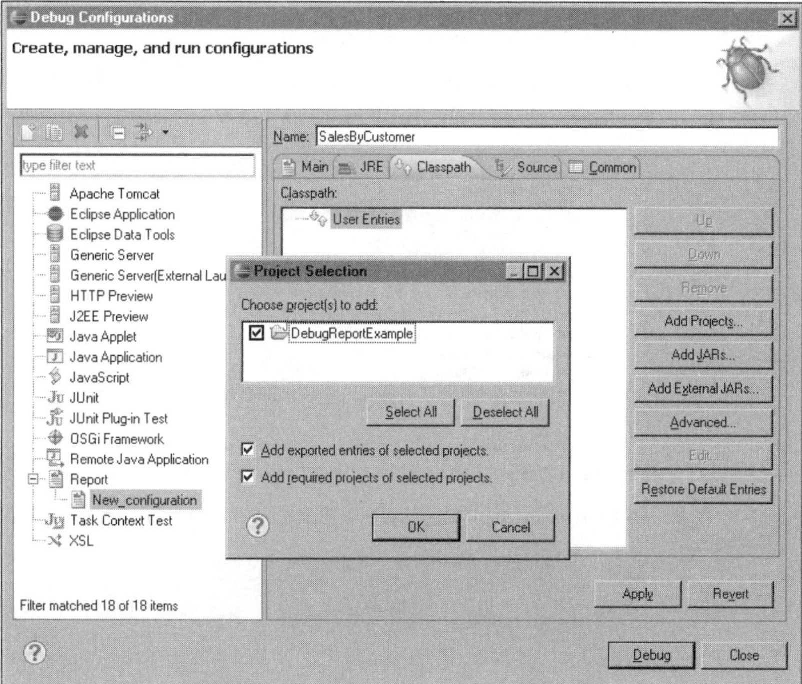

Figure 12-34 Adding a project to the Java classpath

   Choose OK. DebugReportExample is added to the classpath.

7 In Debug configurations, choose Apply to complete the creation of the debug configuration.

Task 5: Debugging the report

Debugging supports performing the following tasks:

- Stepping through the source in the script and Java editors as it executes.
- Managing breakpoints from the script editor and the breakpoints view.
- Examining variable values in the variables view.
- Evaluating expressions and viewing the results.
- Following the output of the program in the console view.

To make programs easier to debug, do not put multiple statements on a single line. Most of the debugger features operate on a line basis. For example, you cannot step over or set line breakpoints on more than one statement in a line.

1 Choose Debug. The debugging environment may take a few moments to start. Debug displays the status of the launch process in the bottom right corner of the screen, as shown in Figure 12-35.

Figure 12-35 Process status

Depending on your setup, the debug process appears in the debug stack view, as shown in Figure 12-36.

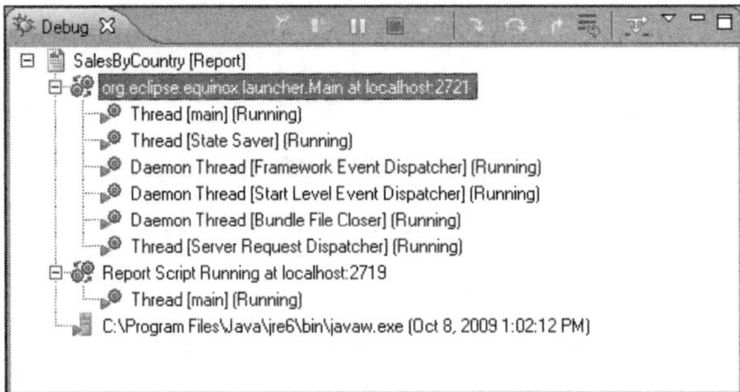

Figure 12-36 Inspecting the Debug view

2 In Input Parameters, select Planes as shown in Figure 12-37.

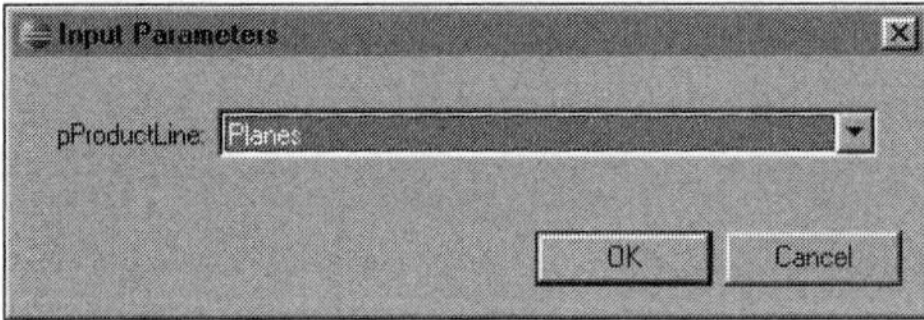

Figure 12-37 Entering the report parameter

Note that in debug mode, Input Parameters displays the parameter names, pProductLine and pStyle, instead of the display text. Displaying the parameter name supports finding the parameter in the Report Design perspective and provides information about values each parameter takes.

Choose OK. The report runs, and in a few seconds, execution stops at the breakpoint in the JavaScript onCreate method, as shown in Figure 12-38.

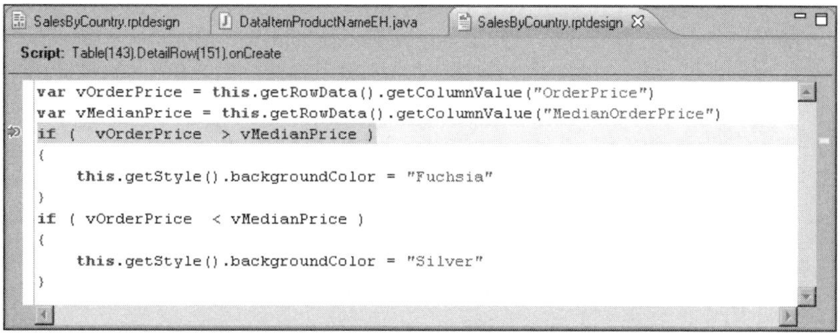
SalesByCountry.rptdesign
DataItemProductNameEH.java
SalesByCountry.rptdesign
Script: Table(143).DetailRow(151).onCreate
var vOrderPrice = this.getRowData().getColumnValue("OrderPrice")
var vMedianPrice = this.getRowData().getColumnValue("MedianOrderPrice")
if (vOrderPrice > vMedianPrice)
{
this.getStyle().backgroundColor = "Fuchsia"
}
if (vOrderPrice < vMedianPrice)
{
this.getStyle().backgroundColor = "Silver"
}

Figure 12-38 Stopping at the JavaScript breakpoint

3 Inspect the Console messages.

1. In Console, scroll down to look at the debug messages. The messages present information about the compiled and executed code in the report. These informational messages are written by different modules in the debug plug-in, org.eclipse.birt.report.debug.internal.core. The first several messages, printed in gray, as shown in Figure 12-39, appear in red on the screen.

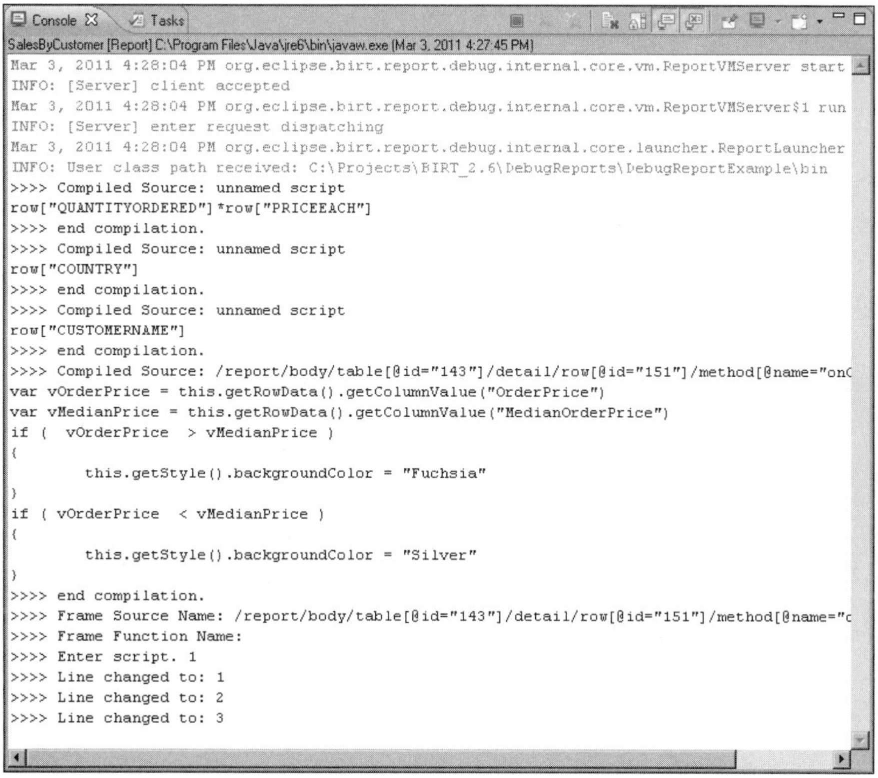
Console
Tasks
SalesByCustomer [Report] C:\Program Files\Java\jre6\bin\javaw.exe (Mar 3, 2011 4:27:45 PM)
Mar 3, 2011 4:28:04 PM org.eclipse.birt.report.debug.internal.core.vm.ReportVMServer start
INFO: [Server] client accepted
Mar 3, 2011 4:28:04 PM org.eclipse.birt.report.debug.internal.core.vm.ReportVMServer$1 run
INFO: [Server] enter request dispatching
Mar 3, 2011 4:28:04 PM org.eclipse.birt.report.debug.internal.core.launcher.ReportLauncher
INFO: User class path received: C:\Projects\BIRT_2.6\DebugReports\DebugReportExample\bin
>>>> Compiled Source: unnamed script
row["QUANTITYORDERED"]*row["PRICEEACH"]
>>>> end compilation.
>>>> Compiled Source: unnamed script
row["COUNTRY"]
>>>> end compilation.
>>>> Compiled Source: unnamed script
row["CUSTOMERNAME"]
>>>> end compilation.
>>>> Compiled Source: /report/body/table[@id="143"]/detail/row[@id="151"]/method[@name="onC
var vOrderPrice = this.getRowData().getColumnValue("OrderPrice")
var vMedianPrice = this.getRowData().getColumnValue("MedianOrderPrice")
if (vOrderPrice > vMedianPrice)
{
this.getStyle().backgroundColor = "Fuchsia"
}
if (vOrderPrice < vMedianPrice)
{
this.getStyle().backgroundColor = "Silver"
}
>>>> end compilation.
>>>> Frame Source Name: /report/body/table[@id="143"]/detail/row[@id="151"]/method[@name="c
>>>> Frame Function Name:
>>>> Enter script. 1
>>>> Line changed to: 1
>>>> Line changed to: 2
>>>> Line changed to: 3

Figure 12-39 Inspecting debug messages in Console

   2 Scroll down and analyze the next set of messages, which appear darker in Figure 12-39. These are compilation messages for the JavaScript expressions and the script in the report's onCreate( ) event.

   3 The last few lines in the console, shown in Figure 12-39, trace the execution of each line of script. Note that the last message points to line 3 in this code snippet. You set the breakpoint at this line, as shown in Figure 12-38.

4 Observe the Debug view, as shown in Figure 12-40. This view shows the current debug target, the thread, and the current stack frame.

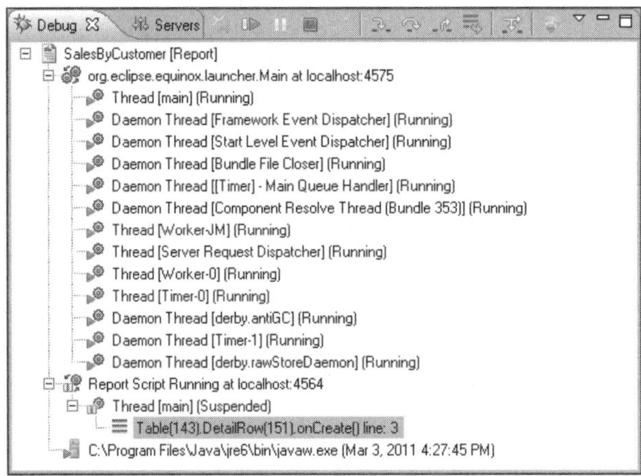

Figure 12-40 Inspecting the Debug view

The status of the current execution is Suspended. The highlighted line in Figure 12-40 shows the location of the suspended thread.

The last line shows the location of javaw.exe. The javaw.exe process is the Java Virtual Machine that runs programs written in the Java programming language.

5 Press <F6> to Step Over to the next line. The current row is highlighted in the script editor. A new message indicating the execution moved to line 7 appears in the Console view.

6 Inspect variable values.

   1 In Variables, note the values of vMedianPrice and vOrderdPrice, as shown in Figure 12-41. Expand the this. variable in the Variables view. The two variables vMedianPrice and vOrderPrice also appear as properties of this.

   Because the two variables contain the same value, 1814.4, the background color of the table row showing this order in the report remains unchanged.

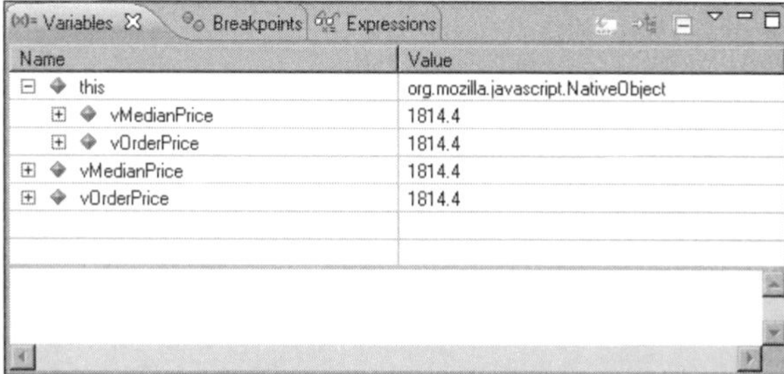

Figure 12-41 Inspecting structures and values in the Variables view

2 To use an alternative way to check variable values, move the mouse pointer over the variable in the script editor as shown in Figure 12-42.

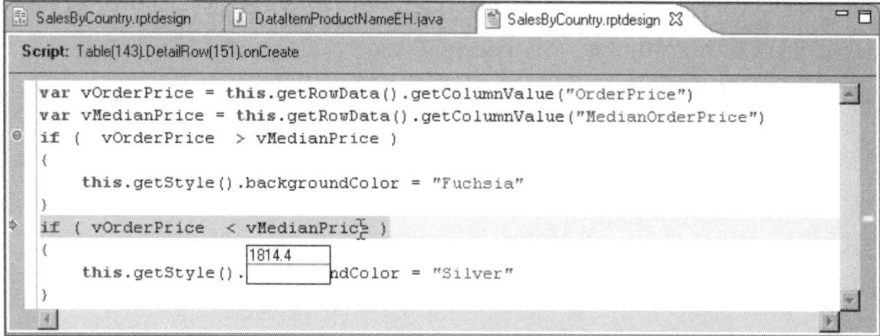

Figure 12-42 Using the mouse pointer to show the value of a variable

3 In the script editor, double-click vMedianPrice to select the text. Then, right-click vMedianPrice and choose Watch from the context menu, as shown in Figure 12-43.

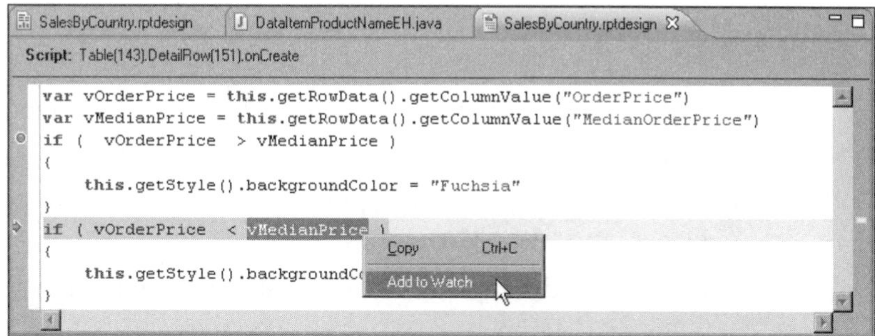

Figure 12-43 Adding a variable to watch

The variable is added to the Expressions view. Expand vMedianPrice, as shown in Figure 12-44.

If the Expressions view is not visible, choose the Show View as a fast view icon in the bottom left corner of the screen. From the list that appears, select Expressions to add the view.

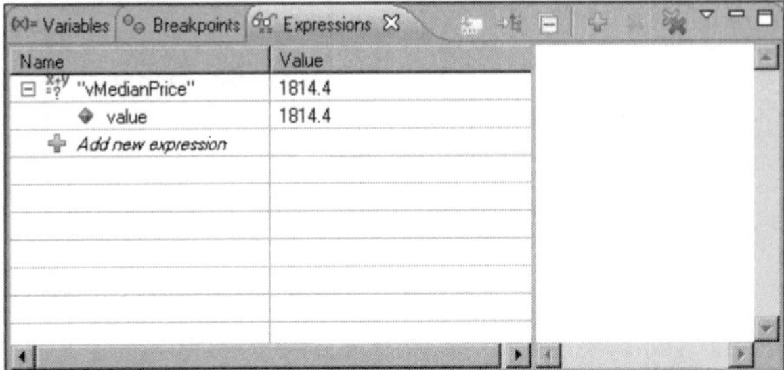

Figure 12-44 Inspecting the Expressions view

7 Press Resume <F8> to restart the report generation. Execution stops again at the breakpoint in the DataItemProductEH.java.

The debugger stops at this breakpoint as many times as there are records returned by the report query.

```
public class DataItemProductNameEH extends DataItemEventAdapter {
    /* (non-Javadoc)
     * @see org.eclipse.birt.report.engine.api.script.eventadapter.DataItemEventAc
     */
    @Override
    public void onCreate(IDataItemInstance data, IReportContext reportContext) {
        try{
            String ProductLine = ( String )data.getRowData( ).getColumnValue( "dsI
            System.out.println( ProductLine );
            String productline = ( String )reportContext.getParameterValue( "pProc
            if( productline.equals( ProductLine ) ) {
                data.getStyle().setFontWeight("bold");
            }
        }catch(ScriptException e){
            e.printStackTrace();
        }catch(Exception e){
            e.printStackTrace();
        }
    }
}
```

Figure 12-45 Stopping at a breakpoint in DataItemProductNameEH.java

8 Press <F6> to Step Over to the next line.

9 Press <F6> again. The current line of code executes and the product line, Planes, appears in Console.

10 In the Java editor, place the cursor at the following line:

```
data.getStyle().setFontWeight("bold");
```

11 Press <CTRL-R> to run the code to the current line. Report execution resumes and stops at the current line.

12 In the Variables view, inspect the available variables in the current context, as shown in Figure 12-46.

The current order is for the product line, Planes, and appears in the report in Bold font.

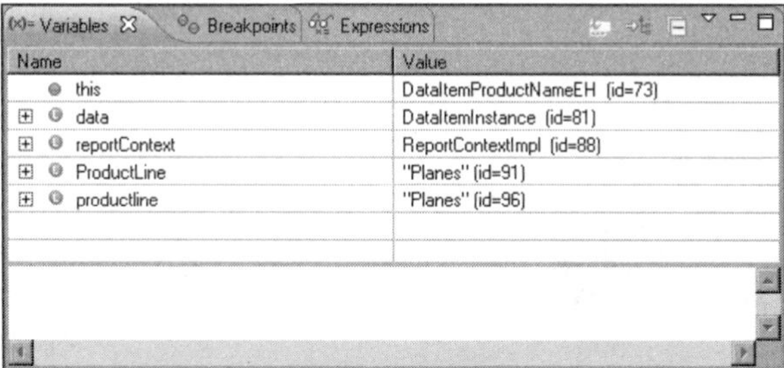

Figure 12-46 Inspecting the variables during report execution

13 In the Java editor, move the mouse pointer over the ProductLine text, as shown in Figure 12-47. The debugger parses the text and shows the value if it is available.

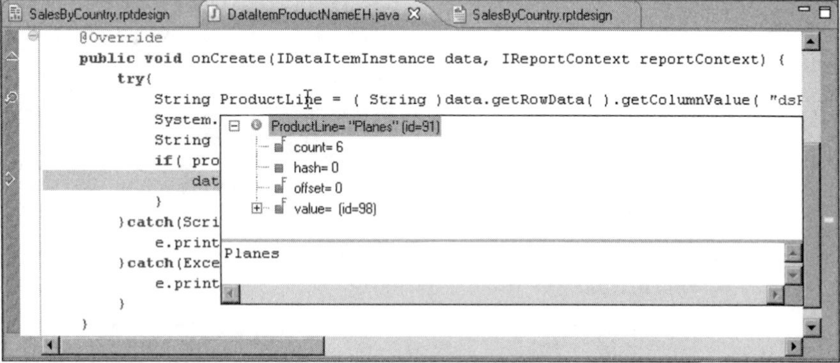

Figure 12-47 Moving the mouse pointer over Java text

14 In the Breakpoint view, deselect the two breakpoints as shown in Figure 12-48. In the next run, the debugger will not suspend execution at these breakpoints.

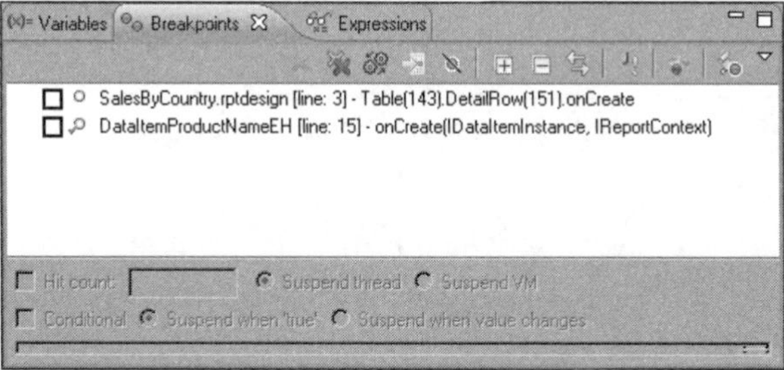

Figure 12-48 Disabling breakpoints

15 Press <F8> to resume the execution. As you selected Open the generated file in the debug options, the file opens after the debug process terminates. A new browser window containing the generated report appears, as shown in Figure 12-49.

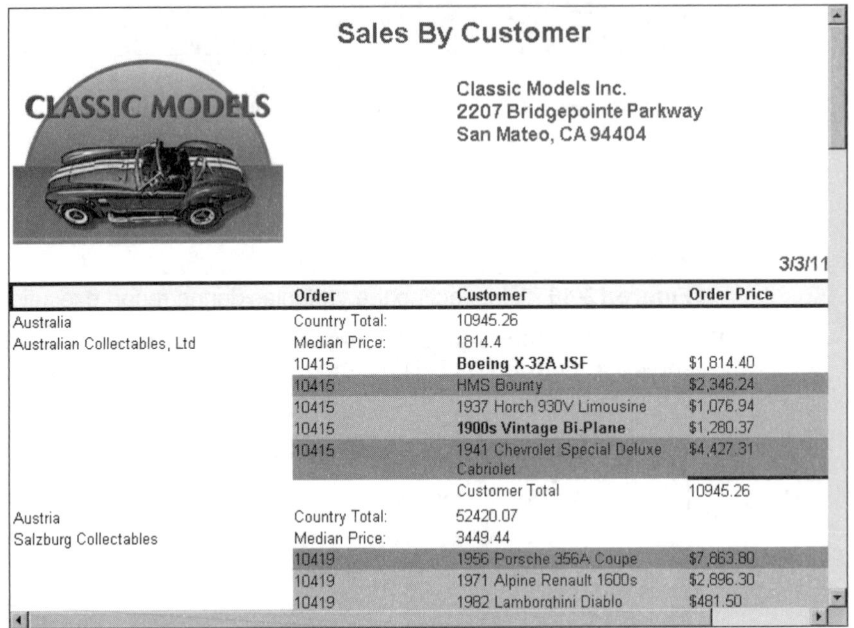

Figure 12-49 Viewing the report in the browser

16 Examine the Debug view for the terminated debug process, as shown in Figure 12-50.

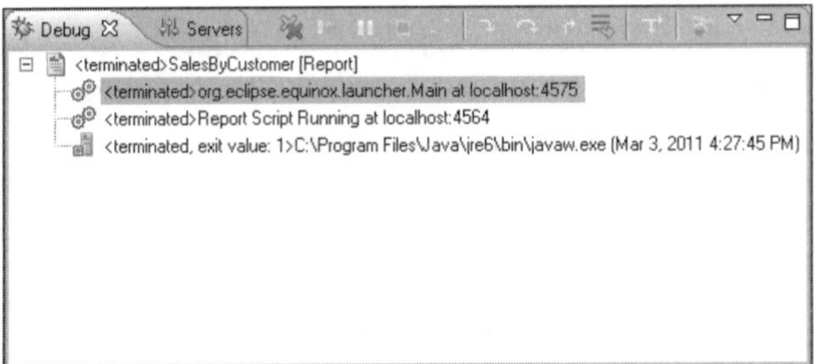

Figure 12-50 Inspecting the final status of the debug process

Part

IV

Integrating BIRT into Applications

Chapter

13

Understanding the BIRT APIs

The Eclipse BIRT code consists of many hundreds of Java classes and interfaces, but most of them are private, for use by contributors to the BIRT open source project. Developers of applications use the classes and interfaces that are in the public API. The public API consists of the classes and interfaces in the following package hierarchies:

- Report Engine API

  The org.eclipse.birt.report.engine.api package hierarchy contains the API that a developer of a custom report generator uses. This API provides the most commonly used functionality for a reporting application. The key class in the Report Engine API is ReportEngine. This class provides access to all the tasks that create a report from a report design or a report document. The Report Engine API also includes the classes and packages that support the scripting capabilities of a report design.

- Design Engine API

  The org.eclipse.birt.report.model.api package hierarchy is by far the larger of the two reporting APIs. This API provides access to the content and structure of a report design, a template, or a library. A reporting application can call this API to change the structure of a design. The Design Engine API is also the API that a developer of a custom report designer uses.

- Chart Engine API

  The org.eclipse.birt.chart package hierarchy contains the API that a developer of a custom chart generator uses. A reporting application can also use this API in conjuction with the Report Engine and Design Engine APIs to create and modify chart elements in a report design.

- Extension APIs

  BIRT provides a set of extension APIs for creating custom report items, custom data sources and data sets, custom rendering formats, and custom charts. Part 5, "Working with the Extension Framework" provides detailed examples of how to use these extensions.

For detailed information about API classes and interfaces, see the Javadoc in the online help in BIRT Programmer Reference➛Reference➛API Reference and BIRT Charting Programmer Reference➛Reference➛API Reference.

Package hierarchy diagrams

This chapter contains hierarchical diagrams for the packages in the BIRT APIs. These diagrams show the hierarchy of the classes in the package and interfaces local to the package or implemented by classes in the package. Classes and interfaces preceded by a package name are not local to the package. In these hierarchical diagrams, the graphics shown in Table 13-1 indicate different attributes and relationships of the classes and interfaces.

Table 13-1 Conventions for the hierarchy diagrams

Item	Symbol
Abstract class	Class
Class that has one or more subclasses	Class
Class that has no subclasses	Class
Final class	Class
Interface	Interface
Solid lines indicate a superclass-subclass relationship	SuperClass SubClass
Broken lines indicate an implementation relationship	Class Interface

Table 13-1 Conventions for the hierarchy diagrams

Item	Symbol
An asterisk indicates too many subclasses to list	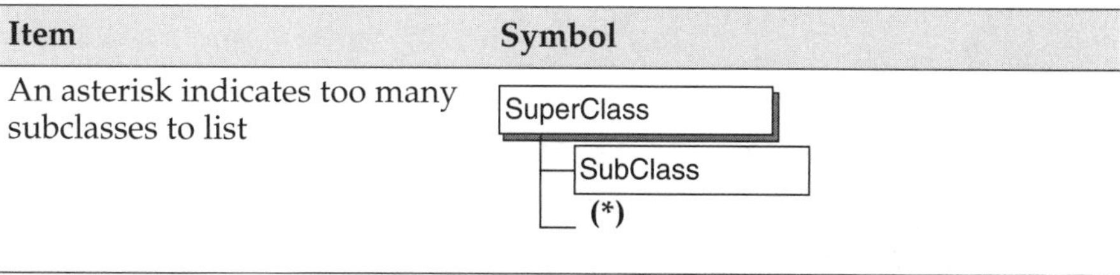

About the BIRT Report Engine API

The BIRT Report Engine supports report generation and rendering in several different environments, such as:

- Stand-alone engine
  A Java developer uses a stand-alone engine to render a BIRT report from an existing report design (.rptdesign) file. In this environment, the Java developer creates a command line application to write a complete report in any of the supported formats.
- BIRT report viewer
  BIRT Report Designer uses the BIRT report viewer to view a report as paginated HTML. The BIRT report viewer is a web application that runs in the Tomcat Application Server, which is embedded in Eclipse. This viewer contains an embedded report engine.
- Custom report designer with an embedded engine
  A custom desktop reporting application integrates the BIRT Report Engine for the purpose of previewing the report.
- Web application that embeds the engine
  A web application similar to the BIRT report viewer can use the BIRT Report Engine to generate a web-based report.

The BIRT Report Engine supports running and rendering reports in these diverse environments. It does not perform environment-dependent processing such as URL construction, image storage, and design file caching. The application using the engine API must provide such context information to the engine.

The BIRT Report Engine API consists of interfaces and implementation classes that support integrating the run-time part of BIRT into an application. The API provides task classes that support the following operations:

- Discovering the set of parameters defined for a report
- Getting the default values for parameters
- Running a report design to produce an unformatted report document

- Running a report design or report document to produce any of the supported output formats
- Extracting data from a report document

Creating the BIRT ReportEngine instance

Each application, whether it is stand-alone or web-based, only needs to create one ReportEngine instance. As the BIRT Report Engine is thread-safe, the single-instance recommendation is not a restriction.

Use an IReportEngineFactory instance and an EngineConfig object to create the ReportEngine instance.

Using the BIRT Report Engine API

The BIRT Report Engine API supports the following key tasks to generate reports:

- Setting options for the report engine using an EngineConfig object
- Starting the Platform
- Creating a ReportEngine object using the ReportEngineFactory
- Opening an existing report design using one of the openReportDesign( ) methods of ReportEngine or opening an existing report document using the openReportDocument( ) method
- Optionally, obtaining design details of the report parameters using an IGetParameterDefinitionTask object
- Running and rendering a report using IRunAndRenderTask or IRunTask followed by IRenderTask
- Cleaning up the report engine by calling destroy( ) on the engine instance to unload extensions and delete temporary files

A few key classes and interfaces provide the core functionality of the BIRT Report Engine. The following sections provide an overview of these classes.

EngineConfig class

The EngineConfig class wraps configuration settings for a report engine. Use the EngineConfig object to set global options for the environment of the report engine, including:

- Specifying the BIRT home, the location of the engine plug-ins and Java archive (.jar) files
- Setting OSGi arguments
- Setting the Platform context
- Setting resource locations

- Adding application-wide scriptable objects
- Setting the directory where the report engine writes temporary files
- Managing logging

ReportEngine class

The ReportEngine class represents the BIRT Report Engine. To instantiate the ReportEngine object, use a factory method that takes an EngineConfig object as an argument. If the configuration object is null, the environment must provide a BIRT_HOME variable that specifies the BIRT home. Use a ReportEngine object to perform the following tasks:

- Getting the configuration object
- Opening a report design or a report document
- Creating an engine task to get parameter definitions
- Creating an engine task to access the data from a report item
- Getting supported report formats and MIME types
- Creating an engine task to run a report or render a report to an output format
- Creating an engine task to extract data from a report document
- Changing the logging configuration
- Cleaning up and destroying the engine

IReportRunnable interface

To use the engine to work with the report design, load the design using one of the openReportDesign( ) methods in the ReportEngine class. These methods return an IReportRunnable instance that represents the engine's view of the report design. Use an IReportRunnable object to perform the following tasks:

- Getting standard report design properties such as the report title
- Getting any images embedded within the report design
- Getting a handle to the report design

IReportDocument interface

To use a report document, load the document using one of the ReportEngine. openReportDocument( ) method. These methods return an IReportDocument instance. Use an IRenderTask object to render the report specified by an IReportDocument object to a supported output format. Use table of contents markers in the IReportDocument to determine pages to render. The IReportDocument interface also supports retrieving page counts, parameter values used while creating the report document, and bookmarks.

IEngineTask interface

The IEngineTask interface provides the framework for the tasks that the report engine performs. The IEngineTask interface manages the scripting context, getting and setting parameter values, setting the report's locale, getting the current status of a task, and cancelling a task. The other task interfaces extend IEngineTask.

IGetParameterDefinitionTask interface

The IGetParameterDefinitionTask interface extends IEngineTask to provide access to information about parameters. Use the engine factory method to create an IGetParameterDefinitionTask object takes an IReportRunnable argument. Parameter definitions provide access to:

- Information that BIRT Report Designer specified at design time
- Static or dynamic selection lists
- User-supplied values
- Grouping structure of the parameters
- Custom XML
- User-defined properties

IDataExtractionTask interface

The IDataExtractionTask interface extends IEngineTask to provide access to the data stored in an IReportDocument object. Use an IDataExtractionTask object to examine the metadata for a set of data rows. Use the metadata to select a set of columns to extract, sort, or filter. This interface can extract the data from:

- The whole report document
- A single report item
- A single instance of a report item

IRunTask interface

The IRunTask interface provides the methods to run a report design. This task saves the result as a report document (.rptdocument) file on disk. An IRunTask object takes parameter values as a HashMap. Call the validateParameters( ) method to validate the parameter values before running the report.

IRenderTask interface

The IRenderTask interface provides the methods to render a report document to one of the supported output formats. This task can save the report to a file on disk or to a stream.

Use the RenderOption class to set options for rendering. Set options specific to particular output formats using subclasses of the RenderOption class. Pass the appropriate render option object to the IRenderTask object before rendering the report.

IRunAndRenderTask interface

The IRunAndRenderTask interface provides the methods to run a report and render it in one of the supported output formats. This task can save the report to disk or to a stream. This task does not create an intermediate report document (.rptdocument) file.

An IRunAndRenderTask object takes parameter values as a HashMap or individually. Call the validateParameters( ) method to validate the parameter values before running the report.

An IRunAndRenderTask object supports setting the same rendering options as an IRenderTask object. Pass the appropriate render option object to the IRunAndRenderTask object before running the report.

Report engine class hierarchy

The class hierarchy in Figure 13-1 illustrates the organization of the classes in the report engine package. Unless otherwise specified, all classes and interfaces in this diagram are in the org.eclipse.birt.report.engine.api package.

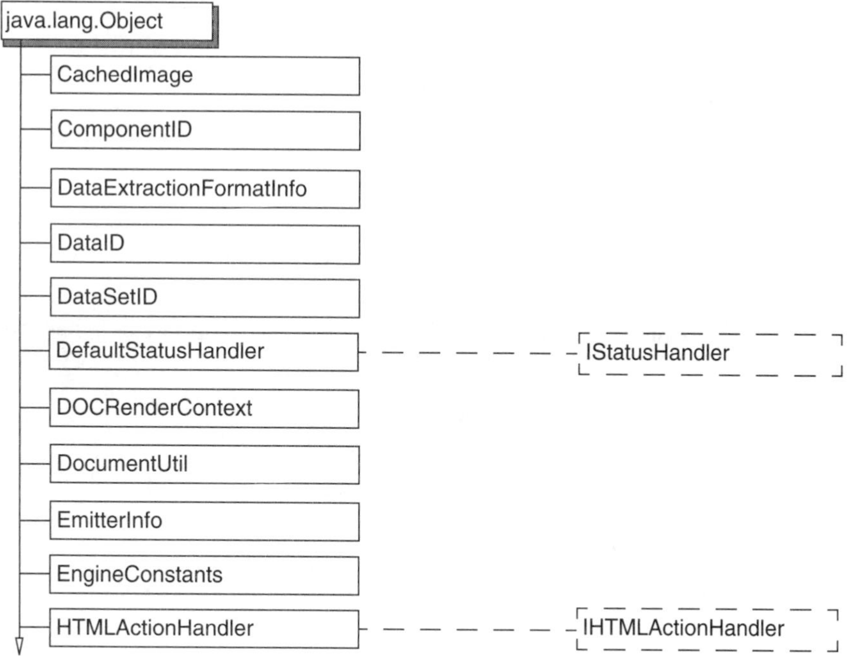

Figure 13-1 Classes within the report engine package

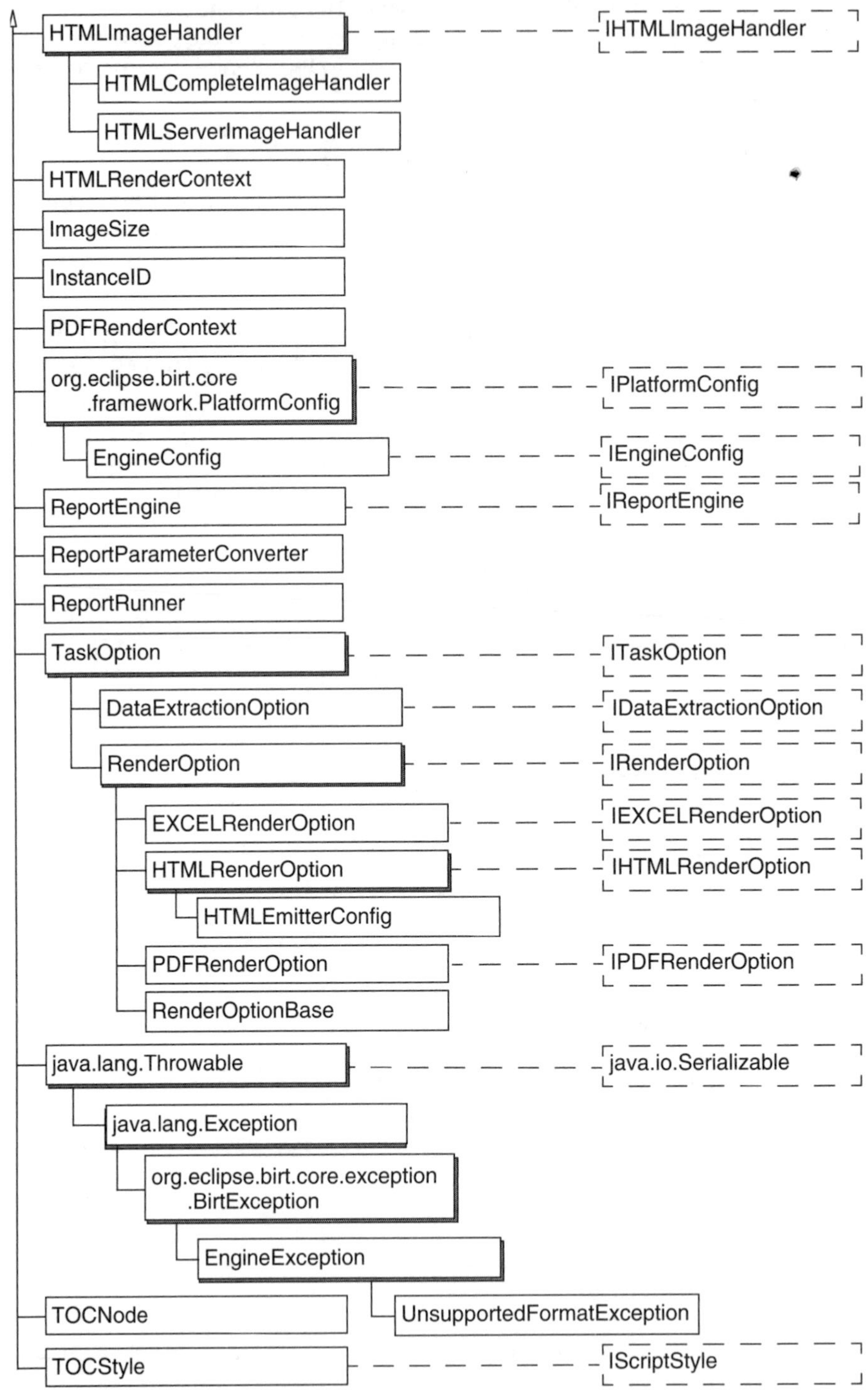

Figure 13-1 Classes within the report engine package

Report engine interface hierarchy

Figure 13-2 contains the interface hierarchy for the Report Engine API. Unless otherwise specified, all interfaces in this diagram are in the org.eclipse.birt.report.engine.api package.

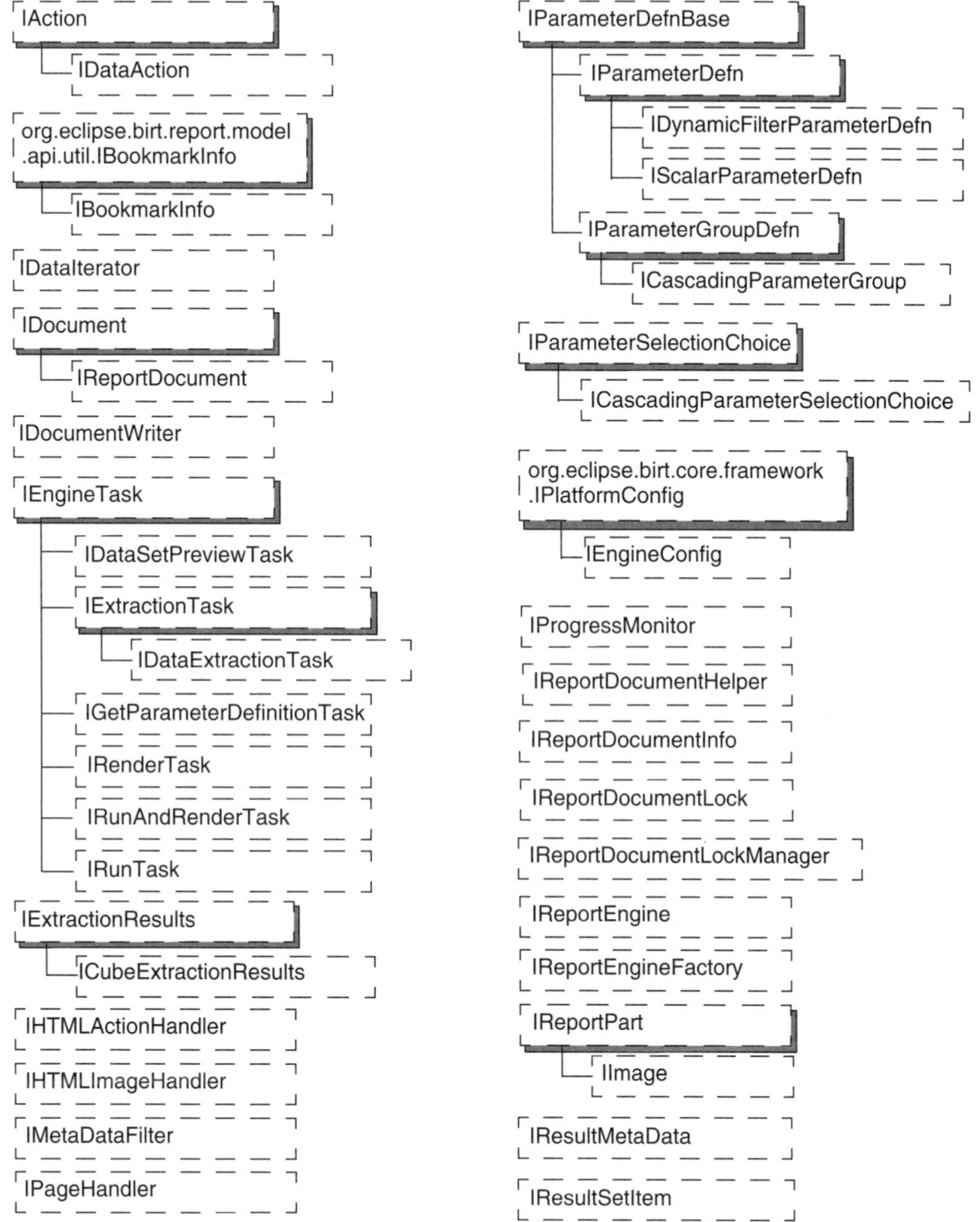

Figure 13-2 Interface hierarchy for the report engine package

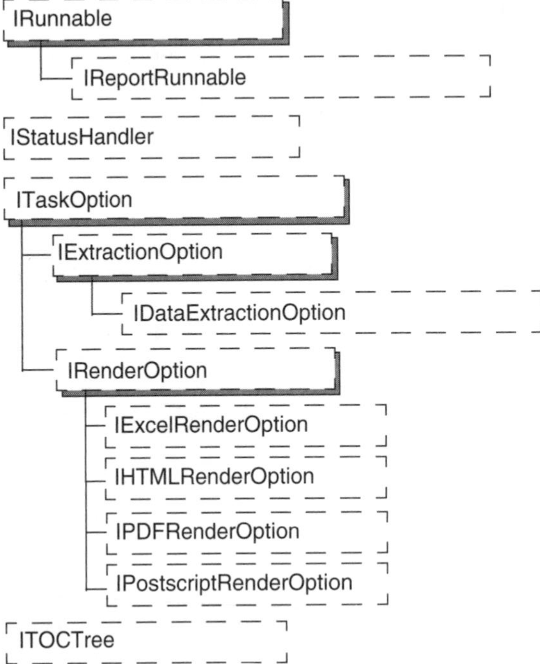

Figure 13-2 Interface hierarchy for the report engine package

About the Design Engine API

The Design Engine API is also known as the report model API. The Design Engine API is the API that a tool writer uses to develop a design tool. The Design Engine API supports creating, accessing, and validating a report design, library, or template.

The org.eclipse.birt.report.model.api package contains the interfaces and classes used to access the design model objects. The Design Engine API supports the following tasks:

- Reading and writing design files
- Maintaining the command history for undo and redo
- Providing a rich semantic representation of the report design
- Providing metadata about the ROM
- Performing property value validation
- Notifying the application when the model changes

Using the BIRT Design Engine API

The purpose of the BIRT Design Engine API is to modify or create a design file that the BIRT report engine can use to generate a report. BIRT Report Designer, for example, uses the BIRT Design Engine API for this purpose. A custom report design tool, written for the same general purpose as BIRT Report Designer, can also use the BIRT Design Engine API to generate a design file. The Design Engine API supports libraries and templates in the same way as report designs. The BIRT Design Engine API does not include any user interface classes. A custom report design tool must provide its own user interface code.

The design engine supports the following tasks to create or modify a BIRT report design:

- Setting options for the design engine by using a DesignConfig object
- Starting the Platform, if not already started
- Creating a DesignEngine object using the DesignEngineFactory
- Beginning a user session by using the DesignEngine.newSessionHandle( ) method to instantiate a SessionHandle object
- Setting session parameters and loading the property definitions of the report elements by using the SessionHandle object to create an instance of the ReportDesignHandle class
- Using the ReportDesignHandle to create an ElementFactory, which can create report elements
- Using the ReportDesignHandle to add new elements to the report design or modify existing elements
- Saving the report design file by using the ReportDesignHandle

The following sections describe the primary classes of the BIRT Design Engine API.

DesignConfig class

The DesignConfig class wraps configuration settings for a design engine. Use a DesignConfig object to set global options for the design engine, including:

- Specifying the location of engine plug-ins and Java archive (.jar) files
- Setting the Platform Context
- Specifying configuration variable
- Set OSGi arguments

DesignEngine class

The DesignEngine class represents the BIRT design engine. Create the DesignEngine with a factory method that takes a DesignConfig object. If the configuration object is null, the environment must provide the path to the BIRT home, the directory that contains the engine plug-ins and JAR files. The DesignEngine class is the gateway to creating the other objects needed to build a report design tool. Use the methods of the DesignEngine class to create a locale-specific SessionHandle object by calling the newSession( ) method. The SessionHandle provides access to report design objects.

SessionHandle class

The SessionHandle class represents the user session. A SessionHandle object provides access to the set of open designs. A session has a set of default values for style properties and a default unit of measure. The session also has methods to create and open report designs, templates, and libraries, as well as setting the path and algorithm used to locate resources. The methods to create or open a report design return a ReportDesignHandle object.

ModuleHandle class

ModuleHandle provides access to the common structure and functionality of report designs, templates, and libraries. The ModuleHandle class is the parent class of the ReportDesignHandle and LibraryHandle classes. ModuleHandle provides access to the generic properties, such as author and comments. Use ModuleHandle for many tasks on the file, including:

- Saving the module to a file
- Accessing the command stack for undo and redo
- Navigating to the various parts of the module
- Retrieving the module location
- Getting configuration variables

Other ModuleHandle methods support getting handles to the individual report items and all the other elements in a report design, template, or library. These elements and supporting components include:

- Report items. These elements are visual report elements such as tables, grids, images, and text elements.
- Code modules. These modules are global scripts that apply to the file as a whole.
- Parameters.
- Data sources, data sets, and cubes.
- Color Palette. This component is a set of custom color names.
- CSS files that the module uses.
- Theme. The theme is a group of styles that the module uses for formatting report elements.

- Master page. This element defines the layout of pages in paginated report output.
- Libraries. Any module can use one or more libraries to provide predefined elements.
- Resources. External files, for example, providing images or lists of messages in localized forms.
- Embedded images.

ReportDesignHandle class

ReportDesignHandle provides access to report design-specific properties such as the scripts that execute when generating or rendering a report. This class also provides access to properties that templates use, such as the cheat sheet, display name, and icon file.

ReportDesignHandle is a subclass of ModuleHandle, so supports all that class's functionality. Use ReportDesignHandle to get handles to individual report items and for many report design-specific tasks, including:

- Navigating to the various parts of the design
- Setting the event-specific scripts that execute when the report engine runs and renders the report

The ReportDesignHandle also has methods to gain access to the following report components:

- Styles, the list of user-defined styles for formatting report elements
- Base directory, the location of file system resources with relative paths
- Body, a list of the report sections and report items in the design
- Scratch Pad, a temporary place to hold report items while restructuring a report

LibraryHandle class

LibraryHandle is a subclass of ModuleHandle, so supports all that class's functionality. LibraryHandle also provides access to the following library-specific properties:

- Name space, the name that a module including a library uses to identify the elements that the library defines
- The set of themes that the library defines
- Imported CSS styles used by themes

DesignElementHandle class

DesignElementHandle is the base class for all report elements, both visual report item elements and non-visual ones, such as data sets and cubes. DesignElementHandle provides generic services for all elements, such as:

- Adding a report item to a slot
- Registering a change event listener
- Getting and setting properties, names, and styles
- Getting available choices for specific properties
- Dropping an element from the design
- Copying, pasting, and moving report items

Individual element handle classes

Element handle classes derive from ReportElementHandle. Each report element has its own handle class. To work with operations unique to a given report element, cast the ReportElementHandle to the appropriate subclass for the element. For example, the CellHandle class provides methods such as getColumn( ), and the DataSourceHandle class has methods such as setBeforeOpen( ).

Design engine class hierarchy

Figure 13-3 illustrates the hierarchy of the classes within the design engine package. Unless otherwise specified, all classes and interfaces in this diagram are in the org.eclipse.birt.report.model.api package.

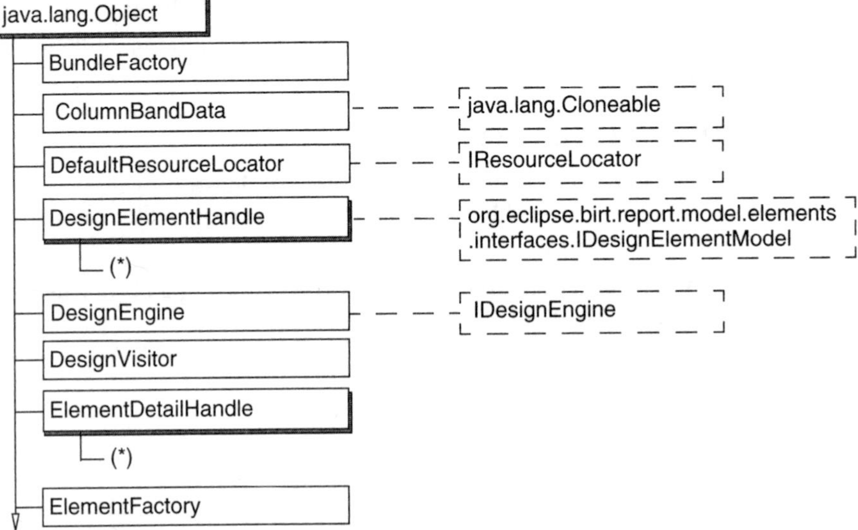

Figure 13-3 Classes within the report model package

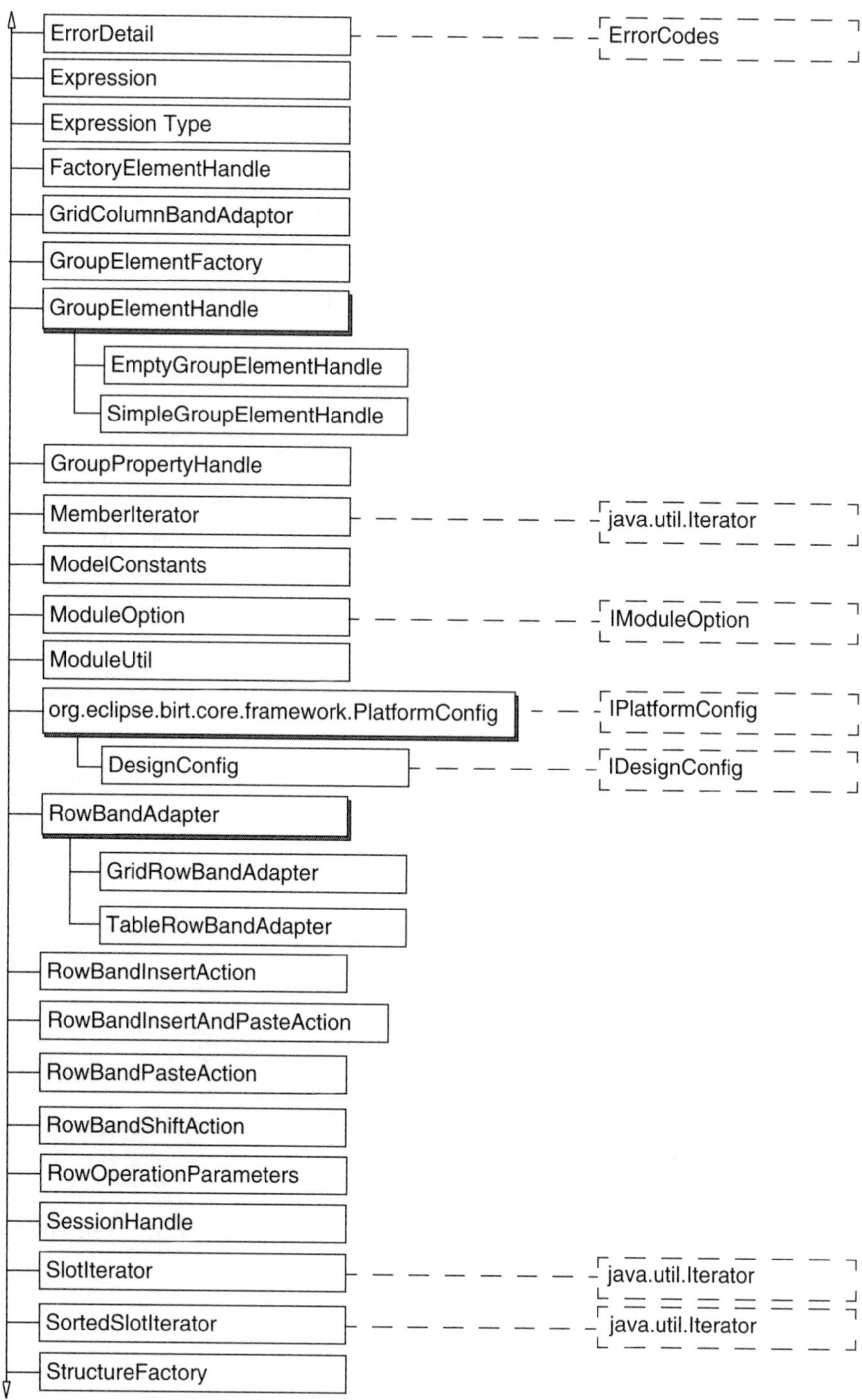

Figure 13-3 Classes within the report model package

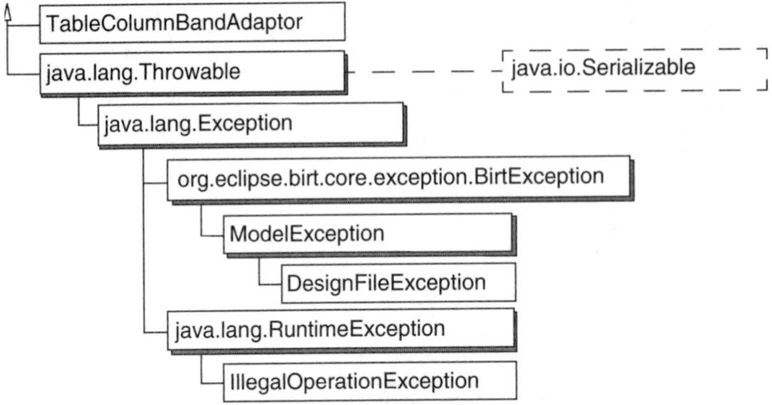

Figure 13-3 Classes within the report model package

DesignElementHandle hierarchy

Figure 13-4 contains the class hierarchy for DesignElementHandle in the org.eclipse.birt.report.model.api package and the classes that derive from it.

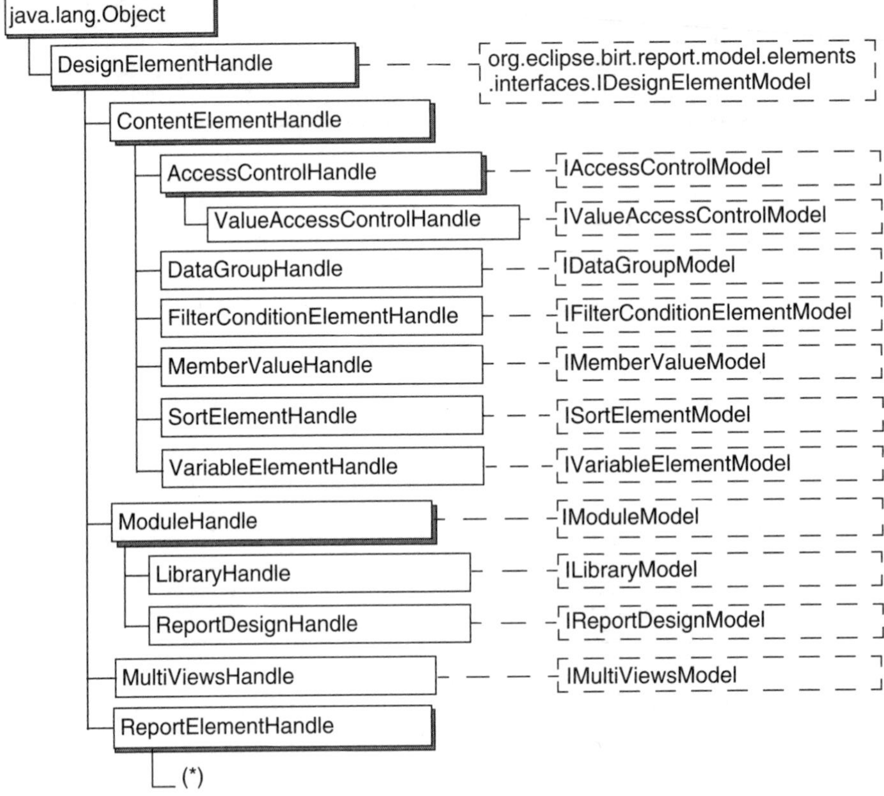

Figure 13-4 DesignElementHandle class hierarchy

ReportElementHandle hierarchy

Figure 13-5 contains the class hierarchy for ReportElementHandle in the org.eclipse.birt.report.model.api package and the classes that derive from it. The interfaces that the classes implement are all in the org.eclipse.birt.report .model.elements.interfaces and org.eclipse.birt.report.model.elements packages. Classes with names that have a prefix of olap are in the org.eclipse. birt.report.model.olap package.

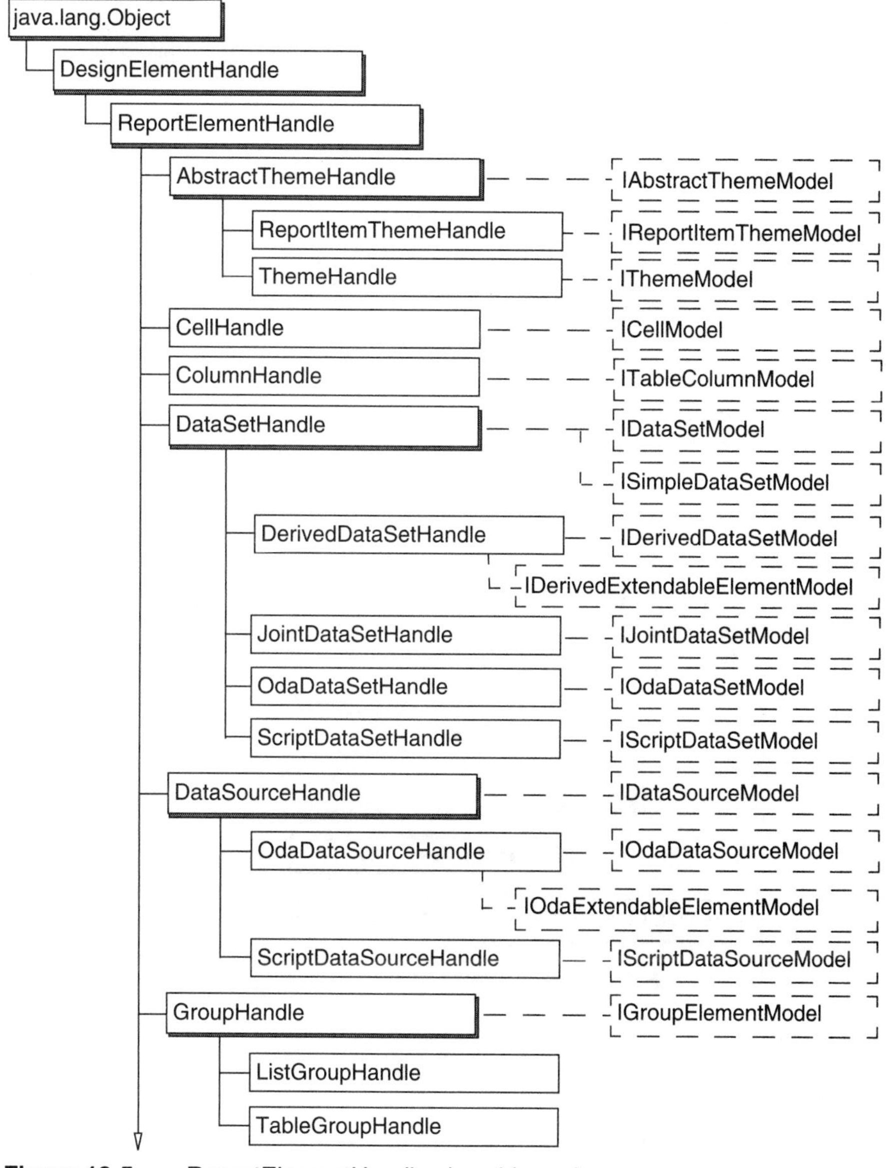

Figure 13-5 ReportElementHandle class hierarchy

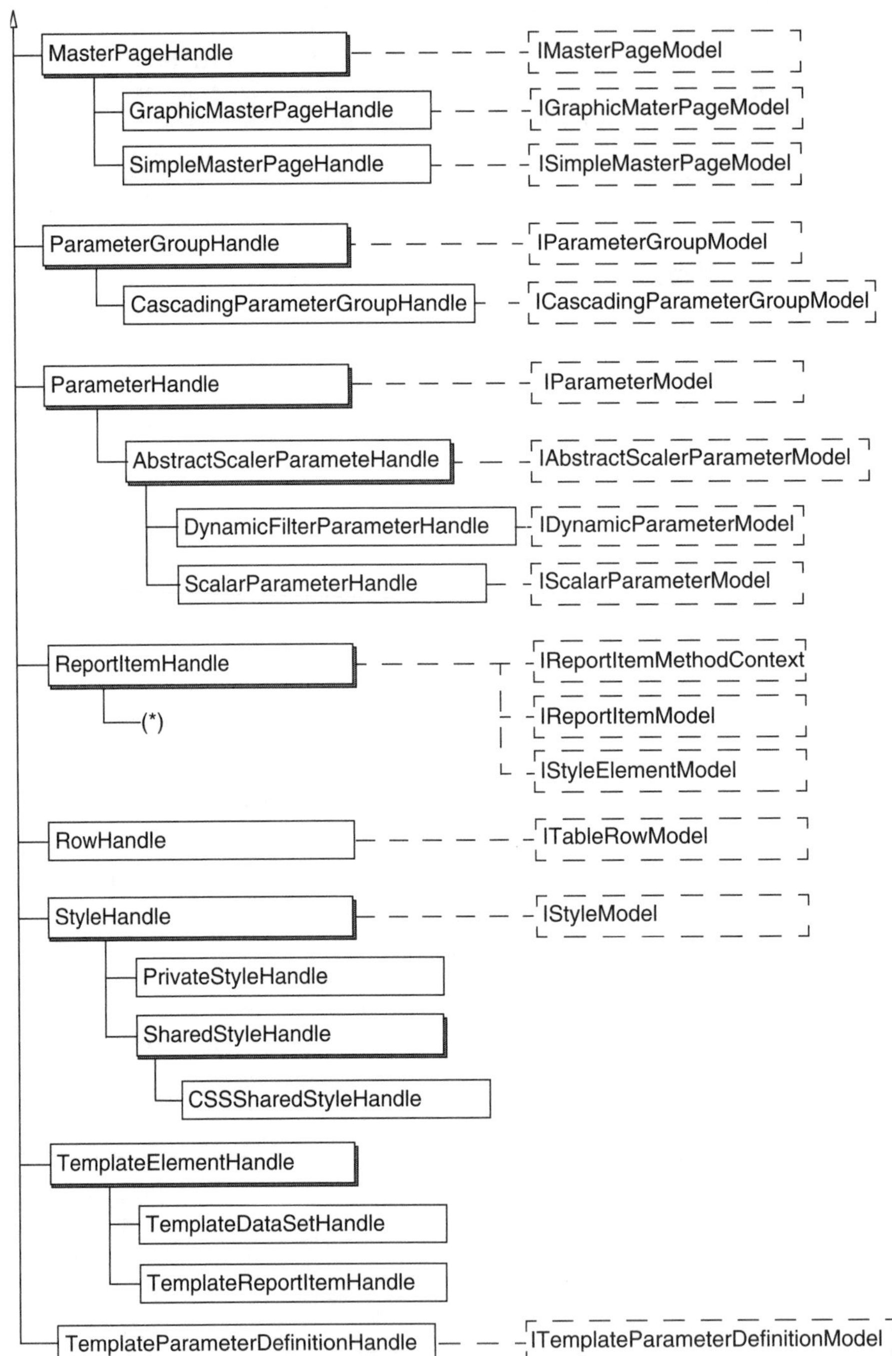

Figure 13-5 ReportElementHandle class hierarchy

ReportItemHandle hierarchy

Figure 13-6 contains the class hierarchy for ReportItemHandle in the org. eclipse.birt.report.model.api package and the classes that derive from it. The interfaces that the classes implement are all in the org.eclipse.birt.report. model.elements.interfaces and org.eclipse.birt.report.model.elements packages.

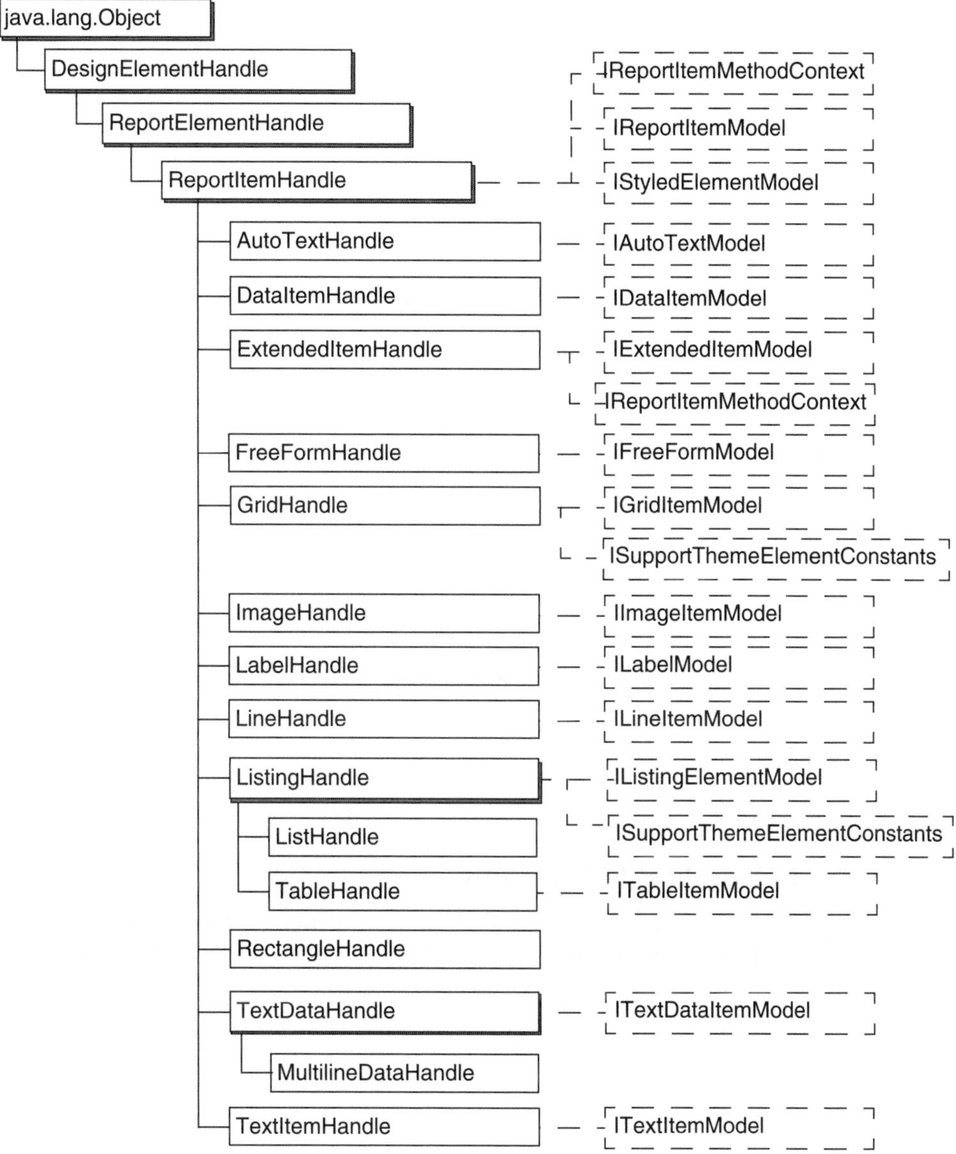

Figure 13-6 ReportItemHandle class hierarchy

ElementDetailHandle hierarchy

Figure 13-7 contains the class hierarchy for ElementDetailHandle in the org.eclipse.birt.report.model.api package and the classes that derive from it.

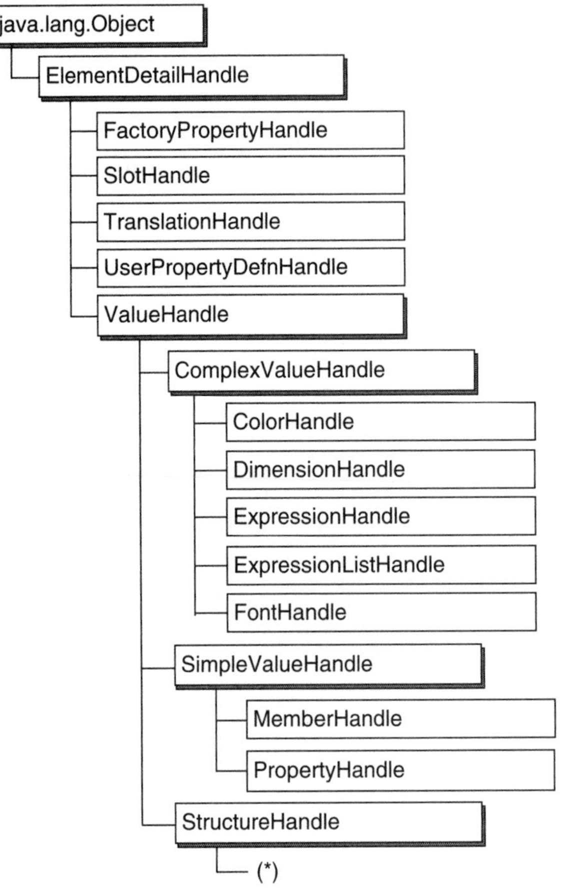

Figure 13-7 ElementDetailHandle class hierarchy

StructureHandle hierarchy

Figure 13-8 contains the class hierarchy for StructureHandle in the org.eclipse.birt.report.model.api package and the classes that derive from it.

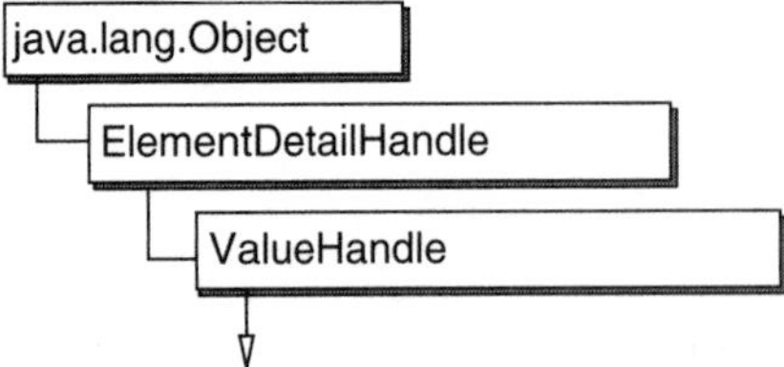

Figure 13-8 StructureHandle class hierarchy

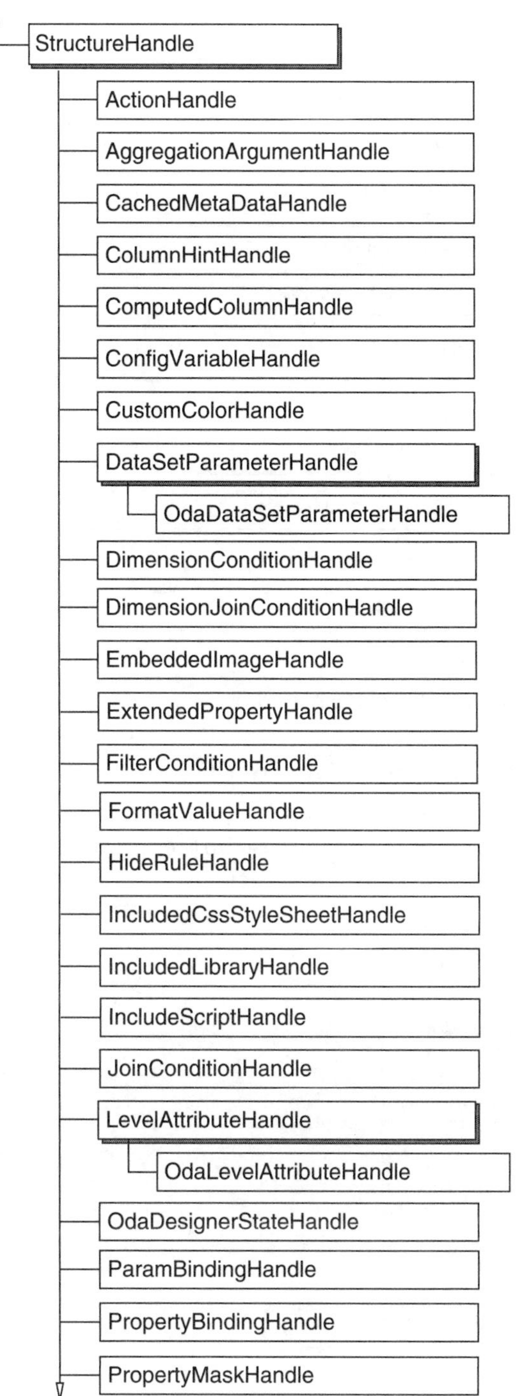

Figure 13-8 StructureHandle class hierarchy

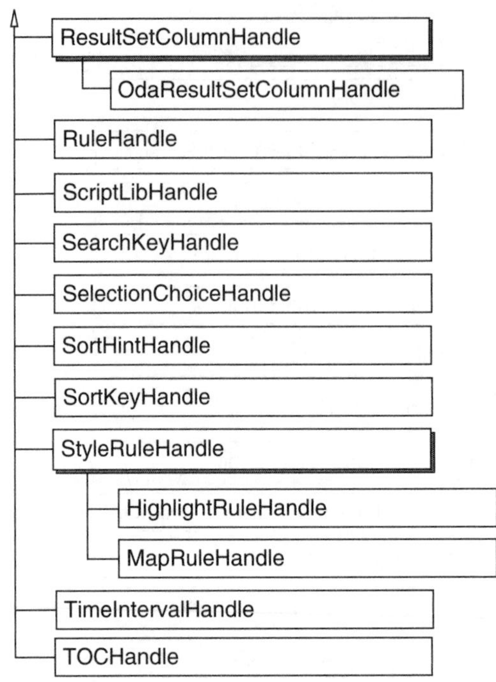

Figure 13-8 StructureHandle class hierarchy

Design engine interface hierarchy

Figure 13-9 contains the interface hierarchy for the Design Engine API. All interfaces in this diagram is in the org.eclipse.birt.report.model.api package

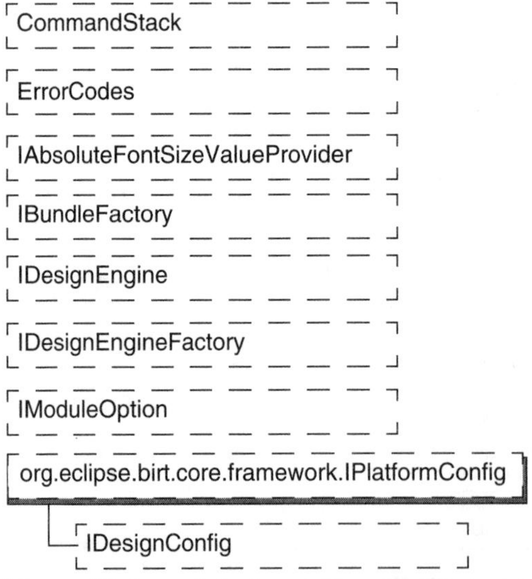

Figure 13-9 Interface hierarchy for design engine package

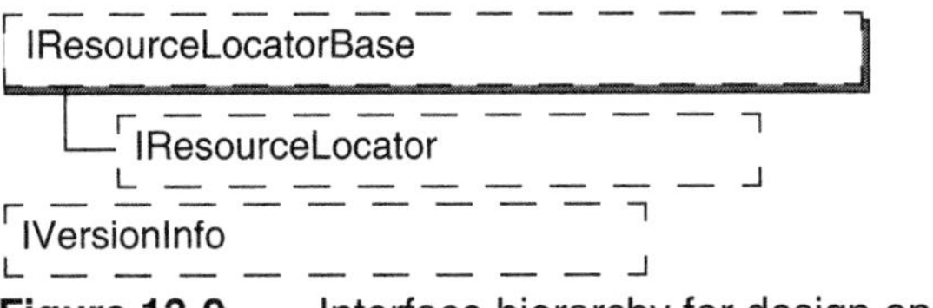

Figure 13-9 Interface hierarchy for design engine package

About the BIRT Chart Engine API

The chart engine API uses the Eclipse Modeling Framework (EMF) as a structured data model. Use the classes and interfaces in the chart engine API to modify chart objects within a BIRT reporting application or in a stand-alone charting application.

The Chart Engine API includes many packages in the org.eclipse.birt.chart hierarchy. The model.* packages contain the core chart model interfaces and enumeration classes generated using EMF. The model.*.impl packages contain the core chart model implementation classes generated using EMF. All other packages are dependencies from and indirect references to the core model. There is a one-to-one correspondence between classes in the impl packages and interfaces in matching model packages. The classes in the impl packages implement the methods in the interfaces of the model classes. The impl classes also contain factory methods used to create an instance of a class.

Using the BIRT Chart Engine API

Although there are over 500 classes and interfaces in the BIRT Chart Engine API, most functionality for creating or modifying a chart is concentrated in a small subset of classes and interfaces. The primary interface in the BIRT Chart Engine API is the Chart interface. An object of the Chart type is called the chart instance object. The Chart interface has two subinterfaces, ChartWithAxes and ChartWithoutAxes. DialChart is a third interface that inherits from ChartWithoutAxes. ChartWithoutAxes defines a pie chart and DialChart defines a meter chart. ChartWithAxes defines all other chart types.

To create a chart instance object, call create( ) in ChartWithAxesImpl, ChartWithoutAxesImpl, or DialChartImp, as in the following statement:

```
ChartWithAxes myChart = ChartWithAxesImpl.create( );
```

To set the basic properties of a chart, such as its orientation and dimensionality, use setter methods of the Chart interface, such as:

```
myChart.setOrientation( Orientation.VERTICAL_LITERAL );
myChart.setDimension( ChartDimension.THREE_DIMENSIONAL );
```

Set more complex properties of a chart, like characteristics of the chart's axes and series by getting an instance of the object to modify and then setting its properties. For example, to set an *x*-axis caption, use the following code:

```
Axis xAxis = myChart.getPrimaryBaseAxes( )[0];
xAxis.getTitle( ).getCaption( ).setValue( "Months" );
```

Although charts are often identified by type, such as a pie chart or a line chart, a chart with multiple series of differing types cannot be classified as one type. A series has a specific type. Use the BIRT Chart Engine API to create a specific type of series by using the create( ) method of one of the SeriesImpl subclasses. For example, the following code creates a bar series:

```
BarSeries barSeries1 = ( BarSeries ) BarSeriesImpl.create( );
```

Chart engine class hierarchy

The diagrams that follow contain hierarchies for the following chart engine packages:

- org.eclipse.birt.chart.aggregate
- org.eclipse.birt.chart.datafeed
- org.eclipse.birt.chart.device
- org.eclipse.birt.chart.event
- org.eclipse.birt.chart.exception
- org.eclipse.birt.chart.factory
- org.eclipse.birt.chart.log
- org.eclipse.birt.chart.model
- org.eclipse.birt.chart.model.attribute
- org.eclipse.birt.chart.model.component
- org.eclipse.birt.chart.model.data
- org.eclipse.birt.chart.model.layout
- org.eclipse.birt.chart.model.type
- org.eclipse.birt.chart.render
- org.eclipse.birt.chart.script
- org.eclipse.birt.chart.util

The hierarchy diagrams for the org.eclipse.birt.chart.model.*.impl packages are not included because they are simply implementations of the interfaces in the corresponding org.eclipse.birt.chart.model.* packages. The model packages, with two exceptions, contain only interfaces.

The first exception is org.eclipse.birt.chart.model, which has one class, ScriptHandler. The second exception is org.eclipse.birt.chart.model.attribute, which has a set of enumeration classes, one for each attribute. Each of the enumeration classes contains only a list of valid values for its attribute.

chart.aggregate class and interface hierarchy

The chart.aggregate package contains the class and interface that support the aggregate functions that produce the values that a chart shows. Figure 13-10 contains the class and interface hierarchy for org.eclipse.birt.chart.aggregate.

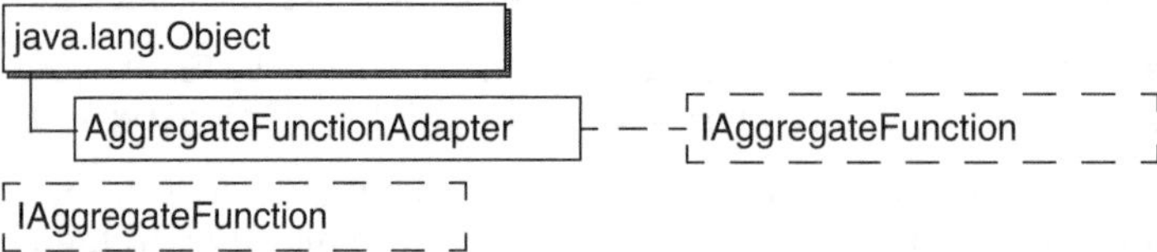

Figure 13-10 Classes and interfaces in org.eclipse.birt.chart.aggregate

chart.datafeed class and interface hierarchy

The chart.datafeed package contains the class and interfaces that support defining a custom data set for a chart. Figure 13-11 contains the class and interface hierarchy for org.eclipse.birt.chart.datafeed.

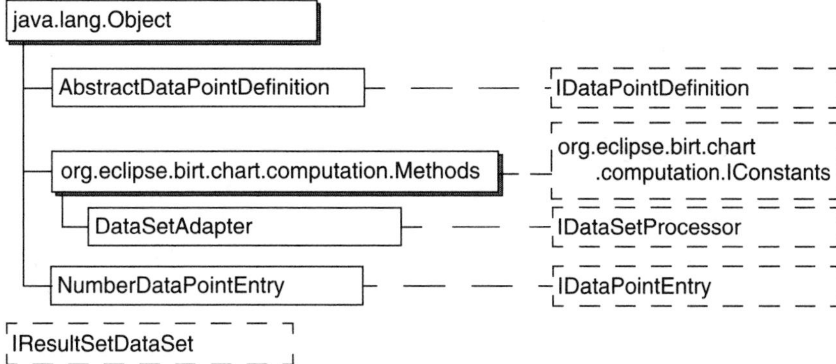

Figure 13-11 Classes and interfaces in org.eclipse.birt.chart.datafeed

chart.device class and interface hierarchy

The chart.device package contains the classes and interfaces that support rendering a chart to a specific output type. Device adapter classes provide the rendered output. These classes process the events defined in the chart.event package. Display adapter classes provide metrics for the output device. Figure 13-12 contains the class hierarchy for org.eclipse.birt.chart.device.

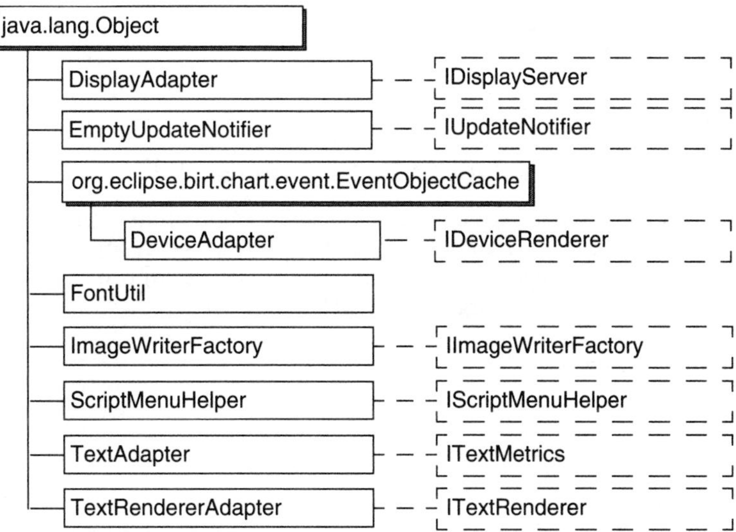

Figure 13-12 Classes in org.eclipse.birt.chart.device

Figure 13-13 contains the interface hierarchy for org.eclipse.birt.chart.device.

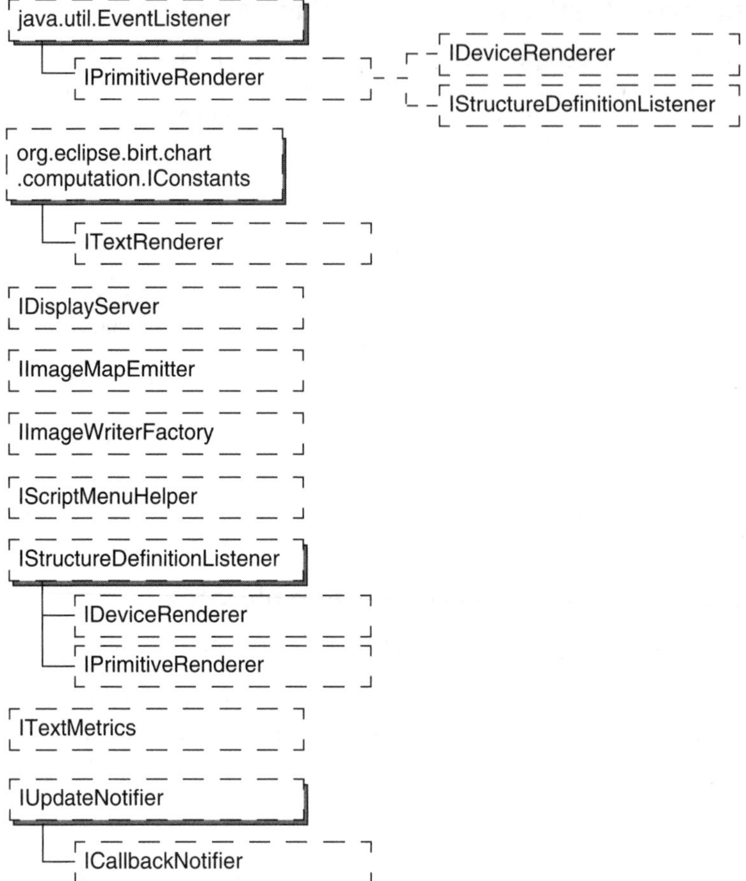

Figure 13-13 Interfaces in org.eclipse.birt.chart.device

chart.event class and interface hierarchy

The chart.event package contains the set of events that a rendering device that extends the chart.device.DeviceAdapter class can support. It also provides structural and caching classes for events. Figure 13-14 contains the interface hierarchy for org.eclipse.birt.chart.event.

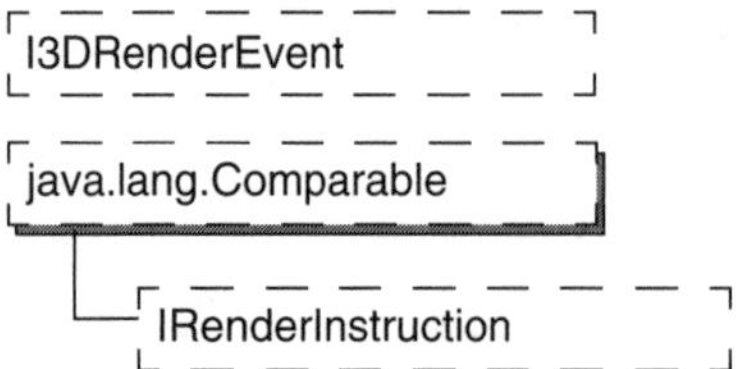

Figure 13-14 Interfaces in org.eclipse.birt.chart.event

Figure 13-15 contains the class hierarchy for org.eclipse.birt.chart.event.

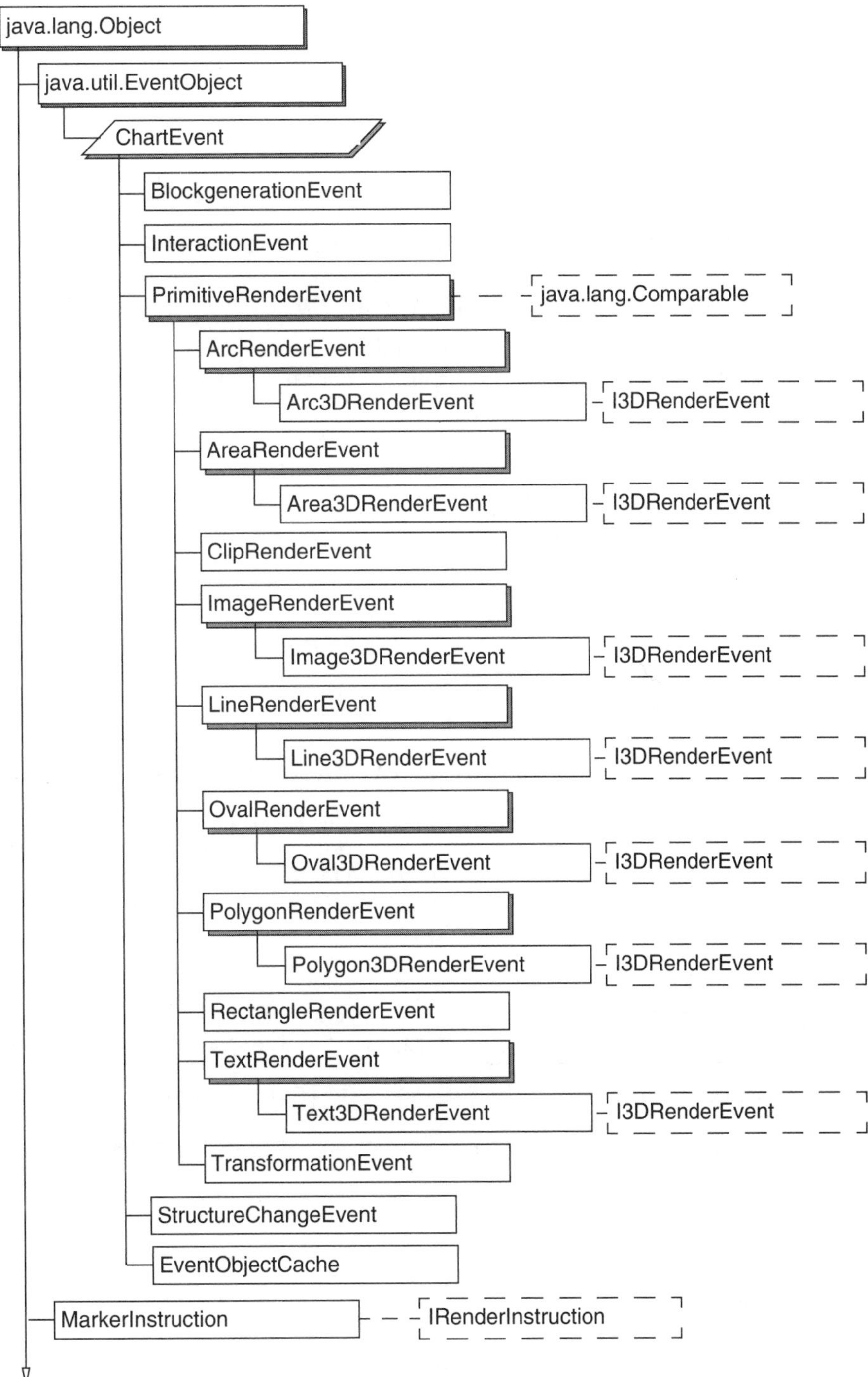

Figure 13-15 Classes in org.eclipse.birt.chart.event package

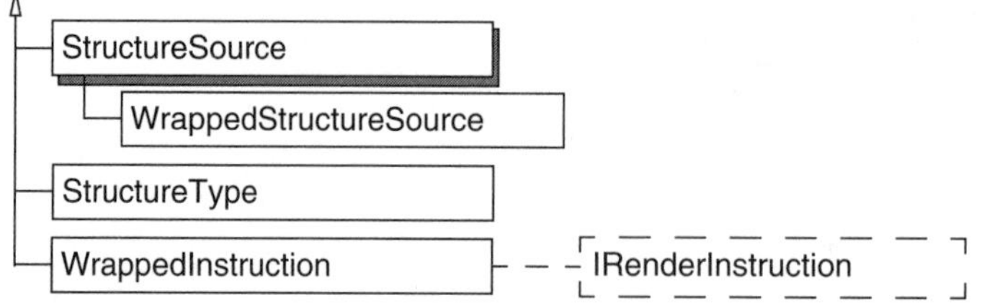

Figure 13-15 Classes in org.eclipse.birt.chart.event package

chart.exception class hierarchy

The chart.exception package contains the single exception class the BIRT Chart Engine defines. Figure 13-16 contains the class hierarchy for org.eclipse.birt.chart.exception.

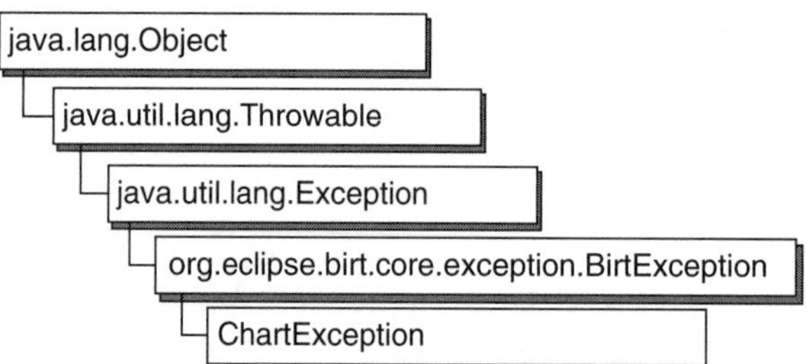

Figure 13-16 Class in org.eclipse.birt.chart.exception

chart.factory class and interface hierarchy

The chart.factory package contains classes and interfaces that build and generate a chart. It also contains a context class that provides information about the environment in which the factory runs, such as the locale and associated localization information. Figure 13-17 contains the class hierarchy for org.eclipse.birt.chart.factory.

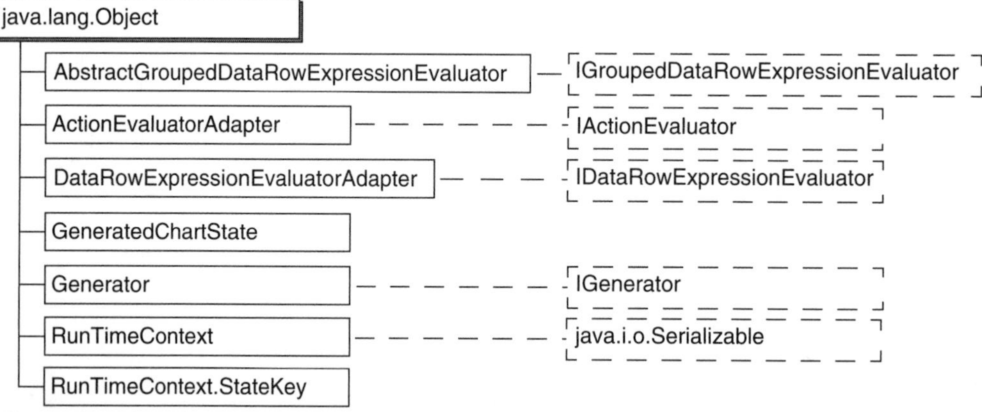

Figure 13-17 Classes in org.eclipse.birt.chart.factory

Figure 13-18 contains the interface hierarchy for org.eclipse.birt.chart.factory.

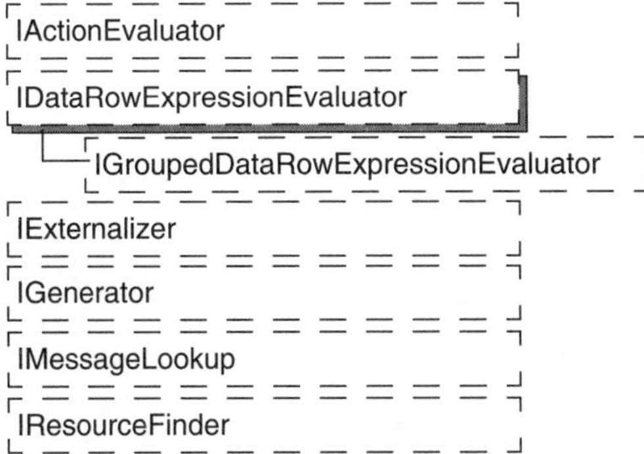

Figure 13-18 Interfaces in org.eclipse.birt.chart.factory

chart.log class and interface hierarchy

The chart.log package contains a single class and an interface to manage logging of the tasks that the BIRT Chart Engine performs. Figure 13-19 contains the class hierarchy for org.eclipse.birt.chart.log.

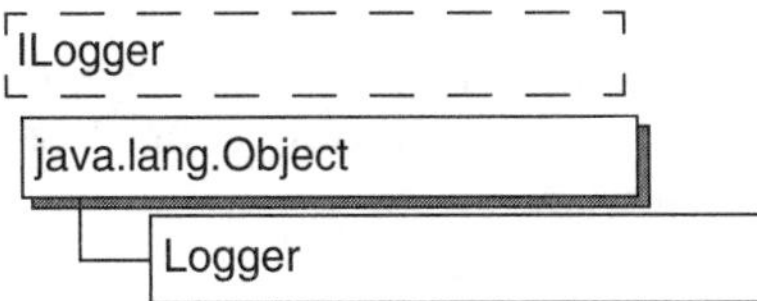

Figure 13-19 Class and interface in org.eclipse.birt.chart.log

chart.model interface hierarchy

The chart.model package contains the interfaces that describe the available chart types and the factory for generating charts. Figure 13-20 contains the interface hierarchy for org.eclipse.birt.chart.model.

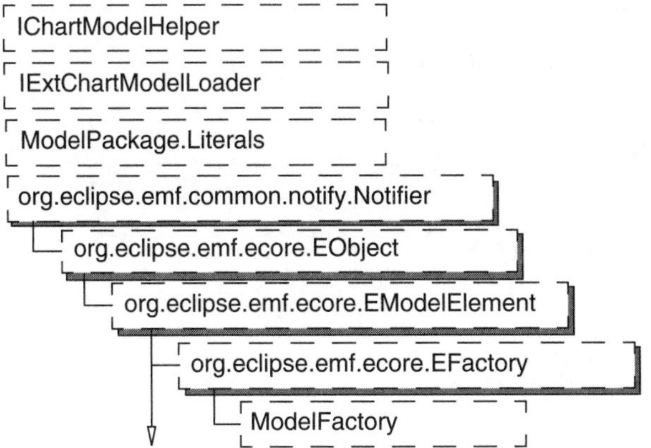

Figure 13-20 Interfaces in org.eclipse.birt.chart.model

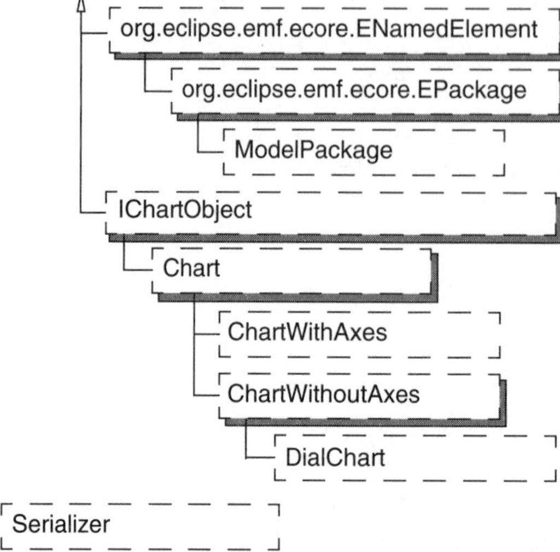

Figure 13-20 Interfaces in org.eclipse.birt.chart.model

chart.model.attribute class and interface hierarchy

The chart.model.attribute package contains classes that define the permitted values for attributes as static fields. Figure 13-21 contains the class hierarchy for org.eclipse.birt.chart.model.attribute.

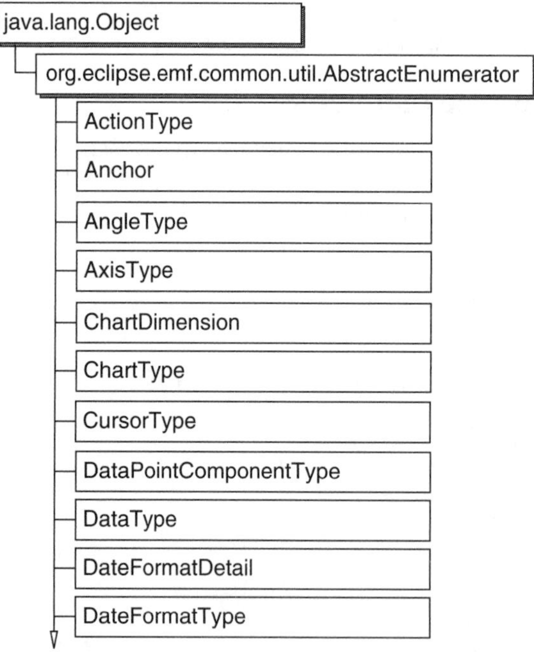

Figure 13-21 Classes in org.eclipse.birt.chart.model.attribute

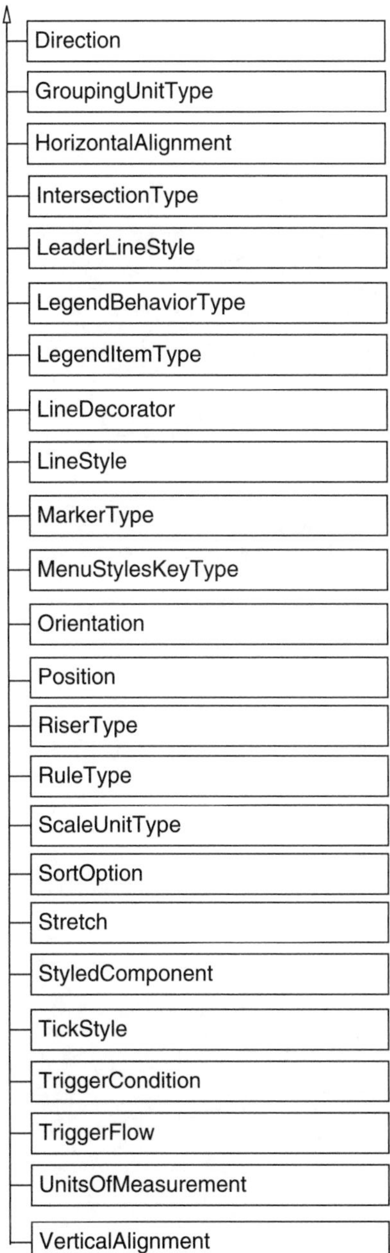

Figure 13-21 Classes in org.eclipse.birt.chart.model.attribute

The interfaces in the chart. model.attribute provide the getter and setter methods that chart engine objects use to test and set the values of the attributes. Figure 13-22 contains the interface hierarchy for org.eclipse.birt. chart.model.attribute.

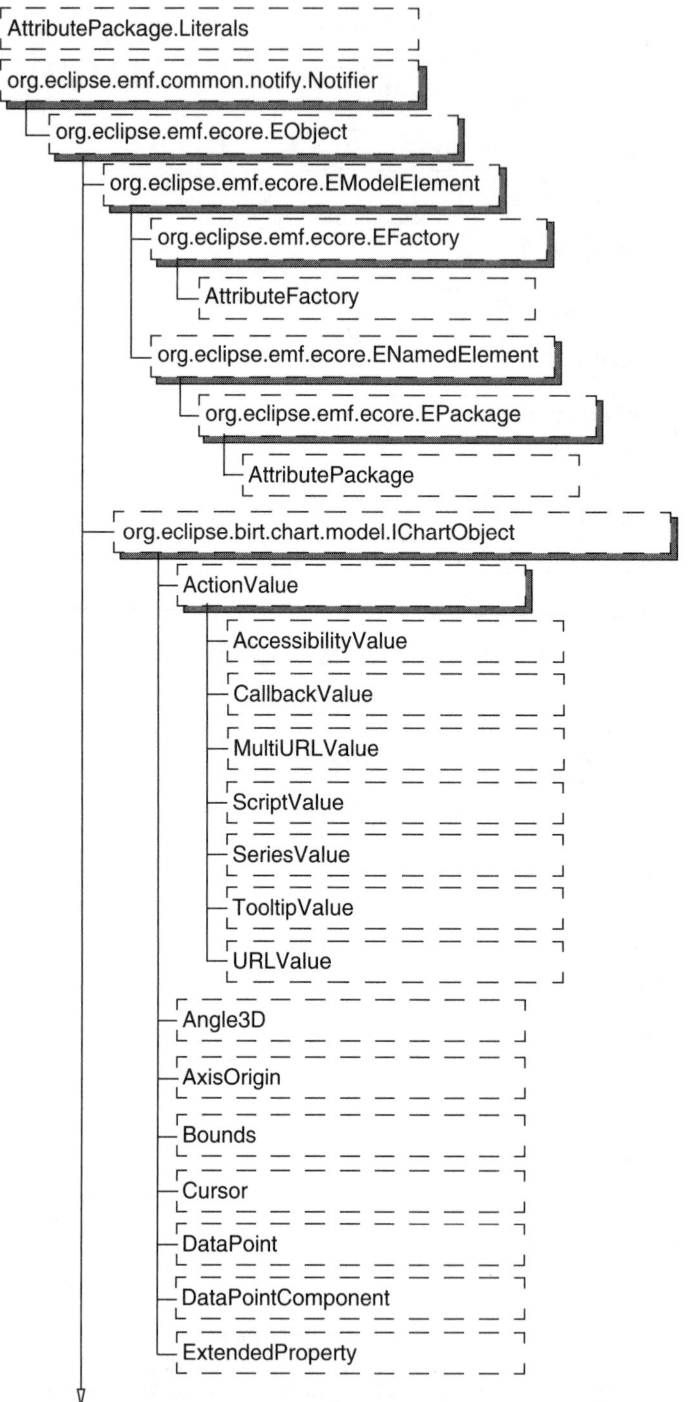

Figure 13-22 Interfaces in org.eclipse.birt.chart.model.attribute

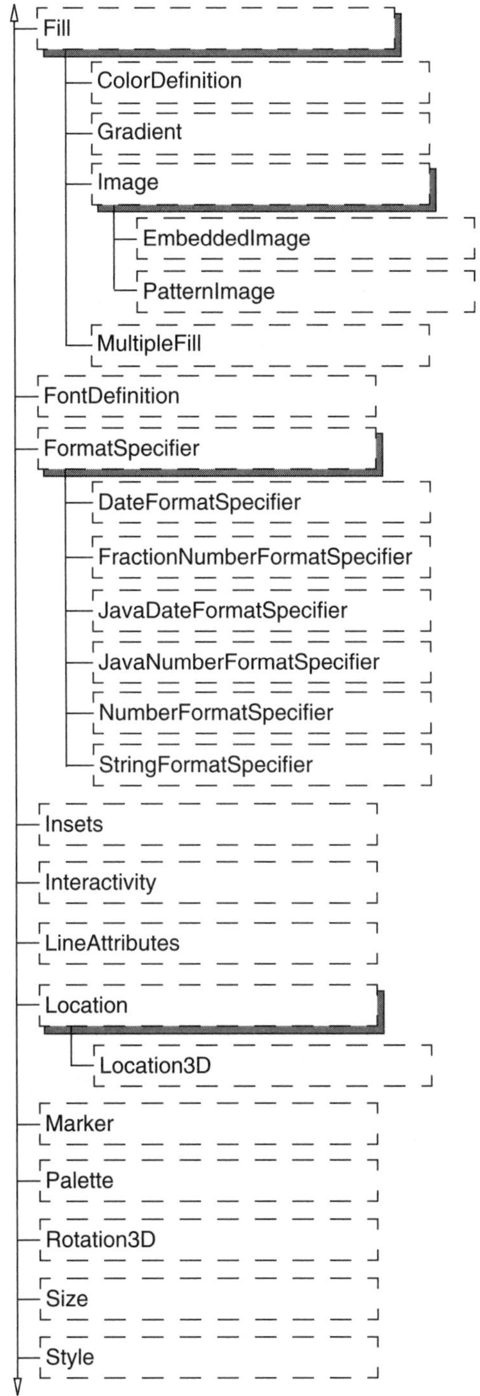

Figure 13-22 Interfaces in org.eclipse.birt.chart.model.attribute

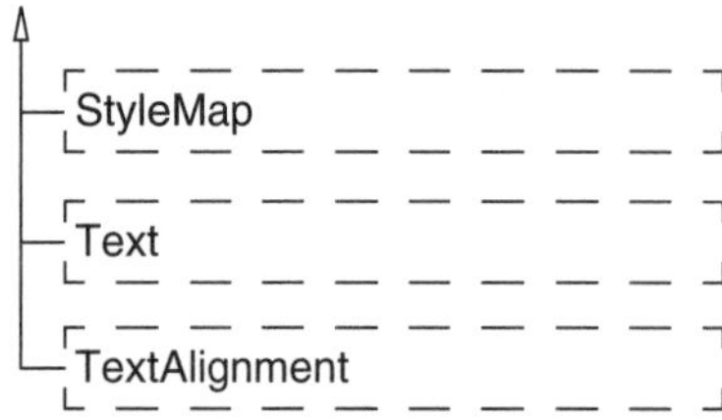

Figure 13-22 Interfaces in org.eclipse.birt.chart.model.attribute

chart.model.component interface hierarchy

The chart.model.component package contains the interfaces that define the behavior of all the components that make up a chart. Figure 13-23 contains the interface hierarchy for org.eclipse.birt.chart.model.component.

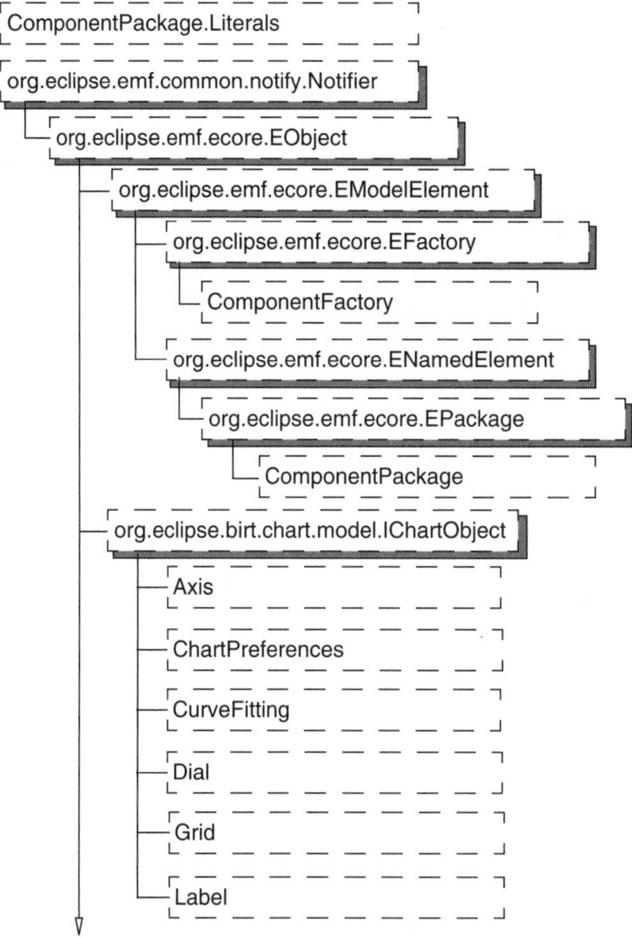

Figure 13-23 Interfaces in org.eclipse.birt.chart.model.component

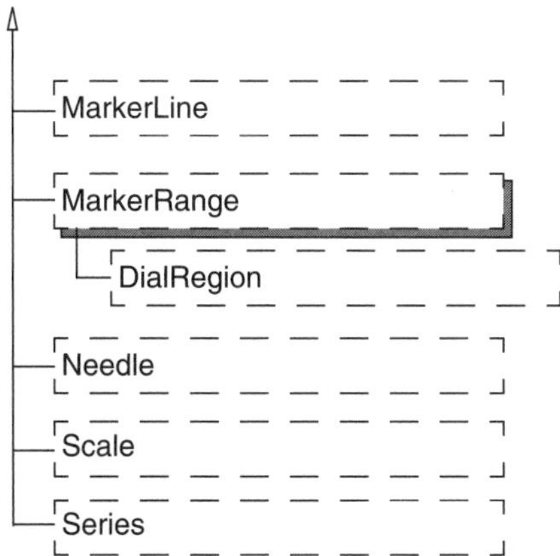

Figure 13-23 Interfaces in org.eclipse.birt.chart.model.component

chart.model.data interface hierarchy

The chart.model.data package contains interfaces that define a data source, a query structure, and the data components for a chart. These interfaces define getter and setter methods for data set properties and the permitted values for these properties as static fields. Figure 13-24 contains the interface hierarchy for org.eclipse.birt.chart.model.data.

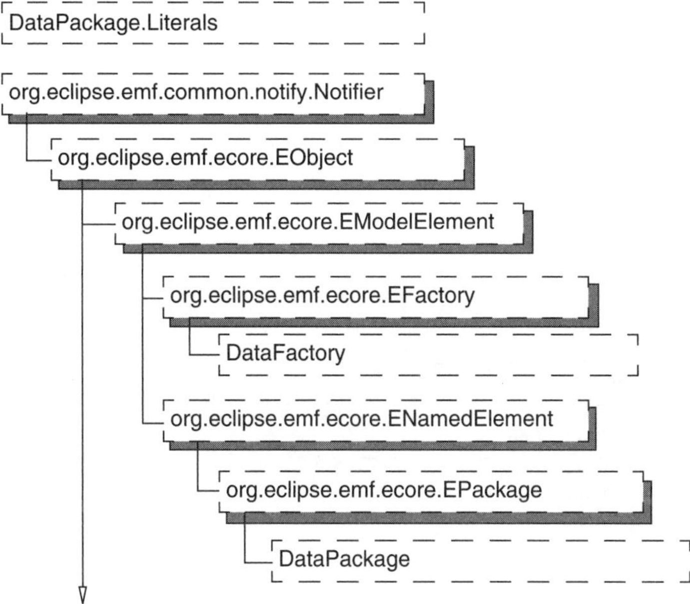

Figure 13-24 Interfaces in org.eclipse.birt.chart.model.data

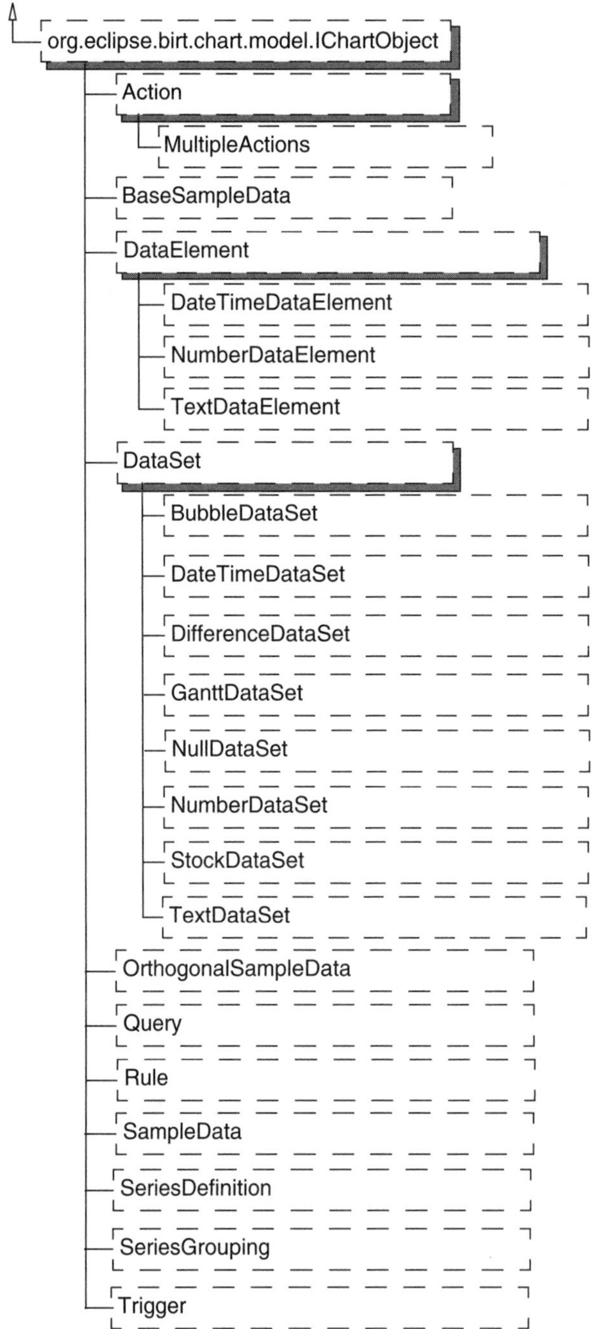

Figure 13-24 Interfaces in org.eclipse.birt.chart.model.data

chart.model.layout interface hierarchy

The chart.model.layout package contains the interfaces that define and arrange the blocks that make up the main components of a chart, such as the plot, title, and legend areas. Figure 13-25 contains the interface hierarchy for org.eclipse.birt.chart.model.layout.

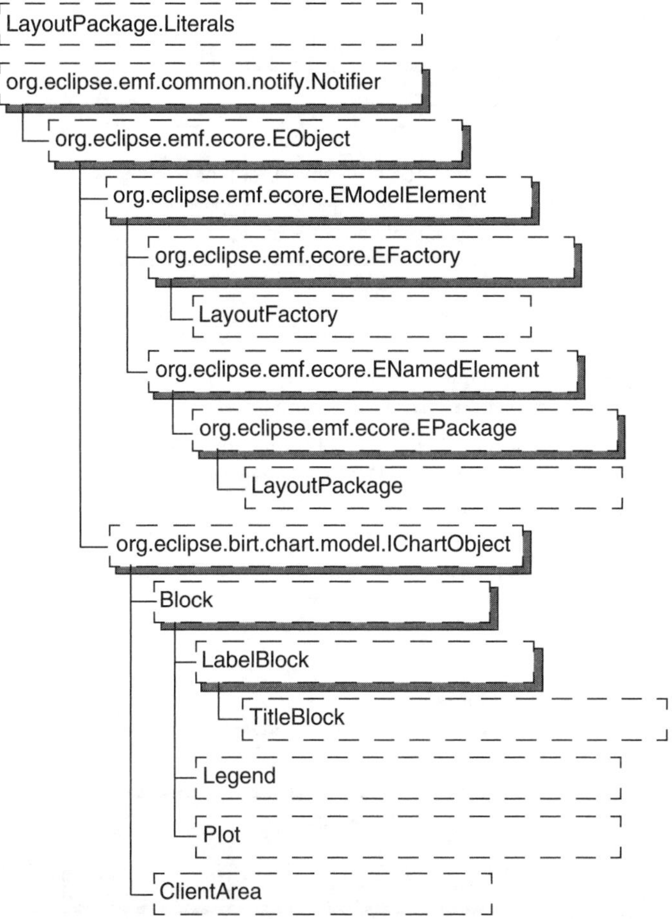

Figure 13-25 Interfaces in org.eclipse.birt.chart.model.layout

chart.model.type interface hierarchy

The chart.model.type package contains the interfaces that define the series for all the available chart types. Figure 13-26 contains the interface hierarchy for org.eclipse.birt.chart.model.type.

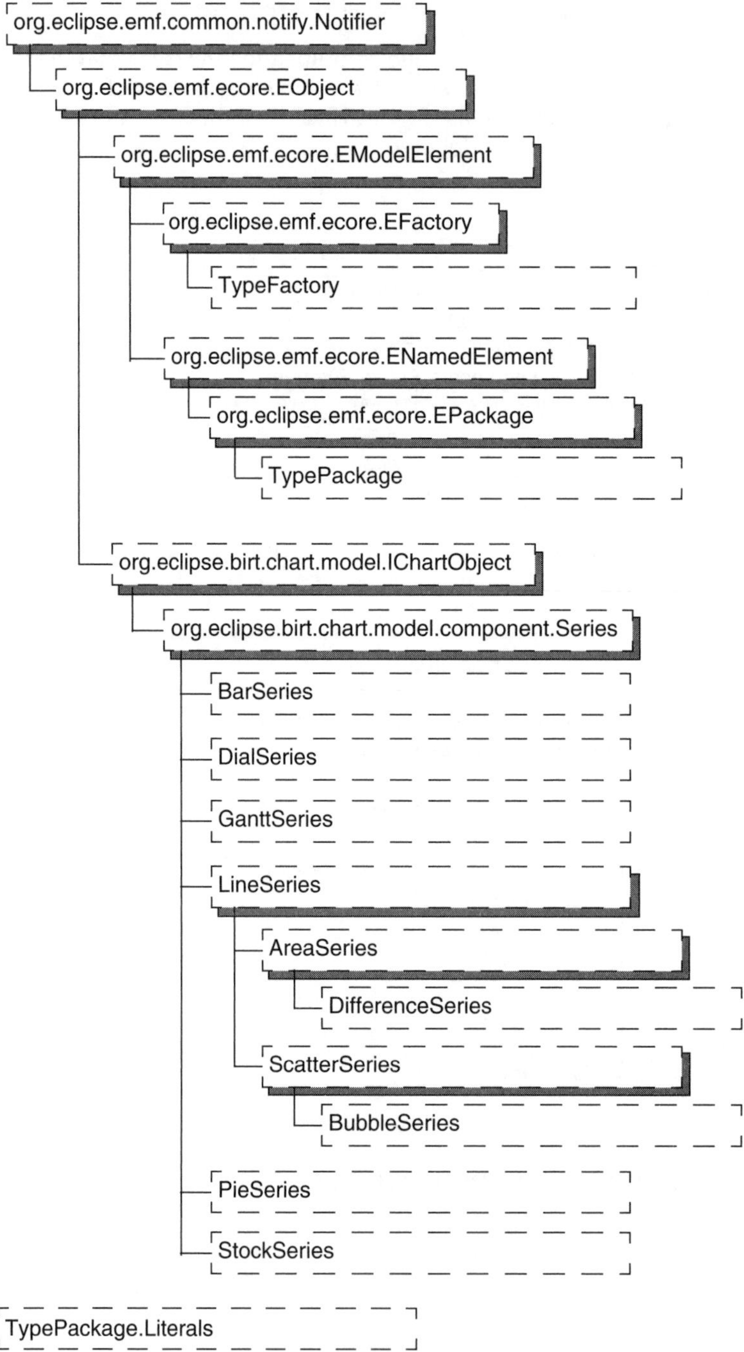

Figure 13-26 Interfaces in org.eclipse.birt.chart.model.type

chart.render class and interface hierarchy

The chart.render package contains classes and interfaces that render a chart. Figure 13-27 contains the interface hierarchy for org.eclipse.birt.chart.render.

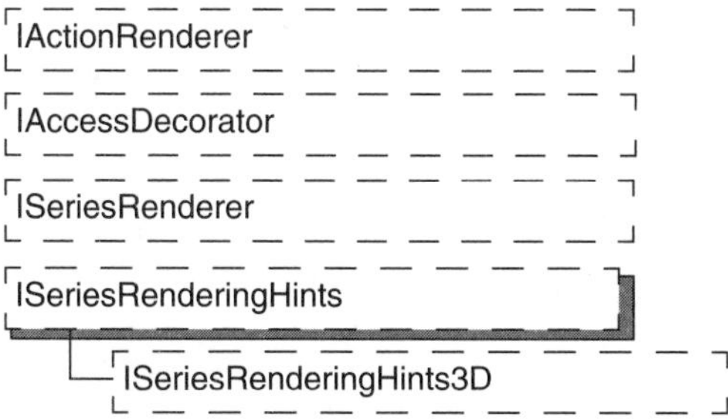

Figure 13-27 Interfaces in org.eclipse.birt.chart.render

Figure 13-28 contains the class hierarchy for org.eclipse.birt.chart.render.

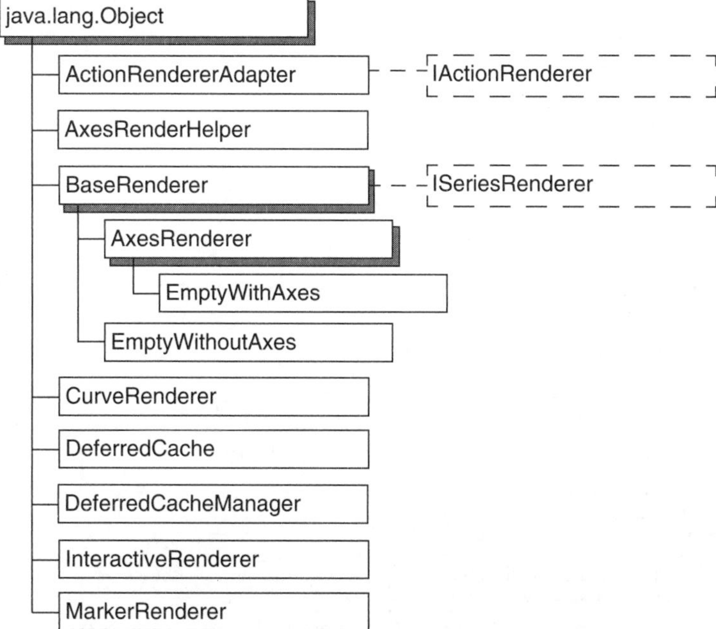

Figure 13-28 Classes in org.eclipse.birt.chart.render

chart.script class and interface hierarchy

The chart.script package contains the classes and interfaces that support script handling for chart developers to write custom code within the chart class itself. Figure 13-29 contains the class and interface hierarchy for org.eclipse.birt.chart.script.

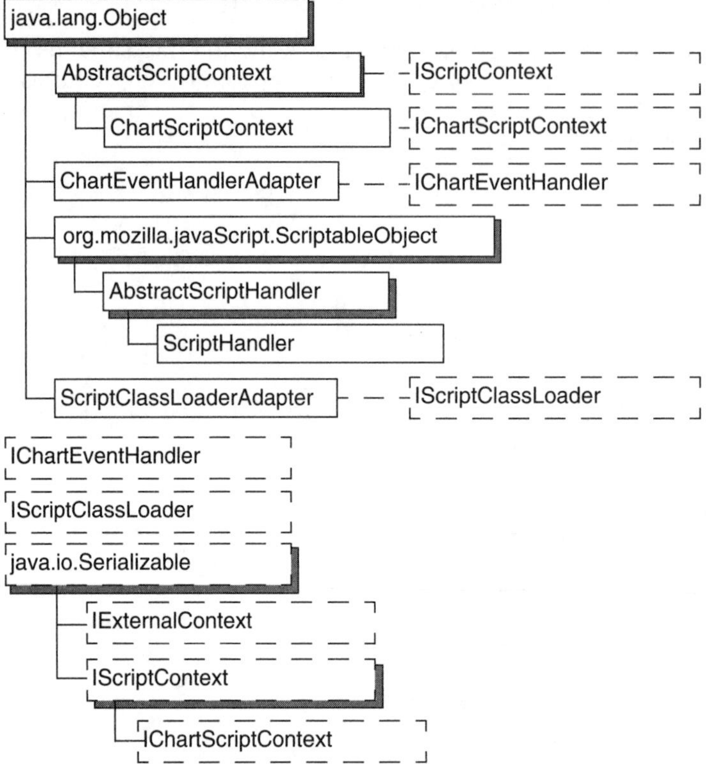

Figure 13-29 Classes and interfaces in org.eclipse.birt.chart.script package

chart.util class hierarchy

The chart.util package contains classes that support data types and looking up attribute and property values in the literal classes. Figure 13-30 contains the class hierarchy for org.eclipse.birt.chart.util.

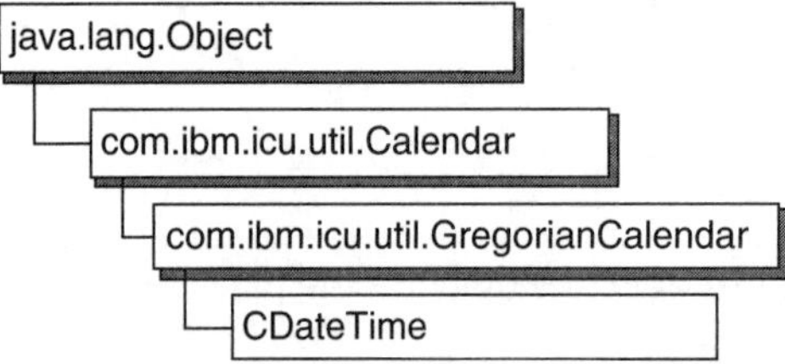

Figure 13-30 Classes in org.eclipse.birt.chart.util

Chapter

14

Programming Using the BIRT Reporting APIs

A reporting application uses the BIRT report engine API to generate reports from report design (.rptdesign) files. Typically, the application produces the report as a formatted file or stream, in HTML or PDF format. Alternatively, the application creates a report document (.rptdocument) file that contains the report content in binary form and renders the report to one of the supported output formats later.

This chapter describes the fundamental requirements of a reporting application and describes the BIRT API classes and interfaces that you use in the application. This chapter also provides detailed information about the tasks that a reporting application performs.

The BIRT APIs in the org.eclipse.birt.report.engine.api package support the process of generating a report from a report design. This package provides the ReportEngine class and supporting interfaces and classes.

Optionally, the reporting application can use the BIRT design engine API to access the structure of report designs, templates, and libraries. Using this API, the application can create and modify report designs before generating a report. This API supports creating and modifying the report items and other elements within designs. The org.eclipse.birt.report.model.api package and its subpackages provide access to all the items that comprise a report design.

For complete information about all the methods and fields of the classes and interfaces in these packages, see the online Javadoc. To view the Javadoc, open the online help and navigate to BIRT ProgrammerReference➛Reference ➛API Reference. Choose Report Engine API Reference for the report engine API and Report Object Model API Reference for the design engine API. The Javadoc also shows supporting packages in the public API.

Building a reporting application

An application that generates a report must complete the required tasks described in the following sections. Additional tasks, such as supplying user-entered values for parameters, are optional.

Creating and configuring a report engine

A single report engine object can generate multiple reports from multiple report designs. Use the Platform.createFactoryObject( ) method to create a ReportEngine object. Set the BIRT home directory, which defines the location of required plug-ins and libraries.

Opening a report design or report document

Use one of the openReportDesign( ) methods of the ReportEngine class to open a report design from a String file name or an input stream. These methods return an IReportRunnable object.

Use the openReportDocument( ) method of the ReportEngine class to open a report document (.rptdocument) file from a String file name. This method returns an IReportDocument object.

Ensuring access to the data source

Ensure the report engine can locate the classes that connect to the data source and supply data to the data set. The report engine can either create a connection to the data source or use a Connection object that the application provides.

Preparing to create a report in the supported output formats

Use an IRenderOption object to set the output format, the output file name or stream, the locale, and format-specific settings. The HTMLRenderOption class supports the HTML output format. For PDF output, use RenderOption.

Generating a report in one of the supported output formats

Use an IRunAndRenderTask object to create the report from the IReportRunnable object. Use an IRenderTask object to create the report from an IReportDocument object.

Alternatively, use a URL to access the report viewer servlet, such as when deploying a BIRT report to an application server, as described earlier in this book. The report viewer can generate a report from either a design file or a document file.

Destroying the engine

Destroy the report engine after the application has generated all required reports.

Optional tasks

The tasks in the following list are optional for a reporting application. Typically, the application performs one or more of these tasks.

- Gather values for parameters.

  If the application uses a report design that has parameters, use the default values for the parameters or set different values.

- Create a report document file.

  A report document file contains the report in a binary storage form. If the application uses a report design, use an IRunTask object to create the report document as an IReportDocument object.

- Export data from a report document.

  Use an IDataExtractionTask object to extract data values from any item or set of items in the report document. Export the data values to a file or another application, or perform further processing on the data.

About the development environment

The development environment for a reporting application must provide access to all the required BIRT plug-ins and API libraries. The key requirement for the application is the path to the BIRT home directory. The BIRT home directory contains the BIRT engine, which is made up of the required BIRT plug-ins and libraries.

Installing the BIRT Report Engine package, as described in Chapter 3, "Installing Other BIRT Packages,"provides a complete BIRT home in the ReportEngine subdirectory.

About plug-ins in BIRT home

The plugins subdirectory of the BIRT home directory contains the org.eclipse.birt and other plug-ins that provide the functionality of a reporting application. Depending on the requirements of your reporting application and the items in your report designs, you can omit plug-ins that provide functionality that the application and designs do not use.

About libraries in BIRT home

The lib subdirectory of the BIRT home directory contains JAR files providing BIRT API classes and classes that support the APIs. This location within the report engine ensures that the class loader of the application server or JVM in which you deploy the report engine can locate the libraries. Depending on the requirements of your reporting application and the items in your report designs, you can omit libraries that provide functionality that the application and designs do not use.

Table 14-1 lists and describes all the JAR files in the lib directory.

Table 14-1 Libraries in the BIRT home lib directory

Library	Description
chartengineapi.jar	Contains chart model and factory API classes. Supports generation of charts in a report.
chartexamplescoreapi.jar	Contains classes providing an example of a charting extension.
chartitemapi.jar	Contains the classes for the chart report item.
com.ibm.icu_<version> .jar	Provides International Components for Unicode to support text in multiple locales.
commons-cli-<version> .jar	Provides command-line parsing. Used by the report.engine. ReportRunner class.
coreapi.jar	Contains framework and utility API classes.
crosstabcoreapi.jar	Contains cross-tab API classes.
dataadapterapi.jar	Contains data adapter classes.
dataaggregationapi.jar	Contains the data aggregation API class.
dataextraction.jar	Contains classes for extracting report contents to comma-separated values (CSV) format.
dteapi.jar	Provides API access to data sources. Transforms data that the data set provides.
emitterconfig.jar	Contains classes to support custom emitters.
engineapi.jar	Contains API classes for generating a report from a design.
flute.jar	Used by the report.model plug-in. Provides access to CSS functionality.
js.jar	Provides scripting functionality.
modelapi.jar	Contains report design element API classes.
modelodaapi.jar	Used for conversions between ROM elements and required Eclipse Data Tools Platform (DTP) Open Data Access (ODA) elements.
odadesignapi.jar	Used when retrieving data.
org.apache.commons .codec-<version>.jar	Used by the report.engine plug-in. Provides encoding and decoding functionality.
org.eclipse.emf.common _<version>.jar	Required for charts.
org.eclipse.emf.ecore .xmi_<version>.jar	Required for charts.
org.eclipse.emf.ecore _<version>.jar	Required for charts.

Table 14-1 Libraries in the BIRT home lib directory

Library	Description
org.w3c.css.sac _<version>.jar	Used by the report.model plug-in. Required for CSS functionality.
scriptapi.jar	Contains API classes for Java-based scripting.

About required JDBC drivers

BIRT applications load JDBC drivers from the BIRT home directory plugins/org.eclipse.birt.report.data.oda.jdbc_<version>/drivers. Place the driver classes or Java archive (.jar) files that you require to access JDBC data sources in this location.

Setting up the build path and accessing Javadoc

To access the BIRT APIs during application development using the Java perspective in the Eclipse Workbench, add API JAR files to the build path. The org.eclipse.birt.chart.doc.isv and org.eclipse.birt.doc.isv plug-ins provide the Javadoc for the public BIRT APIs. Extract the plug-ins' JAR files to a convenient location, for example in your workspace or a resource folder. Then, use the Java Build Path settings in Eclipse to set the Javadoc location for each public API JAR file. Table 14-2 lists the source plug-in and the extracted location of the Javadoc.

Table 14-2 Javadoc locations for BIRT API libraries

API library	Javadoc source plug-in	Javadoc folder
chartengineapi.jar	org.eclipse.birt.chart.doc.isv	chart/api
coreapi.jar	org.eclipse.birt.doc.isv	core/api
dteapi.jar	org.eclipse.birt.doc.isv	data/api
engineapi.jar	org.eclipse.birt.doc.isv	engine/api
modelapi.jar	org.eclipse.birt.doc.isv	model/api
scriptapi.jar	org.eclipse.birt.doc.isv	enginescript/api

How to add BIRT libraries and API Javadoc to a Java application's build path

Use the Java perspective in the Eclipse Workbench to perform these steps on an existing Java project.

1 Install the BIRT Engine package to create a BIRT home.

2 To make the BIRT Javadoc files accessible to the Eclipse Java perspective, navigate to the eclipse\plugins directory. Extract the org.eclipse.birt.chart.doc.isv and org.eclipse.birt.doc.isv plug-in JAR files to a workspace or resource directory.

3 In Package Explorer, right-click the Java project. Choose Build Path➛ Configure Build Path.

4 In Properties for <project name>—Java Build Path, select Libraries. To add a JAR file to the build path, choose Add External JARs.

5 In JAR Selection, navigate to the BIRT home lib directory. Select a required JAR file. Choose Open. The JAR file appears in JARs and class folders on the build path.

6 To associate the Javadoc with the class files in a BIRT API library, perform the following steps:

   1 Expand the API JAR file in JARs and class folders on the build path. Select Javadoc location: (None). Choose Edit.

   2 In Javadoc for <JAR file name>, type or browse to the directory that contains the Javadoc extracted in step 2. Type or browse to the subdirectory specified in Table 14-2.

   3 Choose Validate. Validating Javadoc Location displays a message about whether the specified directory contains Javadoc. Choose OK.

   4 If necessary, correct the path to the Javadoc. In Javadoc for <JAR file name>, choose OK.

7 Repeat steps 4 through 6 for each required BIRT JAR file.

Modifying a report design using the API

A reporting application can modify a report design before generating the report. For example, the application can add or remove items from the report design based on the user who generates the report. To provide further customization of a report, during the generation of the output, a report design can use JavaScript classes or embedded JavaScript code to handle events. The classes in the Design Engine API support making changes to a report design and including or changing scripts. The key Design Engine classes are in the org.eclipse.birt.model.api package.

About the deployment environment

A deployed application must be able to access all the classes required for BIRT, the external data sources, and any other necessary classes. Set up the BIRT home directory and the CLASSPATH for the application.

If you use or customize the BIRT source code, ensure that the version that your application uses matches the version of the plug-ins and libraries in the BIRT home directory. If these versions are not the same, the reporting application is likely to fail.

Generating reports from an application

The key tasks that a reporting application must perform are to set up the report engine, any required parameter values, and the task objects to generate the report document, and finally to render the report. The reporting application does not require the BIRT Report Designer user interface to generate a report.

The org.eclipse.birt.report.engine.api package contains the classes and interfaces that an application uses to generate reports. The main classes and interfaces are ReportEngine, EngineConfig, IReportRunnable, IRenderOption and its descendants, and IEngineTask and its descendants.

Setting up the report engine

A report engine is an instantiation of the ReportEngine class. This object is the key component in any reporting application. It provides access to runnable report designs, parameters, the structure of a report design, and the task for generating a report from a report design. Prepare the report engine's properties with an EngineConfig object. After setting all the required properties, use the BIRT engine factory to create the report engine. The following sections describe the various configuration options and creation of the engine.

Configuring the BIRT home

The BIRT home, which is the location of the BIRT plug-ins and libraries, is the key property that the report engine requires. The report engine cannot parse a report design nor render the report without a defined BIRT home. For a stand-alone application, the BIRT home is an absolute path to a file system location. For an application running from a web archive (.war) file on an application server, the BIRT home is a relative path in the WAR file. To set the BIRT home location, use one of the following techniques:

- For a stand-alone application, use one of the following techniques:
  - Call EngineConfig.setBIRTHome( ) with an argument that is the path to the BIRT home directory, for example:

    ```
    config.setBIRTHome
       ( "C:/birt-runtime-<version>/ReportEngine" );
    ```

  - In the application's environment, set up the BIRT_HOME and CLASSPATH variables to access the required libraries. For example, in a Windows batch file, include commands similar to the following ones before launching the stand-alone application:

    ```
    set BIRT_HOME="C:\birt-runtime-<version>\ReportEngine"
    SET CLASSPATH=%BIRT_HOME%\<required library 1>;
       %BIRT_HOME%\<required library 2 and so on>;
       %CLASSPATH%
    ```

    To develop an application that uses a BIRT_HOME environment variable, set BIRT_HOME in the VM arguments in the Eclipse Run dialog. For example, in VM arguments, type text similar to the following line:

```
-DBIRT_HOME="C:\birt-runtime-<version>\ReportEngine"
```

- For a deployed web application, use one of the following techniques:
  - If the application has a location in the file system, use the servlet context to find the real path of the BIRT home, for example:

    ```
    config.setBIRTHome
       ( servletContext.getRealPath( "/WEB-INF" ) );
    ```

  - If the application runs from a WAR file, use a relative path from the WAR file root, as shown in the following example. This configuration uses PlatformServletContext.

    ```
    config.setBIRTHome( "" );
    ```

- If you use BIRT in an Eclipse-based application, such as an RCP application, and the BIRT plug-ins are located in the application's plugins directory, you do not need to set BIRT_HOME.

Configuring the report engine

Optionally, set other configuration properties using methods on an EngineConfig object. Table 14-3 describes these properties and how to set them using EngineConfig methods. The EngineConfig class also provides getter methods to access these properties.

Table 14-3 EngineConfig properties

Property type	Setting the property
Configuring an emitter	To set the properties for the required report output format, call setEmitterConfiguration( ) with arguments providing the format and a IRenderOption object for that format.
Logging	To set the logging file location and level, call setLogConfig( ). To refine the logging file name and properties, use the other setLogXXX( ) methods.
OSGi (Open Services Gateway Initiative) configuration	To set specific OSGi startup parameters, call setOSGiArguments( ) or setOSGiConfig( ).
Platform context	To indicate whether the application and BIRT home are in a stand-alone environment or packaged as a web archive (.war) file, create an implementation of the IPlatformContext interface. Then, call setPlatformContext( ).
Resource files	To set the location from which the reporting application accesses resource files such as

Table 14-3 EngineConfig properties

Property type	Setting the property
Resource files	libraries and properties files containing localized strings, call setResourcePath( ). To change the algorithm for locating these resources, call setResourceLocator( ).
Scripting configuration	To provide external values to scripting methods, call setProperty( ). To provide additional Java resources to scripting methods, call getAppContext( ) and add the object to the application context object.
Status handling	To provide a custom status handler, create an implementation of the IStatusHandler interface. Then, call setStatusHandler( ).
Temporary file location	To set up a custom location for temporary files, call setTempDir( ).

Setting up a stand-alone or WAR file environment

Two engine configuration properties depend on whether the environment in which the application runs is stand-alone or in a web archive (.war) file on an application server. These properties are the platform context and the HTML emitter configuration. The platform context provides the report engine with the mechanism to access plug-ins. The default platform context provides direct file system access to these plug-ins, as used by a stand-alone application. The HTML emitter configuration provides the functionality to process images and handle hyperlinking and bookmark actions.

Setting up the platform context

Because BIRT is an Eclipse-based application, it uses the OSGi platform to start up the plug-ins that make up the report and design engines. The BIRT application locates the plug-ins in the BIRT home using the platform context, which is an implementation of the org.eclipse.birt.core.framework .IPlatformContext interface. This interface defines the method, getPlatform( ) that returns the location of the plugins directory. Use the IPlatformContext object as the argument to the EngineConfig object's setPlatformContext( ) method.

The BIRT framework provides two implementations of the IPlatformContext interface. These implementations provide all the required functionality for the platform context.

The default implementation, PlatformFileContext, accesses the plug-ins in the BIRT home folder on the file system. If the application sets the BIRT home location in the EngineConfig object or the application environment contains BIRT_HOME, creating a PlatformFileContext object is not necessary.

For a web deployment, such as an application running from a WAR file on an application server, use the PlatformServletContext implementation. This class uses the resource-based access provided by the J2EE ServletContext class to locate the required plug-ins. The constructor for this class takes one argument, a ServletContext object. By default, PlatformServletContext finds plug-ins in the /WEB-INF/platform/ directory by using the ServletContext .getRealPath( ) method. Some application servers return null from this method. In this case, the PlatformServletContext object creates a platform directory in the location defined by the system property, javax.servlet .context.tempdir. The PlatformServletContext object copies the plug-ins and configuration folders to this location. Listing 14-2 sets up a platform context for a reporting application that runs from a WAR file.

If neither of these IPlatformContext implementations meets your needs, implement your own version of IPlatformContext. In the same way as for the built-in platform contexts, call EngineConfig.setPlatformContext( ) to configure the engine to use the new implementation.

Setting up the HTML emitter

To generate a report in HTML format, the report engine uses an org.eclipse .birt.report.engine.api.HTMLRenderOption object to determine how to handle resources that the HTML emitter uses or creates. These resources include new image files for image elements and chart elements, and the locations of jumps from bookmark and drill-through actions. BIRT uses different image handlers for file system-based applications and applications deployed on the web. Use the EngineConfig object to set up the HTML emitter options when creating the report engine, as shown in Listing 14-1, or set the options later when rendering a report to HTML.

To set up the HTML emitter, instantiate an HTMLRenderOption object. Use this object as the argument to ReportEngine.setEmitterConfiguration( ) to define the HTML rendering options when creating the report engine.

Call the HTMLRenderOption.setImageHandler( ) method to configure the image handler. This method determines how to save the image files by using an org.eclipse.birt.report.engine.api.IHTMLImageHandler object. Images defined in a report as a URL are not saved locally. BIRT provides two implementations of the IHTMLImageHandler interface. Both implementations create unique image file names for temporary images.

The default image handler implementation, HTMLCompleteImageHandler, saves images to the file system. Use this implementation for a stand-alone application or for a web application that uses file system deployment on the application server. This image handler finds the location for images by searching first for the image directory set in the HTMLRenderOption object, next the temporary files directory as set by the EngineConfig.setTempDir( ) method, and finally the location set by the system setting, java.io.tmpdir. All images in the generated HTML use file references to the created images.

For a web deployment, such as an application running from a WAR file on an application server, use the HTMLServerImageHandler implementation. This class saves images to the image directory set in the HTMLRenderOption object. The src attribute of images in the generated HTML appends the image name to the base image URL, also set in the HTMLRenderOption object. In this way, the report engine produces the images locally and shares the images using a URL. To use this implementation, set the image directory and the base image URL, as shown in Listing 14-3. The example BIRT Web Viewer in the org.eclipse.birt.report.viewer plug-in uses this implementation.

If neither IHTMLImageHandler meets your needs, create a class that implements IHTMLImageHandler or extends an existing image handler. Typically, HTMLCompleteImageHander provides sufficient functionality for file system access, so an application does not extend the class. For the application server environment, extend from HTMLServerImageHandler. To configure the engine to use the new implementation, in the same way as for the built-in image handlers, call EngineConfig.setEmitterConfiguration( ).

Starting the platform

After setting up the PlatformContext, an application starts the platform by using the org.eclipse.birt.core.framework.Platform class. This class acts as a wrapper around the Eclipse OSGILauncher class and provides the method, startup( ), to start the platform. Calling this synchronized static method uses substantial system resources, so an application should call this method only once. If the report engine is deployed in a web application, call Platform .startup( ) in the servlet's init( ) method or in the first request that uses the platform. To achieve this behavior, wrap the platform start-up code in a singleton, as shown in Listing 14-2. When an application finishes using the platform, call Platform.shutdown( ). If you use the example Web Viewer or deploy the report engine in an Eclipse-based project such as an Rich Client Platform (RCP) application, do not start up or shut down the platform, because these applications control the OSGi start-up and shutdown.

Creating the report engine

BIRT provides a factory service to create the ReportEngine object. Call Platform.createFactoryObject( ) to create this factory, which implements the org.eclipse.birt.report.engine.api.IReportEngineFactory interface. The createFactoryObject( ) method uses a PlatformConfig object. Call IReportEngineFactory.createReportEngine( ) to create the report engine.

How to set up a report engine as a stand-alone application

Listing 14-1 shows an example of setting up a report engine as a stand-alone application on a Windows system. The application uses the BIRT home located in the BIRT run-time directory. The report output format is HTML.

Listing 14-1 Setting up the report engine for a stand-alone application

```
// Create an EngineConfig object.
EngineConfig config = new EngineConfig( );
```

```
// Set up the path to your BIRT home directory.
config.setBIRTHome
   ( "C:/Program Files/birt-runtime-2_6_0/ReportEngine" );
// Start the platform for a non-RCP application.
try
{
   Platform.startup( config );
   IReportEngineFactory factory =
      ( IReportEngineFactory ) Platform.createFactoryObject
      ( IReportEngineFactory.EXTENSION_REPORT_ENGINE_FACTORY );
   // Set up writing images or charts embedded in HTML output.
   HTMLRenderOption ho = new HTMLRenderOption( );
   ho.setImageHandler( new HTMLCompleteImageHandler( ));
   config.setEmitterConfiguration
      ( RenderOption.OUTPUT_FORMAT_HTML, ho );
   // Create the engine.
   IReportEngine engine = factory.createReportEngine( config );
}
catch ( BirtException e ) { e.printStackTrace(); }
```

How to set up a report engine as a web application

1 Set up the platform context, as shown in Listing 14-2.

Listing 14-2 Setting up the platform context for WAR file deployment

```
// Example class to create the report engine
public class BirtEngine
{
   private static IReportEngine birtEngine = null;

   public static synchronized IReportEngine
      getBirtEngine( ServletContext sc )
   {
      if (birtEngine == null) {
         EngineConfig config = new EngineConfig( );
         config.setBIRTHome( "" );
         IPlatformContext context =
            new PlatformServletContext( sc );
         config.setPlatformContext( context );
         try
         {
            Platform.startup( config );
            IReportEngineFactory factory =
               ( IReportEngineFactory )
                Platform.createFactoryObject
( IReportEngineFactory.EXTENSION_REPORT_ENGINE_FACTORY );
            birtEngine =
               factory.createReportEngine( config );
         }
         catch ( Exception e ) { e.printStackTrace( ); }
      }
```

```
        return birtEngine;
    }
}
```

2 Set up further configuration options on the engine after instantiating the class, as shown in Listing 14-3.

Listing 14-3 Setting up HTML options for WAR file deployment

```
// In a different class, get the report engine
IReportEngine reportEngine = BirtEngine.getBirtEngine
   ( request.getSession( ).getServletContext( ));
// Set up the engine
EngineConfig config = reportEngine.getConfig( );
HTMLRenderOption ho = new HTMLRenderOption( );
ho.setImageHandler( new HTMLServerImageHandler( ));
ho.setImageDirectory("output/image");
ho.setBaseImageURL("http://myhost/prependme?image=");
config.setEmitterConfiguration
   ( RenderOption.OUTPUT_FORMAT_HTML, ho );
```

In this listing, request is an HttpServletRequest object.

Using the logging environment to debug an application

BIRT Report Engine uses the java.util.logging classes, Logger and Level, to log information about the processing that the engine performs. When an application runs in the Eclipse workbench, by default, the messages appear in the console. When an application runs outside Eclipse, the default location of the log messages depends on the environment. The default logging threshold is Level.INFO. Typically, you change this level in your application to reduce the number of internal logging messages.

To set up the logging environment to write the engine's log messages to a file, use the EngineConfig.setLogConfig( ) method. This method takes two arguments. The first argument is the directory in which to create the log file. The second argument is the lowest level at which to log information. Set the logging level to a high threshold so that the engine logs fewer messages. Typically, you want to see information at INFO level when you first develop a block of code. Use the ReportEngine.changeLogLevel( ) method to modify the amount of information that the engine logs. This method takes a single argument, which is a Level constant. When the code is stable, you no longer need to see all the engine's INFO messages. At that point, delete or comment out the call to changeLogLevel( ). BIRT Report Engine creates a log file with a name of the format ReportEngine_YYYY_MM_DD_hh_mm_ss.log. To change this name, call EngineConfig.setLogFile( ). Use the EngineConfig methods, setLogRollingSize( ) and setLogMaxLogBackupIndex( ), to control the size and number of log files.

How to use BIRT logging

The following example shows how to use logging in an application. You set up the logging environment and modify it later in your application. The variable, config, is the EngineConfig object that the code's active ReportEngine object, engine, is using.

1 Configure logging on the report engine object.

```
// Set up the location and level of the logging output.
config.setLogConfig( "C:/Temp", Level.SEVERE );
config.setLogFile( "myBIRTApp.log" );
```

2 In any newly written code, increase the amount of logging.

```
engine.changeLogLevel( Level.INFO );
```

Opening a source for report generation

BIRT Report Engine classes generate a formatted report from either a report design or a binary report document. Typically, these files have the extensions RPTDESIGN and RPTDOCUMENT respectively. The engine can also generate a binary report document from a report design.

To open a report design, call one of the openReportDesign( ) methods on ReportEngine. These methods instantiate an IReportRunnable object, using a String that specifies the path to a report design or an input stream. To open a report document, call ReportEngine.openReportDocument( ). This method instantiates an IReportDocument object, using a String that specifies the path to a report document. Handle the EngineException that these methods throw.

Understanding an IReportRunnable object

The IReportRunnable object provides direct access to basic properties of the report design. The names of report design properties are static String fields, such as IReportRunnable.AUTHOR. To access a report design property, use getProperty( ) with a String argument that contains one of these fields.

To generate a report from a design, open the report design as shown in Listing 14-4. Then, perform the tasks shown later in this chapter.

How to access a report design

Listing 14-4 shows how to open a report design and find a property value. If the engine cannot open the specified report design, the code destroys the engine. The variable, engine, is a ReportEngine object.

Listing 14-4 Accessing a report design

```
String designName = "./SimpleReport.rptdesign";
IReportRunnable runnable = null;
try {
   runnable = engine.openReportDesign( designName );
}
```

```
catch ( EngineException e ) {
   System.err.println ( "Design " + designName + " not found!" );
   engine.destroy( );
   System.exit( -1 );
}
// Get the value of a simple property.
String title = ( String ) runnable.getProperty
   ( IReportRunnable.TITLE );
```

Understanding an IReportDocument object

The IReportDocument object provides access to the structure and contents of a binary report document. IReportDocument provides methods to retrieve bookmark, page, and report design information. A bookmark is a String object that locates an instance of a report element in the document and the page on which the element exists. Use page information to render individual pages in the document to an output format. Bookmarks also provide access to the design elements that generated the element instance.

Use the getBookmarks( ) method to get a List object containing all the bookmarks in the document. Call the getBookmarkInstance( ) method with a String argument containing a bookmark to access the instantiated report element. Calling the getReportRunnable( ) method returns an IReportRunnable object, which an application can use to access report design information or generate another report document.

Close the document after use by calling IReportDocument.close( ).

How to access a report document

Listing 14-5 shows how to open a report document and find a page. If the engine cannot open the specified report design, the code logs the error. The variable, engine, is a ReportEngine object.

Listing 14-5 Accessing a report document

```
String dName = "./SimpleReport.rptdocument";
IReportDocument doc = null;
try {
   doc = engine.openReportDocument( dName );
} catch ( EngineException e ) {
   System.err.println( "Document " + dName + " not found!" );
   return;
}
// Get the second bookmark in the document.
java.util.List bookmarks = doc.getBookmarks( );
String bookmark = ( String ) bookmarks.get( 1 );
long pageNumber = doc.getPageNumber( bookmark );
logger.log(Level.INFO, bookmark + " Page number: " + pageNumber);
// Close the document.
doc.close( );
```

Accessing a report parameter

A report parameter is a report element that provides input to a report design before an application generates the report. A report document does not use report parameters to create a formatted report. If an application already has the parameter names and the values to set, or the default values for all report parameters for a report design are always valid, or the report source is a report document, you do not need to perform the tasks in this section.

Report parameters have attributes that a reporting application can access. The most commonly used attributes are name and value. The report engine uses the report design logic and the report parameter values to perform tasks such as filtering a data set or displaying an external value in the report.

After the reporting application sets values for the report parameters, it must pass these values to the task that generates the report, as shown later in this chapter. To access report parameters and their default values and to set user-supplied values to a parameter, the application uses the BIRT report engine API classes and interfaces shown in Table 14-4.

An application can access report parameters by name or using generic code. Use generic code if the application must be able to run any report design, for example, to access report designs from a list that depends on user input. An application that runs only a fixed set of known report designs can access the report parameters by name.

Table 14-4 Classes and interfaces that support report parameters

Class or interface	Use
ReportEngine class	Instantiates the task that accesses report parameters. To create the task object, call the createGetParameterDefinitionTask( ) method. This method returns an instance of IGetParameterDefinitionTask.
IGetParameterDefinition Task interface	Accesses a single report parameter or a collection of all the report parameters in a report design. Also provides access to valid values for parameters that use restricted sets of values, such as cascading parameters.
IParameterDefnBase interface	The base interface for report parameter elements. Scalar parameters implement the derived interface, IScalarParameterDefn. Parameter groups implement the derived interface IParameterGroupDefn. To get information about parameter attributes, use objects implementing these interfaces.
IParameterGroupDefn interface	The base interface for report parameter groups. Cascading parameter groups implement the derived interface ICascadingParameterGroup.
IParameterSelection Choice interface	Defines valid values for a report parameter that uses a restricted set of values, such as a cascading parameter.

Table 14-4 Classes and interfaces that support report parameters

Class or interface	Use
ReportParameter Converter class	Converts a String value provided by a user interface into a locale-independent format.

Creating a parameter definition task object for the report design

A single IGetParameterDefinitionTask object provides access to all parameters in a report design. Create only one of these objects for each report design, by calling ReportEngine.createGetParameterDefinitionTask( ). Close the parameter definition task object after use by calling its close( ) method.

Testing whether a report design has report parameters

To test if a report design has report parameters, call the getParameterDefns( ) method on IGetParameterDefinitionTask. This method returns a Collection. To test whether the Collection has elements call the Collection.isEmpty( ) method. An application that runs only known report designs does not need to perform this task.

Getting the report parameters in a report design

To access a single report parameter of a known name, use the IGetParameterDefinitionTask.getParameterDefn( ) method. This method returns an object of type IParameterDefnBase.

Use the IGetParameterDefinitionTask.getParameterDefns( ) method to return a Collection of IParameterDefnBase objects. The application can then use an Iterator to access each report parameter from this Collection in turn. The getParameterDefns( ) method takes a Boolean argument. For an argument value of false, the method returns an ungrouped set of report parameters. For a value of true, the method returns parameter groups, as defined in the report design. To create a user interface that replicates the parameter group structure, use a value of true.

To check whether a report parameter is a group, the application must call IParameterDefnBase.getParameterType( ). This method returns IParameterDefnBase.PARAMETER_GROUP if the parameter is a group or IParameterDefnBase.CASCADING_PARAMETER_GROUP if the parameter is a cascading parameter group. To access the group's report parameters, use the IParameterGroupDefn.getContents( ) method. This method returns an ArrayList object of objects of type IScalarParameterDefn.

Getting the default value of each report parameter

This task is optional. To get the default value of a single known report parameter, use IGetParameterDefinitionTask.getDefaultValue( ). This method returns an Object. To determine the effective class of the Object, use IScalarParameterDefn.getDataType( ). This method returns an int value, which is one of the static fields in IScalarParameterDefn. Call

IGetParameterDefinitionTask.getDefaultValues( ) to get the default value of all parameters in the report design. This method returns a HashMap object, which maps the report parameter names and their default values.

Getting valid values for parameters using a restricted set of values

Some report parameters accept only values from a restricted list. In some cases, this list is a static list of values, such as RED, BLUE, or GREEN. In other cases, the list is dynamic and a query to a database provides the valid values. For example, a query can return the set of sales regions in a sales tracking database. To determine the list of valid values, call the method, IGetParameterDefinitionTask.getSelectionList( ). This method returns a Collection of IParameterSelectionChoice objects. IParameterSelectionChoice has two methods. getLabel( ) returns the display text and getValue( ) returns the value. If the Collection is null, the report parameter can take any value.

Getting the attributes of each report parameter

This task is optional. To get the attributes of a report parameter, use the IScalarParameterDefn methods. The application can use the attributes to generate a customized user interface. For example, to get the data type of a report parameter, use the getDataType( ) method.

Collecting an updated value for each report parameter

To provide new values for the report parameters, provide application logic such as a user interface or code to retrieve values from a database.

Call IGetParameterDefinitionTask.setParameterValue( ) to set the value of the parameter. If a user interface returns String values to your application for date and number parameters, convert the String into a locale-independent format before setting the value. To perform this task, call the method, ReportParameterConverter.parse( ), before calling setParameterValue( ).

After setting the report parameter values, call the method, IGetParameterDefinitionTask.getParameterValues( ). This method returns a HashMap object containing the current parameter values as set by calls to IGetParameterDefinitionTask.setParameterValue( ). Use this HashMap object to set parameter values for report generation, as described later in this chapter.

How to set the value of a known report parameter

The code sample in Listing 14-6 shows how to set the value of a report parameter that has a known name. The sample creates a HashMap object that contains the parameter values to use later to run the report. The variable, engine, is a ReportEngine object. The variable, runnable, is an object of type IReportRunnable. This sample does not show details of code for retrieving the parameter value from a user interface or a database. The code to perform these tasks depends on your application's requirements.

Listing 14-6 Setting the value of a single parameter

```
// Create a parameter definition task.
IGetParameterDefinitionTask task =
   engine.createGetParameterDefinitionTask( runnable );
// Instantiate a scalar parameter.
IScalarParameterDefn param = (IScalarParameterDefn)
   task.getParameterDefn( "customerID" );
// Get the default value of the parameter. In this case,
// the data type of the parameter, customerID, is Double.
int customerID =
   ((Double) task.getDefaultValue( param )).intValue( );
// Get a value for the parameter. This example assumes that
// this step creates a correctly typed object, inputValue.
// Set the value of the parameter.
task.setParameterValue( "customerID", inputValue );
// Get the values set by the application for all parameters.
HashMap parameterValues = task.getParameterValues( );
// Close the parameter definition task.
task.close( );
```

How to use the Collection of report parameters

The code sample in Listing 14-7 shows how to use the Collection of report parameters. The sample uses the ReportParameterConverter class to convert the String values that the user interface supplies into the correct format for the parameter. The sample creates a HashMap object that contains the parameter values to use later to run the report. The variable, engine, is a ReportEngine object. The variable, runnable, is an IReportRunnable object. This sample does not show details of code for retrieving the parameter values from a user interface or a database. The code to perform these tasks depends on your application's requirements.

Listing 14-7 Setting the values of multiple parameters without grouping

```
// Create a parameter definition task.
IGetParameterDefinitionTask task =
   engine.createGetParameterDefinitionTask( runnable );

// Create a flat collection of the parameters in the design.
Collection params = task.getParameterDefns( false );
// Get the default values of the parameters.
HashMap parameterValues = task.getDefaultValues( );

// Get values for the parameters. Later code in this example
// assumes that this step creates a HashMap object,
// inputValues. The keys in the HashMap are the parameter
// names and the values are those that the user provided.

// Iterate through the report parameters, setting the values
// in standard locale-independent format.
Iterator iterOuter = params.iterator( );
```

```
ReportParameterConverter cfgConverter = new
   ReportParameterConverter( "", Locale.getDefault() );
while ( iterOuter.hasNext( ) ) {
   IScalarParameterDefn param =
      (IScalarParameterDefn) iterOuter.next( );
   String value = (String) inputValues.get( param.getName( ));
   if ( value != null ) {
      parameterValues.put( param.getName( ),
         cfgConverter.parse( value, param.getDataType( ) ) );
   }
}
// Close the parameter definition task.
task.close( );
```

Getting the values for cascading parameters

A cascading parameter group contains an ordered set of parameters that provide lists of acceptable values for the end user to select. The value chosen for the first parameter limits the available values for the second one, and so on. The parameters use one or more queries to retrieve the values to display to the user from a data set. The parameter definition task uses the data rows from the queries to filter the values for each parameter, based on the values of preceding parameters in the group. For example, consider a cascading parameter group that uses the following query:

```
SELECT
   PRODUCTS.PRODUCTLINE,
   PRODUCTS.PRODUCTNAME,
   PRODUCTS.PRODUCTCODE
FROM CLASSICMODELS.PRODUCTS
```

The group has two parameters, ProductLine on PRODUCTS.PRODUCTLINE and ProductCode on PRODUCTS.PRODUCTCODE. The display text for ProductCode uses values from PRODUCTS.PRODUCTNAME. Figure 14-1 shows the appearance of the requester that prompts for values for these parameters when a user previews the report in BIRT Report Designer.

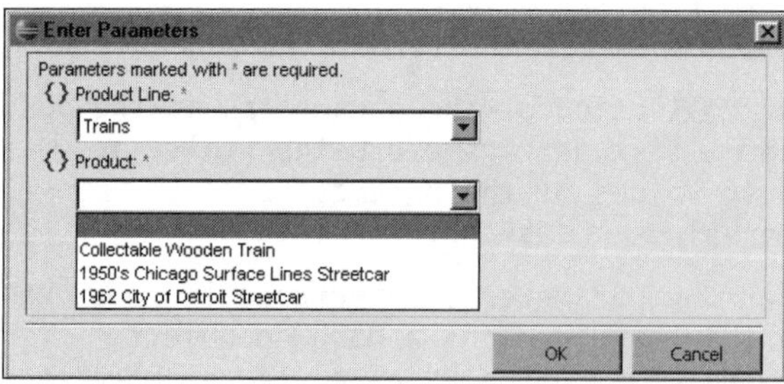

Figure 14-1 Cascading report parameters

To use the report engine API to get the values for cascading parameters, perform the tasks in the following list.

- To populate the list of values for the first report parameter in the group, call IGetParameterDefinitionTask.getSelectionListForCascadingGroup( ). This method takes two parameters, the String name of the parameter group and an array of Object. For the first parameter, this array is empty. The method returns a Collection of IParameterSelectionChoice objects.
- To populate the list of values for further report parameter in the group, call getSelectionListForCascadingGroup( ) again. In this case, the Object[ ] array contains the values for the preceding report parameters in the group. In the example shown in Figure 14-1, the Object[ ] array is:

  ```
  new Object[ ] { "Trains" }
  ```

How to use cascading parameters

The code sample in Listing 14-8 accesses the set of valid values for each parameter in the cascading parameter group in turn. The variable, task, is an object of type IGetParameterDefinitionTask.

Listing 14-8 Getting the valid values for cascading parameters

```
// Create a grouped collection of the design's parameters.
Collection params = task.getParameterDefns( true );

// Iterate through the parameters to find the cascading group.
Iterator iter = params.iterator( );
while ( iter.hasNext( ) ) {
   IParameterDefnBase param = (IParameterDefnBase) iter.next();
   if ( param.getParameterType() ==
      IParameterDefnBase.CASCADING_PARAMETER_GROUP ) {
      ICascadingParameterGroup group =
         (ICascadingParameterGroup) param;
      String groupName = group.getName();
      Iterator i2 = group.getContents( ).iterator( );

      Object[ ] userValues =
         new Object[group.getContents( ).size( )];

      // Get the report parameters in the cascading group.
      int i = 0;
      while ( i2.hasNext( ) ) {tOptio
         IScalarParameterDefn member =
            (IScalarParameterDefn) i2.next( );

         // Get the values for the parameter.
         Object[ ] setValues = new Object[i];
         if ( i > 0 ) {
            System.arraycopy( userValues, 0, setValues, 0, i );
         }
         Collection c = task.getSelectionListForCascadingGroup
               ( group.getName(), setValues );
```

```
      String[ ] choiceValue = new String[c.size( )];
      String[ ] choiceLabel = new String[c.size( )];

      // Iterate through the values for the parameter.
      Iterator i3 = c.iterator();
      for ( int j = 0; j < c.size( ); j++ ) {
         IParameterSelectionChoice s =
            ( IParameterSelectionChoice ) i3.next( );
         choiceValue[j] = ( String ) s.getValue( );
         choiceLabel[j] = s.getLabel( );
      }
      // Get the value for the parameter from the list of
      // choices. This example does not provide the code for
      // this task.
      userValues[i] = inputChoiceValue;
      i++;
   }
}
```

Preparing to generate the report

BIRT provides output emitters for HTML, Adobe PDF, Adobe PostScript (PS), Microsoft Excel (XLS), Microsoft PowerPoint (PPT), and Microsoft Word (DOC) formats. BIRT also supports custom output formats provided by renderers developed from the rendering extension points.

Three task classes support generating a report from a source. Sections earlier in this chapter described how to open the two types of source, a report design and a report document. The following tasks support generating a report from the source:

- IRunAndRenderTask. An object of this type creates a report in one of the supported formats by running a report design directly. To instantiate this object, call the ReportEngine method, createRunAndRenderTask( ).
- IRunTask. An object of this type creates a report document (.rptdocument) file from a report design. To instantiate this object, call the ReportEngine method, createRunTask( ). After creating the binary format report document, create the report output using an IRenderTask object.
- IRenderTask. An object of this type creates a complete report or a set of pages from a report by formatting the contents of a binary report document. To instantiate this object, call the ReportEngine method, createRenderTask( ).

Each type of task object can act on multiple sources. When the application no longer needs the task object, call the task's close( ) method.

Setting the parameter values for running a report design

To set the values for parameters for generating a report, use methods on an IRunAndRenderTask or an IRunTask object. These tasks run a report design to generate output. IRenderTask supports reading but not changing the parameters for a report because its source is a report document. The IRunTask object that created the report document already specified the parameter values.

Call setParameterValues( ) to set values for all the parameters in a report design. This method takes a HashMap as an argument. To create a suitable HashMap, use the techniques shown in Listing 14-6 or Listing 14-7, earlier in this chapter. To set the value for a single parameter when generating a report, call the setParameterValue( ) method. When the task generates the report or the report document, it uses the default values for any parameters having unset values.

Adding to the report engine's class path

Some report designs require access to external Java classes. The BIRT Report Engine uses class path information from various settings in its environment to locate the external classes. BIRT supports defining some of these locations by setting properties programmatically on the application context or on the EngineConfig object, or with the Java System class. To set the properties, use constants from the org.eclipse.birt.report.engine.api.EngineConstants class. To set a property on the application context, use the EngineTask object or the EngineConfig object, as shown in the following lines of code, where MyClass is the class that starts the report engine:

```
configOrTask.getAppContext( ).put
   ( EngineConstants.APPCONTEXT_CLASSLOADER_KEY,
   MyClass.class.getClassLoader( ));
```

To set a CLASSPATH property on the EngineConfig object, use code similar to the following lines. The property value must be a valid CLASSPATH.

```
config.setProperty( EngineConstants.WEBAPP_CLASSPATH_KEY,
   "c:/myjars/jar1.jar;c:/myclasses" );
```

To use the Java System class to set a CLASSPATH property, use code similar to the following lines. The property value must be a valid CLASSPATH.

```
System.setProperty( EngineConstants.WEBAPP_CLASSPATH_KEY,
   "c:/myjars/jar1.jar;c:/myclasses" );
```

BIRT searches locations for external classes in the order shown in the following list:

- The CLASSPATH for the report engine plug-in.
- The CLASSPATH of the parent class loader that is set as the EngineConstants.APPCONTEXT_CLASSLOADER_KEY. Define this property on the application context.
- The CLASSPATH set as EngineConstants.WEBAPP_CLASSPATH_KEY. Define this property using the Java System class or on the EngineConfig object.

- The CLASSPATH set as EngineConstants.PROJECT_CLASSPATH_KEY. Define this property using the Java System class or on the EngineConfig object.
- The CLASSPATH in EngineConstants.WORKSPACE_CLASSPATH_KEY. Define this property using the Java System class or on the EngineConfig object.
- JAR files included in the report design.

Providing an external object to a report design

BIRT supports an application passing previously instantiated objects into the report engine. Using this technique, the engine does not have to provide the code to create the object using information external to BIRT. The calling application can manipulate the object in memory immediately before calling the report engine. A typical use of external objects is in the BIRT scripting environment. After the application passes the object to the report engine, script expressions can reference the object by name at the appropriate stage in the report generation process. To supply an object to the report engine, use the application context, accessed from either the EngineConfig object or the task object, as shown in the code in Listing 14-9.

Listing 14-9 Setting up an external Connection object

```
myConnection mc = DriverManager.getConnection( myURL );
config = new EngineConfig( );
// Get the application context from the config or the task
HashMap hm = configOrTask.getAppContext( );
hm.put( "MyConnectionObject", mc );
configOrTask.setAppContext( hm );

// To refer to this object in a BIRT script
// or expression, use MyConnectionObject.myMethod()
```

Generating a binary report document

A binary report document contains all the information required to create a formatted report. The document contains appearance, data, and pagination information. Generate a binary report document if the same information must be rendered to multiple formats, if the output format is unknown at the time the report runs, or to render a subset of the pages in the report. Call an IRunTask.run( ) method to create a binary report document.

How to generate a binary report document

The code sample in Listing 14-10 shows the use of an IRunTask object to set the output file name. The variable, engine, is a ReportEngine object. The variable, runnable, is an object of type IReportRunnable. The variable, name, is the name of the report design. The variable, str_DateStamp, is a String representing today's date.

Listing 14-10 Using an IRunTask object to create a binary report document

```
// Create a run task object.
IRunTask task = engine.createRunTask( runnable );
String output = name.replaceFirst( ".rptdesign", str_DateStamp +
   ".rptdocument" );

try {
   task.run( output );
   task.close( );
   System.out.println( "Created document " + output + "." );
}
catch ( EngineException e1 ) {
   System.err.println( "Report " + output + " creation failed." );
   System.err.println( e1.toString( ) );
}
```

Preparing to render a formatted report

Render a formatted report from a report design by calling the method IRunAndRenderTask.run( ). Render a formatted report from a binary report document by calling the method IRenderTask.render( ).

Setting up the rendering options

Before rendering a report to one of the supported output formats, the application must set options that determine features of the output. The options must specify either an output file name or a stream. Other configuration settings, such as the type of HTML to generate, are optional. BIRT supports two types of HTML output, HTML and embeddable HTML. Embeddable HTML is suitable for including inside another web page. This format contains no header information nor the <body> or <html> tags.

The application uses a rendering options object to set the output options on an IRunAndRenderTask or an IRenderTask object. Format-specific rendering options classes implement IRenderOption and extend RenderOption. The rendering options class for the Excel format is EXCELRenderOption, for the HTML format is HTMLRenderOption, and for the PDF format is PDFRenderOption. All other output formats use the RenderOption class.

After creating the rendering option object, call the task's setRenderOption( ) method. This method takes a IRenderOption object as an argument. Use the setRenderOption( ) method on an IRenderTask or an IRunAndRenderTask object. This method performs no function on an IRunTask object because this task does not render to an output format. Listing 14-11 includes code that sets the rendering option for HTML.

To apply a rendering setting, use setter methods on the rendering option object. These objects also have getter methods that retrieve render settings. Common option settings are a base URL for hyperlinks, an action handler, an image handler, output format, and supported image output formats.

The supported image formats setting is used for extended report items such as charts or custom extended items. The final rendering environment for the report, such as the browser for a report in HTML format, affects this option value. To set the supported formats, use setSupportedImageFormats( ) with an argument of a String that contains a list of the supported image formats. The image formats are standard types, such as BMP, GIF, JPG, PNG, and SVG. Semicolons separate the items in the list. The method getSupportedImageFormats( ) returns a String of the same format.

Understanding HTML rendering options

Before generating an HTML report that uses images on disk or creates images or charts in a report, the application must provide additional settings. The HTMLRenderOption class provides many ways to customize the emitted HTML. The following list describes some of the commonly used options and how the options interact with each other:

- Image directory. Many reports include either static or dynamic images. For example, charts are dynamic images. HTML reports place all these images in a defined location. To set this location, call the setImageDirectory( ) method.
- Base image URL. For a web deployment, such as a WAR file for the reporting application, the images created in the image directory must be available to a user's web browser. Provide the engine with a URL prefix to apply to the image directory. To set the URL, use the setBaseImageURL( ) method, as shown in Listing 14-3.
- Image handler. Use the setImageHandler( ) method to set up an image handler, as described earlier in this chapter.
- Embeddable HTML. Call the setEmbeddable( ) method with the argument, true, to set this option. The embeddable produced HTML does not have <html> and <body> tags.
- Right to left generation. To set the HTML emitter to generate content right to left, call the setHtmlRtLFlag( ) method with the argument, true.
- Title tag. Use the setHtmlTitle( ) method to write a <title> tag to the produced HTML. This title appears in the title bar of the browser and in the tab on a multi-tabbed browser window.
- Master page content. In a BIRT report design, the developer uses the Master Page to set up page sizes, header and footers. These settings affect the produced HTML. To suppress the master page content, call the setMasterPageContent( ) with the argument, false. The master page content setting affects the results of setting paginated HTML and fixed layout.
- Floating footer. By default, the master page footer appears directly below the content of each HTML page. Pass the argument, false, to the setPageFooterFloatFlag( ) method to force the footer to the bottom of a

fixed-size master page. This setting adds a div statement with a height attribute to the produced HTML.

- Master page margins. Master page margins affect the appearance of the HTML output if the report uses fixed layout or if the value, true, is the argument to the setOutputMasterPageMargins( ) method.
- Paginated HTML. When rendering the report in HTML, the engine supports paginating the results. The report design's master page defines the size of the page and the content of its page headers and footers. To display the entire or partial report as a single HTML page, call the setHtmlPagination( ) method with the argument, false. In this case, setting a render task page range of 5-7 renders pages 5 to 7 as one HTML page. Header and footer information appear several times within this HTML page if you choose to display master page content. For your application to support pagination, you need to set up pagination controls similar to the example Web Viewer.
- Fixed or automatic layout. By default, BIRT generates tables with columns that are fixed in size. When the user changes the width of the browser window, the column widths do not change. BIRT also supports automatic layout, in which column widths adjust according to the width of the window. Fixed layout produces reports with a consistent layout, but this choice can increase rendering time. The table-layout:fixed attribute is applied to all tables. Appropriate div statements set column widths and padding. The div settings are also applied if master page content is used. To change this setting, use the setLayoutPreference( ) method. Pass the LAYOUT_PREFERENCE_AUTO or LAYOUT_PREFERENCE_FIXED value as its argument.
- Style calculation. The setEnableAgentStyleEngine( ) method provides the developer control over how the styles are calculated. Passing a value of true to this method emits the styles directly to the produced HTML. In this case, the browser performs the style calculations. Passing a value of false to the method causes the emitter to use the BIRT style engine to do the calculations. As with the fixed or automatic layout setting, this setting affects the consistency of the report's appearance.
- Base URL. Most BIRT report items have a hyperlink property. When building this hyperlink in the report designer, the report developer uses a URL, an internal bookmark, or a drill-through operation. The report design stores the results of the design session. The setBaseURL( ) method defines the base URL to prefix to the hyperlinks built using the designer. Use this setting for applications deployed in a web environment.
- Action handler. The emitter handles hyperlink, bookmark, and drill-through actions. When rendering the report as HTML, BIRT uses the HTMLActionHandler class to determine how to build the hyperlink for these actions. The HTMLActionHandler class implements the IHTMLActionHandler interface. If the default HTMLActionHandler does not meet your needs, use a custom implementation of IHTMLInterface. To set up the new action handler, use the setActionHandler( ) method.

The HTMLRenderOption class provides equivalent getter methods for the setter methods described in the previous list.

How to configure properties for a report in HTML format

The code sample in Listing 14-11 shows the use of rendering options on an IRunAndRenderTask object to set report parameter values, the output format of the report, and the output file name. The variable, engine, is a ReportEngine object. The variable, runnable, is an object of type IReportRunnable. The variable, name, is the name of the report design.

Listing 14-11 Configuring properties on an IRunAndRenderTask object

```
// Create a run and render task object.
IRunAndRenderTask task =
   engine.createRunAndRenderTask( runnable );
// Set values for all parameters in a HashMap, parameterValues
task.setParameterValues( parameterValues );
// Validate parameter values.
boolean parametersAreGood = task.validateParameters( );
// Set the name of an output file and other HTML options.
HTMLRenderOption options = new HTMLRenderOption( );
String output = name.replaceFirst( ".rptdesign", ".html" );
options.setOutputFileName( output );
options.setImageDirectory( "image" );
options.setEmbeddable( false );
// Apply the rendering options to the task.
task.setRenderOption( options );
```

Understanding Excel rendering options

The EXCELRenderOption class provides the following methods to modify the appearance of the generated spreadsheet:

- setHideGridlines( ) uses a boolean value of true or false to hide or show gridlines in the spreadsheet.
- setOfficeVersion( ) sets the compatibility level of the spreadsheet. Valid values for the String parameter are office2003 and office2007. The default value is office2003.
- setWrappingText( ) uses a boolean value of true or false to set or unset text wrapping in cells in the spreadsheet.

The EXCELRenderOption class provides equivalent getter methods to retrieve the current values of the options.

Using generic methods to access rendering options

The RenderOption class provides getter and setter methods for accessing the most commonly used rendering options. For example, this class provides the getOutputFileName( ) and setOutputFileName( ) methods to get and set the file name of rendered report. RenderOption also provides fields to identify the options. An application accesses the less commonly used options by calling the following generic methods, inherited from TaskOption, using a RenderOption field as an argument:

- getOption( )
  This method returns an Object containing the option value. For boolean or int values, the returned Object is a Boolean or Integer respectively.
- getBooleanOption( ), getIntOption( ), getStringOption( )
  Use these methods if the code is accessing an option of known type. These methods return a boolean value, an int value, and a String object respectively.
- getOptions( )
  This method returns a Hashmap object containing all the rendering options that have been set explicitly using setOption( ).
- hasOption( )
  Use this method to check whether the rendering options object supports a particular option. If the object supports an option, this method returns true even if the value of the option is null.
- setOption( )
  This method takes a second argument, an Object that contains the value of the option. For boolean or int values, use a Boolean or Integer object respectively.

The code sample in Listing 14-12 provides examples of these methods.

Listing 14-12 Using generic rendering options

```
RenderOption ro = new RenderOption( );
if ( ro.getOption( RenderOption.RENDER_DPI ) == null )
{
   ro.setOption( RenderOption.RENDER_DPI, new Integer( 96 ) );
}
ro.setOption( RenderOption.RTL_FLAG, new Boolean( true ) );

// The following line returns:
// INFO: Options: {RenderDpi=96, RTLFlag=true}
logger.log( Level.INFO, "Options: " + ro.getOptions().toString());
```

Rendering formatted output

To generate a formatted report, the application calls the run( ) method on an IRunAndRenderTask or the render( ) method on an IRenderTask object. The application must handle the EngineException that these methods can throw. After generating the report, the application can reuse the report engine and the task to generate further reports. If the application generates only a single report, close the task and destroy the engine after performing the report generation.

The IRunAndRenderTask.run( ) method creates a formatted document containing all the data in the report. The IRenderTask.render( ) method is more versatile. This method supports rendering the whole report or a subset of pages based on a bookmark, a page number, or a page range. A bookmark is a String that identifies a location in the report document. Use a value defined by the report developer using BIRT Report Designer or navigate the table of contents to identify the required portion of a report.

To access table of contents entries, use ITOCTree and TOCNode objects. The ITOCTree interface provides access to the tree of table of contents entries. A TOCNode object defines each table of contents entry. Each entry contains three strings: the identifier, the display value, and the bookmark of the entry. Get an ITOCTree object by calling the IRenderTask.getTOCTree( ) method. Then, use the ITOCTree.getRoot( ) method to retrieve the root TOCNode object. To find the subentries of a table of contents entry, use the TOCNode.getChildren( ) method. This method returns a List of TOCNode objects. Alternatively, call the findTOCByValue( ) method to retrieve a List of all TOCNode objects having a particular value. Use the bookmark String to locate the page to which the bookmark links by calling the getPageNumber( ) method. Using this information, the application calls the setPageNumber( ) or setPageRange( ) methods to specify pages to render to a formatted report.

How to generate a report from a report design

The code sample in Listing 14-13 generates a report from a report design and then closes the task. The variable, task, is an IRunAndRenderTask object. The variable, htmlRO, is an HTMLReportOption object. The variable, name, is the name of the report design. The variable, output, is the name of the output file.

Listing 14-13 Generating a report from a report design

```
task.setRenderOptions( htmlRO );
try {
   task.run( );
   System.out.println( "Created Report " + output + "." );
   task.close( );
}
catch ( EngineException e1 ) {
   System.err.println( "Report " + name + " run failed." );
   System.err.println( e1.toString( ) );
}
```

How to generate a partial report from a binary report document

The code sample in Listing 14-14 generates a single page of a report from a binary report document. The sample shows two techniques to locate the page to generate. The variable, htmlRO, is an HTMLReportOption object. The variable, name, is the name of the report design. The variable, output, is the name of the output file. The variable, engine, is a ReportEngine object.

Listing 14-14 Generating part of a report from a binary report document

```
IReportDocument binaryDoc = engine.openReportDocument(output);
// Create a render task object.
IRenderTask task = engine.createRenderTask( binaryDoc );
// Get the root of the table of contents.
ITOCTree tocTree = task.getTOCTree( );
TOCNode td = tocTree.getRoot();
// Traverse the tree of top-level items in the table of contents.
java.util.List children = td.getChildren( );
long pNumber;
// Loop through the top level table of contents entries.
if ( children != null && children.size( ) > 0 ) {
   for ( int i = 0; i < children.size( ); i++ )
   {
      // Find the required table of contents entry.
      TOCNode child = ( TOCNode ) children.get( i );
      if ( child.getDisplayString( ).equals( "157" ) )
      {
         // Get the number of the page that contains the data.
         pNumber = binaryDoc.getPageNumber( child.getBookmark( ));
         task.setPageNumber( pNumber );
      }
   }
}

// Alternatively, use the first entry having the correct value.
java.util.List desiredNodes = tocTree.findTOCByValue( "157" );
if ( desiredNodes != null && desiredNodes.size( ) > 0 )
{
   TOCNode child = (TOCNode) desiredNodes.get(0);
   pNumber = binaryDoc.getPageNumber( child.getBookmark( ) );
   task.setPageNumber( pNumber );
}

// Render the page. Then, close the document and the task.
output = output.replaceFirst( ".rptdocument", ".html" );
htmlRO.setOutputFileName( output );
task.setRenderOption( htmlRO );
task.render();
binaryDoc.close();
task.close();
```

Accessing the formatted report

After generating a formatted report document as a file on disk, access the file in the same way as any other file. For example, open an HTML document in a web browser and a PDF document using Adobe Reader. If the application sends the report to a stream, the stream must be able to process the content.

Checking the status of a running report task

The BIRT Report Engine supports checking the status of any engine task and cancelling that task. Typically, an application uses a separate thread to perform these actions. To check the status of a running report, use the EngineTask.getStatus( ) method, which returns one of the following values:

- IEngineTask.STATUS_NOT_STARTED. The task has not started.
- IEngineTask.STATUS_RUNNING. The task is currently running.
- IEngineTask.STATUS_SUCCEEDED. The task completed with no errors.
- IEngineTask.STATUS_FAILED. The task failed to execute.
- IEngineTask.STATUS_CANCELLED. The task was cancelled.

Cancelling a running report task

To cancel a running task call the IEngineTask.cancel( ) method. All the tasks that run and render reports implement and extend the IEngineTask interface. If the application cancels a task that is running a report, the task stops generating the report content. If the task has started a query on a database, the database continues to run the query to completion.

How to cancel a running report task

1 Define a thread class as an inner class to cancel the report. In Listing 14-15, the name of this class is CancelReport.

2 Within the code that creates the task, create an instance of the CancelReport class, as shown in the following line:

```
CancelReport cancelThread = new CancelReport( "cancelReport",
   task);
```

3 Test for a condition. Then, use the CancelReport object to cancel the report, as shown in the following line:

```
cancelThread.cancel( );
```

Listing 14-15 Defining a class to cancel an engine task

```
private class CancelReport extends Thread
{
   private IEngineTask eTask;

   public CancelReport( String myName, IEngineTask task )
   {
      super( myName );
      eTask = task;
   }

   public void cancel( )
   {
```

```
        try {
            Thread.currentThread( ).sleep( 100 );
            eTask.cancel( );
            System.out.println( "#### Report cancelled #####" );
        }
        catch( Exception e )
        {
            e.printStackTrace();
        }
    }
}
```

Programming the structure of a report design

A reporting application typically generates reports from report designs. When deploying this type of application, the report designs are deployed with the application. Any changes to the generated reports depend on the values of report parameters and the data from the data set. To access a report design, the application uses an IReportRunnable object.

Sometimes business logic requires changes to the report design before generating the report. Some changes are possible through using parameters and scripting. Other changes can only occur through modification of the report design itself. The API to perform these tasks is known as the model API. The package containing the classes and interfaces to work with the items in a report design, library, or template is org.eclipse.birt.report.model.api.

To access the structure of the report design, the application obtains a ReportDesignHandle object from the design engine. ReportDesignHandle provides access to all properties of the report design and to the elements that the report design contains.

The model API provides handle classes to access all Report Object Model (ROM) elements. For example, a GridHandle object provides access to a grid element in the report design. All ROM element handles, including the report design handle, inherit from DesignElementHandle. Report items inherit from ReportElementHandle and ReportItemHandle.

After making changes to a report design or its elements, the application writes the result to a stream or a file. To generate a formatted report or a binary report document, use the report engine to open an IReportRunnable object on the updated design. Then, use the report engine as described earlier in this chapter. To access the design engine, an application must first instantiate a report engine.

An application typically accesses the items in a report design to perform one of the following tasks:

- Modify an existing report design programmatically to change the contents and appearance of the report output. An application can modify page characteristics, grids, tables, and other report items in the design, the data source, and the data set that extracts data from a data source.

- Build a complete report design and generate report output in a single application.

A reporting application can access and modify the structures in a template or a library file in the same way as the structures in a report design. The techniques described in the rest of this chapter are as applicable to these file types as to report designs. A template has identical functionality to a report design. For this reason, the ReportDesignHandle class provides access to a template. The LibraryHandle class provides access to a library. Both these classes derive from the ModuleHandle class, which provides the fields and methods for the common functionality, such as accessing elements in the file.

About BIRT model API capabilities

A Java developer can use the BIRT model API to write an application that creates and modifies a report design programmatically. This API has the same capabilities as BIRT Report Designer. For example, the following list shows some of the ways in which the BIRT model API supports manipulating a report design programmatically:

- Adding a report item to a report design:
  - Add a simple report item such as a data item, label, or image. Set a value to display in the new report item, such as the expression of a data item or the text in a label item.
  - Create a complex item such as a grid, table, or list. Add other items into the grid, table, or list.
- Changing the properties of a report item in a report design:
  - Change the data set bound to a table or list.
  - Change the expression or other property of a report item.
  - Format a report item, changing the font, font color, fill color, format, alignment, or size.
- Changing the structure of a report design:
  - Add a report parameter.
  - Add or delete a group or column in a table or list.
- Modifying non-visual elements in a report design:
  - Set a design property such as a report title, author, wallpaper, or comment.
  - Set a page property, such as height, width, or margins.
  - Specify a data source for a data set.

Opening a report design for editing

To access a report design and its contents, the application must instantiate first a report engine and secondly a ReportDesignHandle object. The ReportDesignHandle object provides access to the ROM elements in the design opened by the report engine. Instantiate a ReportDesignHandle by calling a method on either the model class, SessionHandle, or the report engine interface, IReportRunnable.

The SessionHandle object manages the state of all open report designs. Use a SessionHandle to open, close, and create report designs, and to set global properties, such as the locale and the units of measure for report elements. The SessionHandle can open a report design from a file or a stream. Create the session handle only once. BIRT supports only a single SessionHandle for a user of a reporting application.

Configuring the design engine to access a design handle

The DesignEngine class provides access to all the functionality of the ROM in the same way that the ReportEngine class provides access to report generation functionality. Before creating a DesignEngine object, create a DesignConfig object to contain configuration settings for the design engine such as the BIRT home location. The BIRT home is the same location that the report engine uses. The DesignConfig object sets up custom access to resources and custom configuration variables for scripting.

Use a factory service to create a DesignEngine in the same way as creating a ReportEngine. After setting configuration properties, create a design engine by calling the Platform.createFactoryObject( ) and the IDesignEngineFactory .createDesignEngine( ) methods. The DesignConfig object defines the settings for this process. If the application has already started the platform in order to set up a report engine, use the same platform instance to create the design engine. If the application runs in an RCP environment, do not start the platform.

Create the SessionHandle object by calling the method, newSessionHandle( ) on the DesignEngine object. To open the report design, call the method, openDesign( ), on the SessionHandle object. This method takes the name of the report design as an argument and instantiates a ReportDesignHandle.

How to open a report design for editing

The code sample in Listing 14-16 creates a DesignEngine object from which to create a SessionHandle object. The code uses the SessionHandle object to open a report design.

Listing 14-16 Opening a report design for editing

```
// Create a design engine configuration object.
DesignConfig dConfig = new DesignConfig( );
dConfig.setBIRTHome( "C:/birt-runtime-2_6_0/ReportEngine" );
```

```
// Start the platform for a non-RCP application.
Platform.startup( dConfig );
IDesignEngineFactory factory =
   ( IDesignEngineFactory ) Platform.createFactoryObject
   ( IDesignEngineFactory.EXTENSION_DESIGN_ENGINE_FACTORY );
IDesignEngine dEngine = factory.createDesignEngine( dConfig );
// Create a session handle, using the system locale.
SessionHandle session = dEngine.newSessionHandle( null );
// Create a handle for an existing report design.
String name = "./SimpleReport.rptdesign";
ReportDesignHandle design = null;
try {
   design = session.openDesign( name );
} catch (Exception e) {
   System.err.println( "Report " + name +
   " not opened!\nReason is " + e.toString( ) );
   return null;
}
```

Using an IReportRunnable object to access a design handle

An alternative way to open a report design is by calling the getDesignHandle( ) method on an IReportRunnable object. Use a design engine to access the elements in this report design in the same way as for any other design handle.

Using a report item in a report design

A report item is a visual element in the report design. Typically, a report developer uses BIRT Report Designer to add a report item to the design by dragging an item from the palette to the layout editor. Sometimes a reporting application must change the properties of certain report items in the design before running the report. The application uses methods on the ReportDesignHandle class to access a report item either by name or from a list of items in a slot in a container report item. These methods return a DesignElementHandle object. All report items derive from this class.

A slot is a logical component of a container report item. A slot holds zero or more members of the appropriate report item type. For example, a table element has four slots: Header, Detail, Footer, and Groups. Each of these slots is a container for further slots. The Header, Detail, and Footer slots all contain elements of type RowHandle. RowHandle has a Cell slot that contains all the cells in the row. The Outline view in BIRT Report Designer provides a visual representation of the slots in an individual report item.

Accessing a report item by iterating through a slot

To access a report item through the report design's structure, first get the slot handle of the report body by calling the ReportDesignHandle.getBody( ) method. This slot handle holds the top-level report items in the report design.

For example, consider a simple report structure that has three top-level items: a grid of header information, a table containing grouped data, and a label that displays a report footer. Figure 14-2 shows its outline view in BIRT Report Designer.

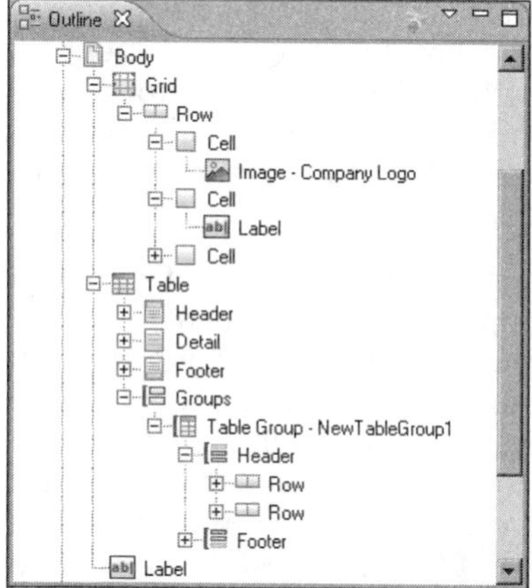

Figure 14-2 Slots in a report design

To access the top-level items in this report design, iterate over the contents of the body slot handle. To access the iterator for a slot handle, call SlotHandle.iterator( ). Each call to Iterator.getNext( ) returns ReportDesignHandle object, which is a handle to a report item or another slot. Alternatively, to access a report item at a known slot index, call SlotHandle.get( ). The slot index number is zero-based.

Accessing a report item by name

To make a report item accessible by name, the item must have a name. Either a report developer sets the name in BIRT Report Designer or an application sets the name programmatically by using the item's setName( ) method. To find a report item by name, use ReportDesignHandle.findElement( ).

Examining a report item

To examine a report item, check the class of the report item and cast the object to its actual class. Then, call methods appropriate to that class. For example, the class of a label element handle is LabelHandle. To get the text that the label displays, call LabelHandle.getText( ).

Some report items, such as a label or a text element, are simple items. Other items, such as a grid or a table element, are structured items. Access properties for the whole of a structured item in the same way as for a simple item. To examine the contents of a structured item, iterate over its slots. Use this technique to determine the contents of a cell in a table. First, call a method to retrieve a slot handle for the table's rows. Next, iterate over the contents of the slot to access the cells. For example, to access the RowHandle objects that make up a table element's footer, call TableHandle.getFooter( ). Table and list elements also have a slot for groups.

Accessing the properties of a report item

To provide information about report items, each class has getter methods specific to the report item type. For example, an image element handle, ImageHandle, has the getURI( ) method. This method returns the URI of an image referenced by URL or file path. The DesignElementHandle class and other ancestor classes in the hierarchy also provide generic getter methods, such as getName( ).

Some properties of a report item are simple properties of a Java type or type wrapper class. An example of a simple property is the name property, which is a String object. Some simple properties, like name, have an arbitrary value. Other simple properties have restricted values from a set of BIRT String constants. The interface, DesignChoiceConstants in the package, org.eclipse.birt.report.model.api.elements, defines these constants. For example, the image source property of an image element can have one of only the values, IMAGE_REF_TYPE_EMBED, IMAGE_REF_TYPE_EXPR, IMAGE_REF_TYPE_FILE, IMAGE_REF_TYPE_NONE, or IMAGE_REF_TYPE_URL.

Other properties are complex properties and the getter method returns a handle object. For example, the DesignElementHandle.getStyle( ) method returns a SharedStyleHandle object and ReportItemHandle.getWidth( ) returns a DimensionHandle object. The handle classes provide access to complex properties of a report item, as described later in this chapter. These classes provide getter methods for attributes of the complex properties. For example, StyleHandle classes provide access to background color, font, and highlights.

How to access a report item by name

The code sample in Listing 14-17 finds an image item by name, checks its type, and examines its URI. The variable, design, is a ReportDesignHandle object.

Listing 14-17 Finding a report item having a given name

```
DesignElementHandle logoImage =
   design.findElement( "Company Logo" );
// Check for the existence of the report item.
if ( logoImage == null) {
   return null;
}
// Check that the report item has the expected class.
if ( !( logoImage instanceof ImageHandle ) ) {
   return null;
}
```

```
// Retrieve the URI of the image.
String imageURI = ( (ImageHandle ) logoImage ).getURI( );
return imageURI;
```

How to use the report structure to access a report item

The code sample in Listing 14-18 finds an image item in a grid, checks its type, and examines its URI. Use this technique for generic code to navigate a report design structure or if to find an item that does not have a name. The variable, design, is a ReportDesignHandle object.

Listing 14-18 Navigating the report structure to access a report item

```
// Instantiate a slot handle and iterator for the body slot.
SlotHandle shBody = design.getBody( );
Iterator slotIterator = shBody.iterator( );

// To retrieve top-level report items, iterate over the body.
while (slotIterator.hasNext( )) {
   Object shContents = slotIterator.next( );
   // To get the contents of the top-level report items,
   // instantiate slot handles.
   if ( shContents instanceof GridHandle ) {
      GridHandle grid = ( GridHandle ) shContents;
      SlotHandle grRows = grid.getRows( );
      Iterator rowIterator = grRows.iterator( );
      while ( rowIterator.hasNext( )) {
         // Get RowHandle objects.
         Object rowSlotContents = rowIterator.next( );
         // To find the image element, iterate over the grid.
         SlotHandle cellSlot =
            ( ( RowHandle ) rowSlotContents ).getCells( );
         Iterator cellIterator = cellSlot.iterator( );

         while ( cellIterator.hasNext( )) {
            // Get a CellHandle object.
            Object cellSlotContents = cellIterator.next( );
            SlotHandle cellContentSlot =
               ( ( CellHandle) cellSlotContents ).getContent( );
            Iterator cellContentIterator =
               cellContentSlot.iterator( );

            while ( cellContentIterator.hasNext( )) {
               // Get a DesignElementHandle object.
               Object cellContents =
                  cellContentIterator.next( );
               // Check that the element is an image.
               if (cellContents instanceof ImageHandle) {
                  String is = ( ( ImageHandle )
                     cellContents ).getSource( );
                  // Check that the image has a URI.
```

```
if ( ( is.equals( DesignChoiceConstants.IMAGE_REF_TYPE_URL ))
|| ( is.equals( DesignChoiceConstants.IMAGE_REF_TYPE_FILE ))) {
                        // Retrieve the URI of the image.
                        String imageURI = ( ( ImageHandle )
                              cellContents ).getURI( );
                  }
               }
            }
         }
      }
   }
}
```

Modifying a report item in a report design

To set the simple properties of report items, each class has setter methods specific to the report item type. For example, an image element handle, ImageHandle, has the setURI( ) method. This method sets the URI of an image referenced by URL or file path. The DesignElementHandle class and other ancestor classes in the hierarchy provide generic setter methods, such as setName( ). Setter methods throw exceptions, such as NameException, SemanticException, and StyleException.

To set attributes of a complex property, such as a style, call methods on a handle object, as described later in this chapter. These classes provide setter methods for related properties. For example, StyleHandle classes provide access to style properties, such as font and background color.

How to change a simple property of a report item

The code sample in Listing 14-19 uses a method on LabelHandle to change the text in a label. The variable, design, is a ReportDesignHandle object. This sample accesses the label by name. Alternatively, access a report item by navigating the report structure.

Listing 14-19 Changing the text property of a label report item

```
// Access the label by name.
LabelHandle headerLabel =
   ( LabelHandle ) design.findElement( "Header Label" );
try {
   headerLabel.setText( "Updated " + headerLabel.getText( ));
} catch ( Exception e ) {
   // Handle the exception
}
```

Accessing and setting complex properties

Complex properties use BIRT handle objects to access data structures. For example, a DimensionHandle object provides access to size and position properties, such as the absolute value and the units of the width of a report item. Some String properties on a handle object, such as font style and text alignment on a style handle, have restricted values defined by constants in the org.eclipse.birt.report.model.api.elements.DesignChoiceConstants interface. For example, the font style property can have one of only the values, FONT_STYLE_ITALIC, FONT_STYLE_NORMAL, or FONT_STYLE_OBLIQUE.

Using a BIRT property handle

To access complex properties, use getter methods on the report item. For example, to access the width of a report item, call the method ReportItemHandle.getWidth( ). This method returns a DimensionHandle object. To work with complex properties, use getter and setter methods on the property handle object. For example, to get and set the size of a dimension, use the DimensionHandle methods getMeasure( ) and setAbsolute( ), respectively. Calling a method on a property handle object to set a value on a complex property affects the report item straight away. You do not call another setter method on the report item itself.

Using styles on a report item

The StyleHandle class provides access to many fundamental properties of a report item, such as margin size, text alignment, background color, borders, font, and so on. StyleHandle provides a full set of getter methods for each style property. For simple properties, StyleHandle provides setter methods. To modify complex properties, use setter methods on the property handle object, not on the style handle itself.

A report item can use two styles; a private style and a shared style. The handle classes for these styles are PrivateStyleHandle and SharedStyleHandle, respectively. Both classes derive from StyleHandle.

A private style contains the settings that the report developer chose in the property editor when designing the report using BIRT Report Designer. Shared styles appear in the Outline view in BIRT Report Designer. Use shared styles to apply the same appearance to multiple items in a report design. Changes to a shared style affect all report items that use the style. Style settings in a private style override the settings in a shared style.

How to change a complex property of a report item

The code sample in Listing 14-20 shows how to use PrivateStyleHandle and ColorHandle objects to change the background color of a label. The variable, design, is a ReportDesignHandle object. This sample accesses the label by name. Alternatively, access a report item by navigating the report structure.

Listing 14-20 Changing a complex property of a report item

```
// Access the label by name.
LabelHandle headerLabel =
   ( LabelHandle ) design.findElement( "Header Label" );
try {
```

```
    // To prepare to change a style property, get a StyleHandle.
    StyleHandle labelStyle = headerLabel.getPrivateStyle();
    // Update the background color.
    ColorHandle bgColor = labelStyle.getBackgroundColor();
    bgColor.setRGB( 0xFF8888 );
} catch ( Exception e ) {
    // Handle the exception
}
```

Understanding property structure objects

Complex property structures represent many optional report element features within BIRT. For example, computed columns, highlight rules, sort keys, and table of contents entries are all optional complex properties of report elements. The classes for these properties all derive directly or indirectly from org.eclipse.birt.report.model.core.Structure. An application can access existing structure property objects on a report element or create new ones.

Using an existing property structure object

Use the property handle, which is an object of class PropertyHandle, to apply a new structure object to a report element's property or to modify an existing property structure. To access the property handle call the method, DesignElementHandle.getPropertyHandle( ), which is available on all report elements. This method takes a String argument that defines the property to access. Class fields having names of the form XXX_PROP define the available property structures for a report element class. The property handle object provides access to one or more property structure objects. Use the PropertyHandle getter methods to access settings on existing property structures.

Typically, the property structure class provides setter methods only for a few key values. Set other values by calling the property structure object's setProperty( ) method. This method takes two arguments: a String that identifies the property and an object that specifies the value. Class fields defined on the property structure class or on the DesignChoiceConstants class provide the values for the property identifier.

How to set values on an existing property structure object

The code sample in Listing 14-21 shows how to change the sort direction value on a table item's first sort key.

Listing 14-21 Changing the sort direction on a table

```
void modSortKey( TableHandle th ) {
    try {
        SortKeyHandle sk;
        PropertyHandle ph =
            th.getPropertyHandle( TableHandle.SORT_PROP );
```

```
      if ( ph.isSet( ) ) {
         sk = ( SortKeyHandle ) ph.get( 0 );
         sk.setDirection
            ( DesignChoiceConstants.SORT_DIRECTION_DESC );
      }
   } catch ( Exception e ) {
      e.printStackTrace( );
   }
}
```

Creating a property structure object

The design engine class, StructureFactory, provides static methods for creating property structure objects. Most StructureFactory methods take the form createXXX, where XXX is the structure to create. After creating a new structure object, set its simple or complex properties using its setter methods. Report element handles provide methods to add key structure properties to their property handles. For example, add a filter condition to a data set object by using the addFilter( ) method. To add other properties to a report element, use the method, PropertyHandle.addItem( ).

How to create a complex property object

The code sample in Listing 14-22 shows how to create a highlight rule object and apply that rule to a row handle. The variable, rh, is a RowHandle object. Because RowHandle does not have a specific method to add a highlight rule property, the code uses the PropertyHandle.addItem( ) method.

Listing 14-22 Adding a highlight rule to a table or grid row

```
try {
   HighlightRule hr = StructureFactory.createHighlightRule( );
   hr.setOperator( DesignChoiceConstants.MAP_OPERATOR_GT );
   hr.setTestExpression( "row[\"CustomerCreditLimit\"]" );
   hr.setValue1( "100000" );
   hr.setProperty
      ( HighlightRule.BACKGROUND_COLOR_MEMBER, "blue" );

   PropertyHandle ph =
      rh.getPropertyHandle( StyleHandle.HIGHLIGHT_RULES_PROP );
   ph.addItem( hr );
} catch ( Exception e  ){ e.printStackTrace(); }
```

The code samples in Listing 14-23 provide further examples of using the structure factory to create complex properties.

Listing 14-23 Various structure factory examples

```
// Use the structure factory to add a sort key to a table.

void addSortKey( TableHandle th ) {
```

```
   try {
      SortKey sk = StructureFactory.createSortKey( );
      sk.setKey( "row[\"CustomerName\"]" );
      sk.setDirection
         ( DesignChoiceConstants.SORT_DIRECTION_ASC );

      PropertyHandle ph =
         th.getPropertyHandle( TableHandle.SORT_PROP );
      ph.addItem( sk );
   } catch ( Exception e ) { e.printStackTrace( ); }
}

// Add a column binding to a table.
void addColumnBinding( TableHandle th ) {
   try {
      ComputedColumn cs1;
      cs1 = StructureFactory.createComputedColumn( );
      cs1.setName( "CustomerName" );
      cs1.setExpression( "dataSetRow[\"CUSTOMERNAME\"]" );
      th.addColumnBinding( cs1, false );
   } catch ( Exception e ) { e.printStackTrace( ); }
}

// Add a filter condition to a table.
void addFilterCondition( TableHandle th ) {
   try {
      FilterCondition fc = StructureFactory.createFilterCond();
      fc.setExpr( "row[\"CustomerCountry\"]" );
      fc.setOperator(DesignChoiceConstants.MAP_OPERATOR_EQ);
      fc.setValue1("'USA'");
      PropertyHandle ph =
         th.getPropertyHandle( TableHandle.FILTER_PROP );
      ph.addItem( fc );
   } catch ( Exception e ) { e.printStackTrace( ); }
}

// Add a filter condition to a data set.
void addFilterCondition( OdaDataSetHandle dh ) {
   try {
      FilterCondition fc = StructureFactory.createFilterCond();
      fc.setExpr( "row[\"COUNTRY\"]" );
      fc.setOperator( DesignChoiceConstants.MAP_OPERATOR_EQ );
      fc.setValue1( "'USA'" );
      // Add the filter to the data set.
      dh.addFilter( fc );
   } catch ( Exception e ) { e.printStackTrace( ); }
}

// Add a hyperlink to a label.
void addHyperlink( LabelHandle lh ) {
   try {
      Action ac = StructureFactory.createAction( );
```

```
      ActionHandle actionHandle = lh.setAction( ac );
      actionHandle.setURI( "'http://www.google.com'" );
      actionHandle.setLinkType
         ( DesignChoiceConstants.ACTION_LINK_TYPE_HYPERLINK );
   } catch ( Exception e ) { e.printStackTrace( ); }
}

// Add a table of contents entry to a data item.
void addToc( DataItemHandle dh ) {
   try {
      TOC myToc = StructureFactory.createTOC
         ( "row[\"CustomerName\"]" );
      dh.addTOC( myToc );
   } catch ( Exception e ) { e.printStackTrace( ); }
}

// Add an embedded image to the report design.
void addImage( ) {
   try {
      EmbeddedImage image =
         StructureFactory.createEmbeddedImage( );
      image.setType
         ( DesignChoiceConstants.IMAGE_TYPE_IMAGE_JPEG );
      image.setData( load( "logo3.jpg" ));
      image.setName( "mylogo" );
      designHandle.addImage( image );
   } catch ( Exception e ) { e.printStackTrace( ); }
}

// Load the embedded image from a file on disk.
public byte[ ] load( String fileName ) throws IOException
{
   InputStream is = null;
   is = new BufferedInputStream
      ( this.getClass( ).getResourceAsStream( fileName ));
   byte data[ ] = null;
   if ( is != null ) {
      try {
         data = new byte[is.available( )];
         is.read( data );
      }
      catch ( IOException e1 ) {
         throw e1;
      }
   }
   return data;
}
```

Adding a report item to a report design

A reporting application can use a simple report design or a template to create more complex designs. The application can add extra report items to the design's structure based on external conditions. For example, based on the user name of the user requesting generation of a report, the application can add extra information to the report for that category of user. To create a design entirely with the API, use the same techniques to add content to the design.

The class that creates new elements, such as report items, in a report design is ElementFactory. This class provides methods of the form, newXXX( ), where XXX is the type of report element to create. The method newElement( ) is a generic method that creates an element of any type. To access the element factory, call the ReportDesign.getElementFactory( ) method.

Place new report items directly in the body slot, within containers such as a cell in a table or grid, or on the master page. The model API supports adding a simple item, such as a label, or complex items, such as a table with contents in its cells. The location of the new report item is a slot, such as the body slot of the report design or a cell slot in a row in a table. To add a report item to a slot, use one of the SlotHandle.add( ) methods. The method has two signatures that support adding the report item to the end of a slot, or to a particular position in a slot.

Table and list elements iterate over the rows that a data set provides. To support access to the data rows for these report item types, bind the item to a data set. The table or list element provides data rows to the report items that it contains. For this reason, bind only the container item to a data set, as described later in this chapter.

How to add a grid item and label item to a report design

The code sample in Listing 14-24 creates a grid item and adds a label item to one of the cells in the grid. An application can create any other report item in a similar manner. The variable, design, is a ReportDesignHandle object.

Listing 14-24 Adding a container item to the body slot

```
// Instantiate an element factory.
ElementFactory factory = design.getElementFactory( );
try {
   // Create a grid element with 2 columns and 1 row.
   GridHandle grid = factory.newGridItem( "New grid", 2, 1 );
   // Set a simple property on the grid, the width.
   grid.setWidth( "50%" );
   // Create a new label and set its properties.
   LabelHandle label = factory.newLabel( "Hello Label" );
   label.setText( "Hello, world!" );

   // Get the first row of the grid.
   RowHandle row = ( RowHandle ) grid.getRows( ).get( 0 );
```

```
    // Add the label to the second cell in the row.
    CellHandle cell = ( CellHandle ) row.getCells( ).get( 1 );
    cell.getContent( ).add( label );

    // Get the body slot. Add the grid to the end of the slot.
    design.getBody( ).add( grid );
} catch ( Exception e ) {
    // Handle any exception
}
```

Accessing a data source and data set with the API

This section shows how to use ROM elements that are not report items. To use other ROM elements, such as the libraries that the report design uses, employ similar techniques as for report items.

Access the report design's data sources and data sets using methods on the ReportDesignHandle instance, in a similar way to other report elements. The model classes that define a data source and data set are DataSourceHandle and DataSetHandle, respectively. A data set provides a report item such as a table with data from a data source. For a report item to access the data set, use the item's setDataSet( ) method.

Use a finder method on the report design handle to access a data source or data set by name. The finder methods are findDataSource( ) and findDataSet( ), respectively. Alternatively, to access all the data sources or data sets, use a getter method that returns a slot handle. The getter methods are getDataSources( ) and getDataSets( ), respectively. To access the individual data sources or data sets in a slot handle, iterate over the contents of the slot handle in the same way as for any other slot handle.

About data source classes

DataSourceHandle is a subclass of ReportElementHandle. Get and set report item properties for a data source in the same way as for any other report element. DataSourceHandle also provides methods to access the scripting methods of the data source.

The two subclasses of DataSourceHandle, OdaDataSourceHandle and ScriptDataSourceHandle, provide the functionality for the two families of BIRT data sources. For more information about ODA data sources, install the Javadoc for the ODA API. The scripting methods for a scripted data source fully define the data source, as described earlier in this book.

About data set classes

DataSetHandle is a subclass of ReportElementHandle. Get and set properties for a data set in the same way as for any other report element. DataSetHandle also provides methods to access properties specific to a data set, such as the data source, the data set fields, and the scripting methods of the data set.

The two subclasses of DataSetHandle, OdaDataSetHandle and ScriptDataSetHandle, provide the functionality for the two families of BIRT data sets. For more information about ODA data sets, see the Javadoc for the ODA API.

Using a data set programmatically

Typically, a reporting application uses data sets and data sources already defined in the report design. Use the data set's setDataSource( ) method to change the data source of a data set. For example, based on the name of the user of the reporting application, access data from the sales database for a particular geographical region, such as Europe or North America.

Changing the properties of a data set

Changing the properties of a data set requires consideration of the impact on the report design. If the application changes the data source of a data set, the type of the data source must be appropriate for the type of the data set. Also ensure that the new data source provides the same data fields as the original data source.

How to change the data source for a data set

The code sample in Listing 14-25 shows how to check for a particular data source and data set in a report design and changes the data source for the data set. The code finds the data source and data set by name. Alternatively, use the getDataSets( ) and getDataSources( ) methods. Then, use the technique for iterating over the contents of a slot handle. The variable, design, is a ReportDesignHandle object.

Listing 14-25 Modifying a data set

```
// Find the data set by name.
DataSetHandle ds = design.findDataSet( "Customers" );

// Find the data source by name.
DataSourceHandle dso = design.findDataSource( "EuropeSales" );

// Check for the existence of the data set and data source.
if ( (dso == null) || ( ds == null ) )
{
   System.err.println( "EuropeSales or Customers not found" );
   return;
}

// Change the data source of the data set.
try {
   ds.setDataSource( "EuropeSales" );
} catch ( SemanticException e1 )
{
   e1.printStackTrace( );
}
```

Changing the data set binding of a report item

Call the report item's setDataSet( ) method to set or change the data set used by a report item. If the application changes the data set used by a report item, ensure that the new data set supplies all the data bindings that the contents of the report item require. If necessary, change the references to data bindings in data elements, text elements, and scripting methods. If the data bindings in the old data set do not match the names or data types of the fields that the new data set provides, the application or a report developer must resolve the data bindings before generating a report from the modified report design.

Use the ReportItemHandle method, columnBindingsIterator( ), to iterate over the column bindings that the report item uses. The items in the list are of type ComputedColumnHandle. This class provides methods to access the name, expression, and data type of the column binding.

To access the data set column and expression that a data item uses, call the methods, getResultSetColumn( ) and getResultSetExpression( ). Then, compare the data type and name with the result-set columns that the data set returns.

How to bind a data set to a table

The code sample in Listing 14-26 shows how to check for a particular data set in a report design and changes the data set for a table. The code finds the table and data set by name. Alternatively, use slot handles to navigate the design structure. The variable, design, is a ReportDesignHandle object.

Listing 14-26 Binding a data set to a report item

```
// Find the table by name.
TableHandle table =
   ( TableHandle ) design.findElement( "Report Data" );

// Find the data set by name.
DataSetHandle ds = design.findDataSet( "EuropeanCustomers" );

// Check for the existence of the table and the data set.
if ( ( table == null ) || ( ds == null ) )
{
   System.err.println( "Incorrect report structure" );
   return;
}

// Change the data set for the table.
try {
   table.setDataSet( ds );
} catch ( Exception e )
{
   System.err.println( "Could not set data set for table" );
}
```

Saving a report design

After making changes to an existing report design or creating a new report design, an application can save the design for archival purposes or for future use. To overwrite an existing report design to which the application has made changes, use the ReportDesignHandle.save( ) method. To save a new report design or to keep the original report design after making changes, use the ReportDesignHandle.saveAs( ) method. Alternatively, saving the changes to the report design is unnecessary, call ReportDesignHandle.serialize( ) method. This method returns an output stream. The report engine can generate a report by opening this stream as an input stream.

If no further changes to the report design are necessary, call the method, ReportDesignHandle.close( ), to close the report design, as shown in the following code. The variable, design, is a ReportDesignHandle object.

```
design.saveAs( "sample.rptdesign" );
design.close( );
```

Creating a report design

The BIRT APIs support using an application to build a report design and generate the report output without using BIRT Report Designer. Use the createDesign( ) method on the session handle class, SessionHandle, to create a report design. Use the other model classes to create its contents, as shown earlier in this chapter.

How to create a new report design

The following code creates a report design:

```
SessionHandle session = DesignEngine.newSession( null );
ReportDesignHandle design = session.createDesign( );
```

Chapter

15

Programming Using the BIRT Charting API

This chapter describes the basic requirements of a charting application and demonstrates how to use the BIRT charting API to create a new chart and modify an existing chart definition. The BIRT chart engine provides the BIRT charting API. Classes and interfaces in this API support:

- Writing Java applications to generate many types of charts, such as bar charts, line charts, pie charts, scatter charts, and stock charts.
- Customizing the properties of a chart to fit the users' requirements.
- Modifying an existing chart item in a BIRT report design or adding a chart to an existing report design.

This chapter shows how to customize an existing chart and create a new chart within a BIRT application. Use of the charting API in a stand-alone application is beyond the scope of this book. For examples of completed charting applications, download the BIRT samples from the BIRT web site.

This chapter discusses only the most important of the more than 400 classes and interfaces in the BIRT charting API. For information about the complete set of charting API classes and interfaces, see the online Javadoc. To view the Javadoc, open the online help and navigate to BIRT Charting Programmer Reference➤Reference➤API Reference.

About the chart engine contents

Downloading and extracting the chart engine archive file from the Eclipse BIRT download page creates the following three folders:

- ChartRuntime, which contains the Eclipse plug-ins required to run, render, and edit charts
- ChartSDK, which contains everything you need to create charting applications, including the following components:
  - All the chart run-time plug-ins and an example plug-in providing sample charting applications including a chart viewer
  - Documentation in the form of online help, context-sensitive help for the user interface components, and Javadoc for the charting API
  - Source code for all the BIRT chart engine packages
- DeploymentRuntime, which contains the JAR files that you need to run a charting application outside Eclipse

About the environment for a charting application

The minimum requirements for creating a basic charting application are:

- The BIRT charting run-time engine
- The BIRT run-time engine, for an application that runs within the BIRT report context
- Java Development Kit 1.5.0 or later
- Deployment Java archive (.jar) files

  To develop or run a Java application that incorporates a BIRT chart, you need to include certain JAR files in the Java CLASSPATH. To be certain that the CLASSPATH includes all the JAR files your application needs, include the following files in the CLASSPATH:

  - All the JAR files in DeploymentRuntime/ChartEngine
  - Any custom extension plug-in JAR files that you use

  Typically, a charting application does not use the functionality from every JAR file in the ChartEngine folder, but having extra JAR files in the CLASSPATH does not affect the performance or size of an application, so the easiest technique is to include them all.

Configuring the chart engine run-time environment

An application using the BIRT chart engine can run either in the context of the BIRT report engine or as a stand-alone application. To deploy charts in a BIRT report, use the BIRT report engine. A stand-alone application does not use the BIRT report engine. Either application produces and consumes charts within itself or passes the chart structure and data to another application. To configure the BIRT chart engine environment, set one and only one of the following two system environment variables:

- STANDALONE

  Create this variable if the application has no need for any extension plug-ins. The variable does not require a value.

- BIRT_HOME

  Create this variable if the application requires the BIRT chart extension plug-ins. Set the value to the directory containing the BIRT report engine plug-ins.

You can set whichever of these two environment variables you need on the command that runs the application. For example, to set the STANDALONE variable, use a command similar to the following one:

```
java -DSTANDALONE ChartingAp
```

If running this command produces an error about an inability to load OSGi, the application is not stand-alone. Instead it requires the BIRT_HOME variable to be set to the location of the run-time engine folder. Use a command line argument similar to the following one to set the variable:

```
-DBIRT_HOME="C:/birt-runtime-2_6_0/ReportEngine"
```

To test a charting application in the Eclipse workbench, set these variables in Run➛Open Run Dialog➛Java Application➛Arguments➛VM Arguments.

Verifying the environment for a charting application

Listing 15-1 illustrates the most basic charting application it is possible to write. The output of this program is a file called myChart.chart, which contains several hundred lines of XML code. This code defines a basic chart with no data, no labels, no series, and no titles. Although this output does not represent a useful chart, compiling and running the program verifies that the environment is configured correctly for a charting application.

Listing 15-1 Basic charting application

```
import java.io.*;
import org.eclipse.birt.chart.model.*;
import org.eclipse.birt.chart.model.impl.*;

public class MyFirstChartProg {

   public static void main( String[ ] args ) {
      Chart myChart = ChartWithAxesImpl.create( );
      Serializer si = SerializerImpl.instance( );
      try {
         si.write( myChart, new FileOutputStream( new File
            ( "C:\\myChart.chart" ) ) );
      } catch ( IOException e ) { e.printStackTrace( ); }
   }
}
```

About the charting API and the chart structure

The chart element in a report design extends the basic BIRT report item through the org.eclipse.birt.report.model.api.ExtendedItemHandle class, so supports the same standard properties and functionality as all other report items. To access the chart item using the design engine API, call the ExtendedItemHandle.getProperty( ) method with an argument of chart.instance. This call returns an org.eclipse.birt.chart.model.Chart object. All chart types implement this interface through one of the classes, ChartWithAxesImpl, ChartWithoutAxesImpl, and DialChartImpl from the org.eclipse.birt.chart.model.impl package. Cast the Chart object to the appropriate class to change its properties.

ChartWithAxesImpl is the most commonly used chart class. This class supports area, bar, bubble, cone, difference, Gantt, line, pyramid, scatter, stock, and tube charts. ChartWithoutAxesImpl supports pie and radar charts. DialChartImpl supports meter charts. Many of these chart types provide subtypes. For example, a bar chart has stacked, percent stacked, and side-by-side subtypes that affect the appearance of a multi-series bar chart.

About chart visual components

The key visual components of a chart are moveable areas known as blocks that are defined by the interface org.eclipse.birt.chart.model.layout.Block. Blocks include the plot, title, and legend areas. A charting application can change the location of the title and legend areas with respect to the plot area.

About chart data

The key data component of a chart is the series. The series controls the set of values to plot and how to group those values. Charts display the values from series as data points in a chart with axes and as slices or pointers in a chart without axes. A charting application can define series values statically as a data set or dynamically as a query. The chart engine also provides extension points to support custom data set types.

Understanding static data

The chart engine requires placing all data in an object that implements the chart org.eclipse.birt.chart.model.data.DataSet interface before generating the chart. The following interfaces in the org.eclipse.birt.chart.model.data .impl package extend the DataSet interface:

- BubbleDataSet
- DateTimeDataSet
- DifferenceDataSet
- GanttDataSet

- NumberDataSet
- StockDataSet
- TextDataSet

Each interface has a corresponding implementation class that supplies a static create method to initialize a data structure. For example, the following code creates a static NumberDataSet for a series in a chart:

```
NumberDataSet seriesOneValues =
   NumberDataSetImpl.create( new double[ ]{ 15, 23, 55, 76 } );
```

The chart engine does not support sorting or grouping on a static data set. A chart displays one data point for every value in a static data set in the order provided.

Understanding dynamic data

The chart engine supports sourcing data from a dynamic source, which includes BIRT data sets and java.sqlResultSet objects. In these cases, the binding phase generates the chart data sets based on the expressions defined in the model for each series in the chart. After completing this phase, each Chart series binds to one of the chart data sets listed in the static data section.

A series is a set of plotted values in a chart. BIRT uses a series definition object to define what data a series contains. For example, row["month"] populates a series with the month column from a BIRT data set bound to a chart. This series definition object results in a run-time series that is bound to a supported chart data set type when the chart generates.

BIRT also supports defining groups and sorting in a series definition. When using these features, BIRT creates additional run time series as necessary, each with its own chart data set.

For example, if a BIRT report contains a data set having three columns, such as the product name, amount sold, and month sold, you can create a bar chart to display the data. The category series contains the product and the value series contains the amount. Using the category series as the *x*-axis and the value series as the *y*-axis, the chart model produces two run-time series when generating the chart. You can add the month to the *y*-axis series to group the data and produce multiple run-time series. The category series and the value series can contain up to twelve run-time series, one for each month.

All run-time series for a chart must have the same number of data points. To get the run-time series for a series, call the getRunTimeSeries( ) method for the specific series definition. Listing 15-2 gets a run-time series and sets the first bar series to have a riser type of triangle.

Some chart types use nested SeriesDefinitions objects. For example, a pie chart creates a top-level series definition that stores category series information. This top-level series definition also contains another nested series definition that stores the information for the value series.

Listing 15-2 Getting a run-time series

```
function beforeGeneration( chart, icsc )
{
   importPackage(
      Packages.org.eclipse.birt.chart.model.attribute );

   var xAxis = chart.getBaseAxes( )[0];
   var yAxis = chart.getOrthogonalAxes( xAxis, true )[0]
   var seriesDef = yAxis.getSeriesDefinitions( ).get( 0 )
   var runSeries = seriesDef.getRunTimeSeries( );
   var firstRunSeries = runSeries.get( 0 );
   firstRunSeries.setRiser( RiserType.TRIANGLE_LITERAL );
}
```

Using the charting API to create a new chart

To create a chart instance object for use in a stand-alone application or a report design, use a static method of one of the chart implementation classes. Depending on which chart implementation object you use, you can either create a chart with or without axes. The following line of code creates a chart with axes:

```
ChartWithAxes newChart = ChartWithAxesImpl.create( );
```

Modifying chart properties

Each of the available chart implementations provides a set of properties. The properties of the chart define everything about a stand-alone chart. Chart properties do not define the integration of a chart object into a chart element in a report design, such as binding a data set to a chart and a chart's ultimate display size. A section later in this chapter describes how to set up a chart as an element in a report design.

The BIRT chart engine API supports changing chart properties. All charts have the properties that the Chart interface provides, such as dimension, which sets the appearance of the chart as two-dimensional, two-dimensional with depth, or three-dimensional, and plot, which is the area that contains the chart itself.

The ChartWithAxesImpl class implements the ChartWithAxes interface, which provides properties related to *x*-, *y*-, and for some chart types, *z*-axes.

The ChartWithoutAxesImpl class implements the ChartWithoutAxes interface, which provides properties for pie slices. The DialChartImpl class implements the ChartWithoutAxes and DialChart interfaces. DialChart supports the superimposition property that meter charts use.

Each interface provides getter and setter methods for its properties, and other methods if necessary. For example, for the dimension property, the Chart interface provides getDimension( ), setDimension( ), isSetDimension( ), and unsetDimension( ) methods.

Understanding simple and complex properties

Some properties, like dimension, are simple properties that take a single value. Some simple properties accept a restricted set of values that the class defines as static fields. Use the Javadoc to find these values.

Other properties, such as a chart's plot or title are complex. A getter method for a complex property returns an object. For example, the Chart.getTitle( ) method returns an org.eclipse.birt.chart.model.layout.TitleBlock object. The chart interfaces do not provide setter methods for complex properties. When code changes the properties of a complex property, the changes take effect on the chart immediately.

Some properties, such as the horizontal spacing of elements within a plot, use values based on the current units of measurement. Call the Chart.setUnits( ) method to set the units that you prefer.

Listing 15-3 shows how to set simple and complex properties and the units of measurement.

Listing 15-3 Getting and setting chart properties

```
// Simple properties
// Set a chart's appearance to two-dimensional
chart.setDimension( ChartDimension.TWO_DIMENSIONAL_LITERAL );

// Set the units of measurement for the chart
chart.setUnits( UnitsOfMeasurement.PIXELS_LITERAL.getLiteral( ) );

// Complex properties
// Set the chart's title
chart.getTitle( ).getLabel( ).getCaption( ).setValue( "Europe" );
// Rotate the text in the chart's title
chart.getTitle( ).getLabel( ).getCaption( ).getFont( )
   .setRotation( 5 );

// Set chart block properties
chart.getBlock( ).setBackground( ColorDefinitionImpl.WHITE( ));
chart.getBlock( ).setBounds( BoundsImpl.create( 0, 0, 400, 250 ));
```

Setting plot properties

All charts have a plot property, which specifies the area in a Chart object that contains the chart itself. The plot is an object that implements the org.eclipse .birt.chart.model.layout.Plot interface. Plot defines horizontal and vertical spacing and the client area, which contains the rendering of the chart. The client area is itself a complex property that defines properties such as the background color and outline of the rendered chart. Plot provides all the properties defined by the Block interface in the same package, such as the background and outline. When setting values for a property that multiple components provide, determine the best class on which to modify the property based on the characteristics of all the classes.

To set properties of the plot, first get a Plot object from the chart instance object. Then, use a setter method of a component of the Plot object. Listing 15-4 illustrates how to get the chart plot and modify its properties.

Listing 15-4 Getting chart plot and modifying its properties

```
Plot plot = chart.getPlot( );
plot.getClientArea().setBackground( ColorDefinitionImpl.CREAM( ));
plot.setHorizontalSpacing( plot.getHorizontalSpacing( ) + 10 );
plot.getOutline( ).setVisible( true );
```

Setting legend properties

All charts have a legend property, which is the area in a Chart object that contains the chart legend. For a chart without axes, the legend identifies the slices on a pie chart or pointers on a meter chart. For a chart with axes, the legend identifies the series that display values on the *x*-axis. For a chart with multiple *y*-series, the legend displays separate sections for each series. Typically, if there is only one *x*-axis group and one *y*-series, do not make the legend visible.

The legend is an object that implements the org.eclipse.birt.chart.model .layout.Legend interface, which extends the Block interface. Legend provides all the Block properties, plus properties specific to Legend, such as position, title, text, and values. The default position of the legend is to the right of the plot area. Within this position, change the location of the legend by setting its anchor property.

To set properties of the chart legend, first get a Legend object from the chart instance object. Then, use a setter method of a component of the Legend object. To set properties of legend lines, use a LineAttribute object from the Legend object. Listing 15-5 illustrates how to get the chart legend and modify its properties.

Listing 15-5 Getting and setting legend properties

```
Legend legend = chart.getLegend( );
legend.getText( ).getFont( ).setSize( 16 );
legend.getInsets( ).set( 10, 5, 0, 0 );
legend.setAnchor( Anchor.NORTH_LITERAL );

// Set the attributes of the legend's outline
legend.getOutline( ).setVisible( false );
LineAttributes lia = legend.getOutline( );
lia.setStyle( LineStyle.SOLID_LITERAL );
```

Setting axes properties

A chart with axes always has at least two axes, the primary base axis and the axis orthogonal to the base axis. A primary base axis is a category axis, which displays values of any data type and is typically an *x*-axis. A chart can have more than one primary base axis. Every base axis has at least one axis that is orthogonal to it. An orthogonal axis is a value axis, which displays numeric values and is typically a *y*-axis.

The org.eclipse.birt.chart.model.component.Axis interface supports both category and value axes.

To set the properties of one or more axes of a chart, cast the Chart object to a type of ChartWithAxes, as shown in the following statement:

```
cwaChart = ( ChartWithAxes ) chart;
```

To access a category axis, call the ChartWithAxes.getPrimaryBaseAxes( ) method. This method returns an array. If there is only one primary base axis, get the first element of the array, as shown in the following code:

```
Axis xAxisPrimary = newChart.getPrimaryBaseAxes( )[0];
```

To access the value axis for a single value-axis chart, call the method, getPrimaryOrthogonalAxis( ). For a chart having multiple value axes, access the list of axes by calling getOrthogonalAxes( ).

Listing 15-6 illustrates the technique for getting the axes of a chart and setting their properties.

Listing 15-6 Getting category and value axes and setting their properties

```
Axis xAxisPrimary = cwaChart.getPrimaryBaseAxes( )[0];
xAxisPrimary.getLabel( ).getCaption( ).getFont( ).setRotation(45);
xAxisPrimary.setType( AxisType.TEXT_LITERAL );
xAxisPrimary.getMajorGrid().setTickStyle(TickStyle.BELOW_LITERAL);
xAxisPrimary.getOrigin( ).setType(IntersectionType.VALUE_LITERAL);
xAxisPrimary.getTitle( ).setVisible( false );

Axis yAxisPrimary =
   cwaChart.getPrimaryOrthogonalAxis( xAxisPrimary );
yAxisPrimary.getMajorGrid( ).setTickStyle(TickStyle.LEFT_LITERAL);
yAxisPrimary.setType( AxisType.LINEAR_LITERAL );
yAxisPrimary.getScale( ).setMax( NumberDataElementImpl.create
   ( 1000 ) );
yAxisPrimary.getScale( ).setMin( NumberDataElementImpl.create(0));
yAxisPrimary.getTitle( ).getCaption( ).setValue( "Sales Growth" );
yAxisPrimary.setFormatSpecifier
   ( JavaNumberFormatSpecifierImpl.create( "$" ) );
```

Using series

All charts use series to define the data values to represent. Series objects contain a list of values to plot on the chart. To instantiate a Series object, call the static create( ) method on org.eclipse.birt.chart.model.component.impl .SeriesImpl. Define the set of values for a series either with a dynamic query that accesses an external data source or with a static data set that is a list of values. A query on the series definition object supports grouping and sorting of the data.

The series for an *x*-axis or for the values that control the number of sectors in a pie can contain non-numeric data values, such as dates or text values. For example, these series can contain the quarters in a range of years, or product codes or countries.

The series for a *y*-axis or for the values that control the size of the sectors in a pie chart must hold numeric values. These series are implementations of specific subinterfaces of the Series interface. Each chart type uses its own series type, to control the chart represents the values. For example, a BarSeries object has riser and riser outline properties to control the appearance of the bars.

Series definition objects provide access to the series objects for the chart and standard properties such as the palette of colors in which to display pie sectors, bars, and other markers. To instantiate a SeriesDefinition object, call the static org.eclipse.birt.chart.model.data.impl.SeriesDefinitionImpl.create( ) method. To add a series to a series definition, get the collection of series and add the series to that collection. To set the color of a series, get a SeriesPalette object and call its shift( ) method.

A series definition supports multiple series. The series do not all have to be the same type. For example, a line chart can use the same axes as a bar chart. Typically, a chart displays extra series on a *y*-axis, not on an *x*-axis.

Listing 15-7 illustrates how to get a series definition from an axis and how to change a property of the series.

Listing 15-7 Getting a series definition and setting a property

```
SeriesDefinition seriesDefX = SeriesDefinitionImpl.create( );
seriesDefX = ( SeriesDefinition )
   xAxisPrimary.getSeriesDefinitions( ).get( 0 );
seriesDefX.getSeriesPalette( ).shift( 1 );
```

Adding a series to a chart

To display values on a chart, add category and value series to a newly created chart or modify the series on an existing chart. For a chart with axes, associate series with both category and value axes.

Creating a category series

On a chart with axes, the category series is the set of values that the category axis displays. On a chart without axes, the category series defines the number of sectors in a pie chart or the number of pointers on a meter chart. To create a category series, use the static create( ) method of the SeriesImpl class, as shown in the following line:

```
Series seriesCategory = SeriesImpl.create( );
```

Creating an orthogonal series

The orthogonal series specifies the representation of the values in the value series. On a chart with axes, the orthogonal series is the set of values that display on the *y*-axis, for example, appearing as bars, bubbles, stock bar-sticks or candle-sticks. On a chart without axes, the orthogonal series sets the size of slices in a pie or the position of a pointer on a meter chart. A chart can have multiple orthogonal series of the same or differing types.

The orthogonal series classes are subclasses of the SeriesImpl class, and are located in the org.eclipse.birt.chart.model.type.impl package. The following classes are available:

- AreaSeriesImpl
- BarSeriesImpl
- BubbleSeriesImpl
- DialSeriesImpl
- DifferenceSeriesImpl
- GanttSeriesImpl
- LineSeriesImpl
- PieSeriesImpl
- ScatterSeriesImpl
- StockSeriesImpl

The BarSeriesImpl class supports bar, cone, pyramid, and tube chart types.

To create an orthogonal series, use the static create( ) method of the series class. The following line shows an example of creating a bar series:

```
BarSeries barSeries2 = ( BarSeries ) BarSeriesImpl.create( );
```

Setting series properties

A category series supports only the properties defined by the SeriesImpl class. A value series supports additional properties defined by the relevant subclass of SeriesImpl. For example, a bar series supports bar stacking and outlines on the risers. A pie series supports slice outlines and exploded slices.

To set the properties of a series, use getter and setter methods of the appropriate series objects, as shown in Listing 15-8, which sets properties on BarSeries and LineSeries objects.

Listing 15-8 Setting the properties of a bar series and line series

```
LineSeries ls1 = ( LineSeries ) LineSeriesImpl.create( );
ls1.getLineAttributes( ).setColor( ColorDefinitionImpl.RED( ) );
BarSeries bs1 = ( BarSeries ) BarSeriesImpl.create( );
bs1.getLabel( ).setVisible( true );
bs1.getLabel( ).getCaption( ).setValue( "Q2" );
```

Associating data with a series

Create either a query or a data set, and add that object to the series data definition. To create a query, use the static create( ) method of the org.eclipse.birt.chart.model.data.impl.QueryImpl class. To create a data set, use the static create( ) method on a subclass of DataSetImpl. The data set type must match the type of values that the axis displays. For example, a category axis displaying date-and-time data values requires a data set of class DateTimeDataSet. Similarly, a bar series requires a numeric data set, of class NumberDataSet. Some series require multiple sets of data. For example, a stock series requires four sets of data, high, low, open, and close. Either add four queries in that order to the series, or add a StockDataSet to the series. Listing 15-9 adds queries and data sets to line, bar, and stock series.

Listing 15-9 Setting a query and a data set on category series

```
// Setting a query on a category series
Series seriesCategory = SeriesImpl.create( );
Query query = QueryImpl.create( "row[\"CATEGORY\"]" );
seriesCategory.getDataDefinition( ).add( query );

// Setting a data set on a category series
Series seBase = SeriesImpl.create( );
DateTimeDataSet dsDateValues =
   DateTimeDataSetImpl.create( new Calendar[ ]{
   new CDateTime( 2011, 12, 21 ),
   new CDateTime( 2011, 12, 20 ),
   new CDateTime( 2011, 12, 19 ),
   new CDateTime( 2011, 12, 18 ),
} );
seBase.setDataSet( dsDateValues );
```

Listing 15-10 illustrates how to create a second value series, set some of its properties, assign data to the series, and add the series to an axis.

Listing 15-10 Creating a series, setting properties, and adding it to an axis

```
SeriesDefinition seriesDefY = SeriesDefinitionImpl.create( );
seriesDefY.getSeriesPalette( ).update( ColorDefinitionImpl
   .YELLOW( ) );
BarSeries barSeries2 = ( BarSeries ) BarSeriesImpl.create( );
barSeries2.setSeriesIdentifier( "Q2" );
barSeries2.setRiserOutline( null );
barSeries2.getLabel( ).setVisible( true );
barSeries2.setLabelPosition( Position.INSIDE_LITERAL );

// Assign data to the series
Query query2 = QueryImpl.create( "row[\"VALUE2\"]" );
barSeries2.getDataDefinition( ).add( query2 );
seriesDefY.getSeries( ).add( barSeries2 );
// Add the new series to the y-axis
yAxisPrimary.getSeriesDefinitions( ).add( seriesDefY );
```

Adding a series definition to a chart

After setting the properties of a SeriesDefinition object, add the object to the chart. For a chart without axes, add the series definitions directly to the chart object's collection of series definitions. The first series definition in the collection defines the category series and the second one defines the orthogonal series. For a chart with axes, add the series definition to each Axis object's collection of series definitions as shown in Listing 15-11.

Listing 15-11 Adding series definitions to a pie chart and a chart with axes

```
ChartWithoutAxes cwoaPie = ChartWithoutAxesImpl.create( );
cwoaPie.getSeriesDefinitions( ).add( sd );
PieSeries sePie = ( PieSeries ) PieSeriesImpl.create( );
sePie.setDataSet( seriesOneValues );
sePie.setSeriesIdentifier( "Cities" );
sd.getSeriesDefinitions( ).add( sdCity );

xAxisPrimary.getSeriesDefinitions( ).add( sdX );
yAxisPrimary.getSeriesDefinitions( ).add( sdY1 );
yAxisPrimary.getSeriesDefinitions( ).add( sdY2 );
```

Setting up the default aggregation for the chart

A chart plots every value that it receives unless an org.eclipse.birt.chart .model.data.SeriesGrouping object defines the type of aggregation to perform. Set up aggregation on the category series to define the value on which to aggregate and the type of aggregation, as shown in Listing 15-12. The chart builder user interface displays the available aggregation types. All orthogonal series use the aggregation type specified by the category series grouping by default.

Listing 15-12 Defining aggregation on the category series

```
SeriesGrouping grouping = sdX.getGrouping( );
grouping.setEnabled( true );
grouping.setGroupType( DataType.TEXT_LITERAL );
grouping.setGroupingUnit( GroupingUnitType.STRING_LITERAL );
grouping.setGroupingInterval( 0 );
grouping.setAggregateExpression( "Sum" );
```

Changing the aggregation for secondary value series

Every value series uses the same aggregation expression to aggregates values to display unless the application changes the aggregation by setting up a SeriesGrouping specific to the series. Change only the grouping properties that differ from the default grouping, as shown in Listing 15-13.

Listing 15-13 Defining aggregation on a value series

```
SeriesGrouping groupingY2 = sdY2.getGrouping( );
groupingY2.setEnabled( true );
groupingY2.setAggregateExpression( "Average" );$
```

Adding a chart event handler

Two kinds of chart event handlers are available to a charting application: a Java event handler or a JavaScript event handler.

Adding a Java chart event handler

To add a Java event handler, create a separate Java class file containing the event handler method or methods. The process for creating a Java event handler class is identical to the process for creating a Java event handler class for any other report item, as described in the chapters on scripting with Java and scripting for charts. The class must include a function for every event handler method of the chart.

To register a Java class in the charting application code, use the setScript( ) method of the chart instance object, as shown in the following statement:

```
chart.setScript
   ( "com.MyCompany.eventHandlers.ChartEventHandlers" );
```

The string argument passed to the setScript( ) method is the fully qualified name of the Java class. Do not include the .class extension in the class name.

Adding a JavaScript chart event handler

To add a JavaScript event handler, code the script as one long string and pass that string to the setScript( ) method of the chart instance object. For example, the statement in Listing 15-14 passes a string to chart.setScript( ) containing event handler script for the beforeDrawDataPointLabel event handler. Line breaks in the JavaScript code are indicated by backslash n (\n), and quotes within the script are indicated by a backslash quote (\"). The JavaScript code consists of several strings concatenated together to form a single string. This technique helps make the script more readable.

Listing 15-14 Adding an event handler script to a bar chart

```
cwaBar.setScript ( "function beforeDrawDataPointLabel"
   + "(dataPoints, label, scriptContext)"
   + "{val = dataPoints.getOrthogonalValue( );"
   +     "clr = label.getCaption( ).getColor( );"
   +     "if ( val < -10 ) clr.set( 32, 168, 255 );"
   +     "else if ( ( val >= -10 ) & ( val <=10 ) )"
   +     "clr.set( 168, 0, 208 );"
   +     "else if ( val > 10 ) clr.set( 0, 208, 32 );}")
```

Using a chart item in a report design

A Java program can open an existing BIRT report design file and alter the content of the report before displaying or saving the report. The chapter on programming BIRT describes how to open a report design file using the BIRT engine and model APIs. This section describes how to use the BIRT charting API to modify an existing chart element in the report design and to create a new chart element. The following sections contain code examples for each step in the process.

Accessing an existing chart item

To get a chart report item from a report design, first perform the following steps using the BIRT core and model APIs, as described earlier in this book:

- On a DesignConfig object, set the BIRT home property to the directory that contains the report engine.
- Start the platform using the configuration object, a design engine factory, and a design engine.
- Use the design engine to create a session handle object.
- Create a design handle object for a report design from the session handle.
- Use the design handle object to access the chart element in the design.

Next, retrieve a Chart object from the chart item. This Chart object supports accessing the BIRT chart engine classes and using BIRT's charting API.

Listing 15-15 illustrates the process of getting a chart report item. This code assumes that the chart is the first report item in a list and that the list is the first report item in the report.

Listing 15-15 Getting a ReportDesignHandle object and a Chart object

```
DesignConfig dConfig = new DesignConfig( );
dConfig.setBIRTHome( "C:/birt-runtime-2_6_0/ReportEngine" );
IDesignEngine dEngine = null;
ReportDesignHandle dHandle = null;

try {
   Platform.startup( dConfig );
   IDesignEngineFactory dFactory = ( IDesignEngineFactory )
      Platform. createFactoryObject( IDesignEngineFactory.
      EXTENSION_DESIGN_ENGINE_FACTORY );
   dEngine = dFactory.createDesignEngine( dConfig );
   SessionHandle sessionHandle =
      dEngine.newSessionHandle( ULocale.ENGLISH );
   dHandle = sessionHandle.openDesign( reportName );
} catch ( BirtException e ) {
   e.printStackTrace( );
```

```
   return;
}
ListHandle li =  ( ListHandle )
   dHandle.getBody( ).getContents( ).get( 0 );
ExtendedItemHandle eihChart1 = ( ExtendedItemHandle )
   li.getSlot( 0 ).getContents( ).get( 0 );
Chart chart = ( Chart ) eihChart1.getProperty( "chart.instance" );
```

Creating a new chart item

Before creating a new chart item in a report design, a charting application performs all the steps to start up the platform and design engine, as described in the previous section. Next, the application creates the Chart object as described earlier in this chapter. Creating a new chart object for use in a report design is identical to creating a chart for a stand-alone application. Finally, the application creates a chart element and sets up the properties required to link the chart object to the element by performing the following tasks. These tasks relate to the appearance and behavior of a chart inside a report design. If the chart is not deployed in a report, the tasks in this section are not required.

- Getting an ElementFactory object

  The ElementFactory object supports creating a new report element.

- Setting the chart type and creating sample data

  The chart type and sample data provide a guide to the appearance of a chart element in a report design in BIRT Report Designer.

- Getting an ExtendedItemHandle object

  The ExtendedItemHandle object is similar to a standard report item handle. The item handle associates the chart object with the report item instance in the report design. The handle is also the object that binds to a data set.

- Setting the chart.instance property on the report item

  The chart.instance property of the report item identifies the chart instance object and links the report item to the chart instance object.

- Getting a data set from the report design

  A chart must bind to data in order to have meaning. The report design provides access to one or more data sets that the report developer defined. The program can create a data set and add it to the design.

- Binding a chart to the data set

  To bind a chart to a data set, specify the data set as a property of the extended item handle object.

- Setting any other report item properties

- Adding the new chart to the report design

The last step is to add the chart to the report design by adding the extended item handle object to the report design.

- Optionally saving the report design

  An application program that creates or modifies a BIRT report design can save the new or modified report design.

The following sections describe these tasks in more detail and provide code examples for every step.

Getting a design engine element factory object

Creating a chart item in a report design requires an ElementFactory object. To get an ElementFactory object, use the getElementFactory( ) method of the ReportDesignHandle object, as shown in the following line of code:

```
ElementFactory ef = dHandle.getElementFactory( );
```

The chapter on programming with the BIRT APIs provides more information about using the Design Engine APIs and how to place a new item in a report design.

Setting the chart type and subtype

A chart's type and subtype determine the appearance of the chart in BIRT Report Designer. In conjunction with sample data, these properties provide a realistic rendering of the chart item in the report design's layout window and in the chart wizard. To ensure that the appearance of this rendered chart is as accurate as possible, set the chart's type so that it matches the series type set on the axis. Many types, such as bar, Gantt, line, and stock, are available for a chart with axes. Charts without axes can be dial, pie, or radar types only.

The bubble, dial, difference, Gantt, and pie classes each support only a single type. The other chart types have multiple subtypes. Set the chart type and subtype by using the Chart methods setType( ) and setSubType( ) respectively. These methods take a single String argument. Table 15-1 shows the available values for chart types and the valid subtypes for each chart type. Because cone, pyramid, and tube charts are merely different representations of a bar chart, they have the same subtypes as a bar chart.

Table 15-1 Chart type and subtype properties

Chart axes	Type	Subtype
With axes	Area Chart	Overlay
		Percent Stacked
		Stacked
	Bar Chart	Percent Stacked
		Side-by-side

(continues)

Table 15-1 Chart type and subtype properties (continued)

Chart axes	Type	Subtype
With axes		Stacked
	Bubble Chart	Standard Bubble Chart
	Cone Chart	Percent Stacked
		Side-by-side
		Stacked
	Difference Chart	Standard Difference Chart
	Gantt Chart	Standard Gantt Chart
	Line Chart	Overlay
		Percent Stacked
		Stacked
	Pyramid Chart	Percent Stacked
		Side-by-side
		Stacked
	Scatter Chart	Standard Scatter Chart
	Stock Chart	Standard Stock Chart
		Bar Stick Stock Chart
	Tube Chart	Percent Stacked
		Side-by-side
		Stacked
Without axes	Meter Chart	Standard Meter Chart
		Superimposed Meter Chart
	Pie Chart	Standard Pie Chart
	Radar	Radar.STANDARD_SUBTYPE_LITERAL
		Radar.SPIDER_SUBTYPE_LITERAL
		Radar.BULLSEYE_SUBTYPE_LITERAL

Listing 15-16 shows how to set a chart type and subtype:

Listing 15-16 Setting a chart's type and subtype

```
ChartWithAxes cwaBar = ChartWithAxesImpl.create( );
cwaBar.setType( "Bar Chart" );
cwaBar.setSubType( "Side-by-side" );
```

Creating sample data

This section describes an optional step in the creation of a chart. Sample data provides visual information in BIRT Report Designer about a chart's appearance. If you omit the code in Listing 15-17, the chart renders correctly when the report generates, but the designer's layout window does not display sample values.

Listing 15-17 Adding sample data to a chart

```
SampleData sdt = DataFactory.eINSTANCE.createSampleData( );
BaseSampleData sdBase =
   DataFactory.eINSTANCE.createBaseSampleData( );
sdBase.setDataSetRepresentation( "A" );
sdt.getBaseSampleData( ).add( sdBase );

OrthogonalSampleData sdOrthogonal =
   DataFactory.eINSTANCE.createOrthogonalSampleData( );
sdOrthogonal.setDataSetRepresentation( "1" );
sdOrthogonal.setSeriesDefinitionIndex( 0 );
sdt.getOrthogonalSampleData( ).add( sdOrthogonal );
newChart.setSampleData( sdt );
```

Getting an extended item handle object

A chart report item extends from the design engine's ReportItemHandle class by further extending the ExtendedItemHandle class. Use the ElementFactory object to create this object by using the newExtendedItem( ) method of the ElementFactory object, as shown in the following line of code:

```
ExtendedItemHandle chartHandle =
   ef.newExtendedItem( null, "Chart" );
```

Setting up the report item as a chart

Set the chart.instance property of the report item object to contain the chart instance object. Get the report item from the extended item handle object, as shown in Listing 15-18.

Listing 15-18 Associating a chart object with an extended item handle

```
ExtendedItemHandle chartHandle =
   ef.newExtendedItem( null, "Chart" );

try {
   chartHandle.getReportItem( ).setProperty
      ( "chart.instance", newChart );
} catch( ExtendedElementException e ) {
   e.printStackTrace( );
}
```

Preparing a data set and data columns

The new chart item still does not have access to data from the report design. The chart item uses data rows from a data set and column bindings that define how to apply values from data set columns to the chart. The names of the column bindings must match the column names used in the chart's series objects.

To access a data set, create a data set or get an existing data set from the report design. Next, set up the columns to bind to the chart by instantiating org.eclipse.birt.report.model.api.elements.structures.ComputedColumn objects. A ComputedColumn object contains an expression that accesses columns from a data set. The code in Listing 15-19 gets the first data set in the report design.

Listing 15-19 Accessing a data set and preparing columns

```
DataSetHandle dataSet =
   ( DataSetHandle ) dHandle.getDataSets( ).get( 0 );
ComputedColumn col1 = StructureFactory.createComputedColumn( );
col1.setName( "VALUE1" );
col1.setExpression( "dataSetRow[\"QUANTITYORDERED\"]") ;
col1.setDataType(
   DesignChoiceConstants.COLUMN_DATA_TYPE_INTEGER );
ComputedColumn col2 = StructureFactory.createComputedColumn( );
col2.setName( "VALUE2" );
col2.setExpression( "dataSetRow[\"PRICEEACH\"]" );
col2.setDataType( DesignChoiceConstants.COLUMN_DATA_TYPE_FLOAT );
ComputedColumn col3 = StructureFactory.createComputedColumn( );
col3.setName( "CATEGORY" );
col3.setExpression( "dataSetRow[\"PRODUCTLINE\"]");
col3.setDataType( DesignChoiceConstants.COLUMN_DATA_TYPE_STRING );
```

Binding the chart to the data set

Use the extended item handle to bind the chart to the data set and data columns, as shown in Listing 15-20.

Listing 15-20 Binding a data set and columns to the chart item

```
try {
   chartHandle.setDataSet( dataSet );
   extendedItemHandle.addColumnBinding( col1, true );

   extendedItemHandle.addColumnBinding( col2, true );
   extendedItemHandle.addColumnBinding( col3, true );
}
catch ( SemanticException e ) {
   e.printStackTrace( );
}
```

Set any other report item properties

The extended report item supports all the properties provided by the org.eclipse.birt.report.model.api.ReportItemHandle class. These properties include a bookmark, dimensions, and a theme. For example, to set the dimensions of the chart report item, use code as shown in Listing 15-21.

Listing 15-21 Setting chart item properties

```
try {
   extendedItemHandle.setHeight( "250pt" );
   extendedItemHandle.setWidth( "400pt" );
} catch ( SemanticException e ) {
   e.printStackTrace( );
}
```

Adding the new chart to the report design

After setting the properties of the chart and binding the chart to data, add the new chart to the report design. Listing 15-22 adds the chart item to the footer of an existing list item.

Listing 15-22 Adding the chart item to the report design

```
ListHandle li =
   ( ListHandle ) dHandle.getBody( ).getContents( ).get( 0 );
try {
   li.getFooter( ).add( chartHandle );
}
catch ( ContentException e3 ) { e3.printStackTrace( ); }
catch ( NameException e3 ) { e3.printStackTrace( ); }
```

Saving the report design after adding the chart

The report design file on disk does not yet contain the chart report item. Typically, you save the modified report design with a new name in order not to overwrite the original report design file.

```
try {
   dHandle.saveAs( "./Test_modified.rptdesign" );
}
catch ( IOException e ) { e.printStackTrace( ); }
dHandle.close( );
```

Putting it all together

The code in Listing 15-23 uses many of the techniques illustrated in this chapter in a complete Java application that creates a chart report item.

Listing 15-23 Adding a chart to the report design

```
import java.io.IOException;

import org.eclipse.birt.chart.model.ChartWithAxes;

import org.eclipse.birt.chart.model.attribute.Anchor;
import org.eclipse.birt.chart.model.attribute.AxisType;
import org.eclipse.birt.chart.model.attribute.DataType;
import org.eclipse.birt.chart.model.attribute.GroupingUnitType;
import org.eclipse.birt.chart.model.attribute.IntersectionType;
import org.eclipse.birt.chart.model.attribute.LineAttributes;
import org.eclipse.birt.chart.model.attribute.LineStyle;
import org.eclipse.birt.chart.model.attribute.MarkerType;
import org.eclipse.birt.chart.model.attribute.TickStyle;

import org.eclipse.birt.chart.model.attribute.impl.BoundsImpl;
import org.eclipse.birt.chart.model.attribute.impl
   .ColorDefinitionImpl;
import org.eclipse.birt.chart.model.component.Axis;
import org.eclipse.birt.chart.model.component.Series;

import org.eclipse.birt.chart.model.component.impl.SeriesImpl;

import org.eclipse.birt.chart.model.data.BaseSampleData;
import org.eclipse.birt.chart.model.data.DataFactory;
import org.eclipse.birt.chart.model.data.OrthogonalSampleData;
import org.eclipse.birt.chart.model.data.Query;
import org.eclipse.birt.chart.model.data.SampleData;
import org.eclipse.birt.chart.model.data.SeriesDefinition;
import org.eclipse.birt.chart.model.data.SeriesGrouping;

import org.eclipse.birt.chart.model.data.impl
   .NumberDataElementImpl;
import org.eclipse.birt.chart.model.data.impl.QueryImpl;
import org.eclipse.birt.chart.model.data.impl
   .SeriesDefinitionImpl;

import org.eclipse.birt.chart.model.impl.ChartWithAxesImpl;

import org.eclipse.birt.chart.model.layout.Legend;
import org.eclipse.birt.chart.model.layout.Plot;

import org.eclipse.birt.chart.model.type.LineSeries;

import org.eclipse.birt.chart.model.type.impl.LineSeriesImpl;

import org.eclipse.birt.core.exception.BirtException;

import org.eclipse.birt.core.framework.Platform;

import org.eclipse.birt.report.engine.api.EngineConfig;

import org.eclipse.birt.report.model.api.DataSetHandle;
import org.eclipse.birt.report.model.api.DesignConfig;
import org.eclipse.birt.report.model.api.ElementFactory;
```

```
import org.eclipse.birt.report.model.api.ExtendedItemHandle;
import org.eclipse.birt.report.model.api.IDesignEngine;
import org.eclipse.birt.report.model.api.IDesignEngineFactory;
import org.eclipse.birt.report.model.api.ListHandle;
import org.eclipse.birt.report.model.api.PropertyHandle;
import org.eclipse.birt.report.model.api.ReportDesignHandle;
import org.eclipse.birt.report.model.api.SessionHandle;
import org.eclipse.birt.report.model.api.StructureFactory;
import org.eclipse.birt.report.model.api.activity
   .SemanticException;

import org.eclipse.birt.report.model.api.command.ContentException;
import org.eclipse.birt.report.model.api.command.NameException;

import org.eclipse.birt.report.model.api.elements
   .DesignChoiceConstants;
import org.eclipse.birt.report.model.api.elements.structures
   .ComputedColumn;
import org.eclipse.birt.report.model.api.extension
   .ExtendedElementException;
import org.eclipse.birt.report.model.api.extension.IReportItem;

import com.ibm.icu.util.ULocale;

/*****************************************************************
 * Read a BIRT report design file, add a chart and write a
 * new report design file containing the added chart.
 * Run this application with the following command line:
 * java ChartReportApp origDesign modifiedDesign
 *****************************************************************/

public class ChartReportApp
{
   private static String birtHome =
      "C:/birt-runtime-2_6_0/ReportEngine";
   private static String reportName = "./test.rptdesign";
   private static String newReportDesign = "./test_new.rptdesign";

   /**************************************************************
   * Get the report design name and the name of the modified
   * report design from the command line if the command line has
   * any arguments.
   * Create an instance of this class, create a new chart,
   * write a new design file containing both the original and
   * the new chart
   **************************************************************/

   public static void main( String[ ] args )
   {
      if( args.length > 0 ) {
         reportName = args[0];
      }
```

```
   if( args.length > 1 ) {
      newReportDesign = args[1];
   }

   ReportDesignHandle dHandle = createDesignHandle(reportName);

   // create an instance of this class
   ChartReportApp cra = new ChartReportApp( );

   // Call the build method of this class.
   cra.build( dHandle, newReportDesign );
}

/**********************************************************
 * The report design handle object is the entry point to
 * the report.

 * Create a report design handle object based on the
 * original design file by performing the following steps:

 * 1) Start the platform using the configuration object
 * 2) Create a design engine factory object from the platform
 * 3) Create a design engine using the factory object
 * 4) Create a session handle object from the design engine
 * 5) Create a design handle object from the session handle

 * The resulting design handle object is the entry point
 * to the report design and thus to the chart.
 **********************************************************/

private static ReportDesignHandle createDesignHandle
   ( String reportName )
{
   EngineConfig config = new EngineConfig( );
   config.setBIRTHome( birtHome );
   DesignConfig dConfig = new DesignConfig( );
   dConfig.setBIRTHome( birtHome );
   IDesignEngine dEngine = null;
   ReportDesignHandle dHandle = null;
   try {
      Platform.startup( config );
      IDesignEngineFactory dFactory =
         ( IDesignEngineFactory ) Platform.createFactoryObject(
         IDesignEngineFactory.EXTENSION_DESIGN_ENGINE_FACTORY );
      dEngine = dFactory.createDesignEngine( dConfig );
      SessionHandle sessionHandle =
         dEngine.newSessionHandle( ULocale.ENGLISH );
      dHandle = sessionHandle.openDesign( reportName );
   }
   catch(BirtException e) {
       e.printStackTrace();
   }
   return dHandle;
```

```
}
/***********************************************************
* Build a chart
***********************************************************/
public void build
   ( ReportDesignHandle dHandle, String newDesignName )
{
   // Create a new chart instance object
   ChartWithAxes newChart = ChartWithAxesImpl.create( );

   // Set the properties of the chart
   newChart.setType( "Line Chart" );
   newChart.setSubType( "Overlay" );

   newChart.getBlock().setBackground(
      ColorDefinitionImpl.WHITE() );
   newChart.getBlock().setBounds(
      BoundsImpl.create( 0, 0, 400, 250 ) );

   Plot p = newChart.getPlot();
   p.getClientArea().setBackground(
      ColorDefinitionImpl.create( 255, 255, 225 ));
   newChart.getTitle().getLabel().getCaption()
      .setValue( "Europe" );

   Legend lg = newChart.getLegend( );
   LineAttributes lia = lg.getOutline( );
   lg.getText().getFont().setSize( 16 );
   lia.setStyle( LineStyle.SOLID_LITERAL );
   lg.getInsets().set( 1, 1, 1, 1 );
   lg.getOutline().setVisible( false );
   lg.setAnchor( Anchor.NORTH_LITERAL );

   Axis xAxisPrimary = newChart.getPrimaryBaseAxes( )[0];
   xAxisPrimary.setType( AxisType.TEXT_LITERAL );
   xAxisPrimary.getMajorGrid().setTickStyle(
      TickStyle.BELOW_LITERAL );
   xAxisPrimary.getOrigin().setType(
      IntersectionType.VALUE_LITERAL );
   xAxisPrimary.getTitle().setVisible( false );

   Axis yAxisPrimary = newChart.getPrimaryOrthogonalAxis(
      xAxisPrimary );
   yAxisPrimary.getMajorGrid().setTickStyle(
      TickStyle.LEFT_LITERAL );
   yAxisPrimary.getScale().setMax(
      NumberDataElementImpl.create( 160 ));
   yAxisPrimary.getScale().setMin(NumberDataElementImpl
      .create( -50 ));
   yAxisPrimary.getTitle().getCaption()
      .setValue( "Sales Growth" );
```

```
// Create sample data.
SampleData sdt =
   DataFactory.eINSTANCE.createSampleData();
BaseSampleData sdBase =
   DataFactory.eINSTANCE.createBaseSampleData();
sdBase.setDataSetRepresentation("A");
sdt.getBaseSampleData().add( sdBase );

OrthogonalSampleData sdOrthogonal =
   DataFactory.eINSTANCE.createOrthogonalSampleData();
sdOrthogonal.setDataSetRepresentation( "1");
sdOrthogonal.setSeriesDefinitionIndex(0);
sdt.getOrthogonalSampleData().add( sdOrthogonal );
newChart.setSampleData(sdt);

// Create the category series.
Series seCategory = SeriesImpl.create();

// Set the data value for X-Series.
Query query = QueryImpl.create( "row[\"CATEGORY\"]" );
seCategory.getDataDefinition().add( query );

// Create the primary data set
LineSeries ls1 = ( LineSeries ) LineSeriesImpl.create();
ls1.setSeriesIdentifier( "Q1" );

// Set dthe ata value for Y-Series 1.
Query query1 = QueryImpl.create( "row[\"VALUE1\"]/1000" );
ls1.getDataDefinition().add( query1 );
ls1.getLineAttributes().setColor(ColorDefinitionImpl.RED());
for ( int i = 0; i < ls1.getMarkers( ).size( ); i++ )
{
   ( ls1.getMarkers( ).get( i ) ).setType(
      MarkerType.TRIANGLE_LITERAL );
}
ls1.getLabel().setVisible( true );

LineSeries ls2 = (LineSeries) LineSeriesImpl.create( );
ls2.setSeriesIdentifier( "Q2" );

// Set the data value for Y-Series 2.
Query query2 = QueryImpl.create( "row[\"VALUE2\"]" );
ls2.getDataDefinition().add( query2 );
ls2.getLineAttributes().setColor(
   ColorDefinitionImpl.YELLOW() );
for ( int i = 0; i < ls2.getMarkers( ).size( ); i++ )
{
   ( ls2.getMarkers( ).get( i ) ).setType(
      MarkerType.CIRCLE_LITERAL );
}
ls2.getLabel().setVisible( true );

SeriesDefinition sdX = SeriesDefinitionImpl.create();
```

```
sdX.getSeriesPalette().shift( 0 );

// Set default grouping.
SeriesGrouping grouping = sdX.getGrouping( );
grouping.setEnabled( true );
grouping.setGroupType( DataType.TEXT_LITERAL );
grouping.setGroupingUnit( GroupingUnitType.STRING_LITERAL );
grouping.setGroupingInterval( 0 );
grouping.setAggregateExpression( "Sum" ); //$NON-NLS-1$
xAxisPrimary.getSeriesDefinitions().add( sdX );
sdX.getSeries().add( seCategory );

SeriesDefinition sdY1 = SeriesDefinitionImpl.create();
sdY1.getSeriesPalette().shift( 0 );
sdY1.getSeries().add( ls1 );
yAxisPrimary.getSeriesDefinitions().add( sdY1 );

SeriesDefinition sdY2 = SeriesDefinitionImpl.create();
sdY2.getSeriesPalette().shift( 0 );
sdY2.getSeries().add( ls2 );
yAxisPrimary.getSeriesDefinitions().add( sdY2 );

// Change the aggregation for Y-Series 2.
SeriesGrouping groupingY2 = sdY2.getGrouping( );
groupingY2.setEnabled( true );
groupingY2.setAggregateExpression( "Average" );//$NON-NLS-1$

// Get a chart implementation object and set its
// chart.instance property
ElementFactory ef = dHandle.getElementFactory( );
ExtendedItemHandle extendedItemHandle =
   ef.newExtendedItem( null, "Chart" );

try{
   IReportItem chartItem =
      extendedItemHandle.getReportItem( );
   chartItem.setProperty( "chart.instance", newChart );
} catch( ExtendedElementException e ) {
      e.printStackTrace( );
}

// Get a data set and bind it to the chart.
DataSetHandle dataSet = ( DataSetHandle )
   dHandle.getDataSets( ).get( 0 );
 ComputedColumn col1 =
   StructureFactory.createComputedColumn( );
 col1.setName( "VALUE1" );
 col1.setExpression( "dataSetRow[\"QUANTITYORDERED\"]") ;
 col1.setDataType(
   DesignChoiceConstants.COLUMN_DATA_TYPE_INTEGER );
 ComputedColumn col2 =
   StructureFactory.createComputedColumn( );
 col2.setName( "VALUE2" );
```

```
        col2.setExpression( "dataSetRow[\"PRICEEACH\"]" );
        col2.setDataType(
          DesignChoiceConstants.COLUMN_DATA_TYPE_FLOAT );
        ComputedColumn col3 =
          StructureFactory.createComputedColumn( );
        col3.setName( "CATEGORY" );
        col3.setExpression( "dataSetRow[\"PRODUCTLINE\"]");
        col3.setDataType(
          DesignChoiceConstants.COLUMN_DATA_TYPE_STRING );

      try {
        extendedItemHandle.setDataSet( dataSet );
        extendedItemHandle.addColumnBinding(col1, true);
        extendedItemHandle.addColumnBinding(col2, true);
        extendedItemHandle.addColumnBinding(col3, true);
        extendedItemHandle.setHeight( "250pt" );
        extendedItemHandle.setWidth( "400pt" );
      } catch ( SemanticException e ) {
          e.printStackTrace( );
      }

      // Add the chart to the report design
      ListHandle li =  (ListHandle) dHandle.getBody( )
         .getContents( ).get( 0 );
      try {
          li.getFooter( ).add( extendedItemHandle );
        } catch ( ContentException e3 ) {
          e3.printStackTrace( );
        } catch ( NameException e3 ) { e3.printStackTrace( ); }

      // Save the report design that now contains a chart
      try {
        dHandle.saveAs( newDesignName );
      } catch ( IOException e ) { e.printStackTrace( ); }
      dHandle.close( );
     Platform.shutdown( );
     System.out.println( "Finished" );
  }
}
```

Using the BIRT charting API in a Java Swing application

The BIRT charting API does not rely on the BIRT design engine or the BIRT report engine, nor does it process a BIRT report design file. You can use the BIRT charting API to generate a chart in any Java application.

The program shown in Listing 15-24 uses the BIRT charting API to build a chart in a Java Swing application. nor does it process a BIRT report design file.

Listing 15-24 Java Swing charting application

```
import java.awt.BorderLayout;
import java.awt.Container;
import java.awt.Dimension;
import java.awt.Graphics;
import java.awt.Graphics2D;
import java.awt.Toolkit;

import java.awt.event.ComponentEvent;
import java.awt.event.ComponentListener;

import java.util.HashMap;
import java.util.Map;

import javax.swing.JFrame;
import javax.swing.JPanel;

import org.eclipse.birt.chart.api.ChartEngine;

import org.eclipse.birt.chart.device.IDeviceRenderer;
import org.eclipse.birt.chart.device.IUpdateNotifier;

import org.eclipse.birt.chart.exception.ChartException;

import org.eclipse.birt.chart.factory.GeneratedChartState;
import org.eclipse.birt.chart.factory.Generator;

import org.eclipse.birt.chart.model.Chart;
import org.eclipse.birt.chart.model.ChartWithAxes;

import org.eclipse.birt.chart.model.attribute.AxisType;
import org.eclipse.birt.chart.model.attribute.Bounds;
import org.eclipse.birt.chart.model.attribute.IntersectionType;
import org.eclipse.birt.chart.model.attribute.LegendItemType;
import org.eclipse.birt.chart.model.attribute.Position;
import org.eclipse.birt.chart.model.attribute.TickStyle;

import org.eclipse.birt.chart.model.attribute.impl.BoundsImpl;
import org.eclipse.birt.chart.model.attribute.impl
   .ColorDefinitionImpl;

import org.eclipse.birt.chart.model.component.Axis;
import org.eclipse.birt.chart.model.component.Series;

import org.eclipse.birt.chart.model.component.impl.SeriesImpl;

import org.eclipse.birt.chart.model.data.NumberDataSet;
import org.eclipse.birt.chart.model.data.SeriesDefinition;
import org.eclipse.birt.chart.model.data.TextDataSet;

import org.eclipse.birt.chart.model.data.impl.NumberDataSetImpl;
```

```
import org.eclipse.birt.chart.model.data.impl
   .SeriesDefinitionImpl;
import org.eclipse.birt.chart.model.data.impl.TextDataSetImpl;

import org.eclipse.birt.chart.model.impl.ChartWithAxesImpl;

import org.eclipse.birt.chart.model.layout.Legend;
import org.eclipse.birt.chart.model.layout.Plot;

import org.eclipse.birt.chart.model.type.BarSeries;

import org.eclipse.birt.chart.model.type.impl.BarSeriesImpl;

import org.eclipse.birt.core.framework.PlatformConfig;

/*
 * The selector of charts in Swing JPanel.
 */

public final class SwingChartingApp extends JPanel implements
      IUpdateNotifier,
      ComponentListener
{
   private static final long serialVersionUID = 1L;
   private boolean bNeedsGeneration = true;
   private GeneratedChartState gcs = null;
   private Chart cm = null;
   private IDeviceRenderer idr = null;
   private Map contextMap;

   /*
    * Create the layout with a container for displaying a chart
    */
   public static void main( String[ ] args )
   {
      SwingChartingApp scv = new SwingChartingApp( );
      JFrame jf = new JFrame( );
      jf.setDefaultCloseOperation( JFrame.DISPOSE_ON_CLOSE );
      jf.addComponentListener( scv );
      Container co = jf.getContentPane( );
      co.setLayout( new BorderLayout( ) );
      co.add( scv, BorderLayout.CENTER );

      Dimension dScreen = Toolkit.getDefaultToolkit( )
         .getScreenSize( );
      Dimension dApp = new Dimension( 800, 600 );
      jf.setSize( dApp );
      jf.setLocation( ( dScreen.width - dApp.width ) / 2,
         ( dScreen.height - dApp.height ) / 2 );
      jf.setTitle( scv.getClass( ).getName( ) + " [device="
         + scv.idr.getClass( ).getName( ) + "]" );//$NON-NLS-1$
      jf.setVisible( true );
   }
```

```
/*
 * Connect with a SWING device to render the graphics.
 */
SwingChartingApp( )
{
   contextMap = new HashMap( );
   try
   {
      PlatformConfig config = new PlatformConfig( );
      config.setProperty( "STANDALONE", "true" ); //$NON-NLS-1$
         //$NON-NLS-2$
      idr = ChartEngine.instance( config ).getRenderer(
         "dv.SWING" );//$NON-NLS-1$
   }
   catch ( ChartException ex )
   {
      ex.printStackTrace( );
   }
   cm = createBarChart( );
}
   /* Build a simple bar chart */
   public static final Chart createBarChart( )
   {
      ChartWithAxes cwaBar = ChartWithAxesImpl.create( );

      /* Plot */
      cwaBar.getBlock( )
         .setBackground( ColorDefinitionImpl.WHITE( ) );
      cwaBar.getBlock( ).getOutline( ).setVisible( true );
      Plot p = cwaBar.getPlot( );
      p.getClientArea( ).setBackground(
          ColorDefinitionImpl.create( 255, 255, 225 ) );
      p.getOutline( ).setVisible( false );

      /* Title */
      cwaBar.getTitle( ).getLabel( ).getCaption( )
         .setValue( "Bar Chart" );

      /* Legend */
      Legend lg = cwaBar.getLegend( );
      lg.getText( ).getFont( ).setSize( 16 );
      lg.setItemType( LegendItemType.CATEGORIES_LITERAL );

      /* X-Axis */
      Axis xAxisPrimary = cwaBar.getPrimaryBaseAxes( )[0];
      xAxisPrimary.setType( AxisType.TEXT_LITERAL );
      xAxisPrimary.getMajorGrid( )
         .setTickStyle( TickStyle.BELOW_LITERAL );
      xAxisPrimary.getOrigin( )
         .setType( IntersectionType.VALUE_LITERAL );
      xAxisPrimary.getTitle( ).setVisible( true );
```

```
      /* Y-Axis */
      Axis yAxisPrimary = cwaBar
         .getPrimaryOrthogonalAxis( xAxisPrimary );
      yAxisPrimary.getMajorGrid( )
         .setTickStyle( TickStyle.LEFT_LITERAL );
      yAxisPrimary.setType( AxisType.LINEAR_LITERAL );
      yAxisPrimary.getLabel( ).getCaption( ).getFont( )
         .setRotation( 90 );

      /* Data Sets */
      TextDataSet categoryValues = TextDataSetImpl
         .create( new String[]{ "Item 1", "Item 2", "Item 3"} );
      NumberDataSet orthoValues = NumberDataSetImpl
         .create( new double[]{ 25, 35, 15 } );

      /* X-Series */
      Series seCategory = SeriesImpl.create( );
      seCategory.setDataSet( categoryValues );

      SeriesDefinition sdX = SeriesDefinitionImpl.create( );
      sdX.getSeriesPalette( ).shift( 0 );
      xAxisPrimary.getSeriesDefinitions( ).add( sdX );
      sdX.getSeries( ).add( seCategory );

      /* Y-Series */
      BarSeries bs = (BarSeries) BarSeriesImpl.create( );
      bs.setDataSet( orthoValues );
      bs.setRiserOutline( null );
      bs.getLabel( ).setVisible( true );
      bs.setLabelPosition( Position.INSIDE_LITERAL );

      SeriesDefinition sdY = SeriesDefinitionImpl.create( );
      yAxisPrimary.getSeriesDefinitions( ).add( sdY );
      sdY.getSeries( ).add( bs );
      return cwaBar;
   }
public void regenerateChart( )
{
   bNeedsGeneration = true;
   repaint( );
}

public void repaintChart( )
{
   repaint( );
}

public Object peerInstance( )
{
   return this;
}
public Chart getDesignTimeModel( )
```

```
{
   return cm;
}

public Object getContext( Object key )
{
   return contextMap.get( key );
}

public Object putContext( Object key, Object value )
{
   return contextMap.put( key, value );
}

public Object removeContext( Object key )
{
   return contextMap.remove( key );
}

public Chart getRunTimeModel( )
{
   return gcs.getChartModel( );
}

public void paint( Graphics g )
{
   super.paint( g );
   Graphics2D g2d = (Graphics2D) g;
   idr.setProperty( IDeviceRenderer.GRAPHICS_CONTEXT, g2d );
   idr.setProperty( IDeviceRenderer.UPDATE_NOTIFIER, this );
   Dimension d = getSize( );
   Bounds bo = BoundsImpl.create( 0, 0, d.width, d.height );
   bo.scale( 72d / idr.getDisplayServer( ).getDpiResolution());
   Generator gr = Generator.instance( );

   if ( bNeedsGeneration ) {
      bNeedsGeneration = false;
      try {
         gcs = gr.build( idr.getDisplayServer( ),
               cm,
               bo,
               null,
               null,
               null );
      }
      catch ( ChartException ex ) {
         System.out.println( ex );
      }
   }
   try {
      gr.render( idr, gcs );
   }
```

```
        catch ( ChartException ex ) { System.out.println( ex ); }
    }

    public void componentHidden( ComponentEvent e ) { }
    public void componentMoved( ComponentEvent e ) { }
    public void componentResized( ComponentEvent e )
    {
        bNeedsGeneration = true;
    }
    public void componentShown( ComponentEvent e ) { }
}
```

Understanding the chart programming examples

The org.eclipse.birt.chart.examples plug-in is a collection of chart programming examples provided in the ChartSDK folder of the chart engine. To access the Java source code of the examples, extract the org.eclipse.birt .chart.examples.source plug-in's JAR file to your workspace. Then, import those files as a project. Include the JAR files in the BIRT home folder and the Java EE JAR file, servlet.jar, in the build path. Add further JAR files from the chart engine's ChartSDK and Eclipse home plugins folders as necessary to resolve build errors in individual examples. To run the examples, use the Eclipse Run dialog to set the VM arguments to include a line of the following form, where <Eclipse home> is the location of eclipse.exe:

```
-DBIRT_HOME="<Eclipse home>"
```

The examples are located in subdirectories of the plug-in's src/org/eclipse /birt/chart/examples directory, called EXAMPLES_ROOT. Most of the examples consist of a Java application that displays a chart. The application classes, which have a main( ) method, are called viewer applications and their class names end in Viewer. Typically, these examples use one or more additional classes to build the chart. The following sections provide brief summaries of the examples in the chart examples plug-in.

api.data examples

The api.data package contains three examples, one that displays charts in a Java Swing environment and two that modify chart items in a report design.

DataCharts example

The DataCharts example consists of DataChartsViewer, a Java Swing application that uses the DataCharts class to build a chart. DataCharts displays hard-coded data values in the charts. Depending on user selection, the application builds one of the following kinds of charts:

- A bar chart that has multiple *y*-axes

- A bar chart that has multiple *y*-series
- A pie chart that has a minimum slice

GroupOnXSeries example

The GroupOnXSeries example is a Java application that reads a BIRT report design and modifies and saves it. The original report design, NonGroupOnXSeries.rptdesign, contains a chart report item that uses data from a scripted data source. The chart item has no grouping on the *x*-series. The GroupOnXSeries Java application modifies the design so that the chart report item does group on the *x*-series. The application saves the modified report design as GroupOnXSeries.rptdesign. Open these report designs and preview the reports to see the effect of this modification.

GroupOnYAxis example

The GroupOnYAxis example is a Java application that reads a BIRT report design and modifies and saves it. The original report design, NonGroupOnYAxis.rptdesign, contains a chart report item that uses data from a scripted data source. The chart item has no grouping on the *y*-axis. The GroupOnYAxis Java application modifies the design so that the chart report item does group on the *y*-axis. The application saves the modified BIRT report design as GroupOnYAxis.rptdesign. Open these report designs and preview the reports to see the effect of this modification.

api.data.autobinding example

This example is an Eclipse SWT application that consists of the AutoDataBindingViewer class. This class instantiates an SWT Display object and adds a chart to it. The application creates data row structures, which it binds to the chart. Then, the application renders the chart.

api.format example

This example is a Java Swing application that consists of the FormatCharts and FormatChartsViewer Java classes. The FormatChartsViewer class displays an interface that presents choices to the user. Based on the user choice, FormatChartsViewer calls static methods in the FormatCharts class to build a chart. FormatChartsViewer then renders the chart. The methods in FormatCharts modify the following chart properties:

- Axis format
- Colored by category
- Legend title
- Percentage value
- Plot format

- Series format

api.interactivity examples

This set of related example applications demonstrate chart interactivity features in the three Java frameworks: SVG, Swing, and SWT. The viewer applications are SvgInteractivityViewer, SwingInteractivityViewer, and SwtInteractivityViewer. The viewer classes display an interface that presents the same interactivity choices to the user. Based on the choice, the viewer class calls static methods in InteractivityCharts to build an interactive chart. Then, the viewer renders the chart. The interactivity types in these charts are:

- Displaying tooltips
- Executing call-back code
- Highlighting a series
- Linking to an external site by using a URL
- Toggling the visibility of a series

api.pdf example

This example is a Java application that builds a simple chart and renders it as a PDF file. The classes in the PDFChartGenerator example are ChartModels and PDFChartGenerator. ChartModels has a single method that builds a simple chart using hard-coded data values. PDFChartGenerator uses the BIRT charting API to render the chart into PDF format. The application saves the PDF file as test.pdf.

api.preference example

This example shows how a Java servlet can process URL parameters to set style preferences for a chart. The servlet class, PreferenceServlet, uses the ChartModels class to generate a chart. The servlet uses the style parameters in the LabelStyleProcessor class to affect the style of a label in the chart. The example also includes a help page, Help.htm, that explains how to:

- Develop chart pages using JSPs and servlets.
- Run the Preference example.
- Set up Eclipse to work with Tomcat.

api.processor example

This example builds a simple chart and applies styles to text in the chart. The example consists of StyleChartViewer, an SWT application, and StyleProcessor, which implements the IStyleProcessor interface to create a style object. StyleChartViewer creates a chart and applies the style to text in the chart. Finally, StyleChartViewer renders the chart.

api.script examples

This example consists of two SWT applications, JavaScriptViewer and JavaViewer. Both applications present the same set of choices to the user. The appearance of the chart that appears for a particular user choice is the same for both viewers. Each choice calls a static method in the ScriptCharts class to create a chart and displays the event handlers that the chart implements. JavaScriptViewer calls ScriptCharts methods to build charts that have JavaScript event handlers. JavaViewer calls ScriptCharts methods to build charts that have Java event handlers.

The ScriptCharts class illustrates techniques for creating charts having report element event handlers. Methods in this class create charts having report element event handlers written in JavaScript. Each JavaScript event handler is defined as a single string in ScriptCharts. A further set of methods creates charts having the same functionality using report element event handlers written in Java. The Java event handlers are Java classes that are located in EXAMPLES_ROOT/api/script/java. The ScriptCharts methods that define a Java event handler pass a string containing the path of the Java class.

api.viewer examples

The api.viewer package contains example applications that create a wide variety of charts. Each class creates and displays a set of charts based on user choices. Each viewer class, except SwingLiveChartViewer.java, calls static methods in the PrimitiveCharts class to create the chart to display. PrimitiveCharts uses hard-coded data values for each chart.

Chart3DViewer example

Chart3DViewer.java is an SWT application that displays the following chart types:

- 3D area chart
- 3D bar chart
- 3D line chart

CurveFittingViewer example

CurveFittingViewer.java is an SWT application that displays the following chart types:

- Curve fitting area chart
- Curve fitting bar chart
- Curve fitting line chart
- Curve fitting stock chart

DialChartViewer example

DialChartViewer.java is an SWT application that displays the following chart types:

- Multiple-dial, multiple-region chart
- Multiple-dial, single-region chart
- Single-dial, multiple-region chart
- Single-dial, single-region chart

SwingChartViewerSelector example

SwingChartViewerSelector.java is a Swing application that supports showing the same data values in different ways. For each chart type, the user can choose to show the chart as two-dimensional or two-dimensional with depth. The user can also choose to display the chart with axes transposed, with the values shown as percentages, or on a logarithmic scale. Some choices are available only for charts with axes. SwingChartViewerSelector displays the following chart types:

- Area chart
- Bar and line stacked chart
- Bar chart
- Bar chart that has two series
- Bubble chart
- Difference chart
- Line chart
- Pie chart
- Pie chart that has four series
- Scatter chart
- Stock chart

SwingLiveChartViewer example

SwingChartLiveChartViewer.java is a Swing application that displays a live, animated chart with scrolling data.

SWTChartViewerSelector example

SWTChartViewerSelector.java is an SWT application that displays the same user interface choices and chart types as SwingChartViewerSelector.java.

builder example

The builder example consists of two Java classes, ChartWizardLauncher and DefaultDataServiceProviderImpl. ChartWizardLauncher attempts to read a chart from testCharts.chart. If the file exists, ChartWizardLauncher modifies that file. If the file does not exist, the application creates a new file. ChartWizardLauncher uses the BIRT chart wizard to create the chart. DefaultDataServiceProviderImpl provides a basic implementation of a simulated data service.

radar.ui example

The radar.ui example consists of the classes that provide the user interface pages for the radar chart.

report.api examples

The three report.api examples are all Java applications that have no user interface. These examples use the BIRT design engine to build a new BIRT report design file in the chart example plug-in's output folder. All the report examples add the following components to the report design file in the order shown:

- Master page
- Data source
- Data set
- A chart element in the body of the report

All the report examples use the BIRT charting API to add a chart to the body slot of the report design. After running these applications, open the new report design file and preview the report to see the chart.

MeterChartExample example

The MeterChartExample example adds a meter chart to the report design. The name of the report design is MeterChartExample.rptdesign.

SalesReport example

The SalesReport example creates styles and adds a pie chart to the report design. The name of the report design is SalesReport.rptdesign.

StockReport example

The StockReport example adds a stock chart to the report design. The name of the report design is StockAnalysis.rptdesign.

report.design examples

The report designs in this folder demonstrate ways to display chart elements in a report design. BarChartWithinTableGroup.rptdesign shows how to use a chart in a table element. BarChartWithJavascript.rptdesign shows how to use JavaScript to modify the rendered chart when a user views the report. DynamicSeriesPieChart.rptdesign shows how to customize a pie chart.

report.design.script examples

The report designs in this folder contain chart elements that use the same JavaScript event handlers that the api.script examples create dynamically. These report designs show how the scripts appear in BIRT Report Designer.

view example

The view folder and its subfolders include the content for the Eclipse view, Chart Examples. To open this view, from the Eclipse main menu, choose Window➛Show View➛Other. On Show View, expand Report and Chart Design, then select Chart Examples and choose OK. By default, the Chart Examples view appears below the main window, in the same position as the console window. To use the Chart Examples view, expand a node on the left of the view, then select an item. The selected chart appears on the right of the view, as shown in Figure 15-1.

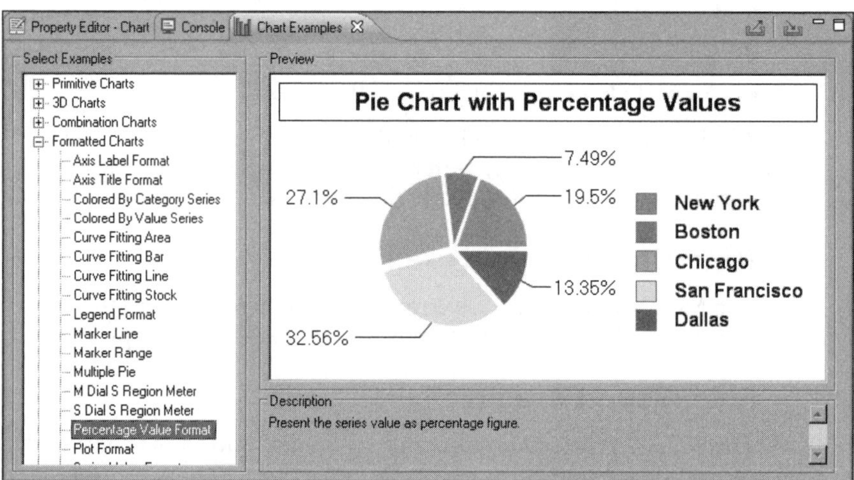

Figure 15-1 Chart Examples view, showing the percentage value format example

To view the source code of the application that generates the selected chart, choose Open Java Source from the toolbar.

To save the XML of the chart item structure, choose Save XML Source from the toolbar.

Part

V

Working with the Extension Framework

Chapter

16

Building the BIRT Project

This chapter explains how to build the BIRT project. The chapter also explains how to build a new web viewer that employs your modifications to BIRT.

This information is primarily for contributors to the BIRT open source project and to those who want to create a custom version of BIRT. The typical user does not need to build BIRT to extend BIRT or to write scripts for BIRT.

After the build process completes, you can explore the BIRT source code and make changes to the code to suit your needs. Any changes made to the BIRT source are immediately implemented in the BIRT Report Designer. To implement your changes in a web application, you must build and export a new web viewer.

About building the BIRT project

Building the BIRT project consists of the following tasks:

- Installing a working version of BIRT Report Designer

  By first installing the same version of BIRT Report Designer that you want to build, you ensure that your Eclipse environment is correct and that you have all the necessary components for building BIRT.

- Configuring Eclipse to compile BIRT

  You may need to change the compiler settings to match those required to build BIRT. Installing the Eclipse SDK is required to use some extension points.

- Downloading and extracting the correct version of the BIRT source code

  Download the BIRT source code from the Eclipse web site. Builds move around as new builds are added, so use search to find the appropriate version. The downloaded version and the working version on your system must be identical.

- Importing and building the BIRT projects

  The act of importing the BIRT projects initiates the build process. The build process takes a few minutes and should complete with no errors.

Installing a working version of BIRT

To ensure that you have all the components that are necessary for building BIRT, first install a working version of BIRT Report Designer. Ensure that all the plug-ins and auxiliary files BIRT requires are present and that these resources are the versions the source code requires.

The simplest and surest way to know that you have all the necessary components of a working BIRT installation is to choose the Full Eclipse Install option. After installing this package, install the BIRT SDK. Follow the instructions in the installation chapters at the beginning of this book.

After installing BIRT, launch Eclipse and open the Report Design perspective. Verify that you can build a simple report and that you can preview the report in both the BIRT previewer and the web viewer. Typically, this test is sufficient to guarantee that you have a valid working version of BIRT. Of course, you can run more extensive tests to confirm access to any custom items in your environment, for example, custom data sources.

Configuring Eclipse to compile BIRT and build the viewer JAR files

Before importing the BIRT source code into a workspace, check that the Java compiler settings on the workspace are compatible with BIRT. The 2.6 version of the BIRT source code uses some features that are only present in JDK version 1.5 and higher. Some plug-ins depend on other modules that require Java version 1.5 and are not compatible with Java version 1.6. In order for BIRT to build successfully, you need to set the Eclipse compiler compliance to Java 1.5. Set this version for your Eclipse workspace by starting Eclipse and setting Eclipse preferences. Ensure that you apply these settings to any workspace you use to work with BIRT.

To build the viewer Java archive (JAR) files, the JAVA_HOME variable in your system must reference the installed JRE specified in the workspace compiler preferences.

In BIRT 2.6, some extension points refer to files that are not present in the BIRT Full Eclipse Install. For these extension points to locate the required files, install the Helios Eclipse SDK.

How to set Eclipse workspace compiler preferences

1 In BIRT Report Designer, choose Window➛Preferences.

2 In Preferences, expand the Java entry in the tree and select Installed JREs. In Installed JREs, select a Java 1.5 JRE, as shown in Figure 16-1.

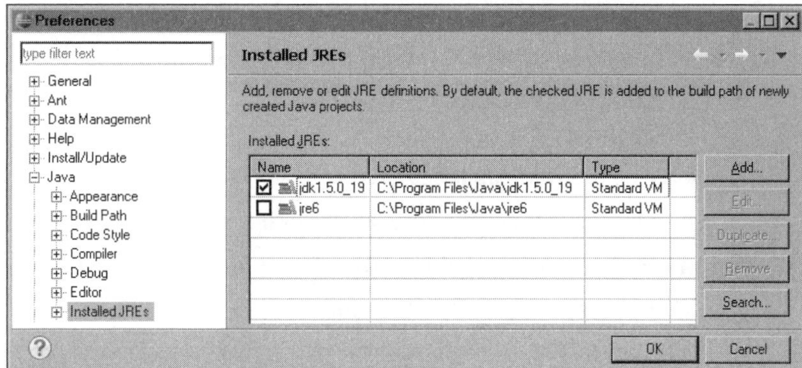

Figure 16-1 Selecting a Java 1.5 JRE

3 Select Compiler. In Compiler, as shown in Figure 16-2, perform the following steps:

- In JDK Compliance, select 1.5 in Compiler compliance level.
- In Classfile Generation, select all the available options.

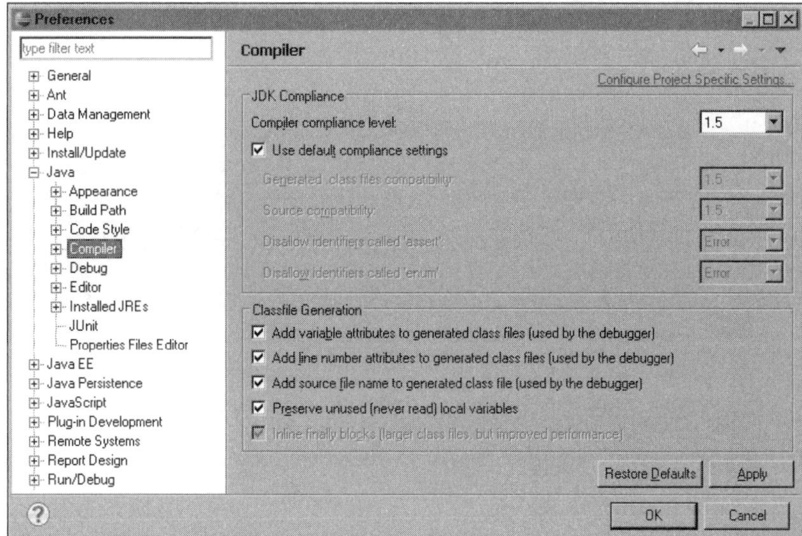

Figure 16-2 Compiler preferences

Choose OK.

If a message appears asking if you want to do a full rebuild now, choose No. This message appears only if you changed the compiler settings and there are Java projects in the workspace.

How to install the Eclipse SDK

Install the Eclipse SDK to avoid missing file references in some extension points in BIRT 2.6.

1. In BIRT Report Designer, choose Help➤Install New Software.
2. In Install, as shown in Figure 16-3, perform the following steps:
   - In Work with, select:

     ```
     The Eclipse Project Updates - http://download.eclipse.org
       /eclipse/updates/3.6
     ```

   - Deselect Show only the latest versions of available software
   - In the list of available software, expand Eclipse SDK. Select:

     ```
     Eclipse SDK 3.6.0.I20100608-0911
     ```

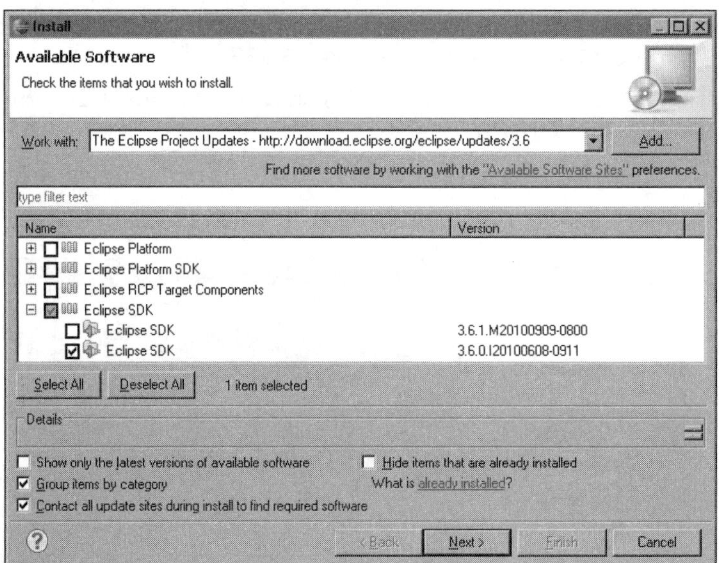

Figure 16-3 Selecting the Eclipse SDK

   Choose Next.

3. Expand the list of software, as shown in Figure 16-4.

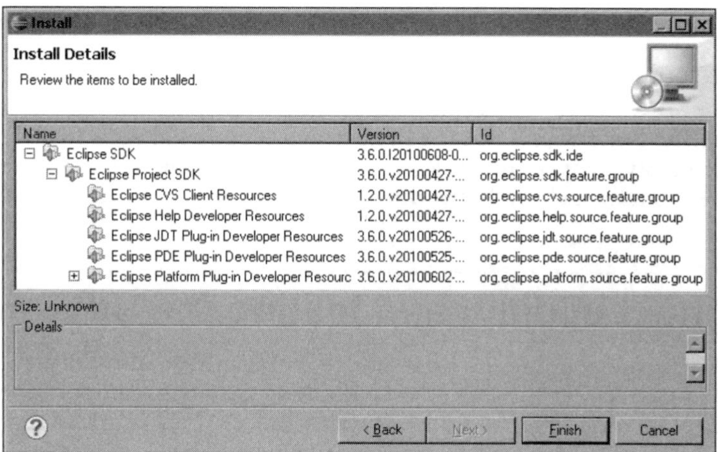

Figure 16-4 Reviewing the list of software to install

Choose Finish. Eclipse installs the new software, as shown in Figure 16-5.

Figure 16-5 Installing the Eclipse SDK

4 In the message that appears, as shown in Figure 16-6, choose Restart Now.

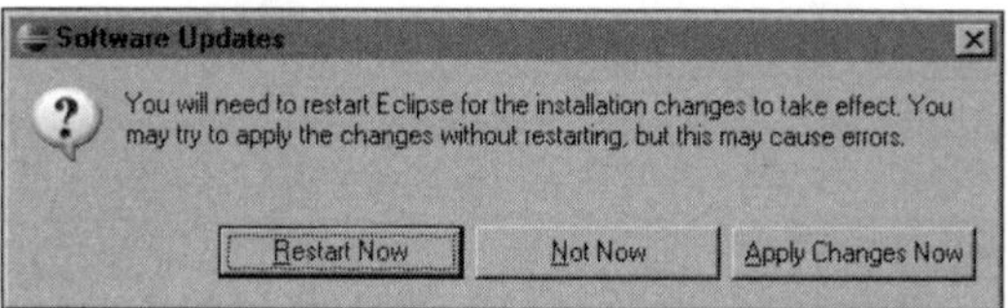

Figure 16-6 Preparing to restart Eclipse

Select the workspace for the BIRT source code when Eclipse restarts.

Downloading and extracting the correct version of the BIRT source code

Download the BIRT source code from the same page from which you downloaded the working version of BIRT. The source archive is in the section labeled BIRT Source Code. The archive file has a name similar to birt-source-2_6_0.zip.

Extract the source code archive into a workspace directory. Typically, you use a workspace for BIRT source code that is separate from workspaces used for report development. A separate workspace is not required, but keeps your report workspace less cluttered. If your workspace contains source code from a BIRT build that is not the same as the plug-ins in your Eclipse home directory, Eclipse runs BIRT using the source code in preference to the plug-ins from the Eclipse home directory.

Importing, building, and testing the BIRT project

After downloading the BIRT source, import the feature files, plug-in files, and source files to your workspace. A single Eclipse import operation imports the source files into a workspace and builds the projects.

How to import and build the BIRT project

Use the Java perspective to import and build the BIRT project.

1 Choose Window➛Perspective➛Other➛Plug-in Development. The Plug-in Development perspective opens.

2 To import the BIRT source-code projects, choose File➛Import.

3 In Import, expand General. Select Existing Projects into Workspace, as shown in Figure 16-7.

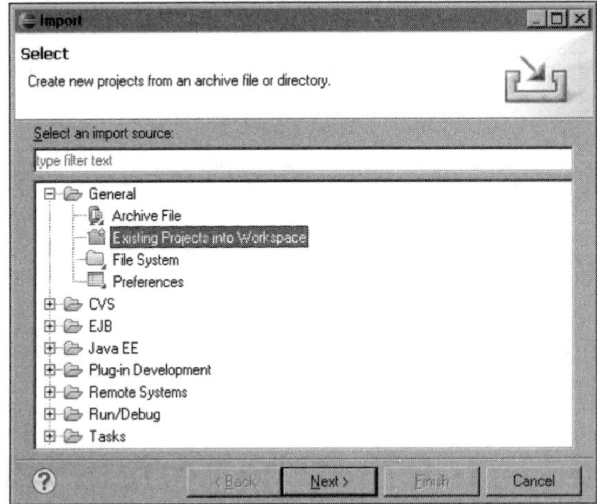

Figure 16-7 Import Project showing expanded General node

Choose Next.

4 In Import Projects, next to Select root directory, choose Browse and navigate to the workspace. A list of all the BIRT source-code projects appears in the Projects pane.

5 Choose Select All, as shown in Figure 16-8. Then, choose Finish.

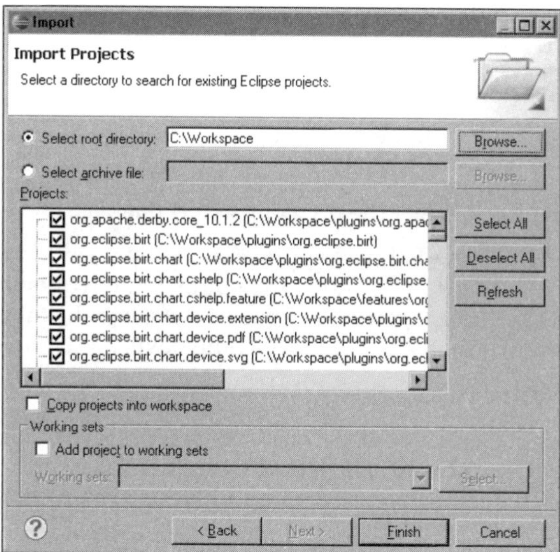

Figure 16-8 Selecting the BIRT source-codeprojects

Eclipse refreshes the workspace, then builds all the projects in a process that can take several minutes. When the build finishes with no errors, the workspace looks like the one shown in Figure 16-9.

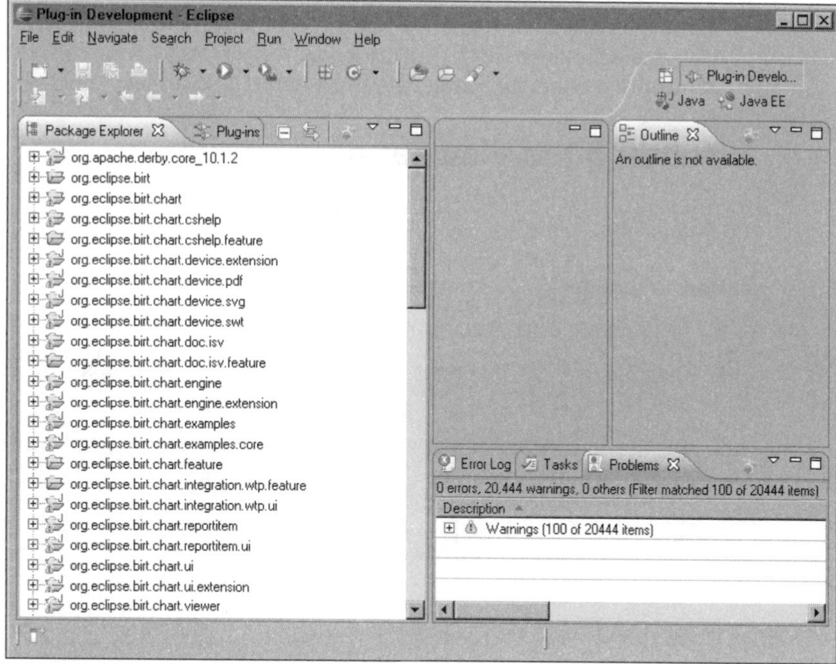

Figure 16-9 Build results showing no errors

If errors appear in the Problems view, use the Eclipse workbench tools to check and correct the project build path.

How to test the BIRT project

To test the BIRT project, run the org.eclipse.birt package as an Eclipse application.

1 In Package Explorer, select the org.eclipse.birt package.

2 Choose Run➛Run As➛Eclipse Application. Eclipse builds a new default workspace. On a Windows system, the name of the workspace is C:\runtime-EclipseApplication. Eclipse opens a new instance of the Eclipse workbench that shows the welcome page.

3 Close the welcome page.

4 Open the Report Design perspective. Choose Window➛Open Perspective➛Report Design. If Report Design is not available, choose Other. On Open Perspective, select Report Design, then choose OK.

   To test this perspective that Eclipse built from the BIRT source code, create report projects and report designs.

Building new JAR files to display BIRT output

To make changes to the BIRT source, recreate the files that the web viewer uses to display the BIRT output. For a report, this file is viewservlets.jar. For stand-alone chart viewing, this file is chart-viewer.jar.

Building the viewservlets.jar file

You build viewservlets.jar in the org.eclipse.birt.report.viewer plug-in project. The following procedure shows how to build this file using Eclipse.

How to regenerate the viewservlets.jar file

1 In Package Explorer, expand org.eclipse.birt.report.viewer.

2 In org.eclipse.birt.report.viewer, expand META-INF and right-click MANIFEST.MF.

3 From the context menu, choose PDE Tools➛Create Ant Build File, as shown in Figure 16-10.

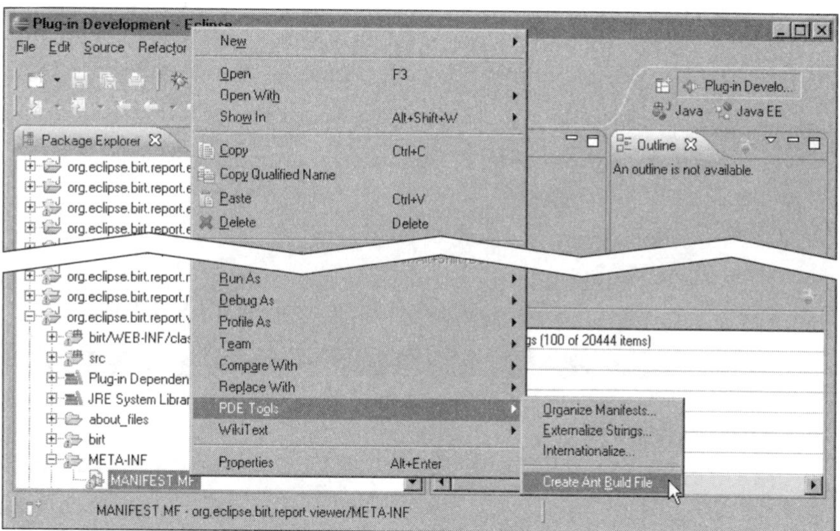

Figure 16-10 Choosing Create Ant Build File

Eclipse creates build.xml in the org.eclipse.birt.report.viewer root folder.

4 In the org.eclipse.birt.report.viewer folder, right-click build.xml and choose Run As➤Ant Build, as shown in Figure 16-11.

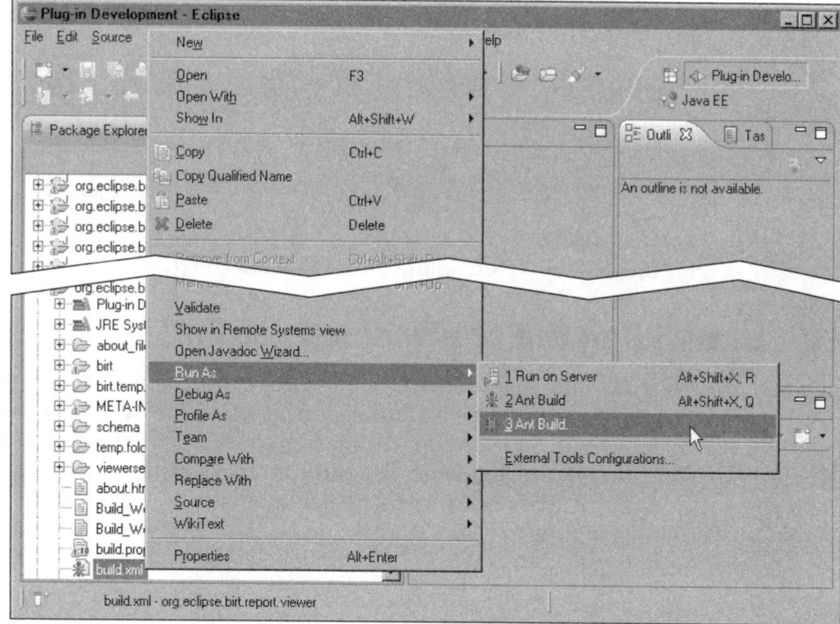

Figure 16-11 Setting up the Ant build to create viewservlets.jar

5 In Edit Configuration, in Arguments, select Main. In Arguments, set the value of buildDirectory to the path to your Eclipse home, by typing a line similar using the following syntax, as shown in Figure 16-12:

```
-DbuildDirectory=<Eclipse home>
```

If the path to your Eclipse home contains spaces, enclose the path in quotation marks.

Choose Apply. Then, choose Run.

The Ant build process takes several minutes and creates viewservlets.jar in org.eclipse.birt.report.viewer/birt/WEB-INF/lib.

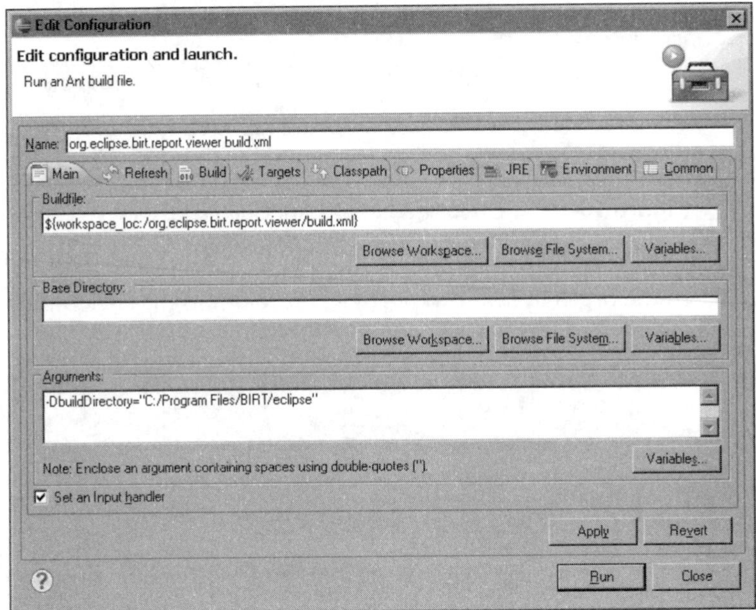

Figure 16-12 Setting the value of buildDirectory

Building the chart-viewer.jar file

If you make changes to the charting source, you typically generate a new chart-viewer.jar file. Use a similar procedure to the one for recreating viewservlets.jar. To build chart-viewer.jar, perform the procedure in org.eclipse.birt.chart.viewer. The build process creates chart-viewer.jar in the org.eclipse.birt.chart.viewer root directory.

Chapter

17

Extending BIRT

This chapter provides an overview of the BIRT extension framework and shows how to create and deploy a BIRT extension using the Eclipse Plug-in Development Environment (PDE).

Overview of the extension framework

BIRT is a set of plug-in extensions that support adding reporting functionality to an application. The BIRT APIs define extension points that support a developer adding custom functionality to this framework. Report developers find the BIRT source code in the Eclipse CVS repository.

In the Eclipse installation, the name of a plug-in directory has an appended version number. For simplicity, this book does not show the version number in the names of the plug-in directories. For example, the book abbreviates the name of the plug-in directory, org.eclipse.birt.report.viewer_2.6.0.v20100605, to org.eclipse.birt.report.viewer.

The following sections provide a general description of how to make an extension to a defined extension point in the BIRT release 2.6 framework.

Understanding the structure of a BIRT plug-in

An Eclipse plug-in implements the following components:

- Extension point schema definition
  An XML document specifying a grammar to follow when defining the elements of a plug-in extension in the Eclipse PDE

- Plug-in manifest

  An XML document describing the plug-in activation framework to the Eclipse run-time environment

- Plug-in run-time class

  A Java class defining the methods to use when starting, managing, and stopping a plug-in instance

The following sections provide detailed descriptions of these Eclipse plug-in components.

Understanding an extension point schema definition file

A plug-in directory typically contains an XML extension point schema definition (.exsd) file in a schema subdirectory. The XML schema documents the elements, attributes, and types used by the extension point. The Eclipse PDE uses this information to describe the elements and attributes in the property editors and other facilities available in the Eclipse platform.

To develop the plug-in content, test, and deploy a plug-in, use the Eclipse PDE. The Eclipse PDE generates the plugin.xml, build.properties, and run-time archive files.

The file, $INSTALL_DIR\eclipse\plugins\org.eclipse.birt.report.designer.ui\schema\reportitemUI.exsd, documents the settings for a report item extension to the BIRT Report Designer user interface. This XML schema file has the following structure:

- <schema> is the root element that sets the target namespace and contains all other elements and their attributes.
- <annotation> contains the following attributes:
  - <appinfo> provides machine-readable metadata that Eclipse uses to identify the plug-in. <appinfo> also provides textual information that appears in the PDE Extensions page and HTML extension point description.
  - <documentation> provides user information that appears in the PDE HTML extension point description.
- <element> declares a reference for the model and optional user interface extensions, such as builder, palette, editor, outline, and description. Each extension element is a complex type containing attributes and annotations, as described below:
  - model is an extension element that specifies the Report Object Model (ROM) name for the report item extension.
  - Each user interface extension element specifies the extension element name and the fully qualified name of the Java class implementing the interface specified for the extension element. For example, builder

implements the interface, org.eclipse.birt.report.designer.ui .extensions.IReportItemBuilderUI.

Listing 17-1 is a partial schema example showing reportitemUI.exsd. The ellipses (…) mark the places in the code where lines are omitted.

Listing 17-1 Partial example schema for Report Item UI

```
<?xml version='1.0' encoding='UTF-8'?>
<!-- Schema file written by PDE -->
<schema targetNamespace="org.eclipse.birt.report.designer.ui"
   xmlns="http://www.w3.org/2001/XMLSchema">
   <annotation>
      <appInfo>
         <meta.schema
            plugin="org.eclipse.birt.report.designer.ui"
            id="reportitemUI"
            name="Report Item UI Extension Point"/>
      </appInfo>
      <documentation>
         This extension point is used in conjunction with the
         Report Item extension point defined in the model. It
         is used to register the GUI to be used for the
         Extended report item.
      </documentation>
   </annotation>
   <element name="extension">
      …
      <complexType>
         <sequence>
            …
            <element ref="model"/>
            <element ref="builder" minOccurs="0" maxOccurs="1"/>
            <element ref="palette" minOccurs="0" maxOccurs="1"/>
            <element ref="editor" minOccurs="0" maxOccurs="1"/>
            <element ref="outline" minOccurs="0" maxOccurs="1"/>
            <element ref="description" minOccurs="0"
               maxOccurs="1"/>
         </sequence>
         <attribute name="point" type="string" use="required">
         …
         </attribute>
      </complexType>
   </element>
   <element name="model">
      <complexType>
         <attribute name="extensionName" type="string"
            use="required">
            <annotation>
               <documentation>
                  The ROM Report Item Extension name that maps
                  to this UI
```

```
            </documentation>
         </annotation>
      </attribute>
   </complexType>
</element>
...
<element name="builder">
   <annotation>
      <documentation>
         Optional Builder for the element inside the Editor.
         Instantiated when a new item is dragged from the
         palette inside the editor.
      </documentation>
   </annotation>
   <complexType>
      <attribute name="class" type="string">
         <annotation>
            <documentation>
               a fully qualified name of the Java class
               implementing org.eclipse.birt.report
               .designer.ui.extensions.IReportItemBuilderUI
            </documentation>
            <appInfo>
               <meta.attribute kind="java"/>
            </appInfo>
         </annotation>
      </attribute>
   </complexType>
</element>
...
</schema>
```

Understanding a plug-in manifest file

Install an Eclipse plug-in in a subdirectory of the $INSTALL_DIR/eclipse /plugins directory. The plug-in manifest file, plugin.xml, describes the plug-in activation framework to the Eclipse run-time environment.

At run time, Eclipse scans the subdirectories in $INSTALL_DIR/eclipse /plugins, parses the contents of each plug-in manifest file, and caches the information in the plug-in registry. If the Eclipse run time requires an extension, Eclipse lazily loads the plug-in, using the registry information to instantiate the plug-in objects. The run-time environment for the BIRT Report Engine functions in a similar way.

The plug-in manifest file declares the required plug-in code and extension points to the plug-in registry. The plug-in run-time class provides the code segment. By lazily loading this code segment, the run-time environment minimizes start-up time and conserves memory resources.

The plug-in manifest file, plugin.xml, has the following structure:

- <plugin> is the root element.
- <extension> specifies extension points, related elements, and attributes that define the processing capabilities of the plug-in component.

Listing 17-2 shows the contents of the plug-in manifest file, org.eclipse.birt.sample.reportitem.rotatedlabel/plugin.xml. This file describes the required classes and extension points for the BIRT report item extension sample, rotated label.

Listing 17-2 Sample plug-in manifest file

```
<?xml version="1.0" encoding="UTF-8"?>
<?eclipse version="3.2"?>
<plugin>
   <extension
      id="rotatedLabel"
      name="Rotated Label Extension"
      point="org.eclipse.birt.report.designer.ui
         .reportitemUI">
      <reportItemLabelUI
         class="org.eclipse.birt.sample.reportitem
            .rotatedlabel.RotatedLabelUI"/>
      <model extensionName="RotatedLabel"/>
      <palette icon="icons/rotatedlabel.jpg"/>
      <editor
         canResize="true"
         showInDesigner="true"
         showInMasterPage="true"/>
      <outline icon="icons/rotatedlabel.jpg"/>
   </extension>
   <extension
      id="rotatedLabel"
      name="Rotated Label Extension"
      point="org.eclipse.birt.report.model.reportItemModel">
      <reportItem
         class="org.eclipse.birt.sample.reportitem
            .rotatedlabel.RotatedLabelItemFactoryImpl"
         extensionName="RotatedLabel">
         <property
            defaultDisplayName="Display Text"
            defaultValue="Rotated Label"
            name="displayText"
            type="string"/>
         <property
            defaultDisplayName="Rotation Angle"
            defaultValue="-45"
            name="rotationAngle"
            type="string"/>
```

```
      </reportItem>
   </extension>
   <extension
      id="rotatedLabel"
      name="Rotated Label Extension
      point="org.eclipse.birt.report.engine.reportitem
         Presentation">
      <reportItem
         class="org.eclipse.birt.sample.reportitem.rotated
            label.RotatedLabelPresentationImpl"
         name="RotatedLabel"/>
   </extension>
   <extension
      point="org.eclipse.birt.report.designer.ui
         .elementAdapters">
         <adaptable
            class="org.eclipse.birt.report.model.api
               .ExtendedItemHandle">
            <adapter
               factory="org.eclipse.birt.sample.reportitem
                  .rotatedlabel.views
                  .RotatedLabelPageGeneratorFactory"
               id="ReportDesign.AttributeView
                  .RotatedLabelPageGenerator"
               priority="1"
               singleton="false"
               type="org.eclipse.birt.report.designer.ui
                  .views.IPageGenerator">
               <enablement>
                  <test
                     forcePluginActivation="true"
                     property="ExtendItemHandle.extensionName"
                     value="RotatedLabel">
                  </test>
               </enablement>
            </adapter>
         </adaptable>
   </extension>
   </plugin>
```

Understanding a plug-in run-time class

A plug-in runs within an instance of a plug-in run-time class. A plug-in run-time class extends org.eclipse.core.runtime.Plugin, the abstract superclass for all plug-in run-time class implementations. The Plugin run-time class defines the methods for starting, managing, and stopping a plug-in instance.

The Plugin run-time class typically contains a reference to an Open Services Gateway Initiative (OSGi) resource bundle that manages the execution context. Plugin implements the interface, org.osgi.framework .BundleActivator, which installs, starts, stops, and uninstalls the OSGi resource bundle. The OSGi resource bundle implements a service registry to support the following services:

- Installing and uninstalling the resource bundle
- Subscribing to an event
- Registering a service object
- Retrieving a service reference

The OSGi platform provides a secure, managed, extensible Java framework for downloading, deploying, and managing service applications. For more information about the OSGi platform, visit the OSGi Alliance web site at http://www.osgi.org/.

Listing 17-3 is a code example showing the life cycle and resource bundle methods for the report item plug-in, rotated label.

Listing 17-3 Sample code for the rotated label report item plug-in

```
package org.eclipse.birt.sample.reportitem.rotatedlabel;
import org.eclipse.core.runtime.Plugin;
import org.osgi.framework.BundleContext;
/**
 * The activator class controls the plug-in life cycle
 */
public class RotatedLabelPlugin extends Plugin {
   // The Plugin ID
   public final static String PLUGIN_ID =
      "org.eclipse.birt.sample.reportitem.rotatedlabel";
   //The shared instance.
   private static RotatedLabelPlugin plugin;
   /**
    * The constructor.
    */
   public RotatedLabelPlugin( ) {
   }
   /**
    * This method is called upon plug-in activation
    */
   public void start(BundleContext context) throws Exception {
      super.start(context);
      plugin = this;
   }
   /**
    * This method is called when the plug-in is stopped
    */
   public void stop(BundleContext context) throws Exception {
      plugin = null;
      super.stop(context);
   }
```

```
    /**
     * Returns the shared instance.
     */
    public static RotatedLabelPlugin getDefault() {
        return plugin;
    }
}
```

Working with the Eclipse PDE

The Eclipse PDE is an integrated design tool used to create, develop, test, debug, and deploy a plug-in. The PDE provides wizards, editors, views, and launchers to assist in developing a plug-in.

The Eclipse PDE provides a wizard, the New Plug-in Project wizard, to assist in setting up a plug-in project and creating the framework for a plug-in extension. The PDE wizard generates the plug-in manifest file, plugin.xml, and optionally, the Java plug-in run-time class.

How to choose the Plug-in Development perspective

To access the PDE, choose the Plug-in Development perspective. To open the Plug-in Development perspective, perform the following tasks:

1 From the Eclipse menu, choose Window➛Open Perspective➛Other. Open Perspective appears.

2 Select Plug-in Development, as shown in Figure 17-1.

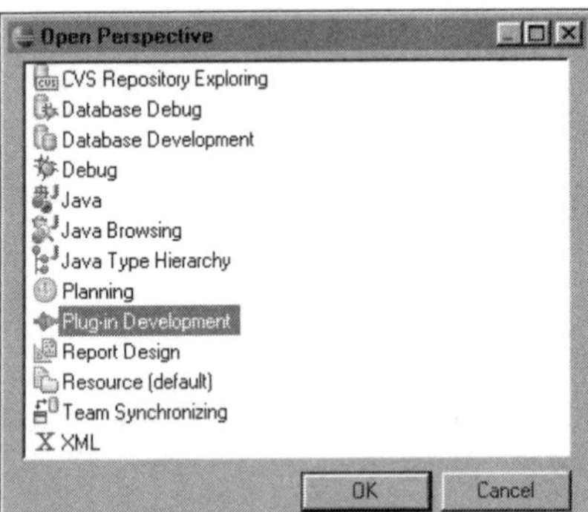

Figure 17-1 Selecting a perspective

Choose OK. The Plug-in Development perspective appears.

How to set up a new plug-in project

To access the New Plug-in Project wizard and create a project, perform the following tasks:

1 From the PDE menu, choose File➛New➛Project. New Project appears.

2 In Wizards, expand Plug-in Development, and select Plug-in Project, as shown in Figure 17-2.

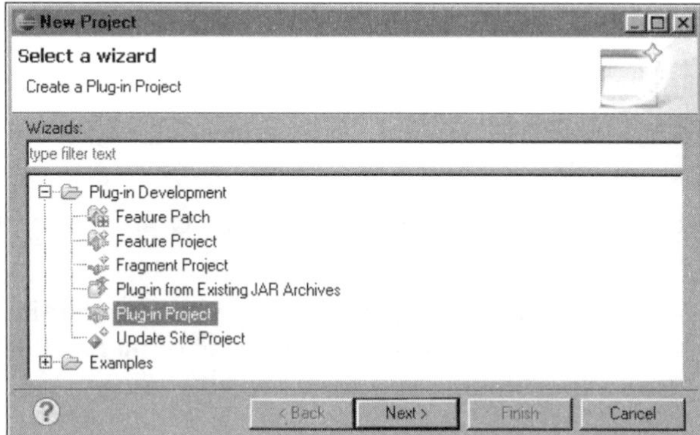

Figure 17-2 Creating a plug-in project

Choose Next. New Plug-in Project appears, as shown in Figure 17-3.

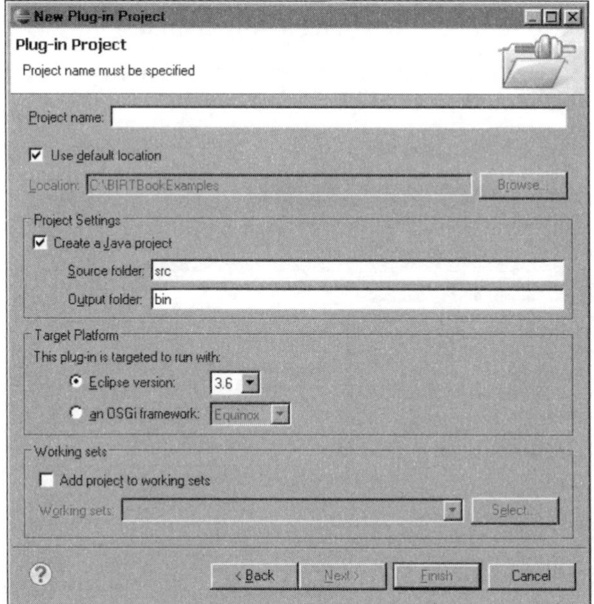

Figure 17-3 Specifying a plug-in project

Understanding plug-in project properties

The New Plug-in Project wizard defines the following properties for the plug-in:

- Project settings
  - Name

   - Location
   - Source and output folders
   - Target platform, specifying the Eclipse version or OSGi framework
- Plug-in content
   - Properties such as ID, version, name, provider, and the run-time library classpath
   - Generation of an activator, a Java class that controls the plug-in's life cycle

Specifying the OSGi framework creates an OSGi bundle manifest, META-INF/ MANIFEST.MF, which contains a set of manifest headers that provide descriptive information about the bundle.

Understanding the Eclipse PDE Workbench

The Eclipse PDE supports host and run-time instances of the workbench project. The host instance provides the development environment. The run-time instance supports launching a plug-in to test it.

Figure 17-4 shows the project for the report item extension sample, rotated label, in the host instance of the PDE Workbench.

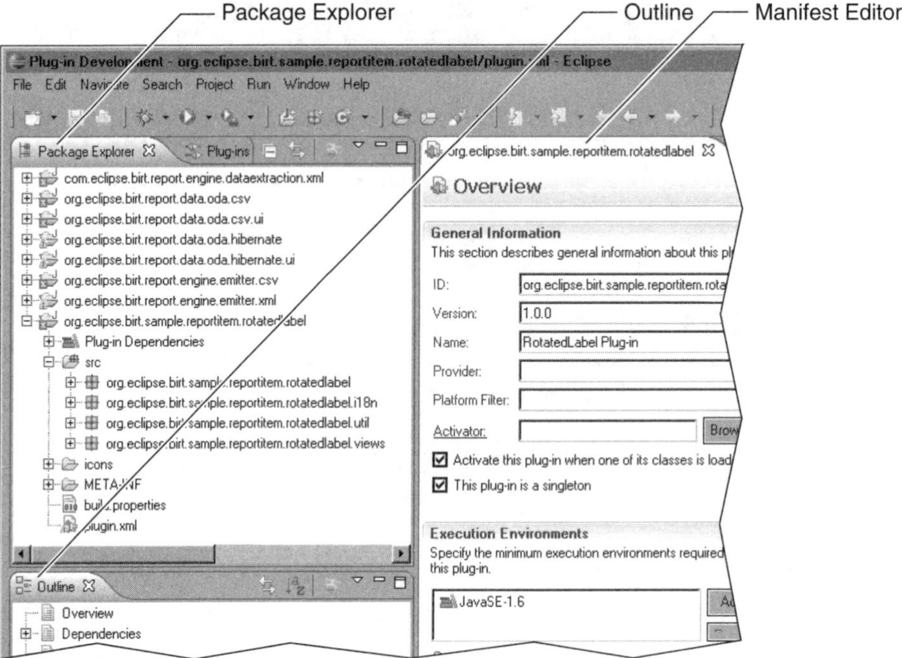

Figure 17-4 Viewing the host instance of the PDE Workbench

In the host instance, the PDE Workbench provides the following view and editor components:

- Package Explorer provides an expandable view of the plug-in package.
- Outline provides an expandable view of the project settings.
- PDE Manifest Editor displays a page containing the project settings for the currently selected item in Outline.

In PDE Manifest Editor, specify project settings and edit related files to create the plug-in framework on the following pages:

- Overview

  List general information such as the plug-in ID, version, name, provider, platform filter, and activator class. This page also contains sections that link to the plug-in content pages, extensions, launchers for testing and debugging, deployment wizards, and the settings for the execution environment.

- Dependencies

  List the plug-ins that must be on the classpath to compile and run.

- Runtime

  Declare the packages the plug-in exposes to clients. Identifies the package visibility to other plug-ins and the libraries and folders in the plug-in classpath.

- Extensions

  Declare the extensions the plug-in makes to the platform and provides extension details, such as the extension point ID, name, description, and schema.

- Extension Points

  Declare the new extension points the plug-in adds to the platform.

- Build

  Displays the build configuration settings. A change to a setting on this page updates the file, build.properties.

- MANIFEST.MF

  Displays an editable page containing the header settings for the manifest file, MANIFEST.MF, that provides descriptive information about an OSGi bundle.

- Plug-in.xml

  Displays an editable page containing settings for the plug-in manifest file, plugin.xml.

- Build.properties

  Displays an editable page containing settings for the file, build.properties.

A modification to a setting in a PDE Manifest Editor page automatically updates the corresponding plug-in manifest or build properties file.

Creating the structure of a plug-in extension

Use the host instance of the PDE Workbench to create the basic structure of a plug-in extension by performing the following tasks:

- Specify the plug-in dependencies
- Verify the plug-in run-time archive
- Specify the plug-in extension

How to specify the plug-in dependencies

1 On PDE Manifest Editor, choose Overview.

2 In Plug-in Content, choose Dependencies.

3 In Required Plug-ins, choose Add.

4 In Plug-in Selection, select a plug-in, such as the following example, as shown in Figure 17-5:

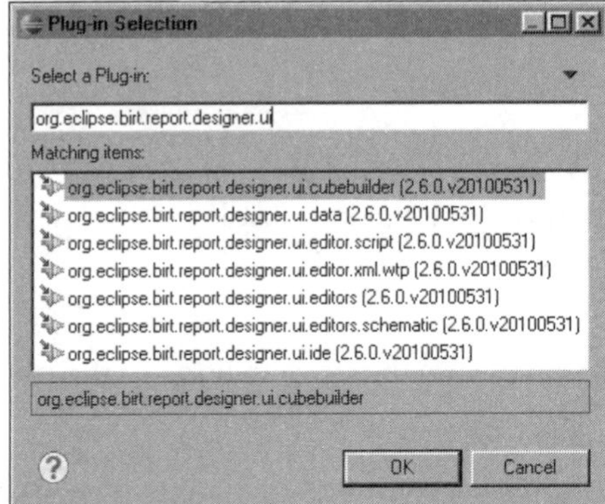

Figure 17-5 Specifying a plug-in dependency

Choose OK.

5 Repeat steps 2 and 3 to add more plug-ins to the list of required plug-ins in the Dependencies page.

In Required Plug-ins, the order of the list determines the sequence in which a plug-in loads at run time. Use Up and Down to change the loading order.

Figure 17-6 shows an example of a list of dependencies for a plug-in extension.

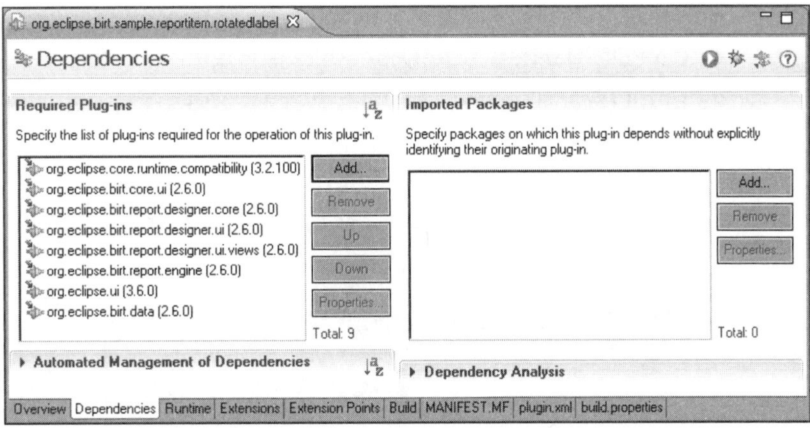

Figure 17-6 Viewing plug-in dependencies

How to verify the plug-in run-time archive

1 On PDE Manifest Editor, choose Runtime. Runtime appears, as shown in Figure 17-7.

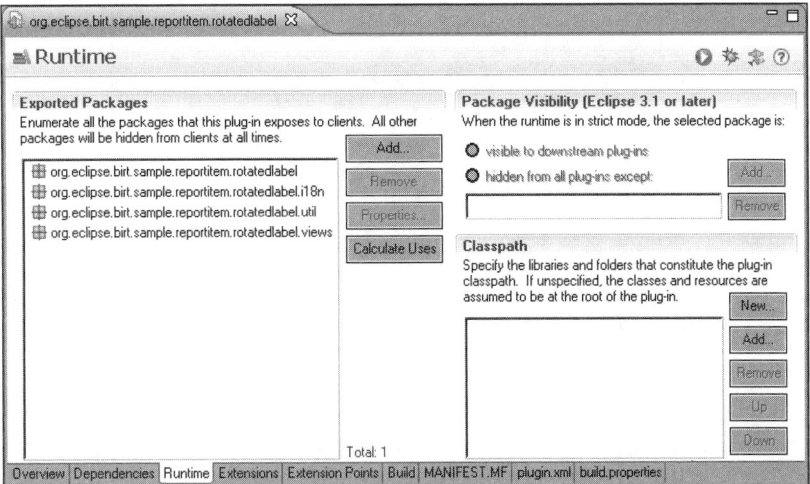

Figure 17-7 Specifying run-time visibility

2 In Runtime, perform the following tasks:

- In Exported Packages, list all the packages that the plug-in exposes to clients.
- In Package Visibility, when the plug-in is in strict run-time mode, indicate whether a selected package is visible to downstream plug-ins or hidden except for the specified plug-ins.
- In Classpath, choose Add to add the name of an archive file or folder to the classpath.

How to specify the plug-in extension

1 On PDE Manifest Editor, choose Extensions.

2 In All Extensions, choose Add. New Extension appears.

3 On Extension Point Selection, in Extension Points, select a plug-in, such as the one in the following example:

```
org.eclipse.birt.report.designer.ui.reportitemUI
```

New Extension appears, as shown in Figure 17-8.

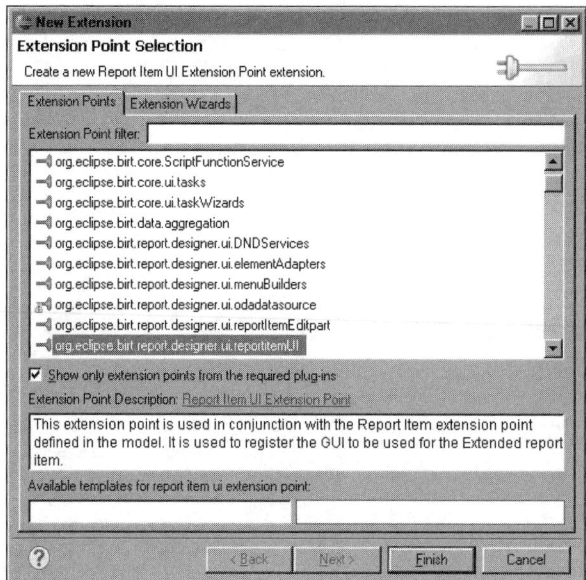

Figure 17-8 Selecting an extension point

Choose Finish. Extensions appears, as shown in Figure 17-9.

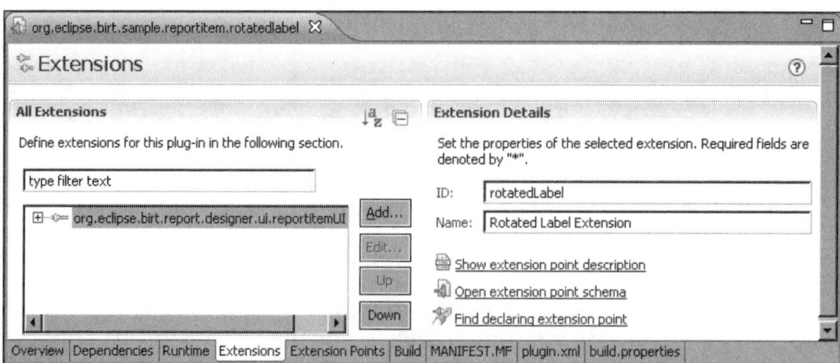

Figure 17-9 Viewing extension point selections

Repeat steps 2 and 3 to add more plug-ins to the list of required extension points in the Extensions page.

Creating the plug-in extension content

The XML schema specifies a grammar to use when creating an extension in the Eclipse PDE. Selecting an extension element in the Extensions page, Eclipse uses the XML schema to populate the Extension Element Details section with a list of valid attributes and values for the element.

In Extensions, as shown in Figure 17-10, if you choose Find declaring extension point, the PDE searches for the extension point currently selected in All Extensions. If you choose Open extension point schema, the PDE opens the .exsd file that contains the XML schema definitions. If you choose Show extension point description, the PDE generates an HTML page containing the information documented in the XML schema and displays the page in a viewer.

This section discusses the following tasks:

- Searching for and viewing extension point information
- Specifying plug-in extension content
- Specifying a build configuration

How to search for and view extension point information

1 In the Eclipse PDE, select a plug-in extension in All Extensions, such as org.eclipse.birt.report.designer.ui.reportitemUI.

2 In Extension Details, choose Find declaring extension point. Search appears. As shown in Figure 17-10, Search lists one match, org.eclipse .birt.report.designer.ui.reportitemUI.

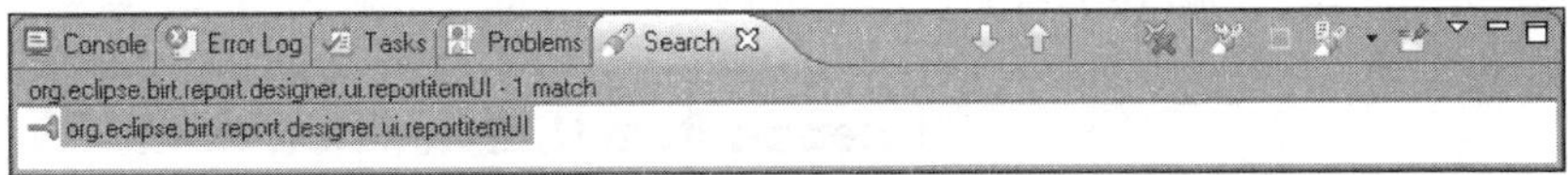

Figure 17-10 Using Search to find a declaring extension point

3 In Search, double-click the match. In PDE Manifest Editor, the contents of the file org.eclipse.birt.report.designer.ui/plugin.xml appear in a new window, as shown in Figure 17-11.

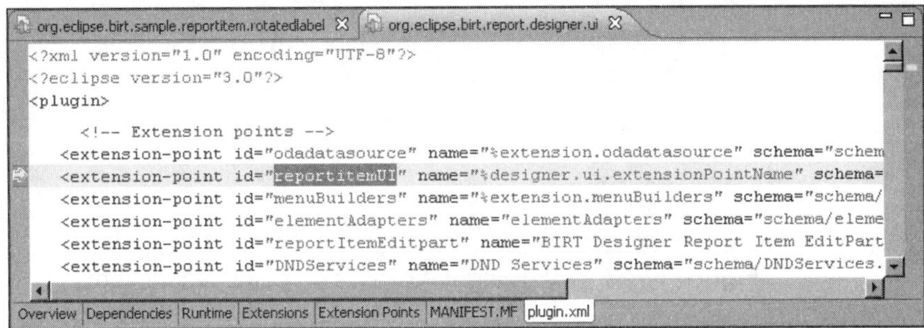

Figure 17-11 Plugin.xml showing extension points

Plugin.xml describes the extension points, odadatasource, reportItemUI, menuBuilders, elementAdapters, reportItemEditpart, and DNDServices.

4 In PDE Manifest Editor, close the window displaying contents of the plugin.xml file.

5 Choose Extensions. In Extension Details, choose Open extension point schema. The PDE Manifest Editor opens the Report Item UI Extension Point schema, as shown in Figure 17-12.

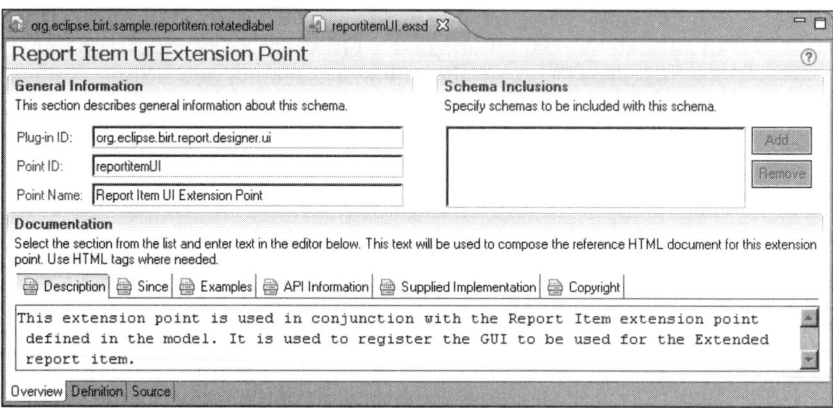

Figure 17-12 Viewing the extension point schema

The schema displays an abstract of the general information, schema inclusions, and documentation.

6 In Extension Details, choose Show extension point description. A viewer opens, displaying the HTML document for the extension point, as shown in Figure 17-13.

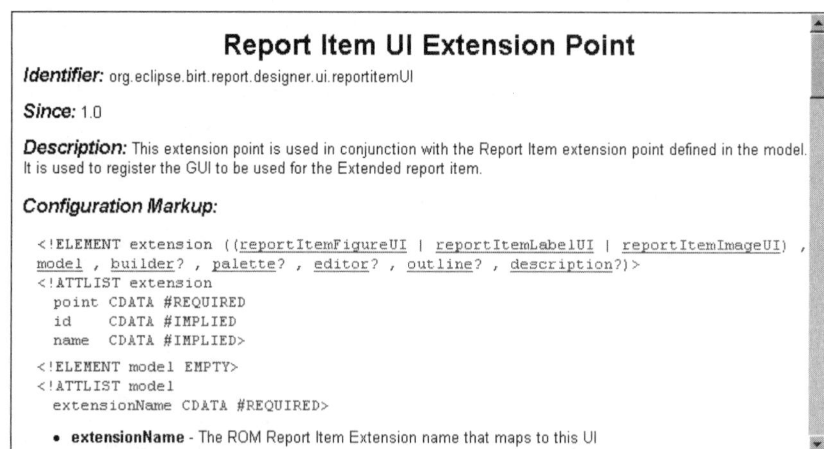

Report Item UI Extension Point
Identifier: org.eclipse.birt.report.designer.ui.reportitemUI
Since: 1.0
Description: This extension point is used in conjunction with the Report Item extension point defined in the model. It is used to register the GUI to be used for the Extended report item.
Configuration Markup:
<!ELEMENT extension ((reportItemFigureUI | reportItemLabelUI | reportItemImageUI) , model , builder? , palette? , editor? , outline? , description?)>
<!ATTLIST extension
point CDATA #REQUIRED
id CDATA #IMPLIED
name CDATA #IMPLIED>
<!ELEMENT model EMPTY>
<!ATTLIST model
extensionName CDATA #REQUIRED>
extensionName - The ROM Report Item Extension name that maps to this UI

Figure 17-13 Viewing the extension point description

In the HTML document, Configuration Markup displays the attribute list for the extension point. Scroll down to view all the contents of the HTML document, including the optional set of user interface elements for the report item extension, such as builder, palette, editor, outline, and description.

How to specify plug-in extension content

1 In PDE Manifest Editor, choose Extensions.

2 In All Extensions, right-click an extension point, such as org.eclipse.birt .report.designer.ui.reportItemUI. Then, choose New➛<extension point element>. The example in Figure 17-14 shows how to select the extension point element, reportItemLabelUI.

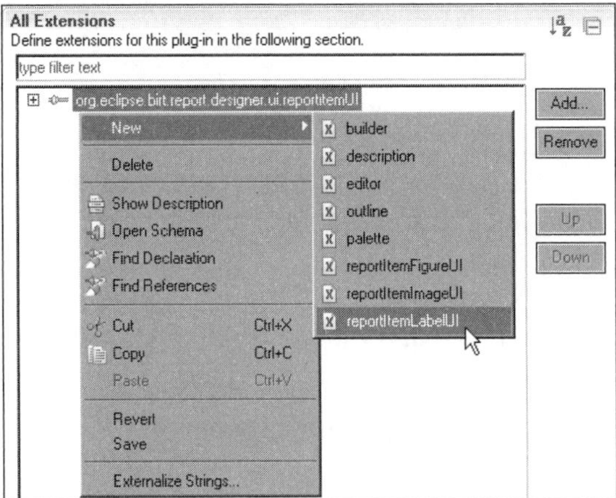

Figure 17-14 Selecting an extension point element

Extensions appears, displaying the extension element and its details, as shown in Figure 17-15.

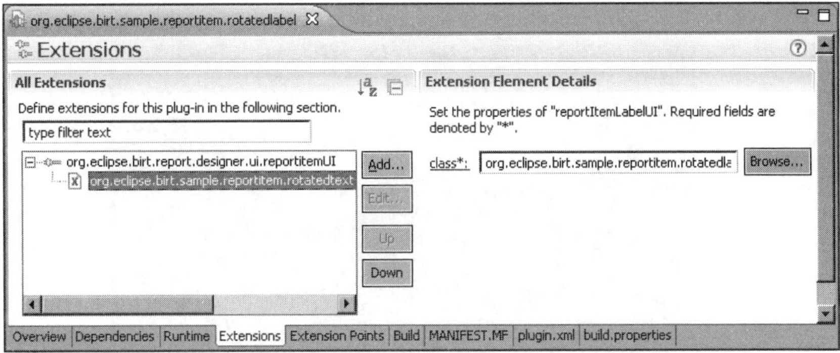

Figure 17-15 Viewing the extension and extension element details

In this example, All Extensions lists the extension, org.eclipse.birt.sample .reportitem.rotatedlabel.RotatedLabelUI (rotatedItemLabelUI), and Extension Element Details lists rotatedItemLabelUI properties. In Extension Element Details, the label for a required attribute, such as class, contains an asterisk.

3 To view the annotation for a property listed in Extension Element Details, place the cursor over the property label.

A Tooltip appears, displaying the annotation for the property from the XML schema. Figure 17-16 shows the annotation for the class property for the example extension element, rotatedItemLabelUI.

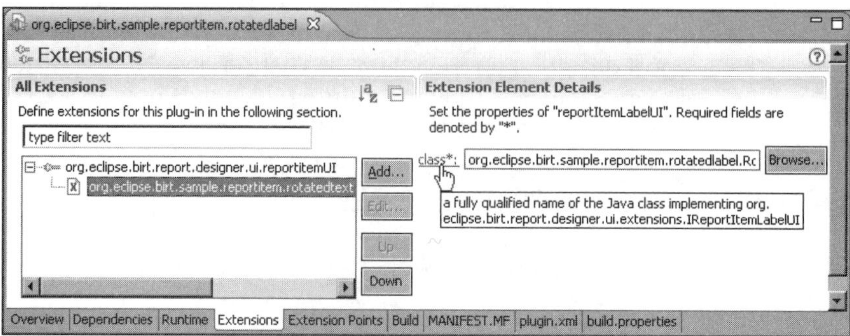

Figure 17-16 Viewing the annotation for an extension element

4 To specify the class attributes for an extension element, choose class in Extension Element Details. If the class file exists, the class file opens in PDE Manifest Editor. If no class file exists, Java Attribute Editor appears, as shown in Figure 17-17.

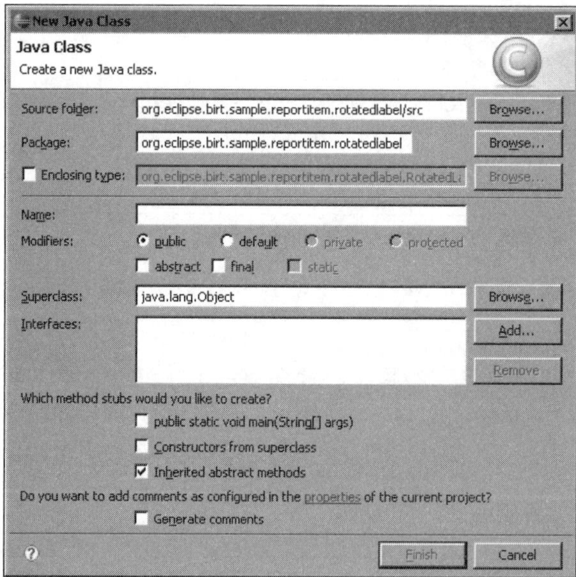

Figure 17-17 Specifying a class in Java Attribute Editor

In Java Attribute Editor, you can modify or add to the settings for the following class properties:

- Source folder

- Package
- Enclosing type
- Class name
- Modifiers, such as public, default, private, protected, abstract, final, and static
- Superclass
- Interfaces
- Method stubs, such as main, constructors, and inherited abstract methods
- Comments

After modifying setting, choose Finish. To add more elements and attributes to a selected extension point, repeat steps 1 and 2.

Figure 17-18 shows the full list of extension points required for the sample report item extension, org.eclipse.birt.sample.reportitem.rotatedlabel.

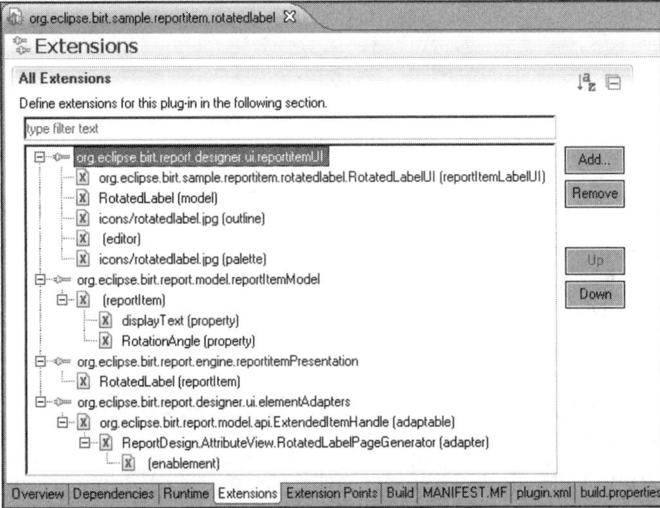

Figure 17-18 Viewing all required extension points for an extension

Building a plug-in extension

In Eclipse PDE Manifest Editor, use Build to specify the build configuration, including the following items:

- Runtime Information

  Defines the libraries, the source folders to compile into each library, and the compilation order.

- Binary Build

  Selects the files and folders to include in the binary build.

- Source Build

  Selects the files and folders to include in the source build. Source Build is not typically required. Source Build uses the org.eclipse.pde.core.source extension point that allows the PDE to find source archives for libraries in other Eclipse plug-ins.

How to specify a build configuration

1 In PDE Manifest Editor, choose Build. Build Configuration appears. Figure 17-19 shows Build Configuration.

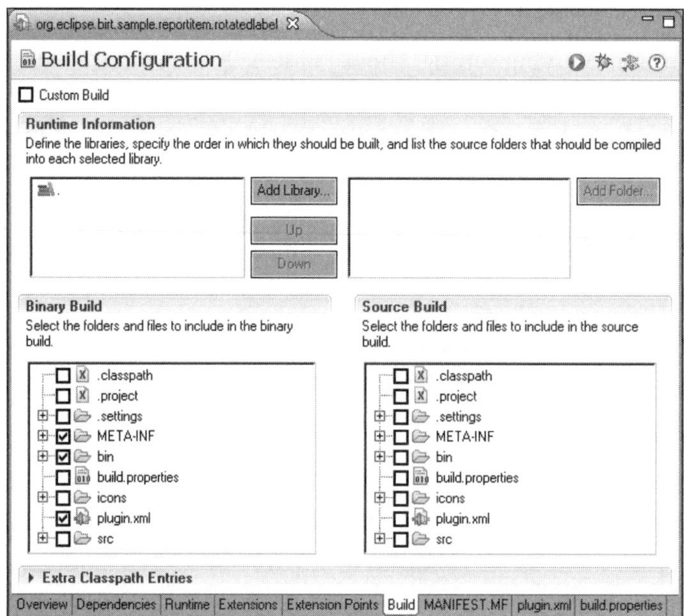

Figure 17-19 Build Configuration

2 In Runtime Information, choose Add Library. Add Entry appears.

3 In Add Entry, type the new library name, as shown in Figure 17-20, or select a run-time library name from the list.

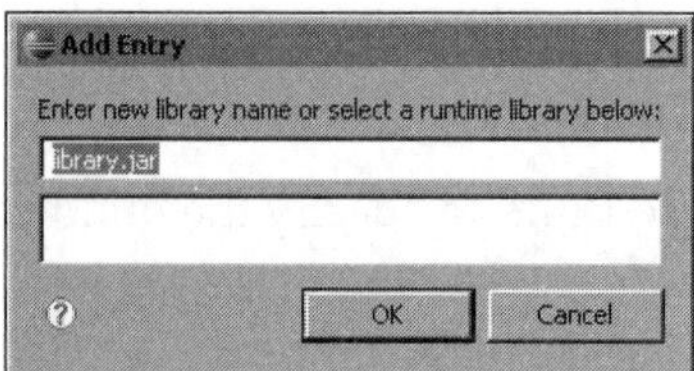

Figure 17-20 Adding a library name

Choose OK. The new library name appears in Runtime Information.

4 To change the compilation order of a library, change its position in the list. In Runtime Information, select the library. Then, choose Up or Down. The example in Figure 17-21 shows mylibrary.jar selected and Down enabled.

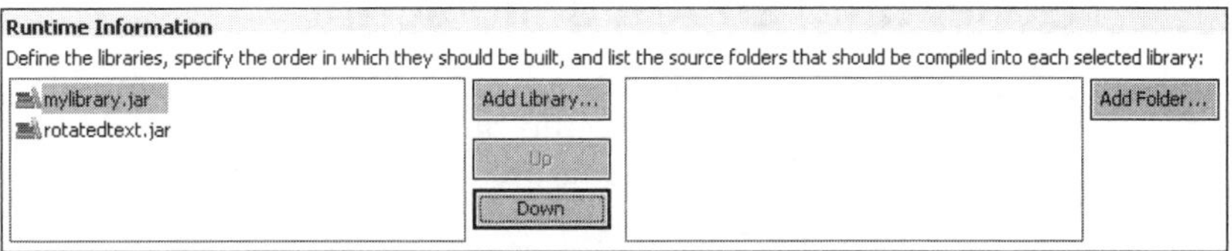

Figure 17-21 Changing the compilation order of a library

5 To add a folder to a library, choose Add Folder.

6 In New Source Folder Select a folder such as src, as shown in Figure 17-22.

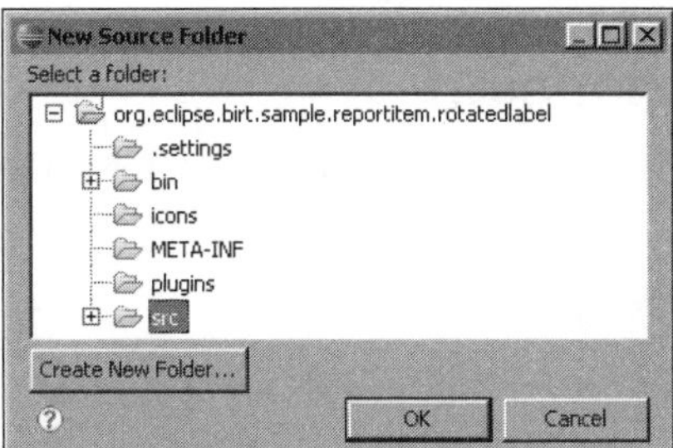

Figure 17-22 Specifying a new source folder

Choose OK. Runtime Information appears, as shown in Figure 17-23.

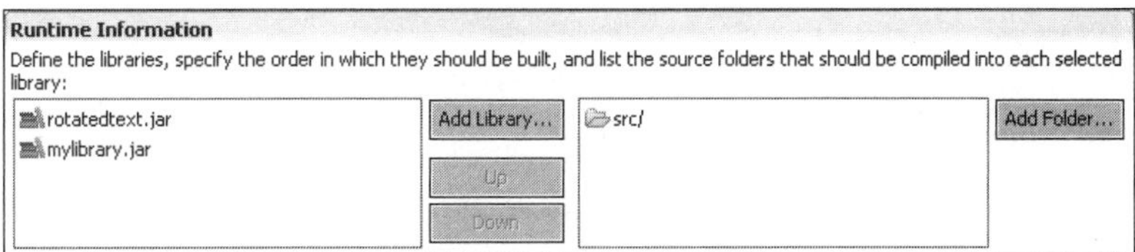

Figure 17-23 Viewing Runtime Information

7 In Binary Build, include a folder in the binary build by selecting the folder. Figure 17-24 shows the icons folder selected.

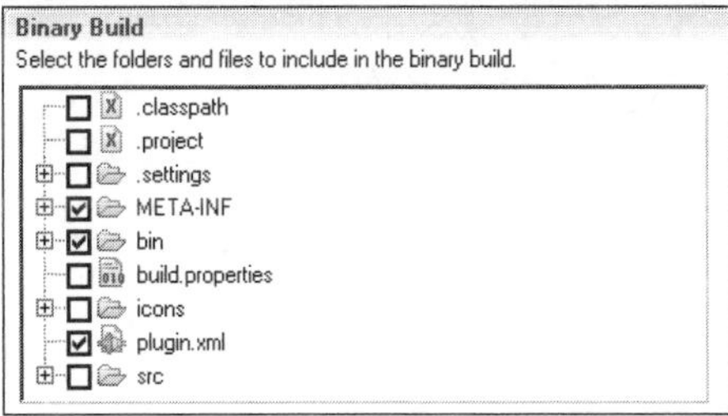

Figure 17-24 Including a folder in Binary Build

8 From the Eclipse menu, choose Project➛Build All, to build a project.

Alternatively, you can choose Project➛Build Automatically to build the project continuously as you make changes to the code.

Generating an Ant build script

The Eclipse PDE can generate an Ant build script to compile plug-in code, based on the settings in the build.properties file. The generated script is an XML file in which the elements are the required tasks for the build operation. The Ant build tool compiles the project, using the specified Java compiler.

How to generate an Ant build script

In Package Explorer, right-click the project's plugin.xml file and choose PDE Tools➛Create Ant Build File. PDE Tools creates an Ant script file, build.xml, in the project folder.

Testing a plug-in extension

You can launch an instance of the run-time workbench to test and debug the plug-in extension.

How to launch a run-time workbench

1 On PDE Manifest Editor, choose Overview. Overview appears as shown in Figure 17-25.

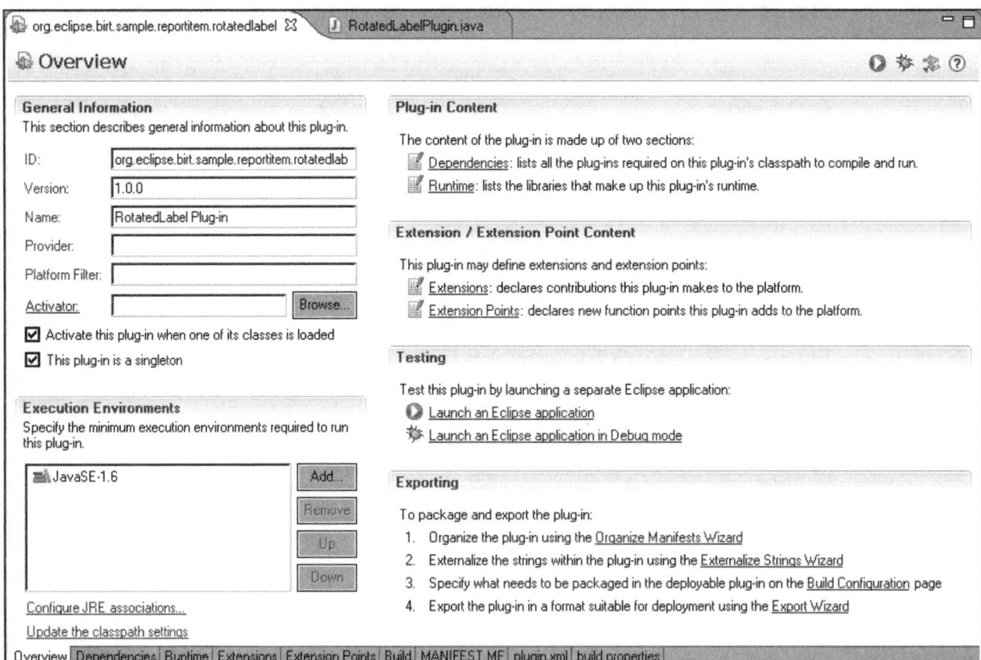

Figure 17-25 Viewing Overview showing testing and debugging options

2 In Testing, choose Launch an Eclipse application. Eclipse launches the run-time workbench.

In the report item extension example, Report Design—Eclipse SDK appears. In the run-time workbench, create a new report design project to use the report label extension.

Deploying the extension plug-in

In the PDE, a plug-in developer can use the Export Wizard to produce a distributable archive file that contains the plug-in code and other resources. A plug-in developer can create and manage an update site using the Update Site Editor in the Eclipse PDE. A user can find software and extract the contents of the archive file to an Eclipse installation using the install new software or update configuration managers.

How to deploy a plug-in extension

1 In the Eclipse PDE Manifest Editor, choose Overview.

2 In Exporting, choose Export Wizard. Export appears.

3 In Available Plug-ins and Fragments, select the plug-in to export. For example, select org.eclipse.birt.sample.reportitem.rotatedlabel.

4 In Export Destination, specify Archive file or Directory. For example, in Directory, type:

```
C:\birt-runtime-2_6_0\ReportEngine\plugins
```

Export appears as shown in Figure 17-26.

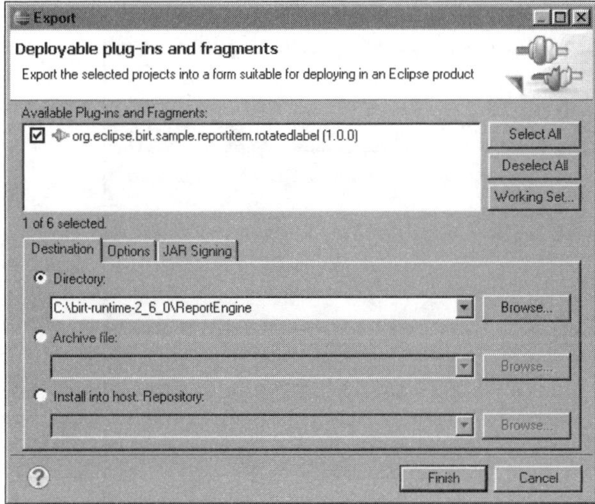

Figure 17-26 Exporting a plug-in

5 In Export Options, select one of the following options, if necessary:

- Include source code
- Package plug-ins as individual JAR archives
- Save as Ant script

Choose Finish to export the plug-in to the specified destination.

Creating an update site project

A plug-in developer can also use a more structured approach and group plug-ins into features. Features contain information that enables the install new software or update configuration managers to locate published updates and discover new related features. Updates are typically published in a special internet directory called an update site, created and managed by a plug-in developer using the Update Site Editor.

A plug-in developer can create an update site by building an update site project in the Eclipse PDE workspace. The update site project contains a manifest file, site.xml, that lists the features and plug-ins packages.

The build operation for an update site puts the JAR files for features in a features folder and the JAR files for plug-ins in a plug-ins folder. The Eclipse PDE also provides support for uploading an update site to a remote server or local file system for distribution.

How to create an update site project

1 From the Eclipse menu, choose File→New→Project. New Project appears.

2 In Wizards, open Plug-in Development and select Update Site Project, as shown in Figure 17-27. Choose Next.

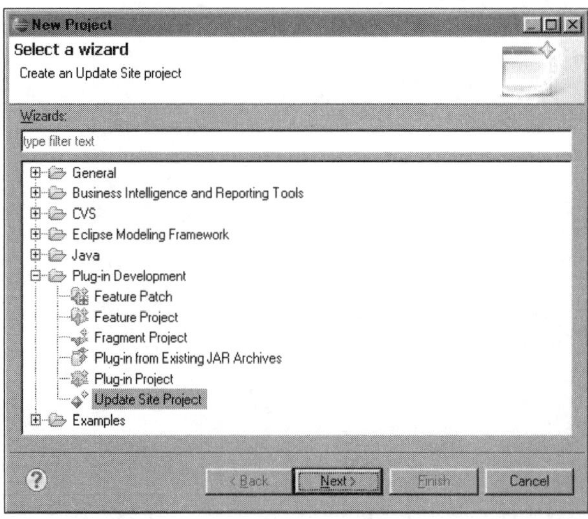

Figure 17-27 Selecting Update Site Project wizard

3 In Update Site Project, specify the following items:

- Project name
- Project contents directory, such as C:/birt-runtime-2_6_0 BIRT Update Site
- Web resources
    - Select the option Generate web page listing of all available features within the site.

      Creates index.html, site.css, and site.xls files to display the contents of the update site.
    - Web resources location.

      Change this setting to the web resources location. The default value is web.

Update Site Project appears as shown in Figure 17-28. Choose Finish.

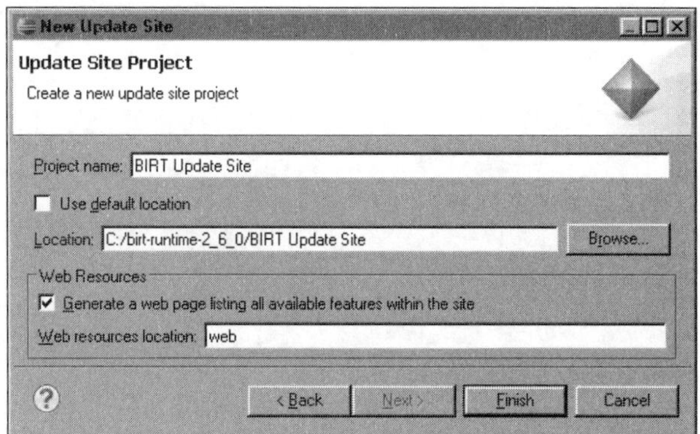

Figure 17-28 Creating a new update site project

Update Site Map appears as shown in Figure 17-29.

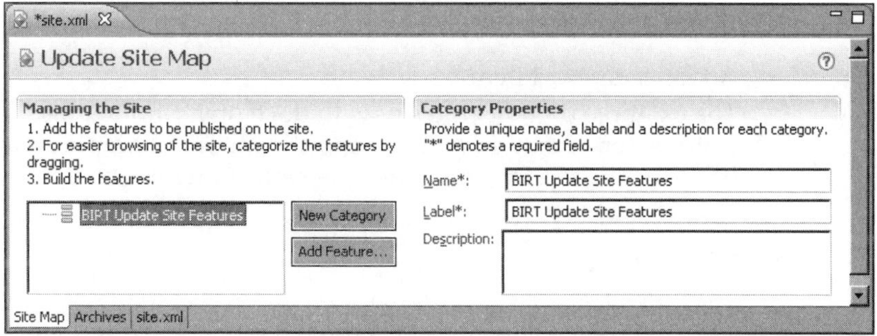

Figure 17-29 Update Site Map

4 Choose New Category to create a feature category.

5 Choose Add Feature to add a feature to a selected category.

Installing available software

If all the dependent resources are available in the new environment, Eclipse can discover and activate the plug-in in the run-time environment. In an unmanaged distribution and installation, the user must find and install updates to the plug-in if a release occurs in the future.

Choose Help→ Install New Software to access available software. Install Software supports searching available sites for updates and new features, as shown in Figure 17-30.

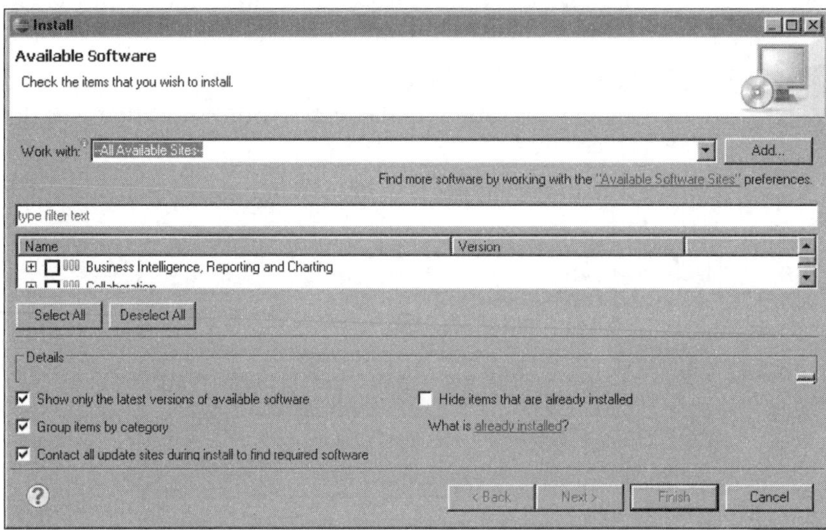

Figure 17-30 Installing new software

Downloading the code for the extension examples

This book provides examples for the following types of BIRT extensions:

- Advanced report item
  The example demonstrates how to develop additional user interface features for a custom, rotated report item. The example shows how to implement a report item builder, a context menu, a custom property page, and data binding.

- ODA drivers
  The CSV ODA driver example is a plug-in that reads data from a CSV file. The Hibernate ODA driver example uses HQL (Hibernate Query Language) to provide a SQL-transparent extension that makes the ODA extension portable to all relational databases.

These examples also show how to develop an ODA extension to the BIRT Report Designer 2.6 user interface so that a report developer can select an extended ODA driver.

- Plug-in fragment

  The plug-in fragment example adds Spanish and Japanese localization features for the BIRT Report Viewer to an existing plug-in.

- Report item

  The example shows how to build a rotated label report item plug-in and add the report item to the BIRT Report Designer using the defined extension points. This plug-in renders the label of a report item as an image. The extension rotates the image in a report design to display the label at a specified angle.

- Report rendering

  The examples show how to extend the emitter interfaces to build and deploy a report rendering plug-in that runs in the BIRT Report Engine environment. The CSV (Comma Separated Values) extension example is a plug-in that writes the table data in a report to a file in CSV format. The XML extension example is a plug-in that writes the table data in a report to a file in XML format.

You can download the source code for these extension examples at http://www.actuate.com/birt/contributions.

Chapter

18

Developing a Report Item Extension

This chapter describes how to create a BIRT extension in the Eclipse PDE using the sample report item extension, rotated label. The BIRT report item extension is presented in the following sections:

- Understanding a report item extension
- Developing the sample report item extension
- Understanding the rotated label report item extension
- Deploying and testing the rotated label report item plug-in
- Developing an advanced report item

Understanding a report item extension

Use a report item extension to add a new report item type to the BIRT framework by implementing multiple extension points. A plug-in defining an extension point typically contains an XML extension point schema definition (.exsd) file in a schema subdirectory. This schema describes the elements, attributes, and types used by the extension point in the Eclipse PDE environment.

To support adding a new report item, a report item extension provides the following extension points:

- Report item model
  org.eclipse.birt.report.model.reportItemModel specifies the report item extension point.

The XML schema file, org.eclipse.birt.report.model/schema/reportItem.exsd describes this extension point.

- Report item user interface

  org.eclipse.birt.report.designer.ui.reportitemUI specifies the report item extension point for the user interface in the report layout editor and report item palette. The XML schema file, org.eclipse.birt.report.designer.ui/schema/reportitemUI.exsd, describes this extension point.

- Report item query

  org.eclipse.birt.report.engine.reportitemQuery specifies the extension point for query preparation support in the BIRT designer and report engine. A query preparation extension is optional. The XML schema file, org.eclipse.birt.report.engine/schema/reportitemQuery.exsd, describes this extension point.

- Report item run time

  org.eclipse.birt.report.engine.reportitemGeneration specifies the extension point for instantiating, processing, and persisting a new report item at report generation time. A run-time extension is optional. The XML schema file, org.eclipse.birt.report.engine/schema/reportitemGeneration.exsd, describes this extension point.

- Report item presentation

  org.eclipse.birt.report.engine.reportitemPresentation specifies the extension point for instantiating, processing, and rendering a new report item at report presentation time. The XML schema file, org.eclipse.birt.report.engine/schema/reportitemPresentation.exsd, describes this extension point.

- Report item UI property page adapters

  org.eclipse.birt.report.designer.ui.elementAdapters specifies the extension points for the adapters for the report item property page UI. The XML schema file, org.eclipse.birt.report.designer.ui/schema/elementAdapters.exsd, describes this extension point.

- Report item emitter

  org.eclipse.birt.report.engine.emitters specifies the extension point for support of a new output format in the presentation engine. An emitter extension is optional. The XML schema file, org.eclipse.birt.report.engine/schema/emitters.exsd, describes this extension point.

At run time, the BIRT Report Engine performs the following processing on a report item before rendering the final output:

- Query preparation

  Gathers the data binding information and expressions defined for the report, passing the information to the report engine. The data engine prepares the data access strategy based on this information.

- Generation
  Creates the instances of report items and fetches the data.
- Presentation
  Renders the report item to a supported data primitive, such as an image, string, HTML segment, or custom data component.
- Emitter
  Converts the output to a specified format, such as HTML or PDF.

This chapter provides an example of a custom report item extension, org.eclipse.birt.sample.reportitem.rotatedlabel.

The standard report item plug-in, chart, is a more complex example of a report item extension. The BIRT chart plug-in implements user interface and report engine extensions that support a report design using any of the bar, line, pie, scatter, stock, or other chart types.

For reference documentation for the report item API, see the Javadoc for the org.eclipse.birt.report.engine.extension package in the BIRT Programmer Reference in Eclipse Help.

Developing the sample report item extension

The Report Item extension framework supports creating a customized report item in the palette of BIRT Report Designer. You can use a report item extension in a report design in the same way that you use a standard report item, such as Label, Text, Grid, Table, or Chart.

The sample code for the rotated label report item extension creates a label element that renders text at a specified angle. To implement the rotated label report item extension, perform the following tasks:

- Configure the plug-in project.
  Build the rotated label report item plug-in manually by following the instructions in this chapter.
- Add the report item to the Report Designer UI.
  Use org.eclipse.birt.report.designer.ui.reportItemUI to extend the Report Item UI extension point.
- Add the report item property pages to the Report Designer UI.
  Use org.eclipse.birt.report.designer.ui.elementAdapters to extend the Report Item UI property page extension point.
- Add the report item definition to the ROM.
  Use org.eclipse.birt.report.model.reportItemModel to extend the Report Item Model extension point.
- Add the report item run-time behavior.

Use org.eclipse.birt.report.engine.reportItemPresentation to extend the Report Item Presentation extension point.

- Deploy the report item extension.

  Export the rotated label report item plug-in folder from your workspace to the eclipse\plugins folder. This step is not necessary to test the extension when you launch it as an Eclipse application in the PDE.

The source code for the rotated label report item extension example is available at http://www.actuate.com/birt/contributions.

The rotated label report item extension depends on the following Eclipse plug-ins:

- org.eclipse.core.runtime.compatibility
- org.eclipse.birt.core.ui
- org.eclipse.birt.data
- org.eclipse.birt.report.designer.core
- org.eclipse.birt.report.designer.ui
- org.eclipse.birt.report.designer.ui.views
- org.eclipse.birt.report.engine
- org.eclipse.ui

Downloading BIRT source code from the CVS repository

Eclipse makes BIRT source code available to the developer community in the CVS repository. BIRT source code is not needed to compile any required plug-ins.

By default, the system uses the JAR files in the $INSTALL_DIR\eclipse \plugin folder. These plug-ins must be in the classpath to compile successfully. To debug, you may need the source code for the required BIRT plug-ins.

BIRT source code is not needed to develop the sample rotated label report item plug-in. You work only with the Java classes in the org.eclipse.birt .sample.reportitem.rotatedlabel package.

Creating a rotated label report item plug-in project

Create a new plug-in project for the rotated label report item extension in the Eclipse PDE.

How to create the plug-in project

1 In the Eclipse PDE, choose File→New→Project. New Project appears.

2 In Select a wizard, select Plug-in Project. Choose Next. New Plug-in Project appears.

3 In Plug-in Project, modify the settings, as shown in Table 18-1.

Table 18-1 Settings for the Report Item Plug-in Project

Section	Option	Value
Plug-in Project	Project name	org.eclipse.birt.sample .reportitem.rotatedlabel
	Use default location	Selected
	Location	Not available when you select Use default location
Project Settings	Create a Java project	Selected
	Source folder	src
	Output folder	bin
Target Platform	Eclipse version	3.6
	OSGi framework	Deselected
Working sets	Add project to working set	Deselected

Plug-in Project appears, as shown in Figure 18-1.

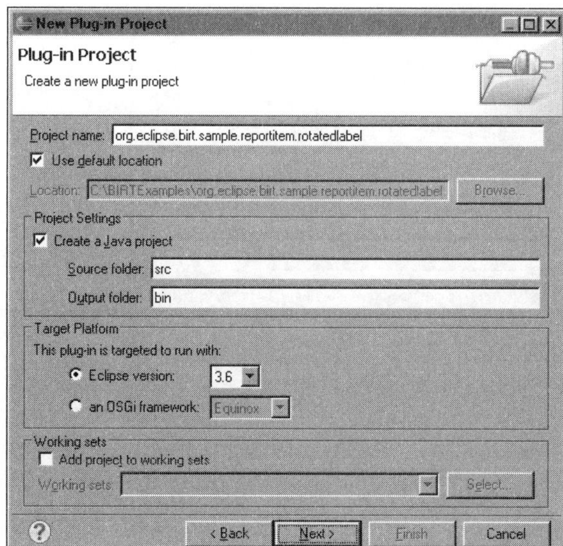

Figure 18-1 Specifying Report Item Plug-in Project settings

Choose Next. Plug-in Content appears.

4 In Plug-in Content, modify the settings as shown in Table 18-2.

Table 18-2 Settings for the Report Item Plug-in Content

Section	Option	Value
Properties	ID	org.eclipse.birt.sample .reportitem.rotatedlabel
	Version	1.0.0
	Name	RotatedLabel
	Provider	yourCompany.com or leave blank
	Execution Environment	JavaSE-1.6
Options	Generate an activator, a Java class that controls the plug-in's life cycle	Deselected
	Activator	Leave blank
	This plug-in will make contributions to the UI	Deselected
	Enable API Analysis	Deselected
Rich Client Application	Would you like to create a rich client application?	No

New Plug-in Content appears, as shown in Figure 18-2. Choose Finish.

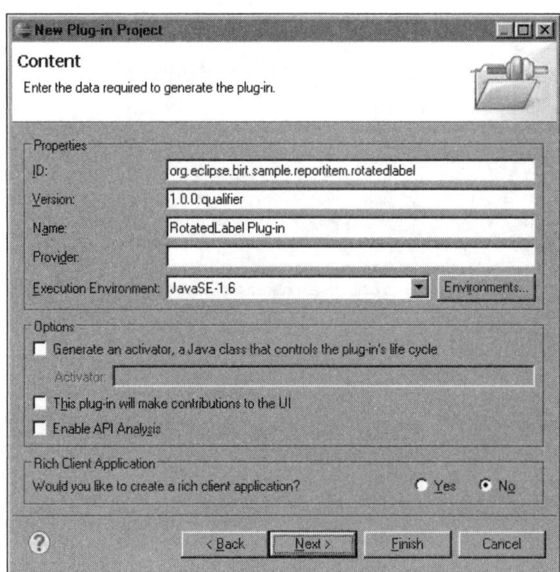

Figure 18-2 Specifying Report Item Plug-in Project content settings

The rotated label report item extension project appears in the Eclipse PDE Workbench, as shown in Figure 18-3.

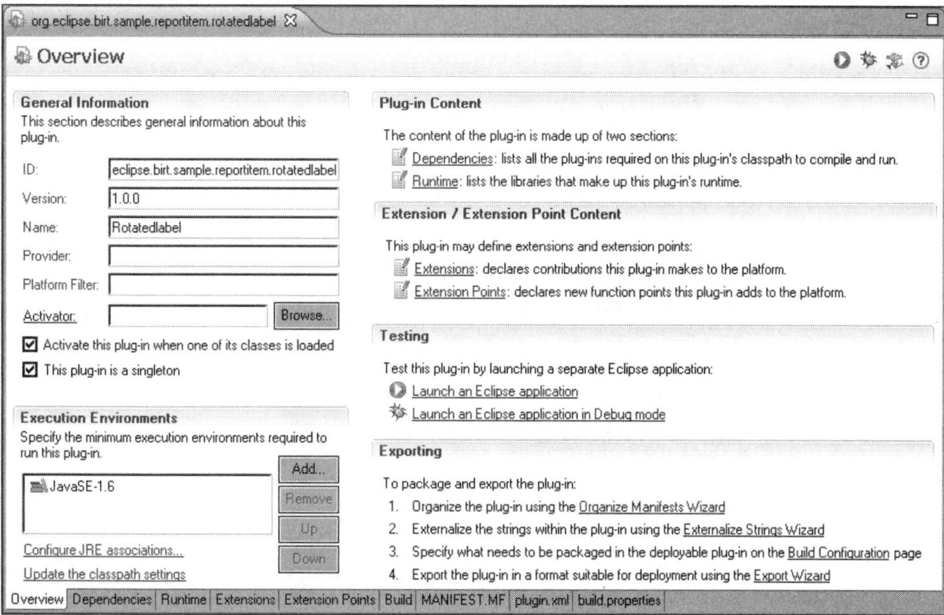

Figure 18-3 Viewing Report Item Plug-in Project Overview

Defining the dependencies for the rotated label report item extension

In this task, specify the list of plug-ins that must be available on the classpath of the rotated label report item extension to compile and run.

How to specify the dependencies

1 On PDE Manifest Editor, choose Overview.

2 In Plug-in Content, choose Dependencies. Required Plug-ins contains the following plug-ins:

```
org.eclipse.core.runtime
```

3 In Required Plug-ins, select org.eclipse.core.runtime and choose Remove. org.eclipse.core.runtime no longer appears in Required Plug-ins.

4 In Required Plug-ins, choose Add. Plug-in Selection appears.

5 In Plug-in Selection, hold down CTRL and select the following plug-ins:

- org.eclipse.birt.core.ui
- org.eclipse.birt.data
- org.eclipse.birt.report.designer.core
- org.eclipse.birt.report.designer.ui

- org.eclipse.birt.report.designer.ui.views
- org.eclipse.birt.report.engine
- org.eclipse.core.runtime.compatibility
- org.eclipse.ui

Choose OK. Dependencies appears, as shown in Figure 18-4.

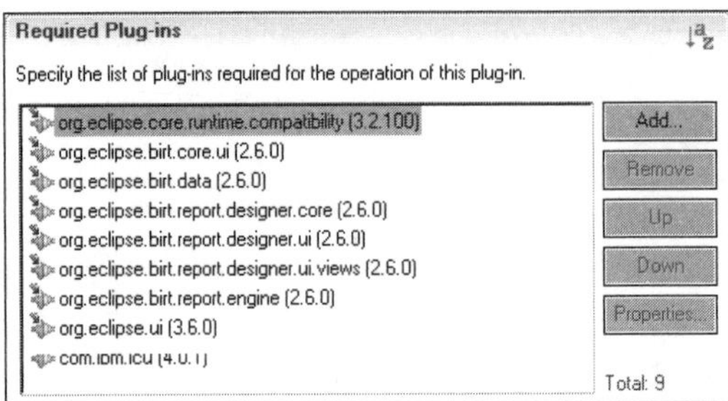

Figure 18-4 Viewing Dependencies showing required plug-ins

The order of the list determines the sequence in which a plug-in loads at run time. Use Up and Down to change the loading order as necessary, as shown in Figure 18-4.

Specifying the run-time package for the rotated label report item extension

On Runtime, specify exported packages, package visibility, libraries, and folders on the plug-in classpath. In the rotated label report item plug-in, make the following packages visible to other plug-ins:

- org.eclipse.birt.sample.reportitem.rotatedlabel
- org.eclipse.birt.sample.reportitem.rotatedlabel.i18n
- org.eclipse.birt.sample.reportitem.rotatedlabel.util
- org.eclipse.birt.sample.reportitem.rotatedlabel.views

On PDE Manifest Editor, choose Runtime. In Exported Packages, verify that the specified packages appear in the list, as shown in Figure 18-5.

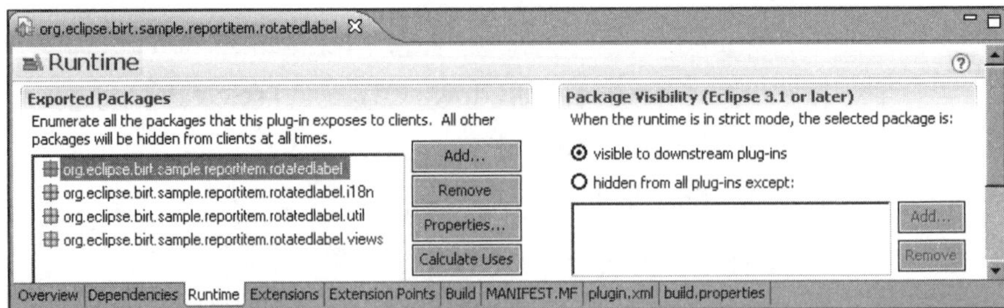

Figure 18-5 The Runtime page

Declaring the report item extension points

Next, specify the extension points required to implement the rotated label report item extension and add the extension element details. The Eclipse PDE uses the XML schema defined for each extension point to provide the list of valid attributes and values specified for the extension elements. The rotated label report item extension implements the following extension points:

- org.eclipse.birt.report.designer.ui.reportitemUI
  Registers the graphical user interface (GUI) to use for the report item extension
- org.eclipse.birt.report.model.reportItemModel
  Specifies how to represent and persist the report item extension in the ROM
- org.eclipse.birt.report.engine.reportitemPresentation
  Specifies how to instantiate, process, and render a new report item at report presentation time
- org.eclipse.birt.report.designer.ui.elementAdapters
  Specifies the adapters for the report item property page UI

The XML schema specifies the following properties that identify each extension point in the run-time environment:

- ID
  Optional identifier of the extension instance
- Name
  Optional name of the extension instance

The extension point, org.eclipse.birt.report.designer.ui.reportitemUI, specifies the following extension elements:

- reportItemFigureUI
  Fully qualified name of the Java class that implements the org.eclipse .birt.report.designer.ui.extensions. IReportItemFigureProvider interface
- reportItemLabelUI
  Fully qualified name of the Java class that gets the display text for the report item component in BIRT Report Designer
- reportItemImageUI
  Fully qualified name of the Java class that implements the org.eclipse .birt.report.designer.ui.extensions.IReportItemImageProvider interface
- model
  ROM report item extension name that maps to this UI component
- builder

Optional component instantiated when a user drags the extended report item from the BIRT Report Designer Palette to the Editor

- palette
  Icon to show and the category in which the icon appears in the Palette
- editor
  Flags indicating whether the editor shows in the MasterPage and Designer UI and is resizable in the Editor
- outline
  Icon to show in the outline view
- description
  Optional element containing text describing what the UI extension does

The extension point, org.eclipse.birt.report.model.reportItemModel, specifies the following extension element properties:

- extensionName
  Internal unique name of the report item extension
- class
  Fully qualified name of the Java class that implements the org.eclipse .birt.report.model.api.extension.IReportItemFactory interface
- defaultStyle
  Predefined style to use for the report item extension
- isNameRequired
  Field indicating whether the report item instance name is required
- displayNameID
  Resource key for the display name
- extendsFrom
  Parent element from which a report item extends
- hasStyle
  Flag that marks whether an extended item can have style

For RotatedLabel, reportItem specifies the following property extension elements:

- displayText
- rotationAngle

These extension elements specify the following properties:

- name
  Internal unique name of the property extension element.

- type
  Data type, such as integer or string.
- displayNameID
  Resource key for the display name.
- detailType
  Detail data type, such as Boolean or string.
- subType
  When the detailType is a list, the subType is required and must be defined as one of the restriction choices. By default the subtype is string.
- canInherit
  Flag indicating whether the property extension element can inherit properties.
- defaultValue
  Default value of the property extension element.
- isEncryptable
  Flag indicating whether the property is encrypted.
- DisplayName
  Display name to use if no localized I18N display name exists.
- isList
  Indicates whether the property value is a single structure or a list.
- hasOwnModel
  Indicates whether the XML property is the extension model.
- allowExpression
  Indicates whether the property can be set as an expression. Each expression contains the value and the type.

The extension point, org.eclipse.birt.report.engine.reportitemPresentation, specifies the following reportItem extension elements:

- name
  Unique name of the report item extension.
- class
  Fully qualified name of the Java class that implements the org.eclipse. birt.report.engine.extension. IReportItemPresentation interface.
- supportedFormats
  Supported rendering formats for this extended item. The value for this attribute is a comma-separated string, such as "HTML,PDF,EXCEL". The string is case-insensitive.

The extension point, org.eclipse.birt.report.designer.ui.elementAdapters, creates an adapter class that implements the IPageGenerator interface. The org.eclipse.birt.report.model.api.ExtendedItemHandle class implements the interfaces which make the extension point adaptable. The adapter specifies the following properties for the property pages:

- id
  Unique name of ReportDesign.AttributeView .RotatedLabelPageGenerator
- type
  Implements org.eclipse.birt.report.designer.ui.views.IPageGenerator
- factory
  Registers and creates the IPageGenerator instance
- singleton
  Indicates whether one or more adapter elements can simultaneously exist
- priority
  Indicates priority in a run-time environment

How to specify the extension points

1 On PDE Manifest Editor, choose Extensions.

2 In All Extensions, choose Add. New Extension appears.

3 In New Extension—Extension Points, Available extension points, select the following plug-in:

```
org.eclipse.birt.report.designer.ui.reportitemUI
```

New Extension—Extension Points appears, as shown in Figure 18-6.

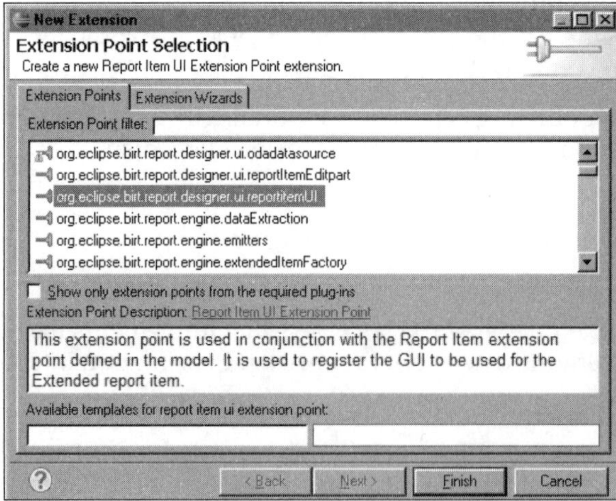

Figure 18-6 Extension points in New Extension

In cases when the plug-in does not appear in the list, uncheck Show only extension points from the required plug-ins box.

Choose Finish.

4 Repeat steps 2 and 3 to add the following extension points to the list of required extension points in the Extensions page:

- org.eclipse.birt.report.model.reportItemModel
- org.eclipse.birt.report.engine.reportitemPresentation
- org.eclipse.birt.report.designer.ui.elementAdapters

Figure 18-7 shows the list of extension points required for the report item extension example.

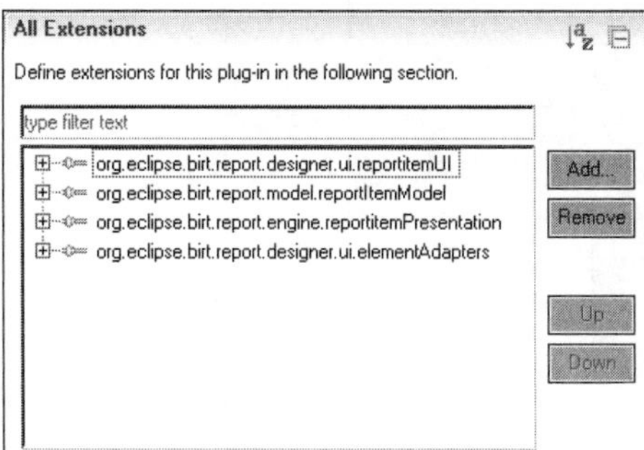

Figure 18-7 Required extension points for a report item extension

How to add the extension details

Perform the following tasks:

1 On Extensions, in All Extensions, select org.eclipse.birt.report.designer.ui .reportitemUI.

2 In Extension Details, set the following property values as shown in Table 18-3.

Table 18-3 Properties for the reportItemUI extension

Property	Value
ID	rotatedLabel
Name	Rotated Label Extension

3 Repeat step 2 to add the property values shown in Table 18-3 to the extension details for the other extension points.

Creating the plug-in extension content

The XML schema specifies a grammar that you must follow when creating an extension in the Eclipse PDE. When you select an element of an extension in the Extensions page of the PDE, Eclipse uses the XML schema to populate the Extension Element Details section with the list of valid attributes and values for the element.

How to specify the plug-in extension content

1 In PDE Manifest Editor, choose Extensions.

2 In All Extensions, right-click org.eclipse.birt.report.designer.ui .reportItemUI and choose New➛reportItemLabelUI, as shown in Figure 18-8.

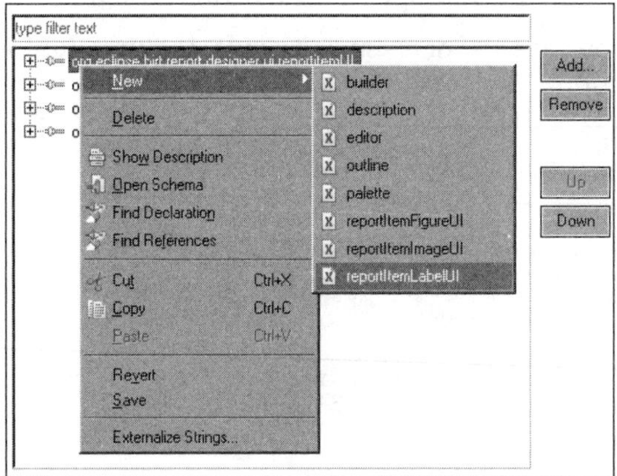

Figure 18-8 Selecting an report item extension element

All Extensions adds the extension, org.eclipse.birt.sample.reportitem .rotatedlabel.ReportItemLabelUI (rotatedItemLabelUI), and Extension Element Details lists rotatedItemLabelUI properties.

3 In Extension Element Details, type the following fully qualified class name:

```
org.eclipse.birt.sample.reportitem.rotatedlabel
   .RotatedLabelUI
```

4 In All Extensions, right-click org.eclipse.birt.report.designer.ui .reportitemUI again and repeatedly choose New➛<extension element> to add the following extension elements, properties, and values, as shown in Table 18-4. Note that the PDE Manifest Editor creates the extension element rotated label model when adding this extension point.

Table 18-4 Properties for other reportitemUI extension elements

Extension element	Property	Value
model	extensionName	RotatedLabel
outline	icon	icons/rotatedlabel.jpg
editor	showInMasterPage	true
	showInDesigner	true

Table 18-4 Properties for other reportitemUI extension elements

Extension element	Property	Value
editor	canResize	true
	menuLabel	
palette	icon	icons/rotatedlabel.jpg
	category	
	categoryDisplayName	

Do not enter a property value in Extension Element Details if the value field for the property in the table is empty. Extension elements appear as shown in Figure 18-9.

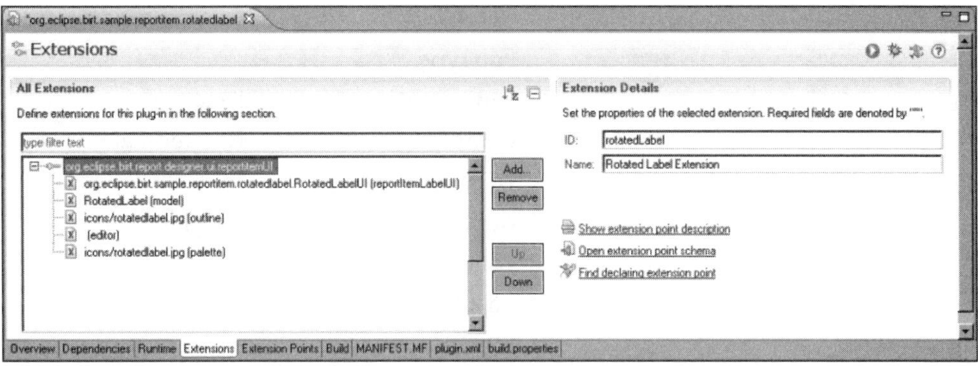

Figure 18-9 Specifying properties for rotatedItemLabelUI

5 In All Extensions, add the org.eclipse.birt.report.model.reportItemModel extension point. Select reportItem. In Extension Element Details, add the reportItem properties shown in Table 18-5.

Table 18-5 Property values for the reportItem

Extension element	Property	Value
reportItem	extensionName	RotatedLabel
	class	org.eclipse.birt.sample .reportitem.rotatedlabel .RotatedLabelItem FactoryImpl
	defaultStyle	
	isNameRequired	false
	displayNameID	
	extendsFrom	ExtendedItem
	hasStyle	true

6 In All Extensions, in org.eclipse.birt.report.model.reportItemModel, perform the following tasks:

1 Right-click reportItem again and choose New→property to create a new extension element property with the settings shown in Table 18-6. The displayText property contains the text that the rotated label displays.

Table 18-6 Property values for the displayText

Extension element	Property	Value
property	name	displayText
	type	script
	displayNameID	
	detailType	
	subType	
	canInherit	true
	defaultValue	Rotated Label
	isEncryptable	false
	defaultDisplayName	Display Text
	isList	false
	hasOwnModel	true
	allowExpression	

2 Right-click reportItem and choose New→property to add an extension element property named rotationAngle. The settings for this property are shown in Table 18-7. As the property name suggests, this property contains the rotation angle of the displayed text.

Table 18-7 Property values for the rotationAngle

Extension element	Property	Value
property	name	rotationAngle
	type	string
	displayNameID	
	detailType	
	subType	
	canInherit	true
	defaultValue	-45
	isEncryptable	false
	defaultDisplayName	Rotation Angle

Table 18-7 Property values for the rotationAngle

Extension element	Property	Value
property	isList	false
	hasOwnModel	true
	allowExpression	

7 In All Extensions, expand org.eclipse.birt.report.engine .reportitemPresentation and choose org.eclipse.birt.sample.reportitem .rotatedlabel.reportItem1(reportItem).

8 In Extension Element Details, modify the reportItem properties to the values shown in Table 18-8.

Table 18-8 Property values for the reportItem

Extension element	Property	Value
reportItem	name	RotatedLabel
	class	org.eclipse.birt.sample .reportitem.rotatedlabel .RotatedLabel PresentationImpl
	supportedFormats	

9 In All Extensions, right-click org.eclipse.birt.report.designer.ui. elementAdapters and choose org.eclipse.birt.sample.reportitem .rotatedlabel.Adaptable1(adaptable).

10 In Extension Element Details, modify the adaptable property to the following class:

```
org.eclipse.birt.report.model.api.ExtendedItemHandle
```

11 In All Extensions, right-click org.eclipse.birt.report.model.api .ExtendedItemHandle (adaptable) and choose New➛adapter.

12 In Extension Element Details, add the adapter properties shown in Table 18-9.

Table 18-9 Property values for the adapter

Extension element	Property	Value
adapter	id	ReportDesign.AttributeView .RotatedLabelPageGenerator
	type	org.eclipse.birt.report.designer.ui.views .IPageGenerator

(continues)

Table 18-9 Property values for the adapter (continued)

Extension element	Property	Value
adapter	class	
	factory	org.eclipse.birt.sample.reportitem . rotatedlabel.views . RotatedLabelPageGeneratorFactory
	singleton	false
	priority	1
	overwrite	
	comments	

Figure 18-10 shows the full list of extension points and elements required for the example, org.eclipse.birt.sample.reportitem.rotatedlabel.

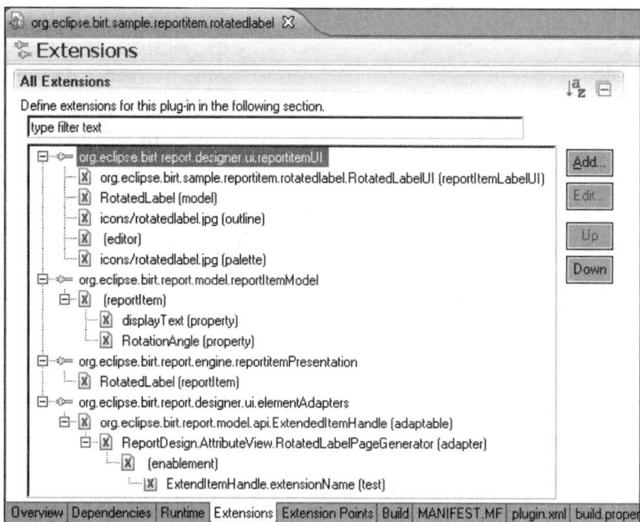

Figure 18-10 Viewing extension points for rotated label report item

Understanding the rotated label report item extension

The rotated label report item plug-in provides the functionality required at run time to render the label of a report item as an image in the report design and display the label at the specified angle. The following sections contain implementation details for the most important classes in the rotated label report item extension.

Understanding RotatedLabelItemFactoryImpl

The RotatedLabelItemFactoryImpl class instantiates a new report item when the user drags a rotated label report item from Palette and drops the report item in the BIRT Report Designer Editor. RotatedLabelItemFactoryImpl extends the adapter class, org.eclipse.birt.report.model.api.extension .ReportItemFactory.

The newReportItem( ) method receives a reference to DesignElementHandle, which provides the interface to the BIRT report model. The newReportItem( ) method instantiates the new report item, as shown in Listing 18-1.

Listing 18-1 The newReportItem( ) method

```
public class RotatedTextItemFactoryImpl
   extends ReportItemFactory implements IMessages
{
   public IReportItem newReportItem( DesignElementHandle deh )
   {
      return  new ReportItem( );
   ...
}
```

Understanding RotatedLabelUI

In the RotatedLabelUI class, the RotatedLabelUI.getLabel( ) method provides the text representation for the label to BIRT Report Designer. RotatedLabelUI extends the adapter class, org.eclipse.birt.report.designer.ui.extensions .ReportItemLabelProvider. Listing 18-2 shows the code for the getLabel( ) method.

Listing 18-2 The getLabel( ) method

```
public class RotatedLabelUI extends ReportItemLabelProvider
{
   public String getLabel( ExtendedItemHandle handle )
   {
      if ( handle.getProperty( "displayText" ) != null ) {
         return ( String ) handle.getProperty( "displayText" );
      } else {
         return "Rotated Label";
      }
   }
```

Understanding RotatedLabelPresentationImpl

The RotatedLabelPresentationImpl class specifies how to process and render the report item at presentation time. RotatedLabelPresentationImpl extends the org.eclipse.birt.report.engine.extension.ReportItemPresentationBase class.

The method, onRowSets( ), renders the rotated label report item as an image, rotated by the angle specified in the report design, as shown in Listing 18-3.

Listing 18-3 The onRowSets( ) method

```
public Object onRowSets(IRowSet[ ] rowSets) throws BirtException
{
   if ( modelHandle == null )
   {
      return null;
   }
      graphicsUtil = new GraphicsUtil( );
      org.eclipse.swt.graphics.Image rotatedImage =
         graphicsUtil.createRotatedText( modelHandle );
      ImageLoader imageLoader = new ImageLoader( );
      imageLoader.data = new ImageData[ ]
         { rotatedImage.getImageData( ) };
      ByteArrayOutputStream baos =
         new ByteArrayOutputStream( );
      imageLoader.save( baos, SWT.IMAGE_JPEG );
      return baos.toByteArray( );
}
```

Understanding GraphicsUtil

The GraphicsUtil class creates the image containing the specified text and rotates the text image to the specified angle, using the following methods:

- createRotatedText( )
  This method performs the following operations:
  - Gets the display text and rotation angle properties
  - Sets the display text font and determines the font metrics
  - Creates an image the same size as the display text String
  - Draws the display text as an image
  - Calls the rotateImage( ) method to rotate the image at the specified angle
  - Disposes of the operating system resources used to render the image
  - Returns the image object

  Listing 18-4 shows the code for createRotatedText( ) method.

  Listing 18-4 The createRotatedText( ) method

```
public Image createRotatedText( ExtendedItemHandle
   modelHandle )
{
   Image stringImage;
```

```
Image image;
GC gc;
   String text = "";
if ( modelHandle.getProperty( "displayText" ) != null ) {
   text = ( String ) modelHandle.getProperty
      ( "displayText" );
}
   Integer angle = -45;
if ( modelHandle.getProperty( "rotationAngle" ) != null ) {
   try {
      angle = Integer.parseInt( (String)
         modelHandle.getProperty( "rotationAngle" ));
   }
   catch( NumberFormatException e ) {
      angle = -45;
   }
}
   String fontFamily = "Arial";
if ( modelHandle.getProperty(Style.FONT_FAMILY_PROP ) !=
   null ) {
   fontFamily = ( String ) modelHandle.getProperty
      ( Style.FONT_FAMILY_PROP );
}
StyleHandle labelStyle = modelHandle.getPrivateStyle();
DimensionHandle fontSize =
   (DimensionHandle) labelStyle.getFontSize();

int height = 12;
String units = fontSize.getUnits( );
if  ( units.compareToIgnoreCase("pt") == 0 )
{
   height = (int) fontSize.getMeasure();
}
if ( display == null ) SWT.error
      ( SWT.ERROR_THREAD_INVALID_ACCESS );

FontData fontData = new FontData( fontFamily, height, 0 );
Font font = new Font( display, fontData );
try
{
   gc = new GC( display );
   gc.setFont( font );
   gc.getFontMetrics( );
   Point pt = gc.textExtent( text );
   gc.dispose( );
   stringImage = new Image( display, pt.x, pt.y );
   gc = new GC( stringImage );
   gc.setFont( font );
   gc.drawText( text, 0, 0 );
```

```
        image = rotateImage( stringImage, angle.doubleValue( ) );
        gc.dispose( );
        stringImage.dispose( );
        return image;
    }
    catch( Exception e )
    {
        e.printStackTrace( );
    }
    return null;
}
```

- rotateImage( )

  This method rotates the image and determines the height, width, and point of origin for the image, as shown in Listing 18-5.

Listing 18-5 The rotateImage( ) method

```
private Image rotateImage ( Image img, double degrees )
{
    double positiveDegrees = ( degrees % 360 ) +
        ( ( degrees < 0 ) ? 360 : 0 );
    double degreesMod90 = positiveDegrees % 90;
    double radians = Math.toRadians( positiveDegrees );
    double radiansMod90 = Math.toRadians( degreesMod90 );
    if ( positiveDegrees == 0 )
        return img;
    int quadrant = 0;
    if ( positiveDegrees < 90 )
        quadrant = 1;
    else if ( ( positiveDegrees >= 90 ) &&
        ( positiveDegrees < 180 ) )
        quadrant = 2;
    else if ( ( positiveDegrees >= 180 ) &&
        ( positiveDegrees < 270 ) )
        quadrant = 3;
    else if ( positiveDegrees >= 270 )
        quadrant = 4;
    int height = img.getBounds( ).height;
    int width = img.getBounds( ).width;
    double side1 = ( Math.sin( radiansMod90 ) * height ) +
        ( Math.cos( radiansMod90 ) * width );
    double side2 = ( Math.cos( radiansMod90 ) * height ) +
        ( Math.sin( radiansMod90 ) * width );
    double h = 0;
    int newWidth = 0, newHeight = 0;
    if ( ( quadrant == 1 ) || ( quadrant == 3) ) {
        h = ( Math.sin( radiansMod90) * height );
        newWidth = ( int )side1;
        newHeight = ( int )side2;
```

```
    } else {
      h = ( Math.sin( radiansMod90 ) * width );
      newWidth = ( int )side2;
      newHeight = ( int )side1;
    }
    int shiftX = ( int )( Math.cos( radians ) * h ) -
      ( ( quadrant == 3 ) || ( quadrant == 4 )
        ? width : 0 );
    int shiftY = ( int )( Math.sin( radians ) * h ) +
      ( ( quadrant == 2) || ( quadrant == 3 )
        ? height : 0 );
    Image newImg = new Image( display, newWidth, newHeight );
    GC newGC = new GC( newImg );
    Transform tr = new Transform( display );
    tr.rotate( ( float )positiveDegrees );
    newGC.setTransform( tr );
    newGC.setBackground( display.getSystemColor
      ( SWT.COLOR_WHITE ) );
    newGC.drawImage( img, shiftX, -shiftY );
    newGC.dispose( );
    return newImg;
  }
```

Understanding RotatedLabelCategoryProvider Factory

In this class, the getCategoryProvider( ) method provides the category information for Property Editor pages such as Bookmark, Borders, Margin, Section, and Table of Contents for the rotated label report item. Listing 18-6 shows the code for the getCategoryProvider( ) method, which specifies the category properties and associated classes.

Listing 18-6 The getCategoryProvider( ) method

```
public ICategoryProvider getCategoryProvider( Object input )
  {
    CategoryProvider provider = new CategoryProvider(
      new String[ ]{
        CategoryProviderFactory.CATEGORY_KEY_GENERAL,
        CategoryProviderFactory.CATEGORY_KEY_BORDERS,
        CategoryProviderFactory.CATEGORY_KEY_MARGIN,
        CategoryProviderFactory.CATEGORY_KEY_ALTTEXT,
        CategoryProviderFactory.CATEGORY_KEY_SECTION,
        CategoryProviderFactory.CATEGORY_KEY_VISIBILITY,
        CategoryProviderFactory.CATEGORY_KEY_TOC,
        CategoryProviderFactory.CATEGORY_KEY_BOOKMARK,
        CategoryProviderFactory.CATEGORY_KEY_USERPROPERTIES,
        CategoryProviderFactory
          .CATEGORY_KEY_NAMEDEXPRESSIONS,
```

```
            CategoryProviderFactory
               .CATEGORY_KEY_ADVANCEPROPERTY,
      }, new String[ ]{
            "General",
            "Borders",
            "Margin",
            "AltText",
            "Section",
            "Visibility",
            "TOC",
            "Bookmark",
            "UserProperties",
            "NamedExpressions",
            "AdvancedProperty",
      }, new Class[ ]{
            RotatedLabelGeneralPage.class,
            BordersPage.class,
            ItemMarginPage.class,
            AlterPage.class,
            SectionPage.class,
            VisibilityPage.class,
            TOCExpressionPage.class,
            BookMarkExpressionPage.class,
            UserPropertiesPage.class,
            NamedExpressionsPage.class,
            AdvancePropertyPage.class,
      } );
      return provider;
   }
```

Understanding RotatedLabelGeneralPage

In this class, the buildUI( ) method creates the content for the General page in the Property Editor, adding the following display text controls:

- Font
- Rotation Angle
- Size

Listing 18-7 shows the code for the buildUI( ) method.

Listing 18-7 The buildUI( ) method

```
public void buildUI( Composite parent )
{
   super.buildUI( parent );
   container.setLayout( WidgetUtil.createGridLayout( 5, 15 ) );

   LibraryDescriptorProvider provider = new
LibraryDescriptorProvider( );
```

```
    librarySection = new TextSection(
  provider.getDisplayName( ),
          container,
          true );
    librarySection.setProvider( provider );
    librarySection.setGridPlaceholder( 2, true );
    addSection( RotatedLabelPageSectionID.LIBRARY,
  librarySection );

// display text property
    separatorSection = new SeperatorSection(
      container, SWT.HORIZONTAL );
    addSection( RotatedLabelPageSectionID.SEPARATOR,
      separatorSection );
    TextPropertyDescriptorProvider nameProvider =
      new TextPropertyDescriptorProvider( "displayText",
        ReportDesignConstants.EXTENDED_ITEM );
    TextSection nameSection = new TextSection(
      "Display text:",
      container,
      true );
    nameSection.setProvider( nameProvider );
    nameSection.setGridPlaceholder( 3, true );
    nameSection.setWidth(200 );
    addSection( RotatedLabelPageSectionID.DISPLAY_TEXT,
      nameSection );

// rotation angle property
    TextPropertyDescriptorProvider angleProvider =
      new TextPropertyDescriptorProvider( "rotationAngle",
        ReportDesignConstants.EXTENDED_ITEM );
    TextSection angleSection =
      new TextSection( "Rotation Angle:",
                                            container,
                                            true );
    angleSection.setProvider( angleProvider );
    angleSection.setGridPlaceholder( 3, true );
    angleSection.setWidth( 200 );
    addSection( RotatedLabelPageSectionID.ROTATION_ANGLE,
      angleSection );

//font family property
    ComboPropertyDescriptorProvider fontFamilyProvider =
      new ComboPropertyDescriptorProvider(
        StyleHandle.FONT_FAMILY_PROP,
        ReportDesignConstants.STYLE_ELEMENT );
    ComboSection fontFamilySection =
      new ComboSection( fontFamilyProvider.getDisplayName( ),
                                            container,
                                              true );
    fontFamilySection.setProvider( fontFamilyProvider );
    fontFamilySection.setLayoutNum( 2 );
```

```
        fontFamilySection.setWidth( 200 );
        addSection( PageSectionId.LABEL_FONT_FAMILY,
                              fontFamilySection );

    //font size property
        FontSizePropertyDescriptorProvider fontSizeProvider =
          new FontSizePropertyDescriptorProvider(
            StyleHandle.FONT_SIZE_PROP,
            ReportDesignConstants.STYLE_ELEMENT );
        FontSizeSection fontSizeSection = new FontSizeSection(
            fontSizeProvider.getDisplayName( ),
            container,
            true );
        fontSizeSection.setProvider( fontSizeProvider );
        fontSizeSection.setLayoutNum( 4 );
        fontSizeSection.setGridPlaceholder( 2, true );
        fontSizeSection.setWidth( 200 );
        addSection( PageSectionId.LABEL_FONT_SIZE,
                              fontSizeSection );
        createSections( );
        layoutSections( );
  }
```

Deploying and testing the rotated label report item plug-in

After building the plug-in, the Eclipse PDE provides support for deploying and testing the plug-in in a run-time environment. The following sections describe the steps to deploy and test the rotated label report item plug-in example.

Deploying a report item extension

To deploy the rotated label report item plug-in and integrate the extension with the BIRT Report Designer, use the Export wizard or manually copy the org.eclipse.birt.sample.reportitem.rotatedtext plug-in from your workspace to the eclipse\plugins directory. For testing, you can create a Run configuration and include the rotated label plug-in from the workspace in the launch plug-in configuration.

Launching the rotated label report item plug-in

On PDE Manifest Editor, in Overview, the Testing section contains links to launch a plug-in as a separate Eclipse application in either Run or Debug mode. Figure 18-11 shows Overview for the rotated label report item extension example in the host instance of the PDE Workbench.

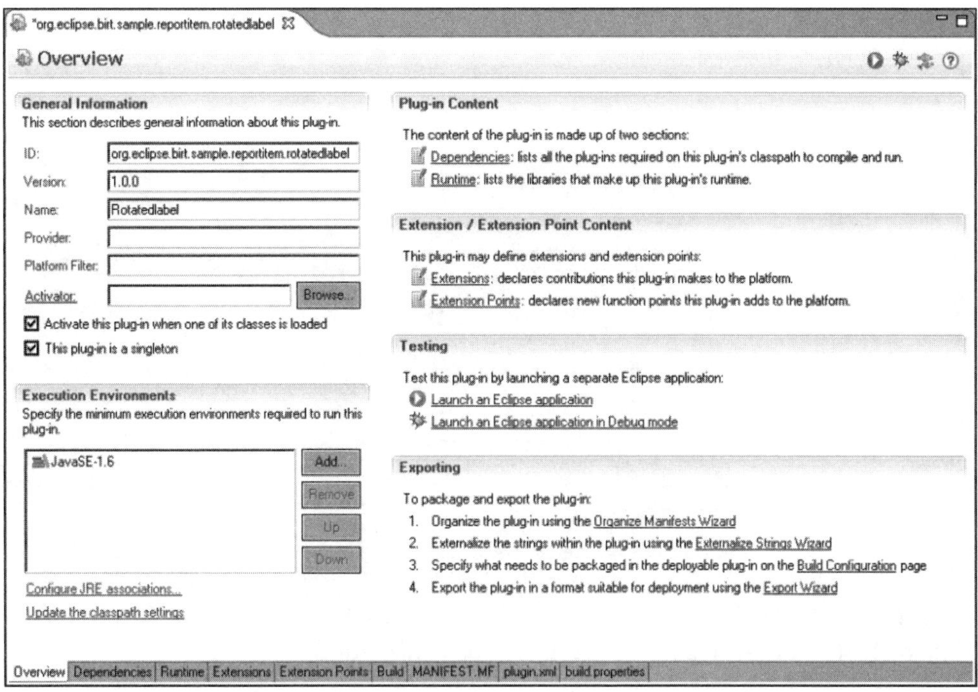

Figure 18-11 Viewing Overview for the rotated label report item extension

How to launch a run-time workbench

1. From the Eclipse SDK menu, choose Run— Run Configurations. In Run Configurations, right-click Eclipse Application. Choose New.
2. Create a configuration to launch an Eclipse application by performing the following tasks:
   1. In Name, type:

      `RotatedLabel`
   2. On Main, in Location, type:

      `C:\Test\TestRotatedLabel`

   Run Configurations appears as shown in Figure 18-12.

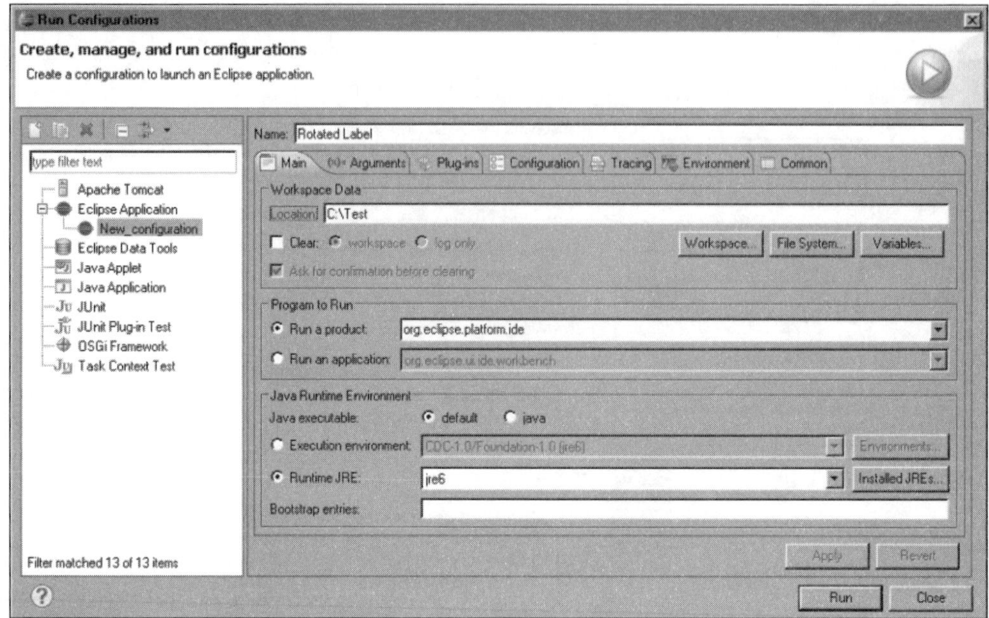

Figure 18-12 Creating the RotatedLabel run configuration

3 Choose the Plug-ins tab to select the list of plug-ins that you want to launch with the Run configuration.

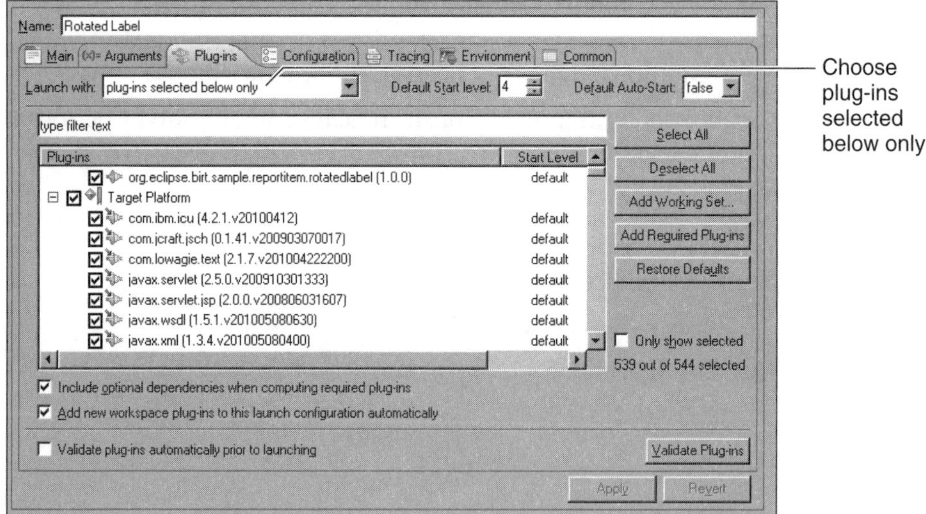

Figure 18-13 Adding the rotated label plug-in to the launch configuration

4 As shown in Figure 18-13, choose

`plug-ins selected below only`

5 Choose Run to launch the run-time workbench.

6 In the run-time workbench, choose the Report Design perspective.

7 In Report Design, choose File➛New➛Project. New Project appears. In Wizards, choose Report Project, as shown in Figure 18-14.

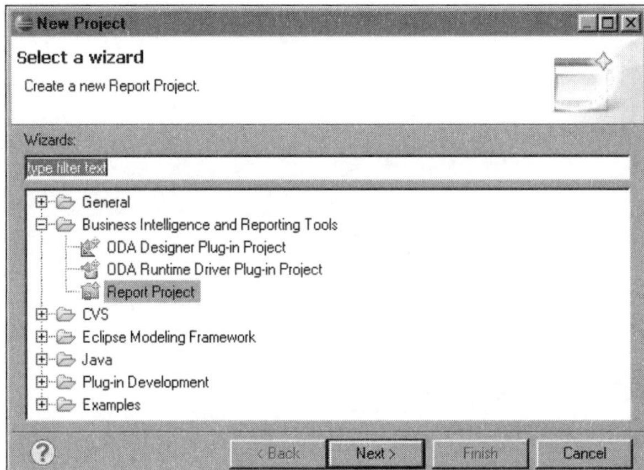

Figure 18-14 Selecting Report Project in New Project

Choose Next. New Report Project appears.

8 In Project name, type:

```
testRotatedLabel
```

Choose Finish.

9 In Report Design—Eclipse Platform, choose File➛New➛Report. New Report appears, as shown in Figure 18-15.

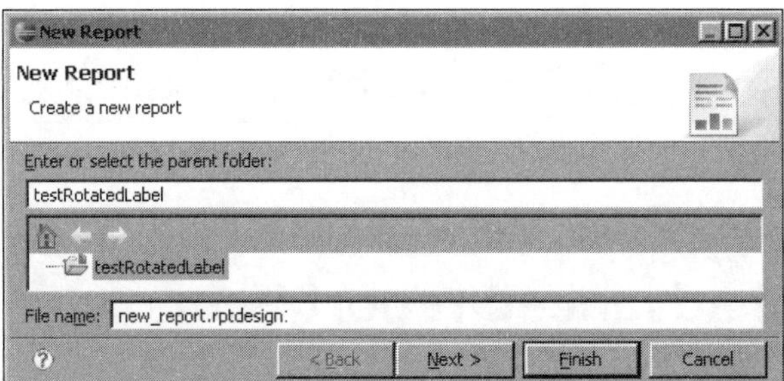

Figure 18-15 Creating a New Report for a rotated label

10 In File name, type a file name to change the default file name. Choose Next. New Report displays the report templates.

11 In Report templates, choose Blank Report. Choose Finish. The layout editor displays the report design, new_report.rptdesign. Palette contains the RotatedText report item.

12 From Palette, drag RotatedLabel to Layout, as shown in Figure 18-16.

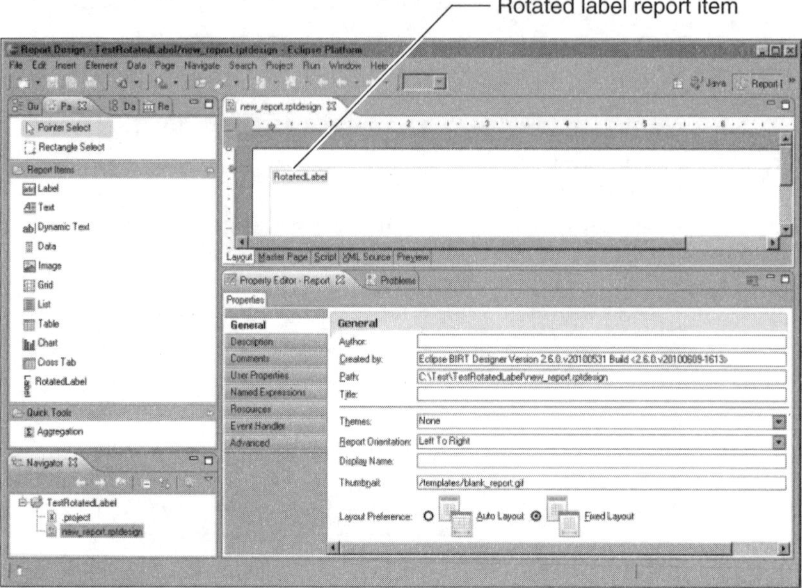

Figure 18-16 Rotated label report item in the report design

13 In new_report.rptdesign, choose Preview. The preview appears, displaying the rotated label report item, as shown in Figure 18-17.

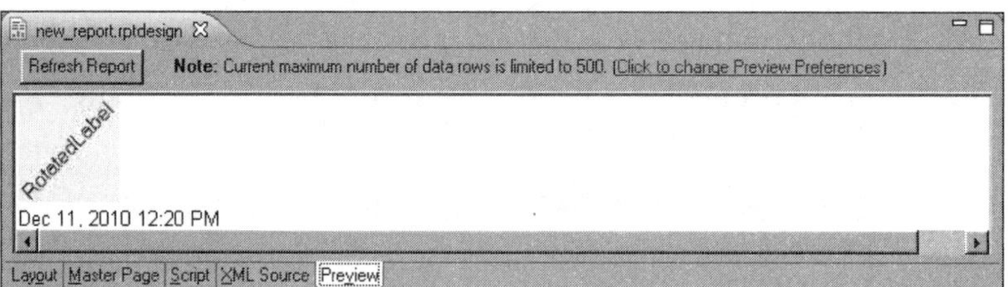

Figure 18-17 The rotated label in the report preview

Developing an advanced report item

The rotated label example, discussed earlier in this chapter in "Developing the sample report item extension," outlines the basic steps in creating a custom report item in BIRT. This section extends that earlier discussion by implementing more advanced functionality to enhance the report item usability and behavior.

The elements of the advanced example demonstrate how to develop additional user interface features for a custom rotated report item. The example shows how to implement a report item builder, a context menu, a custom property page, and data binding.

The example begins by defining a simple report model, design, and behavior. These steps are familiar from the previous example. This example uses more extension points to develop more advanced features. Creating a custom report item involves extending at least these three extension points:

- org.eclipse.birt.report.model.reportItemModel, which provides the report model extensibility
- org.eclipse.birt.report.designer.ui.reportitemUI, which provides the report designer extensibility
- org.eclipse.birt.report.engine.reportitemPresentation, which provides the report engine extensibility

Defining the report item model

The BIRT Report Model provides the org.eclipse.birt.report.model .reportItemModel extension point. As shown in Figure 18-18, defining the report item model involves creating a reportItem element under the extension and specifying the extensionName property as RotatedText. The extension name is the identifier for the extended item and serves as a connection between the report model and the engine and the designer extensions.

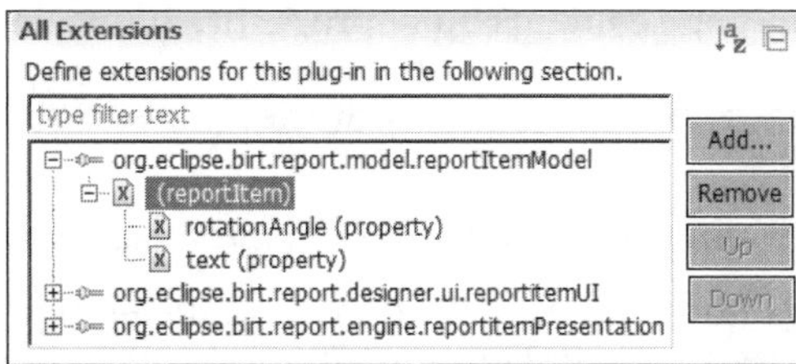

Figure 18-18 Adding the basic extension points

As shown in Figure 18-19, the model factory class org.eclipse.birt.sample. reportitem.rotatedtext.RotatedTextItemFactory must be defined.

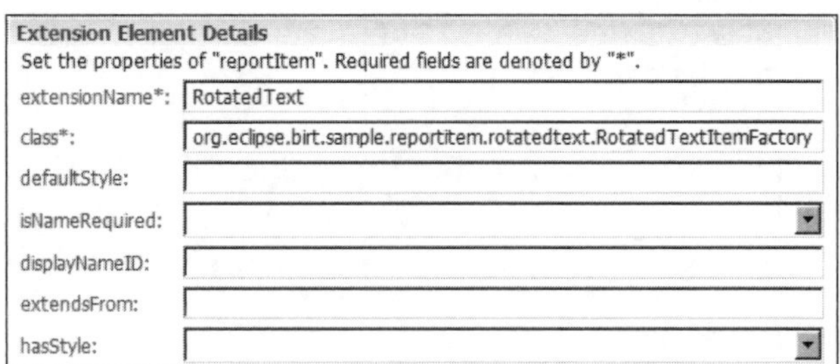

Figure 18-19 Defining the report model

This factory class creates and initializes the IReportItem instance, and provides optional localization support.

Listing 18-8 shows the code for the RotatedTextItemFactory class.

Listing 18-8 RotatedTextItemFactory class

```
public class RotatedTextItemFactory extends ReportItemFactory
{
   public IReportItem newReportItem( DesignElementHandle
   modelHandle )
   {
      if ( modelHandle instanceof ExtendedItemHandle &&
   RotatedTextItem.EXTENSION_NAME.equals( ( (ExtendedItemHandle)
   modelHandle ).getExtensionName( ) ) )
      {
         return new RotatedTextItem( (ExtendedItemHandle)
   modelHandle );
      }
      return null;
   }
   public IMessages getMessages( )
   {
      // TODO implement this to support localization
      return null;
   }
}
```

The reportItem properties page contains more properties like defaultStyle, extendsFrom, hasStyle, and others, which can be used to define additional features. This example does not extend these features; it uses the default values for these properties.

Like the Rotated Label example, the Rotated text element has two properties:

- rotationAngle, which defines the text rotation angle, using type integer and a default value 0, as shown in Figure 18-20.

Extension Element Details

Set the properties of "property". Required fields are denoted by "*".

name*:	rotationAngle
type*:	integer
displayNameID:	
detailType:	
subType:	
canInherit:	
defaultValue:	0
isEncryptable:	
defaultDisplayName:	Rotation Angle
isList:	
hasOwnModel:	
allowExpression:	

Figure 18-20 Defining the rotationAngle properties

- text, which defines the report item text content, using type expression and a default value "Rotated Text", as shown in Figure 18-21.

Extension Element Details

Set the properties of "property". Required fields are denoted by "*".

name*:	text
type*:	expression
displayNameID:	
detailType:	
subType:	
canInherit:	
defaultValue:	"Rotated Text"
isEncryptable:	
defaultDisplayName:	Text Content
isList:	
hasOwnModel:	
allowExpression:	

Figure 18-21 Defining the text properties

These settings complete the report model definition. The next step is to create a class RotatedTextItem. This class defines the basic methods for accessing the report item properties. The code is shown in Listing 18-9.

Listing 18-9 RotatedTextItem class

```
public class RotatedTextItem extends ReportItem
{
   public static final String EXTENSION_NAME = "RotatedText"; //
   $NON-NLS-1$
   public static final String TEXT_PROP = "text"; //$NON-NLS-1$
   public static final String ROTATION_ANGLE_PROP =
   "rotationAngle"; //$NON-NLS-1$

   private ExtendedItemHandle modelHandle;

   RotatedTextItem( ExtendedItemHandle modelHandle )
   {
      this.modelHandle = modelHandle;
   }

   public String getText( )
   {
      return modelHandle.getStringProperty( TEXT_PROP );
   }

   public int getRotationAngle( )
   {
      return modelHandle.getIntProperty( ROTATION_ANGLE_PROP );
   }
```

```
    public void setText( String value ) throws SemanticException
    {
        modelHandle.setProperty( TEXT_PROP, value );
    }

    public void setRotationAngle( int value ) throws
    SemanticException
    {
        modelHandle.setProperty( ROTATION_ANGLE_PROP, value );
    }
}
```

Defining the report item UI design

The Designer provides the org.eclipse.birt.report.designer.ui.reportitemUI extension point to define the user interface of extended report items. Add the org.eclipse.birt.report.designer.ui.reportitemUI extension point and create the design properties to define the user interface, as shown in Figure 18-22.

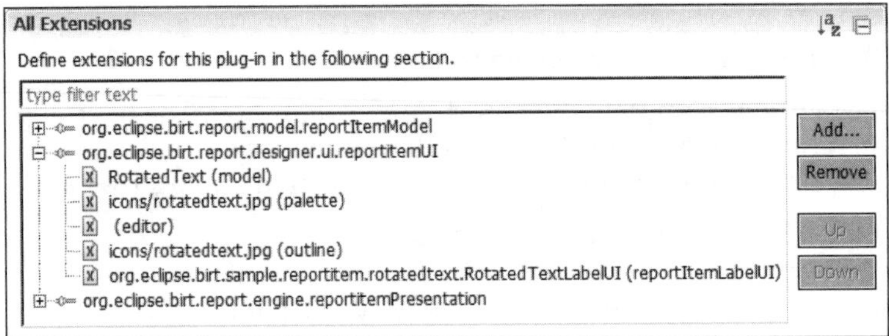

Figure 18-22 Defining the design

The design properties are as follows:

- RotatedText (model)
- palette
- editor
- outline

- The first property, RotatedText (model), binds the Designer extension to the Model extension. The RotatedText's extensionName is RotatedText, the same as the model extension name, as shown in Figure 18-23.

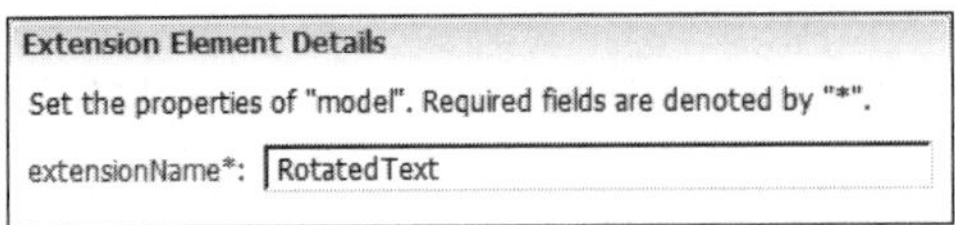

Figure 18-23 RotatedText (model) name

- Palette properties specify the icon displayed in Palette view and the palette category. An empty category value, as shown in Figure 18-24, causes the report item to use the default category of Report Item.

Extension Element Details

Set the properties of "palette". Required fields are denoted by "*".

icon: icons/rotatedtext.jpg

category:

categoryDisplayName:

Figure 18-24 Palette settings

- Editor properties define the report item visibility in different editor pages and whether the resizing control is enabled, as shown in Figure 18-25.

Extension Element Details

Set the properties of "editor". Required fields are denoted by "*".

showInMasterPage: true

showInDesigner: true

canResize: false

menuLabel:

Figure 18-25 Editor settings

- Outline specifies the icon shown in Outline view, as shown in Figure 18-26. Usually the icon is the same as the one in Palette view.

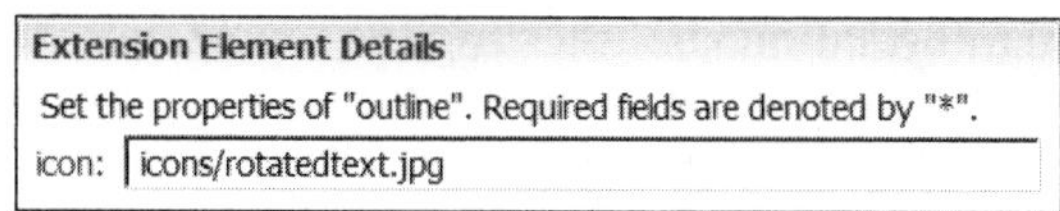

Figure 18-26 Outline settings

- The User Interface (UI) provider defines how to display and interact with the extended report item within the editor. The BIRT designer supports three types of UI providers:
  - The Label UI Provider implements the IReportItemLabelProvider interface, which manipulates and displays a text content.
  - The Image UI Provider implements the IReportItemImageProvider interface, which manipulates and displays an image content.
  - The Figure UI Provider implements the IReportItemFigureProvider, which uses the Figure interface from Graphical Editing Framework (GEF), which provides flexibility and interactivity support.

This example introduces all three providers, starting with the simplest Label UI Provider. The property reportItemLabelUI, created under the extension, registers the Label UI provider, and specifies the implementer class org.eclipse.birt.sample.reportitem.rotatedtext.RotatedTextLabelUI, as shown in Figure 18-27.

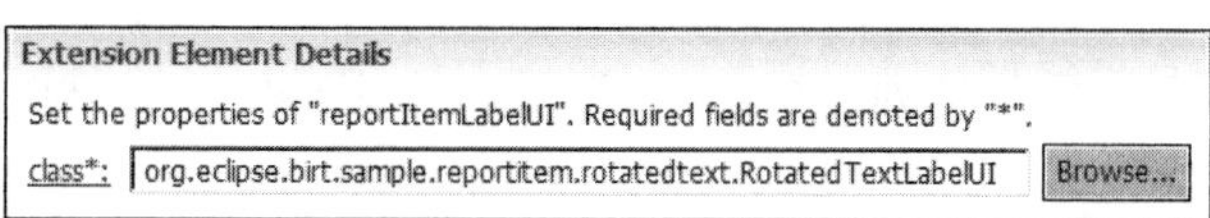

Figure 18-27 reportItemLabelUI setting

The code for RotatedTextLabelUI class, shown in Listing 18-10, reads the text property value from the model and returns it as a string.

Listing 18-10 RotatedTextLabelUI class

```
public class RotatedTextLabelUI implements
   IReportItemLabelProvider
{  public String getLabel( ExtendedItemHandle handle )
   {  try {
         IReportItem item = handle.getReportItem( );
         if ( item instanceof RotatedTextItem )
         {
            return ( (RotatedTextItem) item ).getText( );
         }
      } catch ( ExtendedElementException e )
      {
         e.printStackTrace( );
      }
      return null;
   }
}
```

The final step is to test the completed report item definition in the BIRT Designer. For more information about testing the report item definition, see "Deploying and testing the rotated label report item plug-in," earlier in this chapter. Open a new Eclipse instance in Report Design perspective. Open the Palette view, as shown in Figure 18-28.

The Palette contains the new RotatedText extended report item.

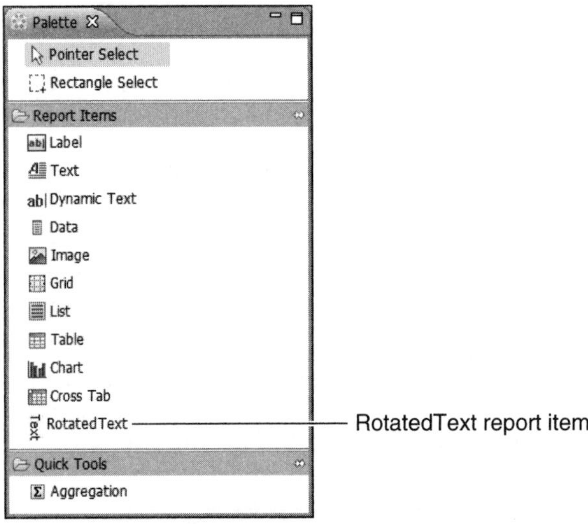

Figure 18-28 Palette view showing the RotatedText report item

Right-click anywhere in the Layout, and the RotatedText item is now also available in the Insert context menu, as shown in Figure 18-29.

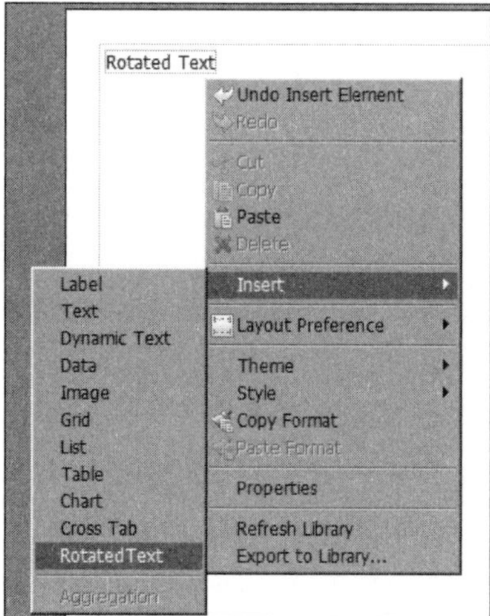

Figure 18-29 Insert context menu showing the RotatedText report item

A RotatedText report item inserted in the layout also appears in the Outline view as shown in Figure 18-30.

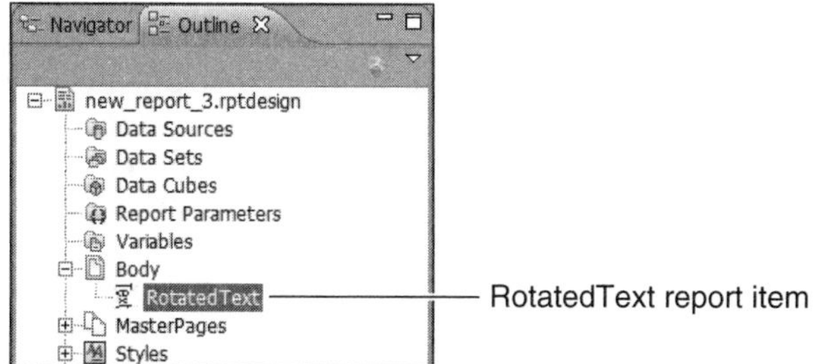

Figure 18-30 Outline view showing a RotatedText report item

Select the RotatedText item in the Layout and open the Properties view. The properties of the item appear as shown in Figure 18-31.

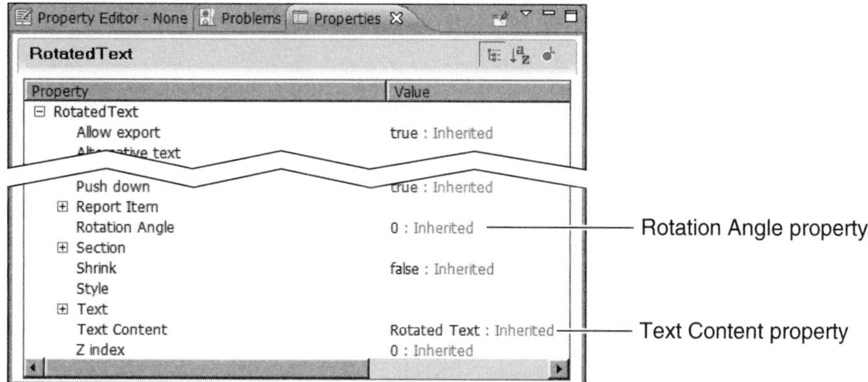

Figure 18-31 Properties view of a RotatedText report item

The Properties view displays all the properties that belong to the RotatedText item. Among them are the Rotation Angle and Text Content properties, as well as other inherited properties. The Properties view supports editing these property values.

Defining the report item presentation

BIRT Report Engine provides the org.eclipse.birt.report.engine .reportitemPresentation extension point, which defines the presentation of extended report items.

The extension property RotatedText binds the engine extension to the model extension. The property name must be set to RotatedText to match the name of the model's RotatedText property.

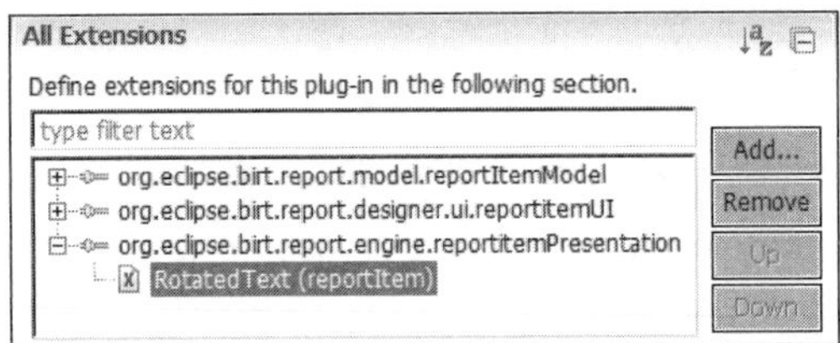

Figure 18-32 Defining the presentation

The presentation implementer class is set to org.eclipse.birt.sample .reportitem.rotatedtext.RotatedTextPresentationImpl and must implement the IReportItemPresentation interface. The implementation of the class creates the text image dynamically, and uses Swing graphics API to render the rotated text. Listing 18-11 shows the code for this class.

Listing 18-11 RotatedTextPresentationImpl class

```
public class RotatedTextPresentationImpl
   extends ReportItemPresentationBase
{
   private RotatedTextItem textItem;
   public void setModelObject( ExtendedItemHandle modelHandle )
   {
      try{
         textItem = (RotatedTextItem) modelHandle.getReportItem();
      }
      catch ( ExtendedElementException e )
      {
         e.printStackTrace( );
      }
   }
   public int getOutputType( )
   {
      return OUTPUT_AS_IMAGE;
   }
```

```
   public Object onRowSets( IRowSet[] rowSets )
   throws BirtException
   {
      if ( textItem == null )
      {
         return null;
      }

      int angle = textItem.getRotationAngle( );
      String text = textItem.getText( );
      BufferedImage rotatedImage =
         SwingGraphicsUtil.createRotatedTextImage( text, angle,
         new Font( "Default", 0, 12 ) ); //$NON-NLS-1$
      ByteArrayInputStream bis = null;

      try
      {
         ImageIO.setUseCache( false );
         ByteArrayOutputStream baos = new ByteArrayOutputStream();
         ImageOutputStream ios =
            ImageIO.createImageOutputStream( baos );
         ImageIO.write( rotatedImage, "png", ios ); //$NON-NLS-1$
         ios.flush( );
         ios.close( );
         bis = new ByteArrayInputStream( baos.toByteArray( ) );
      }
      catch ( IOException e )
      {
         e.printStackTrace( );
      }
      return bis;
   }
}
```

This implementation generates an image dynamically in the onRowSets() method. An in-memory stream returns the image content to the caller. The utility class that implements the key rotation rendering algorithm is shown in Listing 18-12.

Listing 18-12 SwingGraphicsUtil class

```
public class SwingGraphicsUtil
{
   public static BufferedImage createRotatedTextImage(
      String text, int angle, Font ft )
   {
      Graphics2D g2d = null;
      try  {
         if ( text == null || text.trim( ).length( ) == 0 )
         {
            return null;
```

```
      }
      BufferedImage stringImage = new BufferedImage( 1, 1,
         BufferedImage.TYPE_INT_ARGB );
      g2d = (Graphics2D) stringImage.getGraphics( );
      g2d.setFont( ft );
      FontMetrics fm = g2d.getFontMetrics( );
      Rectangle2D bounds = fm.getStringBounds( text, g2d );
      TextLayout tl = new TextLayout( text, ft,
         g2d.getFontRenderContext( ) );
      g2d.dispose( );
      g2d = null;
      return createRotatedImage( tl, (int) bounds.getWidth( ),
         (int) bounds.getHeight( ), angle );
   }
      catch ( Exception e )
   {
      e.printStackTrace( );
      if ( g2d != null )
      {
         g2d.dispose( );
      }
   }
   return null;
}

private static BufferedImage createRotatedImage( Object src,
   int width, int height, int angle )
{
   angle = angle % 360;
   if ( angle < 0 )
   {
      angle += 360;
   }
   if ( angle == 0 )
   {
      return renderRotatedObject( src, 0, width, height, 0, 0);
   }
   else if ( angle == 90 )
   {
      return renderRotatedObject( src, -Math.PI / 2, height,
         width, -width, 0 );
   }
   else if ( angle == 180 )
   {
      return renderRotatedObject( src, Math.PI, width, height,
         -width, -height );
   }
   else if ( angle == 270 )
   {
```

```
        return renderRotatedObject( src, Math.PI / 2, height,
            width, 0, -height );
    }
    else if ( angle > 0 && angle < 90 )
    {
        double angleInRadians = ( ( -angle * Math.PI ) / 180.0 );
        double cosTheta = Math.abs( Math.cos( angleInRadians ) );
        double sineTheta = Math.abs( Math.sin( angleInRadians ));
        int dW = (int) ( width * cosTheta + height * sineTheta );
        int dH = (int) ( width * sineTheta + height * cosTheta );
        return renderRotatedObject( src, angleInRadians, dW, dH,
            -width * sineTheta * sineTheta,
            width * sineTheta * cosTheta );
    }
    else if ( angle > 90 && angle < 180 )
    {
        double angleInRadians = ( ( -angle * Math.PI ) / 180.0 );
        double cosTheta = Math.abs( Math.cos( angleInRadians ) );
        double sineTheta = Math.abs( Math.sin( angleInRadians ));
        int dW = (int) ( width * cosTheta + height * sineTheta );
        int dH = (int) ( width * sineTheta + height * cosTheta );
        return renderRotatedObject( src, angleInRadians, dW, dH,
            -( width + height * sineTheta * cosTheta ),
            -height / 2 );
    }
    else if ( angle > 180 && angle < 270 )
    {
        double angleInRadians = ( ( -angle * Math.PI ) / 180.0 );
        double cosTheta = Math.abs( Math.cos( angleInRadians ) );
        double sineTheta = Math.abs( Math.sin( angleInRadians ));
        int dW = (int) ( width * cosTheta + height * sineTheta );
        int dH = (int) ( width * sineTheta + height * cosTheta );
        return renderRotatedObject( src, angleInRadians, dW, dH,
            -( width * cosTheta * cosTheta ),
            -( height + width * cosTheta * sineTheta ) );
    }
    else if ( angle > 270 && angle < 360 )
    {
        double angleInRadians = ( ( -angle * Math.PI ) / 180.0 );
        double cosTheta = Math.abs( Math.cos( angleInRadians ) );
        double sineTheta = Math.abs( Math.sin( angleInRadians ));
        int dW = (int) ( width * cosTheta + height * sineTheta );
        int dH = (int) ( width * sineTheta + height * cosTheta );
        return renderRotatedObject( src, angleInRadians, dW, dH,
            ( height * cosTheta * sineTheta ),
            -( height * sineTheta * sineTheta ) );
    }
    return renderRotatedObject( src, 0, width, height, 0, 0 );
}
```

```
    private static BufferedImage renderRotatedObject( Object src,
        double angle, int width, int height, double tx, double ty )
    {
        BufferedImage dest = new BufferedImage( width, height,
            BufferedImage.TYPE_INT_ARGB );
        Graphics2D g2d = (Graphics2D) dest.getGraphics( );
        g2d.setColor( Color.black );
        g2d.setRenderingHint( RenderingHints.KEY_TEXT_ANTIALIASING,
            RenderingHints.VALUE_TEXT_ANTIALIAS_ON );
        g2d.setRenderingHint( RenderingHints.KEY_ANTIALIASING,
            RenderingHints.VALUE_ANTIALIAS_ON );
        AffineTransform at = AffineTransform.getRotateInstance(
            angle );
        at.translate( tx, ty );
        g2d.setTransform( at );
        if ( src instanceof TextLayout )
        {
            TextLayout tl = (TextLayout) src;
            tl.draw( g2d, 0, tl.getAscent( ) );
        }
        else if ( src instanceof Image )
        {
            g2d.drawImage( (Image) src, 0, 0, null );
        }
        g2d.dispose( );
        return dest;
    }
}
```

To test the report item, open a new Eclipse instance in the Report Design perspective. Create a report and insert a grid having nine cells. Insert a RotatedText item in each cell, as shown in Figure 18-33, and use the Properties view to set a different rotation angle for each report item.

Figure 18-33 Report layout having nine RotatedText items

A preview of the report as HTML is shown in Figure 18-34.

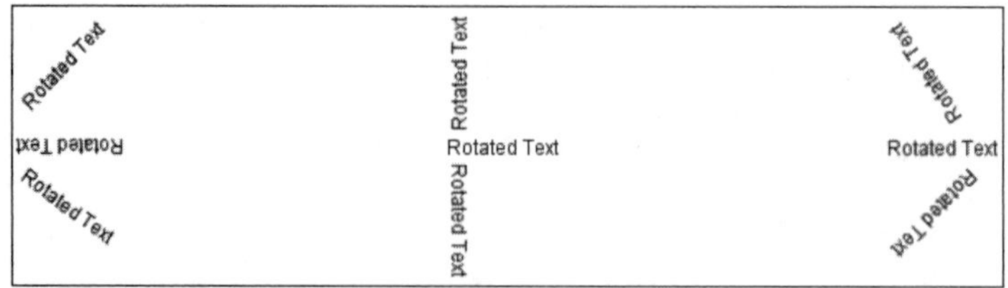

Figure 18-34 Preview in HTML

Improving the report item UI design

As you see in the report layout in Figure 18-33, all RotatedText report items in the report design look the same, displayed as horizontal text. Look at the Properties view to see the different angles at which the text would be displayed in the preview. This inconsistency prevents the report developer from getting an intuitive picture of the final report at the design phase. One obvious improvement is to make the report item image appear in the design in the same way in which it appears in the preview. This technique is called WYSIWYG, the familiar acronym for what you see is what you get, that is adopted by most contemporary editors.

To comply with the WYSIWYG paradigm, change the report item presentation to display the rotated text in the layout. Use the Image UI provider or the Figure UI provider instead of the Label UI Provider to implement this change.

Using the Image UI provider

The Image UI provider requires an image for the UI presentation. The implementation renders the rotated text as an image and returns it to the caller.

To register the Image UI provider, remove the original Label UI provider first, and then add the new Image UI provider extension, as shown in Figure 18-35.

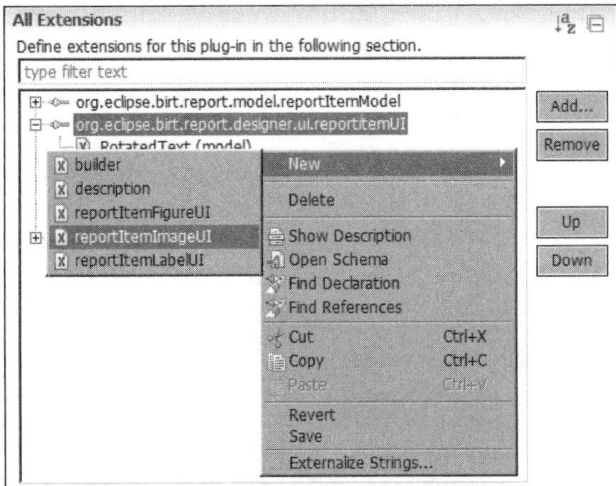

Figure 18-35 Changing the UI provider

The implementer class code is shown in Listing 18-13.

Listing 18-13 RotatedTextImageUI class

```
public class RotatedTextImageUI
   implements IReportItemImageProvider
{
```

```
    public void disposeImage( ExtendedItemHandle handle,
        Image image )
    {
        if ( image != null && !image.isDisposed( ) )
        {
            image.dispose( );
        }
    }

    public Image getImage( ExtendedItemHandle handle )
    {
        try
        {
            IReportItem item = handle.getReportItem( );

            if ( item instanceof RotatedTextItem )
            {
                int angle =
                    ( (RotatedTextItem) item ).getRotationAngle( );
                String text = ( (RotatedTextItem) item ).getText( );

                return SwtGraphicsUtil.createRotatedTextImage( text,
                    angle, null );
            }
        }
        catch ( ExtendedElementException e )
        {
            e.printStackTrace( );
        }
        return null;
    }
}
```

The image handler uses Standard Widget Toolkit (SWT) to process and rotate the image in a new version of the SwingGraphicsUtil class, shown in Listing 18-14.

Listing 18-14 SwingGraphicsUtil class

```
public class SwtGraphicsUtil
{
    public static Image createRotatedTextImage( String text,
        int angle, Font ft )
    {
        GC gc = null;
        try
        {
            if ( text == null || text.trim( ).length( ) == 0 )
            {
                return null;
            }
```

```
      Display display = Display.getCurrent( );

      gc = new GC( display );
      if ( ft != null )
      {
         gc.setFont( ft );
      }

      Point pt = gc.textExtent( text );

      gc.dispose( );

      TextLayout tl = new TextLayout( display );
      if ( ft != null )
      {
         tl.setFont( ft );
      }
      tl.setText( text );

      return createRotatedImage( tl, pt.x, pt.y, angle );
   }
   catch ( Exception e )
   {
      e.printStackTrace( );

      if ( gc != null && !gc.isDisposed( ) )
      {
         gc.dispose( );
      }
   }
   return null;
}

/**
 * @return Returns as [rotatedWidth, rotatedHeight, xOffset,
      yOffset]
 */
public static double[] computedRotatedInfo( int width,
   int height, int angle )
{
   angle = angle % 360;

   if ( angle < 0 )
   {
      angle += 360;
   }

   if ( angle == 0 )
   {
      return new double[]{ width, height, 0, 0 };
   }
   else if ( angle == 90 )
   {
```

```
        return new double[]{ height, width, -width, 0 };
    }
    else if ( angle == 180 )
    {
        return new double[]{ width, height, -width, -height };
    }
    else if ( angle == 270 )
    {
        return new double[]{ height, width, 0, -height };
    }
    else if ( angle > 0 && angle < 90 )
    {
        double angleInRadians = ( ( -angle * Math.PI ) / 180.0 );
        double cosTheta = Math.abs( Math.cos( angleInRadians ) );
        double sineTheta = Math.abs( Math.sin( angleInRadians ));

        int dW = (int) ( width * cosTheta + height * sineTheta );
        int dH = (int) ( width * sineTheta + height * cosTheta );

        return new double[]{ dW, dH,
            -width * sineTheta * sineTheta,
            width * sineTheta * cosTheta };
    }
    else if ( angle > 90 && angle < 180 )
    {
        double angleInRadians = ( ( -angle * Math.PI ) / 180.0 );
        double cosTheta = Math.abs( Math.cos( angleInRadians ) );
        double sineTheta = Math.abs( Math.sin( angleInRadians ));

        int dW = (int) ( width * cosTheta + height * sineTheta );
        int dH = (int) ( width * sineTheta + height * cosTheta );

        return new double[]{ dW, dH,
            -( width + height * sineTheta * cosTheta ),
            -height / 2 };
    }
    else if ( angle > 180 && angle < 270 )
    {
        double angleInRadians = ( ( -angle * Math.PI ) / 180.0 );
        double cosTheta = Math.abs( Math.cos( angleInRadians ) );
        double sineTheta = Math.abs( Math.sin( angleInRadians ));

        int dW = (int) ( width * cosTheta + height * sineTheta );
        int dH = (int) ( width * sineTheta + height * cosTheta );

        return new double[]{ dW, dH,
            -( width * cosTheta * cosTheta ),
            -( height + width * cosTheta * sineTheta ) };
    }
    else if ( angle > 270 && angle < 360 )
    {
```

```
      double angleInRadians = ( ( -angle * Math.PI ) / 180.0 );
      double cosTheta = Math.abs( Math.cos( angleInRadians ) );
      double sineTheta = Math.abs( Math.sin( angleInRadians ));

      int dW = (int) ( width * cosTheta + height * sineTheta );
      int dH = (int) ( width * sineTheta + height * cosTheta );

      return new double[]{ dW, dH,
         ( height * cosTheta * sineTheta ),
         -( height * sineTheta * sineTheta ) };
   }

   return new double[]{ width, height, 0, 0 };
}

private static Image createRotatedImage( Object src, int width,
int height, int angle )
{
   angle = angle % 360;

   if ( angle < 0 )
   {
      angle += 360;
   }

   double[] info = computedRotatedInfo( width, height, angle );

   return renderRotatedObject( src, -angle, (int) info[0],
      (int) info[1], info[2], info[3] );
}

private static Image renderRotatedObject( Object src,
   double angle, int width, int height, double tx, double ty )
{
   Display display = Display.getCurrent( );

   Image dest = null;
   GC gc = null;
   Transform tf = null;

   try
   {
      dest = new Image( Display.getCurrent( ), width, height );
      gc = new GC( dest );

      gc.setAdvanced( true );
      gc.setAntialias( SWT.ON );
      gc.setTextAntialias( SWT.ON );

      tf = new Transform( display );
      tf.rotate( (float) angle );
      tf.translate( (float) tx, (float) ty );

      gc.setTransform( tf );

      if ( src instanceof TextLayout )
```

```
            {
               TextLayout tl = (TextLayout) src;
               tl.draw( gc, 0, 0 );
            }
            else if ( src instanceof Image )
            {
               gc.drawImage( (Image) src, 0, 0 );
            }
         }
         catch ( Exception e )
         {
            e.printStackTrace( );
         }
         finally
         {
            if ( gc != null && !gc.isDisposed( ) )
            {
               gc.dispose( );
            }

            if ( tf != null && !tf.isDisposed( ) )
            {
               tf.dispose( );
            }
         }
         return dest;
      }
   }
```

Run another test and insert a RotatedText item in the layout as shown in Figure 18-36. Specify the rotation angle as 45.

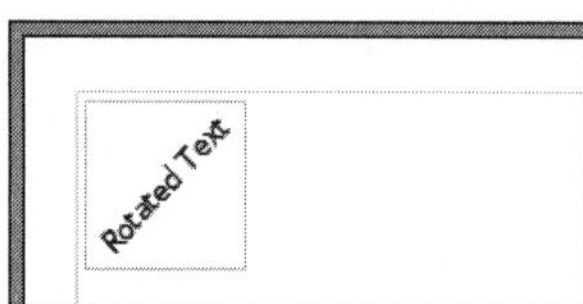

Figure 18-36 Report layout of RotatedText implementing Image UI

After implementing the new Image UI provider, the rotated text item in the report layout appears angled as in the preview, as shown in Figure 18-37.

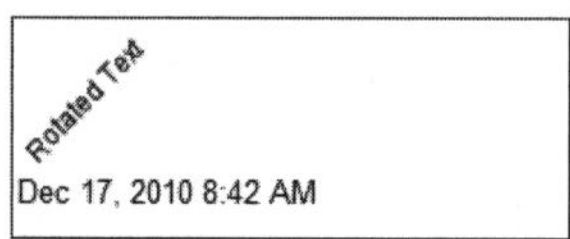

Figure 18-37 Report preview of RotatedText implementing Image UI

Using the Figure UI Provider

The Image UI provides the basic functionality for implementing WYSIWYG support for the rotated report item.

The Figure UI provider is typically used in cases where the requirements are more complex. The Figure UI leverages the IFigure interface from Graphical Editing Framework (GEF) and provides more flexibility and interactivity than the Image UI. Table 18-10 shows a comparison between Figure UI and Image UI.

Table 18-10 Comparing Figure UI and Image UI

Property	Figure UI	Image UI
Interactivity	Supports listeners for UI events.	No interactivity support.
Life Cycle	Three phases: ■ Create ■ Update ■ Dispose Creates the Figure object once. Each time any model state changes, the Update action is invoked. This mechanism supports incremental and selective updates. When Update occurs, the figure instance can check the internal model state and decide what update to execute, full, partial, or none.	Two phases: ■ Create ■ Dispose Each time any model state changes, the Image UI recreates the image presentation.
Presentation	Supports the creation of hierarchical UI structures, controlled by the GEF layout mechanism.	Uses one single Image for presentation.
Usage	Requires knowledge of GEF framework.	Easy to use.

A good use case for the Figure UI Provider is one where a mouse middle-button click controls the report item rotation angle. Each middle-button click adds 45 degrees to the value of the rotation angle.

To implement the Figure UI provider, first remove any existing Label UI or Image UI provider in the extension points. Then, add the new Figure UI provider extension, and specify the implementer class as org.eclipse.birt .sample.reportitem.rotatedtext.RotatedTextFigureUI. The code for the class is in Listing 18-15.

Listing 18-15 RotatedTextFigureUI class

```
public class RotatedTextFigureUI extends ReportItemFigureProvider
{
   public IFigure createFigure( ExtendedItemHandle handle )
   {
      try
      {
         IReportItem item = handle.getReportItem( );

         if ( item instanceof RotatedTextItem )
         {
            return new RotatedTextFigure( (RotatedTextItem) item );
         }
      }
      catch ( ExtendedElementException e )
      {
         e.printStackTrace( );
      }
      return null;
   }

   public void updateFigure( ExtendedItemHandle handle,
      IFigure figure )
   {
      try
      {
         IReportItem item = handle.getReportItem( );

         if ( item instanceof RotatedTextItem )
         {
            RotatedTextFigure fig = (RotatedTextFigure) figure;

            fig.setRotatedTextItem( (RotatedTextItem) item );
         }
      }
      catch ( ExtendedElementException e )
      {
         e.printStackTrace( );
      }
   }

   public void disposeFigure( ExtendedItemHandle handle,
      IFigure figure )
   {
      ( (RotatedTextFigure) figure ).dispose( );
   }
}
```

The Figure UI provider creates a RotatedTextFigure instance. The RotatedTextFigure class implements the rendering following an algorithm similar to the Image UI provider. The only addition is using a listener to handle the mouse middle-button click event. The code for this class is in Listing 18-16.

Listing 18-16 RotatedTextFigure class

```
public class RotatedTextFigure extends Figure
{
   private String lastText;
   private int lastAngle;
   private Image cachedImage;
   private RotatedTextItem textItem;

   RotatedTextFigure( RotatedTextItem textItem )
   {
      super( );

      this.textItem = textItem;

      addMouseListener( new MouseListener.Stub( ) {

         public void mousePressed( MouseEvent me )
         {
            if ( me.button == 2 )
            {
               try
               {
                  RotatedTextFigure.this.textItem.setRotationAngle(
   normalize( RotatedTextFigure.this.textItem.getRotationAngle( )
                     + 45 ) );
               }
               catch ( SemanticException e )
               {
                  e.printStackTrace( );
               }
            }
         }
      } );
   }

   private int normalize( int angle )
   {
      angle = angle % 360;

      if ( angle < 0 )
      {
         angle += 360;
      }

      return angle;
   }

   public Dimension getMinimumSize( int hint, int hint2 )
```

```
{
   return getPreferredSize( hint, hint2 );
}

public Dimension getPreferredSize( int hint, int hint2 )
{
   Display display = Display.getCurrent( );

   GC gc = null;

   try
   {
      String text = textItem.getText( );
      int angle = textItem.getRotationAngle( );

      gc = new GC( display );

      Point pt = gc.textExtent( text == null ? "" : text );
         //$NON-NLS-1$

      double[] info = SwtGraphicsUtil.computedRotatedInfo(
         pt.x, pt.y, angle );

      if ( getBorder( ) != null )
      {
         Insets bdInsets = getBorder( ).getInsets( this );

         return new Dimension(
            (int) info[0] + bdInsets.getWidth( ),
            (int) info[1] + bdInsets.getHeight( ) );
      }
      return new Dimension( (int) info[0], (int) info[1] );
   }
   finally
   {
      if ( gc != null && !gc.isDisposed( ) )
      {
         gc.dispose( );
      }
   }
}

protected void paintClientArea( Graphics graphics )
{
   final Rectangle r = getClientArea( ).getCopy( );

   String text = textItem.getText( );
   int angle = textItem.getRotationAngle( );

   if ( text == null )
   {
      text = ""; //$NON-NLS-1$
   }
```

```
      if ( !text.equals( lastText ) || angle != lastAngle
            || cachedImage == null || cachedImage.isDisposed( ) )
      {
         lastText = text;
         lastAngle = angle;

         if ( cachedImage != null && !cachedImage.isDisposed( ) )
         {
            cachedImage.dispose( );
         }

         cachedImage = SwtGraphicsUtil.createRotatedTextImage(
            text, angle, null );
      }

      if ( cachedImage != null && !cachedImage.isDisposed( ) )
      {
         graphics.drawImage( cachedImage, r.x, r.y );
      }
   }

   void setRotatedTextItem( RotatedTextItem item )
   {
      this.textItem = item;
   }

   void dispose( )
   {
      if ( cachedImage != null && !cachedImage.isDisposed( ) )
      {
         cachedImage.dispose( );
      }
   }
}
```

To test the RotatedText report item, insert a RotatedText item in the layout editor. Each time you middle-click the RotatedText item, the image rotates by 45 degrees.

Creating a report item builder

In the implementation so far, the only way to manipulate the property values of the RotatedText report item is from Property view. Another more sophisticated and user friendly way to set the properties is to use a builder. A builder is a user interface, designed to populate the properties and create a new instance of a selected item. Some of the report items in BIRT, like the Chart, for example, have associated builders. The builders appear every time you double-click or add a report item to the layout.

To create a builder for the RotatedText item, add the builder UI extension and specify the implementer class as org.eclipse.birt.sample.reportitem .rotatedtext.RotatedTextBuilder, as shown in Figure 18-38.

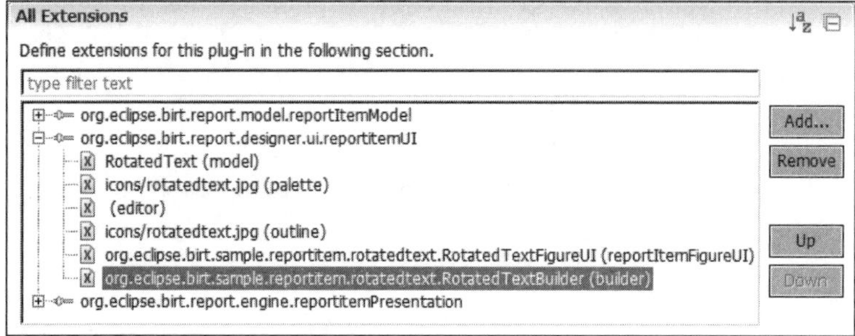

Figure 18-38 Defining the builder support

The class RotatedTextBuilder extends the org.eclipse.birt.report.designer.ui .extensions.IReportItemBuilderUI interface. The code is in Listing 18-17.

Listing 18-17 RotatedTextBuilder class

```
public class RotatedTextBuilder extends ReportItemBuilderUI
{
   public int open( ExtendedItemHandle handle )
   {
      try
      {
         IReportItem item = handle.getReportItem( );

         if ( item instanceof RotatedTextItem )
         {
            RotatedTextEditor editor = new RotatedTextEditor(
               Display.getCurrent( ).getActiveShell( ),
               (RotatedTextItem) item );
            return editor.open( );
         }
      }
      catch ( Exception e )
      {
         e.printStackTrace( );
      }
      return Window.CANCEL;
   }
}
```

The code instantiates an object of RotatedTextEditor class to populate the actual UI. The code of the RotatedTextEditor class is in Listing 18-18.

Listing 18-18 RotatedTextEditor class

```
class RotatedTextEditor extends TrayDialog
{
   protected RotatedTextItem textItem;
   protected Text txtText;
   protected Scale sclAngle;
```

```
protected Label lbAngle;

protected RotatedTextEditor( Shell shell,
   RotatedTextItem textItem )
{
   super( shell );
   this.textItem = textItem;
}

protected void configureShell( Shell newShell )
{
   super.configureShell( newShell );
   newShell.setText( "Rotated Text Builder" ); //$NON-NLS-1$
}

protected void createTextArea( Composite parent )
{
   Label lb = new Label( parent, SWT.None );
   lb.setText( "Text Content:" ); //$NON-NLS-1$

   txtText = new Text( parent, SWT.BORDER );
   GridData gd = new GridData( GridData.FILL_HORIZONTAL );
   gd.horizontalSpan = 2;
   txtText.setLayoutData( gd );
}

protected Control createDialogArea( Composite parent )
{
   Composite composite = new Composite( parent, SWT.NONE );
   GridLayout layout = new GridLayout( 3, false );
   layout.marginHeight = convertVerticalDLUsToPixels(
      IDialogConstants.VERTICAL_MARGIN );
   layout.marginWidth = convertHorizontalDLUsToPixels(
      IDialogConstants.HORIZONTAL_MARGIN );
   layout.verticalSpacing = convertVerticalDLUsToPixels(
      IDialogConstants.VERTICAL_SPACING );
   layout.horizontalSpacing = convertHorizontalDLUsToPixels(
      IDialogConstants.HORIZONTAL_SPACING );
   composite.setLayout( layout );
   composite.setLayoutData(new GridData( GridData.FILL_BOTH ));

   createTextArea( composite );

   Label lb = new Label( composite, SWT.None );
   lb.setText( "Rotation Angle:" ); //$NON-NLS-1$

   sclAngle = new Scale( composite, SWT.None );
   sclAngle.setLayoutData( new GridData(
      GridData.FILL_HORIZONTAL ) );
   sclAngle.setMinimum( 0 );
   sclAngle.setMaximum( 360 );
   sclAngle.setIncrement( 10 );

   lbAngle = new Label( composite, SWT.None );
```

```
        GridData gd = new GridData( );
        gd.widthHint = 20;
        lbAngle.setLayoutData( gd );

        sclAngle.addSelectionListener( new SelectionListener( ) {

            public void widgetDefaultSelected( SelectionEvent e )
            {
                lbAngle.setText( String.valueOf(
                    sclAngle.getSelection( ) ) );
            }

            public void widgetSelected( SelectionEvent e )
            {
                lbAngle.setText( String.valueOf(
                    sclAngle.getSelection( ) ) );
            }
        } );

        applyDialogFont( composite );

        initValues( );

        return composite;
    }

    private void initValues( )
    {
        txtText.setText( textItem.getText( ) );
        sclAngle.setSelection( textItem.getRotationAngle( ) );
        lbAngle.setText( String.valueOf(
            textItem.getRotationAngle( ) ) );
    }

    protected void okPressed( )
    {
        try
        {
            textItem.setText( txtText.getText( ) );
            textItem.setRotationAngle( sclAngle.getSelection( ) );
        }
        catch ( Exception ex )
        {
            ex.printStackTrace( );
        }

        super.okPressed( );
    }
}
```

The RotatedText builder UI, as shown in Figure 18-39, consists of a Text control and a Scale control, corresponding to the text content and rotation angle properties. The builder appears every time you add a RotatedText item to the layout or double-click a RotatedText item in the layout.

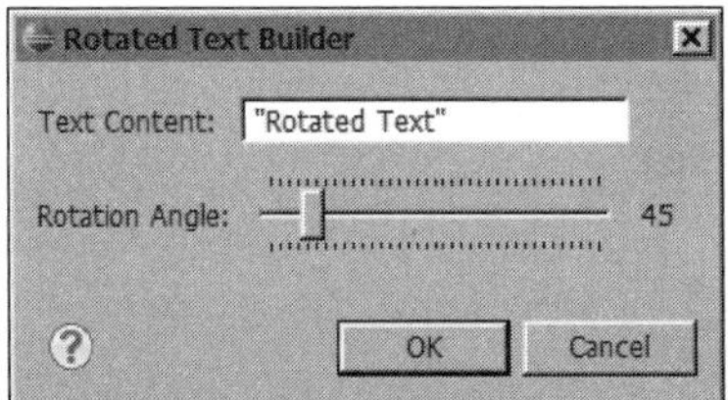

Figure 18-39 RotatedText builder

Creating a context menu

Another attractive and convenient UI feature is the context menu. The context menu displays links to specific actions and appears when a user right-clicks a selected object with the mouse.

To support a custom context menu, implement the extension org.eclipse.birt.report.designer.ui.menuBuilders. The implementer class implements the org.eclipse.birt.report.designer.ui.extensions.IMenuBuilder interface, as shown in Figure 18-40.

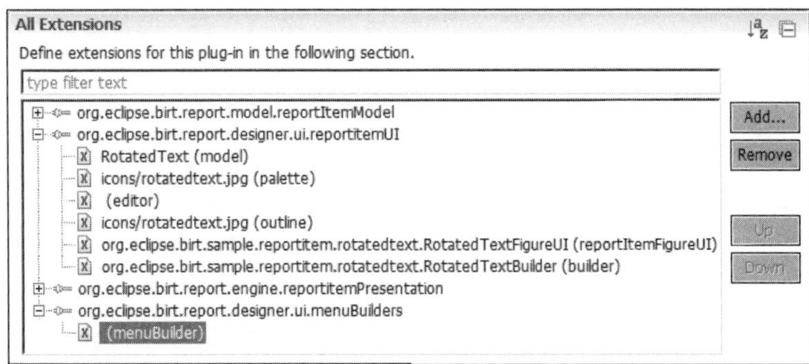

Figure 18-40 Adding the menuBuilders extension

As shown in Figure 18-41, the RotatedText elementName binds menuBuilders extension to the model extension. The implementer class name is org.eclipse.birt.sample.reportitem.rotatedtext.RotatedTextMenuBuilder.

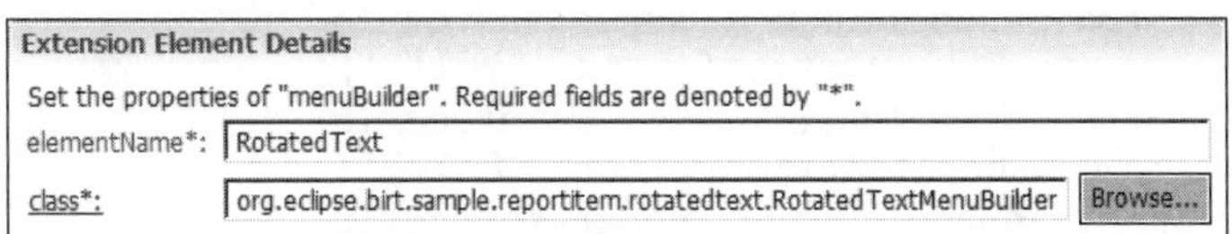

Figure 18-41 Setting the menuBuilder properties

The menu builder extension for RotatedText item contains four custom actions to perform quick rotations at angle values of -90, 90, 0 and 180 degrees. The code is shown in Listing 18-19.

Listing 18-19 RotatedTextMenuBuilder class

```
public class RotatedTextMenuBuilder implements IMenuBuilder
```

```
{
   public void buildMenu( IMenuManager menu, List selectedList )
   {
      if ( selectedList != null && selectedList.size( ) == 1
         && selectedList.get( 0 ) instanceof ExtendedItemHandle )
      {
         ExtendedItemHandle handle =
            (ExtendedItemHandle) selectedList.get( 0 );

         if ( !RotatedTextItem.EXTENSION_NAME.equals(
            handle.getExtensionName( ) ) )
         {
            return;
         }

         RotatedTextItem item = null;
         try {
            item = (RotatedTextItem) handle.getReportItem( );
         } catch ( ExtendedElementException e )
         {
            e.printStackTrace( );
         }

         if ( item == null )
         {
            return;
         }

         Separator separator = new Separator(
            "group.rotatedtext" ); //$NON-NLS-1$
         if ( menu.getItems( ).length > 0 )
         {
            menu.insertBefore( menu.getItems( )[0].getId( ),
               separator );
         }
         else {
            menu.add( separator );
         }

         menu.appendToGroup( separator.getId( ),
            new RotateAction( item, -90 ) );
         menu.appendToGroup( separator.getId( ),
            new RotateAction( item, 90 ) );
         menu.appendToGroup( separator.getId( ),
            new RotateAction( item, 0 ) );
         menu.appendToGroup( separator.getId( ),
            new RotateAction( item, 180 ) );
      }
   }

   static class RotateAction extends Action
   {
      private RotatedTextItem item;
```

```
        private int angle;

        RotateAction( RotatedTextItem item, int angle )
        {
            this.item = item;
            this.angle = angle;

            setText( "Rotate as " + angle + "\u00BA" );
                //$NON-NLS-1$ //$NON-NLS-2$
        }

        public void run( )
        {
            try
            {
                item.setRotationAngle( angle );
            }
            catch ( SemanticException e )
            {
                e.printStackTrace( );
            }
        }
    }
}
```

Run the designer to test the context menu. Right-click any RotatedText report item in the layout editor. The context menu appears as shown in Figure 18-42.

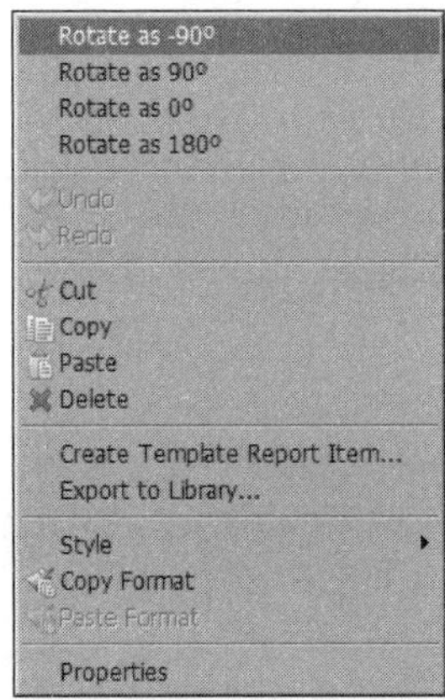

Figure 18-42 Testing the RotatedText item context menu

Creating a property editor

The property editor in BIRT Designer provides a user friendly interface for property editing. The property editor controls two types of settings, generic settings for all report items, and specific settings for each report item.

Property Editor, as shown in Figure 18-43, appears as a separate view having a tabbed style in BIRT Designer.

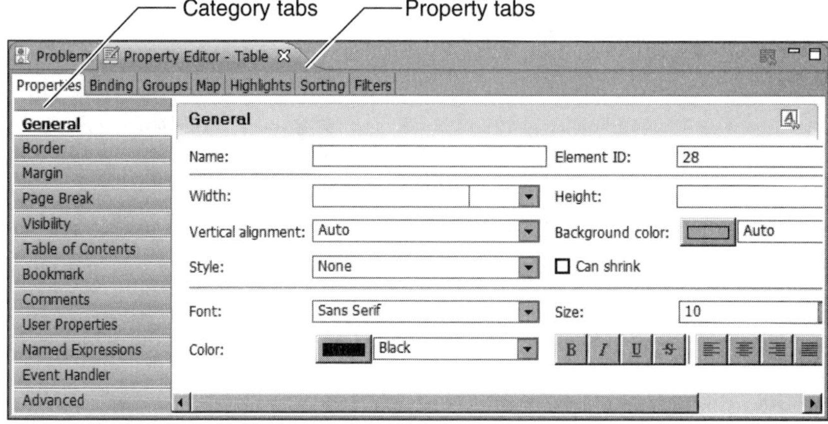

Figure 18-43 Property Editor for a table element

The property tabs, positioned horizontally, organize the property settings into several pages. The category tabs, positioned vertically, group the properties in a single page into different categories. By default, only the first Properties tab supports categories. You can alter the style and overwrite the logic behind this user interface.

You can create a similar Property Editor for the RotatedText report item. The new Property Editor should create a user interface for the rotated text and rotated angle properties and reuse the generic property user interface for report items.

To support custom property pages, implement the org.eclipse.birt.report .designer.ui.elementAdapters extension, as shown in Figure 18-44.

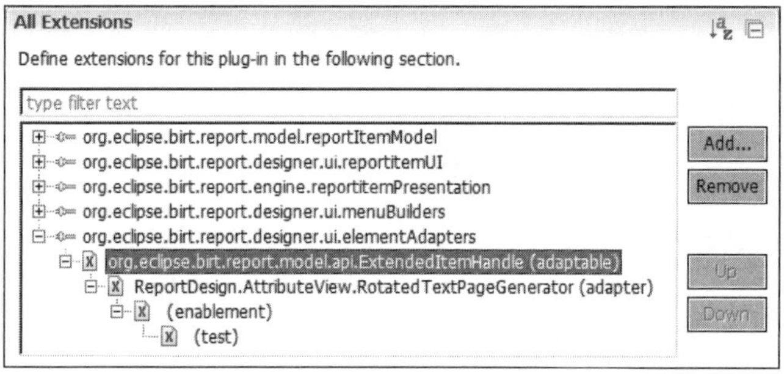

Figure 18-44 Adding the elementAdapters extension

The org.eclipse.birt.report.designer.ui.elementAdapters extension point is a generic extension point used by BIRT Designer to support property page and other UI extensions.

In the BIRT model, the org.eclipse.birt.report.model.api .ExtendedItemHandle class represents all custom extended report items.

Specify the adaptable class as org.eclipse.birt.report.model.api .ExtendedItemHandle.

The next step is to specify the adapter settings, as shown in Figure 18-45.

Extension Element Details

Set the properties of "adapter". Required fields are denoted by "*".

id*:	ReportDesign.AttributeView.RotatedTextPageGenerator	
type*:	org.eclipse.birt.report.designer.ui.views.IPageGenerator	Browse...
class:		Browse...
factory:	org.eclipse.birt.sample.reportitem.rotatedtext.views.RotatedTextPageGeneratorFactory	Browse...
singleton:	false	
priority:		
overwrite:		
comments:		

Figure 18-45 Adapter extension

Table 18-11 lists and explains the adapter settings

Table 18-11 Adapter settings

Property	Value	Description
id	ReportDesign .AttributeView .RotatedTextPageGenerator	The adapter unique identifier.
type	org.eclipse.birt.report .designer.ui.views .IPageGenerator	The Java class type to which this adapter adapts.
class		The Java class for the adapter. The class must have a constructor without any arguments. As you are using the factory mode here, just leave it blank.
factory	org.eclipse.birt.sample .reportitem .rotatedtext.views .RotatedTextPage GeneratorFactory	The Java class for the adapter factory. The class implements the org.eclipse .core.runtime.IAdapterFactory interface.
singleton	false	Specifies whether the adapter object is a singleton. For a singleton, the adapter object is cached and reused for all matching adaptable objects. Here, because you are using the factory mode, just set it to false.
priority		Specifies the priority for the adapter. The user interface uses this priority to sort

(continues)

Table 18-11 Adapter settings (continued)

Property	Value	Description
priority		multiple adapters defined for same adaptable. Use the default value by leaving it blank.
overwrite		Specifies a semicolon separated id list that this adapter overwrites. Leave it blank.
comments		An additional field to contain description text for the adapter.

The adapter settings describe the generic behavior of the property editor. The next step is to create custom property pages for the RotatedText item, and set additional constraints for the adaptable. To accomplish this task, create an enablement element using type test under the adapter node. In the settings, as shown in Figure 18-46, specify the test property as ExtendItemHandle .extensionName and the value as RotatedText. This approach restricts the adaptable object to be the RotatedText report items only.

Extension Element Details

Set the properties of "test". Required fields are denoted by "*".

forcePluginActivation:	true
property:	ExtendItemHandle.extensionName
value:	RotatedText

Figure 18-46 Enablement element settings

The code of the factory class is shown in Listing 18-20.

Listing 18-20 `RotatedTextPageGeneratorFactory class`

```
public class RotatedTextPageGeneratorFactory implements
   IAdapterFactory
{
   public Object getAdapter( Object adaptableObject, Class
   adapterType )
   {
      return new RotatedTextPageGenerator( );
   }

   public Class[] getAdapterList( )
   {
      return new Class[]{
         IPageGenerator.class
      };
   }
}
```

The factory class creates a generator instance per call. Each generator implements the org.eclipse.birt.report.designer.ui.views.IPageGenerator interface. Extend the org.eclipse.birt.report.designer.ui.views.attributes .AbstractPageGenerator class to use the basic support for categorized styles created by this class.

The implementation of the RotatedTextPageGenerator class is shown in Listing 18-21. The class overwrites the General category page in the Properties tab and reuses some of the built-in categories like Border, Margin, and Page Break. The code also adds a Custom property tab to the property editor. The RotatedTextPageGenerator class overwrites three methods, buildItemContent( ), createTabItems( ), and refresh( ). The methods createTabItems( ) and buildItemContent( ) implement the custom logic. The createTabItem( ) method overwrites the creation logic for the General category page to add the reused built-in pages and the new Custom property page. The buildItemContent( ) method contains the code to create the Custom property page.

Listing 18-21 RotatedTextPageGenerator class

```
public class RotatedTextPageGenerator
   extends AbstractPageGenerator
{
   private static final String CUSTOM_PAGE_TITLE = "Custom";
      //$NON-NLS-1$
   private IPropertyTabUI generalPage;

   protected void buildItemContent( CTabItem item )
   {
      if ( itemMap.containsKey( item )
         && itemMap.get( item ) == null )
      {
         String title = tabFolder.getSelection( ).getText( );

         if ( CUSTOM_PAGE_TITLE.equals( title ) )
         {
            TabPage page = new RotatedTextCustomPage( ).getPage( );
            if ( page != null )
            {
               setPageInput( page );
               refresh( tabFolder, page, true );
               item.setControl( page.getControl( ) );
               itemMap.put( item, page );
            }
         }
      }
      else if ( itemMap.get( item ) != null )
      {
         setPageInput( itemMap.get( item ) );
         refresh( tabFolder, itemMap.get( item ), false );
      }
   }
```

```
public void refresh( )
{
   createTabItems( input );

   generalPage.setInput( input );
   addSelectionListener( this );
   ( (TabPage) generalPage ).refresh( );
}

public void createTabItems( List input )
{
   if ( generalPage == null
      || generalPage.getControl( ).isDisposed( ) )
   {
      tabFolder.setLayout( new FillLayout( ) );
      generalPage = AttributesUtil.buildGeneralPage( tabFolder,
         new String[]{
            null,
            AttributesUtil.BORDER,
            AttributesUtil.MARGIN,
            AttributesUtil.SECTION,
            AttributesUtil.VISIBILITY,
            AttributesUtil.TOC,
            AttributesUtil.BOOKMARK,
            AttributesUtil.USERPROPERTIES,
            AttributesUtil.NAMEDEXPRESSIONS,
            AttributesUtil.ADVANCEPROPERTY
         },
         new String[]{ "General" }, //$NON-NLS-1$
         new String[]{ "General" }, //$NON-NLS-1$
         new AttributesUtil.PageWrapper[]{
            new RotatedTextGeneralPage( )
         },
         input );

      CTabItem tabItem = new CTabItem( tabFolder, SWT.NONE );
      tabItem.setText( ATTRIBUTESTITLE );
      tabItem.setControl( generalPage.getControl( ) );
   }

   this.input = input;
   generalPage.setInput( input );
   addSelectionListener( this );
   ( (TabPage) generalPage ).refresh( );

   createTabItem( CUSTOM_PAGE_TITLE, ATTRIBUTESTITLE );

   if ( tabFolder.getSelection( ) != null )
   {
      buildItemContent( tabFolder.getSelection( ) );
   }
}
```

```
}
```

The General category page contains two text controls for editing: one for the text content and one for the rotation angle of the RotatedText report item. Listing 18-22 shows the code.

Listing 18-22 RotatedTextGeneralPage class

```
public class RotatedTextGeneralPage
   extends AttributesUtil.PageWrapper
{
   protected FormToolkit toolkit;
   protected Object input;
   protected Composite contentpane;
   private Text txtText, txtAngle;

   public void buildUI( Composite parent )
   {
      if ( toolkit == null )
      {
         toolkit = new FormToolkit( Display.getCurrent( ) );
         toolkit.setBorderStyle( SWT.NULL );
      }

      Control[] children = parent.getChildren( );

      if ( children != null && children.length > 0 )
      {
         contentpane = (Composite) children[children.length - 1];

         GridLayout layout = new GridLayout( 2, false );
         layout.marginLeft = 8;
         layout.verticalSpacing = 12;
         contentpane.setLayout( layout );

         toolkit.createLabel( contentpane, "Text Content:" );
            //$NON-NLS-1$
         txtText = toolkit.createText( contentpane, "" );
            //$NON-NLS-1$
         GridData gd = new GridData( );
         gd.widthHint = 200;

         txtText.setLayoutData( gd );
         txtText.addFocusListener( new FocusAdapter( ) {

            public void focusLost(
               org.eclipse.swt.events.FocusEvent e )
            {
               updateModel( RotatedTextItem.TEXT_PROP );
            };
         } );

         toolkit.createLabel( contentpane, "Rotation Angle:" );
            //$NON-NLS-1$
```

```
      txtAngle = toolkit.createText( contentpane, "" );
         //$NON-NLS-1$
      gd = new GridData( );
      gd.widthHint = 200;

      txtAngle.setLayoutData( gd );
      txtAngle.addFocusListener( new FocusAdapter( ) {

         public void focusLost(
            org.eclipse.swt.events.FocusEvent e )
         {
            updateModel( RotatedTextItem.ROTATION_ANGLE_PROP );
         };
      } );
   }
}

public void setInput( Object input )
{
   this.input = input;
}

public void dispose( )
{
   if ( toolkit != null )
   {
      toolkit.dispose( );
   }
}

private void adaptFormStyle( Composite comp )
{
   Control[] children = comp.getChildren( );
   for ( int i = 0; i < children.length; i++ )
   {
      if ( children[i] instanceof Composite )
      {
         adaptFormStyle( (Composite) children[i] );
      }
   }
   toolkit.paintBordersFor( comp );
   toolkit.adapt( comp );
}

protected RotatedTextItem getItem( )
{
   Object element = input;

   if ( input instanceof List && ( (List) input ).size( ) > 0 )
   {
      element = ( (List) input ).get( 0 );
   }
```

```
    if ( element instanceof ExtendedItemHandle )
    {
        try
        {
            return (RotatedTextItem) (
                (ExtendedItemHandle) element ).getReportItem( );
        }
        catch ( Exception e )
        {
            e.printStackTrace( );
        }
    }

    return null;
}

public void refresh( )
{
    if ( contentpane != null && !contentpane.isDisposed( ) )
    {
        if ( toolkit == null )
        {
            toolkit = new FormToolkit( Display.getCurrent( ) );
            toolkit.setBorderStyle( SWT.NULL );
        }

        adaptFormStyle( contentpane );

        updateUI( );
    }
}

public void postElementEvent( )
{
    if ( contentpane != null && !contentpane.isDisposed( ) )
    {
        updateUI( );
    }
}

private void updateModel( String prop )
{
    RotatedTextItem item = getItem( );

    if ( item != null )
    {
        try
        {
            if (RotatedTextItem.ROTATION_ANGLE_PROP.equals( prop ))
            {
                item.setRotationAngle(
                    Integer.parseInt( txtAngle.getText( ) ) );
```

```
            }
            else if ( RotatedTextItem.TEXT_PROP.equals( prop ) )
            {
               item.setText( txtText.getText( ) );
            }
         }
         catch ( Exception e )
         {
            e.printStackTrace( );
         }
      }
   }
   protected void updateUI( )
   {
      RotatedTextItem item = getItem( );
      if ( item != null )
      {
         String text = item.getText( );
         txtText.setText( text == null ? "" : text );

         txtAngle.setText( String.valueOf( item.getRotationAngle(
   ) ) );
      }
   }
}
```

The RotatedTextGeneralPage class uses FormToolkit to achieve the same look and feel as the built-in pages in the Property editor. Alternatively, you can design your own UI styles.

The Custom property page, shown in Listing 18-23, implements a read-only version of the General category page just to illustrate the extension mechanism.

Listing 18-23 RotatedTextCustomPage class

```
public class RotatedTextCustomPage extends RotatedTextGeneralPage
{
   private Label lbText, lbAngle;
   public void buildUI( Composite parent )
   {
      if ( toolkit == null )
      {
         toolkit = new FormToolkit( Display.getCurrent( ) );
         toolkit.setBorderStyle( SWT.NULL );
      }
      Control[] children = parent.getChildren( );
      if ( children != null && children.length > 0 )
```

```
        {
            contentpane = (Composite) children[children.length - 1];

            GridLayout layout = new GridLayout( 2, false );
            layout.marginTop = 8;
            layout.marginLeft = 8;
            layout.verticalSpacing = 12;
            contentpane.setLayout( layout );

            toolkit.createLabel( contentpane, "Text Content:" );
               //$NON-NLS-1$
            lbText = toolkit.createLabel( contentpane, "" );
               //$NON-NLS-1$
            GridData gd = new GridData( );
            gd.widthHint = 200;
            lbText.setLayoutData( gd );

            toolkit.createLabel( contentpane, "Rotation Angle:" );
               //$NON-NLS-1$
            lbAngle = toolkit.createLabel( contentpane, "" );
               //$NON-NLS-1$
            gd = new GridData( );
            gd.widthHint = 200;
            lbAngle.setLayoutData( gd );
        }
    }
    protected void updateUI( )
    {
        RotatedTextItem item = getItem( );

        if ( item != null )
        {
            String text = item.getText( );
            lbText.setText( text == null ? "" : text ); //$NON-NLS-1$
            lbAngle.setText( String.valueOf( item.getRotationAngle( )
    ) );
        }
    }
}
```

The newly designed Property editor is shown in Figure 18-47. The General category page displays the two editable properties.

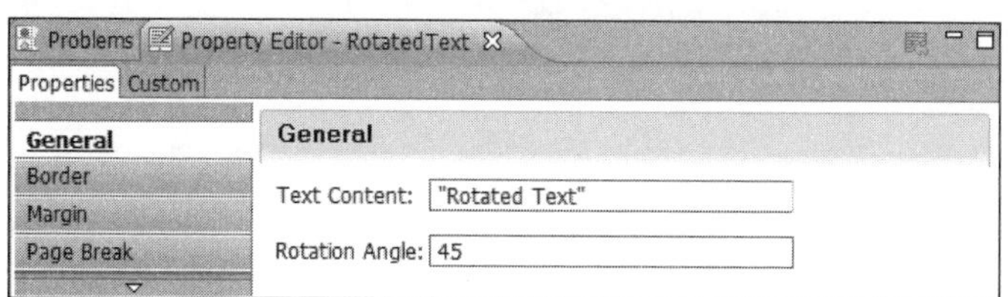

Figure 18-47 General property page for the RotatedText item

The reused Border category brings up the built-in border property page where the report developer can change the report item border settings. The changes immediately appear in the layout editor.

The Custom page, shown in Figure 18-48, displays the read-only properties.

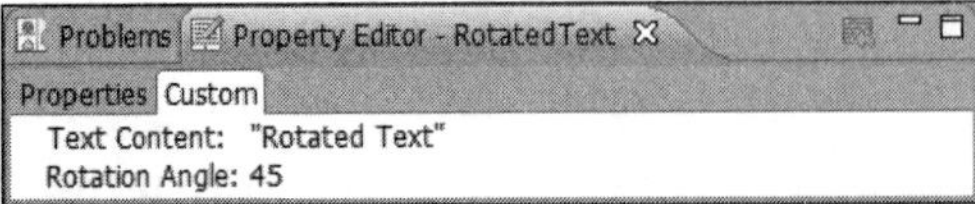

Figure 18-48 Custom property page for the RotatedText item

Binding the report item to data

BIRT report items access data only through column bindings. Column bindings form an intermediate layer between data set data and report items that display data. Column bindings can also access data derived from functions or user-defined formulas.

To support data bindings, the RotatedText property must be binding-aware, so the text value can change dynamically. The implementation involves changes in the model, the presentation, and the user interface of the RotatedText report item. The user interface modifications include changes in the RotatedText item builder and the Property editor.

Changes in the model definition

To support data binding for the text property, change the model extension definition. Change the property type of the text from string to expression by adding quotation marks around the original default value, as shown in Figure 18-49. This change indicates that the property supports expressions. As the original default value, Rotated Text, is not a valid JavaScript expression, change it to use JavaScript literal string syntax.

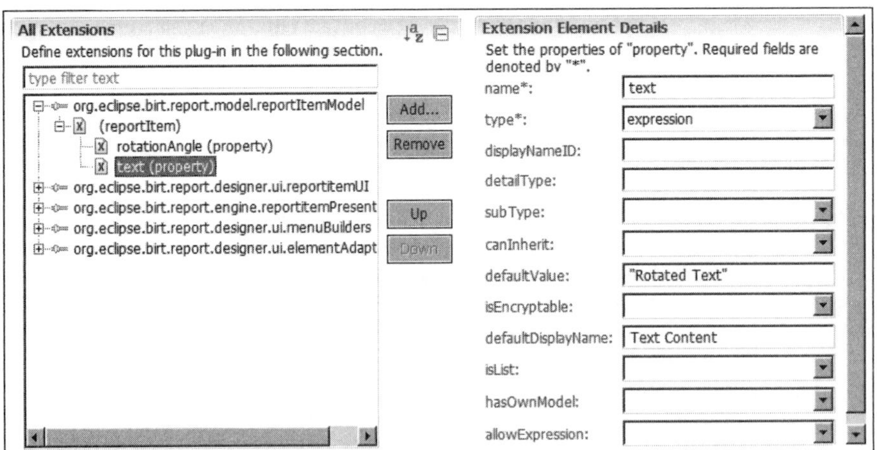

Figure 18-49 Setting the text property definition to an expression

Changes in the report item presentation

To support expressions, the code of the onRowSets( ) method of RotatedTextPresentationImpl class must be changed, as shown in Listing 18-24. The new code adds logic to handle the text property as an expression. The code evaluates the text value under the current engine context to get the final string result.

Listing 18-24 onRowSets method of the RotatedTextPresentationImpl class

```
public Object onRowSets( IBaseResultSet[] results )
   throws BirtException
{
   if ( textItem == null )
   {
      return null;
   }

   int angle = textItem.getRotationAngle( );
   String text = textItem.getText( );
   // XXX added to support expression
   if ( results != null && results.length > 0 )
   {
      if ( results[0] instanceof IQueryResultSet
         && ( (IQueryResultSet) results[0] ).isBeforeFirst( ) )
      {
         ( (IQueryResultSet) results[0] ).next( );
      }
      text = String.valueOf( results[0].evaluate( text ) );
   } else
   {
      text = String.valueOf( context.evaluate( text ) );
   }
   // end new code
   BufferedImage rotatedImage =
      SwingGraphicsUtil.createRotatedTextImage( text, angle,
      new Font( "Default", 0, 12 ) ); //$NON-NLS-1$
   ByteArrayInputStream bis = null;
   try
   {
      ImageIO.setUseCache( false );
      ByteArrayOutputStream baos = new ByteArrayOutputStream( );
      ImageOutputStream ios =
         ImageIO.createImageOutputStream( baos );
      ImageIO.write( rotatedImage, "png", ios ); //$NON-NLS-1$
      ios.flush( );
      ios.close( );
      bis = new ByteArrayInputStream( baos.toByteArray( ) );
   }
   catch ( IOException e ) {
      e.printStackTrace( );
```

```
    }
    return bis;
}
```

Changing the report item UI to support expressions

To update the user interface you must make changes in two places—the builder and the property page.

Adding data binding to the builder

To enable report developers to use the standard BIRT expression builder to construct a data-binding expression, the report item builder must provide a button to lunch the expression builder. Place the button beside the text control, as shown in Figure 18-50.

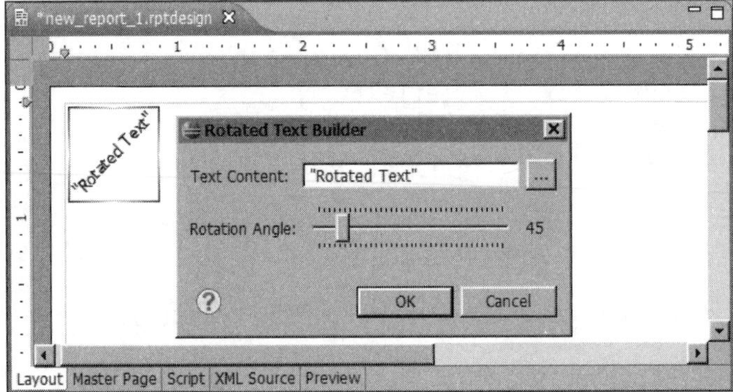

Figure 18-50 RotatedText builder

The standard BIRT expression builder, shown in Figure 18-51, provides JavaScript support.

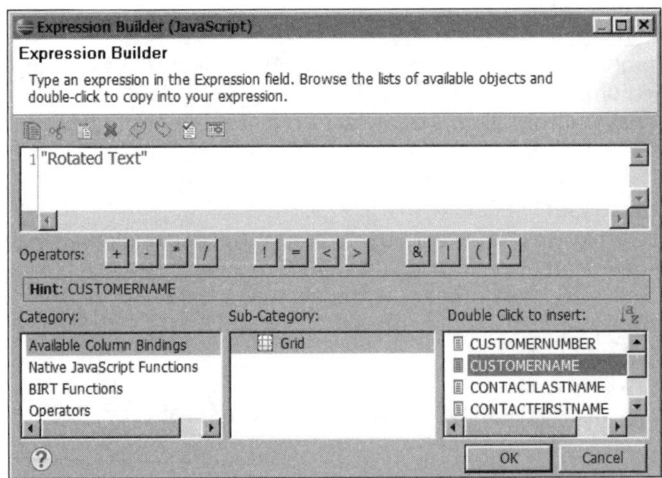

Figure 18-51 BIRT expression builder

The code of the RotatedTextBuilder class changes, as shown in Listing 18-25. The newly created RotatedTextEditor2 class overwrites the UI creation logic for the new expression button.

Listing 18-25 RotatedTextBuilder class

```
public class RotatedTextBuilder extends ReportItemBuilderUI
{
   public int open( ExtendedItemHandle handle )
   {
      try {
         IReportItem item = handle.getReportItem( );

         if ( item instanceof RotatedTextItem )
         {
            RotatedTextEditor editor = new RotatedTextEditor2(
               Display.getCurrent( ).getActiveShell( ),
               (RotatedTextItem) item );
            return editor.open( );
         }
      }
      catch ( Exception e ) {
         e.printStackTrace( );
      }
      return Window.CANCEL;
   }
}

class RotatedTextEditor2 extends RotatedTextEditor
{
   protected RotatedTextEditor2( Shell shell,
      RotatedTextItem textItem )
   {
      super( shell, textItem );
   }

   protected void createTextArea( Composite parent )
   {
      Label lb = new Label( parent, SWT.None );
      lb.setText( "Text Content:" ); //$NON-NLS-1$

      txtText = new Text( parent, SWT.BORDER );
      GridData gd = new GridData( GridData.FILL_HORIZONTAL );
      txtText.setLayoutData( gd );

      Button btnExp = new Button( parent, SWT.PUSH );
      btnExp.setText( "..." ); //$NON-NLS-1$
      btnExp.setToolTipText( "Invoke Expression Builder" );
         //$NON-NLS-1$
      btnExp.addSelectionListener( new SelectionAdapter( ) {
         public void widgetSelected( SelectionEvent event )
         {
```

```
            openExpression( txtText );
         }
      } );
   }
   private void openExpression( Text textControl )
   {
      String oldValue = textControl.getText( );

      ExpressionBuilder eb = new ExpressionBuilder(
         textControl.getShell( ), oldValue );
      eb.setExpressionProvier( new ExpressionProvider(
         textItem.getModelHandle( ) ) );
      String result = oldValue;
      if ( eb.open( ) == Window.OK )
      {
         result = eb.getResult( );
      }
      if ( !oldValue.equals( result ) )
      {
         textControl.setText( result );
      }
   }
}
```

Adding data binding to the property page

A similar change must be made to the Property page. The General property page needs a button, beside the text control, that calls the expression builder. The code implementing the change to the RotatedTextGeneralPage class is shown in Listing 18-26.

Listing 18-26 RotatedTextGeneralPage class

```
public class RotatedTextGeneralPage
   extends AttributesUtil.PageWrapper
{
   //.........
   public void buildUI( Composite parent )
   {
      if ( toolkit == null )
      {
         toolkit = new FormToolkit( Display.getCurrent( ) );
         toolkit.setBorderStyle( SWT.NULL );
      }
      Control[] children = parent.getChildren( );
      if ( children != null && children.length > 0 )
      {
         contentpane = (Composite) children[children.length - 1];
         GridLayout layout = new GridLayout( 3, false );
         layout.marginLeft = 8;
```

```
         layout.verticalSpacing = 12;
         contentpane.setLayout( layout );
         toolkit.createLabel( contentpane, "Text Content:" );
            //$NON-NLS-1$
         txtText = toolkit.createText( contentpane, "" );
            //$NON-NLS-1$
         GridData gd = new GridData( );
         gd.widthHint = 200;
         txtText.setLayoutData( gd );
         txtText.addFocusListener( new FocusAdapter( ) {
            public void focusLost(
               org.eclipse.swt.events.FocusEvent e )
            {
               updateModel( RotatedTextItem.TEXT_PROP );
            };
         } );

         Button btnExp = toolkit.createButton( contentpane, "...",
            SWT.PUSH ); //$NON-NLS-1$
         btnExp.setToolTipText( "Invoke Expression Builder" );
            //$NON-NLS-1$
         btnExp.addSelectionListener( new SelectionAdapter( ) {
            public void widgetSelected( SelectionEvent e )
            {
               openExpression( txtText );
            }
         } );

         toolkit.createLabel( contentpane, "Rotation Angle:" );
            //$NON-NLS-1$
         txtAngle = toolkit.createText( contentpane, "" );
            //$NON-NLS-1$
         gd = new GridData( );
         gd.widthHint = 200;
         gd.horizontalSpan = 2;
         txtAngle.setLayoutData( gd );
         txtAngle.addFocusListener( new FocusAdapter( ) {
            public void focusLost(
               org.eclipse.swt.events.FocusEvent e )
            {
               updateModel( RotatedTextItem.ROTATION_ANGLE_PROP );
            };
         } );
      }
   }

   private void openExpression( Text textControl )
   {
      RotatedTextItem item = getItem( );
      if ( item != null )
      {
```

```
            String oldValue = textControl.getText( );
            ExpressionBuilder eb = new ExpressionBuilder(
               textControl.getShell( ), oldValue );
            eb.setExpressionProvier( new ExpressionProvider(
               item.getModelHandle( ) ) );

            String result = oldValue;
            if ( eb.open( ) == Window.OK )
            {
               result = eb.getResult( );
            }
            if ( !oldValue.equals( result ) )
            {
               textControl.setText( result );
               updateModel( RotatedTextItem.TEXT_PROP );
            }
         }
      }
         //.........
}
```

The new appearance of the General property page is shown in Figure 18-52.

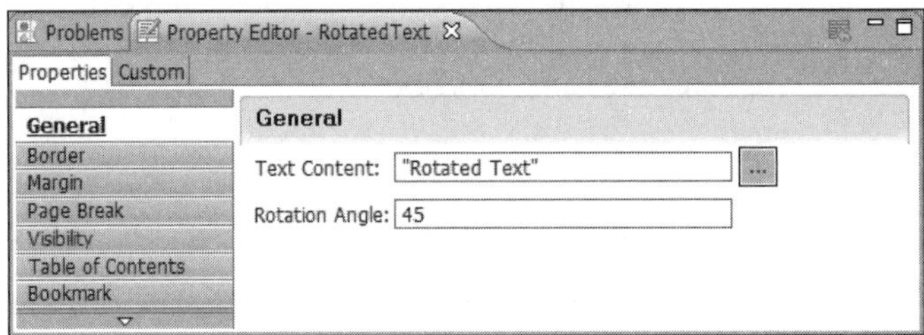

Figure 18-52 Final appearance of the RotatedText item's General property page

To test the implementation, run a new report design instance and create a new report, as explained earlier in this chapter in "Deploying and testing the rotated label report item plug-in." Insert a ClassicModels data source and data set. Create a table having three columns, and bind the table to the data set. Insert one RotatedText report item in the table detail row, and two more data items, as shown in Figure 18-53.

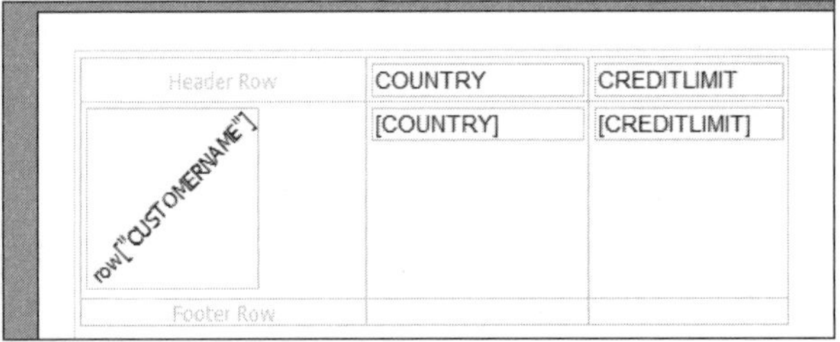

Figure 18-53 Report layout showing the final RotatedText item

Specify the expression of the RotatedText item as shown in Figure 18-54.

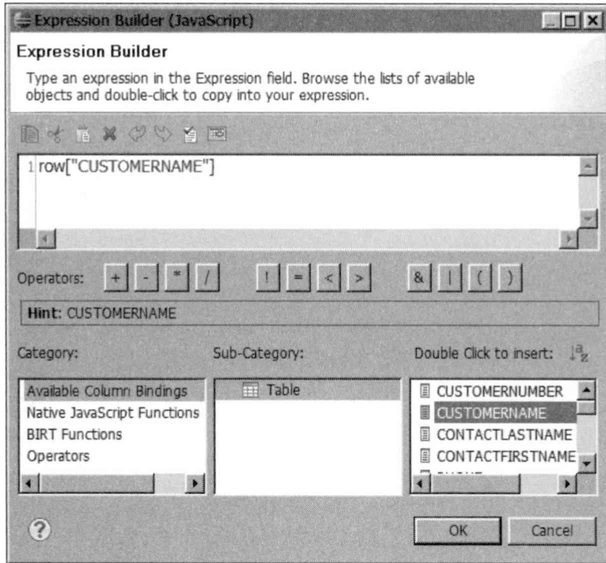

Figure 18-54 Defining a data-binding expression for the RotatedText item

The preview in the Report Designer, shown in Figure 18-55, displays values from the database for the RotatedText report item. The text data comes from the column bindings and automatically changes per row.

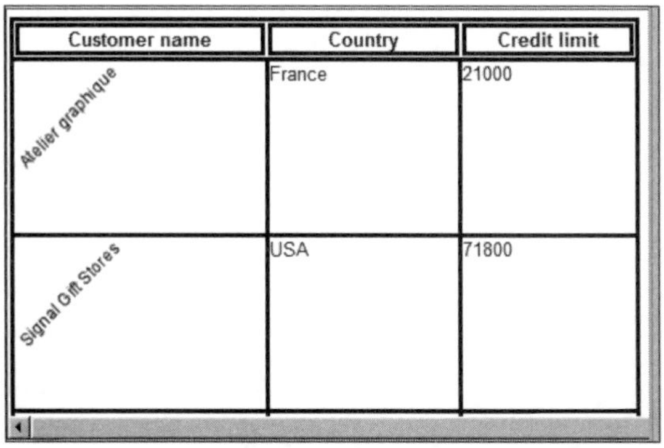

Customer name	Country	Credit limit
Atelier graphique	France	21000
Signal Gift Stores	USA	71800

Figure 18-55 Report preview showing data values in RotatedText items

Chapter

19

Developing a Report Rendering Extension

This chapter describes how to develop a report rendering extension using the Eclipse PDE with sample CSV and XML report rendering extensions as the examples. Developing a BIRT report rendering extension is discussed in the following sections:

- Understanding a report rendering extension
- Developing a CSV report rendering extension
- Developing an XML report rendering extension

Understanding a report rendering extension

BIRT Report Engine provides report rendering extensions that render a report in HTML, PDF, XLS, PostScript, Microsoft Word and PowerPoint. This chapter provides sample implementations of customized CSV and XML report rendering extensions, org.eclipse.birt.report.engine.emitter.csv and org.eclipse.birt.report.engine.emitter.xml. The sample code creates plug-ins that write the data contents of a report to a file in the specified format.

A BIRT plug-in typically loads and runs in the BIRT Report Engine environment rather than the Eclipse run-time environment. BIRT implements a separate plug-in loading framework for the BIRT Report Engine, giving the BIRT Report Engine complete control of report execution. A BIRT engine plug-in extension is functionally similar to an Eclipse plug-in extension.

A rendering extension adds an emitter to the BIRT Report Engine framework by implementing the extension point, org.eclipse.birt.report.engine.emitters.

The XML schema file, org.eclipse.birt.report.engine/schema/emitters.exsd, describes this extension point.

The extension point enables support for a new output format in the presentation engine. The BIRT plug-in registry uses this extension point to discover all supported output formats specified for the report engine environment.

This book uses the customized CSV and XML report rendering extensions in this chapter as examples of how to create a report rendering extension. The BIRT user interface also provides a built-in data extraction feature that can export data from a report document in CSV, TSV (tab-separated values), and XML formats.

You can download the source code for the CSV and XML report rendering extension examples at http://www.actuate.com/birt/contributions. For reference documentation, see the BIRT Report Engine API Javadoc in Eclipse Help for the org.eclipse.birt.report.engine.emitter and org.eclipse.birt.report .engine.content packages.

Developing a CSV report rendering extension

The CSV report rendering extension extends the functionality defined by the org.eclipse.birt.report.engine.emitter package, which is part of the org.eclipse.birt.report.engine plug-in. In developing the CSV report rendering extension, you perform the following tasks:

- Create a CSV report rendering extension project in the Eclipse PDE.
- Define the dependencies.
- Declare the emitters extension point.
- Implement the emitter interfaces.
- Test the extension in the designer and in the run-time environments.

Creating a CSV report rendering plug-in project

Create a new plug-in project for the CSV report rendering extension using the Eclipse PDE.

How to create the CSV report rendering plug-in project

1. From the Eclipse PDE menu, choose File➛New➛Project. New Project appears.
2. In New Project, select Plug-in Project. Choose Next. New Plug-in Project appears.
3. In Plug-in Project, modify the settings, as shown in Table 19-1.

Table 19-1 Values for CSV Emitter Plug-in Project fields

Section	Option	Value
Plug-in Project	Project name	org.eclipse.birt.report .engine.emitter.csv
	Use default location	Selected
	Location	Not available when you select Use default location
Project Settings	Create a Java project	Selected
	Source folder	src
	Output folder	bin
Target Platform	Eclipse version	3.6
	OSGi framework	Not selected
Working sets	Add project to working sets	Not selected

Plug-in Project appears as shown in Figure 19-1. Choose Next. Content appears.

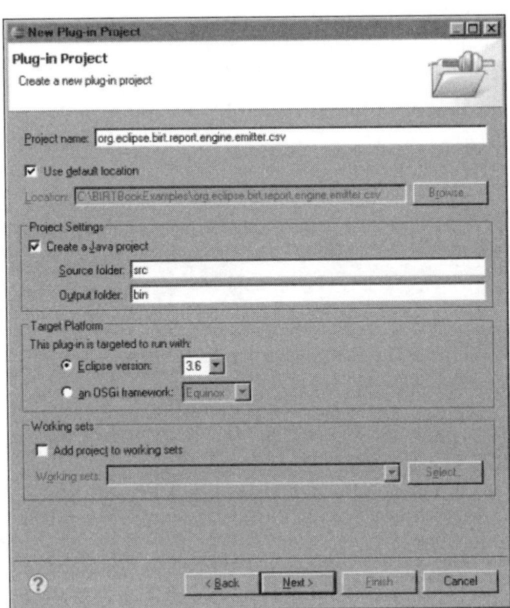

Figure 19-1 Values for CSV Emitter Plug-in Project

4 In Content, modify the settings, as shown in Table 19-2.

Table 19-2 Values for CSV Emitter Content fields

Section	Option	Value
Plug-in Properties	ID	org.eclipse.birt.report .engine.emitter.csv
	Version	1.0.0
	Name	BIRT CSV Emitter
	Provider	yourCompany.com or leave blank
	Execution Environment	JavaSE-1.6
Options	Generate an activator, a Java class that controls the plug-in's life cycle	Selected
	Activator	org.eclipse.birt.report .engine.emitter.csv .CsvPlugin
	This plug-in will make contributions to the UI	Not selected
	Enable API Analysis	Not selected
Rich Client Application	Would you like to create a rich client application?	No

Content appears as shown in Figure 19-2. Choose Finish.

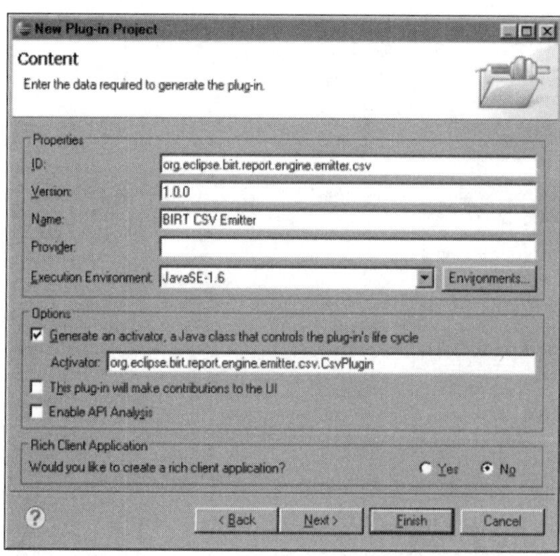

Figure 19-2 Values for Plug-in Content

The CSV report rendering extension project appears in the Eclipse PDE workbench, as shown in Figure 19-3.

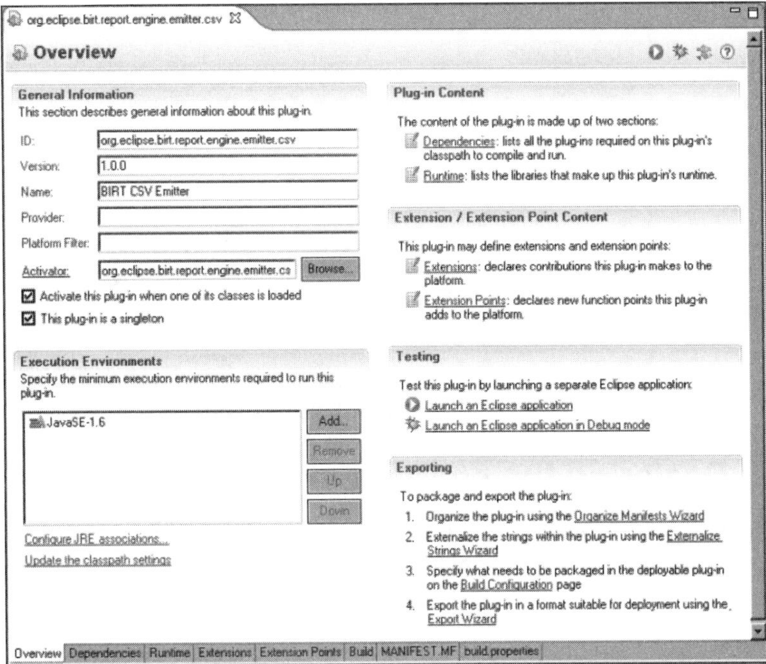

Figure 19-3 CSV report rendering extension project

Defining the dependencies for the CSV report rendering extension

To compile and run the CSV report rendering example, you need to specify the list of plug-ins that must be available on the classpath of the extension.

How to specify the dependencies

1 On PDE Manifest Editor, choose Overview.

2 In Plug-in Content, choose Dependencies. Required Plug-ins contains the following plug-in:

```
org.eclipse.core.runtime
```

3 In Required Plug-ins, perform the following tasks:

   1 Select org.eclipse.core.runtime and choose Remove.

   org.eclipse.core.runtime no longer appears in Required Plug-ins.

   2 Choose Add. Plug-in Selection appears.

   3 In Plug-in Selection, hold down CTRL and select the org.eclipse.birt .report.engine plug-in.

   Choose OK. Dependencies appears as shown in Figure 19-4.

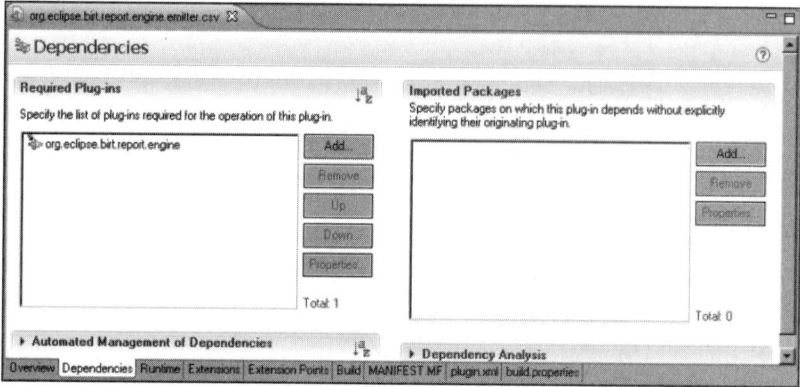

Figure 19-4 The Dependencies page

Declaring the emitters extension point

In this step, you specify the extension point required to implement the CSV report rendering extension and add the extension element details. The extension point, org.eclipse.birt.report.engine.emitters, specifies the following properties that identify the extension point:

- ID
  Optional identifier of the extension instance
- Name
  Optional name of the extension instance

The extension point defines an emitter that specifies the output format for the plug-in, requiring definition of the following extension element properties:

- class
  Java class that implements the IContentEmitter interface
- format
  Output format that the emitter supports, such as csv
- mimeType
  MIME type for the supported output format, such as text/csv
- id
  Optional identifier of the emitter extension
- icon
  Optional icon path of the emitter extension
- pagination
  Optional setting that controls page breaks. When page-break-pagination is set, the pagination is based on the page break configuration. When no-

pagination is set, the report output is on one page. When paper-size-pagination is set, the pagination is based on the content size.

- supportedImageFormats

  The supported format for images. The CSV emitter in this example does not support images.

- outputDisplayNone

  This property controls whether the hidden content is output in the final report. For example, if the user set the display to hidden, the content will not display in the final output.

  On the client side, the user has the option to invoke scripts that reset the display to block or show the hidden content. To choose not to display the output, set outputDisplayNone to true. This setting is valid only for HTML/XHTML.

- isHidden

  Used to determine whether the format is shown in UI. This property is not used in the current release.

- needOutputResultSet

  Represents whether the emitter needs to output the query result set in the final output. If the property is set to true, the emitter implementation can access the result set in the content object.

To specify the extension point and extension element details use the Eclipse PDE.

How to specify the extension point

1 On PDE Manifest Editor, choose Extensions.

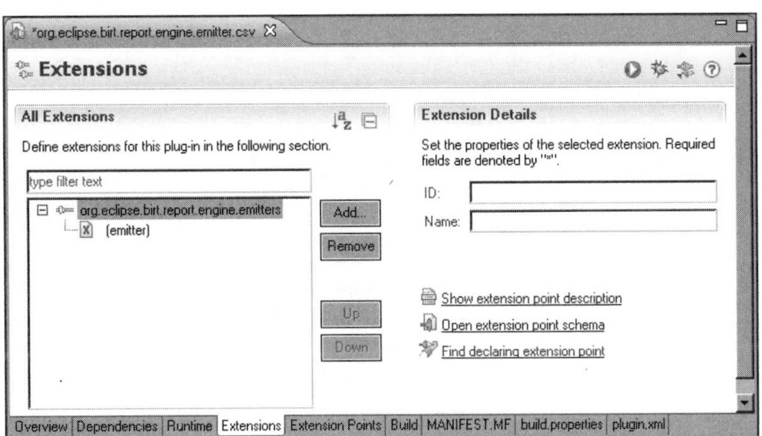

Figure 19-5 Emitter plug-in extension on the Extensions page

2 In All Extensions, choose Add. New Extension—Extension Point Selection appears.

3 In Available extension points, select the following plug-in:

```
org.eclipse.birt.report.engine.emitters
```

Choose Finish. Extensions appears, as shown in Figure 19-5.

All Extensions lists the extension point, org.eclipse.birt.report.engine .emitters, and the extension element, emitter. Extension Element Details contains the element details list specified in the XML schema file, emitters.exsd.

4 In Extension Element Details, specify the properties for the CSV emitter extension element, emitter, as shown in Table 19-3.

Table 19-3 Property values for the CSV Emitter extension element

Property	Value
class	org.eclipse.birt.report.engine.emitter.csv .CSVReportEmitter
format	csv
mimeType	text/csv
id	org.eclipse.birt.report.engine.emitter.csv
icon	
supportedImageFormats	
pagination	
outputDisplayNone	
isHidden	
needOutputResultSet	

Extension Element Details appears as shown in Figure 19-6.

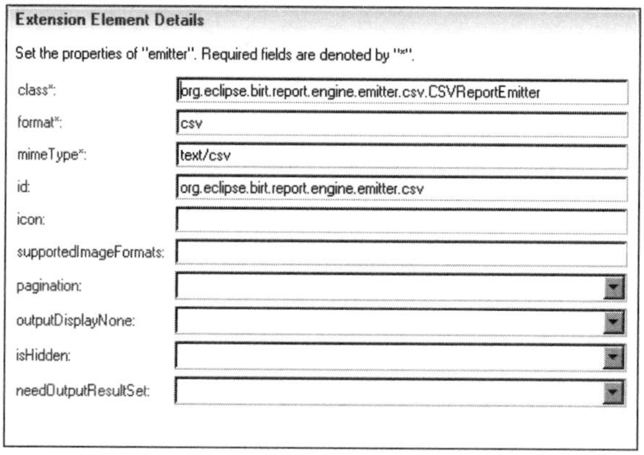

Figure 19-6 Property values for the emitter extension

PDE Manifest Editor automatically updates plugin.xml.

Understanding the sample CSV report rendering extension

The CSV report rendering extension described in this chapter is a simplified example that illustrates how to create a report rendering plug-in using the Eclipse PDE. The extension extends the report emitter interfaces in org.eclipse.birt.report.engine.emitters.

The CSV report rendering extension example exports only the data presented by table elements to a CSV output file. The lines of the CSV output file contain only column data separated by commas. The sample CSV report emitter does not export images, charts, or hyperlinks.

The extension example creates the CSV output file in the same folder as the exported report. The output file name is the name of the report with a .csv extension. The extension example does not support nested tables.

The following section provides a general description of the code-based extensions a developer must make to complete the development of the CSV report rendering extension after defining the plug-in framework in the Eclipse PDE.

Understanding the CSV report rendering extension package

The implementation package for the CSV report rendering extension example, org.eclipse.birt.report.engine.emitter.csv, contains the following classes:

- CSVPlugin
  Defines the methods for starting, managing, and stopping a plug-in instance.

- CSVRenderOption
  Integrates the plug-in with BIRT Report Engine, specifying configuration information. CSVRenderOption extends RenderOption, specifying the output format as CSV.

- CSVReportEmitter
  Extends org.eclipse.birt.report.engine.emitter.ContentEmitterAdapter. CSVReportEmitter handles the start and end processing that renders the report container.

- CSVTags.java
  Defines the comma and new line String settings used when writing to the CSV file.

- CSVWriter
  CSVWriter writes the data and label contents of the report to the CSV file, using a call to java.io.PrintWriter.print( ). CSVWriter also uses

org.eclipse.birt.report.engine.emitter.XMLWriter with java.util.logging .Logger to write log messages at specified levels.

The following sections contain specific information about implementation details for the classes in the CSV report rendering extension package.

Understanding CSVReportEmitter

CSVReportEmitter is the class that extends ContentEmitterAdapter to output the text content of the report items to a CSV file. CSVReportEmitter instantiates the writer and emitter objects.

CSVReportEmitter implements the following methods:

- CSVReportEmitter( ) instantiates the CSV report emitter class as an org.eclipse.birt.report.engine.presentation.ContentEmitterVisitor object, to perform emitter operations, as shown in Listing 19-1.

  Listing 19-1 The CSVReportEmitter( ) constructor

  ```
  public CSVReportEmitter( )
  {
     contentVisitor = new ContentEmitterVisitor( this );
  }
  ```

- initialize( ) performs the following operations required to create an output stream that writes the text contents of the report to the CSV file:

  - Obtains a reference to the IEmitterServices interface. Instantiates the file and output stream objects, using the specified settings.
  - Instantiates the CSV writer object.

  Listing 19-2 shows the initialize( ) method.

  Listing 19-2 The initialize( ) method

  ```
  public void initialize( IEmitterServices services )
  {
     this.services = services;
     Object fd = services.getOption
        ( RenderOptionBase.OUTPUT_FILE_NAME );
     File file = null;
     try
     {
        if ( fd != null )
        {
           file = new File( fd.toString( ) );
           File parent = file.getParentFile( );
           if ( parent != null && !parent.exists( ) )
           {
              parent.mkdirs( );
           }
  ```

```
            out = new BufferedOutputStream( new
               FileOutputStream( file ) );
         }
      }
      catch ( FileNotFoundException e )
      {
         logger.log( Level.WARNING, e.getMessage( ), e );
      }
      if ( out == null )
      {
         Object value = services.getOption
            ( RenderOptionBase.OUTPUT_STREAM );
         if ( value != null && value instanceof OutputStream )
         {
            out = (OutputStream) value;
         } else
         {
            try
            {
               file = new File( REPORT_FILE );
               out =
                  new BufferedOutputStream
                     ( new FileOutputStream( file ) );
            }
            catch ( FileNotFoundException e )
            {
               logger.log( Level.SEVERE, e.getMessage( ), e );
            }
         }
      }
      writer = new CSVWriter( );
   }
```

- start( ) performs the following operations:
  - Obtains a reference to the IReportContent interface.
  - Sets the start emitter logging level and writes to the log file.
  - Opens the output file and specifies the encoding scheme as UTF-8.
  - Starts the CSV writer

  Listing 19-3 shows the start( ) method.

Listing 19-3 The start( ) method

```
public void start( IReportContent report )
{
   logger.log( Level.FINE,
      "[CSVReportEmitter] Start emitter." );
   this.report = report;
```

```
    writer.open( out, "UTF-8" );
    writer.startWriter( );
}
```

- end( ) performs the following operations:
  - Sets the end report logging level and writes to the log file.
  - Ends the write process and closes the CSV writer.
  - Closes the output file.

  Listing 19-4 shows the end( ) method.

  Listing 19-4 The end( ) method

```
public void end( IReportContent report )
{
    logger.log( Level.FINE,
        "[CSVReportEmitter] End report." );
    writer.endWriter( );
    writer.close( );
    if( out != null )
    {
        try
        {
            out.close( );
        }
        catch ( IOException e )
        {
            logger.log( Level.WARNING, e.getMessage( ), e );
        }
    }
}
```

Understanding the other CSVReportEmitter methods

The CSVReportEmitter class defines the following additional methods, called at different phases of the report generation process, that provide access to emitters, render options, and style information to facilitate BIRT Report Engine processing:

- startTable( )

  When writing to the CSV file, the CSV rendering extension must consider the cell position in the row because a comma appears as the last character in all the cells except the last cell in the row.

  The startTable( ) method uses ITableContent.getColumnCount( ) to get information about table column numbers and to initialize the protected columnNumbers variable, as shown in Listing 19-5.

Listing 19-5 The startTable( ) method

```
public void startTable( ITableContent table )
{
   assert table != null;
   tableDepth++;
   columnNumbers = table.getColumnCount( );
...
}
```

- startRow( )

  At the start of each row, startRow( ) performs the following operations:

  - Calls isRowInFooterBand( ) to determine if the row is in the header or footer band of a table or group
  - Sets exportElement to false if the current table element belongs to a table header, footer, or is an image, since this extension exports only label and data elements to the CSV file
  - Sets the currentColumn indicator to 0

  Listing 19-6 shows the startRow( ) code.

  Listing 19-6 The startRow( ) method

```
public void startRow( IRowContent row )
{
   assert row != null;
   if ( tableDepth > 1) {
      logger.log( Level.FINE,
      "[CSVTableEmitter] Nested tables are not supported." );
      return;
   }
   if ( isRowInFooterBand( row ) )
      exportElement = false;

   currentColumn = 0;
}
```

- isRowInFooterBand( )

  If the row is an instance of band content, isRowInFooterBand( ) checks the band type. If the band type is a footer, the method returns true, as shown in Listing 19-7.

  Listing 19-7 The isRowInFooterBand( ) method

```
boolean isRowInFooterBand( IRowContent row )
{
   IElement parent = row.getParent( );
   if ( !( parent instanceof IBandContent ) )
   {
      return false;
```

```
    }
    IBandContent band = ( IBandContent )parent;
    if ( band.getBandType( ) == IBandContent.BAND_FOOTER )
    {
      return true;
    }
    return false;
  }
```

- startText( )
  If the element is exportable, startText( ) writes the text value to the CSV output file, as shown in Listing 19-8.

Listing 19-8 The startText( ) method

```
public void startText( ITextContent text )
{
  if ( tableDepth > 1) {
    logger.log( Level.FINE,
      "[CSVTableEmitter] Nested tables are not supported."
      );
    return;
  }
  String textValue = text.getText( );
  if (exportElement)
  {
    writer.text( textValue );
  }
}
```

- endCell( )
  If the current cell is not the last column in the row and the element is exportable, endCell( ) writes a comma to the CSV output file, as shown in Listing 19-9.

Listing 19-9 The endCell( ) method

```
public void endCell( ICellContent cell )
{
  if ( ( currentColumn < columnNumbers )
    && exportElement )
  {
    writer.closeTag( CSVTags.TAG_COMMA );
  }
}
```

- endRow( )
  At the end of each row, if the element is exportable, endRow( ) writes a new line or carriage return to the CSV output file, as shown in Listing 19-10.

Listing 19-10 The endRow( ) method

```
public void endRow( IRowContent row )
   if ( exportTableElement )
      writer.closeTag( CSVTags.TAG_CR );
   exportElement = true;
}
```

Understanding CSVTags

The CSVTags class defines the contents of the comma and new line tags, as shown in Listing 19-11.

Listing 19-11 The CSVTags class

```
public class CSVTags
{
   public static final String TAG_COMMA = "," ;
   public static final String TAG_CR = "\n" ;
}
```

Understanding CSVWriter

The CSVWriter class writes the closing tags defined in CSVTags, as shown in Listing 19-12.

Listing 19-12 The closeTag( ) method

```
public void closeTag( String tagName )
{
   printWriter.print( tagName );
}
```

Understanding CSVRenderOption

The org.eclipse.birt.report.engine.emitter.csv.CSVRenderOption class extends org.eclipse.birt.report.engine.api.RenderOption to add the CSV rendering option to the BIRT Report Engine run time, as shown in Listing 19-13.

Listing 19-13 The CSVRenderOption class

```
public class CSVRenderOption extends RenderOption  {
   public static final String CSV = "CSV";
      public CSVRenderOption( ) {
   }
}
```

Testing the CSV report rendering plug-in

You can use the new CSV emitter directly in the BIRT Report Designer or programmatically when you run and render reports using the BIRT Report Engine API. This section provides instructions on how to test the CSV emitter in both scenarios.

How to launch the CSV report rendering plug-in

1 From the Eclipse PDE menu, choose Run— Run Configurations. On Run Configurations, right-click Eclipse Application. Choose New.

2 Create a configuration to launch an Eclipse application by performing the following tasks:

   1 In Name, type:

   ```
   CSVEmitter
   ```

   2 On Main, in Location, type:

   ```
   C:\Test\CSVEmitter
   ```

   Run Configurations appears as shown in Figure 19-7.

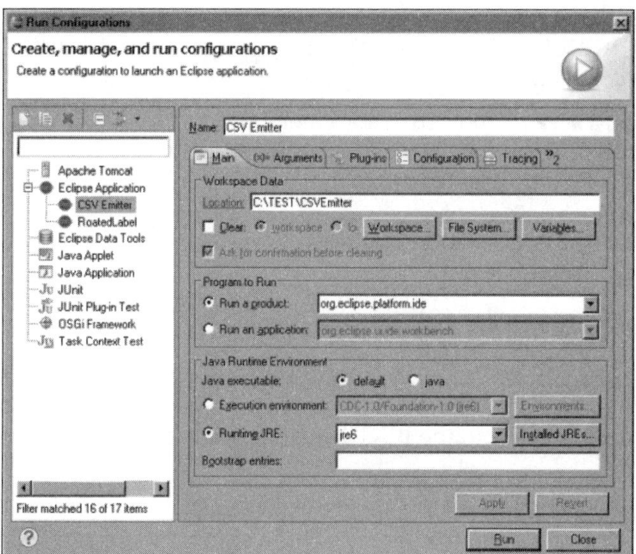

Figure 19-7 Creating the CSVEmitter run configuration

3 Choose the Plug-ins tab to select the list of plug-ins that you want to launch with the Run configuration.

4 In Launch with, choose

```
plug-ins selected below only
```

from the drop-down list, as shown in Figure 19-8.

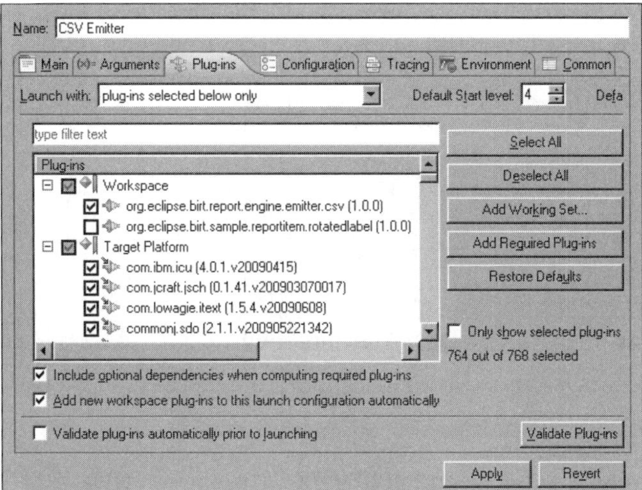

Figure 19-8 Adding the csv emitter plug-in to the launch configuration

5 In Plug-ins, select Workspace and Target Platform.

6 Choose Run to launch the run-time Eclipse workbench. A new instance of Eclipse opens up.

How to preview a BIRT report in CSV format in BIRT Report Designer

The BIRT Report Designer discovers the new CSV custom emitter and displays the new rendering format in the Run➛ViewReport menu.

To preview a BIRT report in CSV format, perform the following tasks:

1 In the new Eclipse workbench, switch to BIRT Report Design perspective.

2 In BIRT Report Designer perspective, open the BIRT report, you want to render in CSV format.

3 Choose Run➛ViewReport➛As CSV from the main menu, as shown in Figure 19-9.

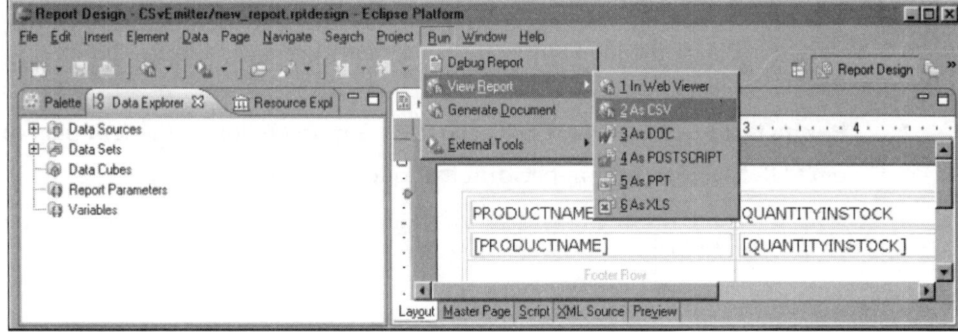

Figure 19-9 Preview a report in CSV format

4 A new browser window opens and a file download message appears, as shown in Figure 19-10.

Figure 19-10 File Download message

5 Choose Save and select the location to save the CSV report.

6 Open the report using any editor or Excel to validate the CSV output.

How to render a BIRT report in CSV format programmatically

To test the CSV report rendering example, you create a Java application that runs a report design in an installation of the BIRT run-time engine. BIRT provides a run-time engine that runs in a stand-alone Java EE application server environment and a preview engine that runs in the BIRT Report Designer.

To test the CSV report rendering plug-in, you perform the following tasks:

- Build the org.eclipse.birt.report.engine.emitter.csv plug-in.
- Deploy the plug-in to the BIRT run-time engine directory.
- Create a report design containing a table that maps to a data source and data set.
- Create a Java application that runs the report design and writes the table data to a CSV file.
- Run the application and examine the output in the CSV file.

The test environment must include the BIRT run-time engine.

The following sections describe the steps required to build and export the plug-ins, create the Java application and report design, and test the plug-in example.

How to build and export the org.eclipse.birt.report.engine.emitter.csv plug-in

On PDE Manifest Editor, perform the following tasks:

1 Choose the Build tab, and specify the binary build configuration for the plug-in to include the following items:

   - META-INF\MANIFEST.MF
   - bin\org.eclipse.birt.report.engine.emitter.csv
   - plugin.xml

2 On Overview, in Exporting, choose the Export Wizard and perform the following tasks:

   1 In Options, choose Package plug-ins as individual JAR archives and Allow for binary cycles in target platform, as shown in Figure 19-11.

Figure 19-11 Exporting a plug-in option

   2 In Destination, choose the directory, $INSTALL_DIR\birt-runtime-2_6_0\ReportEngine, as shown in Figure 19-12. Choose Finish.

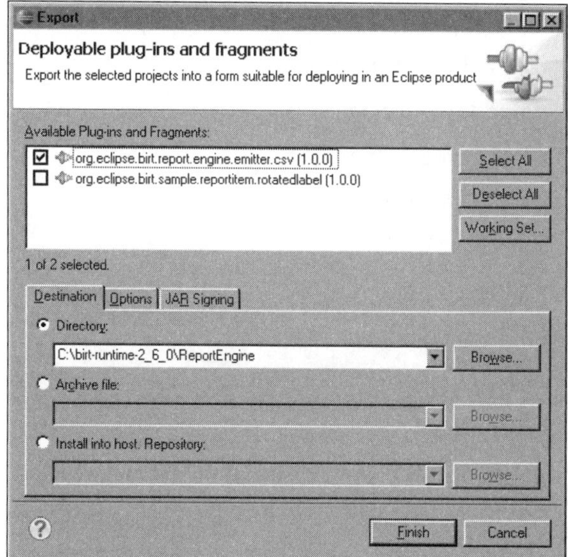

Figure 19-12 Exporting a plug-in to BIRT run-time engine

The org.eclipse.birt.report.engine.emitter.csv JAR file deploys to the $INSTALL_DIR\birt-runtime-2_6_0\ReportEngine\plugins directory.

How to create the report execution Java project

1 In Eclipse workbench, choose File→New→Project. New Project appears.

2 In New Project—Select a wizard, perform the following tasks:

   1 In Wizards, choose Java Project. Choose Next. Create a Java Project appears.

   2 In Create a Java Project, perform the following tasks:

1. In Project name, type:

   ```
   ExecuteCSVReport
   ```

2. Choose Next. Java Settings—Source appears.

3 In Java Settings, choose Libraries. Java Settings—Libraries appears.

4 In Libraries, perform the following tasks:

1. Choose Add External JARS. JAR Selection opens.
2. On JAR Selection, in Look in, navigate to $INSTALL_DIR\birt -runtime-2_6_0\ReportEngine\lib and, holding down CTRL, select the following libraries:

   - chartengineapi.jar
   - com.ibm.icu_4.2.1.<version>.jar
   - commons-cli-1.0.jar
   - coreapi.jar
   - crosstabcoreapi.jar
   - dataadapterapi.jar
   - dataaggregationapi.jar
   - dataextraction.jar
   - dteapi.jar
   - emitterconfig.jar
   - engineapi.jar
   - flute.jar
   - js.jar
   - modelapi.jar
   - modelodaapi.jar
   - odadesignapi.jar
   - org.apache.commons.codec_1.3.0.jar
   - org.eclipse.emf.common_2.6.0.<version>.jar
   - org.eclipse.emf.ecore_2.6.0.<version>.jar
   - org.eclipse.emf.ecore.xmi_2.5.0.<version>.jar
   - org.w3c.css.sac_1.3.0.<version>.jar
   - scriptapi.jar

   Choose Open.

3 On JAR Selection, in Look in, navigate to $INSTALL_DIR\birt-runtime-2_6_0\ReportEngine\plugins and select org.eclipse.birt.report.engine.emitter.csv.jar. Choose Open.

   Choose Finish. In Package Explorer, the ExecuteCSVReport project appears.

How to create the Java report execution class

1. In Eclipse workbench, choose File→New→Class. New Java Class appears.
2. On New Java Class, perform the following tasks:
   1. In Source folder, type:

      `ExecuteCSVReport/src`
   2. In Name, type:

      `ExecuteCSVReport`
   3. In Which method stubs would you like to create?, perform the following tasks:
      1. Select Public static void main(Strings[ ] args).
      2. Deselect Constructors from superclass.
      3. Deselect Inherited abstract methods.

      Choose Finish.

      In Package Explorer, ExecuteCSVReport.java appears in the ExecuteCSVReport project.
3. Open ExecuteCSVReport.java in Java Editor, and add the required code. The ExecuteCSVReport code is discussed later in this chapter.
4. In Eclipse workbench, compile the project by choosing Project→Build Project.

How to run the CSV report rendering extension

To run the CSV report rendering extension, using the ExecuteCSVReport application, perform the following tasks:

1. In Eclipse workbench, right-click ExecuteCSVReport, and choose Run As→Run Configurations. Run Configurations appears.
2. In Run Configurations, perform the following tasks:
   1. In Run Configurations, right-click JavaApplication. Choose New.
   2. A New Configuration appears as shown in Figure 19-13. Keep the values set by default.

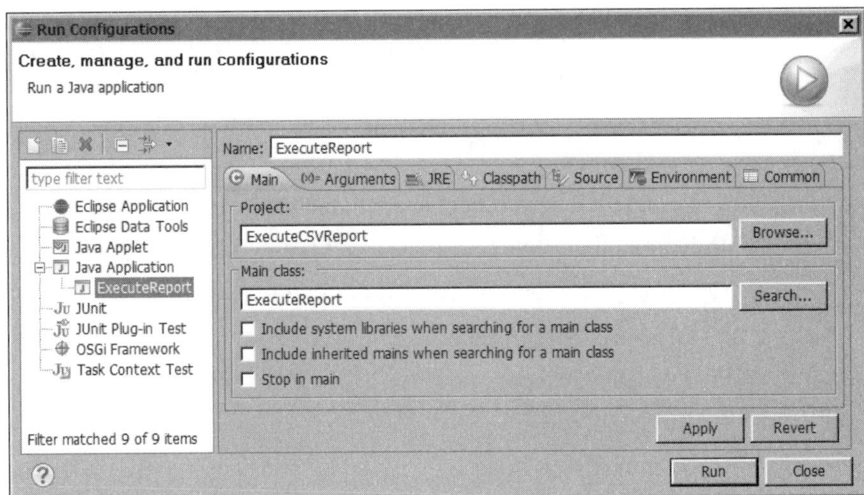

Figure 19-13 Creating the ExecuteCSVReport Run Configuration

   3 Choose Apply.

3 To run the Java application using the launch configuration, choose Run.

How to view the CSV report rendering extension file output

1 In Eclipse, navigate to the directory containing the CSV output file. The output CSV file is saved to the following location:

```
C:\Test\CSVEmitter\ExecuteCSVReport\reports
```

2 Using a text editor or other tool, open the file, and view its contents.

   Figure 19-14 shows the CSV output.

PRODUCTNAME	QUANTITYINSTOCK	MSRP
1969 Harley Davidson Ultimate Chopper	7933	95.7
1952 Alpine Renault 1300	7305	214.3
1996 Moto Guzzi 1100i	6625	118.94
2003 Harley-Davidson Eagle Drag Bike	5582	193.66
1972 Alfa Romeo GTA	3252	136
1962 LanciaA Delta 16V	6791	147.74

Figure 19-14 CSV output

The XML source code for the report design used in this example is discussed later in this chapter.

About ExecuteCSVReport class

The ExecuteCSVReport class uses BIRT Engine API to run a BIRT report and render the output in CSV format. The custom CSV emitter writes the text-based elements of the report to a file. The ExecuteCSVReport class performs the following operations:

- Configures the report engine
- Sets the log configuration and logging level

- Starts the platform and loads the plug-ins
- Gets the report engine factory object from the platform and creates the report engine
- Opens the report design
- Creates a task to run and render the report
- Set the rendering options, such as the output file and format
- Runs the report and destroys the engine
- Shuts down the engine

Listing 19-14 shows the code for the ExecuteCSVReport class in the CSV report rendering extension example.

Listing 19-14 The ExecuteCSVReport class code

```
import java.util.logging.Level;
import org.eclipse.birt.core.framework.Platform;
import org.eclipse.birt.report.engine.api.EngineConfig;
import org.eclipse.birt.report.engine.api.CSVRenderOption;
import org.eclipse.birt.report.engine.api.IReportEngine;
import
   org.eclipse.birt.report.engine.api.IReportEngineFactory;
import org.eclipse.birt.report.engine.api.IReportRunnable;
import org.eclipse.birt.report.engine.api.IRunAndRenderTask;

public class ExecuteCSVReport {

   static void executeCSVReport( ) throws Exception
   {
      IReportEngine engine=null;
      EngineConfig config = null;
      config = new EngineConfig( );
      config.setEngineHome
         ( "C:/birt-runtime-2_6_0/ReportEngine" );
      config.setLogConfig( "c:/birt/logs", Level.FINE );
      Platform.startup( config );
      IReportEngineFactory factory =
         ( IReportEngineFactory ) Platform.createFactoryObject
         ( IReportEngineFactory
            .EXTENSION_REPORT_ENGINE_FACTORY );
      engine = factory.createReportEngine( config );
      engine.changeLogLevel( Level.FINEST );

      IReportRunnable design =
         engine.openReportDesign
            ( "reports/csvTest.rptdesign" );
      IRunAndRenderTask task =
         engine.createRunAndRenderTask( design );
      String format = "CSV";
      CSVRenderOption csvOptions = new CSVRenderOption( );
```

```
        csvOptions.setOutputFormat( format );
        csvOptions.setOutputFileName( "reports/csvTest.csv" );
        task.setRenderOption( csvOptions );
        task.run( );
        task.close( );
        engine.destroy( );
        Platform.shutdown( );
        System.out.println("We are done!!!");
    }
    public static void main(String[] args) {
        try
        {
            executeCSVReport( );
        }
        catch ( Exception e )
        {
            e.printStackTrace();
        }
    }
}
```

About the report design XML code

The XML file for the report design, csvTest.reportdesign, contains the following source code settings, as specified in the report design:

- Data sources, including the ODA plug-in extension ID, driver class, URL, and user
- Data sets, including the ODA JDBC plug-in extension ID, result set properties, and query text
- Page setup, including the page footer
- Body, containing the table structure and properties for the bound data columns, including the header, footer, and detail rows

The report design example specifies a data source that connects to org.eclipse.birt.report.data.oda.sampledb, the BIRT Classic Models sample database. Listing 19-15 shows the XML source code for the report design used to test the CSV rendering example. The sample application runs the report from the reports subfolder in the ExecuteCSVReport project.

Listing 19-15 The report design XML code

```
<?xml version="1.0" encoding="UTF-8"?>
<report xmlns="http://www.eclipse.org/birt/2005/design"
    version="3.2.21" id="1">
    <property name="createdBy">
    Eclipse BIRT Designer Version 2.6.0.v20100531 Build &lt;2.6
    .0.v20100609-1613> </property>
    <property name="units">in</property>
```

```
<data-sources>
   <oda-data-source
      extensionID=
         "org.eclipse.birt.report.data.oda.jdbc"
         name="Data Source" id="2">
         <list-property name="privateDriverProperties">
            <ex-property>
               <name>contentBidiFormatStr</name>
               <value>ILYNN</value>
            </ex-property>
            <ex-property>
               <name>metadataBidiFormatStr</name>
               <value>ILYNN</value>
            </ex-property>
         </list-property>
      <property
         name="odaDriverClass">
         org.eclipse.birt.report.data.oda.sampledb.Driver
      </property>
      <property
         name="odaURL">jdbc:classicmodels:sampledb
      </property>
      <property name="odaUser">ClassicModels</property>
   </oda-data-source>
</data-sources>
<data-sets>
   <oda-data-set
      extensionID=
         "org.eclipse.birt.report.data.oda.jdbc
            .JdbcSelectDataSet" name="Data Set" id="3">
      <list-property name="columnHints">
         <structure>
            <property name=
                  "columnName">PRODUCTNAME</property>
            <text-property name=
               "displayName">PRODUCTNAME</text-property>
            <text-property name=
                  "displayName">PRODUCTNAME</text-property>
         </structure>
         <structure>
            <property name=
                  "columnName">QUANTITYINSTOCK</property>
            <text-property name=
                  "displayName">QUANTITYINSTOCK</text-property>
         </structure>
         <structure>
            <property name="columnName">MSRP</property>
            <text-property name=
               "displayName">MSRP</text-property>
         </structure>
      </list-property>
```

```
<structure name="cachedMetaData">
     <list-property name="resultSet">
        <structure>
           <property name="position">1</property>
           <property name=
              "name">PRODUCTNAME
           </property>
           <property
              name="dataType">string
           </property>
        </structure>
        <structure>
           <property name="position">2</property>
           <property
              name="name">QUANTITYINSTOCK
           </property>
           <property
              name="dataType">integer
           </property>
        </structure>
        <structure>
           <property name="position">3</property>
           <property name="name">MSRP</property>
           <property name="dataType">float</property>
        </structure>
     </list-property>
  </structure>
  <property name="dataSource">Data Source</property>
     <list-property name="resultSet">
           <structure>
                 <property name="position">1</property>
                 <property name="name">PRODUCTNAME
                 </property>
                 <property name=
                       "nativeName">PRODUCTNAME</property>
                 <property name="dataType">string
                 </property>
                 <property name=
                       "nativeDataType">12</property>
           </structure>
           <structure>
                 <property name="position">2</property>
                 <property name="name">QUANTITYINSTOCK
                 </property>
                 <property name=
                       "nativeName">QUANTITYINSTOCK
                       </property>
                 <property name="dataType">integer
                 </property>
                 <property name="nativeDataType">4
                 </property>
           </structure>
           <structure>
                 <property name="position">3</property>
```

```
                    <property name="name">MSRP</property>
                    <property name="nativeName">MSRP
                    </property>
                    <property name="dataType">float
                    </property>
                    <property name="nativeDataType">8
                    </property>
                </structure>
            </list-property>
        <property name="queryText"><![CDATA [
            select CLASSICMODELS.PRODUCTS.PRODUCTNAME,
                   CLASSICMODELS.PRODUCTS.QUANTITYINSTOCK,
                   CLASSICMODELS.PRODUCTS.MSRP
            from CLASSICMODELS.PRODUCTS]]</xml-property>
    </oda-data-set>
</data-sets>
<page-setup>
    <simple-master-page name="Simple MasterPage" id="4">
        <property name="topMargin">1in</property>
        <property name="leftMargin">1.25in</property>
        <property name="bottomMargin">1in</property>
        <property name="rightMargin">1.25in</property>
        <page-footer>
            <text id="5">
                <property name="contentType">html</property>
                <text-property name="content">
                    <![CDATA[<value-of>new Date()</value-of>]]>
                </text-property>
            </text>
        </page-footer>
    </simple-master-page>
</page-setup>
<body>
    <table id="6">
        <property name="width">100%</property>
        <property name="dataSet">Data Set</property>
        <list-property name="boundDataColumns">
            <structure>
                <property name="name">PRODUCTNAME</property>
                <expression
                    name="expression">dataSetRow["PRODUCTNAME"]
                </expression>
            </structure>
            <structure>
                <property
                    name="name">QUANTITYINSTOCK
                </property>
                <expression
                    name="expression">
                    dataSetRow["QUANTITYINSTOCK"]
                </expression>
            </structure>
            <structure>
                <property name="name">MSRP</property>
```

```
<expression
   name="expression">dataSetRow["MSRP"]
</expression>
</structure>
</list-property>
<column id="28"/>
<column id="29"/>
<column id="30"/>
<header>
   <row id="7">
      <cell id="8">
         <property name="colSpan">3</property>
         <property name="rowSpan">1</property>
         <property name="textAlign">center</property>
         <label id="9">
               <property
                  name="fontSize">x-large
               </property>
               <property
                  name="fontWeight">bold
               </property>
               <property
                  name="textAlign">center
               </property>
               <list-property name="visibility">
                     <structure>
                           <property name=
                              "format">all</property>
                           <expression name=
                                 "valueExpr">true
                           </expression>
                     </structure>
               </list-property>
               <text-property
               name="text">Report
               </text-property>
            </label>
      </cell>
   </row>
   <row id="10">
      <cell id="11">
         <label id="12">
            <text-property
               name="text">PRODUCTNAME
            </text-property>
         </label>
      </cell>
      <cell id="13">
         <label id="14">
            <text-property
               name="text">QUANTITYINSTOCK
            </text-property>
         </label>
      </cell>
```

```
                    <cell id="15">
                        <label id="16">
                            <text-property
                                name="text">MSRP
                            </text-property>
                        </label>
                    </cell>
                </row>
            </header>
            <detail>
                <row id="17">
                    <cell id="18">
                        <data id="19">
                            <property
                                name="resultSetColumn">PRODUCTNAME
                            </property>
                        </data>
                    </cell>
                    <cell id="20">
                         <data id="21">
                            <property
                                name="resultSetColumn">QUANTITYINSTOCK
                            </property>
                        </data>
                    </cell>
                    <cell id="22">
                        <data id="23">
                            <property
                                name="resultSetColumn">MSRP
                            </property>
                        </data>
                    </cell>
                </row>
            </detail>
            <footer>
                <row id="24">
                    <cell id="25"/>
                    <cell id="26"/>
                    <cell id="27"/>
                </row>
            </footer>
        </table>
    </body>
</report>
```

BIRT Report Engine can render a report design for output using a standard emitter extension or a customized emitter extension, such as this CSV rendering example.

Developing an XML report rendering extension

The sample XML report rendering extension is a plug-in that can export BIRT report data in XML format. Typically, report developers render BIRT report data to XML to enable sharing data with another application.

For example, business-to-business (B2B) systems must transmit data to customers and trading partners in a consistent way that supports interoperability according to Electronic Data Interchange (EDI) standards. These systems use specialized forms of XML such as Electronic Business eXtensible Markup Language (ebXML). A custom XML report rendering extension can render BIRT report data in a format that is consistent with this established standard.

The sample XML report rendering extension provides the following capabilities:

- Exports BIRT report data in XML format

  The XML report rendering plug-in renders each report element and writes to the output file, <report_name>.xml.

- Defines a public API for rendering BIRT reports in XML format

  The plug-in extends the functionality defined by the org.eclipse.birt .report.engine.emitter extension point defined in the org.eclipse.birt .report.engine plug-in.

- Supports the user specifying an XML schema for formatting output

  During the rendering process, the sample plug-in processes all the elements in the report design, exporting XML properties and related data to the output file. Optionally, the plug-in supports mapping the report elements to an XML schema to provide additional formatting for output.

  The plug-in defines these mappings in the property file, <report_name> .xmlemitter. The plug-in reads the property file at run time and loads the custom tags.

Creating an XML report rendering plug-in project

Create a new plug-in project for the XML report rendering extension using the Eclipse PDE.

How to create the XML report rendering plug-in project

1. From the Eclipse PDE menu, choose File→New→Project. New Project appears.
2. On New Project, select Plug-in Project. Choose Next. New Plug-in Project appears.

3 In Plug-in Project, modify the settings, as shown in Table 19-4.

Table 19-4 Values for XML Emitter Plug-in Project fields

Section	Option	Value
Plug-in Project	Project name	org.eclipse.birt.report .engine.emitter.xml
	Use default location	Selected
	Location	Not available when you select Use default location
Project Settings	Create a Java project	Selected
	Source folder	src
	Output folder	bin
Target Platform	Eclipse version	3.6
	OSGi framework	Not selected
Working sets	Add project to working sets	Not selected

Choose Next. Plug-in Content appears.

4 In Plug-in Content, modify the settings, as shown in Table 19-5.

Table 19-5 Values for XML Emitter Plug-in Content fields

Section	Option	Value
Plug-in Properties	Plug-in ID	org.eclipse.birt.report .engine.emitter.xml
	Plug-in Version	1.0.0
	Plug-in Name	BIRT XML Emitter
	Plug-in Provider	yourCompany.com or leave blank
	Classpath	xmlEmitter.jar or leave blank
Plug-in Options	Generate an activator, a Java class that controls the plug-in's life cycle	Selected
	Activator	org.eclipse.birt.report .engine.emitter.xml .XmlPlugin
	This plug-in will make contributions to the UI	Not selected

(continues)

Table 19-5 Values for XML Emitter Plug-in Content fields (continued)

Section	Option	Value
Plug-in Options	Enable API Analysis	Not selected
Rich Client Application	Would you like to create a rich client application?	No

Choose Finish.

The XML report rendering extension project appears in the Eclipse PDE workbench, as shown in Figure 19-15.

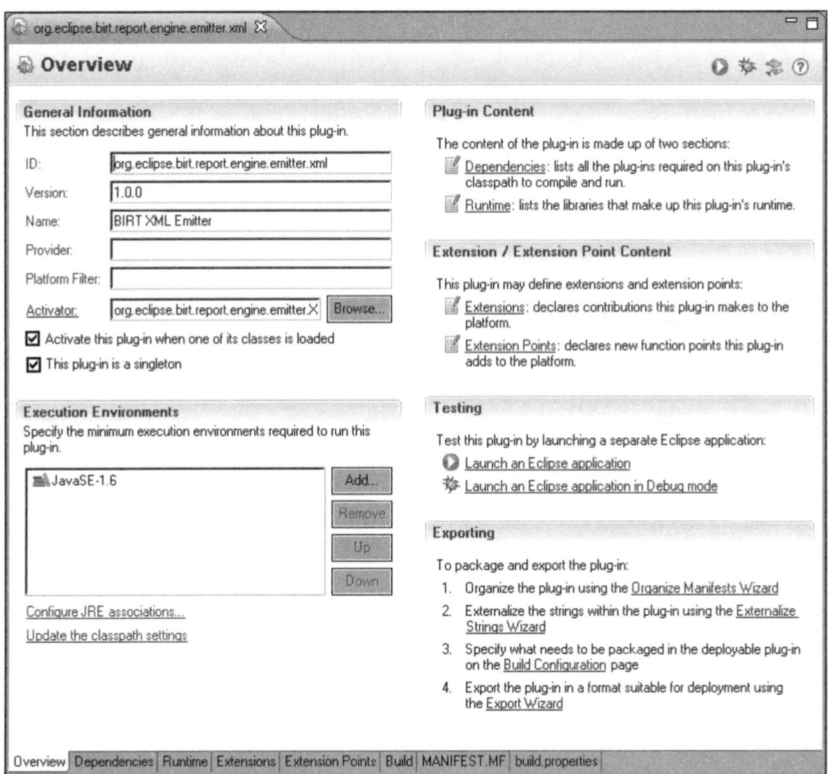

Figure 19-15 XML report rendering extension project

Defining the dependencies for the XML report rendering extension

To compile and run the XML report rendering example, specify the org .eclipse.birt.report.engine plug-in, which must be available on the classpath for the XML rendering extension.

Declaring the emitters extension point

To implement the XML report rendering extension, specify the org.eclipse.birt.report.engine.emitters extension point and add the extension element details.

How to specify the extension point

1 On PDE Manifest Editor, choose Extensions.

2 In All Extensions, choose Add. New Extension—Extension Point Selection appears.

3 In Available extension points, select the following plug-in:

```
org.eclipse.birt.report.engine.emitters
```

Choose Finish.

4 In All Extensions, right-click the extension point, org.eclipse.birt.report.engine.emitters, and choose the extension element, emitter.

5 In Extension Element Details, specify the properties for the XML emitter extension element, emitter, as shown in Table 19-6.

Table 19-6 Property values for the XML Emitter extension element

Property	Value
class	org.eclipse.birt.report.engine.emitter.xml.XMLReportEmitter
format	xml
mimeType	xml
id	org.eclipse.birt.report.engine.emitter.xml

Understanding the sample XML report rendering extension

The XML report rendering extension extends the report emitter interfaces and XML writer in org.eclipse.birt.report.engine.emitter. The extension example provides access to the report container, pages, tables, rows, cells text, labels, data, images, hyperlinks, and other contents at different phases of the report generation process.

The example writes the contents of the report to an XML output file. The example creates the XML file in the same folder as the exported report. The output file name is the name of the report with a .xml extension. The example provides only limited error checking.

The following section provides a general description of the code-based extensions a developer must make to develop an XML report rendering extension after defining the plug-in framework in the Eclipse PDE.

Understanding the XML report rendering extension package

The implementation package for the XML report rendering extension example, org.eclipse.birt.report.engine.emitter.xml, contains the following classes:

- XMLPlugin

  The plug-in run-time class for the report item extension example.

- XMLReportEmitter

  Handles the start and end processing that renders the report container.

- XMLRenderOption

  Integrates the plug-in with BIRT Report Engine, specifying configuration information, including the output format as XML.

- XMLTags.java

  Defines the controls and associated property lists used when writing to the XML file.

- XMLFileWriter

  Writes the XML version, text, image, data, label, and report tag content of the report to the XML output file.

- LoadExportSchema

  Loads the XML schema file, if one exists, to replace the default values specified for the XML version, data, image, label, report tags, and text. An accessor method for each tag returns the value to XMLReportEmitter for output to the export file.

The following section contains more specific information about the implementation details for the classes in the XML report rendering extension package.

Understanding XMLReportEmitter

XMLReportEmitter writes the contents of the report to an XML file. XMLReportEmitter instantiates the writer and emitter objects and handles the start and end processing that renders the report container. XMLReportEmitter exports the XML version, data, image, label, report tag content, and text of the report to the XML output file.

XMLReportEmitter implements the following methods:

- XMLReportEmitter( ) instantiates the XML report emitter class as an org.eclipse.birt.report.engine.presentation.ContentEmitterVisitor object to perform emitter operations.

- initialize( ) performs the following operations required to create an output stream that writes the report contents to the XML file, similar to the CSV report rendering extension:
  - Obtains a reference to the IEmitterServices interface
  - Instantiates the file and output stream objects, using the specified settings
  - Instantiates the XML file writer object
- start( ) performs the following operations:
  - Obtains a reference to the IReportContent interface, containing accessor methods that get the interfaces to the report content emitters
  - Sets the start emitter logging level and writes to the log file
  - If an optional XML schema file exists, start( )
    - locates the XML schema file for the report and
    - instantiates a LoadExportSchema object to read the XML schema file
  - Opens the output file, specifying the encoding scheme as UTF-8
  - Starts the XML writer
  - Writes the start tag, which specifies the <xml> tag, including the version and encoding schema, to the output file
  - Writes the <report> tag, which specifies the report name and other properties in the report property list to the output file

Listing 19-16 shows the start( ) method.

Listing 19-16 The start( ) method

```
public void start( IReportContent report )
{
logger.log( Level.FINE,
   "[XMLReportEmitter] Start emitter." );
String fileName =
   report.getDesign( ).getReportDesign( ).getFileName( );
   int pos = fileName.indexOf("/");
   String fn = fileName.substring(pos+1,fileName.length( ));
   fileName = fn;
   if (fileName.length( ) > 0) {
      pos =  fileName.lastIndexOf(".");
      if ( pos > 0 )
         fileName = fileName.substring(0, pos);

         fileName = fileName + ".xmlemitter";
         pos = fileName.lastIndexOf("/");
```

```
            String propFileName =
               fileName.substring( pos+1 , fileName.length( ) );
            String resourceFolder =
               report.getDesign().getReportDesign( )
                     .getResourceFolder( );
            if ( fileExists(resourceFolder + "/"
               + propFileName))
               exportSchema = new LoadExportSchema(
                     resourceFolder + "/" + propFileName );
            else
               if ( fileExists(fileName))
                     exportSchema =
                           new LoadExportSchema( fileName );
               else exportSchema = new LoadExportSchema( "" );
      }
      this.report = report;
      writer.open( out, "UTF-8" );
      writer.startWriter( );

      writer.closeTag( exportSchema.getExportStartTag( ));
      writer.closeTag( XMLTags.TAG_CR );

      String rp = exportSchema.getExportReportTag( );
      for (int i = 0;i < XMLTags.rPropList.length;i++)
      {
         if (exportSchema.isPropertyRequired(
               XMLTags.rPropList[i], rp))
         {
            String propValue = getReportPropValue(i,report);
            rp = replaceTag( rp, "??"
                           +XMLTags.rPropList[i], propValue );
         }
      }
      writer.writeCode( rp );
      writer.closeTag( XMLTags.TAG_CR );
   }
```

- end( ) performs the following operations, similar to the CSV rendering extension:
  - Sets the end report logging level and writes to the log file
  - Ends the write process and closes the XML writer
  - Closes the output file

Understanding the other XMLReportEmitter methods

The XMLReportEmitter class defines the following additional methods, called at different phases of the report generation process, that provide access to the report container, pages, tables, rows, cells text, labels, data, images, hyperlinks, and other contents. The following examples show the processing for a label:

- startLabel( ) performs the following operations:
  - Calls LoadExportSchema.getExportLabelTag( ) to get the pattern for the <label> tag specified in the <report_name>.xmlemitter property file. If the property file does not exist, the plug-in uses the following default pattern specified in the LoadExportSchema class:

    ```
    <label>??value</label>
    ```

  - Iterates through the following label properties list defined in XMLTags to determine the properties required by the report:

    ```
    static String[ ] lPropList =
       {"Bookmark","Height","Hyperlink","InlineStyle",
          "Name","TOC","Width","X","Y" };
    ```

  - Calls getLabelPropValue( ) to obtain each required property value and substitute the value in the <label> tag expression.
  - Calls startText( ) and XMLFileWriter.closeTag( ) to write the <label> tag to the output file.

  Listing 19-17 shows the startLabel( ) method code.

  Listing 19-17 The startLabel( ) method

  ```
  public void startLabel( ILabelContent label )
  {
     String lbl = exportSchema.getExportLabelTag( );
     int len =  XMLTags.lPropList.length;
     for (int i = 0;i < XMLTags.lPropList.length;i++)
     {
        if (exportSchema.isPropertyRequired(
           XMLTags.lPropList[i], lbl))
        {
           String propValue = getLabelPropValue(i,label);
           lbl = replaceTag( lbl, "??"+XMLTags.lPropList[i],
              propValue );
        }
     }
     startText( label, lbl );
     writer.closeTag( XMLTags.TAG_CR );
  }
  ```

- startText( ) performs the following operations:
  - Sets the start text logging level and writes to the log file
  - Uses getLabelPropValue( ) iteratively to get the label text value
  - Writes the <label> tag to the output file

  Listing 19-18 shows the startText( ) method code.

Listing 19-18 The startText( ) method

```
public void startText( ITextContent text, String exportTag )
{
   logger.log( Level.FINE,
      "[XMLReportEmitter] Start text" );
   String txt = exportSchema.getExportLabelTag();
   int len =  XMLTags.lPropList.length;
   for (int i = 0;i < XMLTags.lPropList.length;i++)
   {
      if (exportSchema.isPropertyRequired(
            XMLTags.lPropList[i], lbl))
      {
         String propValue = getLabelPropValue(i,label);
         lbl = replaceTag( lbl, "??"
               +XMLTags.lPropList[i], propValue );
      }
   }
   String textValue = text.getText( );
   writer.writeCode( replaceTag( exportTag, XMLTags.valueTag,
textValue ) );
}
```

- getLabelPropValue( ) performs the following operations:
  - Calls the appropriate IContent accessor method to obtain the property value
  - Returns the value to startLabel( ) for substitution in the <label> tag and writing the tag to the XML output file

Listing 19-19 shows the getLabelPropValue( ) method code.

Listing 19-19 The getLabelPropValue( ) method

```
private String getLabelPropValue( int property, ILabelContent
label)
{
   String propValue;

   switch (property) {
      case 0: // "Bookmark":
         propValue = label.getBookmark( );
         break;
      case 1: // "Height":
         if ( label.getHeight( ) != null )
            propValue = label.getHeight().toString( );
         else
               propValue = "";
         break;
      case 2: //"Hyperlink":
         if ( label.getHyperlinkAction( ) != null )
            propValue =
                  label.getHyperlinkAction( ).getHyperlink( );
```

```
            else propValue = "";
            break;
         ...
         case 8: //"Y":
            if ( label.getY( ) != null )
               propValue = label.getY( ).toString( );
            else
               propValue = "";
            break;
         default: propValue = "";
            break;
   }
      if ( propValue == null )
         propValue = "";
         return propValue;
   }
```

Understanding XMLTags

The XMLTags class defines the controls and associated property lists used in analyzing the report contents, as shown in Listing 19-20.

Listing 19-20 The XMLTags class

```
public class XMLTags
{
   public static final String TAG_CR = "\n" ;
   static String valueTag = "??value";
   static String labelControl = "label";
   static String textControl = "text";
   static String imageControl = "image";
   static String dataControl = "data";
   static String reportControl = "report";
   static String startControl = "start";
   static String endControl = "end";

   static String[ ] iPropList =
      {"Bookmark","Height","Hyperlink","ImageMap",
         "InlineStyle","MIMEType","Name","Style","TOC","URI",
         "Width","X","Y"};
   static String[ ] dPropList =
         {"Bookmark","Height","Hyperlink","InlineStyle","Name",
            "Style","TOC","Width","X","Y"};
   static String[ ] lPropList =
      {"Bookmark","Height","Hyperlink","InlineStyle","Name",
         "TOC","Width","X","Y" };
   static String[ ] tPropList =
         {"Bookmark","Height","Hyperlink","InlineStyle","Name",
            "Style","Text","TOC","Width","X","Y"}
   static String[ ] rPropList =
         {"TotalPages", "TOCTree", "Name"};
}
```

Understanding XMLFileWriter

The XMLFileWriter class writes the closing tag similar to the CSV report rendering extension.

Understanding XMLRenderOption

The org.eclipse.birt.report.engine.emitter.xml.XMLRenderOption class adds the XML rendering option to the BIRT Report Engine run time, as shown in Listing 19-21.

Listing 19-21 The XMLRenderOption class

```
package org.eclipse.birt.report.engine.emitter.xml;
import org.eclipse.birt.report.engine.api.RenderOption;

public class XMLRenderOption extends RenderOption{
   public static final String XML = "XML";
   public XMLRenderOption( ) {
}
```

Understanding LoadExportSchema

The org.eclipse.birt.report.engine.emitter.xml.LoadExportSchema class optionally loads an XML schema by performing the following operations:

- Specifies the default substitution patterns for the XML tags
- Calls the readSchemaFile( ) method
- Specifies an accessor method for each tag that returns a value to XMLReportEmitter for output to the export file

Listing 19-22 shows the specification of the default substitution patterns for the XML tags and the constructor, which calls the readSchemaFile( ) method.

Listing 19-22 The LoadExportSchema class

```
package org.eclipse.birt.report.engine.emitter.xml;
...
public class LoadExportSchema{
   protected String fileName = "";
   protected String startTag =
      "<?xml version=\"1.0\" encoding=\"UTF-8\"?>";
   protected String textTag = "<text>??value</text>";
   protected String imageTag = "<image>??value</image>";
   protected String dataTag = "<data>??value</data>";
   protected String labelTag = "<label>??value</label>";
   protected String endTag = "</report>";
   protected String reportTag = "<report:??name>";

   public LoadExportSchema(String fileName)
   {
      if ( fileName.length( ) > 0 )
```

```
        {
            this.fileName = fileName;
            readSchemaFile( );
        }
    }
    . . .
```

The readSchemaFile( ) method reads the XML Schema file, one line at a time, replacing the default values for the patterns of the XML version, data, image, label, report tags, and text with the values specified in the XML Schema file.

Listing 19-23 shows the code for the readSchemaFile( ) method.

Listing 19-23 The readSchemaFile( ) method

```
private void readSchemaFile( )
{
   BufferedReader input = null;
   try
   {
      input = new BufferedReader(
            new FileReader(fileName) );
      String line = null; //not declared within while loop
      while (( line = input.readLine( )) != null){
         int pos = line.indexOf("=");
         if ( pos > 0 )
         {
            String index = line.substring(0, pos );
            String indexTag = line.substring(pos + 1,
               line.length( ));
            if ( index.equalsIgnoreCase(
               XMLTags.labelControl ) )
            {
               labelTag = indexTag;
         }
         if ( index.equalsIgnoreCase( XMLTags.imageControl ) )
         {
            imageTag = indexTag;
         }
         if ( index.equalsIgnoreCase( XMLTags.dataControl ) )
         {
            dataTag = indexTag;
         }
         if ( index.equalsIgnoreCase( XMLTags.startControl ) )
         {
            startTag = indexTag;
         }
         if ( index.equalsIgnoreCase( XMLTags.endControl ) )
         {
            endTag = indexTag;
         }
         if ( index.equalsIgnoreCase( XMLTags.reportControl ) )
         {
            reportTag = indexTag;
```

```
            }
         }
         catch (FileNotFoundException ex)
         {
            ex.printStackTrace( );
         }
         catch (IOException ex)
         {
            ex.printStackTrace( );
         }
         finally
         {
            try
            {
               if (input!= null)
               {
                  input.close( );
               }
            }
            catch (IOException ex)
            {
               ex.printStackTrace( );
            }
         }
      }
```

Listing 19-24 shows the values of the patterns for the XML version, data tags, image, label, report, and text specified in the XML Schema file, xmlReport.xmlemitter.

Listing 19-24 The XML Schema file

```
start=<?xml version="1.0" encoding="UTF-8"?>
report=<report name=??name>
label=<label name=??name hyperlink=??hyperlink>??value</label>
text=<text name=??name>??value</text>
image=<image name=??name>??value</image>
data=<data>??value</data>
end=</report>
```

Testing the XML report rendering plug-in

To test the XML report rendering example, create a Java application that runs a report design in an installation of the BIRT run-time engine, similar to the application created to run the CSV report rendering example.

To test the XML report rendering plug-in, perform the following tasks:

- Build the org.eclipse.birt.report.engine.emitter.xml plug-in.
- Deploy the plug-in to the BIRT run-time engine directory.
- Launch a run-time instance of the Eclipse PDE or open an Eclipse workbench.

- Create a Java application that runs the report design and writes the report's data to an XML file.
- Create a report design containing a table that maps to a data source and data set.
- Run the application and examine the XML in the output file.

Figure 19-16 shows the report design used in the XML report rendering example.

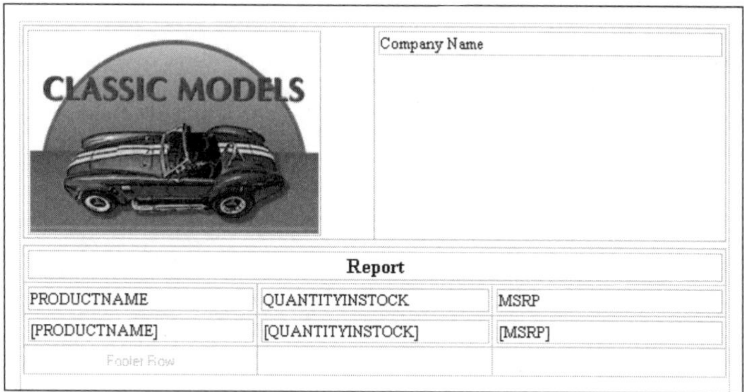

Figure 19-16 Report design for the XML report rendering example

Listing 19-25 shows the contents of the XML output file, containing XML version, report, image, label, and data tags for an executed report.

Listing 19-25 The XML output file

```
<?xml version="1.0" encoding="UTF-8"?>
<report name=
   C:/Test/XMLEmitter/ExecuteXMLReport/reports/
   xmlReport.rptdesign>
   <image name=>
      /9j/4AAQSkZJRgABAgEBLAEsAAD
      /4RVaRXhpZgAATU0AKgAAAAgABwESAAMAAAABAAEAAAEaAAUA
      ...
      7PMv9I9nVo5cj8b7MV9zB/gh8cf/2Q==
   </image>
   <label
      name= hyperlink=http://www.actuate.com>Company Name
   </label>
   <label name= hyperlink=>Report</label>
   <label name= hyperlink=>PRODUCTNAME</label>
   <label name= hyperlink=>QUANTITYINSTOCK</label>
   <label name= hyperlink=>MSRP</label>
   <data>1969 Harley Davidson Ultimate Chopper</data>
   <data>7933</data>
   <data>95.7</data>
   <data>1952 Alpine Renault 1300</data>
   <data>7305</data>
   <data>214.3</data>
```

```
    <data>1996 Moto Guzzi 1100i</data>
    <data>6625</data>
    <data>118.94</data>
    <data>2003 Harley-Davidson Eagle Drag Bike</data>
    <data>5582</data>
    <data>193.66</data>
    ...
    <data>American Airlines: MD-11S</data>
    <data>8820</data>
    <data>74.03</data>
    <data>Boeing X-32A JSF</data>
    <data>4857</data>
    <data>49.66</data>
    <data>Pont Yacht</data>
    <data>414</data>
    <data>54.6</data>
    ...
</report>
```

Chapter

20

Developing an ODA Extension

BIRT uses the Eclipse Data Tools Platform (DTP) open data access (ODA) API to build a driver that connects to a data source and retrieves data for a report. This API defines interfaces and classes that manage the following tasks:

- Connecting to a data source
- Preparing and executing a query
- Handling data and metadata in a result set
- Mapping between the object representation of data and the data source

Eclipse DTP also provides tools and support for SQL development, locales, logging, and other special types of processing. For more information about the Eclipse DTP project, see http://www.eclipse.org/datatools.

The ODA framework is a key component of the DTP. ODA presents the Java developer with a robust architecture to extend the capabilities of BIRT by being able to report on custom data sources. The framework provides new project wizards to create plug-in projects for ODA run-time and designer extensions. The generated plug-in projects include class templates and default implementation. These plug-in projects support expediting the development of customized ODA data source extensions.

This chapter shows how to develop an ODA extension using examples that extend the org.eclipse.datatools.connectivity.oda.dataSource extension point to provide access to the following data sources:

- CSV file

  Uses the new DTP ODA wizards to create a plug-in project that accesses a CSV data source. DTP ODA interfaces are similar to JDBC interfaces with extensions that support retrieving data from relational and non-relational database sources.

- Relational database
  Uses Hibernate Core for Java, an object-oriented software system for generating SQL and handling JDBC result sets. Hibernate Query Language (HQL) provides a SQL-transparent extension that makes the DTP ODA extension portable to all relational databases. Hibernate also supports developing a query in the native SQL dialect of a database.

  Hibernate is free, open-source software licensed under the GNU Lesser General Public License (LGPL). For more information about Hibernate, see http://www.hibernate.org/.

Understanding an ODA extension

A BIRT report design specifies the type of data access and data transformations required to generate a report. All data comes from an external data source. The BIRT data engine supports the DTP ODA framework. The DTP ODA framework provides access to standard and custom data sources using an open API.

Using the DTP ODA framework makes it possible to create a plug-in driver to any external data source. BIRT uses DTP ODA extension points for the report designer and report generation environments.

A DTP ODA extension adds a new data source driver to the BIRT framework by implementing the following extension points:

- ODA data source
  org.eclipse.datatools.connectivity.oda.dataSource supports the extension of BIRT design-time and run-time data source access. The XML schema file, org.eclipse.datatools.connectivity.oda/schema/dataSource.exsd, describes this extension point.

- ODA user interface
  org.eclipse.datatools.connectivity.oda.design.ui.dataSource supports optionally adding an integrated user interface for an ODA driver to BIRT Report Designer. The plug-in can provide user interface support used by a report designer to specify the data source and edit the data set. The XML schema file, org.eclipse.datatools.connectivity.oda.design.ui/schema /dataSource.exsd, describes this extension point.

- ODA connection profile
  org.eclipse.datatools.connectivity.oda.connectionProfile supports optionally adding different types of connection profiles to an ODA driver user interface for BIRT Report Designer. A connection profile can define a category or set of configuration types such as JDBC connection profiles. This user interface defines a corresponding newWizard element used to

create the resource. The XML schema file, org.eclipse.datatools.connectivity/schema/connectionProfile.exsd, describes this extension point.

- ODA connection properties page

  org.eclipse.ui.propertyPages supports optionally adding a page used to edit the properties of a connection profile. The XML schema file, org.eclipse.ui.propertyPages/schema/propertyPages.exsd, describes this extension point.

For more information about the DTP ODA APIs, see the Javadoc for the org.eclipse.datatools.connectivity.oda package hierarchy. The Javadoc is in the DTP Software Development Kit (SDK) available from the Eclipse Data Tools Platform project at http://www.eclipse.org/datatools.

Developing the CSV ODA driver extensions

Eclipse DTP provides two ODA plug-in template wizards, one for ODA data source runtime driver, another for ODA data source designer. Each wizard creates a new plug-in project, generating implementations of related ODA extension points. The auto-generated Java classes implement method stubs that support a single result set and input parameters. The classes have hard-coded result set data so that an ODA extension developer can immediately verify that the generated ODA driver plug-ins work with an ODA consumer, for example, BIRT.

After the ODA wizard generates the plug-ins, modify the TODO tags in the generated source code to customize data source behavior.

To develop the CSV ODA extensions, perform the following tasks:

- Download the required BIRT source code from the Eclipse CVS repository.
- Create two new projects using the ODA wizards in the Eclipse PDE to implement the following plug-ins:
  - CSV ODA driver to access the data source
  - CSV ODA user interface to select the data file and available data columns in BIRT Report Designer
- Extend the source code in the CSV ODA plug-in projects by adding new functionality at the defined extension points.
- Test and deploy the extensions in the run-time environment.

You can download the source code for the CSV ODA driver extension examples at http://www.actuate.com/birt/contributions.

About the CSV ODA plug-ins

The CSV ODA extensions require the following two plug-ins:

- org.eclipse.birt.report.data.oda.csv
  The CSV ODA data source plug-in extends the functionality defined by the extension point, org.eclipse.datatools.connectivity.oda.dataSource, to create the CSV ODA driver. The first row of the CSV input file contains the column names. The remaining rows, separated by new line markers, contain the data fields, separated by commas. The org.eclipse.birt.report .data.oda.csv plug-in contains the database classes and data structures, such as data types, result set, metadata result set, and query used to handle data in a BIRT report.

  The org.eclipse.datatools.connectivity.oda.dataSource extension point is in the Eclipse DTP project and is part of the org.eclipse.datatools .connectivity.oda plug-in. This plug-in is available from the CVS repository in /home/datatools.

- org.eclipse.birt.report.data.csv.ui
  The CSV ODA user interface plug-in extends the functionality defined by the org.eclipse.datatools.connectivity.connectionProfile, org.eclipse.ui .propertyPages, and org.eclipse.datatools.connectivity.oda.design.ui .dataSource extension points. The user interface consists of the following two pages:

  - The data source page, which specifies and validates the path and name of the CSV file.
  - The data set page, which shows the selected data file and columns available in the file. By default, the user interface selects all the columns in the data set.

Downloading BIRT source code from the CVS repository

The CSV ODA driver plug-in, org.eclipse.birt.report.data.oda.csv, requires the following plug-ins:

- org.eclipse.core.runtime
- org.eclipse.datatools.connectivity.oda
- org.eclipse.datatools.connectivity.oda.profile

The CSV ODA user interface extension, org.eclipse.birt.report.data.csv.ui, requires the following plug-ins:

- org.eclipse.birt.report.data.oda.csv
- org.eclipse.core.runtime
- org.eclipse.datatools.connectivity.oda.design.ui

- org.eclipse.ui

For the org.eclipse.birt.report.data.oda.csv plug-in, extend only the Java classes in the org.eclipse.datatools.connectivity.oda plug-in. For the org.eclipse.birt.report.data.csv.ui plug-in, extend the Java classes in the org.eclipse.datatools.connectivity.oda.design.ui plug-in.

Eclipse makes source code available to the developer community in the CVS repository. Compiling does not require the source code for the plug-ins. You can configure the system to use the JAR files in the eclipse\plugins folder. To debug, you may need the source code for all the required BIRT and DTP plug-ins.

Implementing the CSV ODA driver plug-in

This section describes how to implement an ODA driver plug-in, using the CSV ODA driver plug-in as an example. To create an ODA driver plug-in, perform the following tasks:

- Create the ODA driver plug-in project.
- Define the dependencies.
- Specify the run-time archive.
- Declare the ODA extension points.

You can create the CSV ODA driver plug-in project, org.eclipse.birt.report .data.oda.csv, in the Eclipse PDE. This section describes how to create the plug-in project using the New Plug-in Project wizard.

How to create the CSV ODA driver plug-in project

1 From the Eclipse PDE menu, choose File➛New➛Project.

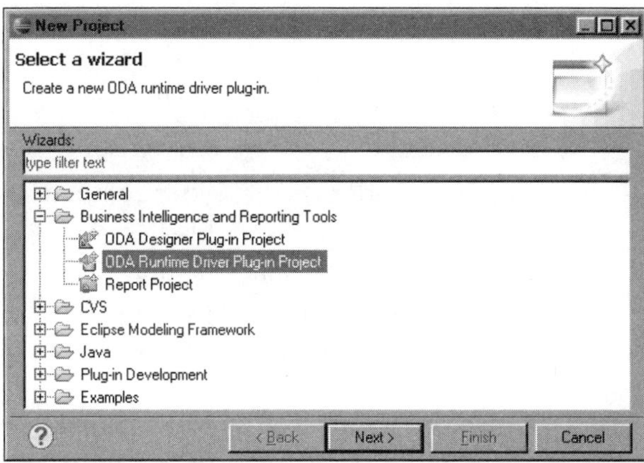

Figure 20-1 Specifying the CSV ODA Runtime Driver Plug-in Project

2 In New Project—Select a wizard, open Business Intelligence and Reporting Tools, and select ODA Runtime Driver Plug-in Project as shown in Figure 20-1. Choose Next. New Plug-in Project appears.

3 In Plug-in Project, modify the settings as shown in Table 20-1.

Table 20-1 Settings for CVS ODA Plug-in Project options

Section	Option	Value
Plug-in Project	Project name	org.eclipse.birt.report.data .oda.csv
	Use default location	Selected
	Location	Not available when you select Use default location
Project Settings	Create a Java project	Selected
	Source folder	src
	Output folder	bin
Target Platform	Eclipse version	3.6
	OSGi framework	Deselected
Working Sets	Add project to working set	Deselected

Choose Next. Plug-in Content appears.

4 In Plug-in Content, modify the settings as shown in Table 20-2.

Table 20-2 Settings for CSV ODA Plug-in Content options

Section	Option	Value
Properties	Plug-in ID	org.eclipse.birt.report.data .oda.csv
	Plug-in Version	1.0.0
	Plug-in Name	CSV ODA Driver
	Plug-in Provider	yourCompany.com or leave blank
	Execution Environment	JavaSE-1.6
Options	Generate an activator, a Java class that controls the plug-in's life cycle	Deselected
	Activator	Not available when you deselect Plug-in Options

Table 20-2 Settings for CSV ODA Plug-in Content options

Section	Option	Value
Options	Plug-in that makes contributions to the user interface	Deselected
	Enable API Analysis	Deselected
Rich Client Application	Would you like to create a rich client application?	No

Choose Next. Templates appears.

5 In Templates, choose ODA Data Source Runtime Driver, as shown in Figure 20-2.

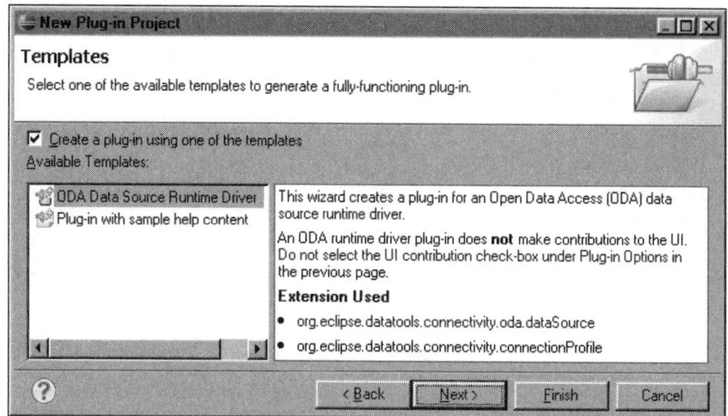

Figure 20-2 Specifying the CSV ODA Data Source Runtime Driver template

Choose Next. ODA Data Source Runtime Driver appears.

6 In ODA Data Source Runtime Driver, specify values for the following options used to generate the ODA plug-in, as shown in Table 20-3.

Table 20-3 Settings for CSV ODA Data Source Runtime Driver options

Option	Value
Java Package Name	org.eclipse.birt.report.data.oda.csv.impl
ODA Data Source Element Id	org.eclipse.birt.report.data.oda.csv
Data Source Display Name	CSV Data Source
Number of Data Source Properties	1
Data Set Display Name	CSV Data Set
Number of Data Set Properties	0

Choose Finish. The CSV ODA driver plug-in project appears in the Eclipse PDE workbench. The project created by the wizard appears as shown in Figure 20-3. The wizard creates all the plug-in files and the main functional Java classes. Customize the default settings as needed and add code to the Java class stubs to implement the desired functionality.

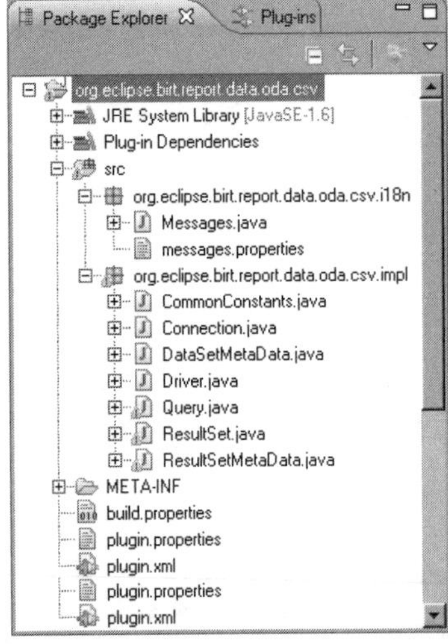

Figure 20-3 Viewing project package structure

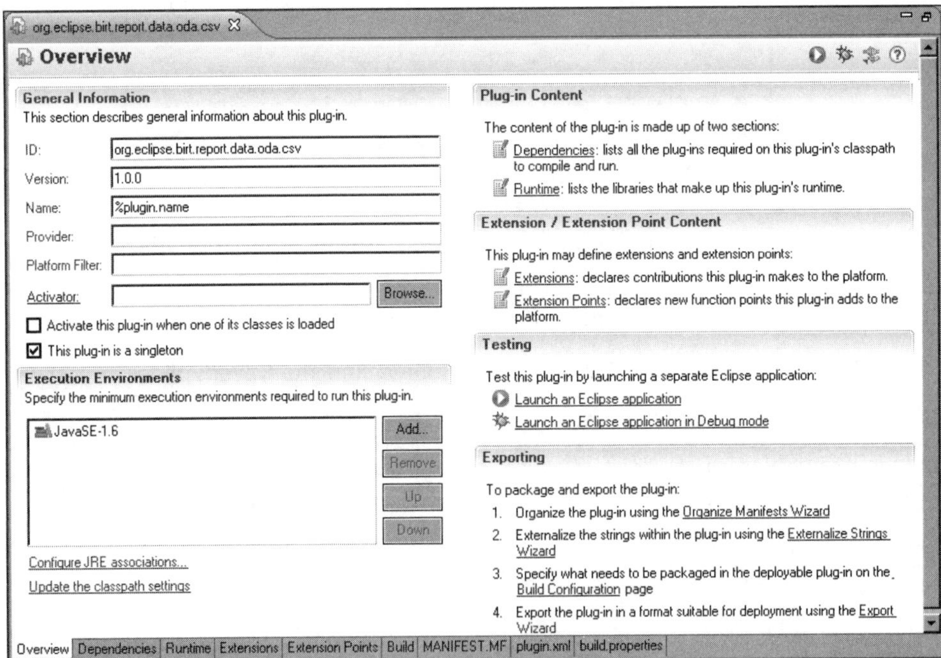

Figure 20-4 PDE Manifest Editor—CSV ODA Overview

7 Choose plugin.xml in Package Explorer and double-click to open PDE Manifest Editor, as shown in Figure 20-4. Using PDE Manifest Editor, you can review and edit all the plug-in settings.

Understanding the ODA data source extension points

In this step you review the extension points added by the wizard. Click the Extensions tab in PDE Manifest Editor to open the Extensions pane in the editor. The PDE Manifest Editor automatically adds the following two extension points:

- org.eclipse.datatools.connectivity.oda.dataSource
- org.eclipse.datatools.connectivity.oda.connectionProfile

Understanding dataSource extension point properties

The ODA data source extension point supports extending design-time and run-time data source access for an application. The extension must implement the ODA Java run-time interfaces defined in the org.eclipse .datatools.connectivity.oda plug-in. Figure 20-5 shows the ODA data source extension points used in the CSV ODA plug-in example.

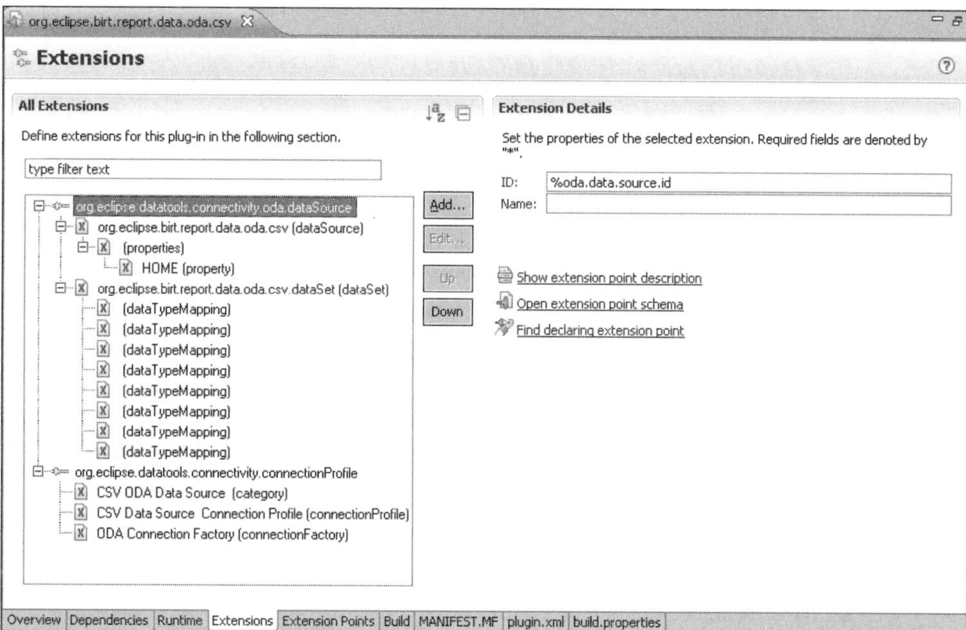

Figure 20-5 PDE Manifest Editor—CSV ODA Extensions

The extension point, org.eclipse.datatools.connectivity.oda.dataSource, specifies the following properties that identify the extension in the run-time environment:

- ID
  Optional identifier of the extension instance.

  The wizard added a reference, %oda.data.source.id, to the extension point ID that you specified in the wizard. The plugin.properties file provides definitions of all the localized variables. The value for the ID, shown in Listing 20-1, is as follows:

  ```
  org.eclipse.birt.report.data.oda.csv
  ```

  Listing 20-1 plugin.properties

  ```
  ##############################################################
  # Copyright (c) 2009 <<Your Company Name here>>
  #
  ##############################################################
  # Plug-in Configuration
  #
  oda.data.source.id=org.eclipse.birt.report.data.oda.csv
  #
  ##############################################################
  # NLS String
  ##############################################################
  #
  plugin.name=CSV ODA Runtime Driver
  data.source.name=CSV ODA Data Source
  data.set.name=CSV ODA Data Set
  ```

- Name
  Optional name of the extension instance. Fully qualified identifier of the extension.

  The extension point defines the extension elements and extension element details for the CSV ODA driver.

The dataSource extension element defines the ODA data source extension type to use at design time and run time. It contains the following properties:

- id
  Fully qualified identifier of an ODA data source extension. The wizard references the externalized id with the notation %oda.data.source.id.

- driverClass
  Java class that implements the org.eclipse.datatools.connectivity.oda .IDriver interface. This interface provides the entry point for the ODA run-time driver extension.

- odaVersion

Version of the ODA interfaces. Specify version 3.1 for an ODA driver developed for BIRT release 2.6.

- defaultDisplayName

  Display name of the ODA data source extension. To externalize the value, use the plugin.properties mechanism.

- setThreadContextClassLoader

  Indicates whether the consumer of the ODA run-time extension plug-in must set the thread context class loader before calling an ODA interface method.

  The OSGi class loader that loads the ODA run-time plug-in is not designed to load additional classes. To load additional classes, an ODA run-time plug-in must provide its own java.net.URLClassLoader object and switch the thread context class loader as required.

The dataSource element also specifies a property, containing the following extension element details:

- name

  Unique name of a property group. Type HOME for a property name.

- defaultDisplayName

  Default display name of a property group. To localize the value, use the plugin.properties mechanism.

  For the default display name, type "CSV File Full Path".

- type

  Data type of the property. The default is String.

- canInherit

  Flag indicating whether the property extension element can inherit properties. Select true.

- defaultValue

  Default value of the property extension element.

- isEncryptable

  Flag indicating whether the property is encrypted. Select false.

- allowsEmptyValueAsNull

  Flag indicating whether an empty value of this property can be treated as a null value. The default value is true.

The dataSet extension element describes the following properties:

- id

  Required identifier of the ODA data set extension.

- defaultDisplayName

Display name of the ODA data set extension.

To localize the value, use the plugin.properties file. The default display name is CSV ODA Data Set, as you can see from Listing 20-1.

The dataSet element also specifies a complex data type, dataTypeMapping, which defines a sequence of data type mappings containing the following properties:

- nativeDataTypeCode
  Integer value that must match one of the data type codes returned in the implementation for the ODA driver interface.

- nativeDataType
  String value specifying the data source native data type.

- odaScalarDataType
  ODA scalar data type that maps to the native type. Supported ODA data types include Date, Double, Integer, String, Time, Timestamp, Decimal, and Boolean. The default supported types set by the wizard are shown in Table 20-4.

Table 20-4 Settings for CSV ODA dataTypeMapping elements

nativeDataType Code	nativeDataType	odaScalar DataType
1	String	String
4	Integer	Integer
8	Double	Double
3	BigDecimal	Decimal
91	Date	Date
92	Time	Time
93	TimeStamp	Timestamp
16	Boolean	Boolean

Understanding ConnectionProfile properties

This extension point supports creating database connections using connections profiles. The CSV ODA plug-in uses the following settings created by the plug-in wizard:

- CSV ODA Data Source (category)
- CSV ODA Data Source Connection Profile (connectionProfile)
- ODA Connection Factory (connectionFactory)

Understanding the dependencies for the CSV ODA driver extension

In Figure 20-6, the Dependencies page shows a list of plug-ins that must be available on the classpath of the CSV ODA driver extension to compile and run.

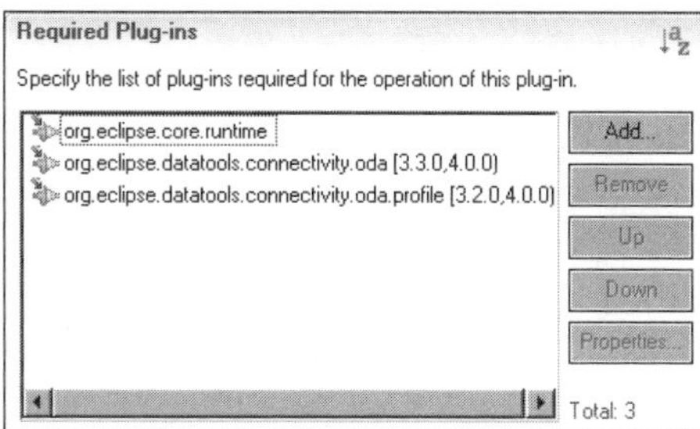

Figure 20-6 The CSV ODA Dependencies page

The ODA Runtime driver wizard adds the following dependencies to your plug-in:

- org.eclipse.datatools.connectivity.oda
- org.eclipse.datatools.connectivity.oda.profile

You can run Organize Manifest wizard at the end of your work to optimize the dependencies settings. Figure 20-7 shows an example of what settings to use when running the wizard.

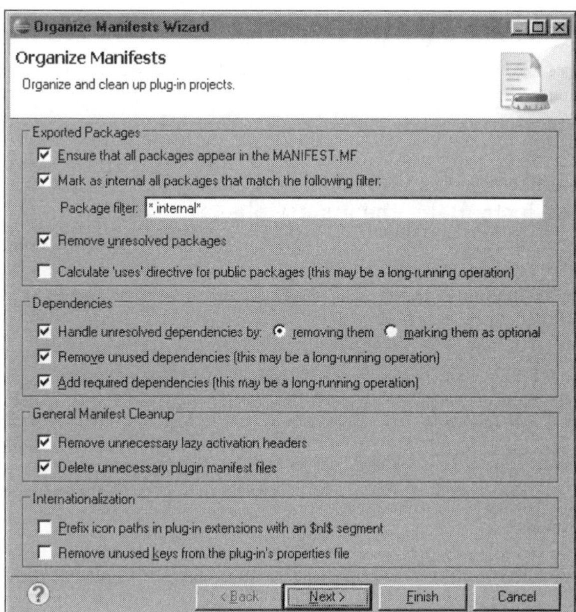

Figure 20-7 Organize Manifests Wizard

The link to this wizard is on the Overview page of the Manifest Editor. The next wizard page displays the changes in the plug-in manifest file. You can review the proposed changes and accept or decline the modifications.

Understanding the sample CSV ODA driver extension

BIRT Data Engine supports the Eclipse DTP ODA framework. The DTP ODA framework supports creating an extension that can plug any external data source into BIRT Report Engine.

The DTP ODA API specifies the interfaces for a run-time driver. BIRT Data Engine uses the data source and data set definitions in a report design to access the ODA run-time driver to execute a query and retrieve data.

The DTP ODA interfaces are similar to JDBC interfaces having extensions that support retrieving data from non-RDBMS sources. An extended ODA driver can implement these interfaces to wrap the API for another data source, such as a CSV file, to retrieve a result set containing data rows.

The CSV ODA driver extension described in this chapter is a simplified example that illustrates how to create an ODA plug-in using the Eclipse PDE. The package for the CSV ODA extension example, org.eclipse.birt.report .data.oda.csv, uses the following classes to implement the ODA plug-in interfaces:

- Driver
  Implements the IDriver interface. Instantiates the connection object for the CSV ODA driver and sets up the log configuration and application context.

- Connection
  Implements the IConnection interface. Opens and closes the connection to the CSV file and instantiates the IQuery object.

- Query
  Implements the IQuery interface. Handles the processing that performs the following operations:
  - Sets up the java.io.File object, containing the file and path names
  - Fetches the data rows from the data file, using the internal class, CSVBufferReader
  - Trims the column data, removing extraneous characters such as commas and quotes
  - Prepares the result set metadata, containing the table and column names

- ResultSet

  Implements the IResultSet interface. Handles the processing that transforms the String value for a column to the specified data type.

- ResultSetMetaData

  Implements the IResultSetMetaData interface. Describes the metadata for each column in the result set.

- DataSetMetaData

  Implements the IDataSetMetaData interface. Describes the features and capabilities of the data set.

- Messages

  Defines the exception messages for the CSV ODA driver.

- CommonConstant

  Defines the constants used in the package, such as the driver name, ODA version, query keywords, and delimiters.

Understanding Driver

The Driver class instantiates the connection object for the CSV ODA driver by calling the getConnection( ) method as shown in Listing 20-2.

Listing 20-2 The getConnection( ) method

```
public IConnection getConnection( String dataSourceType )
      throws OdaException
{
   return new Connection( );
}
```

Understanding Connection

The Connection class opens and closes the connection to the CSV file and calls the newQuery( ) method to instantiate the Query object. Listing 20-3 shows the newQuery( ) method.

Listing 20-3 The newQuery( ) method

```
public IQuery newQuery( String dataSetType )
      throws OdaException
{
   if( !isOpen( ) )
      throw new OdaException(
         Messages.getString(
            "common_CONNECTION_HAS_NOT_OPENED" ) );
   return new Query( this.homeDir, this);
}
```

Understanding Query

The Query class constructor sets up a java.io.File object, containing the file and path names. The constructor supports an application submitting the home directory parameter, homeDir, as a file name as well as a path. Query( ) configures the data source property based on the value of the HOME property specified in the report design, as shown in Listing 20-4.

Listing 20-4 The Query class constructor

```
Query ( String homeDir, IConnection host )
   throws OdaException
{
   if ( homeDir == null || host == null )
      throw new OdaException(Messages.getString
         ("Common.ARGUMENT_CANNOT_BE_NULL"));
   File file = new File(homeDir);
   if (file.isDirectory( )
      this.homeDirectory = homeDir;
   else if (file.isFile( )
      this.homeDirectory = file.getParent( );
   this.connection = host;
}
```

The Query class prepares and executes a query, then retrieves the data. Query implements the following additional methods:

- prepare( ) performs the following operations:
  - Generates query and column information by calling splitQueryText( )
  - Validates the connection by calling validateOpenConnection( )
  - Formats the query String, eliminating redundant spaces and converting all keywords to uppercase, by calling formatQueryText( )
  - Validates the query by calling validateQueryText( )
  - Prepares the metadata required for the execution of the query and retrieval of the query results by calling prepareMetaData( )

  Listing 20-5 shows the prepare( ) method.

  Listing 20-5 The prepare( ) method

```
public void prepare( String queryText )
   throws OdaException
{
   if ( queryText != null )
   {
      String query = splitQueryText(queryText)[0] ;
      String colInfo = splitQueryText( queryText )[1];
      validateOpenConnection( );
      String formattedQuery = formatQueryText( query );
      validateQueryText( formattedQuery );
```

```
      prepareMetaData( formattedQuery, colInfo );
   }
   else
      throw new OdaException( Messages.getString(
         "common_NULL_QUERY_TEXT" ) );
}
```

- prepareMetaData( ) acquires the following metadata:
  - Table name
  - Actual column names read from data file
  - Query column names
  - Query data types

  prepareMetaData( ) then instantiates and configures the ResultSetMetaData object. Listing 20-6 shows the prepareMetaData( ) method.

Listing 20-6 The prepareMetaData( ) method

```
private void prepareMetaData( String query,
      String savedSelectedColInfo )
   throws OdaException
{
   String[ ] queryFragments =
      parsePreparedQueryText( query );
   String tableName = queryFragments[2];
   String[ ] allColumnNames =
      discoverActualColumnMetaData( tableName,NAME_LITERAL );
   String[ ] allColumnTypes =
      createTempColumnTypes( allColumnNames.length );
   String[ ] queryColumnNames = null;
   String[ ] queryColumnTypes = null;
   String[ ] queryColumnLables = null;

   queryColumnNames = allColumnNames;
   queryColumnTypes = allColumnTypes;
   queryColumnLabels = allColumnNames;

   this.resultSetMetaData =
      new ResultSetMetaData( queryColumnNames,
         queryColumnTypes, queryColumnLabels );
   this.currentTableName = tableName;
}
```

- executeQuery( ) performs the following operations:
  - Fetches the data from the file to a Vector object
  - Transfers the data from the Vector to a two-dimensional String array
  - Returns the data rows and metadata in a single ResultSet object

  Listing 20-7 shows the executeQuery( ) method.

Listing 20-7 The executeQuery( ) method

```
public IResultSet executeQuery( ) throws OdaException
{
   Vector v = fetchQueriedDataFromFileToVector( );
   String[ ][ ] rowSet =
      copyDataFromVectorToTwoDimensionArray( v );
return new ResultSet( rowSet, this.resultSetMetaData );
}
```

- The internal class, CSVBufferReader, fetches the data rows from the data file. Listing 20-8 shows the readLine( ) method.

Listing 20-8 The readLine( ) method

```
public String readLine( ) throws IOException
{
   if ( isLastCharBuff( ) && needRefillCharBuff( ) )
      return null;

   if ( needRefillCharBuff( ) )
   {
      charBuffer = newACharBuff( );
      int close = reader.read( charBuffer );
      if ( close == -1 )
         return null;
      if ( close != CHARBUFFSIZE )
         this.eofInPosition = close;
      this.startingPosition = 0;
   }

   String candidate = "";
   int stopIn = CHARBUFFSIZE;
   if ( isLastCharBuff( ) )
   {
      stopIn = this.eofInPosition;
   }

   for ( int i = this.startingPosition; i < stopIn; i++ )
   {
      if ( this.charBuffer[i] == '\n' )
      {
         return readALine( candidate, stopIn, i );
      }
   }

   if ( isLastCharBuff( ) )
   {
      return readLastLine( candidate );
   }
   return readExtraContentOfALine( candidate );
}
```

Understanding ResultSet

The ResultSet class performs the following operations:

- Provides the cursor processing that fetches forward into the buffered result set rows
- Transforms the String value for a column to the specified data type

ResultSet implements the following methods:

- ResultSet( ), the constructor, sets up a two-dimensional array that contains the table data and metadata, as shown in Listing 20-9.

  Listing 20-9 The ResultSet( ) constructor

  ```
  ResultSet( String[ ][ ] sData, IResultSetMetaData rsmd )
  {
     this.sourceData = sData;
     this.resultSetMetaData = rsmd;
  }
  ```

- getRow( ) returns the cursor, indicating the position of the row in the result set, as shown in Listing 20-10.

  Listing 20-10 The getRow( ) method

  ```
  public int getRow( ) throws OdaException
  {
     validateCursorState( );
     return this.cursor;
  }
  ```

- next( ) increments the cursor to point to the next row, as shown in Listing 20-11.

  Listing 20-11 The next( ) method

  ```
  public boolean next( ) throws OdaException
  {

     if ( (this.maxRows <= 0? false:cursor >=
        this.maxRows - 1) || cursor >=
        this.sourceData.length - 1 )
     {
        cursor = CURSOR_INITIAL_VALUE;
        return false;
     }
     cursor++;
     return true;

  }
  ```

- `getString( )` returns the value for a column in the row at the column position specified in the result set, as shown in Listing 20-12.

Listing 20-12 The getString( ) method

```
public String getString( int index )
   throws OdaException
{

validateCursorState( );
String result = sourceData[cursor][index - 1];
if( result.length( ) == 0 )
      result = null;
   this.wasNull = result == null ? true : false;
   return result;

}
```

Understanding ResultSetMetaData

The ResultSetMetaData class describes the metadata for a column in the result set, including the following information:

- Column count in the result set
- Display length
- Label
- Name
- Data type
- Precision
- Scale
- Permits null

getColumnName( ) returns the column name for a column at the row, column position specified in the result set, as shown in Listing 20-13.

Listing 20-13 The getColumnName( ) method

```
public String getColumnName( int index ) throws OdaException
{
   if ( index > getColumnCount( ) || index < 1 )
      throw new OdaException( Messages.getString(
         "resultSetMetaData_INVALID_COLUMN_INDEX" ) + index );

   return this.columnNames[index - 1].trim( );
}
```

Understanding DataSetMetaData

The DataSetMetaData class describes the features and capabilities of the data set, including the following:

- Indicating whether the data set supports multiple result sets

- Providing information about the sort mode for columns
- Returning a reference to the data source connection

getConnection( ) returns a reference to a data source connection, as shown in Listing 20-14.

Listing 20-14 The getConnection( ) method

```
public IConnection getConnection( ) throws OdaException
{
   return m_connection;
}
```

Understanding Messages

The Messages class defines the exception messages for the CSV ODA driver.

getString( ) returns a message from the resource bundle using the key value, as shown in Listing 20-15.

Listing 20-15 The getString( ) method

```
public static String getString(String key) {
   try {
      return RESOURCE_BUNDLE.getString(key);
   }
   catch (MissingResourceException e) {
      return '!' + key + '!';
   }
}
```

Understanding CommonConstants

The CommonConstants class defines the constants used in the package, such as the driver name, ODA version, query keywords, and delimiters. Listing 20-16 shows these definitions.

Listing 20-16 The CommonConstants class

```
final class CommonConstants
{
   public static final String DELIMITER_COMMA = ",";
   public static final String DELIMITER_SPACE = " ";
   public static final String DELIMITER_DOUBLEQUOTE = "\"";
   public static final String KEYWORD_SELECT = "SELECT";
   public static final String KEYWORD_FROM = "FROM";
   public static final String KEYWORD_AS = "AS";
   public static final String KEYWORD_ASTERISK = "*";
   public static final String DRIVER_NAME =
      "ODA CSV FILE DRIVER";

   public static final int MaxConnections = 0;
```

```
    public static final int MaxStatements = 0;
    public static final String CONN_HOME_DIR_PROP = "HOME";
    public static final String CONN_DEFAULT_CHARSET = "UTF-8";
    public static final String PRODUCT_VERSION = "3.0";
}
```

Developing the CSV ODA user interface extension

The data source extension point, org.eclipse.datatools.connectivity.oda .design.ui.dataSource, supports adding a new data source to a user interface, such as BIRT Report Designer. For each data source, the extension implements the following optional components:

- A wizard for creating the data source
- A set of pages for editing the data source
- The list of data sets that the data source supports

For each data set, the extension implements the following optional components:

- A wizard for creating the data set
- A set of pages for editing the data set

The data source editor page must implement the extension point, org.eclipse .ui.propertyPages, by extending the abstract class, org.eclipse.datatools .connectivity.oda.design.ui.wizards.DataSourceEditorPage.

The data set editor page must implement the extension point, org.eclipse.ui .propertyPages, by extending the abstract class, org.eclipse.datatools .connectivity.oda.design.ui.wizards.DataSourceEditorPage.

The ODA data source and data set user interface extensions extend these base classes to create customized property pages with page control and other behavior.

This section describes how to implement a BIRT ODA user interface plug-in, using the CSV ODA driver plug-in as an example.

To create an ODA driver plug-in, perform the following tasks:

- Create the CSV ODA user interface plug-in project.
- Define the dependencies.
- Specify the run-time archive.
- Declare the ODA user interface extension points.

Creating the CSV ODA user interface plug-in project

You can create the CSV ODA user interface plug-in project, org.eclipse.birt.report.data.oda.csv.ui, using the Eclipse PDE. The Eclipse PDE provides a wizard to assist you in setting up a plug-in project and creating the framework for a plug-in extension.

The New Plug-in Project wizard simplifies the process of specifying a plug-in project, automatically adds the required extension points, and sets the dependencies. The wizard also generates the plug-in manifest file, plugin.xml, and optionally, the Java plug-in run-time class.

The wizard creates all the implementation Java classes. It also puts TODO tags in the generated source code for customizing code along with guiding comments.

After using the wizard to create the plug-in, review the settings, make adjustments to the settings, and add the code to the Java class stubs to implement the desired functionality.

The following section describes how to create the plug-in project using the New Plug-in Project wizard.

How to create the CSV ODA user interface plug-in project

1 From the Eclipse menu, choose File➛New➛Project. New Project appears.

2 On New Project—Select a wizard, open Business Intelligence and Reporting Tools, and select ODA Designer Plug-in Project as shown in Figure 20-8.

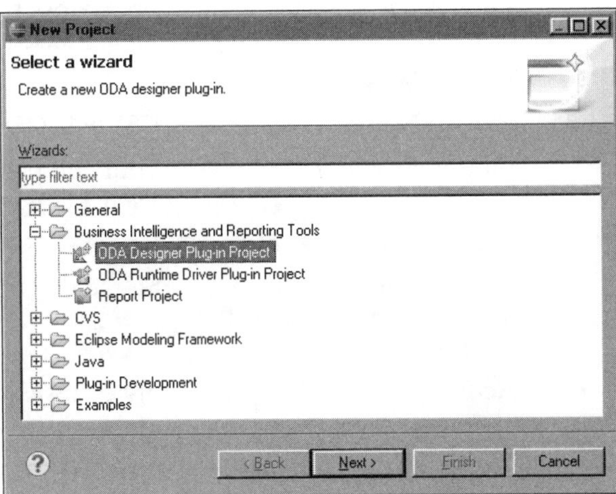

Figure 20-8 Specifying the CSV ODA Designer Plug-in Project

3 Choose Next. New Plug-in Project appears.

4 In Plug-in Project, modify the settings as shown in Table 20-5. Choose Next. Plug-in Content appears.

Table 20-5 Settings for CSV ODA user interface Plug-in Project options

Section	Option	Value
Plug-in Project	Project name	org.eclipse.birt.report.data .oda.csv.ui
	Use default location	Selected
	Location	Not available when you select Use default location
Project Settings	Create a Java project	Selected
	Source folder	src
	Output folder	bin
Target Platform	Eclipse version	3.6
	OSGi framework	Deselected
Working Sets	Add project to working set	Deselected

5 In Plug-in Content, modify the settings, where needed, as shown in Table 20-6. Choose Finish.

Table 20-6 Settings for CSV ODA user interface Plug-in Content options

Section	Option	Value
Properties	Plug-in ID	org.eclipse.birt.report .data.oda.csv.ui
	Plug-in Version	1.0.0
	Plug-in Name	CSV File ODA
	Plug-in Provider	yourCompany.com or leave blank
	Execution Environment	JavaSE-1.6
Options	Generate an activator, a Java class that controls the plug-in's life cycle	Selected
	Activator	org.eclipse.birt.report .data.oda.csv.ui.UiPlugin
	This plug-in will make contributions to the user interface	Selected
Rich Client Application	Would you like to create a rich client application?	No

6 In Templates, choose ODA Data Source Designer as shown in Figure 20-9. Choose Next. ODA Data Source Designer appears.

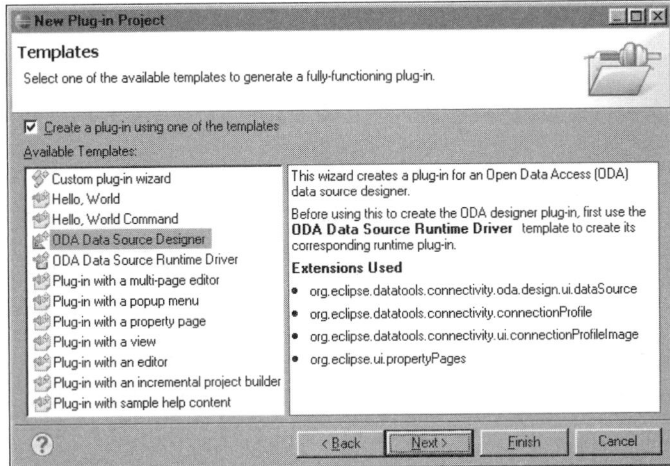

Figure 20-9 Specifying the CSV ODA Data Source Designer template

The wizard warns you to create ODA Data Source Runtime Driver first, then create the designer user interface. The wizard also lists the extension points that are automatically included in the default implementation.

- org.eclipse.datatools.connectivity.connectionProfile
- org.eclipse.datatools.connectivity.ui.connectionProfileImage
- org.eclipse.ui.propertyPages
- org.eclipse.datatools.connectivity.oda.design.ui.dataSource

7 In ODA Data Source Designer, specify values for the following options used to generate the ODA plug-in, as shown in Table 20-7. Choose Finish.

Table 20-7 Settings for CSV ODA UI Plug-in Content options

Option	Value
Java Package Name	org.eclipse.birt.report.data.oda.csv.ui.impl
ODA Runtime Driver Plug-in Id	org.eclipse.birt.report.data.oda.csv
ODA Runtime Data Source Element Id	org.eclipse.birt.report.data.oda.csv
ODA Runtime Driver Class	org.eclipse.birt.report.data.oda.csv.impl.Driver
ODA Runtime Data Set Element Id	org.eclipse.birt.report.data.oda.csv.dataSet
Data Source Display Name	CSV File ODA Data Source
Data Set Display Name	CSV File ODA Data Set

The CSV ODA user interface plug-in project appears in Eclipse Package Explorer, as shown in Figure 20-10.

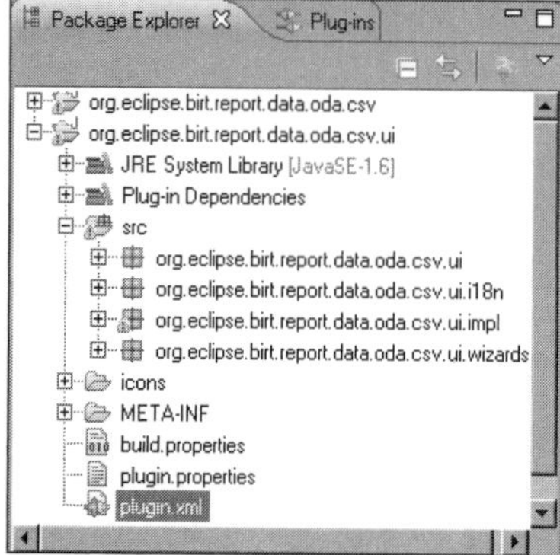

Figure 20-10 Viewing the CSV ODA user interface plug-in project

Double-click plugin.xml to open it in PDE Manifest Editor. The plug-in Overview page looks like the one shown on Figure 20-11.

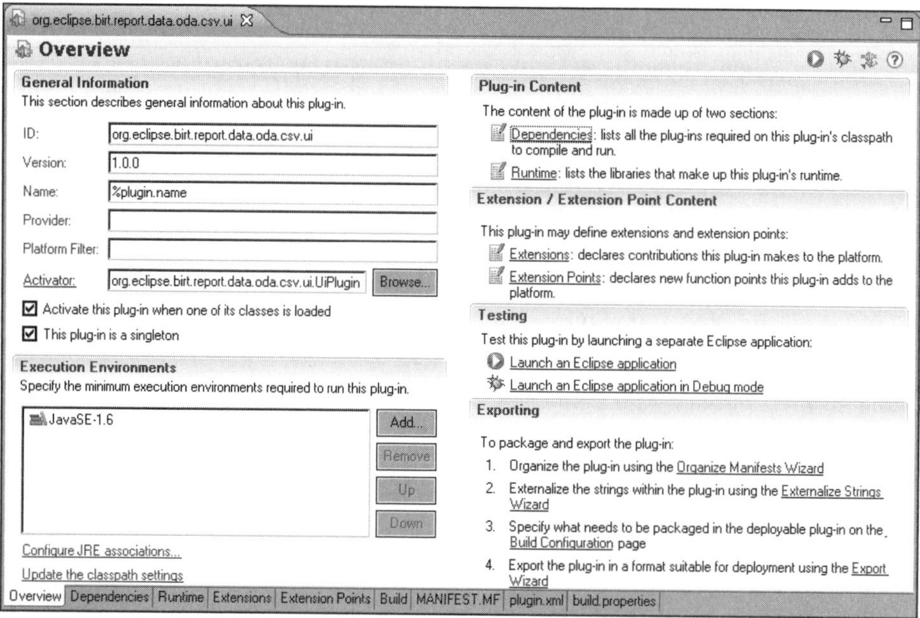

Figure 20-11 Viewing the CSV ODA user interface plug-in

Understanding the ODA data source user interface extension points

In this next step, you review the extension points added by the wizard to implement the CSV ODA user interface extension and add the extension element details. Figure 20-12 shows the list of CSV ODA user interface extension points.

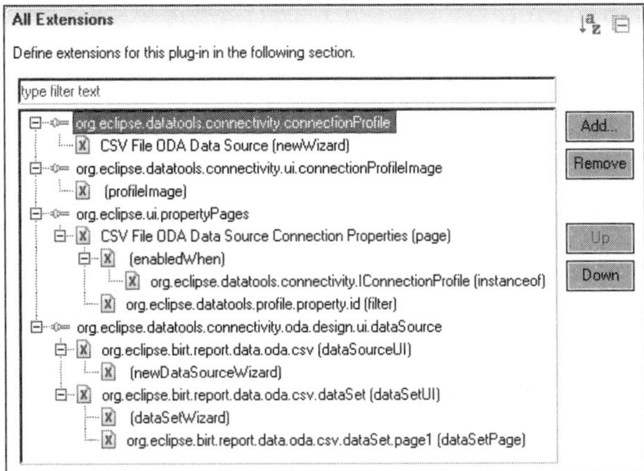

Figure 20-12 CSV ODA user interface extension points

The CSV ODA user interface plug-in extends the functionality defined by the following extension points:

- org.eclipse.datatools.connectivity.connectionProfile
  Provides support for adding a connection profile
- org.eclipse.datatools.connectivity.connectionProfileImage
  The connection profile image extension point supports adopters using multiple icons from their main connection profile extension into a separate plug-in for user interface code and resources.
- org.eclipse.ui.propertyPages
  Adds a property page that displays the properties of an object in a dialog box
- org.eclipse.datatools.connectivity.oda.design.ui.dataSource
  Extends the ODA Designer user interface framework to support creating a dialog page so a user can specify an ODA data source and a related data set

The extension points specify the following properties that identify the extensions in the run-time environment:

- ID
  Optional identifier of the extension instance
- Name
  Optional name of the extension instance

Understanding the ConnectionProfile extension point

The connectionProfile extension point specifies the newWizard, which creates the connection profile.

Understanding the propertyPages extension point

The propertyPages extension point specifies the following extension elements:

- page
  Defines a property page. Specifies properties such as id, display name, category, icon, object class, filter, and category. The id and the display name are localized in the plugin.properties file, as shown in Listing 20-17.

  Listing 20-17 plugin.properties

  ```
  ########################################################
  Copyright (c) 2009 <<Your Company Name here>>
  ########################################################
  # Plug-in Configuration
  #
  oda.data.source.id=org.eclipse.birt.report.data.oda.csv
  #
  ########################################################
  # NLS strings
  #
  plugin.name=CSV File ODA
  data.source.name=CSV File Data Source
  connection.profile.name=CSV File Data Source Connection Profile
  newwizard.name=CSV File Data Source
  newwizard.description=Create a CSV File Data Source
     connection profile
  wizard.window.title=New CSV File Data Source Profile
  wizard.data.source.page.title=CSV File Data Source
  profile.propertypage.name=CSV File Data Source Connection
     Properties
  wizard.data.set.window.title=New CSV File Data Set
  wizard.data.set.page.title=Query
  ```

  The ODA user interface framework provides a default implementation that creates a text control for each property value, which is why there is no need to provide a custom implementation. By default, the wizard sets the page.class in the following org.eclipse.ui.propertyPages extension point:

  ```
  page.class=org.eclipse.datatools.connectivity.oda.design.ui
     .pages.impl.DefaultDataSourcePropertyPage
  ```

- filter
  Specifies an action filter that evaluates the attributes of each object in a current selection. If an object has the specified attribute state, a match

occurs. Each object must implement the org.eclipse.ui.IActionFilter interface.

Understanding the dataSource extension point

The dataSource extension point specifies the following extension elements:

- dataSourceUI
  Adds user interface support for specifying an extended data source.
- dataSetUI
  The dataSetUI extension element defines the following extension elements and details:
  - id
    Fully qualified name of the data set, such as org.eclipse.birt.report.data .oda.csv.dataSet. This name must be the same as the name for the ODA extension driver data set.
  - dataSetWizard
    Wizard class used to specify a data set in the BIRT Report Designer user interface. This class must use or extend org.eclipse.datatools .connectivity.oda.design.ui.wizards.DataSetWizard. Localize the window title, %wizard.data.set.window.title, in the plug-in properties file.
  - dataSetPage
    Specifies an editor page to add to the editor dialog for a data set. The data set user interface adds editor pages to a dialog in the order in which the pages are defined. This class must use or extend org.eclipse .datatools.connectivity.oda.design.ui.wizards.DataSetWizardPage. The implementation code is in org.eclipse.birt.report.data.oda.csv.ui .impl.CustomDataSetWizardPage. The wizard provides a default implementation code.

    The page display name, %wizard.data.set.page.title, is externalized in the plugin.properties tile.

Understanding the sample CSV ODA user interface extension

The CSV ODA user interface extension described in this chapter illustrates how to create an ODA user interface plug-in using the Eclipse PDE. The following section describes the code-based extensions a developer must make to complete the development of the CSV ODA user interface extension, after defining the plug-in framework in the Eclipse PDE.

The CSV ODA user interface plug-in contains the following packages:

- org.eclipse.birt.report.data.oda.csv.ui
  Contains the UiPlugin class, which is automatically generated by the PDE Manifest Editor when you create the plug-in project.

- org.eclipse.birt.report.data.oda.csv.ui.i18n
  Contains the Messages class and the properties file, messages.properties, to generate the messages displayed in the user interface. The localized versions for these messages are in files that use the following naming syntax:

  ```
  messages_<locale>.msg
  ```

- org.eclipse.birt.report.data.oda.csv.ui.impl
  Contains the CustomDataSetWizardPage class, an automatically generated implementation of an ODA data set designer page, which supports creating or editing an ODA data set.

- org.eclipse.birt.report.data.oda.csv.ui.wizards
  The wizards package contains the classes that create the user interface pages used to choose a data source and data set in BIRT Report Designer.

Implementing the ODA data source and data set wizards

In BIRT release 2.1, BIRT Report Designer adopted the Eclipse Data Tools Platform (DTP) ODA design-time framework. BIRT release 2.6 further extends the DTP ODA design-time framework by adding new wizards to automatically generate customizable implementations. The DTP ODA framework defines two of the three extension points used in the CSV ODA user interface plug-in:

- Connection profile
  Defined in org.eclipse.datatools.connectivity.connectionProfile

- Data source and data set wizards
  Defined in org.eclipse.datatools.connectivity.oda.design.ui.dataSource

The CSV ODA user interface plug-in also must implement the extension point for property pages defined in org.eclipse.ui.propertyPages.

The CSV ODA user interface plug-in uses the following abstract base classes in the org.eclipse.datatools.connectivity.oda.design.ui.wizards package to create the wizards that specify the data source and data set pages. An ODA user interface plug-in must extend these classes to provide the wizard pages with page control and related behavior:

- DataSourceEditorPage
  Provides the framework for implementing an ODA data source property page

- DataSourceWizardPage
  Provides the framework for implementing an ODA data source wizard page
- DataSetWizardPage
  Provides the framework for implementing an ODA data set wizard page

Understanding the org.eclipse.birt.report.data .oda.csv.ui.impl package

This customizable page provides a simple Query Text control for user input. The page extends org.eclipse.datatools.connectivity.oda.design.ui.wizards .DataSetWizardPage in the DTP ODA design-time framework to support updating an ODA data set design instance using query metadata.

Understanding the org.eclipse.birt.report.data.oda .csv.ui.wizards package

The org.eclipse.birt.report.data.oda.csv.ui.wizards package in the CSV ODA user interface extension example implements the following classes:

- Constants
  Defines the constants for the data source connection properties defined in the run-time drive implementation, org.eclipse.birt.report.data.oda.csv.
- CSVFilePropertyPage
  Extends DataSourceEditorPage. This class creates and initializes the editor controls for the property page used to specify the ODA data source. The class updates the connection profile properties with the values collected from the page.
- CSVFileSelectionPageHelper
  Specifies the page layout and sets up the control that listens for user input and verifies the location of the CSV data source file.
- CSVFileSelectionWizardPage
  Extends DataSourceWizardPage. This class creates and initializes the controls for the data source wizard page. The class sets the select file message and collects the property values.
- FileSelectionWizardPage
  Extends DataSetWizardPage. This class creates and initializes the controls for the data set wizard page and specifies the page layout. The class connects to the data source, executes a query, retrieves the metadata and result set, and updates the date-set design.

Understanding Constants

The Constants class defines the following variables for the data source connection properties defined in org.eclipse.birt.report.data.oda.csv:

- ODAHOME specifies the CSV ODA file path constant, HOME
- ODA_DEFAULT_CHARSET specifies the default character set as 8-bit Unicode Transformation Format (UTF-8)
- DEFAULT_MAX_ROWS sets the default maximum number of rows that can be retrieved from the data source

Listing 20-18 shows the code for the Constants class.

Listing 20-18 The Constants class

```
public class Constants {

   public static String ODAHOME="HOME";
   public static String ODA_DEFAULT_CHARSET = "UTF-8";
   public static int DEFAULT_MAX_ROWS = 1000;

}
```

Understanding CSVFilePropertyPage

CSVFilePropertyPage extends the DataSourceEditorPage class, implementing the following methods to provide page editing functionality for the CSV ODA data source property page:

- createAndInitCustomControl( ) method performs the following tasks:
  - Instantiates a CSVFileSelectionPageHelper object
  - Specifies the page layout and sets up the editing control by calling CSVFileSelectionPageHelper.createCustomControl( ) and initCustomControl( ) methods

  Listing 20-19 shows the code for the createAndInitCustomControl( ) method.

  Listing 20-19 The createAndInitCustomControl( ) method

```
protected void createAndInitCustomControl
   ( Composite parent, Properties profileProps )
{
   if( m_pageHelper == null )
      m_pageHelper =
         new CSVFileSelectionPageHelper( this );
   m_pageHelper.createCustomControl( parent );
   m_pageHelper.initCustomControl( profileProps );
   if( ! isSessionEditable( ) )
      getControl( ).setEnabled( false );
}
```

- collectCustomProperties( ) updates the connection profile properties with the values collected from the page by calling CSVFileSelectionPageHelper .collectCustomProperties( ) method, as shown in Listing 20-20.

Listing 20-20 The collectCustomProperties( ) method

```
public Properties collectCustomProperties
   ( Properties profileProps )
{
   if( m_pageHelper == null )
      return profileProps;
   return m_pageHelper.collectCustomProperties
      ( profileProps );
}
```

Understanding CSVFileSelectionPageHelper

CSVFileSelectionPageHelper provides auxiliary processing for the CSVFilePropertyPage and CSVFileSelectionWizardPage classes. CSVFileSelectionPageHelper implements the following methods:

- createCustomControl( ) performs the following tasks:
  - Sets up the composite page layout
  - Calls the setupFileLocation( ) method that sets up a control to listen for user input and verify the location of the CSV data source file

  Listing 20-21 shows the code for the createCustomControl( ) method.

  Listing 20-21 The createCustomControl( ) method

```
void createCustomControl( Composite parent )
{
   Composite content = new Composite( parent, SWT.NULL );
   GridLayout layout = new GridLayout( 2, false );
   content.setLayout(layout);
   setupFileLocation( content );
}
```

- setupFileLocation( ) performs the following tasks:
  - Sets up the label and the grid data object in the page layout
  - Sets up the control that listens for user input and verifies the location of the CSV data source file

  Listing 20-22 shows the code for the setupFileLocation( ) method.

  Listing 20-22 The setupFileLocation( ) method

```
private void setupFileLocation( Composite composite )
{
   Label label = new Label( composite, SWT.NONE );
```

```
    label.setText( Messages.getString
      ( "label.selectFile" ) );

    GridData data = new GridData( GridData.FILL_HORIZONTAL );

    fileName = new Text( composite, SWT.BORDER );
    fileName.setLayoutData( data );
    setPageComplete( false );

    fileName.addModifyListener(
      new ModifyListener( )
          {
            public void modifyText( ModifyEvent e )
            {
                   verifyFileLocation();
            }
            } );
}
```

- collectCustomProperties( ) sets the data source directory property in the connection profile, as shown in Listing 20-23.

Listing 20-23 The collectCustomProperties( ) method

```
Properties collectCustomProperties( Properties props )
{
    if( props == null )
      props = new Properties( );
      props.setProperty( CommonConstants.CONN_HOME_DIR_PROP,
        getFolderLocation( ) );
    return props;
}
```

- initCustomControl( ) initializes the data source wizard control to the location of the data source file, as shown in Listing 20-24.

Listing 20-24 The initCustomControl( ) method

```
void initCustomControl( Properties profileProps )
{
    if( profileProps == null || profileProps.isEmpty( ) ||
      fileName == null )
    return;
    String folderPath = profileProps.getProperty(
      CommonConstants.CONN_HOME_DIR_PROP );
    if( folderPath == null )
      folderPath = EMPTY_STRING;
      fileName.setText( folderPath );
      verifyFileLocation( );
}
```

Understanding CSVFileSelectionWizardPage

The CSVFileSelectionWizardPage class extends the DataSourceWizardPage class, implementing the following methods to provide the functionality for the CSV ODA data source wizard page:

- The createPageCustomControl( ) method performs the following tasks:
  - Instantiates a CSVFileSelectionPageHelper object
  - Specifies the page layout and sets up the wizard page control by calling CSVFileSelectionPageHelper.createCustomControl( ) method
  - Calls CSVFileSelectionPageHelper.initCustomControl( ) to initialize the control to the location of the data source file

  Listing 20-25 shows the code for the createPageCustomControl( ) method.

  Listing 20-25 The createPageCustomControl( ) method

```
public void createPageCustomControl( Composite parent )
{
   if( m_pageHelper == null )
         m_pageHelper =
            new CSVFileSelectionPageHelper( this );
      m_pageHelper.createCustomControl( parent );
      m_pageHelper.initCustomControl( m_csvFileProperties );
}
```

- The collectCustomProperties( ) method instantiates a Properties object to contain the CSV data source properties information, as shown in Listing 20-26.

  Listing 20-26 The collectCustomProperties( ) method

```
public Properties collectCustomProperties( )
{
   if( m_pageHelper != null )
      return m_pageHelper.collectCustomProperties(
         m_csvFileProperties );
   return ( m_csvFileProperties != null ) ?
      m_csvFileProperties : new Properties( );
}
```

Understanding FileSelectionWizardPage

The FileSelectionWizardPage class extends the DataSetWizardPage class, implementing the following methods to provide the functionality for the CSV ODA data set wizard page:

- The createPageControl( ) method performs the following tasks:
  - Specifies the page layout and sets up the wizard page control
  - Gets the data source properties

- Calls populateAvailableList( ) to update the data set design

Listing 20-27 shows the code for the createPageControl( ) method.

Listing 20-27 The createPageControl( ) method

```
private Control createPageControl( Composite parent )
{
   Composite composite = new Composite( parent, SWT.NULL );
   FormLayout layout = new FormLayout( );
   composite.setLayout( layout );
   FormData data = new FormData( );
   data.left = new FormAttachment( 0, 5 );
   data.top = new FormAttachment( 0, 5 );
   fileName = new Text( composite, SWT.BORDER );
   fileName.setLayoutData( data );
   Properties dataSourceProps =
      getInitializationDesign( ).getDataSourceDesign( )
      .getPublicProperties( );
   fileName.setText( ( String )(
      dataSourceProps.getProperty( Constants.ODAHOME )));
   data = new FormData( );
   data.top = new FormAttachment(
      fileName, 10, SWT.BOTTOM );
   data.left = new FormAttachment( 0, 5 );
   data.right = new FormAttachment( 47, -5 );
   data.bottom = new FormAttachment( 100, -5 );
   data.width = DEFAULT_WIDTH;
   data.height = DEFAULT_HEIGHT;
   m_availableList = new List( composite,
      SWT.MULTI | SWT.BORDER |
      SWT.H_SCROLL | SWT.V_SCROLL );
   m_availableList.setLayoutData( data );
   m_selectedFile =
      new File(( String )(
      dataSourceProps.getProperty( Constants.ODAHOME )));
   populateAvailableList( );
   return composite;
}
```

- getQuery( ) method builds the query for the data set by performing the following tasks:
  - Gets the table name from the file object
  - Appends the table name to a query that selects all the columns using a wildcard
  - Appends the column list then the table name to a query that selects specific columns
  - Returns the query text

  Listing 20-28 shows the code for the getQuery( ) method.

Listing 20-28 The getQuery( ) method

```
private String getQuery( )
{
   String tableName = null;
   StringBuffer buf = new StringBuffer( );
   File file = m_selectedFile;
   if(file != null)
   {
      tableName = file.getName( );
   }
   if(tableName != null)
   {
      if(m_availableList.getItemCount( ) == 0)
      {
         buf.append("select * from ").append(tableName);
      }
      else
      {
         buf.append("select ");
         String[ ] columns = m_availableList.getItems( );
         for(int n = 0; n < columns.length; n++)
         {
            buf.append(columns[n]);
            if(n < columns.length - 1)
            {
               buf.append(", ");
            }
         }
      buf.append(" from ").append(tableName);
      }
   }
return buf.toString( );
}
```

- getQueryColumnNames( ) method performs the following tasks:
  - Instantiates the CSVFileDriver
  - Prepares the query and gets the results set metadata using the CSV ODA run-time driver and data source connection properties settings
  - Gets the column count
  - Iterates through the metadata results to get the column names and return the results

Listing 20-29 shows the code for the getQueryColumnNames( ) method.

Listing 20-29 The getQueryColumnNames( ) method

```
private String[ ] getQueryColumnNames(
   String queryText, File file )
{
```

```
   IDriver ffDriver = new CSVFileDriver( );
   IConnection conn = null;

   try
   {
      conn = ffDriver.getConnection( null );

      IResultSetMetaData metadata =
         getResultSetMetaData( queryText, file, conn );
      int columnCount = metadata.getColumnCount( );

      if( columnCount == 0 )
         return null;
      String[ ] result = new String[columnCount];

      for( int i = 0; i < columnCount; i++)
         result[i] = metadata.getColumnName( i + 1 );
      return result;
   }
   catch( OdaException e )
   {
      setMessage( e.getLocalizedMessage( ), ERROR );
      disableAll( );
      return null;
   }
   finally
   {
      closeConnection( conn );
   }
}
```

- getResultSetMetaData( ) method performs the following tasks:
  - Sets up the Properties object with the location of the data source file
  - Opens the connection to the data source
  - Sets up a Query object and prepares the query text
  - Executes the query
  - Returns the metadata

Listing 20-30 shows the code for the getResultSetMetaData( ) method.

Listing 20-30 The getResultSetMetaData( ) method

```
private IResultSetMetaData getResultSetMetaData(
   String queryText, File file, IConnection conn )
   throws OdaException
{
   java.util.Properties prop = new java.util.Properties( );
   prop.put( CommonConstants.CONN_HOME_DIR_PROP,
      file.getParent( ) );
   conn.open( prop );
   IQuery query = conn.newQuery( null );
   query.setMaxRows( 1 );
```

```
    query.prepare( queryText );
    query.executeQuery( );
    return query.getMetaData( );
}
```

- setResultSetMetaData( ) method updates the data set page design with metadata returned by the query by performing the following tasks:
  - Calls the DesignSessionUtil.toResultSetColumnsDesign( ) method to convert the run-time metadata to a design-time ResultSetColumns object
  - Obtains a ResultSetDefinition object from the design factory to use in populating the data set page design with the metadata definitions
  - Calls the resultSetDefn.setResultSetColumns( ) method to set the reference to ResultSetColumns object, containing the metadata content
  - Assigns the result set definition to the data set design

  Listing 20-31 shows the code for the setResultSetMetaData( ) method.

  Listing 20-31 The setResultSetMetaData( ) method

```
private void setResultSetMetaData(
    DataSetDesign dataSetDesign,IResultSetMetaData md )
    throws OdaException
{
    ResultSetColumns columns =
        DesignSessionUtil.toResultSetColumnsDesign( md );
    ResultSetDefinition resultSetDefn =
        DesignFactory.eINSTANCE.createResultSetDefinition( );
    resultSetDefn.setResultSetColumns( columns );
    dataSetDesign.setPrimaryResultSet( resultSetDefn );
    dataSetDesign.getResultSets().setDerivedMetaData( true );
}
```

- savePage( ) method performs the following tasks:
  - Instantiates the CSVFileDriver
  - Gets the result set metadata
  - Updates the data set design with the metadata
  - Closes the connection

  Listing 20-32 shows the code for the savePage( ) method.

  Listing 20-32 The savePage( ) method

```
private void savePage( DataSetDesign dataSetDesign )
{
    String queryText = getQuery( );
    dataSetDesign.setQueryText( queryText );
```

```
    IConnection conn = null;
    try
    {
        IDriver ffDriver = new CSVFileDriver( );
        conn = ffDriver.getConnection( null );
        IResultSetMetaData metadata =
            getResultSetMetaData( queryText, m_selectedFile,
            conn );
        setResultSetMetaData( dataSetDesign, metadata );
    }
    catch( OdaException e )
    {
        dataSetDesign.setResultSets( null );
    }
    finally
    {
        closeConnection( conn );
    }
}
```

Testing the CSV ODA user interface plug-in

On PDE Manifest Editor, in Overview, the Testing section contains links to launch a plug-in as a separate Eclipse application in either Run or Debug mode.

How to launch the CSV ODA user interface plug-in

1. From the Eclipse SDK menu, choose Run—Run Configurations. In Run Configurations, right-click Eclipse Application. Choose New.
2. Create a configuration to launch an Eclipse application by performing the following tasks:
    1. In Name, type:

       `CSV ODA Test`
    2. In Main, in Location, type:

       `C:\Test`

       Run Configurations appears, as shown in Figure 20-13.
3. Choose the Plug-ins tab to select the list of plug-ins that you want to launch with the Run configuration.
4. In Launch with, choose

   `plug-ins selected below only`

   from the drop-down list, as shown in Figure 20-14.

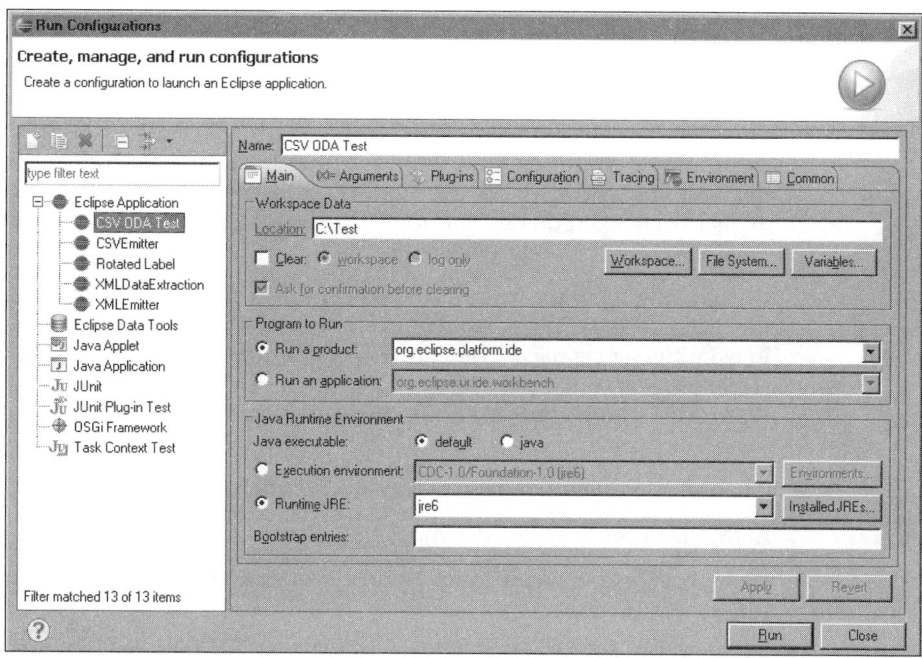

Figure 20-13 Creating a configuration to launch an Eclipse application

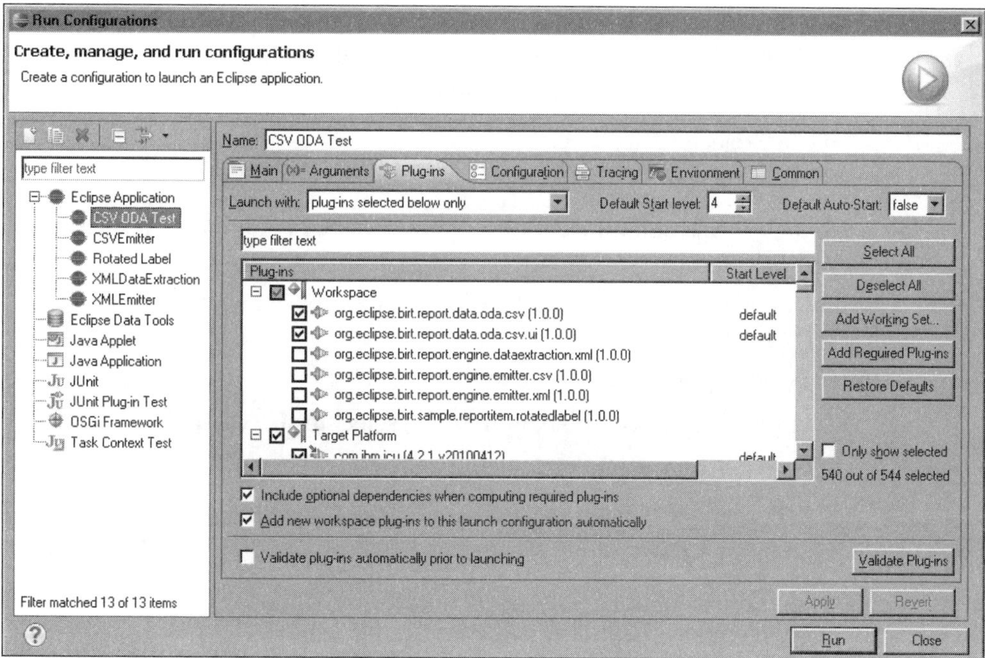

Figure 20-14 Including the ODA plug-ins in the launch configuration

5 In Plug-ins check the following plug-ins

```
org.eclipse.birt.data.oda.csv
org.eclipse.birt.data.oda.csv.ui
```

The plug-ins selected below only option supports configuring an environment that uses a subset of the plug-ins from the workspace and the target platform. The target platform consists of all the plug-ins that are explicitly checked on the Window > Preferences... > Plug-in Development > Target Platform preference page.

When using the plug-ins selected below only option you must ensure that the list of selected plug-ins is up-to-date when you add or remove a plug-in from the workspace. There are several buttons available to help you select plug-ins, including an Add Required Plug-ins button. The Add Required Plug-ins button should be used often to ensure the selected subset of plug-ins is complete.

6 Choose Run to launch the run-time workbench.

7 In the run-time workbench, choose the Report Design perspective.

8 In Report Design, create a new report project and create a new blank report.

How to create a report design

1 In Report Design, choose File➛New➛Project.

2 Expand Business Intelligence and Reporting Tools and choose Report Project. Choose Next. New Report Project appears.

3 In Report Project, perform the following tasks:

   1 In Project name, type:

   ```
   testCSVODA
   ```

   2 Select Use default location. Choose Finish. In Navigator, testCSVODA appears.

4 In Navigator, right-click testCSVODA and choose File➛New➛Report. New Report appears.

5 In New Report, perform the following tasks:

   1 In Enter or select the parent folder, select testCSVODA.

   2 In file name, type:

   ```
   new_report.rptdesign
   ```

   Choose Next.

   3 In Report Templates, select Blank Report. Choose Finish. In Navigator, new_report_1.rptdesign appears in the testCSVODA project folder.

6 Right-click new_report.rptdesign and choose Open. new_report .rptdesign appears in Report Design, as shown in Figure 20-15.

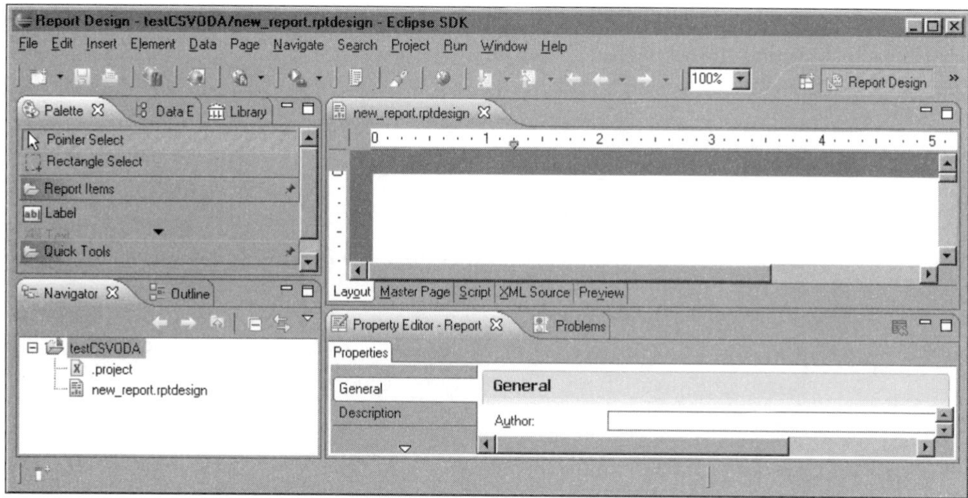

Figure 20-15 new_report.rptdesign in the report design environment

How to specify a data source

1 In Report Design, choose Data➛New Data Source. On New Data Source, choose CSV ODA Data Source, as shown in Figure 20-16. Choose Next.

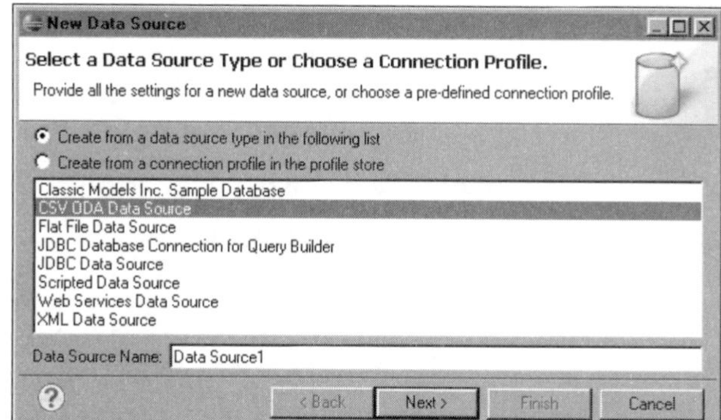

Figure 20-16 Choosing CSV ODA Data Source

2 In Select File, enter the path and file name of the directory that contains the CSV data source file, as shown in Figure 20-17. Choose Finish. Report Design appears.

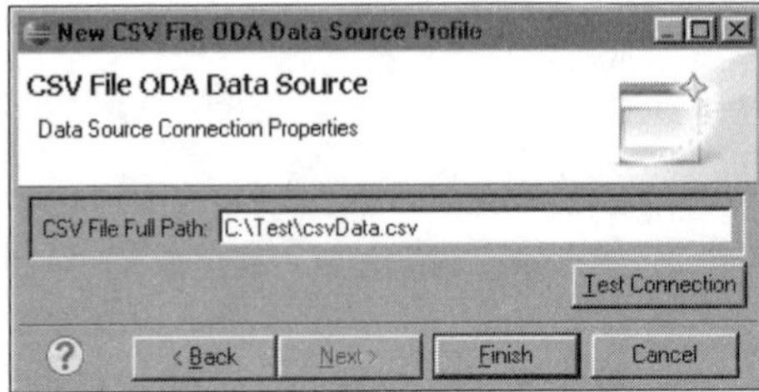

Figure 20-17 Specifying path to the CSV ODA data source file directory

How to select a new data set

1 In Report Design, choose Data➛New Data Set. New Data Set appears, as shown in Figure 20-18. Choose Next. Query appears.

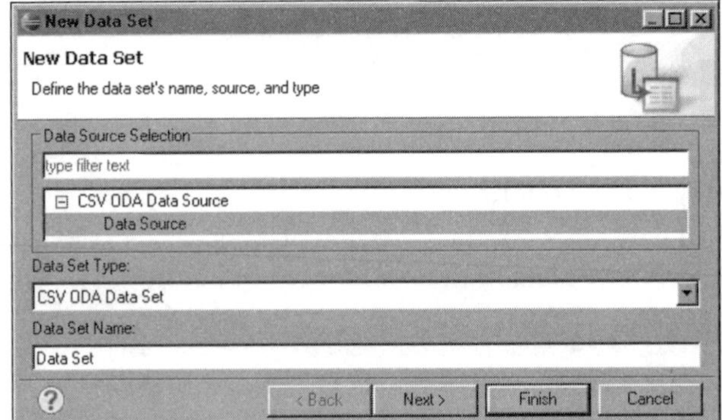

Figure 20-18 New Data Set for the CSV ODA data source

2 In Query, select all the columns, as shown in Figure 20-19. Choose Finish.

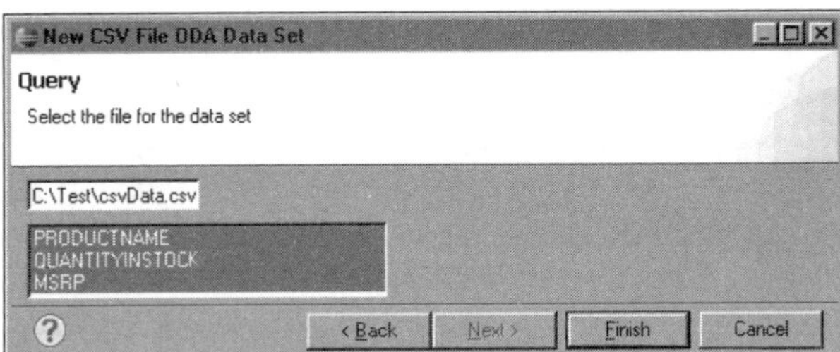

Figure 20-19 Selecting columns

Edit Data Set appears, as shown in Figure 20-20.

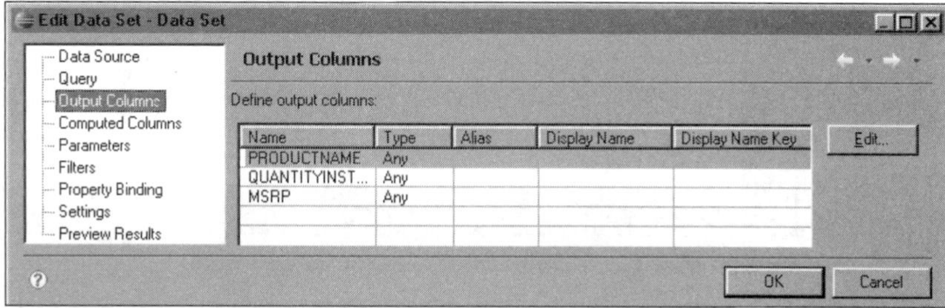

Figure 20-20 Edit Data Set

3 Choose Preview Results. Preview Results appears as shown in Figure 20-21. Choose OK.

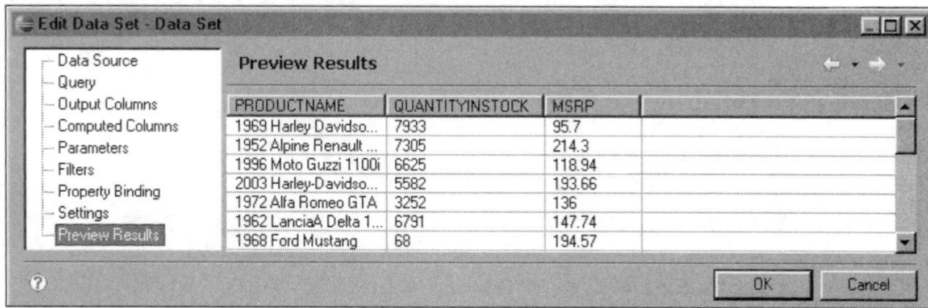

Figure 20-21 Data preview

4 In Data Explorer, expand Data Sources and Data Sets. Data Explorer appears as shown in Figure 20-22.

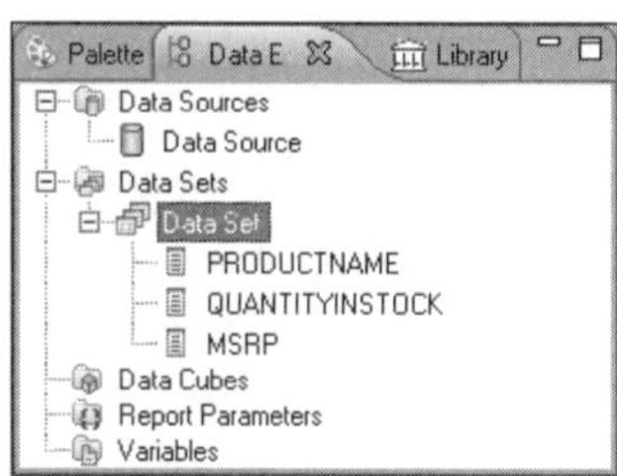

Figure 20-22 Data Set in Data Explorer

How to run a report design using CSV ODA user interface and driver extensions

1 To build the report, drag Data Set from Data Explorer to the layout editor. Layout appears as shown in Figure 20-23.

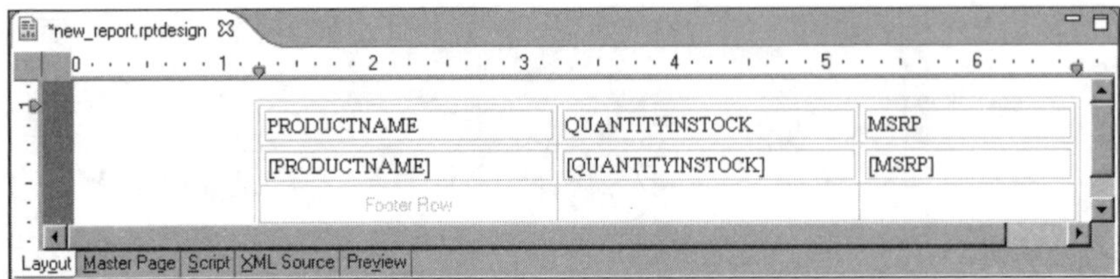

Figure 20-23 Report design in the layout editor

2 To run the report design, choose Preview. new_report_1.rptdesign runs, displaying the data set from the CSV data source, as shown in Figure 20-24.

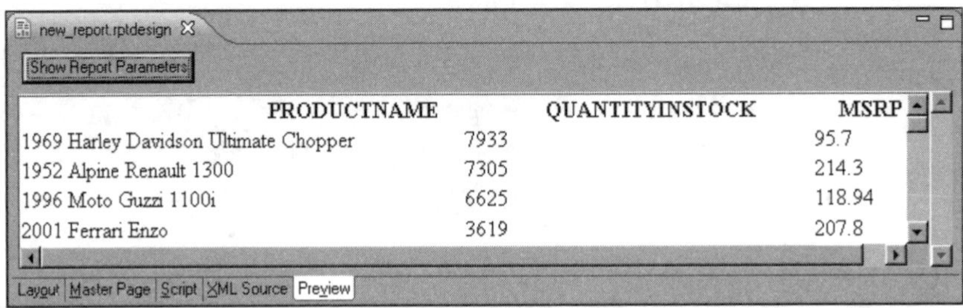

Figure 20-24 Preview of the data set from the CSV ODA data source

Developing a Hibernate ODA extension

To develop the Hibernate ODA extension create two new projects in the Eclipse PDE. These two projects implement the following plug-ins:

- org.eclipse.birt.report.data.oda.hibernate

  The Hibernate ODA driver accesses a relational data source using HQL. The Hibernate ODA data source plug-in extends the functionality defined by the org.eclipse.datatools.connectivity.oda.dataSource extension point to create the Hibernate ODA driver.

- org.eclipse.birt.report.data.oda.hibernate.ui

  The Hibernate ODA user interface plug-in for BIRT Report Designer selects a Hibernate data source and supports creation of an HQL statement to retrieve data from the available tables and columns. The Hibernate ODA user interface plug-in extends the functionality defined by the org.eclipse.datatools.connectivity.oda.design.ui.dataSource, org.eclipse.ui.propertyPages, and org.eclipse.datatools.connectivity.connectionProfile extension points.

  The user interface consists of the following pages:

  - Data source page

Includes the Hibernate data source in the list of available data sources. The Hibernate ODA driver contains the preconfigured Hibernate configuration and mapping files that connect to the MySQL version of the BIRT demonstration database, ClassicModels.

- Data set page

  Creates an HQL statement that selects the data set and embeds the HQL statement in the report design.

In BIRT Report Designer, the Hibernate ODA data source wizard supports selecting a Hibernate ODA driver containing preconfigured Hibernate configuration and mapping files. The Hibernate ODA driver searches for these configuration and mapping files in the plug-in's hibfiles directory.

The Hibernate ODA driver also searches in the hibfiles directory for JAR and ZIP files and the org.eclipse.birt.report.data.oda.jdbc plug-in for JDBC drivers to add to the classpath. This approach prevents the need to copy drivers to multiple locations. Note that changing the configuration causes the Hibernate ODA driver plug-in to rebuild the Hibernate SessionFactory, which is a machine-intensive operation.

Once the Hibernate ODA driver creates the data source configuration, a data set can be created. The Hibernate data set wizard allows the user to enter HQL statements. The Hibernate ODA user interface example supports only simple queries, such as the following types of statements:

```
From Customer
```

or:

```
Select ord.orderNumber,cus.customerNumber, cus.customerName
   from Orders as ord, Customer as cus
   where ord.customerNumber = cus.customerNumber and
   cus.customerNumber = 363
```

In the Hibernate ODA plug-in, there is an exampleconfig directory. This directory contains a sample Hibernate configuration file, mapping files, and Java classes that connect to the BIRT sample MySQL database. Test the plug-in using these files as follows:

- Modify the hibernate.cfg.file to connect to your database configuration.
- Copy these files to the hibfiles directory.
- Create a JAR file containing the Java classes.

You can test and deploy the extensions in the Eclipse PDE run-time environment.

The following sections describe how to create and deploy the Hibernate ODA driver and user interface plug-in projects. To download the source code for the Hibernate ODA driver and user interface extension examples go to http://www.actuate.com/birt/contributions.

Creating the Hibernate ODA driver plug-in project

Create the Hibernate ODA driver plug-in project, org.eclipse.birt.report.data .oda.hibernate, using the New Plug-in Project wizard in the Eclipse PDE.

How to create the Hibernate ODA driver plug-in project

1 From the Eclipse PDE menu, choose File→New→Project.

2 In New Project—Select a wizard, open Business Intelligence and Reporting Tools and select ODA Runtime Driver Plug-in Project. Choose Next. New Plug-in Project appears.

3 In Plug-in Project, modify the settings as shown in Table 20-8.

Table 20-8 Settings for Hibernate ODA Plug-in Project options

Section	Option	Value
Plug-in Project	Project name	org.eclipse.birt.report.data .oda.hibernate
	Use default location	Selected
	Location	Not available when you select Use default location
Project Settings	Create a Java project	Selected
	Source folder name	src
	Output folder name	bin
Target Platform	Eclipse version	3.6
	OSGi framework	Deselected
Working sets	Add project to working sets	Not selected

4 On Plug-in Content, modify the settings as shown in Table 20-9.

Table 20-9 Settings for Hibernate ODA Plug-in Content options

Section	Option	Value
Properties	Plug-in ID	org.eclipse.birt.report.data .oda.hibernate
	Plug-in Version	2.0.0
	Plug-in Name	BIRT ODA-Hibernate Driver
	Plug-in Provider	yourCompany.com or leave blank
	Execution Environment	JavaSE-1.6

Table 20-9 Settings for Hibernate ODA Plug-in Content options

Section	Option	Value
Options	Generate an activator, a Java class that controls the plug-in's life cycle	Selected
	Activator	org.eclipse.birt.report.data .oda.hibernate.Activator
	This plug-in will make contributions to the user interface	Deselected
	Enable API Analysis	Deselected
Rich Client Application	Would you like to create a rich client application?	No

Choose Next. Templates appears.

5 In Templates, choose ODA Data Source Runtime Driver. Choose Next. ODA Data Source Runtime Driver appears.

6 In ODA Data Source Runtime Driver, specify values for the following options used to generate the ODA plug-in, as shown in Table 20-10.

Table 20-10 Settings for ODA Data Source Runtime Driver options

Option	Value
Java Package Name	org.eclipse.birt.report.data.oda.hibernate
ODA Data Source Element Id	org.eclipse.birt.report.data.oda.hibernate
Data Source Display Name	Hibernate Data Source
Number of Data Source Properties	2
Data Set Display Name	Hibernate Data Set
Number of Data Set Properties	0

Choose Finish. The Hibernate ODA driver plug-in project appears in the Eclipse PDE workbench.

How to specify the properties of the Hibernate ODA plug-in project

1 Using the Eclipse PDE Manifest Editor, in Dependencies, specify the following required plug-ins in the following order:

- org.eclipse.core.runtime

- org.eclipse.datatools.connectivity.oda
- org.eclipse.birt.report.data.oda.jdbc

2 In Runtime, in Exported Packages, verify that the following packages that the plug-in exposes to clients appear in the list:

- antlr
- antlr.actions.cpp
- antlr.actions.csharp
- antlr.actions.java
- antlr.actions.python
- antlr.ASdebug
- antlr.build
- antlr.collections
- antlr.collections.impl
- antlr.debug
- antlr.debug.misc
- antlr.preprocessor
- javax.transaction
- javax.transaction.xa
- net.sf.cglib.beans
- net.sf.cglib.core
- net.sf.cglib.proxy
- net.sf.cglib.reflect
- net.sf.cglib.transform
- net.sf.cglib.transform.hook
- net.sf.cglib.transform.impl
- net.sf.cglib.util
- net.sf.ehcache
- net.sf.ehcache.config
- net.sf.ehcache.hibernate
- net.sf.ehcache.store
- org.apache.commons.collections
- org.apache.commons.collections.comparators

- org.apache.commons.collections.iterators
- org.apache.commons.logging
- org.apache.commons.logging.impl
- org.apache.tools.ant.taskdefs.optional
- org.dom4j
- org.dom4j.bean
- org.dom4j.datatype
- org.dom4j.dom
- org.dom4j.dtd
- org.dom4j.io
- org.dom4j.jaxb
- org.dom4j.rule
- org.dom4j.rule.pattern
- org.dom4j.swing
- org.dom4j.tree
- org.dom4j.util
- org.dom4j.xpath
- org.dom4j.xpp
- org.eclipse.birt.report.data.oda.hibernate
- org.hibernate
- org.hibernate.action
- org.hibernate.cache
- org.hibernate.cache.entry
- org.hibernate.cfg
- org.hibernate.classic
- org.hibernate.collection
- org.hibernate.connection
- org.hibernate.context
- org.hibernate.criterion
- org.hibernate.dialect
- org.hibernate.dialect.function
- org.hibernate.engine

- org.hibernate.engine.query
- org.hibernate.engine.transaction
- org.hibernate.event
- org.hibernate.event.def
- org.hibernate.exception
- org.hibernate.hql
- org.hibernate.hql.antlr
- org.hibernate.hql.ast
- org.hibernate.hql.ast.exec
- org.hibernate.hql.ast.tree
- org.hibernate.hql.ast.util
- org.hibernate.hql.classic
- org.hibernate.id
- org.hibernate.impl
- org.hibernate.intercept
- org.hibernate.jdbc
- org.hibernate.jmx
- org.hibernate.loader
- org.hibernate.loader.collection
- org.hibernate.loader.criteria
- org.hibernate.loader.custom
- org.hibernate.loader.entity
- org.hibernate.loader.hql
- org.hibernate.lob
- org.hibernate.mapping
- org.hibernate.metadata
- org.hibernate.param
- org.hibernate.persister
- org.hibernate.persister.collection
- org.hibernate.persister.entity
- org.hibernate.pretty
- org.hibernate.property

- org.hibernate.proxy
- org.hibernate.secure
- org.hibernate.sql
- org.hibernate.stat
- org.hibernate.tool.hbm2ddl
- org.hibernate.tool.instrument
- org.hibernate.transaction
- org.hibernate.transform
- org.hibernate.tuple
- org.hibernate.type
- org.hibernate.usertype
- org.hibernate.util
- org.objectweb.asm
- org.objectweb.asm.attrs

3 On Runtime, in Classpath, add the following JAR files to the plug-in classpath:

- odahibernate.jar
- lib/ant-antlr-1.6.5.jar
- lib/antlr-2.7.6rc1.jar
- lib/asm.jar
- lib/asm-attrs.jar
- lib/cglib-2.1.3.jar
- lib/commons-collections-2.1.1.jar
- lib/commons-logging-1.0.4.jar
- lib/dom4j-1.6.1.jar
- lib/ehcache-1.1.jar
- lib/hibernate3.jar
- lib/jta.jar

These JAR files must have been previously imported into the lib directory in the Hibernate ODA plug-in. These JAR files can also be put in a new plug-in that the Hibernate ODA plug-in references.

4 On Extensions, add the extension point, org.eclipse.datatools.connectivity .oda.dataSource, and the following elements and details for:

- dataSource

  Add the extension element details, as shown in Table 20-11.

Table 20-11 Property settings for the Hibernate dataSource extension element

Property	Value
id	org.eclipse.birt.report.data.oda .hibernate
driverClass	org.eclipse.birt.report.data.oda .hibernate.HibernateDriver
odaVersion	3.0
defaultDisplayName	Hibernate Data Source
setThreadContextClassLoader	true

  The dataSource extension has an attribute named setThreadContextClassLoader, which, if set to true, sets the thread context class loader to the Hibernate ODA plug-in class loader. In this example, this attribute is set to true to avoid potential class conflicts with classes loaded with the Eclipse Tomcat plug-in.

- dataSet

  Add the extension element details, as shown in Table 20-12.

Table 20-12 Property settings for the Hibernate dataSet extension element

Property	Value
id	org.eclipse.birt.report.data.oda .hibernate.dataSet
defaultDisplayName	Hibernate Data Set

5 In Extensions, select dataSource and add the following properties and element details:

- HIBCONFIG, as shown in Table 20-13.

Table 20-13 HIBCONFIG property settings

Property	Value
name	HIBCONFIG
defaultDisplayName	Hibernate Configuration File
type	string
canInherit	true

- MAPDIR, as shown in Table 20-14.

Table 20-14 MAPDIR property settings

Property	Value
name	MAPDIR
defaultDisplayName	Hibernate Mapping Directory
type	string
canInherit	true

6 In Extensions, select dataSet and add the list of dataTypeMapping elements, as shown in Table 20-15.

Table 20-15 Settings for Hibernate dataTypeMapping elements

nativeDataType	nativeDataTypeCode	odaScalarDataType
BIGINT	-5	Decimal
BINARY	-2	String
BIT	-7	Integer
BLOB	2004	Blob
BOOLEAN	16	Integer
CHAR	1	String
CLOB	2005	Clob
DATE	91	Date
DECIMAL	3	Decimal
DOUBLE	8	Double
FLOAT	6	Double
INTEGER	4	Integer
LONGVARBINARY	-4	String
LONGVARCHAR	-1	String
NUMERIC	2	Decimal
REAL	7	Double
SMALLINT	5	Integer
TIME	92	Time
TIMESTAMP	93	Timestamp
TINYINT	-6	Integer
VARBINARY	-3	String
VARCHAR	12	String

Understanding the sample Hibernate ODA driver extension

The package for the Hibernate ODA extension example, org.eclipse.birt .report.data.oda.hibernate, implements the following classes using the ODA plug-in interfaces defined in the DTP plug-in, org.eclipse.datatools .connectivity.oda, and the extension points defined in the XML schema file, datasource.exsd. The package implements the following classes:

- Activator

  Extends org.eclipse.core.runtime.Plugin. Defines the methods for starting, managing, and stopping a plug-in instance.

- HibernateDriver

  Implements the IDriver interface. Instantiates the connection object for the Hibernate ODA driver, which provides the entry point for the Hibernate ODA plug-in.

- Connection

  Implements the IConnection interface. Opens and closes the connection to the Hibernate ODA data source and instantiates the IQuery object.

- Statement

  Implements the IQuery interface. Prepares the result set metadata containing the table and column names, executes the query, and fetches the data rows from the data source.

- ResultSet

  Implements the IResultSet interface. Provides access to the data rows in the result set, maintaining a cursor that points to the current row. Handles the processing that gets the value for a column as the specified data type.

- ResultSetMetaData

  Implements the IResultSetMetaData interface. Describes the metadata for each column in the result set.

- DataSetMetaData

  Implements the IDataSetMetaData interface. Describes the features and capabilities of the driver for the data set.

- Messages

  Defines the exception messages for the Hibernate ODA driver.

- DataTypes

  Defines, validates, and returns the data types supported by the Hibernate ODA driver.

- CommonConstant

  Defines the constants used in the package, such as the driver name, ODA version, query keywords, and delimiters.

- HibernateUtil

  Manages the Hibernate SessionFactory that provides the session or run-time interface between the Hibernate service and the ODA driver. This class is built based on the example HibernateUtil, available at http://www.hibernate.org.

  The Hibernate ODA driver plug-in supports specifying the Hibernate configuration file and mapping files directory in the data source wizard. The plug-in creates the Hibernate SessionFactory from these settings. The example project has an exampleconfig directory that contains a Hibernate configuration and mapping files for use with the BIRT MySQL example database, ClassicModels.

The following sections describe the classes where there are important differences between the implementation of Hibernate ODA driver and the earlier example, the CSV ODA driver.

Understanding HibernateDriver

The HibernateDriver class instantiates the Connection object for the Hibernate ODA driver. This class implements the IDriver interface, but does not provide any processing for the methods that configure logging and set the application context. Listing 20-33 shows the getConnection( ) method.

Listing 20-33 The getConnection( ) method

```
public IConnection getConnection( String connectionClassName )
      throws OdaException
{
   return new Connection( );
}
```

getMaxConnections( ) returns 0, imposing no limit on the number of connections to the ODA data source from the application. Listing 20-34 shows the getMaxConnections( ) method.

Listing 20-34 The getMaxConnections( ) method

```
public int getMaxConnections( ) throws OdaException
{
   return( 0 );
}
```

Understanding Connection

The Connection class implements the following methods:

- open( )

  Opens a Hibernate session and sets the Boolean variable, isOpen, to true. The open( ) method uses the HibernateUtil class to obtain a session from a Hibernate SessionFactory, providing the run-time interface between the Hibernate service and the ODA driver.

The open( ) method retrieves the locations for the Hibernate configuration file and mapping files directory from connection properties. The open( ) method calls HibernateUtil.constructSessionFactory( ), which attempts to build the SessionFactory with these settings. If the SessionFactory already exists, the plug-in does not recreate the SessionFactory unless the Hibernate configuration file or the mapping directory have changed.

Listing 20-35 shows the code for the open( ) method.

Listing 20-35 The open( ) method

```
public void open( Properties connProperties )
   throws OdaException
{
   try
   {
      configfile =
         connProperties.getProperty( "HIBCONFIG" );
      mapdir = connProperties.getProperty( "MAPDIR" );
      HibernateUtil
         .constructSessionFactory( configfile, mapdir );
      Session testSession = HibernateUtil.currentSession( );
      this.isOpen = true;
   }catch( Exception e )
   {
      throw new OdaException( e.getLocalizedMessage( ) );
   }
}
```

- newQuery( )

  Opens a new query by returning an instance of a Statement object, the class that implements the IQuery interface. The connection can handle multiple result set types, but the Hibernate ODA example uses only one and ignores the dataSetType parameter, as shown in Listing 20-36.

  Listing 20-36 The newQuery( ) method

```
public IQuery newQuery( String dataSetType )
   throws OdaException
{
   if ( !isOpen( ) )
      throw new OdaException( Messages.getString
         ( "Common.CONNECTION_IS_NOT_OPEN" ) );
   return new Statement( this );
}
```

- getMetaData( )

  Returns an IDataSetMetaData object of the data set type, as shown in Listing 20-37.

Listing 20-37 The getMetaData( ) method

```
public IDataSetMetaData getMetaData( String dataSetType )
   throws OdaException
{
   return new DataSetMetaData( this );
}
```

- getMaxQueries( )

  Indicates the maximum number of queries the driver supports. The getMaxQueries( ) method returns 1, indicating that the Hibernate ODA driver does not support concurrent queries, as shown in Listing 20-38.

  Listing 20-38 The getMaxQueries( ) method

```
public int getMaxQueries( ) throws OdaException
{
   return 1;
}
```

- commit( ) and rollback( )

  Handle transaction processing. The Hibernate ODA driver example does not support transaction operations. In the Connection class, the commit( ) and rollback( ) methods throw UnsupportedOperationException. Listing 20-39 shows the code for the commit( ) method.

  Listing 20-39 The commit( ) method

```
public void commit( ) throws OdaException
{
   throw new UnsupportedOperationException ( );
}
```

- close( )

  Closes the Hibernate session, as shown in Listing 20-40.

  Listing 20-40 The close( ) method

```
public void close( ) throws OdaException
{
   this.isOpen = false;
   try{
      HibernateUtil.closeSession( );
   }catch(Exception e){
      throw new OdaException( e.getLocalizedMessage( ) );
   }
}
```

Understanding DataSetMetaData

The DataSetMetaData class describes the features and capabilities of the data source for the specified data set. The Hibernate ODA driver example returns true or false to indicate support for a feature. The Hibernate ODA driver example does not support input or output parameters, named parameters, or multiple result sets.

The following code example indicates that the Hibernate ODA driver does not support multiple result sets, as shown in Listing 20-41.

Listing 20-41 The supportsMultipleResultSets( ) method

```
public boolean supportsMultipleResultSets( ) throws OdaException
{
   return false;
}
```

A method such as getSQLStateType( ), which has no implementation, simply throws UnsupportedOperationException, as shown in Listing 20-42.

Listing 20-42 The getSQLStateType( ) method

```
public int getSQLStateType( ) throws OdaException
{
   throw new UnsupportedOperationException ( );
}
```

Understanding Statement

The Statement class implements the IQuery interface. This class prepares and executes the query. Statement also handles parameters and retrieves the result set and result set metadata.

The Statement class implements the following methods:

- prepare( )
  The ODA framework calls the prepare( ) method before executing the query. The ODA framework uses the query saved in the report design.

  The Hibernate ODA user interface plug-in also calls prepare( ) to verify the columns used in the report design. The user interface plug-in passes an HQL statement that gets the columns from the result set object.

  prepare( ) sets up the result-set metadata and stores the query in an object variable for use by the executeQuery( ) method. The ODA run time uses the result-set metadata to retrieve the data. BIRT Report Designer also uses the result-set metadata to display the columns in the user interface.

  The prepare( ) method performs the following operations:

  - Sets up array lists to contain the columns, column types, and column classes

- Trims the query String
- Creates a Hibernate Query object, using the HQL query
- Gets the Hibernate column names, types, and classes for the query
- Instantiates a ResultSetMetaData object, passing in the column names and data types
- Saves the query for execution

Listing 20-43 shows the code for the prepare( ) method.

Listing 20-43 The prepare( ) method

```
public void prepare( String query ) throws OdaException
{
   Query qry = null;
   testConnection( );
   ArrayList arColsType = new ArrayList( );
   ArrayList arCols = new ArrayList( );
   ArrayList arColClass = new ArrayList( );

   String[ ] props = null;
   try
   {
      Session hibsession = HibernateUtil.currentSession( );
      query = query.replaceAll( "[\\n\\r]+"," " );
      query = query.trim( );
      qry = hibsession.createQuery( query );
      Type[ ] qryReturnTypes = qry.getReturnTypes( );
      if( qryReturnTypes.length > 0
         && qryReturnTypes[0].isEntityType( ) )
      {
         for( int j=0; j< qryReturnTypes.length; j++ )
         {
            String clsName=qryReturnTypes[j].getName( );
            props =
               HibernateUtil.getHibernateProp( clsName );
            for( int x = 0; x < props.length; x++ )
            {
               String propType =
                  HibernateUtil.getHibernatePropTypes
                     ( clsName, props[x] );
               if( DataTypes.isValidType( propType ))
               {
                  arColsType.add( propType );
                  arCols.add( props[x] );
                  arColClass.add( clsName );
               }
               else
               {
```

```
                    throw new OdaException
                       ( Messages.getString
                       ( "Statement.SOURCE_DATA_ERROR" ) );
                 }
              }
           }
        }
        else
        {
           props = extractColumns( qry.getQueryString( ) );
           for( int t=0; t < qryReturnTypes.length; t++)
           {
              if( DataTypes.isValidType
                 (qryReturnTypes[t].getName( )))
              {
                 arColsType.add( qryReturnTypes[t].getName( ));
                 arCols.add( props[t] );
              }
              else
              {
                 throw new OdaException
                    ( Messages.getString
                       ("Statement.SOURCE_DATA_ERROR") );
              }
           }
        }
     }
     catch( Exception e )
     {
        throw new OdaException( e.getLocalizedMessage( ) );
     }
     this.resultSetMetaData = new ResultSetMetaData
        (( String[ ])arCols.toArray
           ( new String[arCols.size( )] ),
           (String[ ])arColsType.toArray
              ( new String[arColsType.size( )] ),
           (String[ ])arCols.toArray
              ( new String[arCols.size( )] ),
           (String[ ])arColClass.toArray
              ( new String[arColClass.size( )] ));
     this.query = query;
  }
```

- getMetaData( )

  The BIRT framework calls getMetaData( ) after the prepare( ) method to retrieve the metadata for a result set. The BIRT framework uses the metadata to create the data set in the report.

  Listing 20-44 shows the code for the getMetaData( ) method.

Listing 20-44 The getMetaData( ) method

```
public IResultSetMetaData getMetaData( ) throws OdaException
{
   return this.resultSetMetaData;
}
```

- executeQuery( )

  The executeQuery( ) method executes the prepared query and retrieves the results. The executeQuery( ) method returns an IResultSet object, which is created using the list results, result-set metadata, and Hibernate types returned from the HQL query. The ODA framework uses the IResultSet object to iterate over the results.

  The executeQuery( ) method performs the following operations:

  - Sets up an array of org.hibernate.type.Type to map Java types to JDBC data types
  - Sets up a list to contain the results set
  - Trims the query String
  - Instantiates a Hibernate Query object, creating the HQL query
  - Executes the HQL query, returning the query result set in a List
  - Gets the Hibernate types for the query result set
  - Instantiates a ResultSet object, passing in the data, metadata, and Hibernate types

  Listing 20-45 shows the code for the executeQuery( ) method.

Listing 20-45 The executeQuery( ) method

```
public IResultSet executeQuery( ) throws OdaException
{
   Type[ ] qryReturnTypes = null;
   List rst = null;
   try
   {
      Session hibsession = HibernateUtil.currentSession( );
      String qryStr = this.query;
      qryStr = qryStr.replaceAll( "[\\n\\r]+"," " );
      qryStr.trim( );
      Query qry = hibsession.createQuery( qryStr );
      rst = qry.list( );
      qryReturnTypes = qry.getReturnTypes( );

   }
   catch( Exception e )
   {
      throw new OdaException( e.getLocalizedMessage( ) );
```

```
    }
    return new ResultSet
       ( rst, getMetaData( ), qryReturnTypes );
}
```

- close( )

  The close( ) method clears the Connection and ResultSetMetaData objects. In the Connection object, the close( ) method closes the Hibernate session.

  Listing 20-46 shows the code for the Statement.close( ) method.

  Listing 20-46 The Statement.close( ) method

```
public void close( ) throws OdaException
{
    connection = null;
    resultSetMetaData = null;
}
```

Understanding ResultSet

The ResultSet class implements the IResultSet interface. When this class is instantiated, it stores the list.iterator( ) passed from the Statement object. It uses the iterator when the ODA driver framework calls the next( ) method.

The iterator points to the next available row of data from the HQL query results. The framework calls the accessor methods that get the data types for the columns in the current row. For example, if the first column is a String, the framework calls getString( ). This method calls the getResult( ) method, which interprets the HQL query results.

The getResult( ) method parses the results in one of the following ways, depending on whether the query returns a Hibernate EntityType or just an array of values:

- If the query uses HQL and each return type is an EntityType, getResult( ) gets each Column class and uses the Hibernate ClassMetaData methods to retrieve the value.
- If the query returns standard data types, getResult( ) gets each value or values, returning an Object containing the simple value or an array of Objects containing the multiple values.

Listing 20-47 shows the code for the getResult( ) method.

Listing 20-47 The getResult( ) method

```
private Object getResult( int rstcol ) throws OdaException
   {
      Object obj = this.currentRow;
      Object value = null;
```

```
        try
           {
           if( qryReturnTypes.length >
              0 && qryReturnTypes[0].isEntityType( ))
           {
              String checkClass =
              (( ResultSetMetaData )getMetaData( ))
                 .getColumnClass(rstcol);
              Object myVal =
              HibernateUtil.getHibernatePropVal( obj,
                 checkClass,
                 getMetaData( ).getColumnName( rstcol ));
              value = myVal;
           }
           else
           {
              if( getMetaData( ).getColumnCount( ) == 1)
              {
              value = obj;
           }
           else
           {
              Object[ ] values = ( Object[ ])obj;
              value = values[rstcol-1];
           }

           }
        }
        catch( Exception e )
        {
           throw new OdaException( e.getLocalizedMessage( ) );
        }
     return( value );
}
```

Understanding HibernateUtil

HibernateUtil is a utility class that provides the run-time interface between the Hibernate service and the application. The HibernateUtil class example derives from the class provided with the Hibernate documentation. HibernateUtil performs the following operations:

- Initializes the SessionFactory
- Builds the Hibernate SessionFactory
- Opens and closes a session
- Returns information on Hibernate classes and properties
- Registers the JDBC driver with the DriverManager

Connection.open( ) calls HiberFnateUtil.constructSessionFactory( ), which creates a SessionFactory if one does not already exist. The constructSessionFactory( ) method closes and rebuilds the SessionFactory if the location of the configuration file or mapping files directory has changed.

The SessionFactory construction process creates the ClassLoader. The ClassLoader adds the drivers directory in the org.eclipse.birt.report.data.oda .jdbc plug-in and the hibfiles directory in the Hibernate ODA plug-in to classpath. This process also registers the JDBC driver specified in the Hibernate config file with the DriverManager.

The HibernateUtil class implements the following methods:

- initSessionFactory( )

  This method creates the SessionFactory object from the configuration settings in the hibernate.cfg.xml file.

  Listing 20-48 shows the code for the initSessionFactory( ) method.

  Listing 20-48 The initSessionFactory( ) method

```
private static synchronized void initSessionFactory
   ( String hibfile, String mapdir)
   throws HibernateException
   {
   if( sessionFactory == null)
   {
      Thread thread = Thread.currentThread( );
         try
      {
         oldloader = thread.getContextClassLoader( );
         refreshURLs( );
         ClassLoader changeLoader = new URLClassLoader
            ( ( URL [ ])URLList.toArray
               ( new URL[0]),thread
                  .getContextClassLoader( ));
         thread.setContextClassLoader( changeLoader );
         Configuration cfg =
            buildConfig( hibfile,mapdir );
         Class driverClass =
            changeLoader.loadClass( cfg.getProperty
               ( "connection.driver_class" ));
         Driver driver =
            ( Driver ) driverClass.newInstance( );
            WrappedDriver wd =
               new WrappedDriver( driver,
               cfg.getProperty
               ( "connection.driver_class" ));
            boolean foundDriver = false;
            Enumeration drivers =
               DriverManager.getDrivers( );
```

```
        while ( drivers.hasMoreElements( ))
        {
           Driver nextDriver =
              ( Driver )drivers.nextElement( );
           if ( nextDriver.getClass( ) == wd.getClass( ))
           {
              if( nextDriver.toString( )
                 .equals(wd.toString( )) )
              {
                 foundDriver = true;
                 break;
              }
           }
        }

        if( !foundDriver )
        {
           DriverManager.registerDriver( wd );
        }
        sessionFactory = cfg.buildSessionFactory( );
        configuration = cfg;
        HibernateMapDirectory = mapdir;
        HibernateConfigFile = hibfile;
     }
        catch( Exception e)
        {
           e.printStackTrace( );
           throw new HibernateException
              ( "No Session Factory Created " +
                 e.getLocalizedMessage( ));
        }
        finally
        {
           thread.setContextClassLoader( oldloader );
        }
     }
  }
```

- constructSessionFactory

  This method checks to see if a configuration change occurred. If a change occurred, the method closes the session and SessionFactory and calls the initSessionFactory to rebuild the SessionFactory.

  Listing 20-49 shows the code for the constructSessionFactory( ) method.

Listing 20-49 The constructSessionFactory( ) method

```
public static void constructSessionFactory
   ( String hibfile, String mapdir)
   throws HibernateException
   {
      if( hibfile == null)
      {
```

```
            hibfile = "";
        }

        if( mapdir == null)
        {
            mapdir = "";
        }

        if( sessionFactory == null)
        {
            initSessionFactory( hibfile, mapdir);
            return;
        }

        if( HibernateMapDirectory.equalsIgnoreCase
            ( mapdir ) && HibernateConfigFile
                .equalsIgnoreCase( hibfile ))
        {
            return;
        }
        synchronized( sessionFactory )
        {
            Session s = ( Session ) session.get( );

            if ( s != null )
            {
            closeSession( );
            }

            if ( sessionFactory != null &&
                !sessionFactory.isClosed( ))
            {
                closeFactory( );
            }
            sessionFactory = null;
            initSessionFactory( hibfile, mapdir);
}
```

- currentSession( )

  This method opens a session when called by the Connection.open( ) method, as shown in Listing 20-50.

  Listing 20-50 The currentSession( ) method

```
public static Session currentSession( )
    throws HibernateException {
    Session s = ( Session ) session.get( );
    if ( s == null ) {
        s = sessionFactory.openSession( );
        session.set( s );
    }
        return s;
    }
```

Other methods in this class return information on a particular class and its properties. The getHibernateProp( ) method returns the properties for a class. The getHibernatePropTypes( ) method returns the data type for a property of a class.

Building the Hibernate ODA driver plug-in

To build and deploy the org.eclipse.birt.report.data.oda.hibernate plug-in using the Eclipse PDE Manifest Editor, perform the following tasks:

- In Build, specify the Build Configuration to include the following items:
  - In Runtime Information, add the odahibernate.jar file.
  - In Binary Build, select the following files and folders:
    - META-INF
    - exampleconfig
    - hibfiles
    - lib
    - plugin.xml
- In Overview, in Exporting, choose Export Wizard and perform the following tasks:
  - In Available Plug-ins and Fragments, select org.eclipse.birt.report .data.oda.hibernate.
  - In Options, verify that Package plug-ins as individual JAR archives is not selected.

In Destination, choose the directory, $INSTALL_DIR\birt-runtime-2_6_0 \Report Engine.The Hibernate ODA example uses MySQL as the database. The BIRT sample database and the MySQL installation scripts can be downloaded from http://www.eclipse.org/birt/db. For information about the required Hibernate libraries, please refer to the Hibernate web site at http://www.hibernate.org.

Developing the Hibernate ODA user interface extension

To use the data retrieved by the Hibernate ODA driver in a BIRT report design, you must extend the DTP design user interface. To implement the Hibernate ODA user interface, you extend the following extension points:

- org.eclipse.datatools.connectivity.oda.design.ui.dataSource

  The dataSource extension point defines and implements the user interface for new data source and data set wizards. These wizards use the Hibernate ODA driver plug-in to extend the functionality available in the Data Explorer of BIRT Report Designer.

- org.eclipse.ui.propertyPages

  The propertyPages extension displays and manipulates the Hibernate configuration file and mapping files directory locations.

- org.eclipse.datatools.connectivity.connectionProfile

  The connectionProfile extension shares a data source connection between applications.

To start developing the Hibernate ODA user interface plug-in, create the plug-in project, org.eclipse.birt.report.data.oda.hibernate.ui.

How to create the Hibernate ODA user interface plug-in project

1 From the Eclipse menu, choose File➛New➛Project. New Project appears.

2 On New Project—Select a wizard, open Business Intelligence and Reporting Tools and select ODA Designer Plug-in Project. Choose Next. New Plug-in Project appears.

3 In Plug-in Project, modify the settings as shown in Table 20-16. Choose Next. Plug-in Content appears.

Table 20-16 Settings for Hibernate ODA UI Plug-in Project options

Section	Option	Value
Plug-in Project	Project name	org.eclipse.birt.report.data .oda.hibernate.ui
	Use default location	Selected
	Location	Not available when you select Use default location
Project Setting	Create a Java project	Selected
	Source folder name	src
	Output folder name	bin
Target Platform	Eclipse version	3.6
	OSGi framework	Deselected
Working sets	Add project to working sets	Not selected

4 In Plug-in Content, modify the settings as shown in Table 20-17. Choose Finish.

Table 20-17 Settings for Hibernate ODA UI Plug-in Content options

Section	Option	Value
Properties	Plug-in ID	org.eclipse.birt.report.data .oda.hibernate.ui
	Plug-in Version	2.0.0

Table 20-17 Settings for Hibernate ODA UI Plug-in Content options

Section	Option	Value
Properties	Plug-in Name	BIRT Hibernate user interface Plug-in
	Plug-in Provider	yourCompany.com or leave blank
	Execution Environment	JavaSE-1.6
Options	Generate an activator, a Java class that controls the plug-in's life cycle	Selected
	Activator	org.eclipse.birt.report.data .oda.hibernate.ui .Activator
	This plug-in will make contributions to the user interface	Deselected
	Enable API Analysis	Deselected
Rich Client Application	Would you like to create a rich client application?	No

5 In Templates, choose ODA Data Source Designer. Choose Next. ODA Data Source Designer appears, as shown in Figure 20-25.

6 In ODA Data Source Designer, specify new values for the following options used to generate the Hibernate ODA user interface plug-in, as shown in Table 20-18. Choose Finish.

Table 20-18 Settings for Hibernate ODA Data Source Designer options

Option	Value
Java Package Name	org.eclipse.birt.report.data.oda.hibernate.ui
ODA Runtime Driver Plug-in Id	org.eclipse.birt.report.data.oda.hibernate
ODA Runtime Data Source Element Id	org.eclipse.birt.report.data.oda.hibernate
ODA Runtime Driver Class	org.eclipse.birt.report.data.oda.hibernate .Driver
ODA Runtime Data Set Element Id	org.eclipse.birt.report.data.oda.hibernate .dataSet
Data Source Display Name	ODA Hibernate File Designer Data Source
Data Set Display Name	ODA Hibernate File Designer Data Set

The Hibernate ODA user interface plug-in project appears in the Eclipse PDE workbench.

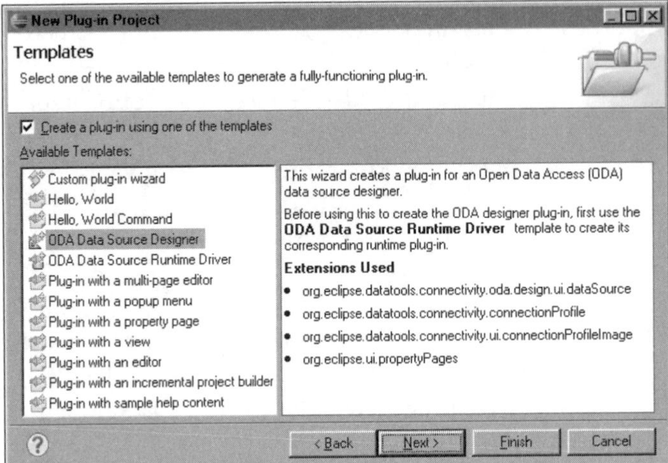

Figure 20-25 Specifying the ODA Data Source Designer template

How to specify the Hibernate ODA user interface dependencies

On the Eclipse PDE Manifest Editor, in Dependencies, specify the required plug-ins in the following order:

- org.eclipse.core.runtime
- org.eclipse.ui
- org.eclipse.datatools.connectivity.oda.design.ui
- org.eclipse.birt.report.data.oda.hibernate

How to specify the Hibernate ODA user interface runtime

On Runtime, in Exported Packages, add org.eclipse.birt.report.oda .hibernate.ui to the list of packages that this plug-in exposes to clients.

How to specify the Hibernate ODA user interface extension points

1 On the PDE Manifest Editor, choose Extensions.

2 In All Extensions, choose Add. New Extension appears.

3 On New Extension—Extension Points, in the list of extension points, select the following plug-in:

```
org.eclipse.datatools.connectivity.oda.design.ui.dataSource
```

Choose Finish.

4 Repeat steps 2 and 3 to add the following extension points to the list on the Extensions page:

- org.eclipse.ui.propertyPages

- org.eclipse.datatools.connectivity.connectionProfile

How to add the extension details

1 In Extensions, select the extension point, org.eclipse.datatools.connectivity.oda.design.ui.dataSource, and add the following elements and element details:

- dataSourceUI

  Add the following id:

  ```
  org.eclipse.birt.report.data.oda.hibernate
  ```

  Add the following extension element to dataSourceUI:

  ```
  newDataSourceWizard
  ```

  Add the extension element details for the extension element, newDataSourceWizard, as shown in Table 20-19.

  Table 20-19 Property settings for the Hibernate newDataSourceWizard

Property	Value
pageClass	org.eclipse.birt.report.data.oda.hibernate.ui.HibernateDataSourceWizard
windowTitle	Hibernate Data Source
includesProgressMonitor	false
pageTitle	Hibernate Data Source

- dataSetUI

  Add the extension element details for the extension element, dataSetUI, as shown in Table 20-20.

  Table 20-20 Property settings for the Hibernate dataSetUI extension element

Property	Value
id	org.eclipse.birt.report.data.oda.hibernate.dataSet
initialPageId	org.eclipse.birt.report.data.oda.hibernate.ui.HibernatePage
supportsInParameters	true
supportsOutParameters	false

2 In Extensions, select dataSetUI and add the following properties and element details:

- dataSetWizard, as shown in Table 20-21

Table 20-21 Property settings for the Hibernate dataSetWizard extension element

Property	Value
class	org.eclipse.datatools.connectivity.oda .design.ui.wizards.DataSetWizard
windowTitle	Hibernate Data Set

- dataSetPage, as shown in Table 20-22

Table 20-22 Property settings for the Hibernate dataSetPage extension element

Property	Value
id	org.eclipse.birt.report.data.oda.hibernate .ui.HibernatePage
wizardPageClass	org.eclipse.birt.report.data.oda.hibernate .ui.HibernateHqlSelectionPage
displayName	Enter HQL
path	/

3 In Extensions, select org.eclipse.ui.propertyPages and add the following ODA Hibernate Data Source Connection Properties (page) property and extension element details, as shown in Table 20-23.

Table 20-23 Property settings for the Hibernate page extension element

Property	Value
id	org.eclipse.birt.report.data.oda.hibernate
name	ODA Hibernate Data Source Connection Properties
class	org.eclipse.birt.report.data.oda.hibernate.ui .HibernatePropertyPage
objectClass	org.eclipse.datatools.connectivity .IConnectionProfile

4 In Extensions, select page and add the following filter property and extension element details, as shown in Table 20-24.

Table 20-24 Property settings for the Hibernate filter extension element

Property	Value
name	org.eclipse.datatools.profile.property.id

Table 20-24 Property settings for the Hibernate filter extension element

Property	Value
value	org.eclipse.birt.report.data.oda.hibernate

5 In Extensions, select org.eclipse.datatools.connectivity.connectionProfile, and add the following properties and element details:

- category, as shown in Table 20-25

Table 20-25 Property settings for the Hibernate category extension element

Property	Value
id	org.eclipse.birt.report.data.oda.hibernate
parentCategory	org.eclipse.datatools.connectivity.oda .profileCategory
name	Hibernate Data Source

- connectionProfile, as shown in Table 20-26

Table 20-26 Property settings for the Hibernate connectionProfile extension element

Property	Value
id	org.eclipse.birt.report.data.oda.hibernate
category	org.eclipse.birt.report.data.oda.hibernate
name	ODA Hibernate Data Source Connection Profile
pingFactory	org.eclipse.datatoools.connectivity.oda.profile .OdaConnectionFactory

- connectionFactory, as shown in Table 20-27

Table 20-27 Property settings for the Hibernate connectionFactory extension element

Property	Value
id	org.eclipse.datatools.connectivity.oda.IConnection
class	org.eclipse.datatools.connectivity.oda.profile .OdaConnectionFactory
profile	org.eclipse.birt.report.data.oda.hibernate
name	ODA Connection Factory

- newWizard, as shown in Table 20-28

Table 20-28 Property settings for the Hibernate newWizard extension element

Property	Value
id	org.eclipse.birt.report.data.oda.hibernate
name	ODA Hibernate Data Source
class	org.eclipse.datatools.connectivity.oda.design.ui .wizards.NewDataSourceWizard
profile	org.eclipse.birt.report.data.oda.hibernate
description	Create an ODA Hibernate connection profile

Understanding the sample Hibernate ODA user interface extension

The following sections describe the code-based extensions a developer must make to complete the development of the Hibernate ODA user interface extension, after defining the plug-in framework in the Eclipse PDE.

The Hibernate ODA user interface plug-in implements the following classes:

- HibernatePropertyPage
  Creates and initializes the editor controls for the property page that specify the ODA data source. This class updates the connection profile properties with the values collected from the page. HibernatePropertyPage extends org.eclipse.datatools.connectivity.oda .design.ui.wizards.DataSourceEditorPage, the abstract base class for implementing a customized ODA data source property page.

- HibernatePageHelper
  Implements the user interface that specifies data source properties. This utility class specifies the page layout, sets up the controls that listen for user input, verifies the location of the Hibernate configuration file, and sets up the location of the mapping directory. The HibernateDataSourceWizard and HibernatePropertyPage classes use HibernatePageHelper. HibernatePageHelper also extends org.eclipse .datatools.connectivity.oda.design.ui.wizards.DataSourceEditorPage.

- HibernateDataSourceWizard
  Creates and initializes the controls for the data source wizard page. The class sets the configuration file message and collects the property values. In the extension element settings for newDataSourceWizard, the pageClass property specifies this class as the implementation class for the dataSourceUI wizard. The HibernateDataSourceWizard class extends org.eclipse.datatools.connectivity.oda.design.ui.wizards .DataSourceWizardPage, the abstract base class for implementing a customized ODA data source wizard page.

- HibernateHqlSelectionPage

  Creates the user interface that specifies an HQL statement. The Hibernate ODA user interface plug-in calls HibernateHqlSelectionPage when creating or modifying the data set for a data source. In the extension element settings for dataSetPage, the wizardPageClass property specifies this class as the implementation class for the dataSetUI page wizard. HibernateHqlSelectionPage also extends org.eclipse.datatools .connectivity.oda.design.ui.wizards.DataSourceWizardPage.

- Messages

  This class and the related properties file, messages.properties, generate the messages displayed in the Hibernate ODA user interface.

Understanding HibernatePageHelper

This class creates the components that select the Hibernate configuration file and a mapping files directory using the following methods:

- createCustomControl( )

  Builds the user interface for the data source

- initCustomControl( )

  Sets the initial property values

- collectCustomProperties( )

  Returns the modified properties to the ODA framework

When the data source page displays, the Finish button becomes available when the setPageComplete( ) method indicates the page is complete.

HibernateDataSourceWizard.createPageCustomControl( ) and HibernatePropertyPage.createAndInitCustomControl( ) call HibernatePageHelper. The createCustomControl( ) method is the entry point for this class.

Listing 20-51 shows the code for the createCustomControl( ) method.

Listing 20-51 The createCustomControl( ) method

```
void createCustomControl( Composite parent )
   {
      Composite content = new Composite( parent, SWT.NULL );
      GridLayout layout = new GridLayout( 3, false );
      content.setLayout(layout);
      setupConfigLocation( content );
      setupMapLocation( content );
   }
```

The setupConfigLocation( ) method sets up the configuration file location. The setupMapLocation( ) method sets up the mapping folder. These two methods perform similar tasks.

Listing 20-52 shows the code for the setupConfigLocation( ) method. This method adds a label, a text entry component, and a button. The text entry component has a ModifyListener( ) method, which verifies that the file selected exists, and the button has a SelectionAdapter( ) method, which uses the FileDialog( ) method to access the configuration file.

Listing 20-52 The setupConfigLocation( ) method

```
private void setupConfigLocation( Composite composite )
   {
      Label label = new Label( composite, SWT.NONE );
      label.setText("Select Hibernate Config File" );
      GridData data =
         new GridData( GridData.FILL_HORIZONTAL );
      m_configLocation = new Text( composite, SWT.BORDER );
      m_configLocation.setLayoutData( data );
      setPageComplete( true );
      m_configLocation.addModifyListener
         ( new ModifyListener( )
            {
               public void modifyText( ModifyEvent e )
               {
                  verifyConfigLocation( );
               }
            } );
   m_browseConfigButton = new Button( composite, SWT.NONE );
   m_browseConfigButton.setText( "..." );
   m_browseConfigButton.addSelectionListener
      ( new SelectionAdapter( )
      {
         public void widgetSelected( SelectionEvent e )
         {
            FileDialog dialog = new FileDialog
               ( m_configLocation.getShell( ) );
            if( m_configLocation.getText( ) != null &&
               m_configLocation.getText( )
                  .trim( ).length( ) > 0 )
               {
                  dialog.setFilterPath
                     ( m_configLocation.getText() );
               }
               dialog.setText
                  ( "Select Hibernate Config File" );
               String selectedLocation = dialog.open( );
               if( selectedLocation != null )
               {
                  m_configLocation.setText
                     ( selectedLocation );
               }
            }
         } );
   }
```

The initCustomControl( ) method initializes the properties settings. The plug-in passes the properties to the method from the createPageCustomControl( ) and setInitialProperties( ) methods of the HibernateDataSourceWizard class and the createAndInitCustomControl( ) method of the HibernatePropertyPage class.

The initCustomControl( ) method retrieves the properties for the Hibernate configuration file and mapping files directory and sets text component values.

Listing 20-53 shows the code for the initCustomControl( ) method.

Listing 20-53 The initCustomControl( ) method

```
void initCustomControl( Properties profileProps )
   {
      setPageComplete( true );
      setMessage( DEFAULT_MESSAGE, IMessageProvider.NONE );
      if( profileProps == null || profileProps.isEmpty() ||
         m_configLocation == null )
         return;
      String configPath =
         profileProps.getProperty( "HIBCONFIG" );
      if( configPath == null )
      configPath = EMPTY_STRING;
      m_configLocation.setText( configPath );
      String mapPath = profileProps.getProperty( "MAPDIR" );
      if( mapPath == null )
         mapPath = EMPTY_STRING;
      m_mapLocation.setText( mapPath );
      verifyConfigLocation( );
   }
```

When the user presses the Finish or Test Connection button, the plug-in calls the collectCustomProperties( ) method to retrieve the new values for the Hibernate configuration file and mapping files directory. The HibernateDataSourceWizard and HibernatePropertyPage classes call the HibernatePageHelper.collectCustomProperties( ) method from their collectCustomProperties( ) methods.

Listing 20-54 shows the code for the collectCustomProperties( ) method.

Listing 20-54 The collectCustomProperties( ) method

```
Properties collectCustomProperties( Properties props )
   {
      if( props == null )
         props = new Properties( );
      props.setProperty( "HIBCONFIG",
         getConfig( ) );
      props.setProperty( "MAPDIR", getMapDir( ) );
      return props;
   }
```

Understanding HibernateDataSourceWizard

The HibernateDataSourceWizard class extends the DTP DataSourceWizardPage by implementing three methods that the ODA framework calls:

- createPageCustomControl( )
  Constructs the user interface
- setInitialProperties( )
  Sets the initial values of the user interface
- collectCustomProperties( )
  Retrieve the modified values

This class creates the HibernatePageHelper class, and uses the methods described earlier to handle these three methods. The ODA framework uses this class to create a new data source.

Understanding HibernatePropertyPage

The HibernatePropertyPage class extends the DTP DataSourceEditorPage by implementing two methods that the ODA framework calls:

- createAndInitCustomControl( )
  Constructs the user interface and sets the initial values
- collectCustomProperties( )
  Retrieves the modified values

This class creates the HibernatePageHelper class and uses the methods described earlier to handle these two methods. The ODA framework uses this class to create a new data source.

Understanding HibernateHqlSelectionPage

The HibernateHqlSelectionPage class extends DataSetWizardPage to define the page controls and related functionality for the Hibernate ODA data set wizard. HibernateHqlSelectionPage allows the user to create an HQL statement that selects the data set and embeds the HQL statement in the report design. This page links to the Hibernate ODA through the wizardPageClass attribute of the dataSetPage element within the dataSource extension.

The HibernateHqlSelectionPage class implements the following methods:

- createPageControl( )

  This method performs the following operations:

  - Sets up a composite set of controls using a series of GridLayout and GridData objects to create the data set editor user interface

- Sets the user prompt to enter an HQL statement and verify the query
- Adds a text control to allow the user to enter and modify text
- Adds a ModifyListener to the text control to detect user input
- Sets up the Verify Query button and adds a SelectionListener to detect when the user selects the button
- Returns the composite page control

Listing 20-55 shows the code for the createPageControl( ) method.

Listing 20-55 The createPageControl( ) method

```
public Control createPageControl( Composite parent )
   {
      Composite composite = new Composite
      ( parent, SWT.NONE );
   GridLayout layout = new GridLayout( );
   layout.numColumns = 1;
   composite.setLayout( layout );
   Label label = new Label( composite, SWT.NONE );
   label.setText( Messages.getString
      ( "wizard.title.selectColumns" ));
   GridData data = new GridData( GridData.FILL_BOTH );
   queryText = new Text( composite,SWT.MULTI |
      SWT.WRAP | SWT.V_SCROLL );
   queryText.setLayoutData( data );

   queryText.addModifyListener( new ModifyListener( )
   {
      public void modifyText( ModifyEvent e )
      {
         if( m_initialized == false)
         {
            setPageComplete(true);
            m_initialized = true;
         }
         else
         {
            setPageComplete(false);
         }
         }
   } );
   setPageComplete( false );
   Composite cBottom = new Composite
      ( composite, SWT.NONE );
   cBottom.setLayoutData
      ( new GridData( GridData.FILL_HORIZONTAL ) );
   cBottom.setLayout( new RowLayout( ) );
   queryButton = new Button( cBottom, SWT.NONE );
   queryButton.setText(Messages.getString
      ( "wizard.title.verify" ));
   queryButton.addSelectionListener
```

```
    ( new SelectionAdapter( ))
{
public void widgetSelected( SelectionEvent event )
{
            verifyQuery( );
     }
} );
return composite;
   }
```

- initializeControl( )

  The plug-in calls this method to retrieve the HQL query from the current design and initializes the HQL text component with this value. initializeControl( ) also reads the Hibernate configuration file and mapping files directory from the report design and stores them in member variables for use when building a query.

  Listing 20-56 shows the code for the initializeControl( ) method.

  Listing 20-56 The initializeControl( ) method

```
private void initializeControl( )
{
   Properties dataSourceProps =
      getInitializationDesign( ).getDataSourceDesign( )
         .getPublicProperties( );

   m_hibconfig =
         dataSourceProps.getProperty( "HIBCONFIG" );
   m_mapdir = dataSourceProps.getProperty( "MAPDIR" );

   DataSetDesign dataSetDesign =
         getInitializationDesign( );
   if( dataSetDesign == null )
         return;

   String queryTextTmp = dataSetDesign.getQueryText( );
   if( queryTextTmp == null )
      return;

   queryText.setText( queryTextTmp );
   this.m_initialized = false;
   setMessage( "", NONE );
}
```

- verifyQuery( )

  This method is the selection event called when the user chooses the Verify Query button. verifyQuery performs the following operations:

  - Opens a connection to the run-time environment.
  - Instantiates a Query object and gets the query text entered by the user.
  - Prepares the query.

- Checks the column to determine if the query prepare was successful. Depending on the success of the query prepare, verifyQuery( ) indicates that page processing is complete or incomplete.
- Re-enables the Verify Query button.
- Closes the connection.

Listing 20-57 shows the code for the verifyQuery( ) method.

Listing 20-57 The verifyQuery( ) method

```
boolean verifyQuery( )
{
   setMessage( "Verifying Query", INFORMATION );
   setPageComplete( false );
   queryButton.setEnabled( false );
   Connection conn = new Connection( );
   try
   {
      Properties prop = new Properties( );
      if( m_hibconfig == null)m_hibconfig = "";
      if( m_mapdir == null)m_mapdir = "";
      prop.put("HIBCONFIG", m_hibconfig );
         prop.put("MAPDIR", m_mapdir);
      conn.open( prop );
      IQuery query = conn.newQuery( "" );
      query.prepare( queryText.getText( ) );
      int columnCount =
         query.getMetaData( ).getColumnCount( );
      if ( columnCount == 0 )
      {
         setPageComplete( false );
         return false;
      }
      setPageComplete( true );
      return true;
   }
   catch ( OdaException e )
   {
      System.out.println( e.getMessage( ) );
      showError( "ODA Verify Exception", e.getMessage( ) );
      setPageComplete( false );
      return false
   }
   catch ( Exception e )
   {
      System.out.println( e.getMessage( ) );
      showError( "Verify Exception", e.getMessage( ) );
      setPageComplete( false );
      return false;
   }
   finally
   {
      try
```

```
            {
               queryButton.setEnabled( true );
               conn.close( );
            }
            catch ( OdaException e )
            {
               System.out.println( e.getMessage( ) );
               setMessage( e.getLocalizedMessage( ),
               ERROR );e.getMessage( ) );
               setPageComplete( false );
               return false;
         }
      }
   }
```

- savePage( )

  The savePage( ) method is called when the ODA framework calls the collectDataSetDesign( ) method. This action occurs when the user presses the Finish button on the new data set wizard or the OK button on the data set editor is pressed. The savePage( ) method saves the query to the report, as shown in Listing 20-58.

  Listing 20-58 The savePage( ) method

```
private boolean savePage( )
{
   IConnection conn = null;
   try
   {
      IDriver hqDriver = new HibernateDriver( );
      conn = hqDriver.getConnection( null );
      IResultSetMetaData metadata =
         getResultSetMetaData( dataSetDesign
            .getQueryText( ), conn );
      setResultSetMetaData( dataSetDesign, metadata );
   }
   catch( OdaException e )
   {
      dataSetDesign.setResultSets( null );
   }
   finally
   {
      closeConnection( conn );
   }
}
```

- getResultSetMetaData( )

  The savePage( ) method calls the getResultSetMetaData( ) method when saving the report design. This method retrieves the query metadata that setResultSetMetaData( ) uses to create the data set columns.

  Listing 20-59 shows the code for the getResultSetMetaData( ) method.

Listing 20-59 The getResultSetMetaData( ) method

```
private IResultSetMetaData getResultSetMetaData
   ( String queryText, IConnection conn )
   throws OdaException
{
         java.util.Properties prop =
            new java.util.Properties( );

         if( m_hibconfig == null) m_hibconfig = "";
         if( m_mapdir == null) m_mapdir = "";

         prop.put( "HIBCONFIG", m_hibconfig );
         prop.put( "MAPDIR", m_mapdir );
         conSn.open( prop );

         IQuery query = conn.newQuery( null );
         query.prepare( queryText );
         return query.getMetaData( );
}
```

- setResultSetMetaData( )

  The savePage( ) method calls the setResultSetMetaData( ) method when saving the report design. This method uses the DataSetDesign and the ResultSetMetaData objects for the query to create the columns in the data set for use in the report design.

  Listing 20-60 shows the code for the setResultSetMetaData( ) method.

Listing 20-60 The setResultSetMetaData( ) method

```
private void setResultSetMetaData
   ( DataSetDesign dataSetDesign,
      IResultSetMetaData md ) throws OdaException
{
ResultSetColumns columns =
      DesignSessionUtil.toResultSetColumnsDesign( md );

   ResultSetDefinition resultSetDefn =
      DesignFactory.eINSTANCE
      .createResultSetDefinition( );

   resultSetDefn.setResultSetColumns( columns );
   dataSetDesign.setPrimaryResultSet( resultSetDefn );
   dataSetDesign.getResultSets().setDerivedMetaData( true );
}
```

- collectDataSetDesign( )

  The plug-in calls this method when creating or modifying the query finishes. The plug-in passes the current design to this method. collectDataSetDesign( ) then verifies that a query exists and sets the design query to the value of the query text. The savePage( ) method saves the design and creates the columns in the data set.

Listing 20-61 shows the code for the collectDataSetDesign( ) method.

Listing 20-61 The collectDataSetDesign( ) method

```
protected DataSetDesign collectDataSetDesign
   ( DataSetDesign design )
{
if( ! hasValidData( ) )
      return design;

   design.setQueryText( queryText.getText( ) );
   savePage( design );
   return design;
}
```

Building the Hibernate ODA user interface plug-in

To build the org.eclipse.birt.report.data.oda.hibernate.ui plug-in using the Eclipse PDE Manifest Editor, perform the following tasks:

- In Build, specify the Build Configuration to include the following items:
  - In Runtime Information, add the hibernateodaui.jar file.
  - In Binary Build, select the following files and folders:
    - META-INF
    - plugin.xml

  Build Configuration appears, as shown in Figure 20-26.

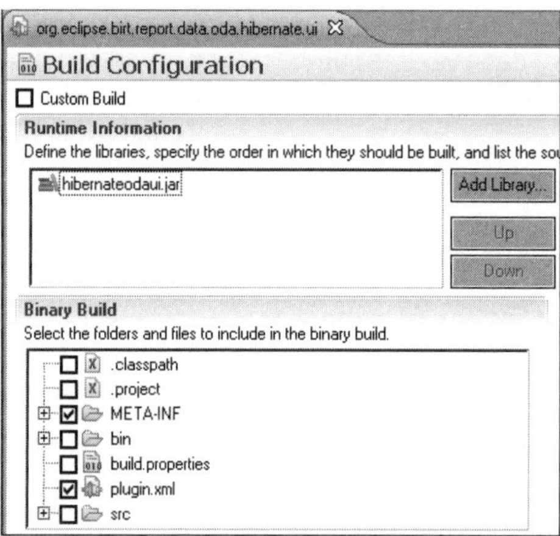

Figure 20-26 Build Configuration settings

Testing the Hibernate ODA user interface plug-in

To test the Hibernate ODA user interface plug-in, after exporting it, use a run-time configuration of the Eclipse PDE workbench.

How to launch the Hibernate ODA user interface plug-in

1 From the Eclipse SDK menu, choose Run—Run Configurations. On Run Configurations, right-click Eclipse Application. Choose New.

2 Create a configuration to launch an Eclipse application by performing the following tasks:

   1 In Name, type:

   ```
   Hibernate ODA Test
   ```

   2 On Main, in Location, type:

   ```
   C:\Test\Hibernate
   ```

   Run Configurations appears as shown in Figure 20-27.

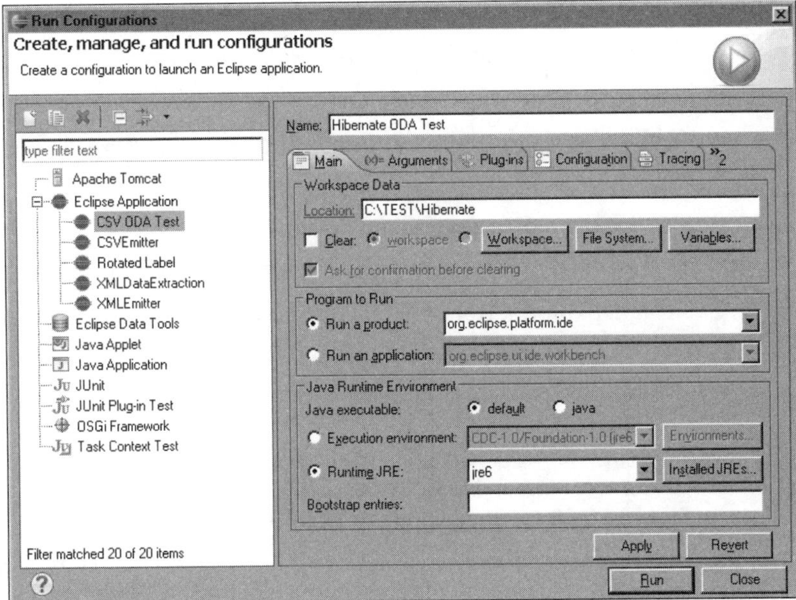

Figure 20-27 Creating a configuration to launch an Eclipse application

3 Add the Hibernate ODA plug-ins to the launch configuration.

   1 In Run Configurations, choose Plug-ins.

   2 In Launch with, choose

   ```
   plug-ins selected below only
   ```

   from the drop-down list as shown in Figure 20-28.

   3 In Plug-ins, check the following plug-ins:

   ```
   org.eclipse.birt.data.oda.hibernate
   org.eclipse.birt.data.oda.hibernate.ui
   ```

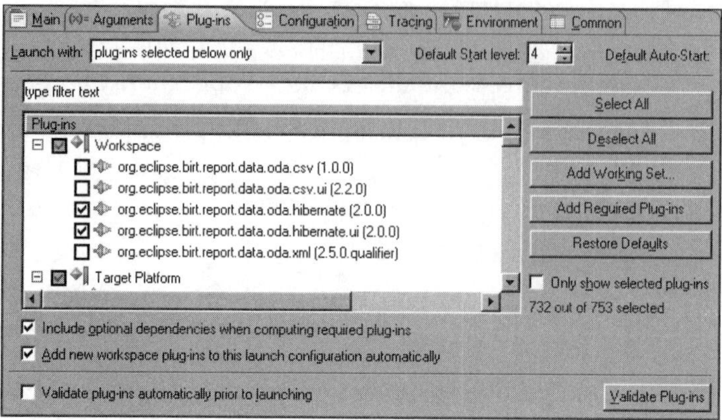

Figure 20-28 Adding Hibernate ODA plug-ins to launch configuration

4 Choose Run to launch the run-time workbench.

5 In the run-time workbench, choose the Report Design perspective.

6 In Report Design, create a new report project and create a new blank report.

How to specify a data source and data set

1 In Report Design, choose Data Explorer. Data Explorer appears.

2 In Data Explorer, right-click Data Sources and choose New Data Source, as shown in Figure 20-29. New Data Source appears.

Figure 20-29 Choosing New Data Source

In New Data Source, choose Create from a data source type in the following list and select Hibernate Data Source as the data source type, as shown in Figure 20-30. Choose Next.

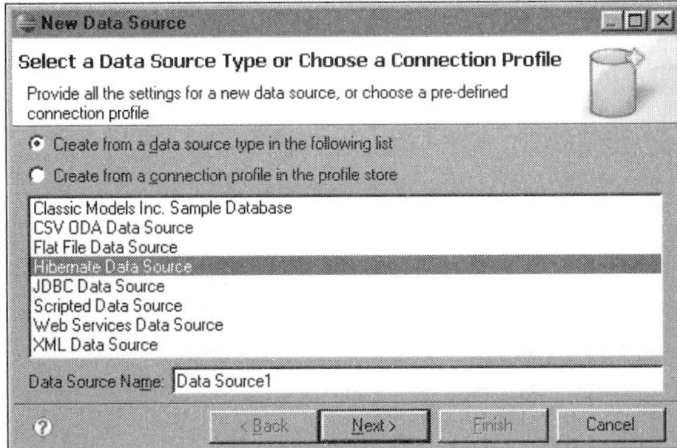

Figure 20-30 Selecting Hibernate Data Source

Hibernate Data Source appears, as shown in Figure 20-31. In Hibernate Data Source, select the Hibernate configuration file and mapping directory or leave these items blank if you use the hibfiles directory. Choose Finish.

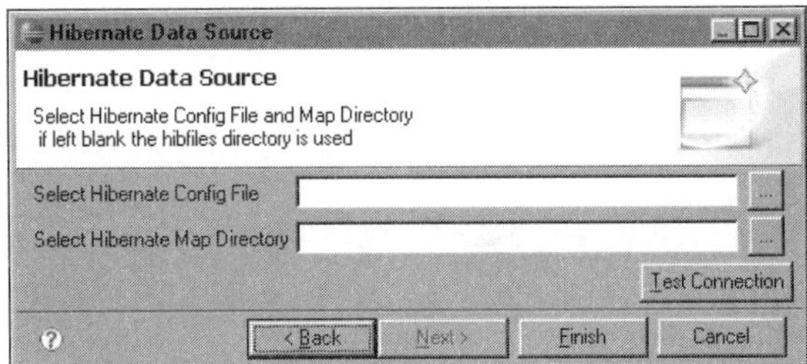

Figure 20-31 Configuring the Hibernate Data Source

Data Explorer appears with the new data source in Data Sources, as shown in Figure 20-32.

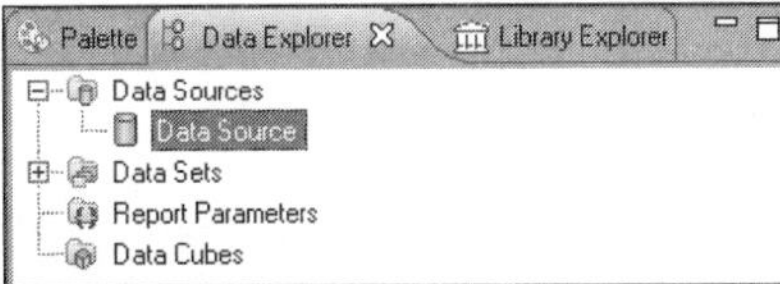

Figure 20-32 New data source in Data Explorer

3 In Data Explorer, right-click Data Sets and choose New Data Set, as shown in Figure 20-33.

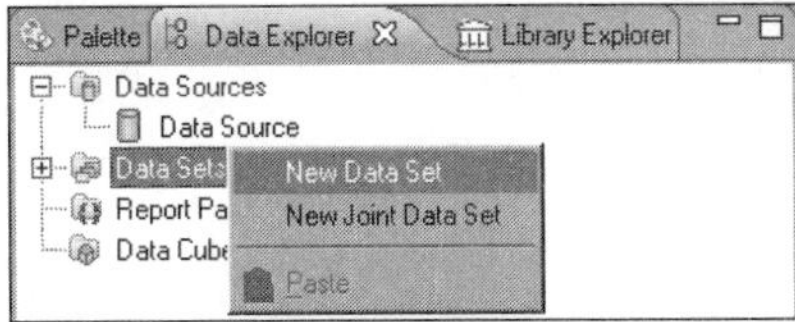

Figure 20-33 Choosing New Data Set

New Data Set appears, as shown in Figure 20-34.

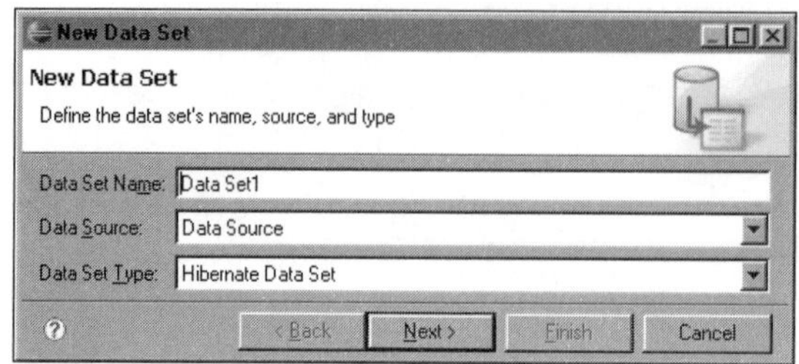

Figure 20-34 New Data Set

Choose Next. Hibernate Data Set appears.

4 In Edit Data Set, perform the following tasks:

1 In Enter HQL and Verify Query, type:

```
select ord.orderNumber, cus.customerNumber,
        cus.customerName
from Orders as ord, Customer as cus
where  ord.customerNumber = cus.customerNumber
and cus.customerNumber = 363
```

Edit Data Set displays the query, as shown in Figure 20-35.

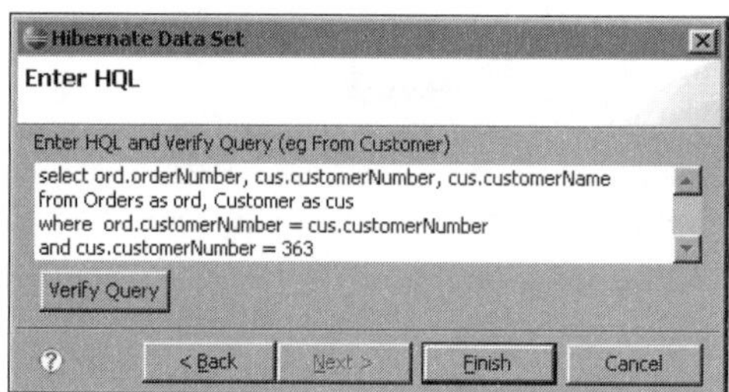

Figure 20-35 Editing the HQL query

2 Choose Verify Query.

3 Choose Finish. Edit Data Set appears. Choose Preview Results. Preview Results appears as shown in Figure 20-36.

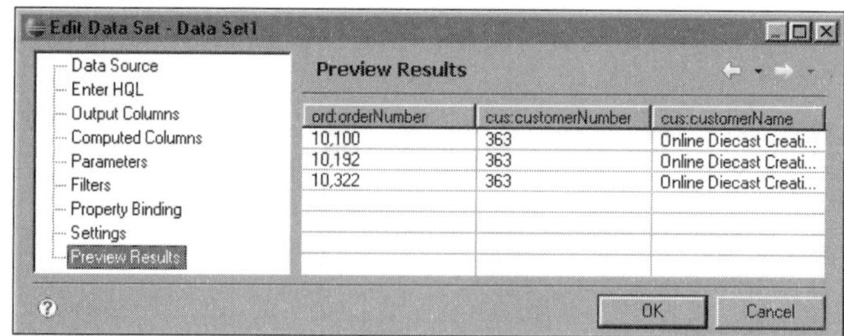

Figure 20-36 Previewing the data set

Choose OK. Data Explorer appears.

5 In Data Explorer, expand Data Sets. The new data set lists three columns, as shown in Figure 20-37.

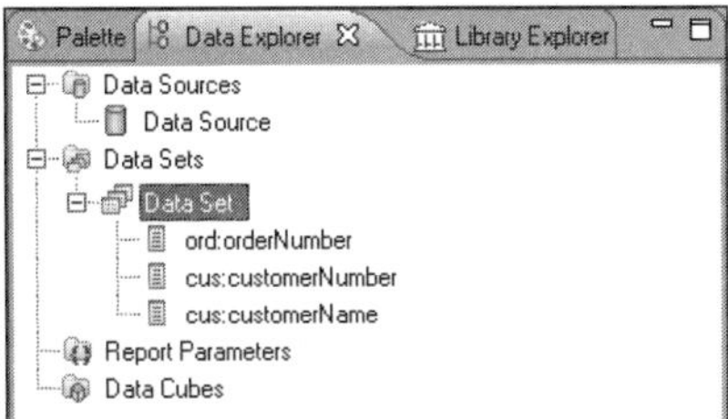

Figure 20-37 Data set in Data Explorer

6 To build a report that uses the data set, perform the following tasks:

1 In Data Explorer, drag Data Set to the layout editor. The layout appears, as shown in Figure 20-38.

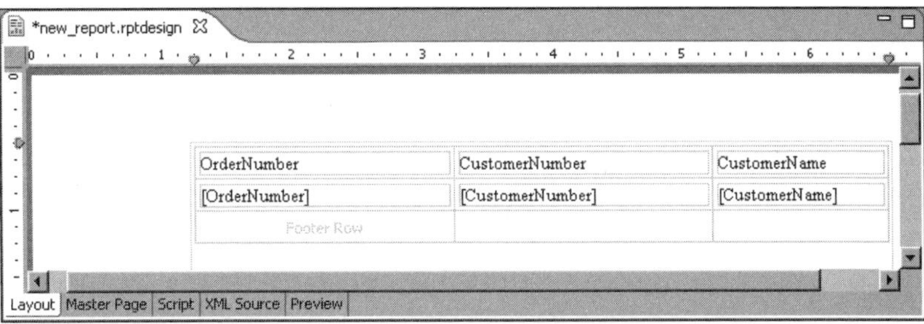

Figure 20-38 Report design in the layout editor

2 To view the output for new_report_1.rptdesign, choose Preview. The Preview, appears as shown in Figure 20-39.

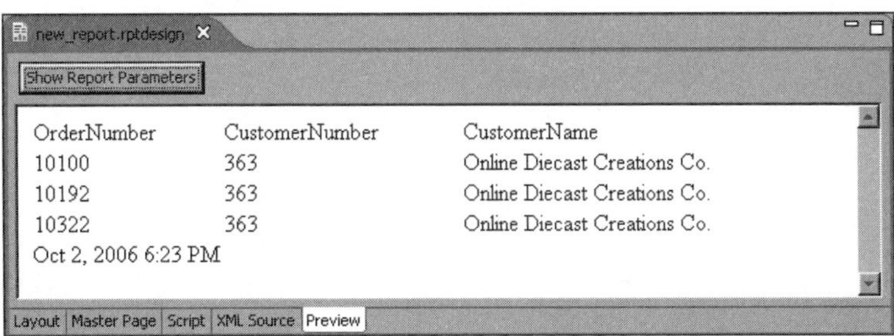

Figure 20-39 Preview of the report design

Chapter

21

Developing a Data Extraction Extension

This chapter describes how to develop a report data extraction extension using the Eclipse PDE. The data extraction example exports report data to XML format. The Eclipse PDE provides the basis for the extension.

Understanding a data extraction extension

BIRT Report Engine provides a data extraction extension point that supports developing a new plug-in for exporting report data to a custom format. The BIRT user interface also provides a built-in data extraction feature that can export data from a report document in CSV format. This functionality is available in the BIRT Web Viewer. The Data Export feature is available in the BIRT Web Viewer toolbar, as shown in Figure 21-1.

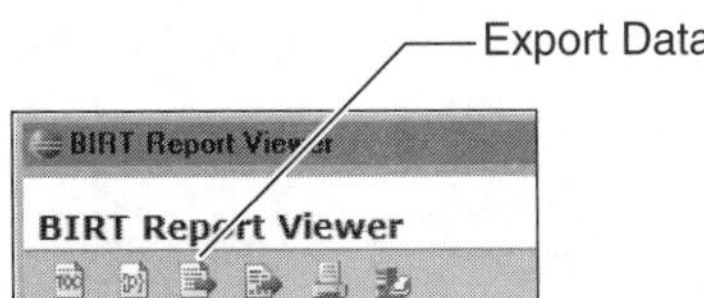

Figure 21-1 BIRT Web Viewer toolbar

The user can select the data columns for the export, the export format, the data encoding, and other properties using Export Data, as shown in Figure 21-2.

A data extraction extension adds a plug-in to the BIRT Report Engine framework by implementing the extension point, org.eclipse.birt.report

.engine.dataExtraction. The XML schema file, org.eclipse.birt.report.engine /schema/dataExtraction.exsd, describes this extension point.

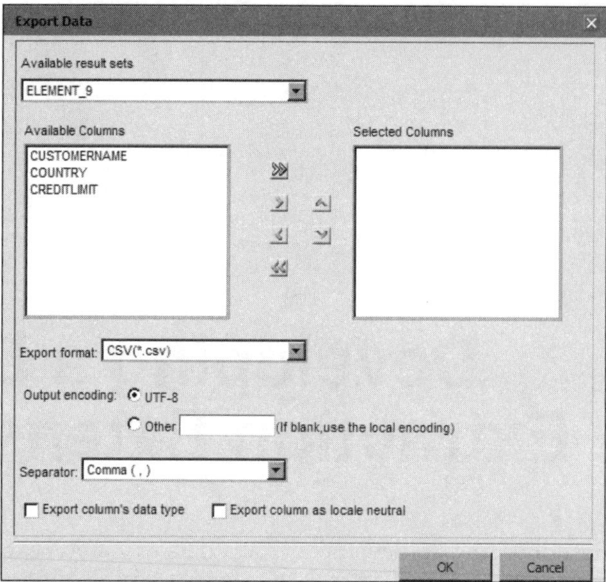

Figure 21-2 Export Data menu

The data extraction extension point enables support for new output formats in the presentation engine. The BIRT plug-in registry uses this extension point to discover all supported output formats specified for the report engine environment. The Export Data menu lists the available formats in the Export format list.

The XML data extraction extension in this chapter provides an example of how to create a data extraction extension.

You can download the source code for the XML data extraction extension example at http://www.actuate.com/birt/contributions. For reference documentation, see the BIRT Report Engine API Javadoc in Eclipse Help for the org.eclipse.birt.report.engine.dataextraction and org.eclipse.birt.report .engine.content packages.

Developing an XML data extraction extension

The sample XML data extraction extension is a plug-in that can export BIRT report data in XML format. Typically, report developers render BIRT report data to XML to enable sharing data with another application. The XML data extraction extension extends the functionality defined by the org.eclipse.birt .report.engine.dataExtraction package, which is part of the org.eclipse.birt

.report.engine.dataextraction plug-in. In the course of developing the XML data extraction extension, you perform the following tasks:

- Create an XML data extraction extension project in the Eclipse PDE
- Define the dependencies
- Declare the plug-in extension point
- Implement the plug-in interfaces
- Test the extension

Creating an XML data extraction plug-in project

Create a new plug-in project for the XML data extraction extension using the Eclipse PDE.

How to create the XML data extraction plug-in project

1 From the Eclipse PDE menu, choose File➛New➛Project. New Project appears.

2 In New Project, select Plug-in Project. Choose Next. New Plug-in Project appears.

3 In Plug-in Project, modify the settings, as shown in Table 21-1.

Table 21-1 Settings for the XML Data Extraction Plug-in Project

Section	Option	Value
Plug-in Project	Project name	org.eclipse.birt.report .engine.dataextraction .xml
	Use default location	Selected
	Location	Not available when you select Use default location
Project Settings	Create a Java project	Selected
	Source folder	src
	Output folder	bin
Target Platform	Eclipse version	3.6
	OSGi framework	Not selected
Working sets	Add project to working sets	Not selected

Plug-in Project appears as shown in Figure 21-3. Choose Next. Plug-in Content appears.

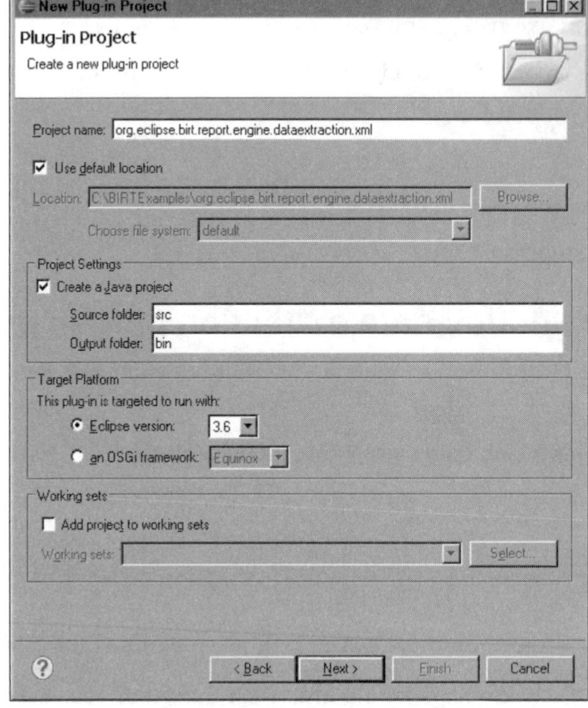

Figure 21-3 Specifying Plug-in Project settings

4 In Plug-in Content, modify the settings, as shown in Table 21-2.

Table 21-2 Settings for the XML Data Extraction Plug-in Content

Section	Option	Value
Plug-in Properties	ID	org.eclipse.birt.report .engine.dataextraction. xml
	Version	1.0.0
	Name	XML Data Extraction Plug-in
	Provider	yourCompany.com or leave blank
	Execution Environment	JavaSE-1.6
Options	Generate an activator, a Java class that controls the plug-in's life cycle	Not selected
	Activator	Not selected
	This plug-in will make contributions to the UI	Not selected

Table 21-2 Settings for the XML Data Extraction Plug-in Content

Section	Option	Value
Options	Enable API Analysis	Not selected
Rich Client Application	Would you like to create a rich client application?	No

Plug-in Content appears as shown in Figure 21-4. Choose Finish.

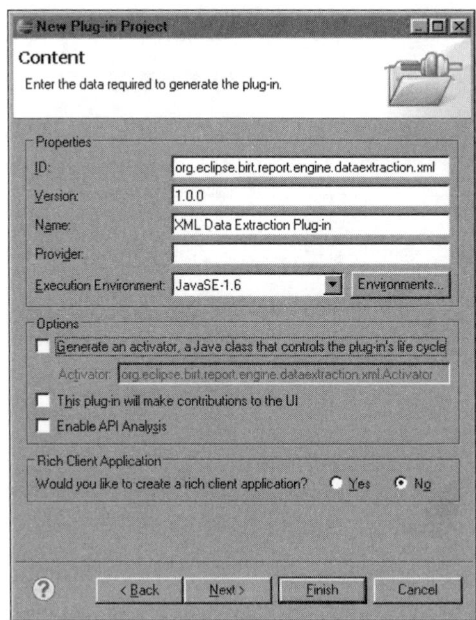

Figure 21-4 Specifying Plug-in Content settings

The XML data extraction extension project appears in the Eclipse PDE workbench, as shown in Figure 21-5.

Defining the dependencies for the XML data extraction extension

To compile and run the XML data extraction example, specify the list of plug-ins that must be available on the classpath of the extension.

How to specify the dependencies

1 On PDE Manifest Editor, choose Overview.

2 In Plug-in Content, choose Dependencies.

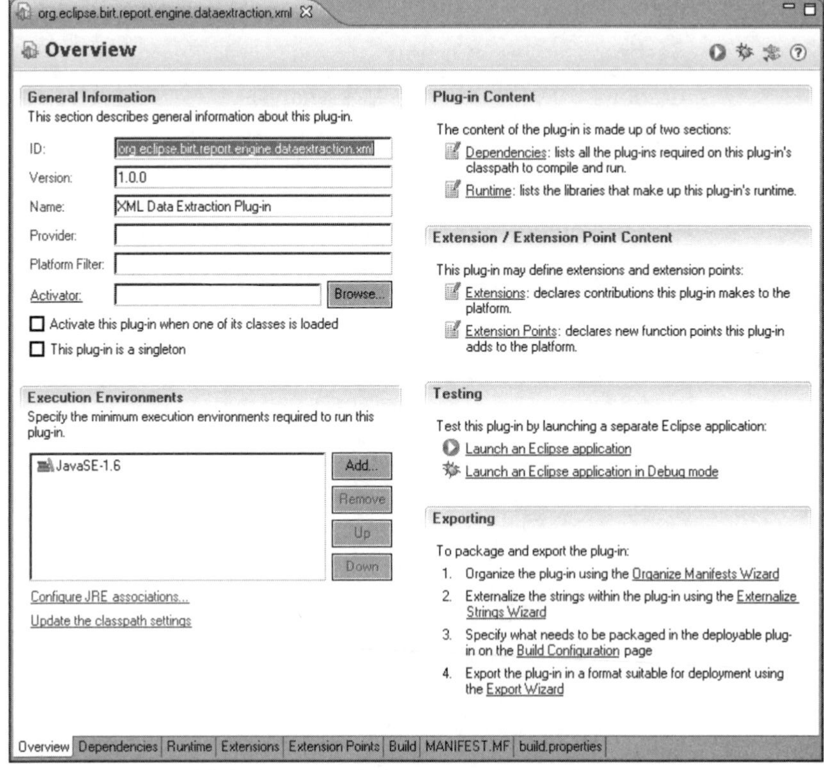

Figure 21-5 CSV report rendering extension project

3 In Plug-in Dependences, choose Add. Plug-in Selection appears.

1. In Plug-in Selection, hold down CTRL and select the org.eclipse .birt.report.engine following plug-ins:
   - org.eclipse.birt.report.engine.dataextraction
   - org.eclipse.birt.report.engine
   - com.ibm.icu
2. Choose OK. Dependencies appear as shown in Figure 21-6.

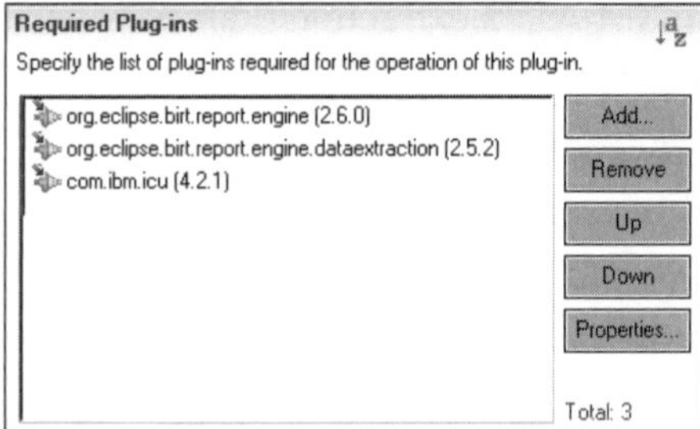

Figure 21-6 The Dependencies page

Declaring the data extraction extension point

In this step, specify the extension point required to implement the XML data extraction extension and add the extension element details. The extension point, org.eclipse.birt.report.engine.dataExtraction, sets the following properties for the extension point:

- ID
  Optional identifier of the extension instance
- Name
  Optional name of the extension instance

The extension point defines how to create a new data extraction extension to extract data in a custom way. The extension point defines the following extension element properties:

- id
  Optional identifier for the data extraction extension
- format
  Supported format of this data extraction extension
- class
  Java class, that implements the IDataExtractionExtension
- mimeType
  MIME type of the supported file output format, such as xml
- name
  Name of the extension
- isHidden
  Used to determine whether format is shown in UI

Use the Eclipse PDE to specify the extension point and extension element details.

How to specify the extension point

1 On PDE Manifest Editor, choose Extensions.

2 In All Extensions, choose Add. New Extension—Extension Point Selection appears.

3 In Available extension points, select the following extension point:

```
org.eclipse.birt.report.engine.dataExtraction
```

Extensions appears, as shown in Figure 21-7. Choose Finish.

All Extensions lists the extension point, org.eclipse.birt.report.engine .dataExtraction. Extension Details contains the list of extension details specified in the XML schema file, dataExtraction.exsd.

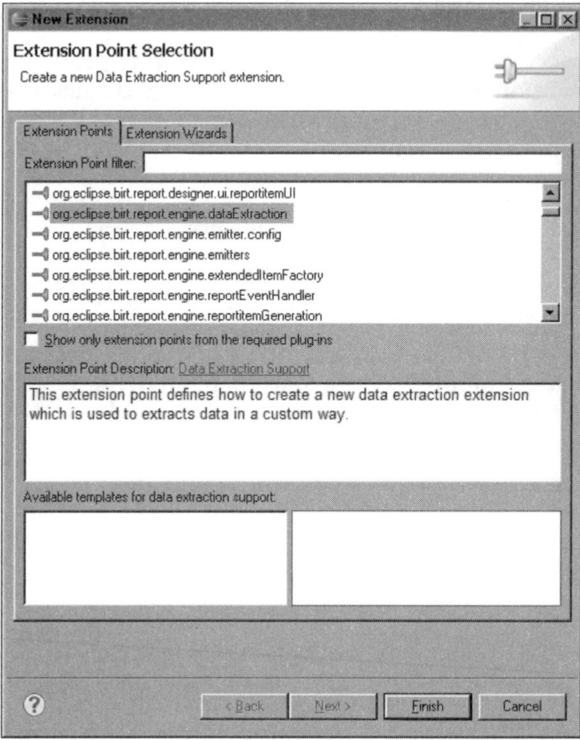

Figure 21-7 Selecting the data extraction extension point

4 In All Extensions, choose the extension point, org.eclipse.birt.report .engine.dataExtraction.The Extension Element Details appear.

5 In Extension Element Details, specify the properties for the data extraction extension element, as shown in Table 21-3.

Table 21-3 Property values for the data extraction extension element

Property	Value
id	org.eclipse.birt.report.engine.dataextraction.xml
format	xml
class	org.eclipse.birt.report.engine.dataextraction.xml .XMLDataExtractionImpl
mimeType	xml
name	XML
isHidden	false

Extension Element Details appears as shown in Figure 21-8. The PDE Manifest Editor automatically updates plugin.xml.

Extension Element Details

Set the properties of "dataExtraction". Required fields are denoted by "*".

id*:	com.eclipse.birt.report.engine.dataextraction.xml
format*:	xml
class*:	com.eclipse.birt.report.engine.dataextraction.xml.XMLDataExtractionIm
mimeType*:	xml
name*:	XML
isHidden:	false

Figure 21-8 Property values for the emitter extension

Understanding the XML data extraction extension

The XML data extraction extension example described in this chapter illustrates how to create a plug-in extension that converts all or part of report data to XML format. The XML data extraction extension example exports only the data selected in the export data menu to an output file. The export data feature is available in the BIRT Web Viewer.

This extension example creates the XML output stream and sends the stream to the browser. Typically the browser shows a download message that prompts the user to select to view or save the XML output.

This behavior depends on the browser and how it is configured to work with XML MIME type files. If the user changes the MIME type in the plug-in's extension properties to text/plain, the browser displays the xml file instead of displaying a download message.

The following section provides a general description of the code a developer must write to complete the development of an XML data extraction extension.

Implementing the data extraction interfaces

The org.eclipse.birt.report.engine.api and org.eclipse.birt.report.engine .dataextraction plug-ins define the data extraction interfaces used to extract and format data to a specified format. The XML data extraction extension implements the following interfaces and classes:

- org.eclipse.birt.report.engine.extension.IDataExtractionExtension

  Defines three methods to initialize the resources, output extracted data, and release allocated resources during the data extraction process.

  The purpose of the output method is to process the metadata in the result set and format the output in the desired format. Extending the implementation class of the interface DataExtractionExtensionBase instead of the interface itself is a recommended best practice.

- org.eclipse.birt.report.engine.api.IExtractionResults

  Provides the API for retrieving metadata for the result set.

- org.eclipse.birt.report.engine.api.IDataExtractionOption
  Defines the basic properties of the data extraction and related get and set methods. Basic properties include elements such as output format, output file, and output stream.
- org.eclipse.birt.report.engine.dataextraction .ICommonDataExtractionOption
  Extends the IDataExtractionOption interface to define the basic properties and related get and set methods for a common data extraction plug-in. The XML data extraction extension uses this interface, since most of the properties defined for the common data extraction apply to the XML extraction as well.

  The implementation class for this interface is org.eclipse.birt.report.engine .dataextraction.impl.CommonDataExtractionImpl. The class provides utility methods that are initialized according to the data extraction options. The basic properties for the data extraction option are:

  - Output locale
  - Output timezone
  - Output encoding, such as UTF-8, UTF-16LE, or ISO-8859-1
  - Output date format
  - Selected columns for export
  - Indicator of whether to export the columns data type
  - Indicator of whether to export the locale neutral format value
  - User-defined parameters

Understanding the XML document format

The implementation package for the XML data extraction extension, org.eclipse.birt.report.engine.dataextraction.xml, contains only the class XMLDataExtractionImpl.java.

The XMLDataExtractionImpl extends org.eclipse.birt.report.engine .dataextraction.impl.CommonDataExtractionImpl class and implements private methods that create an XML document.

The XML document schema contains the following elements:

- <Report>
  <Report> encloses the other elements of the XML document
- <Properties>
  Contents include information about the following report properties:
  - <ReportName>
    Full path and the report name

- <Locale>

  Report locale for display. If the locale is null, the default is locale en_US, displaying American English.

- <Encoding>

  Specifies an option in the Export Data user interface allowing users to select the encoding for exported report data. By default, the encoding is set to UTF-8. The text content of <Encoding> displays the selected encoding.

- <Parameters>

  This tag includes all parameters passed in the URL used to run the report in the Web Viewer. These parameters are referred as user parameters, which are different from report parameters. These items appear in separate <Parameter> tags. The parameter name is shown in a name attribute and the value is displayed as text in the <Parameter> node.

  The exact number and values of the parameters depend on the report design and the environments in which the report runs. The user parameter names are self-documenting.

  The following list displays the most common user parameters:

  - __asattachment
  - __cubememsize
  - __dpi
  - __exportdatatype
  - __exportencoding
  - __extractextension
  - __format
  - __locale
  - __localeneutral
  - __masterpage
  - __report
  - __resourceFolder
  - __resultsetname
  - __rtl
  - __selectedcolumn0
  - __selectedcolumn1
  - __selectedcolumn2

- __selectedcolumnnumber
- __sep=0
- __sessionId
- __svg
- __timezone

- <isLocaleNeutral>
  Users have the option to export data in a locale neutral format. Numbers are exported as neutral string values. Date format columns are exported in ISO8601 format, such as YYYY-MM-DD or YYYYMMDD for example.

- <Columns>
  Lists the columns in the data row. Column type is an attribute of <Column>. The type attribute is optional and appears in an XML document only if the user selects to export the data types in the Data Export dialog.
- <Row>
  Contains the data for a single data row. <Data> displays the column values.

Listing 21-1 shows an example of an exported XML document.

Listing 21-1 An exported XML document

```
<?xml version="1.0" encoding="UTF-8" standalone="no"?>
<Report>
   <!--Extract report data in XML format-->
   <!--Lists the report properties, such as name, locale,
   encoding, user parameters-->
   <Properties>
      <ReportName>C:\TEST\XMLDataExtraction\
   XMLDataExtraction.rptdesign</ReportName>
      <Locale>English</Locale>
      <isLocaleNeutral>true</isLocaleNeutral>
      <Encoding>UTF-8</Encoding>
      <Parameters>
         <Parameter name="__exportencoding">UTF-8</Parameter>
         <Parameter name="__svg">false</Parameter>
         <Parameter name=
            "__selectedcolumn1">COUNTRY</Parameter>
         <Parameter name=
            "__selectedcolumn2">CREDITLIMIT</Parameter>
         <Parameter name="__rtl">false</Parameter>
         <Parameter name=
            "__extractextension">com.eclipse.birt.report
            .engine.dataextraction.xml</Parameter>
```

```
        <Parameter name=
          "__report">C:\TEST\XMLDataExtraction\
          XMLDataExtraction.rptdesign</Parameter>
        <Parameter name="__masterpage">true</Parameter>
        <Parameter name=
          "__sessionId">20090923_110444_204</Parameter>
        <Parameter name="__format">html</Parameter>
        <Parameter name="__asattachment">true</Parameter>
        <Parameter name="__selectedcolumnnumber">3</Parameter>
        <Parameter name="__localeneutral">true</Parameter>
        <Parameter name="__sep">0</Parameter>
        <Parameter name=
          "__timezone">America/Los_Angeles</Parameter>
        <Parameter name="1069371071"/>
        <Parameter name="__locale">en_US</Parameter>
        <Parameter name="__cubememsize">10</Parameter>
        <Parameter name="__exportdatatype">true</Parameter>
        <Parameter name="__resultsetname">ELEMENT_9</Parameter>
        <Parameter name=
          "__selectedcolumn0">CUSTOMERNAME</Parameter>
        <Parameter name=
          "__resourceFolder">C:\TEST\XMLDataExtraction
        </Parameter>
        <Parameter name="__dpi">100</Parameter>
      </Parameters>
    </Properties>
    <Columns>
      <Column type="String">CUSTOMERNAME</Column>
      <Column type="String">COUNTRY</Column>
      <Column type="Float">CREDITLIMIT</Column>
    </Columns>
    <Row>
      <Data>Signal Gift Stores</Data>
      <Data>USA</Data>
      <Data>71800.0</Data>
    </Row>
    <Row>
      <Data>Mini Gifts Distributors Ltd.</Data>
      <Data>USA</Data>
      <Data>210500.0</Data>
    </Row>
    <Row>
      <Data>Mini Wheels Co.</Data>
      <Data>USA</Data>
      <Data>64600.0</Data>
    </Row>
</Report>
```

Understanding XMLDataExtractionImpl methods

XMLDataExtractionImpl extends CommonDataExtractionImpl.

The class creates private variables to store the output XML document, the output stream where the document streams as a string, and the properties of the report. These properties are exported in the <properties> tag of the output XML file.

The variable declarations are shown in Listing 21-2.

Listing 21-2 XML data extraction option variables

```
public class XMLDataExtractionImpl extends
   CommonDataExtractionImpl {
   public static final String PLUGIN_ID =
   "org.eclipse.birt.report.engine.dataextraction.xml";
   public static final String DEFAULT_ENCODING =
      Charset.defaultCharset( ).name( );
   private Document outDocument;
   private OutputStream outputStream;
   private String encoding;
   private String selectedColumnNames;
   private boolean isExportDataType;
   private boolean isLocaleNeutral;
   private Locale locale;
   private String reportName;
   private Map pUserParameters;
```

The XMLDataExtractionImpl class uses Java API defined in org.w3c.dom package for the XML processing. Table 21-4 describes the exported properties variables.

Table 21-4 Report properties variables

Property	Variable	Description
Report name	reportName	Name of BIRT report.
Locale	locale	Locale in which the report runs.
Encoding	encoding	Encoding used in report. User selects the value in the Export Data menu.
Selected column names	selectedColumnNames	The columns selected for export.
User parameters	pUserParameters	Parameters passed in the Web Viewer URL by the report engine.

Table 21-4 Report properties variables

Property	Variable	Description
Export the data types	isExportDataType	Variable that defines whether to export the data type of the columns to the output XML document. User selects the value in the Export Data menu.
Neutral local	isLocaleNeutral	Variable that defines whether to use a neutral local format for the data types columns. User defines the value in the Export Data menu.

The following XMLDataExtractionImpl methods set up and implement the data extraction:

- initialize( )

  Defined by the org.eclipse.birt.report.engine.extension .IDataExtractionExtension interface class. Initializes context and options objects and calls the private initXMLOptions( ) method to initialize local variables.

  Listing 21-3 initialize( )

```
public void initialize( IReportContext context,
   IDataExtractionOption options )
   throws BirtException
{
   super.initialize( context, options );
   initXMLOptions( options );
}
```

- initXMLOptions( )

  Called at the beginning of each data extraction to perform the following operations:

  - Creates the output stream that writes the text contents of the report to the XML file.
  - Obtains a reference to the CommonDataExtractionOption object xmlOption, containing accessor methods that get the IDataExtractionOption interface options for the plug-in.
  - Uses the data extraction API methods to initialize report property values, such as encoding, locale, iLocaleNeutral, selected columns, isExportDataType, user parameters, and report name.

Listing 21-4 initXMLOptions( )

```
private void initXMLOptions( IDataExtractionOption options ){
   outputStream = options.getOutputStream( );

   CommonDataExtractionOption xmlOption;
   if ( options instanceof CommonDataExtractionOption ){
      xmlOption = (CommonDataExtractionOption)options;
      }
      else {
         xmlOption =
            (CommonDataExtractionOption)
            new CommonDataExtractionOption(
               options.getOptions( ));
      }
      encoding = xmlOption.getEncoding( );
      if ( encoding == null || "".equals(encoding.trim( ))){
         encoding = null;
      }
      else {
         encoding = encoding.trim( );
      }
      if ( encoding == null ){
         encoding = DEFAULT_ENCODING;
      }
      isLocaleNeutral = xmlOption.isLocaleNeutralFormat( );
      locale = (Locale) xmlOption.getLocale( );
      if ( locale == null ){
         locale = Locale.getDefault( );
      }
      selectedColumnNames = xmlOption.getSelectedColumns( );
      isExportDataType = xmlOption.isExportDataType( );
      pUserParameters = xmlOption.getUserParameters( );
      getReportName( pUserParameters );
   }
```

- getReportName( )

  Called by the initXMLOptions( ) method to extract the report name and path from the user parameters.

Listing 21-5 getReportName( )

```
private void getReportName( Map pUserParameters ){
   Map uParameters = pUserParameters;
   \\Iterate over the keys, values in the map
   if ( uParameters != null ){
      java.util.Iterator it = null;
      for ( it =(java.util.Iterator)
            uParameters.keySet( ).iterator( );
            ((java.util.Iterator) it).hasNext( ); ) {
         Object key = it.next( );
```

```
            Object value = uParameters.get(key);
            if (key.toString( )
                  .equalsIgnoreCase("__report")){
               reportName = value.toString( );
            }
         }
      }
   }
```

- output( )

  Interface method called to format the output stream for the data extraction. Uses the Document Object Model (DOM) component API to create the output XML document.

  The data set result set is passed to the output( ) method through the IExtractionResults results input parameter. The code iterates through the result set to extract the data for only the selected columns. At the end the code converts the XML document to a string and writes the string to the output stream.

Listing 21-6 output( )

```
public void output( IExtractionResults results )
   throws BirtException{
   String[ ] columnNames = (String[ ]) selectedColumnNames;
   try {
      outDocument = createNewDocument ( );
   } catch (Exception e) {
      e.printStackTrace();
}
//create root element of output XML document
   Element rootElement =
      outDocument.createElement( "Report" );
   rootElement.appendChild( outDocument.createComment(
         "Extract report data in XML format" ));
   outDocument.appendChild( rootElement );

   Element pRow =
      outDocument.createElement( "Properties" );
   rootElement.appendChild( outDocument.createComment(
      "Lists the report properties, such as name, locale,
         encoding, user parameters" ));
   rootElement.appendChild( pRow );

   Element nodeReportName =
      outDocument.createElement( "ReportName" );
   nodeReportName.appendChild(
      outDocument.createTextNode( reportName ));
   pRow.appendChild( nodeReportName );

   Element nodeLocale =
      outDocument.createElement( "Locale" );
```

```
nodeLocale.appendChild(outDocument.createTextNode(
locale.getDisplayLanguage( ) ));
pRow.appendChild( nodeLocale );

Element nodeEncoding =
   outDocument.createElement( "Encoding" );
nodeEncoding.appendChild( outDocument
   .createTextNode( encoding ));
pRow.appendChild( nodeEncoding );

Element nodeParameters =
   outDocument.createElement( "Parameters" );
nodeParameters.appendChild(
   outDocument.createTextNode( userParameters ));
pRow.appendChild(nodeParameters);

try {
 // if selected columns are null or empty,
   returns all columns
      if ( columnNames == null || columnNames.length <= 0 ){
            int count =
            results.getResultMetaData( ).getColumnCount( );
            columnNames = new String[ count ];
            for ( int i = 0; i < count; i++ ){
               String colName =
               results.getResultMetaData( ).getColumnName(i);
                  columnNames[i] = colName;
            }
   }
   IDataIterator iData = null;
      if ( results != null ){
         iData = results.nextResultIterator( );
         if ( iData != null && columnNames.length > 0 ){
            String[ ] values =
                  new String[ columnNames.length ];
               while ( iData.next( ) ){
                        Element row =
                  outDocument.createElement( "Row" );
                  rootElement.appendChild( row );
                  for (int i = 0; i < columnNames.length;
                        i++){
                     String columnName =
                        results.getResultMetaData( )
                           .getColumnName( i );
                     values[i] = getStringValue(iData
                        .getValue( columnNames[i] ),
                        isLocaleNeutral, locale );
                     Element node =
                        outDocument.createElement(
                           columnName);
```

```
                        node.appendChild(
                        outDocument.createTextNode(
                           values[ i ] ));
                        row.appendChild( node );
                     }
                 }
              }
           }
        if ( encoding != null &&
           encoding.trim( ).length( ) > 0 ){
           outputStream.write(
              serialize( outDocument ).getBytes(
                 encoding.trim( )));
           }
        else{
           outputStream.write( serialize( outDocument )
              .getBytes( ));
        }
     }
     catch ( Exception e ){
     }
  }
```

- getColumnTypes( )
  Extracts the data types from the result set metadata. The column data types export to the XML document only when the user selects this option in the Export Data dialog.

Listing 21-7 getColumnTypes( )

```
private String[ ] getColumnTypes( String[ ] columnNames,
   IExtractionResults results ) throws BirtException {
      Map<String,Integer> typesMap =
         new HashMap<String,Integer>( );
      int count =
         results.getResultMetaData( ).getColumnCount( );
      for ( int i = 0; i < count; i++ ){
         String colName = results.getResultMetaData( )
            .getColumnName( i );
         int colType = results.getResultMetaData( )
            .getColumnType( i );
         typesMap.put( colName, colType );
      }
      int[ ] types = new int[ columnNames.length ];
      String[ ] typeNames = new String[ columnNames.length ];
      for ( int i = 0; i < columnNames.length; i++ ){
         types[i] = typesMap.get( columnNames[i] ).intValue( );
         typeNames[i] = DataType.getName( types[i] );
      }
   return typeNames;
}
```

- exportIntoString( )

  Converts XML document to a string in order to write to the output stream and send to the browser. The exportIntoString( ) method uses the javax .xml.transform package API to convert the XML document to a string.

Listing 21-8 exportIntoString( )

```
public String exportIntoString( ) throws Exception {
   try {
      ByteArrayOutputStream byteArrayOutputStream =
         new ByteArrayOutputStream( );
      TransformerFactory transformerFactory =
         TransformerFactory.newInstance( );
      Transformer transformer =
         transformerFactory.newTransformer( );
      Properties props = new Properties( );
      props.setProperty( OutputKeys.INDENT, "yes" );
      transformer.setOutputProperties( props );
      Source source = new DOMSource( outDocument );
      StreamResult streamResult =
         new StreamResult( byteArrayOutputStream );
      transformer.transform( source, streamResult );
      return byteArrayOutputStream.toString( encoding );
      //output is always in UTF-8
   } catch ( Exception e ) {
      System.out.println( "error in doExportIntoString" );
      throw e;
   }
}
```

Testing the XML data extraction plug-in

You can run the new XML data extraction plug-in directly in BIRT Report Designer or programmatically when you run and render a report using the Web Viewer. This section describes how to test the XML data extraction plug-in in BIRT Report Designer.

How to launch the XML data extraction plug-in

1. From the Eclipse SDK menu, choose Run—Run Configurations. In Run Configurations, right-click Eclipse Application. Choose New.
2. Create a configuration to launch an Eclipse application by performing the following tasks:
   1. In Name, type:

      `XMLDataExtraction`
   2. On Main, in Location, type:

      `C:\Test`

3 Run Configurations appears as shown in Figure 21-9.

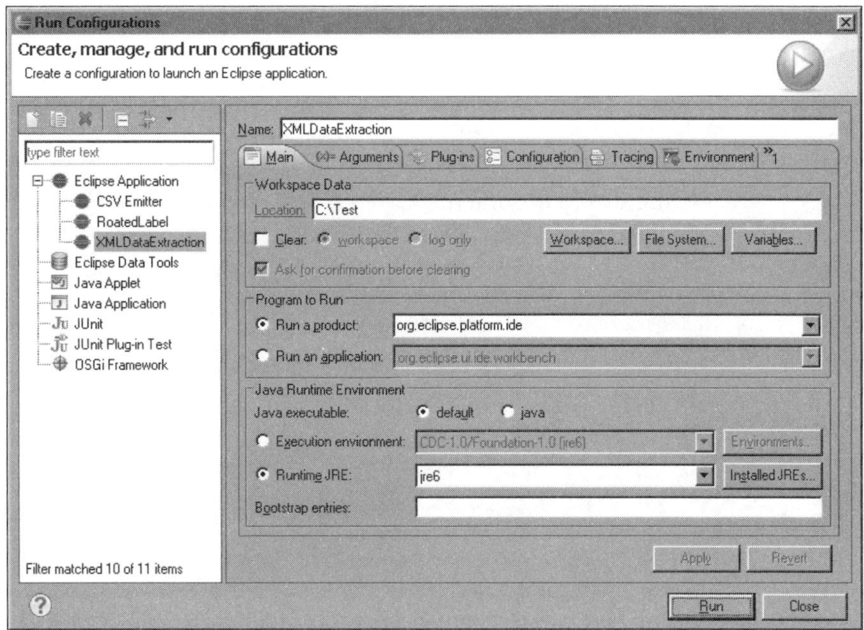

Figure 21-9 Creating the XMLDataExtraction run configuration

4 Choose the Plug-ins tab to select the list of plug-ins to launch with the Run configuration.

5 In Launch with, choose:

```
plug-ins selected below only
```

from the drop-down list, as shown in Figure 21-10.

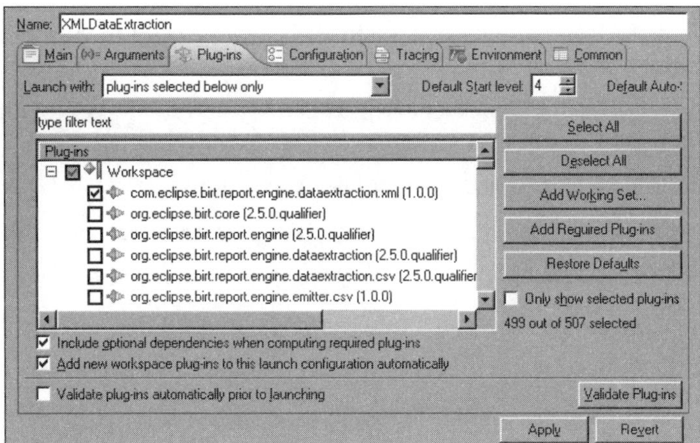

Figure 21-10 Selecting the XMLDataExtraction plug-in

In some configurations, you can get an error message related to insufficient memory. The error is:

```
java.lang.OutOfMemoryError: PermGen space
```

To fix the error, add the following VM argument in the run configuration:

```
-XX:MaxPermSize=256M
```

In Run Configuration, choose Arguments and enter the MaxPermSize setting in VM arguments to avoid this problem, as shown in Figure 21-11.

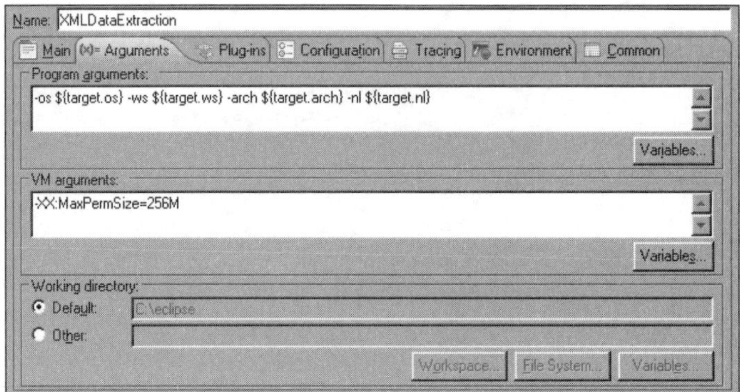

Figure 21-11 Setting the VM argument

6 Choose Run to launch the run-time Eclipse workbench. A new instance of Eclipse opens up.

How to extract data from a BIRT report to XML format

The BIRT Report Designer discovers the new XML data extraction plug-in and displays the new XML format in the Export Data menu.

1 In the new Eclipse workbench, open the BIRT Report Design perspective.

2 In BIRT Report Designer perspective, open a BIRT report.

3 Choose Run➛View Report➛In Web Viewer from the main menu, as shown in Figure 21-12.

4 In the Web Viewer, select Export Data from the viewer toolbar, as shown in Figure 21-13.

5 In Export Data, choose the following options:

    1 In Available Columns, press <CTRL> and select the columns to export.

    2 Choose the arrow to move the columns to the Selected Columns list.

    Use the double arrow to select and move all the columns in the dataset.

    Use the up and down arrows to change the order in which the columns appear in the output file.

    3 In the Export format, select XML(*.xml) from the list.

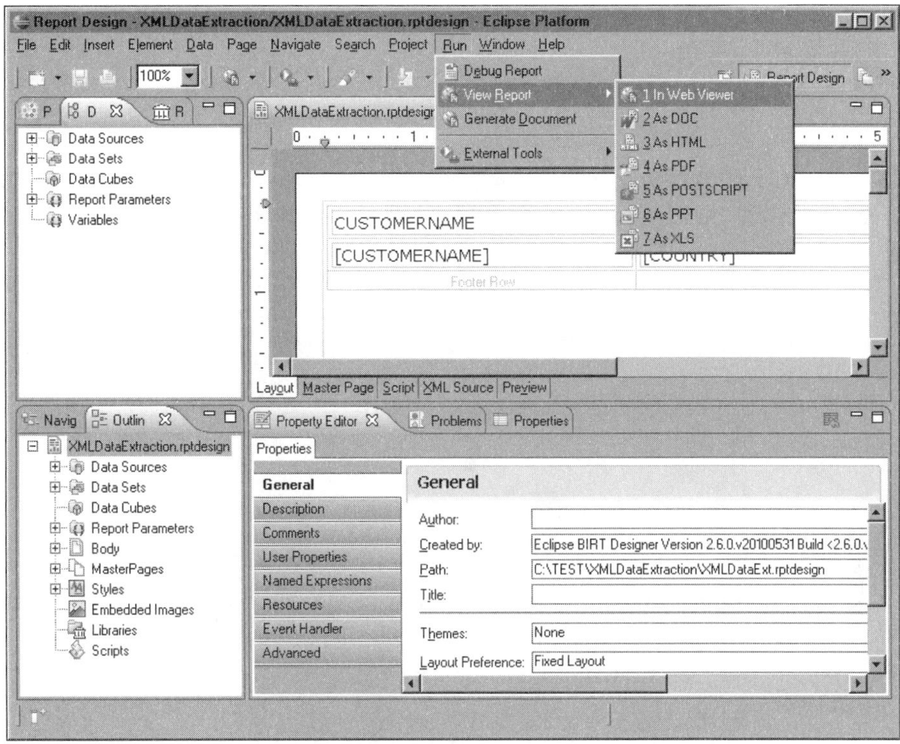

Figure 21-12 Previewing a report in CSV format

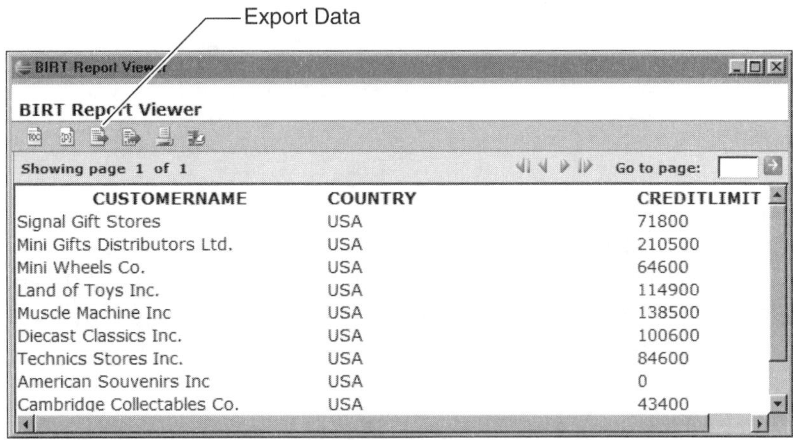

Figure 21-13 Selecting the Export Data feature

4 Select the Export column data type and Export column as locale neutral, as shown in Figure 21-14.

5 Choose OK to start the export.

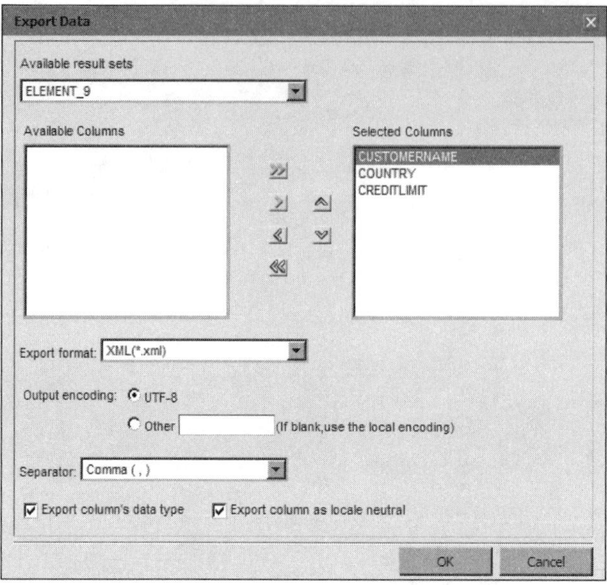

Figure 21-14 Setting the Export Data properties

6 File Downloads opens with the message, Do you want to open or save this file?, as shown in Figure 21-15.

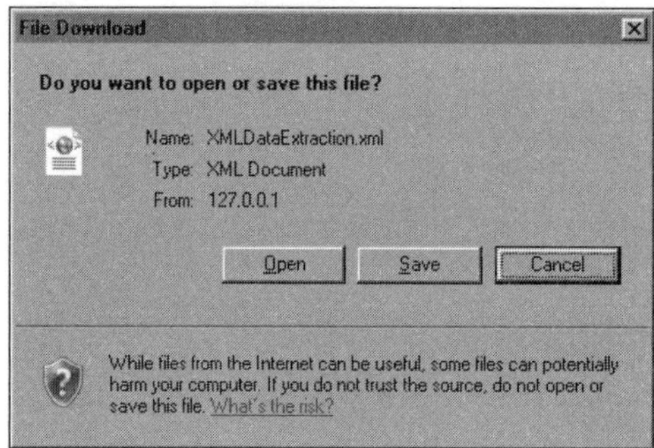

Figure 21-15 Saving the exported XML data

7 Choose Save and select the location to save the XML report or Open to view the report in the browser.

8 Open a saved report using any editor. Listing 21-9 shows a partial listing of exported data from an example report.

Listing 21-9 Partial listing of exported report data

```
<?xml version="1.0" encoding="UTF-8" standalone="no"?>
<Report>
<!--Extract report data in XML format-->
<!--Lists the report properties, such as name, locale,
   encoding, user parameters-->
```

```
<Properties>
<ReportName>C:\TEST\XMLDataExtraction\
  XMLDataExtraction.rptdesign</ReportName>
<Locale>English</Locale>
<isLocaleNeutral>true</isLocaleNeutral>
<Encoding>UTF-8</Encoding>
<Parameters>
<Parameter name="__exportencoding">UTF-8</Parameter>
<Parameter name="__svg">false</Parameter>
<Parameter name="__selectedcolumn1">COUNTRY</Parameter>
<Parameter name="__selectedcolumn2">CREDITLIMIT</Parameter>
<Parameter name="__rtl">false</Parameter>
<Parameter
  name="__extractextension">com.eclipse.birt.report.engine
  .dataextraction.xml</Parameter>
<Parameter name="__report">C:\TEST\XMLDataExtraction\
  XMLDataExtraction.rptdesign</Parameter>
<Parameter name="__masterpage">true</Parameter>
<Parameter name="__sessionId">20090923_110444_204</Parameter>
<Parameter name="__format">html</Parameter>
<Parameter name="__asattachment">true</Parameter>
<Parameter name="__selectedcolumnnumber">3</Parameter>
<Parameter name="__localeneutral">true</Parameter>
<Parameter name="__sep">0</Parameter>
<Parameter name="__timezone">America/Los_Angeles</Parameter>
<Parameter name="1069371071"/>
<Parameter name="__locale">en_US</Parameter>
<Parameter name="__cubememsize">10</Parameter>
<Parameter name="__exportdatatype">true</Parameter>
<Parameter name="__resultsetname">ELEMENT_9</Parameter>
<Parameter name="__selectedcolumn0">CUSTOMERNAME</Parameter>
<Parameter name="__resourceFolder">C:\TEST\XMLDataExtraction
  </Parameter>
<Parameter name="__dpi">100</Parameter>
</Parameters>
</Properties>
<Columns>
<Column type="String">CUSTOMERNAME</Column>
<Column type="String">COUNTRY</Column>
<Column type="Float">CREDITLIMIT</Column>
</Columns>
<Row>
<Data>Signal Gift Stores</Data>
<Data>USA</Data>
<Data>71800.0</Data>
</Row>
<Row>
<Data>Mini Gifts Distributors Ltd.</Data>
<Data>USA</Data>
```

```
<Data>210500.0</Data>
</Row>
<Row>
<Data>Mini Wheels Co.</Data>
<Data>USA</Data>
<Data>64600.0</Data>
</Row>
...
</Report>
```

About the report design XML code

The XML file for the report design, new_report.rpdesign, contains the following source code settings, as specified in the report design:

- Data sources, including the ODA plug-in extension ID, driver class, URL, and user
- Data sets, including the ODA JDBC plug-in extension ID, result set properties, and query text
- Page setup, including the page footer
- Body, containing the table structure and properties for the bound data columns, including the header, footer, and detail rows

The report design example specifies a data source that connects to org.eclipse.birt.report.data.oda.sampledb, the BIRT Classic Models sample database. Listing 21-10 shows the XML source code for the report design used to test the XML data extraction example.

Listing 21-10 The report design XML code

```
<?xml version="1.0" encoding="UTF-8"?>
<report xmlns="http://www.eclipse.org/birt/2005/design"
   version="3.2.21" id="1">
   <property name="createdBy">Eclipse BIRT Designer Version
      2.6.0.v20100531 Build &lt;2.6.0.v20100609-0613>
   </property>
   <property name="units">in</property>
   <property name=
      "iconFile">/templates/blank_report.gif</property>
   <property name="bidiLayoutOrientation">ltr</property>
   <parameters>
      scalar-parameter name="country" id="31">
         <property name="valueType">dynamic</property>
         <property name="dataSetName">Data Set</property>
         <expression name=
            "valueExpr">dataSetRow["COUNTRY"]</expression>
         <expression name=
            "labelExpr">dataSetRow["COUNTRY"]</expression>
```

```
<expression name=
   "sortByColumn">dataSetRow["COUNTRY"]</expression>
<property name="sortDirection">asc</property>
<property name="dataType">string</property>
<simple-property-list name="defaultValue">
   <value type="constant">USA</value>
</simple-property-list>
<property name="paramType">simple</property>
<property name="controlType">list-box</property>
<property name="mustMatch">true</property>
<property name="fixedOrder">false</property>
<property name="distinct">true</property>
   <structure name="format">
      <property name="category">Unformatted</property>
   </structure>
</scalar-parameter>
</parameters>
<data-sources>
   <oda-data-source extensionID=
      "org.eclipse.birt.report.data.oda.jdbc"
         name="Data Source" id="7">
      <property name="odaDriverClass">
         org.eclipse.birt.report.data.oda.sampledb.Driver
      </property>
      <property name="odaURL">jdbc:classicmodels:sampledb
      </property>
      <property name="odaUser">ClassicModels</property>
   </oda-data-source>
</data-sources>
<data-sets>
   <oda-data-set
      extensionID=
         "org.eclipse.birt.report.data.oda.jdbc
            .JdbcSelectDataSet" name="Data Set" id="8">
      <list-property name="columnHints">
         <structure>
            <property name="columnName">CUSTOMERNAME
            </property>
            <property name="displayName">CUSTOMERNAME
            </property>
            </structure>
            <structure>
            <property name="columnName">COUNTRY</property>
            <property name="displayName">COUNTRY</property>
         </structure>
         <structure>
            <property name="columnName">CREDITLIMIT
            </property>
```

```
        <property name="displayName">CREDITLIMIT
        </property>
      </structure>
    </list-property>
    <list-property name="parameters">
      <structure>
        <property name="name">param_1</property>
        <property name="paramName">country</property>
        <property name="nativeName"></property>
        <property name="dataType">string</property>
        <property name="nativeDataType">12</property>
        <property name="position">1</property>
        <property name="isOptional">true</property>
        <property name="allowNull">true</property>
        <property name="isInput">true</property>
        <property name="isOutput">false</property>
      </structure>
    </list-property>
    <structure name="cachedMetaData">
      <list-property name="resultSet">
        <structure>
          <property name="position">1</property>
          <property name="dataType">string</property>
        </structure>
        <structure>
          <property name="position">2</property>
          <property name="name">COUNTRY</property>
          <property name="dataType">string</property>
        </structure>
        <structure>
          <property name="position">3</property>
          <property name="name">CREDITLIMIT</property>
          <property name="dataType">float</property>
        </structure>
      </list-property>
    </structure>
      <property name="dataSource">Data Source</property>
        <list-property name="resultSet">
          <structure>
            <property name="position">1</property>
            <property name="name">CUSTOMERNAME
              </property>
            <property name="nativeName">CUSTOMERNAME
              </property>
            <property name="dataType">string</property>
            <property name="nativeDataType">12</property>
          </structure>
```

```
      <structure>
         <property name="position">2</property>
         <property name="name">COUNTRY</property>
         <property name="nativeName">COUNTRY</property>
         <property name="dataType">string</property>
         <property name="nativeDataType">12</property>
      </structure>
      <structure>
         <property name="position">3</property>
         <property name="name">CREDITLIMIT</property>
         <property name="nativeName">CREDITLIMIT
            </property>
         <property name="dataType">float</property>
         <property name="nativeDataType">8</property>
      </structure>
   </list-property>
<xml-property name="queryText">
   <![CDATA[select CLASSICMODELS.CUSTOMERS
            .CUSTOMERNAME,
            CLASSICMODELS.CUSTOMERS.COUNTRY,
            CLASSICMODELS.CUSTOMERS.CREDITLIMIT
         from CLASSICMODELS.CUSTOMERS
         where country=?]]>
</xml-property>
<xml-property name="designerValues">
   <![CDATA[<?xml version="1.0" encoding="UTF-8"?>
   <model:DesignValues xmlns:design=
        "http://www.eclipse.org/datatools/
        connectivity/oda/design" xmlns:model=
        "http://www.eclipse.org/birt/report/model/
        adapter/odaModel">
      <Version>1.0</Version>
   <design:DataSetParameters>
      <design:parameterDefinitions>
         <design:inOutMode>In</design:inOutMode>
         <design:attributes>
            <design:name></design:name>
            <design:position>1</design:position>
            <design:nativeDataTypeCode>12
               </design:nativeDataTypeCode>
            <design:precision>50</design:precision>
            <design:scale>0</design:scale>
            <design:nullability>Nullable
               </design:nullability>
         </design:attributes>
         <design:inputAttributes>
            <design:elementAttributes>
            <design:optional>true</design:optional>
            </design:elementAttributes>
         </design:inputAttributes>
```

```
      </design:parameterDefinitions>
    </design:DataSetParameters>
    <design:ResultSets derivedMetaData="true">
      <design:resultSetDefinitions>
      <design:resultSetColumns>
        <design:resultColumnDefinitions>
          <design:attributes>
            <design:name>CUSTOMERNAME</design:name>
            <design:position>1</design:position>
            <design:nativeDataTypeCode>12
              </design:nativeDataTypeCode>
            <design:precision>50</design:precision>
            <design:scale>0</design:scale>
            <design:nullability>Nullable
              </design:nullability>
            <design:uiHints>
              <design:displayName>CUSTOMERNAME
                  </design:displayName>
            </design:uiHints>
          </design:attributes>
          <design:usageHints>
            <design:label>CUSTOMERNAME</design:label>
            <design:formattingHints>
              <design:displaySize>50
                </design:displaySize>
            </design:formattingHints>
          </design:usageHints>
        </design:resultColumnDefinitions>
        <design:resultColumnDefinitions>
          <design:attributes>
            <design:name>COUNTRY</design:name>
            <design:position>2</design:position>
            <design:nativeDataTypeCode>12
              </design:nativeDataTypeCode>
            <design:precision>50</design:precision>
            <design:scale>0</design:scale>
            <design:nullability>Nullable
              </design:nullability>
            <design:uiHints>
              <design:displayName>COUNTRY
                </design:displayName>
            </design:uiHints>
          </design:attributes>
          <design:usageHints>
            <design:label>COUNTRY</design:label>
            <design:formattingHints>
              <design:displaySize>50
                </design:displaySize>
            </design:formattingHints>
```

```
                      </design:usageHints>
                    </design:resultColumnDefinitions>
                    <design:resultColumnDefinitions>
                      <design:attributes>
                        <design:name>CREDITLIMIT</design:name>
                        <design:position>3</design:position>
                        <design:nativeDataTypeCode>8
                          </design:nativeDataTypeCode>
                         <design:precision>15</design:precision>
                        <design:scale>0</design:scale>
                        <design:nullability>Nullable
                          </design:nullability>
                        <design:uiHints>
                            <design:displayName>CREDITLIMIT
                              </design:displayName>
                        </design:uiHints>
                      </design:attributes>
                      <design:usageHints>
                        <design:label>CREDITLIMIT</design:label>
                        <design:formattingHints>
                          <design:displaySize>22
                            </design:displaySize>
                        </design:formattingHints>
                      </design:usageHints>
                    </design:resultColumnDefinitions>
                  </design:resultSetColumns>
                </design:resultSetDefinitions>
              </design:ResultSets>
            </model:DesignValues>]]></xml-property>
          </oda-data-set>
        </data-sets>
        <styles>
          <style name="report" id="4">
            <property name="fontFamily">"Verdana"</property>
            <property name="fontSize">10pt</property>
          </style>
          <style name="crosstab-cell" id="5">
            <property name="borderBottomColor">#CCCCCC</property>
            <property name="borderBottomStyle">solid</property>
            <property name="borderBottomWidth">1pt</property>
            <property name="borderLeftColor">#CCCCCC</property>
            <property name="borderLeftStyle">solid</property>
            <property name="borderLeftWidth">1pt</property>
            <property name="borderRightColor">#CCCCCC</property>
            <property name="borderRightStyle">solid</property>
            <property name="borderRightWidth">1pt</property>
            <property name="borderTopColor">#CCCCCC</property>
            <property name="borderTopStyle">solid</property>
```

```
         <property name="borderTopWidth">1pt</property>
      </style>
      <style name="crosstab" id="6">
         <property name="borderBottomColor">#CCCCCC</property>
         <property name="borderBottomStyle">solid</property>
         <property name="borderBottomWidth">1pt</property>
         <property name="borderLeftColor">#CCCCCC</property>
         <property name="borderLeftStyle">solid</property>
         <property name="borderLeftWidth">1pt</property>
         <property name="borderRightColor">#CCCCCC</property>
         <property name="borderRightStyle">solid</property>
         <property name="borderRightWidth">1pt</property>
         <property name="borderTopColor">#CCCCCC</property>
         <property name="borderTopStyle">solid</property>
         <property name="borderTopWidth">1pt</property>
      </style>
   </styles>
   <page-setup>
      <simple-master-page name="Simple MasterPage" id="2">
         <page-footer>
            <text id="3">
            <property name="contentType">html</property>
               <text-property name="content">
                  <![CDATA[<value-of>new Date()</value-of>]]>
               </text-property>
            </text>
         </page-footer>
      </simple-master-page>
   </page-setup>
   <body>
      <table id="9">
         <property name="dataSet">Data Set</property>
         <list-property name="boundDataColumns">
            <structure>
               <property name="name">CUSTOMERNAME</property>
               <property name="displayName">CUSTOMERNAME
                  </property>
               <expression
                  name="expression">dataSetRow["CUSTOMERNAME"]
                     </expression>
               <property name="dataType">string</property>
            </structure>
            <structure>
               <property name="name">COUNTRY</property>
               <property name="displayName">COUNTRY</property>
               <expression
                  name="expression">dataSetRow["COUNTRY"]
                  </expression>
```

```
            <property name="dataType">string</property>
         </structure>
         <structure>
            <property name="name">CREDITLIMIT</property>
            <property name="displayName">CREDITLIMIT
               </property>
            <expression name="expression">
               dataSetRow["CREDITLIMIT"]</expression>
            <property name="dataType">float</property>
         </structure>
      </list-property>
      <column id="28"/>
      <column id="29"/>
      <column id="30"/>
         <header>
            <row id="10">
               <cell id="11">
                  <label id="12">
                     <text-property name="text">CUSTOMERNAME
                        </text-property>
                  </label>
               </cell>
               <cell id="13">
                  <label id="14">
                     <text-property name="text">COUNTRY
                        </text-property>
                  </label>
               </cell>
               <cell id="15">
                  <label id="16">
                     <text-property name="text">CREDITLIMIT
                        </text-property>
                  </label>
               </cell>
            </row>
         </header>
         <detail>
            <row id="17">
               <cell id="18">
                  <data id="19">
                     <property
                           name="resultSetColumn">CUSTOMERNAME
                     </property>
                  </data>
               </cell>
               <cell id="20">
                  <data id="21">
                     <property name="resultSetColumn">COUNTRY
                        </property>
                  </data>
```

```
                    </cell>
                    <cell id="22">
                       <data id="23">
                          <property
                             name="resultSetColumn">CREDITLIMIT
                          </property>
                       </data>
                    </cell>
                 </row>
              </detail>
              <footer>
                 <row id="24">
                    <cell id="25"/>
                    <cell id="26"/>
                    <cell id="27"/>
                 </row>
              </footer>
        </table>
     </body>
  </report>
```

Chapter

22

Developing a Fragment

The BIRT Report Engine environment supports plug-in fragments. A plug-in fragment is a separately loaded package that adds functionality to an existing plug-in, such as a specific language translation in a National Language Support (NLS) localization application.

The Eclipse Babel Project provides language packs that support the translation of strings in the Eclipse user interface. For BIRT, the Babel Project provides an NLS plug-in for most major languages. For more information about the Babel Project and to download language packs, navigate to:

`http://babel.eclipse.org/babel/`

The example in this chapter creates a Java resource bundle that adds translations to the messages defined in the messages.properties files for the org.eclipse.birt.report.viewer plug-in.

Understanding a fragment

A fragment does not define its own plugin.xml file or a plug-in class. The related plug-in controls all processing. A fragment loads along the classpath of the related plug-in, providing access to all classes in the plug-in package.

A fragment inherits all the resources specified in the requires element of the plug-in manifest. A fragment can also specify additional libraries, extensions, and other resources.

The fragment's optional manifest file, fragment.xml, contains the attributes that associate the fragment with the plug-in. A fragment.xml file can specify the following tags and associated attributes:

- <fragment>

Specifies the following attributes:

- name
  Display name of the extension.
- id
  Unique identifier for the fragment extension.
- plugin-id
  The plug-in associated with the fragment.
- version
  Version of the fragment extension, such as 2.6.0.
- type
  Specification of a code or a resource file contained in the fragment. The default is code.

- <runtime>
  Specifies a list of one or more libraries required by the fragment runtime. The name attribute for the <library> element can specify an archive, directory, or substitution variable.

Developing the sample fragment

The fragment example in this chapter creates an XML specification that loads additional messages.properties files that contain the translations of messages in the resource bundle for the org.eclipse.birt.report.viewer plug-in. This section describes the steps required to implement the sample org.eclipse.birt .report.viewers.nl1 project, using the Eclipse Plug-in Development Environment (PDE).

To implement the sample fragment, perform the following tasks:

- Configure the fragment project.
  To build the sample fragment plug-in project, follow the instructions in this chapter.
- Add the translations contained in the message properties files to the org.eclipse.birt.report.resource bundle.
  The name of each message properties file uses the following pattern:
  ```
  Messages_<lower-case language symbol>.properties
  ```
  For example, Messages_es.properties indicates the message properties file for Spanish (Español).
- Build, deploy, and test the fragment.

Build the fragment and export the fragment package from your workspace to the eclipse\plugins folder. Test the fragment by starting Eclipse using a specific language setting and creating a report in the BIRT report designer.

Creating a fragment project

You can create the fragment project for the NL1 fragment sample in the PDE.

How to create the fragment project

1 In the Eclipse PDE, choose File➛New➛Project.

2 In New Project, in Select a wizard, expand Plug-in Development and select Fragment Project. Choose Next. New Fragment Project appears.

3 In Fragment Project modify the settings, as shown in Table 22-1.

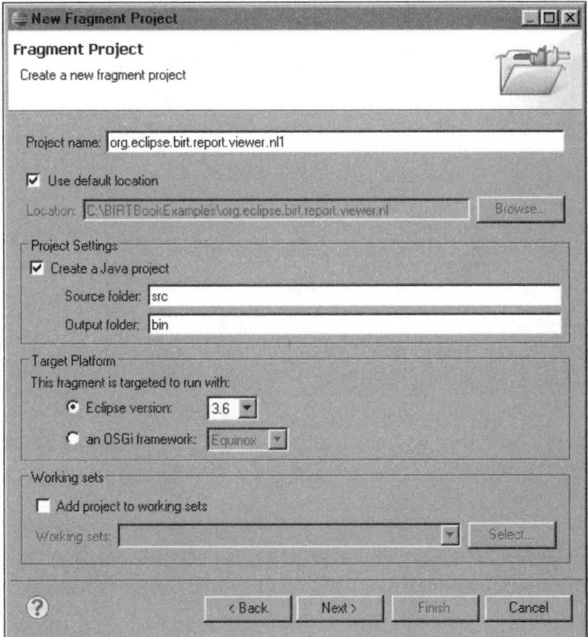

Figure 22-1 Fragment Project settings

Fragment Project appears, as shown in Figure 22-1. Choose Next.

Table 22-1 Settings for Fragment Project fields

Section	Option	Value
Fragment Project	Project name	org.eclipse.birt.report.viewer.nl1

(continues)

Table 22-1 Settings for Fragment Project fields (continued)

Section	Option	Value
Fragment Project	Use default location	Selected
	Location	Not available when you select Use default location.
Project Settings	Create a Java project	Selected
	Source folder	src
	Output folder	bin
Target Platform	Eclipse version	3.6
	OSGi framework	Deselected

4 In Fragment Content, modify the settings as shown in Table 22-2.

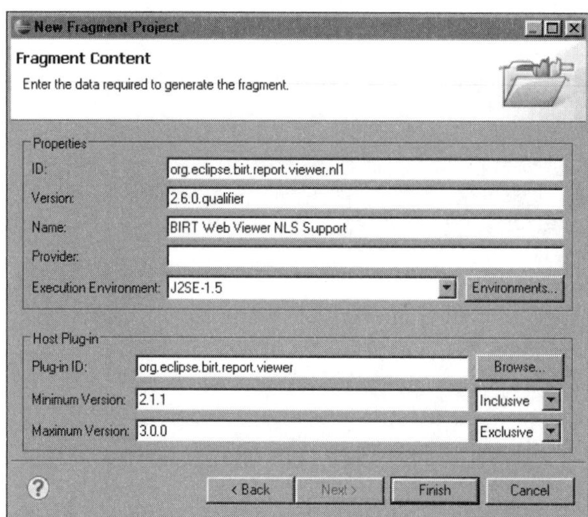

Figure 22-2 Fragment Content settings

Fragment Content appears, as shown in Figure 22-2. Choose Finish.

Table 22-2 Fragment Content settings

Section	Option	Value
Fragment Properties	Fragment ID	org.eclipse.birt.report .viewer.nl1
	Fragment Version	2.6.0.qualifier

Table 22-2 Fragment Content settings

Section	Option	Value
Fragment Properties	Fragment Name	BIRT Web Viewer NLS Support
	Fragment Provider	yourCompany.com or leave blank
	Execution Environment	JavaSE-1.6
Host plug-in	Plug-in ID	org.eclipse.birt.report.viewer
	Minimum Version	2.1.1 Inclusive
	Maximum Version	3.0.0 Exclusive

The fragment project appears in the Eclipse PDE Workbench, as shown in Figure 22-3.

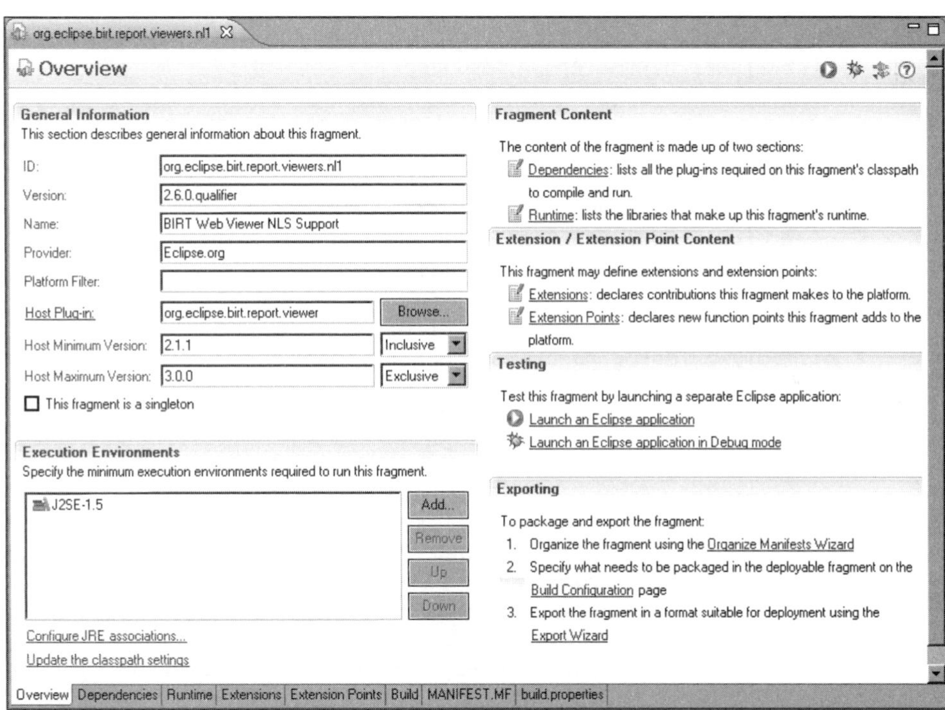

Figure 22-3 Fragment project in the Eclipse PDE Workbench

Understanding the sample fragment

The fragment provides the functionality required at run-time to display the messages seen in the BIRT Report Viewer in alternative languages. The fragment implements NLS messages.properties files in org.eclipse.birt.report.resource.

Listing 22-1 shows an excerpt from the Spanish language version of BIRT Report Viewer messages from the file, Messages_es.properties.

Listing 22-1 Contents of Messages_es.properties

```
##############################################################
birt.viewer.title=BIRT Report Viewer
birt.viewer.title.navigation=Navegación
birt.viewer.title.error=Error
birt.viewer.title.complete=Completado
birt.viewer.title.message=Mensaje

birt.viewer.parameter=Parámetro
birt.viewer.runreport=Ejecutar informe
birt.viewer.required=Los parámetros marcados con
   <FONT COLOR="red">*</FONT> son obligatorios.

birt.viewer.viewinpdf=Ver en PDF
birt.viewer.maximize=Ocultar parámetros de informe
birt.viewer.restore=Mostrar parámetros de informe

birt.viewer.error=Mensaje de error
birt.viewer.error.noparameter=No hay ningún parámetro para este
   informe.
birt.viewer.error.parameter.invalid=El parámetro"{0}" no es
   válido.
birt.viewer.error.noprinter=No se puede encontrar ninguna
   impresora disponible compatible con el formato postscript.
birt.viewer.error.unknownerror=Error desconocido.
birt.viewer.error.generatereportfirst=Se debe generar antes un
   documento de informe.
birt.viewer.error.parameterrequired=No se ha especificado el valor
   del parámetro necesario [{0}].
birt.viewer.error.parameternotallowblank=El parámetro "{0}" no
   puede estar en blanco.
birt.viewer.error.parameternotselected=Seleccione un valor para el
   parámetro"{0}".
birt.viewer.error.noviewingsession=La sesión de visualización no
   está disponible o ha caducado.
birt.viewer.error.viewingsessionexpired=La sesión de visualización
   ha caducado.
birt.viewer.error.viewingsessionlocked=La sesión de visualización
   está bloqueada y no se puede finalizar.
```

```
birt.viewer.error.viewingsessionmaxreached=Se ha alcanzado el
   máximo de sesiones de visualización.
birt.viewer.message.taskcanceled=La operación en proceso se ha
   cancelado.

#################################################################
# Toolbar
#################################################################
birt.viewer.toolbar.print=Imprimir informe como PDF
birt.viewer.toolbar.printserver=Imprimir informe en el servidor
birt.viewer.toolbar.toc=Mostrar tabla de contenido
birt.viewer.toolbar.parameter=Ejecutar informe
birt.viewer.toolbar.export=Exportar datos
birt.viewer.toolbar.font=Cambiar fuente
birt.viewer.toolbar.enableiv=Llamar a Interactive Viewer
birt.viewer.toolbar.exportreport=Exportar informe
...
```

Building, deploying, and testing a fragment

Build the fragment after generating and modifying the build.xml file to specify the conversion of .msg files from native to ASCII format as .properties files. Listing 22-2 shows the contents of the build.xml file with the NativeToAscii specification.

Listing 22-2 Contents of build.xml file

```
<?xml version="1.0" encoding="UTF-8"?>
   <project
      name="org.eclipse.birt.report.viewer.nl" default="Jar"
         basedir=".">
      <description>
         NL Fragment for org.eclipse.birt.report.viewer
      </description>
      <property file="META-INF/MANIFEST.MF" />
      <property name="dir.src" value="src" />
      <property name="dir.bin" value="bin" />
      <property name="nl.group" value="1" />
      <property name="module.name"
         value="org.eclipse.birt.report.viewer.nl" />
      <property name="jar.name"
         value=
            "${module.name}${nl.group}_${Bundle-Version}.jar" />
      <target name="Clean">
         <delete>
            <fileset dir="${dir.src}"
               includes="**/*_??_??.properties" />
            <fileset dir="." includes="${jar.name}" />
         </delete>
```

```
    </target>
    <target name="NativeToAscii"
      description="Execute native2ascii for *.msg files">
      <native2ascii encoding="Cp1252"
        src="${dir.src}"
        dest="${dir.src}"
        ext=".properties"
        includes="**/*_de_DE.msg,
          **/*_fr_FR.msg, **/*_es_ES.msg"/>
      <native2ascii encoding="GBK"
        src="${dir.src}"
        dest="${dir.src}"
        ext=".properties"
        includes="**/*_zh_CN.msg"/>
      <native2ascii encoding="SJIS"
        src="${dir.src}"
        dest="${dir.src}"
        ext=".properties"
        includes="**/*_ja_JP.msg"/>
      <native2ascii encoding="MS949"
        src="${dir.src}"
        dest="${dir.src}"
        ext=".properties"
        includes="**/*_ko_KR.msg"/>
    </target>
    <target name="nl-jar">
      <jar destfile="${jar.name}"
        manifest="./META-INF/MANIFEST.MF">
      <zipfileset dir="${dir.src}"
        includes="**/*.properties"/>
        <fileset dir="."
          includes="plugin_??_??.properties"/>
      </jar>
    </target>
    <target
      name="Jar" depends="NativeToAscii, nl-jar" >
    </target>
    <target name="Export">
      <copy todir="${export.dir}">
        <fileset dir="." includes="${jar.name}"/>
      </copy>
    </target>
</project>
```

If you set the fragment version number to 2.6.0.qualifier, the Eclipse PDE generates a JAR file with the following name:

```
org.eclipse.birt.report.viewer.nl1_2.6.0.qualifier.jar
```

Before building the fragment, change qualifier to the BIRT Report Viewer plug-in build number, such as v20100605. The Eclipse PDE generates a JAR file with the following name:

```
org.eclipse.birt.report.viewer.nl1_2.6.0.v20100605.jar
```

The Eclipse PDE provides support for deploying the plug-in in a run-time environment. To deploy the fragment to the BIRT Report Viewer example, use the Export wizard as shown in Figure 22-4 or manually copy the org.eclipse.birt.report.viewer.nl1 JAR file from your workspace to the eclipse/plugins folder.

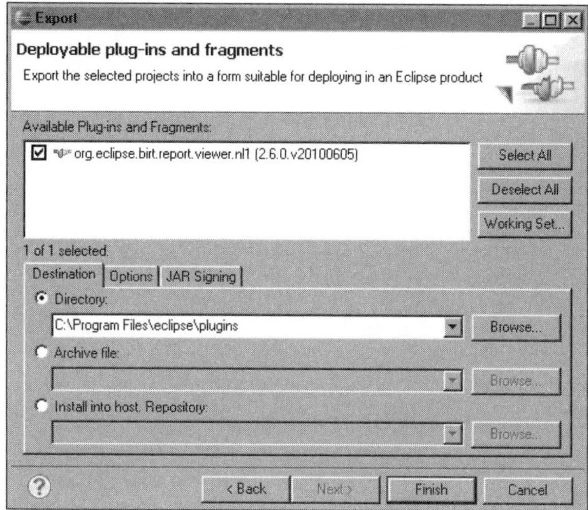

Figure 22-4 Deploying a fragment using the Export wizard

Test the fragment after deploying it by starting Eclipse using the -nl argument with the desired language setting. Listing 22-3 shows the command to start Eclipse using the -nl argument with the lowercase symbol for Spanish, as specified in the name of the Spanish messages.properties file, Messages_es.properties.

Listing 22-3 Starting Eclipse using the -nl setting for Spanish

```
eclipse -nl es
```

In Eclipse, open BIRT Report Designer, or in Spanish, Diseño de informe perspective, as shown in Figure 22-5.

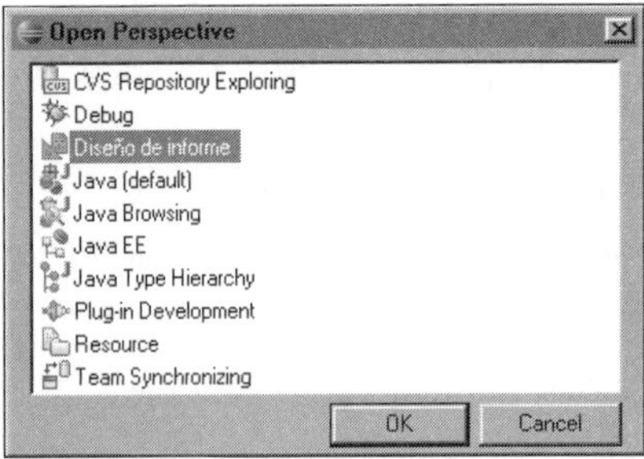

Figure 22-5 Opening the BIRT perspective using Spanish NL1 settings

The BIRT Report Designer appears with the Spanish language settings specified in the NL1 language pack. Figure 22-6 shows the Palette with the names of the report items appearing in Spanish.

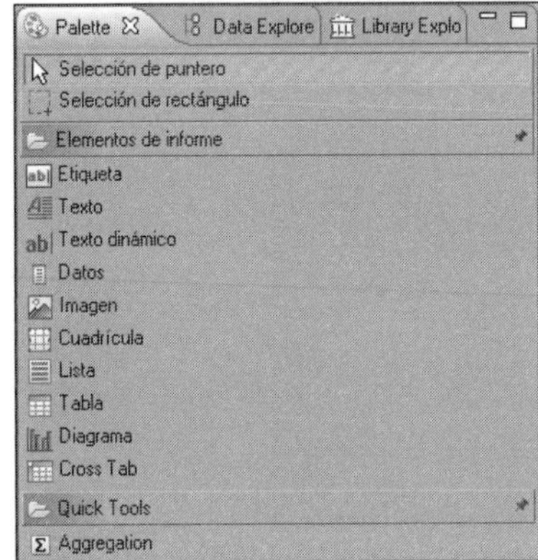

Figure 22-6 The Palette using Spanish NL1 settings

Figure 22-7 shows the Property Editor with the names of the Properties categories and the settings for General appearing in Spanish.

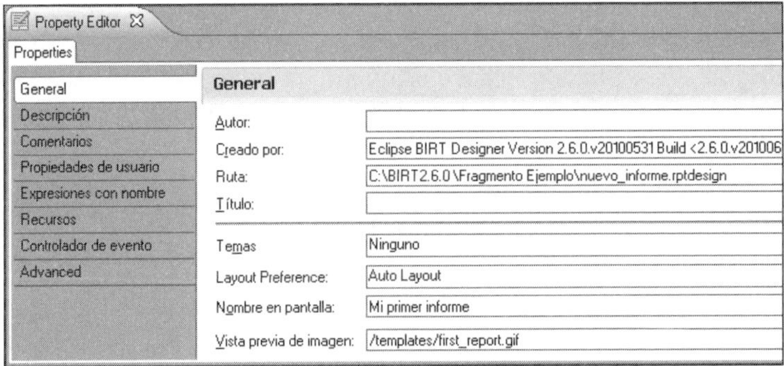

Figure 22-7 The Property Editor using Spanish NL1 settings

Run the report using BIRT Web Viewer by choosing View Report→View report in Web Viewer or, in Spanish, Ver informe en Web Viewer, as shown in Figure 22-8.

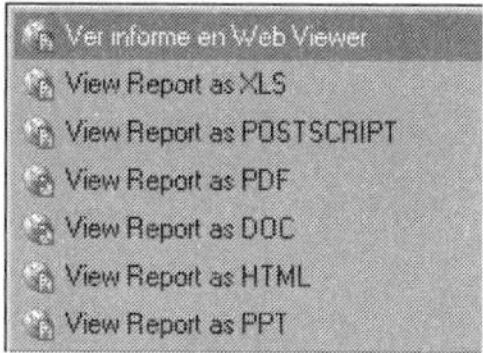

Figure 22-8 Running a report in Web Viewer using Spanish NL1 settings

Figure 22-9 shows the Editor with the names of the Editor tabs appearing in Spanish.

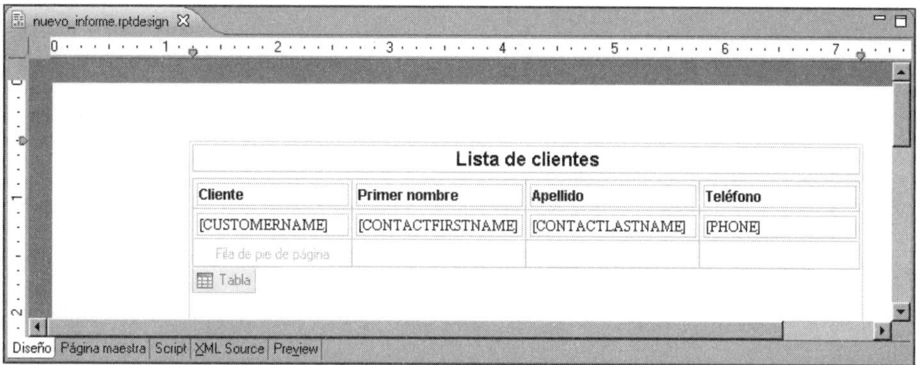

Figure 22-9 The Editor using Spanish NL1 settings

Figure 22-10 shows the report with the BIRT Web Viewer page prompts, such as Showing page appearing in Spanish as Mostrando página.

BIRT Report Viewer

BIRT Report Viewer

Mostrando página 1 de 1

Ir a la página:

Lista de clientes

Cliente	Primer nombre	Apellido	Teléfono
Atelier graphique	Carine	Schmitt	40.32.2555
Signal Gift Stores	Jean	King	7025551838
Australian Collectors, Co.	Peter	Ferguson	03 9520 4555
Baane Mini Imports	Jonas	Bergulfsen	07-98 9555
Mini Gifts Distributors Ltd.	Susan	Nelson	4155551450

Figure 22-10 The Web Viewer using Spanish NL1 settings

The NLS language pack configures only elements in the BIRT Report Designer and Viewer user interfaces. For example, in Figure 22-9 and Figure 22-10, the elements in the report design and output, such as the table title and column names, are user-defined and not part of the NL1 language pack configuration.

Chapter

23

Developing a Charting Extension

This chapter discusses the process of adding a new chart type to the BIRT chart engine. BIRT provides a radar chart type with the chart engine as an example of how to build new chart types. This chapter describes how to create this radar chart example.

A radar chart, also known as a spider chart, displays multiple data points proportionately using equidistant radii. This chart type allows the simultaneous comparison of multiple data points in a series. Each data point value determines the magnitude of each radius.

The number of data points in the chart determines the number of radials. The data points can be connected by lines, except for the first and last data points, or all the lines can be connected and the space filled to form a polygon.

The background for a radar chart can be blank, circular, or polygonal. Some chart generators support additional background types, but the following examples support only these three backgrounds, as shown in Figure 23-1 and Figure 23-2.

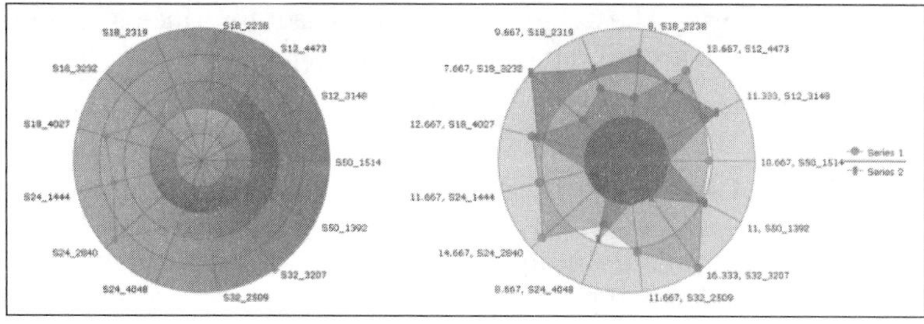

Figure 23-1 Images of possible radar charts

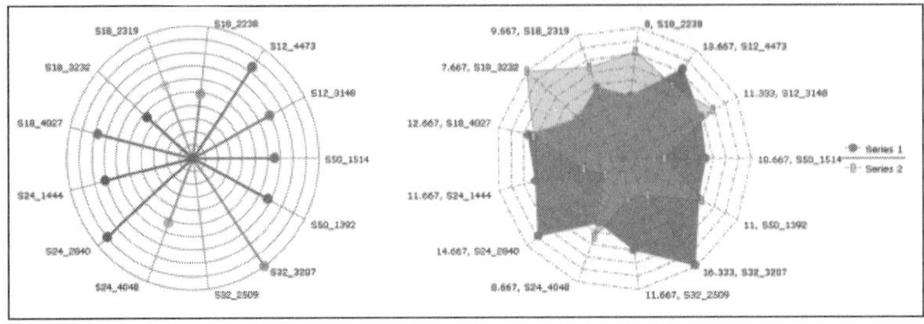

Figure 23-2 More images of possible radar charts

The radar chart example presented in this discussion uses BIRT chart engine version 2.6.

About BIRT charting extension points

The chart engine, like most components in BIRT, defines extension points for adding new features. Table 23-1 is a partial list of the primary extension points with brief descriptions..

Table 23-1 BIRT charting extension points

Extension point	Description
org.eclipse.birt.chart .engine .modelrenderers	Used to render a specific series type. For example, the bar chart renders rectangles on a Cartesian grid. The extending class implements the ISeriesRenderer interface. This class also extends AxesRenderer for chart types that require axes and BaseRenderer for charts that do not implement axes. A model renderer draws using object primitives.
org.eclipse.birt.chart .ui.types	Used to register a chart type so that it appears for selection in the chart wizard. The registered class must implement the org.eclipse.birt.chart.ui.swt.interfaces.IChartType interface. This class defines the subtypes and user interface images, supported dimensions, and other chart type features such as whether the chart can combine with other chart types.
org.eclipse.birt.chart .ui.seriescomposites	Used to build a custom user interface for a particular series type. The developer uses this user interface to customize the wizard for a particular chart type.
org.eclipse.birt.chart .engine.charttypes	Used to load the custom model for a new chart type.
org.eclipse.birt.chart .engine .datasetprocessors	Used to specify a class to process each row of data for a specific series type. The class uses a query result set to populate a unique set of values for a series type. Use this extension point only if the chart requires a unique data-point type, such as the stock chart type, where each data point represents four values.

Table 23-1 BIRT charting extension points

Extension point	Description
org.eclipse.birt.chart .engine .devicerenderers	Used to define a class that implements the drawing primitives used by the model renderer for a specific output device. For example, the core engine supports SWT, Swing, PNG, JPG, BMP, SVG, and PDF device renderers. Drawing primitives include methods such as drawArc, fillPolygon, and drawText. The device renderer must also handle user events for the new output format. All device renderers extend org.eclipse.birt .chart.device.DeviceAdapter.
org.eclipse.birt.chart .engine .displayservers	Used to function with the devicerenderers extension point to provide generic services, such as retrieving font metrics, loading images, configuring DPI, and setting the graphics context. The BIRT core currently supports SWT and Swing display servers. All display servers must extend org.eclipse .birt.chart.device.DisplayAdapter.
org.eclipse.birt.chart .engine .datapointdefinitions	Used to define an individual data point in a series, such as a stock chart type containing high, low, open, and close values for each data point. This extension point returns the point types and display text for a data point in a particular series.
org.eclipse.birt.chart .ui.uisheets	Used to add user interface panels to the tree view in the chart wizard.
org.eclipse.birt.chart .engine .aggregatefunctions	Used to add custom aggregate functions to the chart engine. These functions, such as sum and count, appear in the chart builder. The functions aggregate data for display in a chart. The extending class implements the IAggregateFunction interface.

The radar chart example implements some of the extension points described in Table 23-1. The example uses a category and value for each data point, so no special treatment of the individual points is required as occurs, for example, in a stock chart

The implementation of the example requires two plug-ins. The first plug-in implements the user interface in the design-time wizard, shown in Figure 23-3. The second plug-in implements the run-time version of a radar chart that appears in a rendered document.

The radar chart example requires unloose default implementation of the org.eclipse.birt.chart.engine.datasetprocessors extension point because the data for this chart type is not unique. The example also adds a new chart type, which requires implementing the org.eclipse.birt.chart.ui.types and org.eclipse.birt.chart.engine.charttypes extension points.

The example implements the org.eclipse.birt.chart.engine.modelrenderers extension point to do the drawing and the org.eclipse.birt.chart.ui

.seriescomposites extension point to implement a radar-specific series sheet for the chart builder.

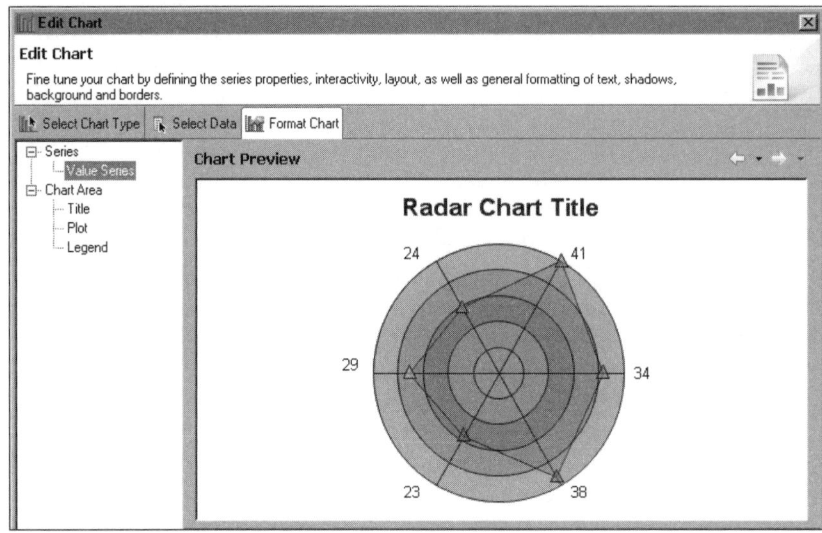

Figure 23-3 Viewing radar series attributes

The example implements the following extension points listed in Table 23-2.

Table 23-2 BIRT radar source plug-ins

Plug-in	Extension Point
org.eclipse.birt.chart .examples	org.eclipse.birt.chart.ui.types
	org.eclipse.birt.chart.ui.seriescomposites
org.eclipse.birt.chart .examples.core	org.eclipse.birt.chart.engine.modelrenderers
	org.eclipse.birt.chart.engine.datasetprocessors
	org.eclipse.birt.chart.engine.charttypes

Note that these plugins contain other chart examples. For example, the org.eclipse.birt.chart.examples plug-in contains chart engine API examples.

Setting up the build environment

The example requires an initial workspace setup. The chart engine uses an XSD SDK to generate an EMF model. The example requires the BIRT chart engine plug-ins. These components must be present in the environment. Obtain the required plug-ins by downloading the Eclipse IDE for Java and Report Developers from http://www.eclipse.org/downloads. Unzip the downloaded file to a suitable location and launch eclipse.exe located in the \eclipse directory. Create a new workspace and provide a name, such as C:\work\workspaces\2.6workspaces\examplechart. Next, add the EMF and XSD plug-ins manually or use the update manager. To use the update manager, select the Help➤Install New Software, as shown in Figure 23-4.

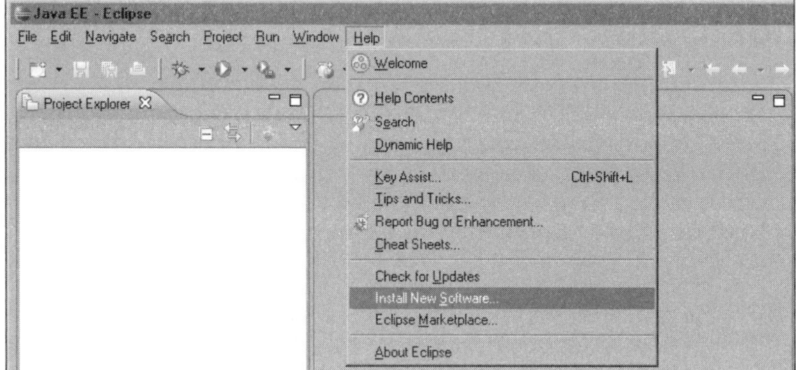

Figure 23-4 Using the update manager to install new software

In Install, in Work with, select an update site. For example, select Helios - http://download.eclipse.org/releases/helios. In the list of available updates, expand Modeling and select EMF – Eclipse Modeling Framework SDK and XSD – XML Schema Definition SDK items, as shown in Figure 23-5.

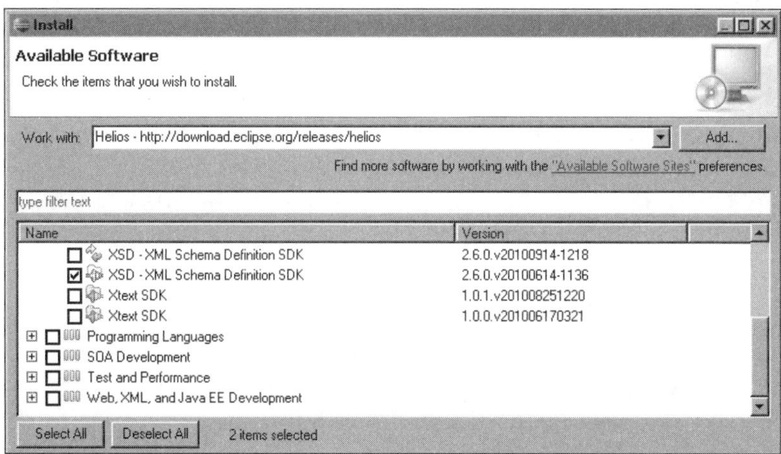

Figure 23-5 Selecting an update site and the EMF and XSD items

Choose Next. Install calculates dependencies and presents a summary of the items to install, as shown in Figure 23-6.

Name	Version	Id
☑ EMF - Eclipse Modeling Framework SDK	2.6.0.v2010061...	org.eclipse.emf.sdk.feature.group
☑ XSD - XML Schema Definition SDK	2.6.0.v2010061...	org.eclipse.xsd.sdk.feature.group

Figure 23-6 Modeling components to install

Choose Next, accept the license, then choose Finish.

After downloading the EMF and XSD plug-ins, restart Eclipse. Then, create a new plug-in project, as described in the following section.

Extending the chart model

After setting up the workspace, you can develop the new chart type. As stated earlier, BIRT uses XSD files to define the chart model. These XSD files are in the org.elcipse.birt.chart.engine plug-in. You can download the plug-in from CVS or obtain it from the source download. Technically, only the xsd directory and the existing EMF model are required, although it is useful to have the chart engine source for debugging purposes.

The xsd directory in the chart engine plug-in contains the schema files, listed in Table 23-3. The schemas meet all the requirements for other chart elements, such as data types. A radar chart requires extending only the type schema.

Table 23-3 XSD schema files in the chart engine plug-in

Schema	Description
attribute.xsd	Defines attributes associated with various components that make up the chart, such as line attributes, date formats, and markers.
component.xsd	Defines the components of a chart, such as scales, axis, and base-level series.
data.xsd	Defines the data types used in the chart, including basic data types and extended data types such as StockDataSet.
layout.xsd	Defines the layout of the various blocks that make up a chart, including Legend, Plot, and Title blocks.
model.xsd	Defines the chart model and common properties of a chart, which currently include the following top-level items: ■ Chart Contains properties associated with all chart types. All charts extend from this model. ■ ChartWithAxes Extends Chart, adding axis information. ■ ChartWithoutAxes Extends Chart, adding information associated with a non-axis-based chart, such as pie chart. ■ DialChart Extends ChartWithoutAxes, adding dial information.

Table 23-3 XSD schema files in the chart engine plug-in

Schema	Description	
type.xsd	Defines each series type supported by the engine. Each type extends from the base-series type defined in the component schema, which currently includes the following series types:	
	■ AreaSeries	■ GanttSeries
	■ BarSeries	■ LineSeries
	■ BubbleSeries	■ PieSeries
	■ DialSeries	■ ScatterSeries
	■ DifferenceSeries	■ StockSeries

Figure 23-7 shows the new radar chart type and the settings in the type schema required for a radar series. For example, the boolean value, FillPolys, determines whether a polygon drawn in the radar chart is filled.

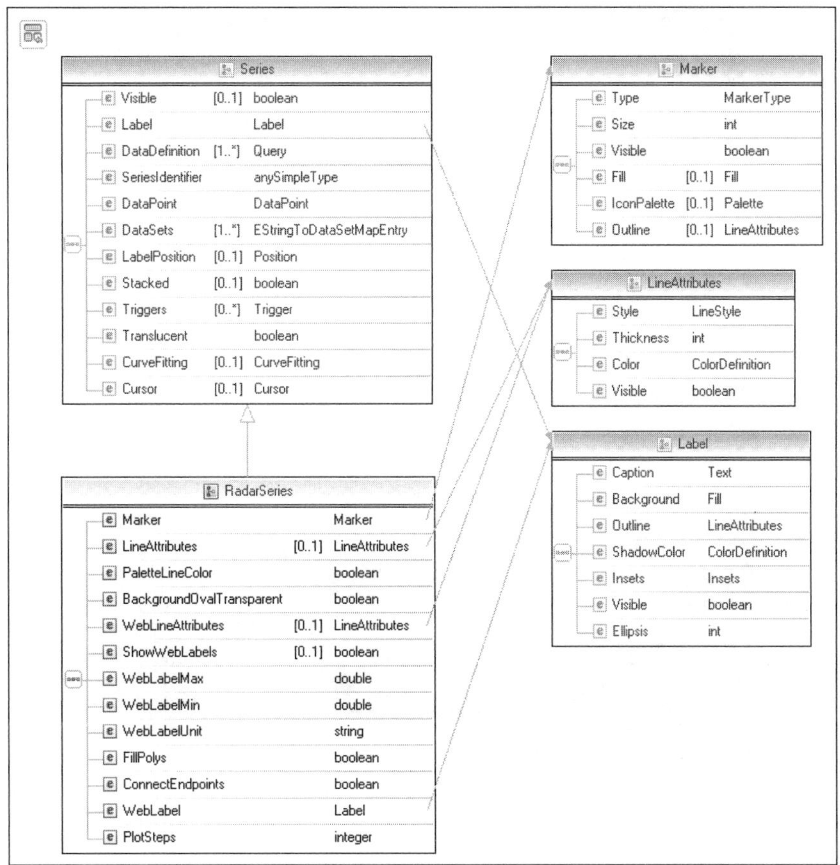

Figure 23-7 Viewing the schema for the radar chart type

An example of this type schema for the chart and the schema file is the file named radar.xsd, which is located in the org.eclipse.birt.chart.examples .radar.model package in the org.eclipse.birt.chart.examples.core plug-in.

In the schema file, the xsd:import statement imports the existing schema files from the chart engine plug-in, such as the type schema, using the following code:

```
<xsd:import namespace="http://www.birt.eclipse.org/ChartModelType"
   schemaLocation="../../../../../../../../
   org.eclipse.birt.chart.engine/xsd/type.xsd"/>
```

Creating an EMF model

First, create a plug-in project. Then, create a folder or package in the project for the model. The next step is to create an EMF model for the series type based on the schema. To create an EMF Generator Model, choose File➛New ➛Other. In New, expand Eclipse Modeling Framework and select EMF Generator Model, as shown in Figure 23-8.

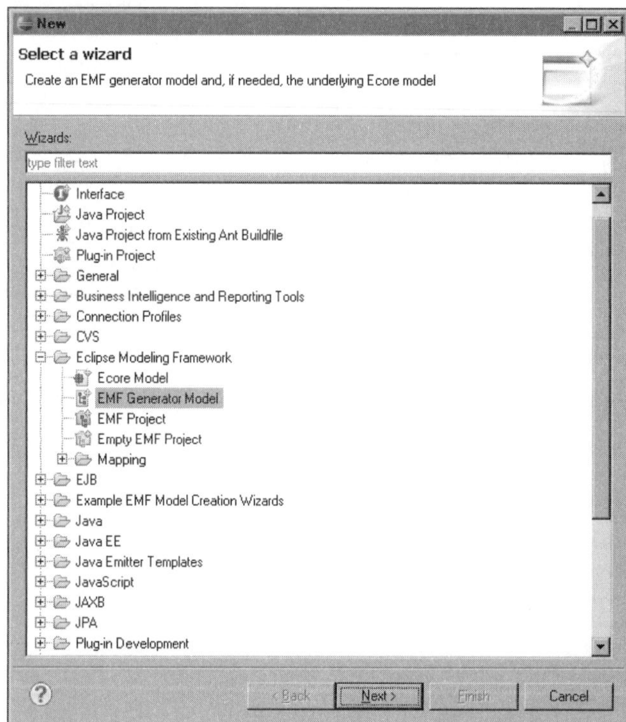

Figure 23-8 Selecting an EMF generator model

Choose Next. Type a name for the model class. In Figure 23-9, showing the radar example, the model is in the org.eclipse.birt.chart.examples.radar .model package.

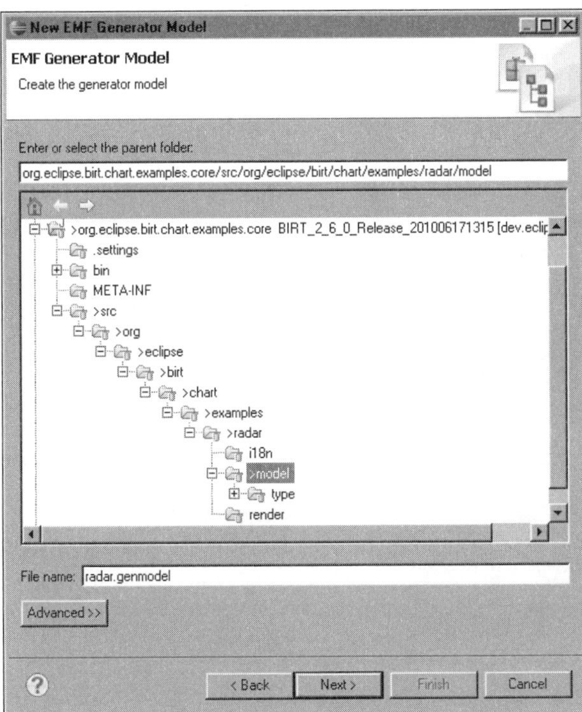

Figure 23-9 Creating an EMF model for the radar-series type

Choose Next. Select the XML Schema as the model importer, as shown in Figure 23-10.

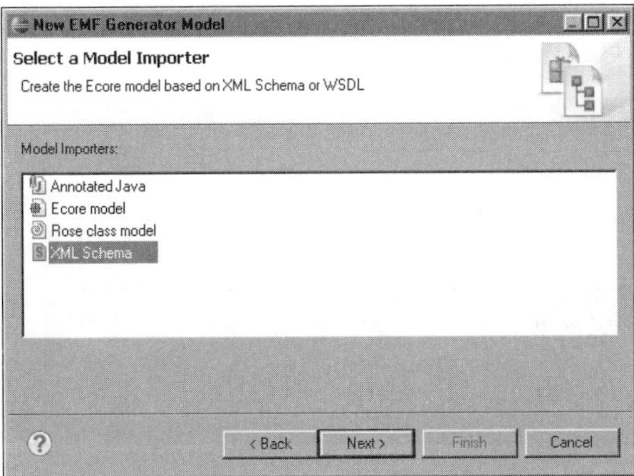

Figure 23-10 Creating an XML schema for the radar-series type

Choose Next. The wizard prompts for the location of the schema files to use in creating the model. Select Browse Workspace and select the XSD file created earlier, as shown in Figure 23-11.

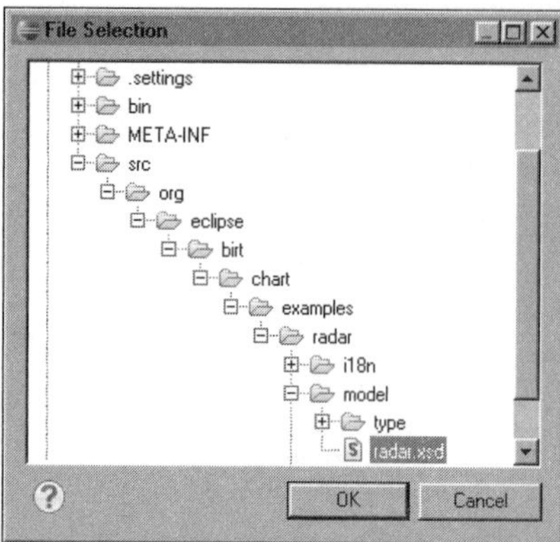

Figure 23-11 Selecting the location of the schema file

Choose OK. The XSD file appears in the wizard, as shown in Figure 23-12.

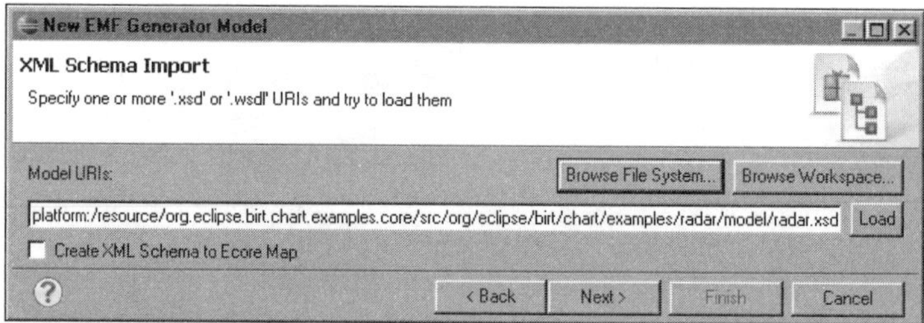

Figure 23-12 Checking the location of the schema files

Choose Next. In Package Selection, select the package of the new type, which in the radar example is the org.actuate.birt.radar.chart.model.type. You can also change the name of the ecore file. The example in Figure 23-13 shows the file name changed to radar.ecore.

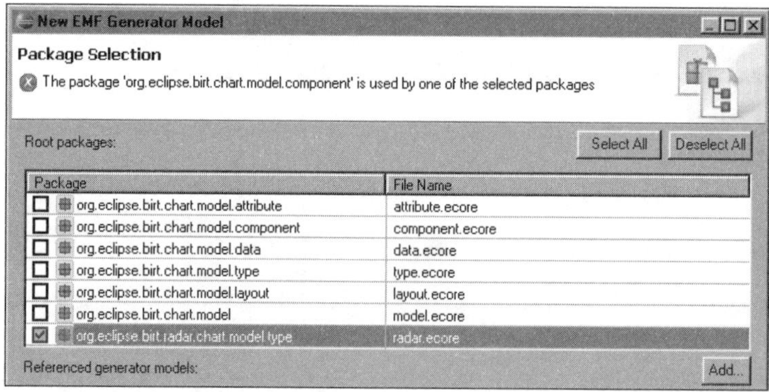

Figure 23-13 Selecting the new type

To reference the existing chart model, choose Add. In File Selection, select the generator model to reference, as shown in Figure 23-14. The existing generator model is in the src/model directory of the chart engine plug-in.

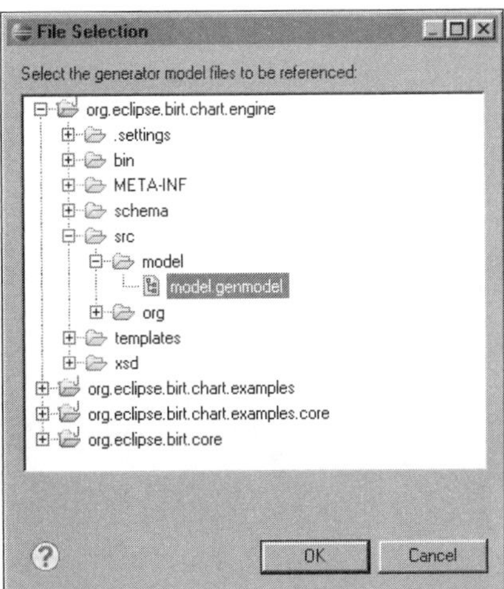

Figure 23-14 Selecting the new EMF generator model

After these steps, New EMF Generator Model displays all the referenced chart model packages and the root package of the new type to create, as shown in Figure 23-15.

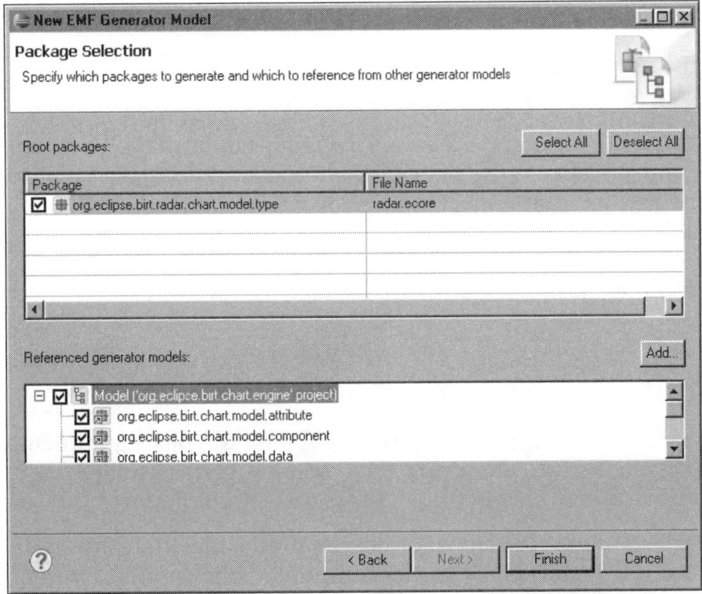

Figure 23-15 Selecting the new EMF generator model

Choose Finish. This operation creates the genmodel and ecore files.

To change the model, change the XSD file and reload the model. To perform this task, right-click the genmodel file and choose Reload. To generate source code based on this model, right-click genmodel and choose Open with EMF Generator. Next, right–click the top node and choose Generate Model Code, as shown in Figure 23-16.

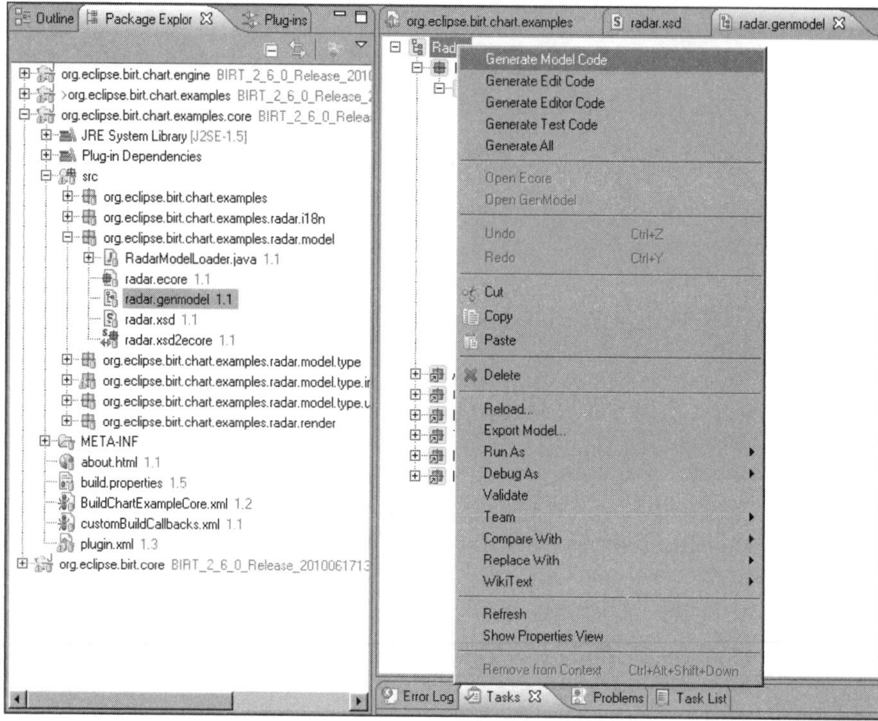

Figure 23-16 Choosing Generate Model Code

These operations generate the basic code for manipulating the model. Note that Eclipse constructs the package names using the targetNamespace attribute defined in the schema, as shown in the following example:

```
targetNamespace="http://www.birt.eclipse.org/RadarChartModelType"
```

In the radar example, these packages have been refactored for more suitable names.

Completing the new SeriesImpl

After creating the basic code for manipulating the model, implement the extensions that create the series. First, add methods to the newly created SeriesImpl class. In this example, the class is RadarSeriesImpl.

Although EMF provides most of the required code, there are a few methods in the org.eclipse.birt.chart.model.component.Series interface that may need to be written manually. These methods can include canBeStacked, which determines whether multiple series of the same type can be stacked, and canParticipateInCombination, which determines if the chart type can participate in a combination chart. In most cases, such as this example, the default implementation provides adequate functionality and a custom implementation is not required.

The method, getDisplayName( ), which returns a user-friendly string name for the chart, typically needs to be implemented. In the example, the org.eclipse.birt.chart.examples.radar.i18n package handles all messages.

The following code implements the getDisplayName( ) method in the radar chart:

```
public String getDisplayName( )
{
   return Messages.getString( "RadarSeriesImpl.displayName" );
}
```

It is also necessary to override several methods in the new SeriesImpl class. The first is the create( ) method, which allows an instance of the SeriesImpl class to be created and initialized, as shown in the following code:

```
public static final RadarSeries create( )
{
   final RadarSeries se =
   org.eclipse.birt.chart.examples.radar.model.type
      .RadarTypeFactory.eINSTANCE.createRadarSeries( );
   ( (RadarSeriesImpl) se ).initialize( );
   return se;
}
```

When adding the create( ) method, verify that the TypeFactory class is from the org.eclipse.birt.chart.examples.radar.model.type package and not from the org.eclipse.birt.chart.model.type package.

The second method is the initialize( ) method. In the example, this method sets several default attributes for the radar series, including setting the radar-line attributes and the web-radar, background-line attributes, as shown in Listing 23-1.

Listing 23-1 initialize method

```
protected void initialize( )
{
   super.initialize( );
   final LineAttributes lia =
   AttributeFactory.eINSTANCE.createLineAttributes( );
   ( (LineAttributesImpl) lia ).set( null,
         LineStyle.SOLID_LITERAL,
         1 );
   lia.setVisible( true );
   setLineAttributes( lia );
   final LineAttributes weblia =
   AttributeFactory.eINSTANCE.createLineAttributes( );
   ( (LineAttributesImpl) weblia ).set( null,
         LineStyle.SOLID_LITERAL,
         1 );
   weblia.setVisible( true );
   setWebLineAttributes( weblia );
```

```
    final Marker m = AttributeFactory.eINSTANCE.createMarker( );
    m.setType( MarkerType.BOX_LITERAL );
    m.setSize( 4 );
    m.setVisible( true );
    LineAttributes la =
    AttributeFactory.eINSTANCE.createLineAttributes( );
    la.setVisible( true );
    m.setOutline( la );
    setMarker( m );
}
```

Note that additional imports are required. See the source-code example for the complete list of packages to import.

The final two methods to override copy an instance of the radar series. These methods are copyInstance( ) and set( ), as shown in Listing 23-2:

Listing 23-2 copyInstance( ) method

```
public RadarSeries copyInstance( )
{
   RadarSeriesImpl dest = new RadarSeriesImpl( );
   dest.set( this );
   return dest;
}
protected void set( RadarSeries src )
{
   super.set( src );
   // children
   if ( src.getMarker( ) != null )
   {
      setMarker( src.getMarker( ).copyInstance( ) );
   }
   if ( src.getLineAttributes( ) != null )
   {

   setLineAttributes( src.getLineAttributes( ).copyInstance( ) );
   }
   if ( src.getWebLineAttributes( ) != null )
   {
      setWebLineAttributes( src.getWebLineAttributes( ).copyInstan
         ce( ) );
   }
   if ( src.getWebLabel( ) != null )
   {
      setWebLabel( src.getWebLabel( ).copyInstance( ) );
   }
   // attributes
   paletteLineColor = src.isPaletteLineColor( );
   paletteLineColorESet = src.isSetPaletteLineColor( );
   backgroundOvalTransparent = src.isBackgroundOvalTransparent( );
```

```
    backgroundOvalTransparentESet =
    src.isSetBackgroundOvalTransparent( );
    showWebLabels = src.isShowWebLabels( );
    showWebLabelsESet = src.isSetShowWebLabels( );
    webLabelMax = src.getWebLabelMax( );
    webLabelMaxESet = src.isSetWebLabelMax( );
    webLabelMin = src.getWebLabelMin( );
    webLabelMinESet = src.isSetWebLabelMin( );
    webLabelUnit = src.getWebLabelUnit( );
    webLabelUnitESet = src.isSetWebLabelUnit( );
    fillPolys = src.isFillPolys( );
    fillPolysESet = src.isSetFillPolys( );
    connectEndpoints = src.isConnectEndpoints( );
    connectEndpointsESet = src.isSetConnectEndpoints( );
    plotSteps = src.getPlotSteps( );
    plotStepsESet = src.isSetPlotSteps( );
}
```

These two methods are called any time the engine makes a copy of the radar series, for example, when run-time series are created based on the design-time series. The copyInstance( ) method also needs to be defined in the generated Series interface. In this example, the following code was added to the org.eclipse.birt.chart.examples.radar.model.type.RadarSeries interface:

```
RadarSeries copyInstance( );
```

Implementing the extension points

The following section describes the design-time extension points first, then the run-time extension points. The EMF-generated code described earlier in the chapter must be in the run-time plug-in.

Design-time plug-in extensions

The design-time extensions for the chart builder and the radar chart user interfaces are implemented in the org.eclipse.birt.chart.examples plug-in. The following sections discuss each extension point, starting with the design-time extension points, org.eclipse.birt.chart.ui.types and org.eclipse.birt .chart.ui.seriescomposites.

Chart UI-types extension point

Use the UI-types extension point to register new chart types. To use this extension point, create a class that implements the org.eclipse.birt.chart.ui .swt.interfaces.IChartType interface. In this example, we are technically creating a new series renderer, not a new chart type. However, this type shows up as a new chart type in the user interface.

Most of the methods in this interface are used extensively in the chart builder. In the chart engine, there is a default implementation of the IChartType interface from which most chart types extend, the org.eclipse.birt

.chart.ui.swt.DefaultChartTypeImpl class. The example extends from this class. The following list describes the interface methods along with a brief description of when to call each method:

- getName( )
  Returns the name of the Chart.
- getDisplayName( )
  Returns the name to display in the chart builder wizard.
- getImage( )
  Returns the icon image to display in the chart builder for a specific chart type.
- getChartSubtypes( )
  Returns a collection of chart subtypes that the chart supports. A collection should contain an image and a name for each subtype supported.
- getModel( )
  Returns the model for the current chart under development. This method is called when the user selects a different chart type, to handle converting between chart types. For example, when the user selects a bar chart in the first tab, then selects a pie chart, this method is called to convert from a chart with axes to a chart without axes.
- getSupportedDimensions( )
  Called to determine how many dimensions the chart type supports. Currently, the engine can process 2D, 2D with depth, and 3D. If a chart type supports more than 2D, additional rendering code must be written, which is discussed later in this chapter.
- getDefaultDimension( )
  Returns the default dimension for a chart type.
- supportsTransposition( )
  Determines if the chart dimensions can be transposed, such as swapping the x- and y- axes. Transposition can be specific to a supported dimension type. For example, a 2Dchart can support transposition, but a 3D chart may not.
- getDefaultOrientation( )
  Returns the default orientation of a chart, vertical or horizontal. No implementation defaults to vertical.
- getBaseUI( )
  Constructs the base series user interface in the chart builder, which sets the data values for the chart type.
- isDimensionSupported( )
  Determines if a chart type supports a specific dimension.

- getSeries( )

  Creates an initial series type for a specific chart. Called whenever a list of series types is pre-populated within the user interface. In most cases, implementing this method only requires calling the create( ) method of the series implementation class, such as RadarSeriesImpl.create( ).

- canCombine( )

  Determines if a chart type can be combined with another chart type, such as a Bar-and-Line combination chart.

Before implementing this extension point, create a 16 x 16 pixel GIF icon to represent the chart in the first chart builder tab. In addition, create a 71 x 71 pixel GIF icon for each subtype of the new chart type. Note that you should have at least one 71 x 71 image for the default chart subtype.

This example implements three subtypes. Each subtype determines what type of background to render, currently a circular and polygon non-filled background, and a circular-filled background.

To include the images in the workspace, create an icons directory in the plug-in and import the images to this directory. Open the build tab on the Plug-in Manifest Editor and select the icons checkbox to include this new directory in the build, as shown in Figure 23-17.

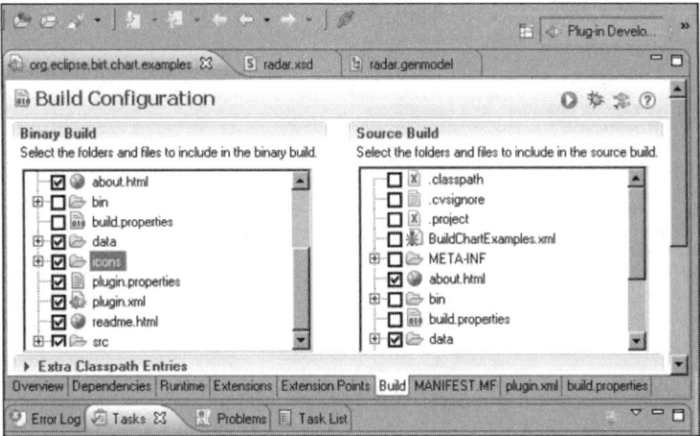

Figure 23-17 Adding an icons directory to the workspace

Next add the org.eclipse.birt.chart.ui.types extension to the plugin.xml. The example adds the following extension to the org.eclipse.birt.chart.examples plug-in, as shown in the following code:

```
<extension
   id="ChartWizardContext"
   name="Chart example types"
   point="org.eclipse.birt.chart.ui.types">
   <chartType
      classDefinition=
         "org.eclipse.birt.chart.examples.radar.ui.type
```

```
            .RadarChart"
        name="Radar Chart"/>
</extension>
```

Use ChartWizardContext as the identifier. The chart builder uses the identifier to display which chart types are supported. Under the chartType element, the classDefinition attribute specifies the class that implements the IChartType interface. The class org.eclipse.birt.chart.examples.ui.type .RadarChart implements the IChartType interface by extending the DefaultChartTypeImpl class.

Select Dependencies. Then, add the following dependencies to your plug-in:

- org.eclipse.birt.chart.engine.extension
- org.eclipse.birt.chart.ui
- org.eclipse.birt.chart.ui.extension
- com.ibm.icu

Figure 23-18 shows these dependencies.

Figure 23-18 Adding dependencies to the plug-in

In the radar chart example, com.ibm.icu is in a dependent plug-in and does not show in this image.

Create the class and package that you specified in the classDefinition attribute of the extension point. The radar chart uses org.eclipse.birt.chart.ui .examples.radar.ui.type package and a class named RadarChart:

```
public RadarChart( )
{
   chartTitle =
   Messages.getString( "RadarChart.Txt.DefaultRadarChartTitle" );
}
```

See the source-code example for a complete listing of the RadarChart class.

The constructor for this class sets the title for the chart. The getImage( ) method reads the 16x16 pixel icon image into an org.eclispe.swt.graphics. Image variable, which returns the value when the framework calls the getImage( ) method, as shown in the following code:

```
public Image getImage( )
{
   return UIHelper.getImage( "icons/obj16/Radar16.gif" );
}
```

The getName( ) and getDisplayName( ) methods return the strings Radar Chart and Radar Series respectively, as shown in the following code:

```
public String getName( )
{
   return Radar.TYPE_LITERAL;
}
public String getDisplayName( )
{
   return Messages.getString( "RadarChart.Txt.DisplayName" );
}
```

The getChartSubtypes( ) method creates a collection of sub-chart types. For each subtype of the chart, instantiate an instance of the DefaultChartSubTypeImpl class, passing the chart type name, the image read from the icons directory, a description, and a display name, as shown in Listing 23-3.

Listing 23-3 getChartSubtypes( ) method

```
public Collection<IChartSubType> getChartSubtypes( String
   sDimension,
      Orientation orientation )
{
   Vector<IChartSubType> vSubTypes = new Vector<IChartSubType>( );
   // Do not respond to requests for unknown orientations
   if ( !orientation.equals( Orientation.VERTICAL_LITERAL ) )
   {
      return vSubTypes;
   }
   if ( sDimension.equals( TWO_DIMENSION_TYPE )
         ||
   sDimension.equals( ChartDimension.TWO_DIMENSIONAL_LITERAL
      .getName( ) ) )
   {
         vSubTypes.add( new
   DefaultChartSubTypeImpl( Radar.STANDARD_SUBTYPE_LITERAL,
         UIHelper.getImage( "icons/wizban/Radar71.gif" ),
         sStandardDescription,
         Messages.getString( "RadarChart.SubType.Standard" ) ) );
         vSubTypes.add( new
DefaultChartSubTypeImpl( Radar.SPIDER_SUBTYPE_LITERAL,
```

```
            UIHelper.getImage( "icons/wizban/spiderweb.gif" ),
            sSpiderDescription,
            Messages.getString( "RadarChart.SubType.Spider" ) ) );
         vSubTypes.add( new
   DefaultChartSubTypeImpl( Radar.BULLSEYE_SUBTYPE_LITERAL,
            UIHelper.getImage( "icons/wizban/bullseye.gif" ),
            sBullseyeDescription,
Messages.getString( "RadarChart.SubType.Bullseye" ) ) );
   }
   return vSubTypes;
}
```

The getModel( ) method converts an existing chart model to a Radar Chart or creates a new one if the wizard has not yet created one. As stated earlier, this method is called by the chart builder when constructing a new chart or converting an existing one, as shown in Listing 23-4.

Listing 23-4 getModel( ) method

```
public Chart getModel( String sSubType, Orientation orientation,
      String sDimension, Chart currentChart )
{
   ChartWithoutAxes newChart = null;
   if ( currentChart != null )
   {
      newChart = (ChartWithoutAxes)
   getConvertedChart( currentChart,
            sSubType,
            sDimension );
      if ( newChart != null )
      {
         return newChart;
      }
   }
   newChart = ChartWithoutAxesImpl.create( );
   newChart.setType( Radar.TYPE_LITERAL );
   newChart.setSubType( sSubType );
   newChart.setDimension( getDimensionFor( sDimension ) );
   newChart.setUnits( "Points" );
   if ( newChart.getDimension( ).equals(
      ChartDimension.TWO_DIMENSIONAL_WITH_DEPTH_LITERAL ) )
   {
      newChart.setSeriesThickness( 15 );
   }
   newChart.getLegend( ).setItemType( LegendItemType
      .SERIES_LITERAL );
   SeriesDefinition sdX = SeriesDefinitionImpl.create( );
   sdX.getSeriesPalette( ).shift( 0 );
   Series categorySeries = SeriesImpl.create( );
   sdX.getSeries( ).add( categorySeries );
```

```
    sdX.getQuery( ).setDefinition( "Base Series" );
    newChart.getTitle( )
        .getLabel( )
        .getCaption( )
        .setValue( getDefaultTitle( ) );
    SeriesDefinition sdY = SeriesDefinitionImpl.create( );
    sdY.setZOrder( 1 );
    sdY.getSeriesPalette( ).shift( 0 );
    RadarSeries valueSeries = RadarSeriesImpl.create( );
    LineAttributes lia =
    LineAttributesImpl.create( ColorDefinitionImpl.GREY( ),
        LineStyle.SOLID_LITERAL,
        1 );
    valueSeries.setWebLineAttributes( lia );
    valueSeries.getLabel( ).setVisible( true );
    valueSeries.setSeriesIdentifier( "Series 1" );
    sdY.getSeries( ).add( valueSeries );
    sdX.getSeriesDefinitions( ).add( sdY );
    newChart.getSeriesDefinitions( ).add( sdX );
    addSampleData( newChart );
    return newChart;
}
```

The private getConvertedChart( ) method is called by getModel( ) in the chart builder when switching between chart types, allowing changes to the model to be preserved during a design session. Most of the code in this method focuses on copying element values for one type of chart to another, as shown in Listing 23-5.

Listing 23-5 getConvertedChart( ) method

```
private Chart getConvertedChart( Chart currentChart, String
    sNewSubType,
        String sNewDimension )
{
    Chart helperModel = (Chart) EcoreUtil.copy( currentChart );
    helperModel.eAdapters( ).addAll( currentChart.eAdapters( ) );
    // Cache series to keep attributes during conversion
    ChartCacheManager.getInstance( )
    .cacheSeries( ChartUIUtil.getAllOrthogonalSeriesDefinitions(
        helperModel ) );
    if ( currentChart instanceof ChartWithAxes )
    {
        if ( !ChartPreviewPainter.isLivePreviewActive( ) )
        {
            helperModel.setSampleData( getConvertedSampleData(
                helperModel.getSampleData( ),
            ( ( (ChartWithAxes) currentChart ).getAxes( )
                .get( 0 ) ).getType( ),
                AxisType.LINEAR_LITERAL ) );
```

```
}
// Create a new instance of the correct type
   and set initial properties
currentChart = ChartWithoutAxesImpl.create( );
currentChart.setType( Radar.TYPE_LITERAL );
currentChart.setSubType( sNewSubType );
currentChart.setDimension( getDimensionFor(
   sNewDimension ) );
// Copy generic chart properties from the old chart
currentChart.setBlock( helperModel.getBlock( ) );
currentChart.setDescription( helperModel
   .getDescription( ) );
currentChart.setGridColumnCount( helperModel
   .getGridColumnCount( ) );
if ( helperModel.getInteractivity( ) != null )
{
   currentChart.getInteractivity( )
   .setEnable( helperModel.getInteractivity( )
      .isEnable( ) );
   currentChart.getInteractivity( )
   .setLegendBehavior( helperModel.getInteractivity( )
   .getLegendBehavior( ) );
}
currentChart.setSampleData( helperModel.getSampleData( ) );
currentChart.setScript( helperModel.getScript( ) );
currentChart.setUnits( helperModel.getUnits( ) );
if ( helperModel.getGridColumnCount( ) > 0 )
{
   currentChart.setGridColumnCount( helperModel
      .getGridColumnCount( ) );
}
else
{
   currentChart.setGridColumnCount( 1 );
}
// Copy series definitions from old chart
( (ChartWithoutAxes) currentChart ).getSeriesDefinitions( )
   .add( ( ( (ChartWithAxes) helperModel ).getAxes( )
   .get( 0 ) ).getSeriesDefinitions( ).get( 0 ) );
Vector<SeriesDefinition> vOSD =
   new Vector<SeriesDefinition>( );
// Only convert series in primary orthogonal axis.
Axis primaryOrthogonalAxis =
   ( (ChartWithAxes) helperModel ).getAxes( )
   .get( 0 ).getAssociatedAxes( ).get( 0 );
EList<SeriesDefinition> osd =
   primaryOrthogonalAxis.getSeriesDefinitions( );
for ( int j = 0; j < osd.size( ); j++ )
{
   SeriesDefinition sd = osd.get( j );
```

```
      Series series = sd.getDesignTimeSeries( );
      sd.getSeries( ).clear( );
      sd.getSeries( ).add( getConvertedSeries( series, j ) );
      vOSD.add( sd );
   }
   ( ( (ChartWithoutAxes)currentChart )
      .getSeriesDefinitions( ).get( 0 ) )
      .getSeriesDefinitions( ).clear( );
   ( ( (ChartWithoutAxes)currentChart )
      .getSeriesDefinitions( )
      .get( 0 ) ).getSeriesDefinitions( ).addAll( vOSD );
   currentChart.getLegend( )
      .setItemType( LegendItemType.SERIES_LITERAL );
   currentChart.getTitle( )
      .getLabel( ).getCaption( )
      .setValue( getDefaultTitle( ) );
}
else if ( currentChart instanceof ChartWithoutAxes )
{
   if ( currentChart.getType( ).equals( Radar.TYPE_LITERAL ) )
   {
      currentChart.setSubType( sNewSubType );
      if ( !currentChart.getDimension( )
         .equals( getDimensionFor( sNewDimension ) ) )
      {
         currentChart.setDimension(
            getDimensionFor( sNewDimension ) );
      }
   }
   else
   {
      // Create a new instance of the correct type
      and set initial
      // properties
      currentChart = ChartWithoutAxesImpl.create( );
      currentChart.setType( Radar.TYPE_LITERAL );
      currentChart.setSubType( sNewSubType );
      currentChart.setDimension(
         getDimensionFor( sNewDimension ) );
      // Copy generic chart properties from the old chart
      currentChart.setBlock( helperModel.getBlock( ) );
      currentChart.setDescription(
         helperModel.getDescription( ) );
      currentChart.setGridColumnCount( helperModel
         .getGridColumnCount( ) );
      currentChart.setSampleData(
         helperModel.getSampleData( ) );
      currentChart.setScript( helperModel.getScript( ) );
      currentChart.setUnits( helperModel.getUnits( ) );
      if ( helperModel.getInteractivity( ) != null )
```

```
            {
               currentChart.getInteractivity( )
               .setEnable( helperModel.getInteractivity( )
                  .isEnable( ) );
               currentChart.getInteractivity( )
                  .setLegendBehavior( helperModel.getInteractivity( )
                  .getLegendBehavior( ) );
            }
            // Clear existing series definitions
            ( (ChartWithoutAxes)
               currentChart ).getSeriesDefinitions( ).clear( );
            // Copy series definitions
            ( (ChartWithoutAxes)
               currentChart ).getSeriesDefinitions( )
               .add( ( (ChartWithoutAxes)helperModel )
               .getSeriesDefinitions( ).get( 0 ) );
            // Update the series
            EList<SeriesDefinition> seriesdefinitions =
               ( ( (ChartWithoutAxes) currentChart )
               .getSeriesDefinitions( ).get( 0 ) )
               .getSeriesDefinitions( );
            for ( int j = 0; j < seriesdefinitions.size( ); j++ )
            {
               Series series = seriesdefinitions.get( j )
               .getDesignTimeSeries( );
               series = getConvertedSeries( series, j );
               // Clear any existing series
               seriesdefinitions.get( j ).getSeries( ).clear( );
               // Add the new series
               seriesdefinitions.get( j ).getSeries( ).add( series );
            }
            currentChart.getLegend( )
            .setItemType( LegendItemType.SERIES_LITERAL );
            currentChart.getTitle( )
            .getLabel( )
            .getCaption( )
            .setValue( getDefaultTitle( ) );
         }
      }
      else
      {
         return null;
      }
      return currentChart;
   }
```

The private method getConvertedSeries( ) is called by the getConvertedModel( ) method to preserve series changes between model changes, for example, customizing a line chart, changing it to a bar chart, then changing it back again to a line chart.

Without these methods, the series has to be created again for every change, as shown in the following code:

```
private Series getConvertedSeries( Series series, int
   seriesIndex )
{
   // Do not convert base series
   if ( series.getClass( ).getName( ).equals( SeriesImpl
      .class.getName( ) ) )
   {
      return series;
   }

   RadarSeries radarseries = (RadarSeries)
   ChartCacheManager.getInstance( )
         .findSeries( RadarSeriesImpl.class.getName( ),
   seriesIndex );
   if ( radarseries == null )
   {
      radarseries = RadarSeriesImpl.create( );
   }
   // Copy generic series properties
   ChartUIUtil.copyGeneralSeriesAttributes( series, radarseries );
   return radarseries;
}
```

The private method addSampleData( ) is called by getModel( ) to provide sample data for the chart. This sample data displays a chart for review until real data is selected. To display the chart using real data instead of sample data, enable the chart live preview preference. The chart builder enables the live preview preference by default.

```
private void addSampleData( Chart newChart )
{
   SampleData sd = DataFactory.eINSTANCE.createSampleData( );
   sd.getBaseSampleData( ).clear( );
   sd.getOrthogonalSampleData( ).clear( );
   // Create Base Sample Data
   BaseSampleData sdBase =
      DataFactory.eINSTANCE.createBaseSampleData( );
   sdBase.setDataSetRepresentation( "A, B, C, D" );
   sd.getBaseSampleData( ).add( sdBase );
   // Create Orthogonal Sample Data (with simulation count of 2)
   OrthogonalSampleData oSample =
   DataFactory.eINSTANCE.createOrthogonalSampleData( );
   oSample.setDataSetRepresentation( "5, 4, 12, 16" );
   oSample.setSeriesDefinitionIndex( 0 );
   sd.getOrthogonalSampleData( ).add( oSample );
   newChart.setSampleData( sd );
}
```

The getSupportedDimensions( ) method determines how many possible dimension choices a specific chart type supports. This example supports only two dimensions.

The wizard calls the getDefaultDimension( ) method when first populating the dimension choices for a specific chart type or when first creating a working model of the specific chart type. Whenever switching between chart types, use the getModel( ) method to call the getDimensionFor( ) private method. This method uses the current dimension of the previously selected chart.

In the process, the chart type automatically specifies a dimension based on the current working session. For example, when a 3D bar chart is created and the user changes the type to an area chart, the new chart also becomes 3D. In the example, the chart dimension is set to 2D to override any dimension passed to the method since the example supports only 2D, as shown in the following code:

```
private static final String[ ] saDimensions = new String[ ]{
   TWO_DIMENSION_TYPE
};
public String[ ] getSupportedDimensions( )
{
   return saDimensions;
}
public String getDefaultDimension( )
{
   return saDimensions[0];
}
   private ChartDimension getDimensionFor( String sDimension )
{
   return ChartDimension.TWO_DIMENSIONAL_LITERAL;
}
```

The getBaseUI( ) method sets up the base series user interface in the chart builder to attach the data to the chart. In the example, an instance of the DefaultBaseSeriesComponent( ) constructs the user interface. Currently, all chart types use the default. Figure 23-19 shows the portion of the user interface handled by this method.

Figure 23-19 Building the user interface for the category series

This user interface must be shared across the defined value series. For example, a combination chart that uses a Bar series and a Line series must use the same category series, as shown in the following code:

```
public ISelectDataComponent getBaseUI( Chart chart,
   ISelectDataCustomizeUI selectDataUI, ChartWizardContext
   context,String sTitle )
```

```
    {
    DefaultBaseSeriesComponent component =
       new DefaultBaseSeriesComponent( ChartUIUtil
       .getBaseSeriesDefinitions( chart ).get( 0 ),context,
       sTitle );
    component.setLabelText( Messages.getString(
       "RadarBaseSeriesComponent.Label.CategoryDefinition" ) );
    component.setTooltipWhenBlank( Messages.getString(
    "RadarChart.Tooltip.InputExpression" ) );
    return component;
    }
    // Copy generic series properties
    ChartUIUtil.copyGeneralSeriesAttributes(series, radarseries);
    return radarseries;
}
```

The getSeries( ) method instantiates a RadarSeriesImpl object using the create( ) method described earlier, as shown in the following code:

```
public Series getSeries( )
{
    return (RadarSeries) RadarSeriesImpl.create( );
}
```

Series composite extension point

The series composite extension point constructs custom user interface elements for use in the chart builder. The series composite element for this extension point has two attributes, seriesType and seriesUIProvider. The seriesType attribute specifies the composite type. The seriesUIProvider attribute specifies the class that implements the ISeriesUIProvider interface. This extension point is implemented in the second and third tabs of the chart builder.

The ISeriesUIProvider interface has the following methods:

- getSeriesAttributeSheet( )
  Constructs the composite used to manipulate the series properties.
- getSeriesDataComponent( )
  Builds elements that appear in chart builder by returning user interface items for the value series and the optional value series grouping.
- getSeriesClass( )
  Returns the series class for which the ISeriesUIProvider is implemented.
- validateSeriesBindingType( )
  Verifies that series has the proper data type. For example, text values are not allowed for value types in some chart types.
- isValidAggregationType( )
  Determines if a particular aggregate function is acceptable for a series.

Functions similar to the validateSeriesBindingType( ) method. Currently, the only chart that implements this method is the Gantt chart, which supports only First, Last, Min, and Max aggregates.

- getCompatibleAxisType( )

  Called for Charts that contain axes. Determines if a specific axis type is supported for a value series. For example, a Gantt chart supports only date-time values for an orthogonal axis. A Bar chart supports logarithmic, linear, or date time values.

- validationIndex( )

  Provides the framework with information about the number of data definitions that must have values for a particular series type. For example, a Bar chart requires only one value in a query definition while a stock chart requires four values.

The chart engine provides an extensible class, DefaultSeriesUIProvider, that provides a default implementation for most methods. The example extends this class by adding the following specification to plugin.xml:

```
<extension point="org.eclipse.birt.chart.ui.seriescomposites">
   <seriescomposite
      seriesUIProvider=
         "org.eclipse.birt.chart.examples.radar.ui.series
            .RadarSeriesUIProvider"
      seriesType=
         "org.eclipse.birt.chart.examples.radar.model.type
            .impl.RadarSeriesImpl"/>
</extension>
```

To implement the class, create the class and package specified in the seriesUI Provider attribute. The radar example uses the org.eclipse.birt.chart .examples.radar.ui.series package and the class, RadarSeriesUIProvider. See the source-code example for a complete listing of the RadarSeriesUIProvider class. Extend this class from the DefaultSeriesUIProvider class. The getSeries Class( ) method returns the RadarSeriesImpl class name, as shown in the following code:

```
private static final String SERIES_CLASS =
   RadarSeriesImpl.class.getName( );
   public String getSeriesClass( )
   {
   return SERIES_CLASS;
}
```

The getSeriesDataComponent( ) method constructs parts of the data select tab in chart builder. The radar example uses the code shown in Listing 23-6.

Listing 23-6 getSeriesDataComponent( ) method

```
public ISelectDataComponent getSeriesDataComponent(
   int seriesType,SeriesDefinition seriesDefn,
   ChartWizardContext context, String sTitle )
```

```
{
   if ( seriesType == ISelectDataCustomizeUI.ORTHOGONAL_SERIES )
   {
   return new BaseDataDefinitionComponent(
      BaseDataDefinitionComponent.BUTTON_AGGREGATION,sTitle,
         seriesDefn,ChartUIUtil.getDataQuery( seriesDefn, 0 ),
         context, sTitle );
   }
   else if ( seriesType ==
      ISelectDataCustomizeUI.GROUPING_SERIES )
   {
   BaseDataDefinitionComponent ddc =
      new YOptionalDataDefinitionComponent(
         BaseDataDefinitionComponent.BUTTON_GROUP,
         ChartUIConstants.QUERY_OPTIONAL,seriesDefn,
         seriesDefn.getQuery( ),context,sTitle );
   return ddc;
   }
   return new DefaultSelectDataComponent( );
}
```

The getSeriesDataComponent( ) method is called for the orthogonal series and the optional grouping user interface portions, as shown in Figure 23-20.

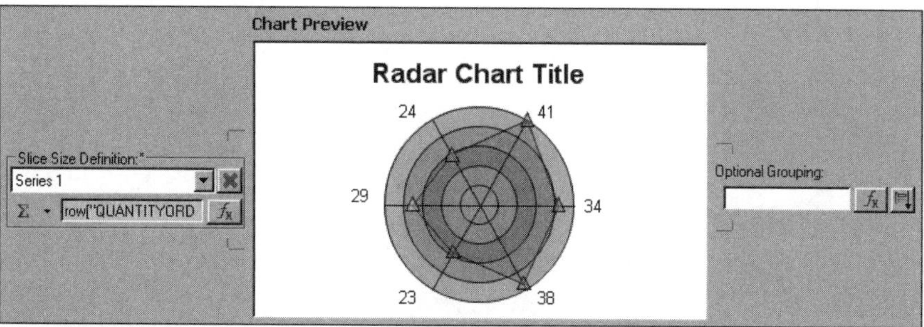

Figure 23-20 Building the user interface for value series and optional grouping

The radar chart cannot use text or date time values for an orthogonal series. The validateSeriesBindingType( ) method verifies that the value series data is a numeric type, as shown in Listing 23-7.

Listing 23-7 validateSeriesBindingType( ) method

```
public void validateSeriesBindingType( Series series,
   IDataServiceProvider idsp ) throws ChartException
{
   Iterator<Query> iterEntries =
      series.getDataDefinition( ).iterator( );
   while ( iterEntries.hasNext( ) )
   {
      Query query = iterEntries.next( );
      DataType dataType =
         idsp.getDataType( query.getDefinition( ) );
      if ( dataType == DataType.TEXT_LITERAL
```

```
            || dataType == DataType.DATE_TIME_LITERAL )
        {
            throw new ChartException( ChartUIExtensionPlugin.ID,
            ChartException.DATA_BINDING,
            query.getDefinition( ) );
            }
        }
    }
```

The getSeriesAttributeSheet method returns an SWT Composite to configure the series in Format Chart in the chart builder. When constructing the user interface, the framework calls this specification for a series, as shown in Figure 23-21.

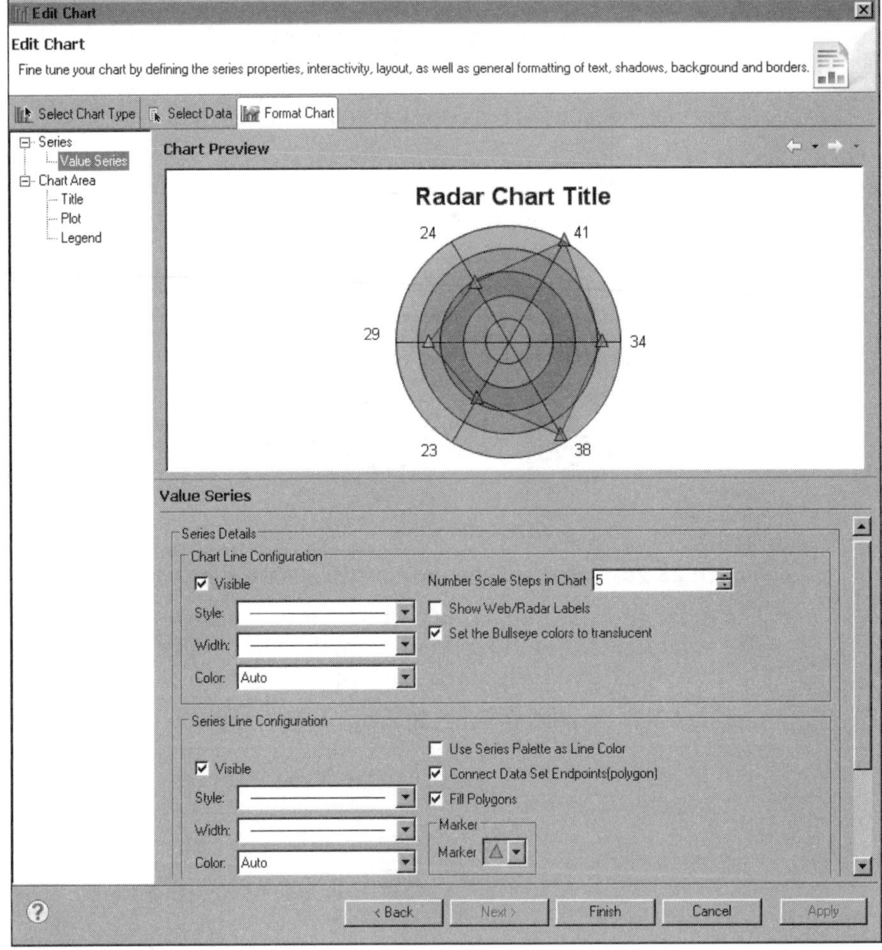

Figure 23-21 Building the user interface for the Value Series

In this example, a new class, RadarSeriesAttributeComposite, performs the actual composite building.

```
public Composite getSeriesAttributeSheet( Composite parent,
   Series series, ChartWizardContext context )
{
   return new RadarSeriesAttributeComposite( parent,
         SWT.NONE,
         context,
         series );
}
```

Add a new class to the package to implement the composite. The radar chart example uses the RadarSeriesAttributeComposite class. This class must extend the org.eclipse.swt.widgets.Composite class and implement the SelectionListener and Listener interfaces from that package, as shown in the following code:

```
public class RadarSeriesAttributeComposite extends Composite
   implements SelectionListener, Listener
```

The constructor for this class verifies the correct series type for the composite and sets the chart model and chart builder context. The call to init( ) sets the height and width for the composite based on the parent container, as shown in Listing 23-8.

Listing 23-8 RadarSeriesAttributeComposite( ) constructor

```
public RadarSeriesAttributeComposite( Composite parent, int style,
   ChartWizardContext context, Series series )
{
   super( parent, style );
   if ( !( series instanceof RadarSeriesImpl ) )
   {
      try
      {
         throw new ChartException( ChartUIExtensionPlugin.ID,
            ChartException.VALIDATION,
            RadarSeriesAttributeComposite.Exception
               .IllegalArgument,
            new Object[ ]{series.getClass( ).getName( )},
            Messages.getResourceBundle( ) );
      }
      catch ( ChartException e )
      {
         logger.log( e );
         e.printStackTrace( );
      }
   }
   this.series = (RadarSeries) series;
   this.context = context;
   this.chart =
      (ChartWithoutAxes) context.getModel( );
   init( );
   placeComponents( );
   ChartUIUtil.bindHelp( parent,
```

```
      ChartHelpContextIds.SUBTASK_YSERIES_LINE );
   }
   private void init( )
   {
   this.setSize( getParent( ).getClientArea( ).width,
      getParent( ).getClientArea( ).height );
   }
   ...
```

The final call in the constructor is placeComponents( ) method, which creates the user interface. Each Radar Series contains line-attribute definitions, which are defined earlier for actual values as well as the background web radar. This example uses only the first series definition to determine how the web-radar background looks.

Before building the complete composite, the implementation checks to see if the series is the first or a subsequent series.Figure 23-22 shows the details of the chart line GUI construction.

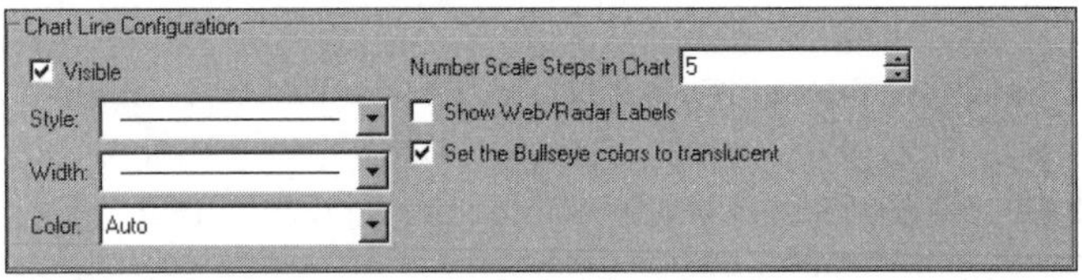

Chart Line Configuration
Visible
Style:
Width:
Color: Auto
Number Scale Steps in Chart 5
Show Web/Radar Labels
Set the Bullseye colors to translucent

Figure 23-22 Building the user interface for the chart line

This portion of the user interface controls the background grid of the chart and is only visible when selecting the first series. The user interface has the standard line attributes to control the web-radar line. The user interface also contains a spinner element to set the number of scale steps in the background, a check box that shows a percentage label at each step, and a check box to determine whether the background color of a bull's-eye radar element is translucent. The rendering process uses these values. The chart uses values from the EMF model.

The code in Listing 23-9 shows how the radar chart example implements the placeComponents( ) method:

Listing 23-9 placeComponents( ) method

```
private void placeComponents( )
{
   boolean show_web_attributes = false;
   RadarSeries rsd = (RadarSeries) chart.getSeriesDefinitions( )
      .get( 0 ).getSeriesDefinitions( ).get( 0 )
      .getDesignTimeSeries( );
   if ( rsd.equals( this.series ) )
   {
      // SeriesIdentifier is not unique
      if( firstSeries.equals(
         this.series.getSeriesIdentifier() ) )
      {
```

```
   show_web_attributes = true;
}
// Main content composite
this.setLayout( new GridLayout( ) );
if ( show_web_attributes )
{
   grpLine = new Group( this, SWT.NONE );
   GridLayout glLine = new GridLayout( 3, false );
   grpLine.setLayout( glLine );
   grpLine.setLayoutData(
      new GridData( GridData.FILL_BOTH ) );
   grpLine.setText( Messages.getString(
      "RadarSeriesMarkerSheet.Label.Web" ) );
   wliacLine = new LineAttributesComposite( grpLine,
      SWT.NONE,
      context,
      series.getWebLineAttributes( ),
      true,
      true,
      true );
   GridData wgdLIACLine = new GridData( );
   wgdLIACLine.widthHint = 200;
   wgdLIACLine.verticalSpan = 3;
   wliacLine.setLayoutData( wgdLIACLine );
   wliacLine.addListener( this );
   lblWebStep = new Label( grpLine, SWT.NONE );
{
lblWebStep.setText( Messages.getString(
   "Radar.Composite.Label.ScaleCount" ) );
lblWebStep.setToolTipText( Messages.getString(
   "Radar.Composite.Label.ScaleCountToolTip" ) );
}
iscScaleCnt = new Spinner( grpLine, SWT.BORDER );
GridData gdISCLeaderLength = new GridData( );
gdISCLeaderLength.widthHint = 100;
iscScaleCnt.setLayoutData( gdISCLeaderLength );
iscScaleCnt.setMinimum( 1 );
iscScaleCnt.setMaximum( MAX_STEPS );
iscScaleCnt.setSelection(
   series.getPlotSteps( ).intValue( ) );
iscScaleCnt.addSelectionListener( this );
   btnWebLabels = new Button( grpLine, SWT.CHECK );
{
   btnWebLabels.setText(
      Messages.getString(
         "RadarSeriesAttributeComposite.Lbl.ShowWeb" ) );
   btnWebLabels.setSelection( series.isShowWebLabels( ) );
   btnWebLabels.addSelectionListener( this );
   GridData gd = new GridData( GridData.FILL_HORIZONTAL );
   gd.horizontalSpan = 2;
   btnWebLabels.setLayoutData( gd );
}
btnTranslucentBullseye = new Button( grpLine, SWT.CHECK );
{
```

```
         btnTranslucentBullseye.setText(
         Messages.getString(
            "Radar.Composite.Label.bullsEye" ) );
         btnTranslucentBullseye.setSelection(
            series.isBackgroundOvalTransparent( ) );
         btnTranslucentBullseye.addSelectionListener( this );
         GridData gd = new GridData( GridData.FILL_HORIZONTAL );
         gd.horizontalSpan = 2;
         gd.verticalAlignment = SWT.TOP;
         btnTranslucentBullseye.setLayoutData( gd );
         btnTranslucentBullseye.setVisible(
            chart.getSubType( ).equals(
            Radar.BULLSEYE_SUBTYPE_LITERAL ) );
      }
   }
   grpLine2 = new Group( this, SWT.NONE );
   GridLayout glLine2 = new GridLayout( 2, false );
   glLine2.horizontalSpacing = 0;
   grpLine2.setLayout( glLine2 );
   grpLine2.setLayoutData( new GridData( GridData.FILL_BOTH ) );
   grpLine2.setText( Messages.getString(
      "RadarSeriesMarkerSheet.Label.Series" ) );
   liacLine =
      new LineAttributesComposite( grpLine2,
      SWT.NONE,
      context,
      series.getLineAttributes( ),
      true,
      true,
      true );
   GridData gdLIACLine = new GridData( );
   gdLIACLine.verticalSpan = 4;
   gdLIACLine.widthHint = 200;
   liacLine.setLayoutData( gdLIACLine );
   liacLine.addListener( this );
   Composite cmp = new Composite( grpLine2, SWT.NONE );
   cmp.setLayoutData( new GridData( GridData.FILL_BOTH ) );
   cmp.setLayout( new GridLayout( ) );
   btnPalette = new Button( cmp, SWT.CHECK );
   {
   btnPalette.setText( Messages.getString(
      "RadarSeriesAttributeComposite.Lbl.LinePalette" ) );
   btnPalette.setSelection( series.isPaletteLineColor( ) );
   btnPalette.addSelectionListener( this );
   }
   btnConnectEndPoints = new Button( cmp, SWT.CHECK );
   {
   btnConnectEndPoints.setText(
   Messages.getString(
      "RadarSeriesAttributeComposite.Lbl.ConnectPoints" ) );
   btnConnectEndPoints.setSelection(
      series.isConnectEndpoints( ) );
   btnConnectEndPoints.addSelectionListener( this );
   }
```

```
   btnFillPoly = new Button( cmp, SWT.CHECK );
   {
   btnFillPoly.setText(
      Messages.getString(
         "RadarSeriesAttributeComposite.Lbl.FillPoly" ) );
   btnFillPoly.setSelection( series.isFillPolys( ) );
   btnFillPoly.addSelectionListener( this );
   btnFillPoly.setEnabled( btnConnectEndPoints.getSelection( ) );
   }
   Group grpMarker = new Group( cmp, SWT.NONE );
   grpMarker.setText( Messages.getString(
      "RadarSeriesMarkerSheet.GroupLabel.Markers" ) );
   grpMarker.setLayout( new GridLayout( 2, false ) );
   // Layout for marker
   Label lblMarker = new Label( grpMarker, SWT.NONE );
   lblMarker.setText( Messages.getString(
      "RadarSeriesMarkerSheet.Label.Markers" ) );
   mec = new MarkerEditorComposite( grpMarker,
      series.getMarker( ) );
   enableLineSettings( series.getWebLineAttributes( )
      .isVisible( ) );
   enableLineSettings( series.getLineAttributes( ).isVisible( ) );
}
```

The place components method in the previous code also populates the user interface with the specific series values, as shown in Figure 23-23. If the series is the first series on the radar, the user interface portion is placed below the radar-web user interface.

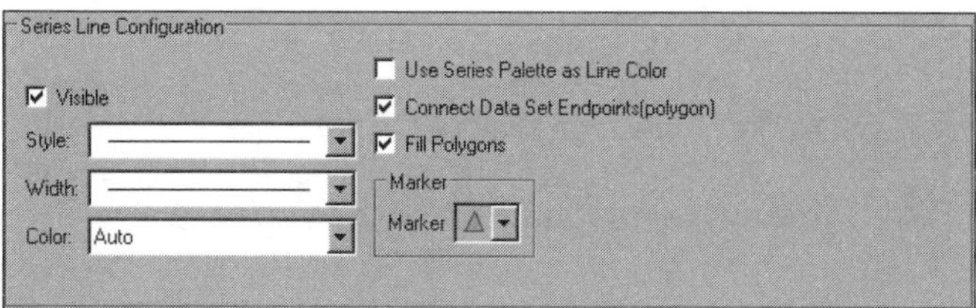

Figure 23-23 Building the series line user interface

The standard line attributes user interface configures the actual line attributes of the radar series. In addition, a check box determines if the series palette color can be used as the line color for the radar. A fill polygons check box determines if the radar series must be filled. A connect data set endpoints check box determines if the first and last data point are connected, which creates a polygon. In addition, a configuration drop-down box can select a specific marker. Note that user interface items are pre-populated with values from the current working model.

The widgetSelected( ) method in this class handles changes to the check boxes and the spinner. This method alters the current series model with the values selected in the user interface, as shown in Listing 23-10.

Listing 23-10 widgetSelected( ) method

```
public void widgetSelected( SelectionEvent e )
{
   if ( e.getSource( ).equals( btnPalette ) )
   {
      series.setPaletteLineColor( btnPalette.getSelection( ) );
   }
   else if ( e.getSource( ).equals( btnFillPoly ) )
   {
      series.setFillPolys( btnFillPoly.getSelection( ) );
   }
   else if ( e.getSource( ).equals( btnConnectEndPoints ) )
   {

   series.setConnectEndpoints( btnConnectEndPoints.getSelection( )
    );

   btnFillPoly.setEnabled( btnConnectEndPoints.getSelection( ) );
   }
   else if ( e.getSource( ).equals( btnTranslucentBullseye ) )
   {

   series.setBackgroundOvalTransparent( btnTranslucentBullseye.get
   Selection( ) );
   }

   else if ( e.getSource( ).equals( mec ) )
   {
      series.setMarker( mec.getMarker( ) );
   }
   else if ( e.getSource( ).equals( iscScaleCnt ) )
   {

   series.setPlotSteps( BigInteger.valueOf( iscScaleCnt.getSelecti
   on( ) ) );
   }
   else if ( e.getSource( ).equals( btnWebLabels ) )
   {
      series.setShowWebLabels( btnWebLabels.getSelection( ) );
   }

}
```

The handleEvent( ) method tracks changes when the series line attributes are altered or when the radar-web background line attributes are changed. As with the widgetSelected( ) method, this method alters the current working radar series model, as shown in Listing 23-11.

Listing 23-11 handleEvent( ) method

```
public void handleEvent( Event event )
{
   if ( event.widget.equals( liacLine ) )
   {
      if ( event.type ==
   LineAttributesComposite.VISIBILITY_CHANGED_EVENT )
      {
         series.getLineAttributes( )
               .setVisible( ( (Boolean)
   event.data ).booleanValue( ) );

   enableLineSettings( series.getLineAttributes( ).isVisible( ) );
      }
      else if ( event.type ==
   LineAttributesComposite.STYLE_CHANGED_EVENT )
      {
         series.getLineAttributes( ).setStyle(
            (LineStyle) event.data );
      }
      else if ( event.type ==
                  LineAttributesComposite.WIDTH_CHANGED_EVENT )
      {
         series.getLineAttributes( )
               .setThickness( ( (Integer)
   event.data ).intValue( ) );
      }
      else if ( event.type ==
   LineAttributesComposite.COLOR_CHANGED_EVENT )
      {
         series.getLineAttributes( )
               .setColor( (ColorDefinition) event.data );
      }
   }
   else if ( event.widget.equals( wliacLine ) )
   {
      if ( event.type ==
   LineAttributesComposite.VISIBILITY_CHANGED_EVENT )
      {
         series.getWebLineAttributes( )
               .setVisible( ( (Boolean)
   event.data ).booleanValue( ) );
         enableLineSettings( series.getWebLineAttributes( )
            .isVisible( ) );
      }
      else if ( event.type ==
   LineAttributesComposite.STYLE_CHANGED_EVENT )
      {
         series.getWebLineAttributes( )
```

```
               .setStyle( (LineStyle) event.data );
      }
      else if ( event.type ==
   LineAttributesComposite.WIDTH_CHANGED_EVENT )
      {
         series.getWebLineAttributes( )
               .setThickness( ( (Integer)
   event.data ).intValue( ) );
      }
      else if ( event.type ==
   LineAttributesComposite.COLOR_CHANGED_EVENT )
      {
         series.getWebLineAttributes( )
               .setColor( (ColorDefinition) event.data );
      }
   }
}
```

The enableLineSettings( ) method disables or enables the series palette as line color check box. If the line series configuration user interface is not visible, the default behavior is to use the series palette as the line color and the check box is disabled. If the line series configuration user interface is visible, the check box is enabled.

```
private void enableLineSettings( boolean isEnabled )
{
   if ( btnPalette != null )
   {
      btnPalette.setEnabled( isEnabled );
   }
}
```

Run-time Plug-in extensions

The run-time extensions should be implemented in the plug-in that extends the chart model described in the first part of this chapter. In the radar example, these extension points are implemented in the org.eclipse.birt.chart .examples.core plug-in. The following sections discuss each of the extension points, org.eclipse.birt.chart.engine.modelreneerers, org.eclipse.birt.chart .engine.datasetprocessors, and org.eclipse.birt.chart.engine.charttypes.

Chart model types extension point

The chart engine framework uses the charttypes extension point to load the custom model. This example implements this extension point with the RadarModelLoader class located in the org.eclipse.birt.chart.examples.radar .model package. This class has only one method which creates an instance of the RadarTypePackage.

```
public class RadarModelLoader implements IExtChartModelLoader
{
   public EPackage getChartTypePackage( )
   {
      return RadarTypePackage.eINSTANCE;
   }
}
```

The plugin.xml snippet for the extension point is shown below:

```
<extension
    point="org.eclipse.birt.chart.engine.charttypes">
    <chartType
      modelLoader=
      "org.eclipse.birt.chart.examples.radar.model
         .RadarModelLoader"
      namespaceURI=
         "http://www.birt.eclipse.org/RadarChartModelType"
   </chartType>
</extension>
```

Data processor extension point

The data set processors extension point supports setting up a processor class to handle row navigation and population of data sets for a chart series. This example requires only the default data set processor, because there are only two values per data point.

To specify the default data set processor, open plugin.xml and add the following code:

```
<extension
    point="org.eclipse.birt.chart.engine.datasetprocessors">
    <datasetProcessor
      processor=
         "org.eclipse.birt.chart.extension.datafeed
            .DataSetProcessorImpl"
      series=
         "org.eclipse.birt.chart.examples.radar.model.type.impl
            .RadarSeriesImpl"/>
</extension>
```

Model Renderer Extension Point

The model renderer extension point is the final extension point in this example. This extension point renders a series. All the previous processing creates and modifies the series model. This extension point focuses on the actual mechanics of drawing the series.

All model renderers must extend from one of two abstract classes, AxesRenderer or BaseRenderer. When a series renderer does not require axes or the axes are drawn in the series renderer, extend the BaseRenderer class. If the model renderer requires axes and needs the framework to generate these axes, extend AxesRenderer.

In a radar-web chart, the axes render in a radial fashion, which the AxesRenderer class currently does not handle, so this example extends the BaseRenderer class. The following code shows the plugin.xml snippet for this extension point:

```
<extension
   point="org.eclipse.birt.chart.engine.modelrenderers">
   <modelRenderer
      renderer=
         "org.eclipse.birt.chart.examples.radar.render.Radar"
       series=
         "org.eclipse.birt.chart.examples.radar.model.type.impl
            .RadarSeriesImpl"/>
</extension>
```

The modelRenderer element has two attributes, series and renderer. The series attribute contains the series class used with the renderer. The renderer attribute declares the class that extends one of the renderer classes. Add this snippet to the plugin.xml and create the package and class specified in the renderer attribute. In the radar example, the Radar class located in the org.eclipse.bir.chart.examples.radar.render package is used and extends from the BaseRenderer class.

The BaseRenderer class implements the ISeriesRenderer interface, providing a set of convenience methods for use by a model renderer. The convenience methods are not discussed in this chapter. See the Javadoc for more details.

The ISeriesRenderer interface contains the following methods, which a series renderer must implement, since an implementation does not exist in the abstract BaseRenderer class:

- Compute( )

  Called by the chart engine framework in the chart engine build( ) method just before returning the GenerateChartState object used for rendering the chart. This method gives the series renderer the opportunity to do pre-processing on the data to be rendered.

- renderLegendGraphic( )

  Called when rendering the legend graphic. For example, rendering a legend line in a line chart using the specified series color and marker.

- renderSeries( )

  Called by the framework for each series when rendering the series graphics for the series type.

Before discussing the actual implementation of these methods, this section provides a small primer about how the drawing framework for the chart engine works. All model renderers are passed an instance of an object that implements the IPrimitiveRenderer interface. This object renders the primitives by implementing the org.eclipse.birt.chart.engine.devicerenderers extension point.

The IPrimitiveRenderer interface describes methods such as drawCircle( ), drawRectangle( ), and fillOval( ). This approach insulates the model renderer from the underlying mechanics of writing the actual output for a chart. The new model renderers function in existing frameworks, such as BIRT, which use the chart engine.

Each of the primitive render methods requires a parameter that defines the object to draw. For example, drawing a line requires start and end points. This parameter object is an instance of an object that extends the abstract class, PrimitiveRenderEvent.

PrimitiveRenderEvent contains information used with all object types, such as the background color and line attributes, which the concrete classes must implement. Each primitive render method has an associated, specific class that extends the PrimitiveRenderEvent class.

Currently BIRT supplies device renderers for the SWT, Swing, BMP, JPG, PNG, SVG and PDF formats, as shown in Figure 23-24.

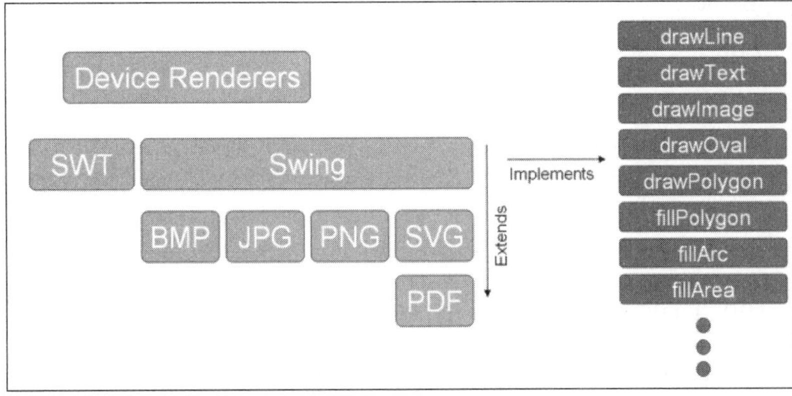

Figure 23-24 Implementing and extending device renderers

For example, the drawLine( ) method is passed a LineRenderEvent object. This class defines the start and end points for a line as well as properties like the line attributes. Refer to the Javadoc to find all the required methods to set for a particular render event object.

Assume that a model renderer is passed the ipr object, which is an instance of the SWTRendererImpl class that implements the IPrimitiveRenderer interface. A line can be drawn by first setting up a LineRenderEvent (myLre) event then calling ipr.drawLine(myLre).

To increase performance, the chart engine also uses an event object cache. This cache stores previously created RenderEvent objects for reuse and is encapsulated in the EventObjectCache class. The device renderer provides a convenience method to retrieve objects from the cache. If the event object does not exist in the cache, it is created, stored in the cache, and returned.

The method, getEventObject( ), takes two parameters, source and type. The source parameter identifies the part of the rendering framework from which the event originates. The type parameter specifies the class that implements the event.

To create the source parameter, BIRT provides the StructureSource class that has methods for creating the various framework sources. For example, when rendering the legend, the source parameter can be created using the StructureSource.createLegend( ) method. When rendering the series, the StructureSource.createSeries( ) method is used.

The source parameter is used by various aspects of the framework, such as interactivity functions. The StructureSource class is also extended by the WrappedStructureSource class, which provides details for a subcomponent of the StructureSource. For example, when rendering a data point, the WrappedStructureSource.createSeriesDataPoint( ) method is used, passing the series as well as the specific data point values for the source. See the Javadoc for StructureSource and WrappedStructureSource to find what specific sources can be created.

A line-render event in the renderLegendGraphic( ) method can be created, as shown in the following code:

```
final LineRenderEvent lre = (LineRenderEvent) ((EventObjectCache)
   ipr).getEventObject(StructureSource.createLegend(lg),
   LineRenderEvent.class);
```

The render event object can then be populated with the appropriate values and passed as a parameter to the drawLine( ) method of the primitive renderer object.

For a design-time series, many run-time series can be generated. For example, when the series are grouped, this situation often requires the copying or creation of new objects defined in the chart EMF model.

To assist in quickly creating these objects, BIRT provides a factory class GObjectFactory that provides creation and copy methods for portions of the chart model. To get access to the object factory, an instance method is provided. The following line is used in the example:

```
protected final static IGObjectFactory goFactory =
   GObjectFactory.instance();
```

The chart engine also provides two utility classes that can be used by model renderers to control z-ordering within and between series. These classes are DeferredCache and DeferredCacheManager.

The DeferredCacheManager is set up during the render phase of chart creation and the one instance can be used by all model renders and the framework in many instances. This class is designed to manipulate one or more DeferredCached instances, allowing drawing events for one or more series to be cached and flushed at appropriate times.

A DeferredCache instance is created for each run-time series for 2D charts or one instance is used with 3D, 2D with depth, and 2D series that are specifically defined to only use one cache. The DeferredCache class provides utility methods to add rendering events to the cache, like addLine( ), addPlane( ), or addLabel( ). Where appropriate these methods allow passing in a z-order value.

The model renderer can call specific flush methods to draw the elements at specific times during processing. To simplify the radar chart example, the deferred cache mechanisms are not often used.

The first method implemented in the Radar class is the renderLegendGraphic ( ) method. As stated earlier, this method is called anytime the legend is rendered. This method is called by the framework for every element that is rendered in the legend.

In the radar chart, render the marker used and optionally a line through the marker. First, verify the bounds that are passed to the method. The bounds object is the area for rendering the particular legend graphic.

Next, retrieve the current series by using a convenience method from the BaseRenderer class named getSeries. Use this method to retrieve the line attributes that are configured for the series.

If the line is visible, draw a line in the legend. To draw the line, a LineRenderEvent event is used, as described earlier. Once the event is created, set the line attributes, start and end points based on the bounds, then draw the line, as shown in Listing 23-12.

Listing 23-12 renderLegendGraphic( ) method

```
public void renderLegendGraphic( IPrimitiveRenderer ipr,
   Legend lg,
   Fill fPaletteEntry, Bounds bo ) throws ChartException
{
   if ( ( bo.getWidth( ) == 0 ) && ( bo.getHeight( ) == 0 ) )
   {
      return;
   }
   final ClientArea ca = lg.getClientArea( );
   final LineAttributes lia = ca.getOutline( );
   final RadarSeries ls = (RadarSeries) getSeries( );
   if ( fPaletteEntry == null )
   {
      fPaletteEntry = ColorDefinitionImpl.RED( );
   }
   final RectangleRenderEvent rre = ( (EventObjectCache)
   ipr ).getEventObject( StructureSource.createLegend( lg ),
        RectangleRenderEvent.class );
   rre.setBackground( ca.getBackground( ) );
   rre.setOutline( lia );
   rre.setBounds( bo );
```

```
ipr.fillRectangle( rre );
LineAttributes liaMarker = ls.getLineAttributes( );
if ( !liaMarker.isSetVisible( ) )
{
   throw new ChartException( ChartEngineExtensionPlugin.ID,
         ChartException.RENDERING,
         exception.unspecified.marker.linestyle.visibility,
         Messages.getResourceBundle( getRunTimeContext( )
            .getULocale( ) ) );
}
if ( liaMarker.isVisible( ) )
{
   final LineRenderEvent lre =
      ( (EventObjectCache) ipr )
         .getEventObject( StructureSource.createLegend( lg ),
            LineRenderEvent.class );

   if ( fPaletteEntry instanceof ColorDefinition &&
      ( ls.isSetPaletteLineColor( ) &&
         ls.isPaletteLineColor( ) ) )
   {
      liaMarker = goFactory.copyOf( liaMarker );
      liaMarker.setColor( goFactory.copyOf( FillUtil.getColor(
         fPaletteEntry ) ) );
   }
   lre.setLineAttributes( liaMarker );
   lre.setStart( LocationImpl.create( bo.getLeft( ) + 1,
      bo.getTop( )#NAME?/ 2 ) );
   lre.setEnd( LocationImpl.create( bo.getLeft( ) +
      bo.getWidth( ) - 1,
      bo.getTop( ) + bo.getHeight( ) / 2 ) );
   ipr.drawLine( lre );
}
...
```

Next, the markers are rendered using a convenience method provided by the base renderer class that handles drawing markers. This method is named renderMarker( ) and is passed various values like the bounds, palette entry, and device renderer. The code for this continuing portion of the renderLegendGraphic( ) method is presented in Listing 23-13.

Listing 23-13 renderLegendGraphic( ) (continued)

```
SeriesDefinition sd = getSeriesDefinition( );

final boolean bPaletteByCategory = isPaletteByCategory( );

if ( bPaletteByCategory && ls.eContainer( )
   instanceof SeriesDefinition )
{
   sd = (SeriesDefinition) ls.eContainer( );
}
```

```
   int iThisSeriesIndex = sd.getRunTimeSeries( ).indexOf( ls );
   if ( iThisSeriesIndex < 0 )
   {
      throw new ChartException( ChartEngineExtensionPlugin.ID,
            ChartException.RENDERING,
            exception.missing.series.for.palette.index,
            new Object[ ]{
               ls, sd },
            Messages.getResourceBundle(
               getRunTimeContext( ).getULocale( ) ) );
      }
   Marker m = null;
   // need
   m = ls.getMarker( );
   double width = bo.getWidth( ) / getDeviceScale( );
   double height = bo.getHeight( ) / getDeviceScale( );
   int markerSize = (int) ( ( ( width > height ? height : width )
      - 2 ) / 2 );
   if ( markerSize <= 0 )
   {
      markerSize = 1;
   }
   if ( m != null && m.isVisible( ) )
   {
      renderMarker( lg, ipr, m,
         LocationImpl.create( bo.getLeft( ) + bo.getWidth( ) / 2,
         bo.getTop( ) + bo.getHeight( ) / 2 ),
         ls.getLineAttributes( ),
         fPaletteEntry,
         null,
         new Integer( markerSize ),
            false,
            false );
   }
}
```

The compute( ) method is called prior to any of the render methods during the build phase of the chart. This method gives the model renderer an opportunity to do pre-calculations or validation of data.

In the example, the radar compute( ) method validates that the number of data points for the base series and the orthogonal series is equal using the validateDataSetCount( ) method of BaseRenderer. It also validates the scale used by the chart as shown in Listing 23-14.

Listing 23-14 compute method

```
public void compute( Bounds bo, Plot p, ISeriesRenderingHints
   isrh )
      throws ChartException
{
   final SeriesRenderingHints srh = (SeriesRenderingHints) isrh;
```

```
// VALIDATE CONSISTENT DATASET COUNT BETWEEN BASE AND
ORTHOGONAL
try
{
   validateDataSetCount( isrh );
}
catch ( ChartException vex )
{
   throw new ChartException( ChartEngineExtensionPlugin.ID,
         ChartException.GENERATION,
         vex );
}

// SCALE VALIDATION
try
{
   dpha = srh.getDataPoints( );

   double[ ] da = srh.asPrimitiveDoubleValues( );

   if ( dpha == null || da == null ||
      dpha.length < 1 || da.length < 1 )
   {
      throw new ChartException( ChartEngineExtensionPlugin.ID,
            ChartException.RENDERING,
            exception.invalid.datapoint.dial,
org.eclipse.birt.chart.engine.extension.i18n.Messages
   .getResourceBundle( getRunTimeContext( ).getULocale( ) ) );
   }

   // Currently only using the base series to store
   // web/radar-specific information
   RadarSeries rsd = getFirstSeries( );
   int psc = rsd.getPlotSteps( ).intValue( );
   if ( psc > 20 )
   {
      psc = 20;
   }
   if ( psc < 1 )
   {
      psc = 1;
   }
   scaleCount = psc;

   // Set on Plot dialog
   double cvr =
      ( (ChartWithoutAxes) getModel( ) ).getCoverage( );
   if ( cvr <= 0 )
   {
      cvr = 0.8;
   }
```

```
      percentReduce = 1 - cvr;
      dSafeSpacing *= getDeviceScale( );
   }
   catch ( Exception ex )
   {
      ex.printStackTrace( );
      throw new ChartException( ChartEngineExtensionPlugin.ID,
            ChartException.GENERATION,ex );
   }
}
```

The chart engine calls the renderSeries( ) method for every generated run-time series. This method calculates the data set min and max values and stores them in a class variable. These values are used to scale the radar. The render method for the series is then called. The code in Listing 23-15 shows the getDsMinMax( ) method and the renderSerie( ) methods which implement this functionality.

Listing 23-15 getDsMinMax( ) and renderSeries( ) methods

```
private void getDsMinMax( )
{
   PluginSettings ps = PluginSettings.instance( );
   IDataSetProcessor iDSP = null;
   DataSet dst;

   EList<SeriesDefinition> el =
      ( (ChartWithoutAxes) getModel( ) ).getSeriesDefinitions( );
   ArrayList<Series> al =
      new ArrayList<Series>( );
   ( (ChartWithoutAxesImpl)getModel( ) ).recursivelyGetSeries(
         el,al,0, 0 );
   final Series[ ] sea = al.toArray( new Series[al.size( )] );

   for ( int i = 0; i < sea.length; i++ )
   {
      try
      {
         iDSP = ps.getDataSetProcessor( sea[i].getClass( ) );
         dst = sea[i].getDataSet( );
         Double min = (Double) iDSP.getMinimum( dst );
         Double max = (Double) iDSP.getMaximum( dst );

         if ( min != null && min < axisMin )
         {
            this.axisMin = min;
         }
         if ( max != null && max > axisMax )
         {
            this.axisMax = max;
         }
      }
```

```
        catch ( Exception e )
        {
            e.printStackTrace( );
        }
    }
}

public void renderSeries( IPrimitiveRenderer ipr, Plot p,
    ISeriesRenderingHints isrh ) throws ChartException
{
    SeriesDefinition sd = getSeriesDefinition( );
    ChartWithoutAxes cwoa = (ChartWithoutAxes) getModel( );
    if ( cwoa.getDimension( ) !=
        ChartDimension.TWO_DIMENSIONAL_LITERAL )
    {
        throw new ChartException( ChartEngineExtensionPlugin.ID,
            ChartException.RENDERING,
            exception.dial.dimension,
            new Object[ ]{cwoa.getDimension( ).getName( )},
            Messages.getResourceBundle(
                getRunTimeContext( ).getULocale( ) ) );
    }

    logger.log( ILogger.INFORMATION,
            Messages.getString( "info.render.series",
                    getRunTimeContext( ).getULocale( ) )
                    + getClass( ).getName( )
                    #NAME?
                    + iSeriesCount );

    getDsMinMax( );

    render( getDevice( ),
            srh.getClientAreaBounds( true ),
            (RadarSeries) getSeries( ),
            sd );
}
```

The render method draws the actual radar. This method uses values from the model to determine how to display the chart.

The render method first calculates the center point and radial sizes of the radar chart. If the series is a bulls-eye chart the ovals are rendered. The data points are iterated and markers and labels are rendered. The points are then used in the renderPolys( ) method to render each of the lines and polygons. Finally, the method renders the web labels if the series is the last in the axes. The code for the render method is shown in Listing 23-16.

Listing 23-16 render method

```
private final void render( IDeviceRenderer idr, Bounds bo,
    RadarSeries se, SeriesDefinition sd ) throws ChartException
```

```
{
   List<Series> rts = sd.getRunTimeSeries( );
   int iThisSeriesIndex = rts.indexOf( se );

   if ( iThisSeriesIndex == -1 )
      iThisSeriesIndex = getSeriesIndex( );

   int totalSeriesCnt = getSeriesCount( );
   int currSeriesIdx = getSeriesIndex( );

   final EList<Fill> elPalette =
   sd.getSeriesPalette( ).getEntries( );
   final AbstractScriptHandler<?> sh =
   getRunTimeContext( ).getScriptHandler( );
   dc = getDeferredCache( );

   // render polys biggest to least
   // render axes
   // render labels
   // render markers

   Bounds boCA = goFactory.copyOf( bo );

   double dh = boCA.getHeight( ) - ( boCA.getHeight( ) *
   percentReduce );
   double dl = boCA.getLeft( ) + ( boCA.getWidth( ) *
   percentReduce ) / 2;
   double dt = boCA.getTop( ) + ( boCA.getHeight( ) *
   percentReduce ) / 2;
   double dw = boCA.getWidth( ) - ( boCA.getWidth( ) *
   percentReduce );
   double centrePointX = Math.round( dl + dw / 2 );
   double centrePointY = Math.round( dt + dh / 2 );
   double mag = dh / 2;

   Location cntpt = LocationImpl.create( centrePointX,
   centrePointY );

   if ( currSeriesIdx == 1 )
   {
      if ( BULLSEYE_SUBTYPE_LITERAL.equals(
         getModel( ).getSubType( ) ) )
      {
         renderOvalBackgrounds( idr, cntpt, se, mag );
      }
   }

   PolarCoordinate pc = new PolarCoordinate( cntpt,
         dpha.length,
         getSeriesCount( ) - 1,
```

```
        getSeriesIndex( ) - 1 );

    final boolean bPaletteByCategory = isPaletteByCategory( );
    Fill fPaletteEntry = null;
    if ( !bPaletteByCategory )
    {
      fPaletteEntry = FillUtil.getPaletteFill( elPalette,
          iThisSeriesIndex );
      updateTranslucency( fPaletteEntry, se );
    }

    Location loAxis =
      LocationImpl.create( centrePointX, centrePointY );
    List<Location> loList = new LinkedList<Location>( );

    for ( int index = 0; index < dpha.length; index++ )
    {
      DataPointHints dph = dpha[index];

      if ( isNaN( dph.getOrthogonalValue( ) ) )
      {
        continue;
      }

      double currval = ( (Double)
    dph.getOrthogonalValue( ) ).doubleValue( );

      if ( currval < 0 )
      {
        continue;
      }

      pc.computeLocation( loAxis, index, mag );
      Location lo = pc.createLocation( index, mag
          * ( currval / getAxisMax( ) ) );
      loList.add( lo );

      if ( bPaletteByCategory )
      {
        fPaletteEntry = FillUtil.getPaletteFill( elPalette,
          index );
        updateTranslucency( fPaletteEntry, se );
      }

      LineAttributes llia = se.getLineAttributes( );
      if ( se.isPaletteLineColor( ) && index == 0 )
      {
        llia.setColor( goFactory.copyOf( FillUtil
          .getColor( fPaletteEntry ) ) );
```

```
    }

    Marker m = se.getMarker( );
    if ( m != null )
    {
       ScriptHandler.callFunction( sh,
             ScriptHandler.BEFORE_DRAW_DATA_POINT,
                dph,
                fPaletteEntry,
                getRunTimeContext( ).getScriptContext( ) );
       getRunTimeContext( ).notifyStructureChange(
          IStructureDefinitionListener
             .BEFORE_DRAW_DATA_POINT, dph );
       renderMarker( se,
             idr,
             m,
             lo,
             llia,
             fPaletteEntry,
             dph,
             m.getSize( ),
             true,
             false );
       ScriptHandler.callFunction( sh,
          ScriptHandler.AFTER_DRAW_DATA_POINT,
             dph,
             fPaletteEntry,
             getRunTimeContext( ).getScriptContext( ) );
       getRunTimeContext( ).notifyStructureChange(
          IStructureDefinitionListener.AFTER_DRAW_DATA_POINT,
          dph );
    }

    drawSeriesLabel( idr, pc, dph, loAxis );
 }

 renderPolys( idr,
       loList.toArray( new Location[loList.size( )] ),
       se,
       sd );

 // last for rendering
 if ( currSeriesIdx == ( totalSeriesCnt - 1 ) )
 {
    if ( se.getWebLineAttributes( ) != null
          && se.getWebLineAttributes( ).isVisible( ) )
    {
       renderAxes( idr, pc, se, mag );
    }

    RadarSeries rsd = getFirstSeries( );
    if ( rsd.isShowWebLabels( ) )
```

```
        {
            Location loLabel = LocationImpl.create( 0, 0 );
            for ( int sc = 0; sc <= scaleCount; sc++ )
            {
                final TextRenderEvent stre =
                    ( (EventObjectCache) idr ).getEventObject(
                        StructureSource.createSeries( se ),
                        TextRenderEvent.class );
                Label la = goFactory.copyOf( rsd.getLabel( ) );
                la.setVisible( true );
                stre.setTextPosition( TextRenderEvent.RIGHT );
                // use this to set the direction
                rsd.getLabelPosition();
                double lblperc = ( (double) sc / scaleCount ) * 100;
                DecimalFormat decform = new DecimalFormat( "#.##" );
                lblperc = Double.valueOf( decform.format( lblperc ) );

                la.getCaption( ).setValue( lblperc + "%" );
                stre.setLabel( la );

    stre.setAction( TextRenderEvent.RENDER_TEXT_AT_LOCATION );
                double ycord = mag * sc / scaleCount;
                ycord = Math.round( centrePointY - ycord );
                double xcord = Math.round( centrePointX - 10 );
                loLabel.set( xcord, ycord );
                stre.setLocation( loLabel );
                dc.addLabel( stre );
            }
        }
    }
}
```

The renderSeries( ) method of the Radar class calls the render( ) method when the chart engine needs to render a radar series. For each series, the render( ) method creates a location array that contains all the points then renders the appropriate graphic.

The render( ) method first retrieves the current series index and the total number of series. These variables are used to determine when to render specific items.

The render( ) method receives the bounds for the area where the series is rendered. These bounds are modified by the coverage plot setting and new top, left, width, and height variables are created. In addition, the center point of the plot is created.

If the chart is a bulls-eye subchart type and is the first radar series to render, the renderOvalBackgrounds( ) method is called, which is discussed later in this chapter. It draws the banded circles in the background of the chart. Then the render( ) method begins to loop through all data points for the series.

For each new data point, a theta is calculated based on radians that split the entire radar chart into equidistant radials. An x- and y- coordinate is calculated for the individual point. The polar coordinates are handled using a private class within the Radar class. See the source code for more information. If the series is the last, the axes are rendered.

The renderOvalBackgrounds( ) method is only called for bulls-eye subchart types. This method draws a filled-oval background for each band in the radar. The palette color is based on the palette for the first series and incremented by one for every step. The bands are optionally rendered translucent, as shown in Listing 23-17.

Listing 23-17 renderOvalBackgrounds( ) method

```
private void renderOvalBackgrounds( IDeviceRenderer idr,
   Location center,
      Series se, double magnitude )
{

   final OvalRenderEvent ore =
      ( (EventObjectCache)idr ).getEventObject(
         StructureSource.createSeries( se ),
         OvalRenderEvent.class );

   LineAttributes lia = null;
   LineAttributes wlia =
      ( (RadarSeries) se ).getWebLineAttributes( );
   if ( wlia == null )
   {
      lia =
         LineAttributesImpl.create( ColorDefinitionImpl.GREY( ),
         LineStyle.SOLID_LITERAL, 1 );
   }
   else
   {
      lia = wlia;
   }
   ore.setBackground( lia.getColor( ) );
   ore.setOutline( lia );

   for ( int sc = scaleCount; sc >= 1; sc-- )
   {
      double spiderMag = magnitude * sc / scaleCount;
      ore.setBounds( goFactory.createBounds( center.getX( ) -
         spiderMag,
         center.getY( ) - spiderMag,
         spiderMag * 2,
         spiderMag * 2 ) );

      Fill wPaletteEntry = null;
      Palette pa = sd.getSeriesPalette( );
      int ps = pa.getEntries( ).size( );
```

```
        int tscnt = getSeriesCount( );
        int palcnt = ps + tscnt + sc;
        if ( palcnt > ps )
          palcnt = 1;

        wPaletteEntry =
          FillUtil.getPaletteFill( pa.getEntries( ), sc + 1 );
        if ( wPaletteEntry instanceof ColorDefinition )
        {
          RadarSeries rsd = getFirstSeries( );
          if ( rsd.isBackgroundOvalTransparent( ) )
          {
            wPaletteEntry =
            goFactory.translucent(
              (ColorDefinition) wPaletteEntry );
          }
        }
        // ore.setBounds( goFactory.copyOf( bo ) );
        ore.setBackground( wPaletteEntry );
        try
        {
          idr.fillOval( ore );
        }
        catch ( Exception e )
        {
          e.printStackTrace( );
        }
    }
}
```

The renderPolys( ) method is called for every series when the final data point is processed. The prelocation array contains all the points for the series. How the array is drawn depends on settings made in the chart builder. For example, the chart can be rendered as a non-filled polygon, filled polygon, or a disconnected line.

This method uses the PolygonRenderEvent event and calls drawPolygon( ) and fillPolygon( ) for series that require filled polygons. The method uses a LineRenderEvent( ) and drawLine( ) to draw the disconnected line radar series, as shown in Listing 23-18.

Listing 23-18 renderPolys( ) method

```
private void renderPolys( IDeviceRenderer idr, Location[ ]
  prelo, Series se, SeriesDefinition sd )
{
  int iThisSeriesIndex = sd.getRunTimeSeries( ).indexOf( se );
  if ( iThisSeriesIndex == -1 )
    iThisSeriesIndex = getSeriesIndex( );
  final EList<Fill> elPalette =
  sd.getSeriesPalette( ).getEntries( );
```

```
Fill fPaletteEntry = FillUtil.getPaletteFill( elPalette,
     iThisSeriesIndex );

LineAttributes llia = ( (RadarSeries)
se ).getLineAttributes( );

final PolygonRenderEvent pre =
   ( (EventObjectCache) idr ).getEventObject(
      StructureSource.createSeries( se ),
      PolygonRenderEvent.class );
final LineRenderEvent lre =
   ( (EventObjectCache) idr ).getEventObject(
      StructureSource.createSeries( se ),
      LineRenderEvent.class );

if ( se.isSetTranslucent( ) && se.isTranslucent( ) )
{
   if ( fPaletteEntry instanceof ColorDefinition )
   {
      fPaletteEntry = goFactory.translucent(
         (ColorDefinition) fPaletteEntry );
   }
}
// Disconnected Lines
if ( !( (RadarSeries) se ).isConnectEndpoints( ) )
{
   lre.setLineAttributes( llia );
   for ( int i = 0; i < ( prelo.length - 1 ); i++ )
   {
      lre.setStart( prelo[i] );
      lre.setEnd( prelo[i + 1] );
      try
      {
         idr.drawLine( lre );
      }
      catch ( Exception e )
      {
         e.printStackTrace( );
      }
   }
}
else
{
   pre.setBackground( fPaletteEntry );
   pre.setPoints( prelo );
   pre.setOutline( llia );
   try
   {
      idr.drawPolygon( pre );
      if ( ( (RadarSeries) se ).isFillPolys( ) )
```

```
            {
               idr.fillPolygon( pre );
            }
         }
         catch ( Exception e )
         {
            e.printStackTrace( );
         }
      }
   }
```

The drawSeriesLabel( ) method is called by the render( ) method and uses TextRenderEvent to render the labels for a specific data point in the series. The code for this method is shown in Listing 23-19.

Listing 23-19 drawSeriesLabel( ) method

```
private final void drawSeriesLabel( IDeviceRenderer idr,
      PolarCoordinate pc, DataPointHints dph, Location lo )
      throws ChartException
{
   if ( se.getLabel( ).isVisible( ) )
   {
      double space = dSafeSpacing / 2;
      Label la = goFactory.copyOf( se.getLabel( ) );
      la.getCaption( ).setValue( dph.getDisplayValue( ) );
      Location loLabel = lo;

      final TextRenderEvent tre = ( (EventObjectCache) idr )
         .getEventObject( WrappedStructureSource
         .createSeriesDataPoint( se,
            dph ),
            TextRenderEvent.class );
      tre.setLabel( la );
      tre.setAction( TextRenderEvent.RENDER_TEXT_AT_LOCATION );

      int degree = pc.getDegree( dph.getIndex( ) );

      if ( Math.abs( degree ) > 90 )
      {
         tre.setTextPosition( TextRenderEvent.LEFT );
      }
      else
      {
         tre.setTextPosition( TextRenderEvent.RIGHT );
      }

      double dX = -Math.signum( Math.abs( degree ) - 90 ) * space;
      double dY = -Math.signum( degree ) * space;
      loLabel.translate( dX, dY );
      tre.setLocation( loLabel );
```

```
        // Text render event must be either cached or copied here
    for correct interactivity.
        dc.addLabel( tre );
    }
}
```

The final method in this example is the renderAxes( ) method. This method is called by the render( ) method on the last series.

The vertical radials are first drawn and appear on all sub-types. Next, if the chart is a bulls-eye or standard radar chart sub-type, a set of ovals is drawn for each band or step.

If the chart subtype is a spider type, then a set of polygons is drawn using line segments to create the bands. The x- and y- coordinates for each line segment are calculated similar to the way the main data value locations described earlier in this chapter. The code in Listing 23-20 shows the renderAxes( ) method.

Listing 23-20 renderAxes( ) method

```
private void renderAxes( IDeviceRenderer idr, PolarCoordinate pc,
   Series se, double magnitude )
{
   Location center = pc.getCenter( );
   int iSeriesCount = getSeriesCount( ) - 1;
   int iCount = pc.getCount( ) * iSeriesCount;
   pc = new PolarCoordinate( center, iCount, 1, 0 );
   Location lo = center.copyInstance( );

   LineAttributes lia = null;
   LineAttributes wlia = null;
   RadarSeries rsd = getFirstSeries( );
   wlia = rsd.getWebLineAttributes( );
   if ( wlia == null )
   {
      lia = LineAttributesImpl.create(
         ColorDefinitionImpl.GREY( ),
         LineStyle.SOLID_LITERAL,1 );
   }
   else
   {
      lia = wlia;
   }
   final LineRenderEvent lre = ( (EventObjectCache)
      idr ).getEventObject( StructureSource.createSeries( se ),
      LineRenderEvent.class );
   final OvalRenderEvent ore = ( (EventObjectCache) idr )
      .getEventObject( StructureSource.createSeries( se ),
      OvalRenderEvent.class );
   lre.setLineAttributes( lia );
```

```
    // Radials
    lre.setStart( center );
    try
    {
       for ( int i = 0; i < iCount; i++ )
       {
          pc.computeLocation( lo, i, magnitude );
          lre.setEnd( lo );
          idr.drawLine( lre );
       }
       String subType = getModel( ).getSubType( );
       if ( STANDARD_SUBTYPE_LITERAL.equals( subType )||
          BULLSEYE_SUBTYPE_LITERAL.equals( subType ) )
          ore.setBackground( lia.getColor( ) );
          ore.setOutline( lia );
          Bounds bo = BoundsImpl.create( 0, 0, 0, 0 );
          for ( int sc = 1; sc <= scaleCount; sc++ )
          {
             double spiderMag = magnitude * sc / scaleCount;
             ore.setBounds( pc.computeBounds( bo, spiderMag ) );
             idr.drawOval( ore );
          }
       }
       else if ( SPIDER_SUBTYPE_LITERAL.equals( subType ) )
       {
          Location lo1 = lo.copyInstance( );
          for ( int sc = 1; sc < scaleCount + 1; sc++ )
          {
             double spiderMag = magnitude * sc / scaleCount;
             pc.computeLocation( lo1, 0, spiderMag );
             for ( int index = 1; index < iCount + 1; index++ )
             {
                lo.set( lo1.getX( ), lo1.getY( ) );
                pc.computeLocation( lo1, index, spiderMag );
                lre.setStart( lo );
                lre.setEnd( lo1 );
                idr.drawLine( lre );
             }
          }
       }

    }
    catch ( Exception e )
    {
       e.printStackTrace( )3;
    }
 }
```

Debugging this example

When debugging this example, verify that the max perm size setting is set to 256M or greater. This setting is available in the VM arguments entry box in Debug Configuration, as shown in Figure 23-25.

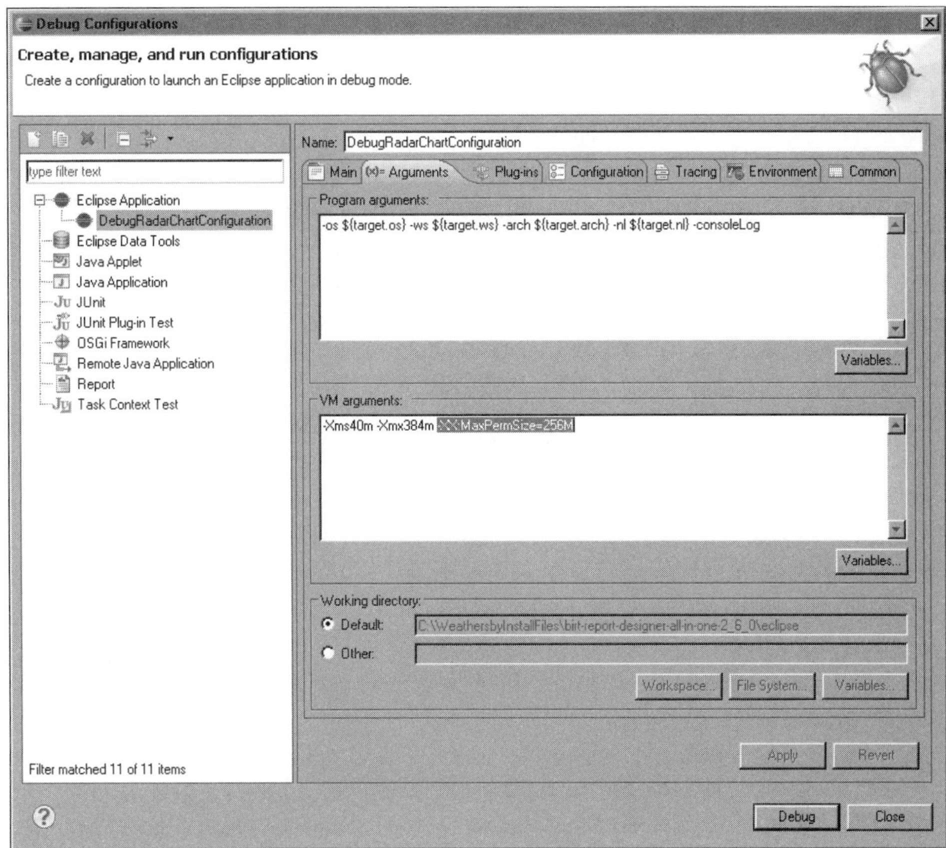

Figure 23-25 Debugging the new Chart Type

Glossary

abstract base class

A class that defines the requirements and behavior of descendant classes by specifying methods and variables. An abstract base class does not support the creation of instances.

Related terms
class, descendant class, method, variable

Contrast with
object

abstraction

A technique that reduces duplication of program code. Abstraction provides a framework for related classes in an object-oriented system.

Related terms
class, object-oriented programming

aggregate function

A function that performs a calculation over a set of data rows. For example, SUM calculates the sum of values of a specified numeric field over a set of data rows. Examples of aggregate functions include AVERAGE, COUNT, MAX, MIN, and SUM.

Related terms
data row, field, function, value

Contrast with
aggregate row, aggregate value

aggregate row

A single row that summarizes data from a group of rows returned by a query. A SQL (Structured Query Language) query that includes an aggregate expression and a Group By clause returns one or more aggregate rows. For example, a row that totals all orders made by one customer is an aggregate row.

Related terms
data, group, query, row, SQL (Structured Query Language)

Contrast with
aggregate value, data row, SQL SELECT statement

aggregate value

The result of applying an aggregate function to a set of data rows. For example, a set of data rows has a field, SPEED, which contains values: 20, 10, 30, 15, 40. Applying the aggregate function MAX to dataSetRow("SPEED"), produces the aggregate value, 40, which is the maximum value for the field.

Related terms
aggregate function, data row, field, value

alias An alternative name:

1 In a SQL SELECT statement, a name given to a database table or column.

2 A name given to a data-set column for use in an expression or in code in a script method.

Related terms
column, data set, database, expression, method, SQL SELECT statement, table

Contrast with
display name

analytics

The iterative process of analyzing data to inform and plan business decisions. Analytics uses drill-down and statistical techniques to examine the same information in both detail and overview forms. Analytics tools promote business intelligence goals by supporting inspection, cleaning, and transformation of data.

Related term
data

ancestor class

A class in the inheritance hierarchy from which a particular class directly or indirectly derives.

Related terms
class, inheritance, hierarchy

Contrast with
class hierarchy, descendant class, subclass, superclass

applet A small desktop application that performs a simple task, for example, a Java program that runs directly from the web browser.

Related terms
application, Java

application

A complete, self-contained program that performs a specific set of related tasks.

Contrast with
applet

application programming interface (API)

A set of routines, including functions, methods, and procedures, that exposes application functionality to support integration and extend applications.

Related terms
application, function, method, procedure

argument

A constant, expression, or variable that supplies data to a function or method.

Related terms
constant, data, expression, function, method, variable

Contrast with
parameter

array A data variable consisting of sequentially indexed elements that have the same data type. Each element has a common name, a common data type, and a unique index number identifier. Changes to an element of an array do not affect other elements.

Related terms
data, element, data type, string, variable

assignment statement

A statement that assigns a value to a variable. For example:

```
StringToDisplay = "My Name"
```

Related terms
statement, value, variable

attribute

A property of an element defined as a name-value pair. For example, in the following line, the attribute defines a Universal Resource Identifier (URI) that links to a web page:

```
<a href="http://www.eclipse.org">
```

Related terms
element, property, Universal Resource Identifier (URI), web page

Contrast with
Extensible Markup Language (XML)

base unit

A unit of time displayed on a time-scale axis in a chart.

Related term
chart

Contrast with
tick

bidirectional text

Text written in multiple languages, at least one of which reads from right-to-left (RTL) and one of which reads from left-to-right (LTR). When right-to-left text, such as Arabic, mixes with left-to-right text, such as English, in the same paragraph, each type of text is written in its own direction.

BigDecimal class

A Java class used for numeric calculations requiring decimal, floating point arithmetic. A BigDecimal value consists of an arbitrary precision integer and a 32-bit integer scale, for example 1024x10 to the power of 3. This class provides accessor methods that support getting and setting the value.

Related terms
class, Java, method, value

Contrast with
Double class, Float class, Integer class

BIRT See Business Intelligence and Reporting Tools (BIRT).

BIRT extension

See Business Intelligence and Reporting Tools (BIRT) extension.

BIRT Report Designer

See Business Intelligence and Reporting Tools (BIRT) Report Designer.

BIRT technology

See Business Intelligence and Reporting Tools (BIRT) technology.

bookmark

An expression that identifies a report element. For example, a table of contents uses a bookmark to navigate to a topic.

Related terms
Business Intelligence and Reporting Tools (BIRT) technology, expression, report element, table of contents

Boolean expression

An expression that evaluates to True or False. For example, Total > 3000 is a Boolean expression. If the condition is met, the condition evaluates to True. If the condition is not met, the condition evaluates to False.

Related term
expression

Contrast with
conditional expression, numeric expression

breakpoint

In BIRT Report Designer, a place marker in a program being debugged. At a breakpoint, execution pauses so the report developer can examine and edit data values.

Related terms
Business Intelligence and Reporting Tools (BIRT) Report Designer, data, debug, value

bridge driver

A driver that maps the functionality of a driver to one with similar behavior in a different system. For example, a JDBC-ODBC bridge driver enables an application that uses the standard Java Database Connectivity (JDBC) protocol to communicate with a database that uses the open database connectivity (ODBC) protocol.

Related terms
application, database, driver, Java Database Connectivity (JDBC), open database connectivity (ODBC), protocol

Business Intelligence and Reporting Tools (BIRT)

An analytics and reporting platform built on Eclipse, the industry standard for open-source software development. BIRT provides a complete solution for extracting data and presenting the results in a formatted document.

Related terms
analytics, data, Eclipse, report

Contrast with
Business Intelligence and Reporting Tools (BIRT) extension

Business Intelligence and Reporting Tools (BIRT) Chart Engine

A tool that supports designing and deploying charts outside a report design. Using this engine, Java developers embed charting capabilities into an application. BIRT Chart Engine is a set of Eclipse plug-ins and Java archive (.jar) files. The chart engine is also known as the charting library.

Related terms
application, Business Intelligence and Reporting Tools (BIRT), chart, design, Java, Java archive (.jar) file, library, plug-in, report

Contrast with
Business Intelligence and Reporting Tools (BIRT) Report Engine

Business Intelligence and Reporting Tools (BIRT) Demo Database

A sample database used in tutorials for BIRT Report Designer and BIRT RCP Report Designer. This package provides this sample database in Derby, Microsoft Access, and MySQL Enterprise formats.

Related terms
Business Intelligence and Reporting Tools (BIRT), Business Intelligence and Reporting Tools (BIRT) Report Designer, Business Intelligence and Reporting Tools (BIRT) Rich Client Platform (RCP) Report Designer, database

Business Intelligence and Reporting Tools (BIRT) extension

A related set of extension points that adds custom functionality to the BIRT platform. BIRT extensions include

- Charting extension

- Rendering extension
- Report item extension

Related terms
Business Intelligence and Reporting Tools (BIRT), charting extension, extension, extension point, rendering extension, report item extension

Business Intelligence and Reporting Tools (BIRT) Report Designer

A tool that builds BIRT report designs and previews reports generated from the designs. BIRT Report Designer is a set of plug-ins to the Eclipse platform and includes BIRT Chart Engine, BIRT Demo Database, and BIRT Report Engine. A report developer who uses this tool can access the full capabilities of the Eclipse platform.

Related terms
Business Intelligence and Reporting Tools (BIRT), Business Intelligence and Reporting Tools (BIRT) Chart Engine, Business Intelligence and Reporting Tools (BIRT) Demo Database, Business Intelligence and Reporting Tools (BIRT) Report Engine, design, Eclipse platform, plug-in, report

Contrast with
Business Intelligence and Reporting Tools (BIRT) Rich Client Platform (RCP) Report Designer

Business Intelligence and Reporting Tools (BIRT) Report Engine

A component that supports deploying BIRT charting, reporting, and viewing capabilities as a stand-alone application or on an application server. BIRT Report Engine consists of a set of Eclipse plug-ins, Java archive (.jar) files, web archive (.war) files, and web applications.

Related terms
application, Business Intelligence and Reporting Tools (BIRT), chart, Eclipse, Java archive (.jar) file, plug-in, report, view, web archive (.war) file

Contrast with
Business Intelligence and Reporting Tools (BIRT) Chart Engine

Business Intelligence and Reporting Tools (BIRT) Rich Client Platform (RCP) Report Designer

A stand-alone tool that builds BIRT report designs and previews reports generated from the designs. BIRT RCP Report Designer uses the Eclipse Rich Client Platform. This tool includes BIRT Chart Engine, BIRT Demo Database, and BIRT Report Engine. BIRT RCP Report Designer supports report design and preview functionality without the additional overhead of the full Eclipse platform. BIRT RCP Report Designer does not support the Java-based scripting and the report debugger functionality the full Eclipse platform provides. BIRT RCP Report Designer can use, but not create, BIRT extensions.

Related terms
Business Intelligence and Reporting Tools (BIRT), Business Intelligence and Reporting Tools (BIRT) Chart Engine, Business Intelligence and Reporting Tools (BIRT) Demo Database, Business Intelligence and Reporting Tools (BIRT) extension, Business Intelligence and Reporting Tools (BIRT) Report

Engine, debug, design, Eclipse platform, Eclipse Rich Client Platform (RCP), extension, Java, report

Contrast with
Business Intelligence and Reporting Tools (BIRT) Report Designer

Business Intelligence and Reporting Tools (BIRT) Samples

A sample of a BIRT report item extension and examples of BIRT charting applications. The report item extension sample is an Eclipse platform plug-in. The charting applications use BIRT Chart Engine. Java developers use these examples as models of how to design custom report items and embed charting capabilities in an application.

Related terms
application, Business Intelligence and Reporting Tools (BIRT), Business Intelligence and Reporting Tools (BIRT) Chart Engine, chart, design, Eclipse platform, Java, plug-in, report, report item, report item extension

Business Intelligence and Reporting Tools (BIRT) technology

A set of Java applications and application programming interfaces (API) that support the design and deployment of a business report. BIRT applications include BIRT Report Designer, BIRT RCP Report Designer, and a report viewer web application servlet. The BIRT Java APIs provide programmatic access to BIRT functionality.

Related terms
application, application programming interface (API), Business Intelligence and Reporting Tools (BIRT), Business Intelligence and Reporting Tools (BIRT) Report Designer, Business Intelligence and Reporting Tools (BIRT) Rich Client Platform (RCP) Report Designer, design, Java, report, report viewer servlet

cascading parameters

Report parameters that have a hierarchical relationship, for example:

```
Country
   State
      City
```

In a group of cascading parameters, each report parameter displays a set of values. When a report user selects a value from the top-level parameter, the selected value determines the values that the next parameter displays, and so on. Cascading parameters display only relevant values to the user. Figure G-1 shows cascading parameters as they appear to a report user.

Related terms
hierarchy, parameter, report, value

cascading style sheet (CSS)

A file containing a set of rules that attaches formats and styles to specified HyperText Markup Language (HTML) elements. For example, a cascading style sheet can specify the color, font, and size of an HTML heading.

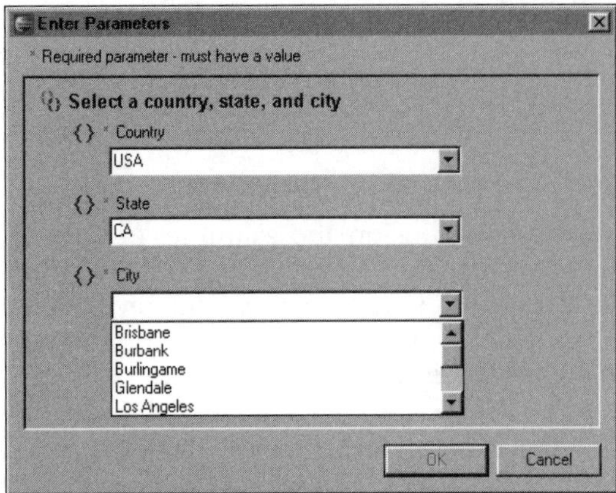

Figure G-1 Cascading parameters

Related terms
element, font, format, HyperText Markup Language (HTML), style

Contrast with
template

case sensitivity

A condition in which the letter case is significant for the purposes of comparison. For example, "McManus" does not match "MCMANUS" or "mcmanus" in a case-sensitive environment.

category

1. In an area, bar, line, step, or stock chart, one of the discrete values that organizes data on an axis that does not use a numerical scale. Typically, the x-axis of a chart displays category values. In a pie chart, category values are called orthogonal axis values and define which sectors appear in a pie.
2. A set of values that can be organized into a hierarchy.

Related terms
chart, data, hierarchy, value

Contrast with
series

cell

The intersection of a row and a column that displays a value in a cross tab, grid element, or table element. Figure G-2 shows a cell.

Related terms
column, cross tab, grid element, row, table element, value

character

An elementary mark that represents data, usually in the form of a graphic spatial arrangement of connected or adjacent strokes, such as a letter or a digit. A character is independent of font size and other display properties. For example, an uppercase C is a character.

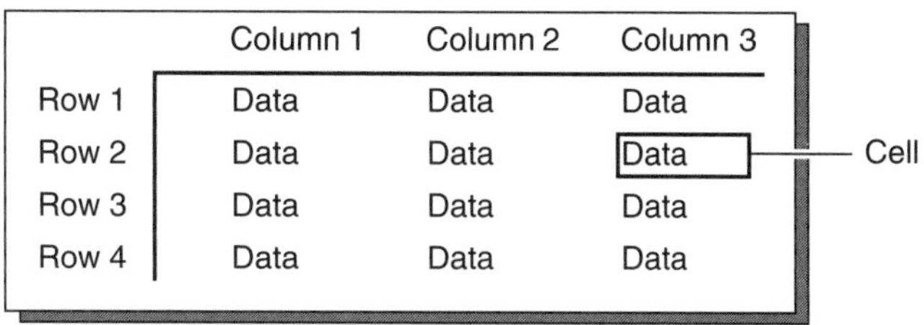

Figure G-2 Cells in a cross tab

Related terms
data, font, property

Contrast with
character set, glyph, string

character set

A mapping of specific characters to code points. For example, in most character sets, the letter A maps to the hexadecimal value 0x21.

Related terms
character, code point

Contrast with
locale

chart

A graphic representation of data or the relationships among sets of data, for example a bar, bubble, line, meter, pie, radar, or stock chart.

Related term
data

Contrast with
chart element

chart element

A report item that displays values from a data set in the form of a chart.

Related terms
chart, data set, report item, value

Contrast with
charting extension

chart engine

See Business Intelligence and Reporting Tools (BIRT) Chart Engine.

charting extension

An extension that adds a new chart type, a new component to an existing chart type, or a new user interface component to the BIRT chart engine.

Related terms
Business Intelligence and Reporting Tools (BIRT) Chart Engine, chart, extension

Contrast with
report item extension

charting library

See Business Intelligence and Reporting Tools (BIRT) Chart Engine.

class

A set of methods and variables that defines the properties and behavior of an object. All objects of a given class are identical in form and behavior, but can contain different data in their variables.

Related terms
data, method, object, property, variable

Contrast with
subclass, superclass

class hierarchy

A tree structure representing inheritance relationships among a set of classes.

Related terms
class, inheritance

class name

A unique name for a class that permits unambiguous references to its public methods and variables.

Related terms
class, method, variable

class variable

A variable that all instances of a class share. An object-oriented environment makes only one copy of a class variable. The value of the class variable is the same for all instances of the class, for example, the taxRate variable in an Order class.

Related terms
class, object-oriented programming, value, variable

code point

A hexadecimal value in a character set. Every character in a character set is represented by a code point. The computer uses the code point to process the character.

Related terms
character, character set, value

column

1 A vertical sequence of cells in a cross tab, grid element, or table element. Figure G-3 shows a column in a cross tab.

	Column 1	Column 2	Column 3
Row 1	Data	Data	Data
Row 2	Data	Data	Data
Row 3	Data	Data	Data

Column of cells

Figure G-3 Column in a cross tab

2 A named field in a database table or query. For each data row, the column can have a different value, called the column value. The term column refers to the definition of the column, not to any particular value. Figure G-4 shows the names of columns in a database table.

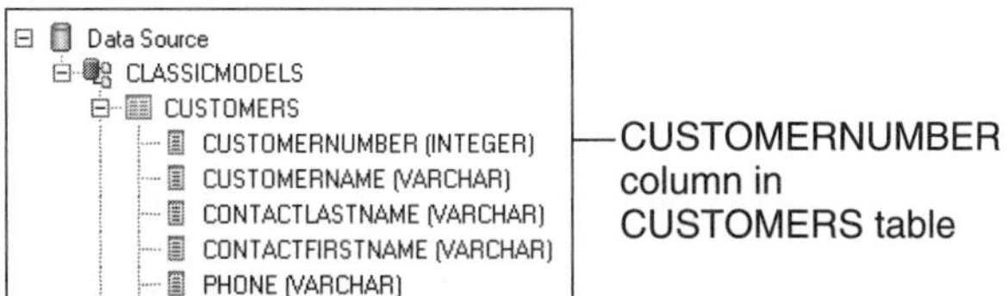

Figure G-4 Columns in a database table

Related terms
cell, cross tab, data row, database, field, grid element, query, table, table element, value

column binding

A named column that defines an expression specifying what data to return. For each piece of data to display in a report, there must be a column binding. Column bindings form a required intermediate layer between data-set data and report elements.

Related terms
column, data, data set, expression, report, report element

column key

An expression used to group data rows into columns and sub-columns in a cross-tab element.

Related terms
column, cross-tab element, data row, expression, group

Contrast with
row key

combination chart

A chart in which multiple data series appear as different chart types. In Figure G-5, for example, the data series for 2004 appears as a line, which stands out as the year of highest annual revenue.

Related terms
chart, data, series

Contrast with
chart element

comma-separated values (CSV) file

A flat file format that stores data in a tabular structure, separating the rows by new-line characters, the column values by commas, and delimiting the column values containing special characters by quotation marks.

Related terms
column, data, flat file, format, row, value

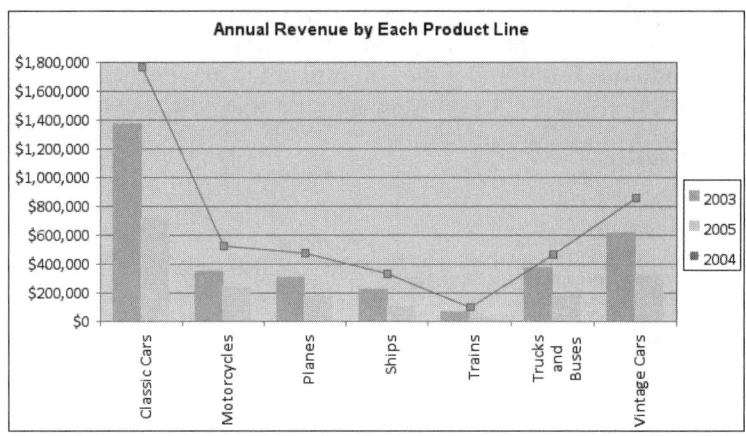

Figure G-5 Combination chart

computed field

A field that displays the result of an expression.

Related terms
expression, field

Contrast with
computed value

computed value

The result of a calculated expression. To display a computed value in a report, use a data element.

Related terms
data element, expression, report, value

Contrast with
computed field

conditional expression

An expression that returns value A or value B depending on whether a Boolean expression evaluates to True or False.

Related terms
Boolean expression, expression, value

conditional format

A format that applies to a cell when a specified condition is met.

Related terms
cell, format

configuration file

An Extensible Markup Language (XML) file containing the parameters and settings used to set run-time values in a program environment. For example, BIRT connection profiles and Eclipse plug-ins use configuration files.

Related terms
Business Intelligence and Reporting Tools (BIRT), Eclipse, parameter, plug-in, run time, value

Connection

A Java object that provides access to a data source.

Related terms
data source, Java, object

constant

An unchanging, predefined value. A constant does not change while a program is running, but the value of a field or variable can change.

Related terms
field, value, variable

constructor code

Code that initializes an instance of a class.

Related term
class

Contrast with
object

container

1 An application that acts as a master program to hold and execute a set of commands or to run other software routines. For example, an application server provides a container that supports communication between an application and an Enterprise JavaBean.

2 A data structure that holds one or more different types of data. For example, a grid element can contain label elements and other report items.

Related terms
application, data, Enterprise JavaBean (EJB), grid element, label element, report item

containment

A relationship among instantiated objects in a report. One object, the container, defines the scope of other objects, the contents.

Related terms
container, instantiation, object, report, scope

containment hierarchy

A hierarchy of objects in a report.

Related terms
hierarchy, object, report

content

See structured content.

converter

A tool that converts data from one format to another format. BIRT technology provides an Excel converter, PDF converter, PostScript converter, PowerPoint converter, Word converter, and an XML converter.

Related terms

Business Intelligence and Reporting Tools (BIRT) technology, data, Excel converter, format, PDF converter, PostScript converter, PowerPoint converter, Word converter, XML converter

cross tab

A report that arranges data into a concise summary for analysis. Data values appear in a matrix of rows and columns. Every cell in a cross tab contains an aggregate value. A cross tab shows how one item relates to another, such as monthly sales revenues aggregated by product line. Figure G-6 shows a cross tab.

Year/QTR/Month 2004			Classic Cars	Motorcycles	Planes	Ships	Trains	Trucks and Buses	Vintage Cars	Grand Total
	1	1	$109,562	$39,987	$31,159	$26,310	$6,387		$42,909	$256,315
		2	$108,232	$45,694	$34,000	$24,894	$4,763	$35,749	$48,688	$302,021
		3	$99,512			$15,559	$9,879	$32,193	$45,252	$202,395
	2	4	$89,998	$32,229	$33,882	$10,808			$33,352	$200,269
		5	$70,698	$47,873	$35,898	$3,440	$4,862	$31,729	$38,536	$233,036
		6	$46,025			$16,472		$41,967	$48,110	$152,574
	3	7	$139,040	$65,156	$43,256	$20,260	$8,985	$36,967	$72,418	$386,082
		8	$140,458	$55,640	$32,083	$23,485	$7,132	$32,147	$65,019	$355,964
		9	$140,177	$6,515	$30,634	$23,114	$5,611	$37,720	$62,984	$306,755
	4	10	$210,010	$69,147	$31,081	$40,881	$13,781	$68,620	$107,121	$540,642
		11	$397,834	$121,934	$97,607	$43,535	$12,148	$78,998	$183,657	$935,713
		12	$131,433	$43,069	$68,654	$43,838	$13,350	$52,612	$75,882	$428,838
	Total		$1,682,980	$527,244	$438,255	$292,595	$86,897	$448,703	$823,928	$4,300,603
Grand Total			$1,682,980	$527,244	$438,255	$292,595	$86,897	$448,703	$823,928	$4,300,603

Figure G-6 Cross tab displaying order totals

Related terms

aggregate value, cell, column, data, report, row, table, value

Contrast with

aggregate function, analytics, cross-tab element, grid

cross-tab element

A report item that displays a cross tab. A cross tab displays aggregate values in a matrix of rows and columns. Figure G-7 shows a cross-tab element.

Related terms

aggregate value, column, cross tab, report item, row

Contrast with

analytics

cross-tabulation

See cross tab.

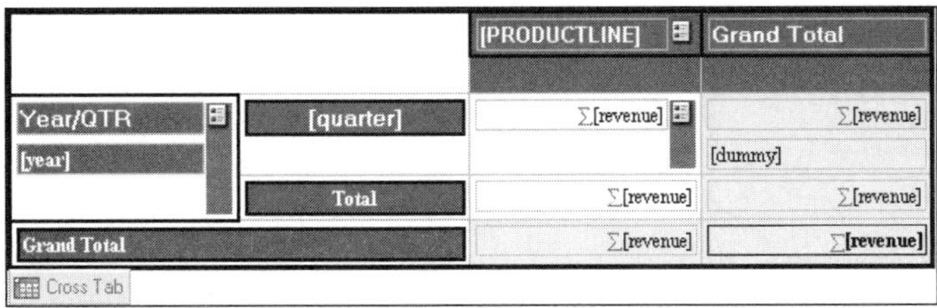

Figure G-7 Cross-tab element

CSS See cascading style sheet (CSS).

cube A multidimensional data structure that provides multiple dimensions and multiple measures to access and analyze large quantities of data. BIRT uses a cube to structure data for display in a cross-tab element.

Related terms
Business Intelligence and Reporting Tools (BIRT), cross-tab element, data, dimension, measure, multidimensional data

Contrast with
analytics

custom data source

See open data access (ODA).

data Information stored in databases, flat files, or other data sources.

Related terms
data source, database, flat file

Contrast with
metadata

data analysis

See analytics.

data binding

See column binding.

data element

A report item that displays a computed value or a value from a data set field.

Related terms
computed value, data set, field, report item, value

Contrast with
label element, Report Object Model (ROM) element, text element

Data Explorer

An Eclipse view that shows the data cubes, data sets, data sources, and report parameters used in a report. Use Data Explorer to create, edit, or delete these items. Figure G-8 shows Data Explorer.

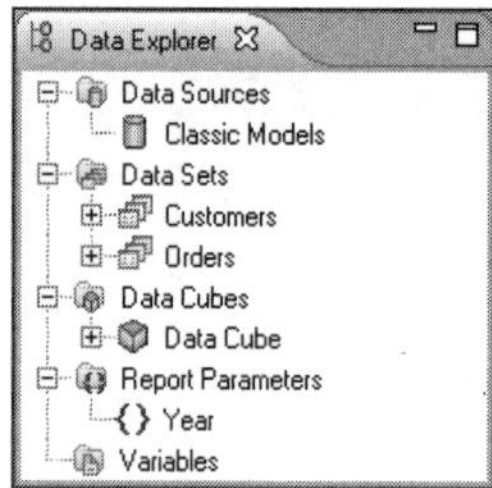

Figure G-8 Data Explorer

Related terms
cube, data set, data source, Eclipse view, parameter, report

data point

A point on a chart that corresponds to a particular pair of *x*- and *y*-axis values.

Related terms
chart, value

Contrast with
data row, data set

data row

One row of data that a data set returns. A data set typically returns many data rows.

Related terms
data, data set, row

Contrast with
data point, data source, filter

data set

A definition of the data to retrieve or compute from a data source.

Related terms
data, data source

Contrast with
data element, data point, data row

data set parameter

A parameter associated with a data set column that restricts the number of data rows that a data set supplies to a report.

Related terms
column, data row, data set, parameter, report

Contrast with
report parameter

data source

1 A relational database or other data repository. For example, an Extensible Markup Language (XML) file, a flat file, or any other source of

information can be a data source. A report can include any of these types of data. This data source provides data rows to a report through a data source element.

2 A design construct that retrieves data rows from a relational database or other data repository.

Related terms
data, data row, database, Extensible Markup Language (XML), flat file, data source element, report

Contrast with
data set

data source element

An item containing connection information for a data source.

Related term
data source

Contrast with
data row, data set

data type

The structure of a value that constrains its characteristics, such as the information the values can hold and permitted operations. In report development, three processes use data types: accessing data, internal processing of data, and formatting output as a report.

Internal data types used by BIRT include Date, Double, Varchar, Time, and Timestamp. These data types map to the Java constants declared in Java.sql.Types, such as DATE, DOUBLE, INT, and STRING. BIRT maps the data types from supported data sources to these internal data types. To format values in a report, BIRT provides date-and-time, number, and string data types.

Related terms
Business Intelligence and Reporting Tools (BIRT), Date data type, date-and-time data type, double data type, Java, number data type, String data type, Time data type, Timestamp data type, value, Varchar data type

database

An integrated collection of logically related records that provides data for information application platforms, such as BIRT. The database model most commonly used is the relational model. Other typical models are entity-relationship, hierarchical, network, object, and object-relational.

Related terms
application, data

database connection

See data source.

database management system (DBMS)

Software that organizes simultaneous access to shared data. Database management systems store relationships among various data elements.

Related term
data, database, element

database schema

See schema.

Date data type

A Java data type used for date-and-time calculations. The base Date data type, java.util.Date, is a class that encapsulates a millisecond date value from January 1, 1970 00:00:00.000 GMT through the year 8099. This Date class provides accessor methods that support getting and setting the value.

Related terms
class, data type, Java, method, value

Contrast with
Time data type, Timestamp data type

date-and-time data type

A data type used to display date, date-and-time, or time values. Report items that contain expressions or fields having a date-and-time data type display the values in the report document. The appearance of these values depends on locale and format settings specified by your computer and the report design.

Related terms
data type, design, expression, field, format, locale, report, report item, value

Contrast with
Date data type, Time data type, Timestamp data type

debug To detect, locate, and fix errors in a computer program. Typically, debugging involves executing specific portions of the program and analyzing the operation of those portions.

declaration

The definition of a class, constant, method, or variable that specifies the name and, if appropriate, the data type.

Related terms
class, constant, data type, method, variable

declarations section

That portion of Java code that contains constant, data type, and global variable declarations.

Related terms
constant, data type, declaration, Java, variable

deploy To bundle and distribute a software package, such as an Eclipse plug-in or a web application, to a run-time environment.

Related terms
application, Eclipse, package, plug-in, run time

derived class

See descendant class.

descendant class

A class that extends another class to provide additional functionality.

Related term
class

Contrast with
subclass, superclass

design A report specification or the act of creating a report specification. Designing a report includes selecting data, laying out the report visually, and saving the layout in a report design file.

Related terms
data, layout, report

Contrast with
file types

design time

The period of time in which a report developer creates a report specification.

Related term
report

Contrast with
design, run time, view time

DHTML (Dynamic Hypertext Markup Language)

See Dynamic HyperText Markup Language (DHTML).

dimension

In a cube, a category containing measures. For example, a dimension, such as orders, can include average cost and total units of products.

Related terms
category, cube, measure

Contrast with
analytics, multidimensional data

display name

An alternative name for a chart series, report parameter, table column, or user-defined Report Object Model (ROM) property. This name can contain any character, including punctuation and spaces. For example, BIRT Report Designer displays this alternative name as a column heading in a report.

Related terms
Business Intelligence and Reporting Tools (BIRT) Report Designer, character, chart, column, property, report, report parameter, Report Object Model (ROM), series, table

Contrast with
alias

document object model (DOM)

A model that defines the structure of a document such as an Extensible Markup Language (XML) or HyperText Markup Language (HTML) document. The DOM defines interfaces that dynamically create, access, and manipulate the internal structure of the document. The Uniform Resource Locator (URL) to the World Wide Web Consortium (W3C) document object model is:

```
www.w3.org/DOM/
```

Related terms
Extensible Markup Language (XML), HyperText Markup Language (HTML), interface, Uniform Resource Locator (URL), World Wide Web Consortium (W3C)

Contrast with
document type definition (DTD), structured content

document type definition (DTD)

A set of Extensible Markup Language (XML) elements and attributes that defines a schema describing the structure of an XML document.

Related terms
attribute, element, Extensible Markup Language (XML), schema

Contrast with
document object model (DOM), structured content

domain name

A name that defines a node on the internet. For example, the domain name of the Eclipse Foundation is eclipse. The Uniform Resource Locator (URL) is:

```
www.eclipse.org
```

Related terms
Eclipse, node, Uniform Resource Locator (URL)

Double class

A Java class that encapsulates the primitive data type, double. The class provides accessor methods that support getting and setting the value.

Related terms
class, data type, double data type, Java, method, value

Contrast with
BigDecimal class, Float class, Integer class, number data type

double data type

A Java data type that stores a double-precision 64-bit IEEE 754 floating point number, from 4.9065645841246544E-324 to 1.79769313486231570E+308 in value.

Related terms
data type, Java, value

Contrast with
Double class, float data type, int data type, number data type

driver An interface that supports communication between an application and another application or a peripheral device such as a printer.

Related terms
application, bridge driver, interface

Dynamic HyperText Markup Language (DHTML)

A HyperText Markup Language (HTML) extension providing enhanced viewing capabilities and interactivity in a web page. The Document Object Model (DOM) Group of the World Wide Web Consortium (W3C) develops DHTML standards.

Related terms
document object model (DOM), HyperText Markup Language (HTML), web page, World Wide Web Consortium (W3C)

dynamic text element

A report item that adjusts its size to display varying amounts of HyperText Markup Language (HTML) or plain text. Figure G-9 shows a dynamic text element in a generated report.

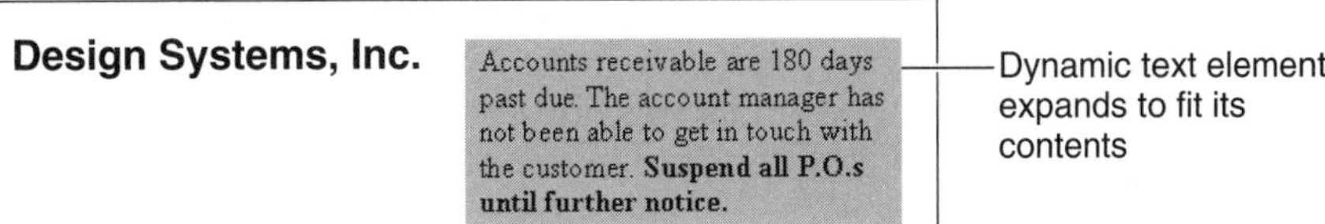

Figure G-9 A report displaying text in a dynamic text element

Related terms
HyperText Markup Language (HTML), report, report item

Contrast with
text element

dynamic variable

A variable that changes during program execution. The program requests the memory allocation for a dynamic variable at run time.

Related terms
run time, variable

Eclipse An open-source development platform, written in Java. The Eclipse platform consists of a plug-in framework, run-time environments, and tools.

Related terms
Eclipse platform, framework, Java, plug-in, run time

Contrast with
Business Intelligence and Reporting Tools (BIRT)

Eclipse launcher

A tool that supports testing an Eclipse project without the need to package the project as a JAR file. For example, the Eclipse Plug-in Development Environment provides a launcher to test new plug-ins.

Related terms
Eclipse, Eclipse Plug-in Development Environment (PDE), Eclipse project, Java archive (.jar) file, plug-in

Eclipse Modeling Framework (EMF)

A Java framework and code generation facility that uses a structured model to build tools and other applications. EMF uses Extensible Markup Language (XML) schemas to generate the EMF model of a plug-in. For example, a BIRT chart type uses EMF to represent the chart structure and properties.

Related terms
application, Business Intelligence and Reporting Tools (BIRT) technology, chart, Eclipse, Extensible Markup Language (XML), framework, Java, plug-in, property, schema

Eclipse perspective

A visual container that includes a set of views and editors. Eclipse Workbench provides a series of perspectives, such as the BIRT Report Designer, Java Development Environment, and Plug-in Development Environment (PDE). A developer can switch between perspectives to work on different tasks. Figure G-10 shows the Eclipse Java perspective.

Related terms
Business Intelligence and Reporting Tools (BIRT) Report Designer, Eclipse, Eclipse Plug-in Development Environment (PDE), Eclipse view, Eclipse Workbench, Java

Contrast with
Eclipse platform, view

Eclipse platform

The framework of the Eclipse application development system. The design-time environment provides user interfaces for specifying application components. The run-time environment provides an extensible system of plug-ins that load and run as needed.

Related terms
application, design time, Eclipse, framework, interface, plug-in, run time

Contrast with
Eclipse perspective, Eclipse view, Eclipse Workbench, extension

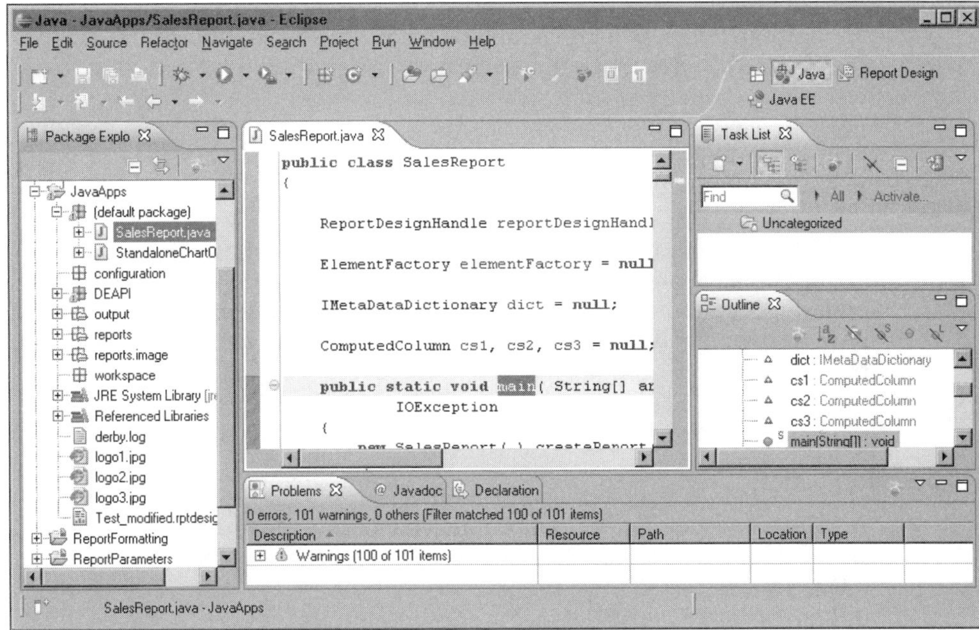

Figure G-10 Eclipse Java perspective

Eclipse Plug-in Development Environment (PDE)

An integrated design tool for creating, developing, testing, debugging, and deploying a plug-in. The Eclipse PDE provides wizards, editors, views, and launchers to support plug-in development. The Eclipse PDE supports design and run-time environments.

Related terms

debug, deploy, design, design time, Eclipse, Eclipse launcher, Eclipse view, plug-in, run time

Contrast with

Eclipse Modeling Framework (EMF), Eclipse platform

Eclipse project

A top-level directory within an Eclipse workspace. An Eclipse project contains folders and files used for builds, resource organization, sharing, and version management.

Related terms

Eclipse, Eclipse workspace, resource

Eclipse Rich Client Platform (RCP)

An Eclipse framework for supporting a client application that uses a minimal set of plug-ins. An Eclipse rich client application is typically a specialized user interface such as the report development tools in BIRT Rich Client Platform (RCP).

Related terms
application, Business Intelligence and Reporting Tools (BIRT) Rich Client Platform (RCP) Report Designer, Eclipse, framework, interface, plug-in, report

Contrast with
Eclipse platform

Eclipse view

A dockable window on the Eclipse Workbench. An Eclipse view can be an editor, the Navigator, a report item palette, a graphical report designer, or any other functional component that an Eclipse perspective provides. A view can have its own menus and toolbars. Multiple views can be visible at one time.

Related terms
design, Eclipse, Eclipse perspective, Eclipse Workbench, Navigator, Palette, report, report item

Eclipse Workbench

A graphical development environment containing perspectives used to create, edit, and view a project, such as the report design perspective.

Related terms
design, Eclipse, Eclipse perspective, Eclipse project, report

Contrast with
Eclipse platform

Eclipse workspace

A file system directory containing one or more projects used to manage resources in Eclipse Workbench.

Related terms
Eclipse project, Eclipse Workbench, resource

EJB See Enterprise JavaBean (EJB).

element

1 A single item of data.

2 A logical structure in an Extensible Markup Language (XML) or HyperText Markup Language (HTML) document specifying a type and optionally one or more attributes and a value. For example, the following code specifies a ConnectionParam element that has three attributes, Name, Display, and Type, and no value:

```
<ConnectionParam Name="username"
  Display="User name"
  Type="string"
/>
```

Related terms
attribute, data, Extensible Markup Language (XML), HyperText Markup Language (HTML), value

Contrast with
report item, Report Object Model (ROM) element

ellipsis

 A button that opens tools that you use to perform tasks, such as navigating to a file or specifying localized text.

encapsulation

A technique that bundles related functions and subroutines. Encapsulation compartmentalizes the structure and behavior of a class so that parts of an object-oriented system do not depend upon or affect each other's internal details.

Related terms
class, function, object, object-oriented programming

enterprise

An integrated set of computers running on multiple platforms in a network environment. Typical software products in an enterprise environment include applications, browsers, databases, and servers that support an information warehouse.

Related terms
application, database, platform

Contrast with
enterprise reporting

enterprise archive (.ear) file

A compressed file format used to deploy Java EE web applications.

Related terms
application, Java Platform Enterprise Edition (Java EE)

Contrast with
Java archive (.jar) file, web archive (.war) file

Enterprise JavaBean (EJB)

A server component used to encapsulate application logic. A client application makes a remote procedure call (RPC) to the server to run an EJB. Enterprise JavaBeans (EJB) are a standards-based framework designed to provide persistence, security, and transactional integrity to enterprise applications.

Related terms
application, enterprise, framework, JavaBean

enterprise reporting

A system that delivers a high volume of complex structured documents that include data from a variety of data sources.

Related terms
data, data source

Contrast with
enterprise, structured content

event An action external to a program that requires handling, such as a mouse click. An event handler in the program collects information about the event and responds.

Related term
event handler

Contrast with
event listener

event handler

A function or method that executes when an event occurs. Report items, data sets, and data sources have event handlers for which a developer can provide code.

Related terms
data set, data source, event, function, method, report, report item

Contrast with
event listener

event listener

An interface that detects when a particular event occurs and calls a function or method to respond to the event.

Related terms
event, function, interface, method

Contrast with
event handler

Excel converter

A module that converts a report or report data to a Microsoft Excel spreadsheet (.xls) file.

Related terms
converter, data, report

exception

An abnormal situation that a program encounters. The program handles some exceptions and returns a message to the user or application running the program. In other cases, the program cannot handle the exception, and the program ends.

Related term
application

executable file

A file that generates report output when run in a report designer or web application. For example, a BIRT report executable (.rptdesign) file generates BIRT report output.

Related terms
application, file types, report, report design (.rptdesign) file

expression

A combination of constants, functions, literal values, names of fields, and operators that evaluate to a single value.

Related terms
constant, field, expression builder, function, operator, value

Contrast with
regular expression

expression builder

A tool for selecting data fields, functions, and operators to write expressions. Figure G-11 shows the expression builder in BIRT Report Designer.

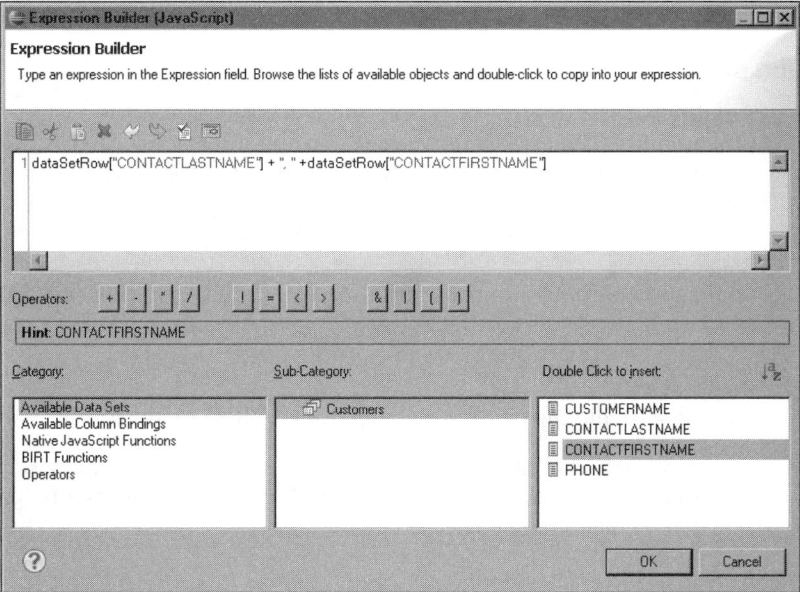

Figure G-11 Expression builder

Related terms
Business Intelligence and Reporting Tools (BIRT) Report Designer, data, expression, field, function, operator

Extensible Markup Language (XML)

A markup language that supports the interchange of data among applications and data sources. Using XML, a wide variety of applications, databases, and legacy systems can exchange information. The World Wide Web Consortium (W3C) specifies the standard for XML schema and documents. XML documents must be well-formed.

Related terms
application, data, data source, database, schema, well-formed XML, World Wide Web Consortium (W3C)

Contrast with
Dynamic HyperText Markup Language (DHTML), HyperText Markup Language (HTML)

extension

A module that adds functionality to an application. For example, BIRT consists of a set of extensions, called plug-ins, which add report development functionality to the Eclipse platform.

Related terms
application, Business Intelligence and Reporting Tools (BIRT), Eclipse platform, plug-in, report

Contrast with
Business Intelligence and Reporting Tools (BIRT) extension, extension point

extension point

A defined place in an application where a developer adds custom functionality. The application programming interfaces (API) in BIRT support adding custom functionality to the BIRT framework. In the Eclipse Plug-in Development Environment (PDE), a developer views the extension points in the PDE Manifest Editor to guide and control plug-in development tasks.

Related terms
application, application programming interface (API), Business Intelligence and Reporting Tools (BIRT), Eclipse Plug-in Development Environment (PDE), extension, framework, plug-in

Contrast with
Business Intelligence and Reporting Tools (BIRT) extension

field The smallest identifiable part of a database table structure. In a relational database, a field is also called a column. Figure G-12 shows a field in a table.

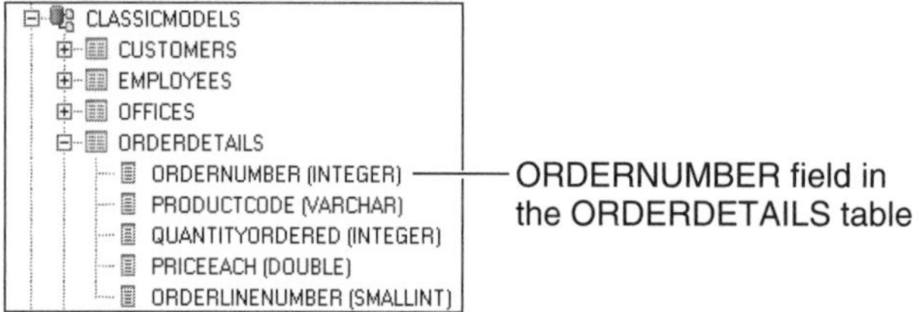

Figure G-12 Fields and tables displayed in a query editor

Related terms
column, database, query editor, table

field variable

In Java, a member variable having public visibility.

Related terms
Java, member, variable

file types

BIRT provides file types to store information used and created by report designs. Table 24-1 lists the report designer's file types.

Table 24-1 File types

Display name	File extension
BIRT Report Design	RPTDESIGN
BIRT Report Design Library	RPTLIBRARY
BIRT Report Design Template	RPTTEMPLATE
BIRT Report Document	RPTDOCUMENT

Related terms
library (.rptlibrary) file, report design (.rptdesign) file, report document (.rptdocument) file, report template (.rpttemplate) file

filter A mechanism that enables a user to reduce the number of items in a list.

flat file A file that contains data in the form of text.

Related term
data

Contrast with
data source

Float class

A Java class that encapsulates the primitive data type, float. The class provides accessor methods that support getting and setting the value.

Related terms
class, data type, float data type, Java, value

Contrast with
BigDecimal class, Double class, Integer class

float data type

A Java data type that stores a single-precision 32-bit IEEE 754 floating point number, ranging in value from 1.40129846432481707E-45 to 3.40282346638528860E+38.

Related terms
data type, Java, value

Contrast with
double data type, Float class, int data type, number data type

font A family of characters of a given style. A font contains information that specifies posture, typeface, type size, and weight.

Related term
character

footer A logically separate unit of information that appears after the main body of content. For example, a page footer typically contains a page number. A group footer aggregates group data.

Related terms
data, group

Contrast with
header

format

1 A specification that describes layout and properties of rich information, such as HyperText Markup Language (HTML), PDF, PostScript, PowerPoint, RTF, or spreadsheet.

2 A set of standard options with which to display and print currency values, dates, numbers, strings, and times.

Related terms
data, HyperText Markup Language (HTML), layout, property, string, value

Contrast with
style

fragment

See plug-in fragment.

framework

A set of interrelated classes that provide an architecture for building an application, such as the chart engine.

Related terms
application, Business Intelligence and Reporting Tools (BIRT) Chart Engine, class

function

A set of interrelated classes that provide an architecture for building an application. A code module containing a set of instructions that operate as a subroutine in a program. To invoke the function, include its name as an instruction anywhere in the program. BIRT provides JavaScript and other functions to support building expressions.

Related terms
Business Intelligence and Reporting Tools (BIRT), expression, JavaScript

Contrast with
method

global variable

A variable available at all levels in an application. A global variable stays in memory in the scope of all executing subroutines until the application terminates.

Related terms
application, scope, variable

glyph

1 An image that is the visual representation of a character.

2 A specific letter form from a specific font. For example, an uppercase C in Palatino font is a glyph.

Related terms
character, font

grandchild class

See descendant class.

grandparent class

See ancestor class.

grid See grid element.

grid element

A report item that contains and arranges other report elements in a static row and column format. A grid element aligns cells horizontally and vertically. Figure G-13 shows a report title section containing an image and two text elements in a grid element. This grid element has one row and two columns.

Investment Report
January 1, 2004 - December 31, 2004
Grid

Figure G-13 Grid element

Related terms
cell, column, image element, report, report item, row, text element

Contrast with
list element, table element

group A set of data rows organized by one or more common values. For example, in a sales report, a group consists of all the orders placed by a single customer.

Related terms
data row, report, value

Contrast with
group key, grouped report

group footer

See footer.

group header

See header.

grouped report

A report that organizes data by common values. Figure G-14 shows a grouped report organized by customer name.

Related terms
data, report, value

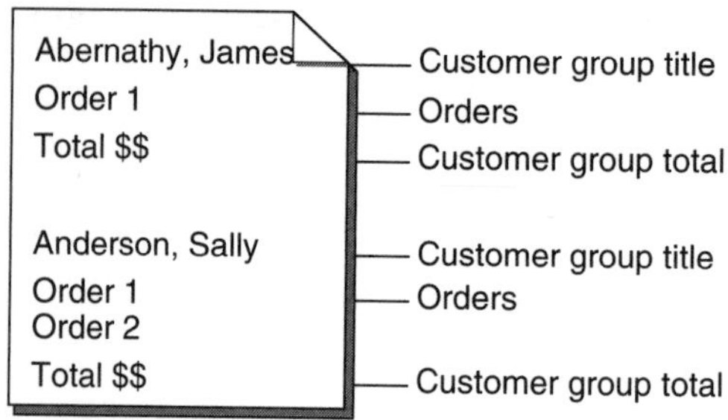

Figure G-14 Grouped report

Contrast with
group

group key

An expression that groups and sorts data. For example, a report developer can group and sort customers by credit rank.

Related terms
data, expression, group, sort

header A logically separate unit of information that appears before the main body of content. For example, a page header typically contains a document title. A group header typically contains key information about the group. For example, a group header in a sales report can contain the country name.

Related terms
group, page

Contrast with
footer

hexadecimal number

A number in base 16. A hexadecimal number uses the digits 0 through 9 and letters A through F. Each place represents a power of 16. By comparison, base 10 numbers use the digits 0 through 9. Each place represents a power of 10.

Contrast with
character set

hierarchy

Any tree structure that has a root and branches that do not converge. Figure G-15 shows an example hierarchy of classes.

Related term
class

HTML See HyperText Markup Language (HTML).

HTML element

See element.

HTTP See HyperText Transfer Protocol (HTTP).

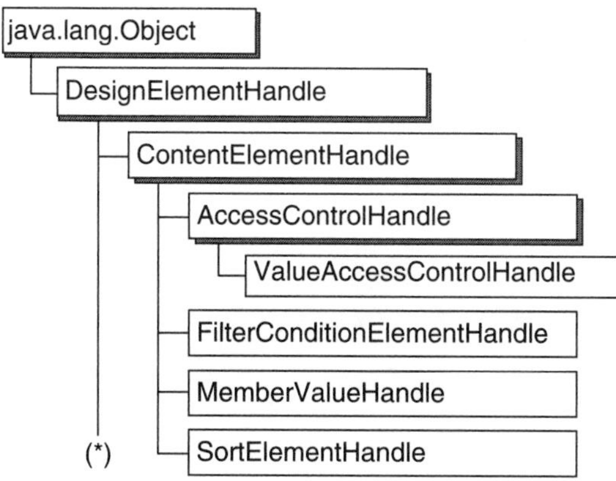

Figure G-15 Hierarchy of classes

hyperchart

A chart that supports linking to report data or other related information. For example, a pie chart segment representing the sales amount for the Boston office links to the report data for that office.

Related terms
chart, data, report

Contrast with
hyperlink

hyperlink

An active connection in a online document that supports access to related information in the same document or an external source. The document can be an e-mail, PDF, report, spreadsheet, or web page. A change from the standard cursor shape to a cursor shaped like a hand indicates a hyperlink.

Related terms
report, web page

Contrast with
hyperchart

HyperText Markup Language (HTML)

A standards-based specification that determines the layout of a web page. HTML is the markup language that a web browser parses to display a web page. The World Wide Web Consortium (W3C) specifies the standard for HTML.

Related terms
layout, web page, World Wide Web Consortium (W3C)

Contrast with
Dynamic HyperText Markup Language (DHTML), Extensible Markup Language (XML)

HyperText Markup Language page

See web page.

HyperText Transfer Protocol (HTTP)

A standard that supports request-response communication between two applications on a network. The World Wide Web Consortium (W3C) specifies the standard for HTTP.

Related terms
application, request, World Wide Web Consortium (W3C)

Contrast with
protocol

identifier

A name assigned to an item in a program, for example a class, function, or variable.

Related terms
class, function, variable

image

A graphic that appears in a report. BIRT supports .gif, .jpg, and .png file types.

Related terms
Business Intelligence and Reporting Tools (BIRT), report

Contrast with
image element

image element

A report item that adds an image to a report design.

Related terms
design, image, report, report item

inheritance

A mechanism whereby one class of objects can be defined as a special case of a more general class and includes the method and variable definitions of the general class, known as a base or superclass. The superclass serves as the baseline for the appearance and behavior of the descendant class, which is also known as a subclass. In the subclass, the appearance, behavior, and structure can be customized without affecting the superclass. Figure G-16 shows an example of inheritance.

Related terms
class, descendant class, method, object, subclass, superclass, variable

Contrast with
abstract base class, hierarchy, object-oriented programming

inner join

A type of join that returns records from two tables using specified values in the join fields. For example, joining customer and order tables where the customer IDs are equal produces a result set that excludes records for customers who have no orders.

Related terms
field, join, result set, table, value

Contrast with
outer join

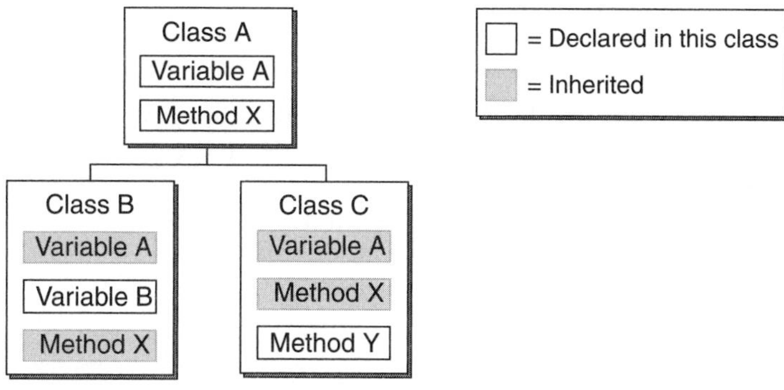

Figure G-16 Inheritance

Input Method Editor (IME) file

A Java class file that sets the keyboard mapping for a character set. BIRT uses this mechanism to support non-ASCII characters. Place the IME file in the jre\lib\ext directory to make it accessible to the Java environment.

Related terms
Business Intelligence and Reporting Tools (BIRT) Report Designer, character, character set, class, Java

input source

See data source.

instance

See object.

instance variable

A variable that other instances of a class do not share. The run-time system creates a new copy of an instance variable each time the system instantiates the class. An instance variable can contain a different value in each instance of a class, for example, the customerID variable in a Customer class.

Related terms
class, run time, value, variable

instantiation

In object-oriented programming, the process of creating an object in a run-time environment based on the class definition.

Related terms
class, object, object-oriented programming, run time

int data type

A 32-bit Java data type that stores whole numbers, ranging in value from -2,147,483,648 to 2,147,483,647.

Related terms
data type, Java, value

Contrast with
double data type, float data type, Integer class

Integer class

A Java class that encapsulates the primitive data type, int. This class provides accessor methods that support getting and setting the value.

Related terms
class, data type, int data type, Java, method, value

Contrast with
BigDecimal class, Double class, Float class

interface

A software component that supports access to computer resources. For example, in Java, a set of methods that provides a mechanism for classes to communicate in order to execute particular actions.

Related terms
class, Java, method

internationalization

The process of designing an application to work correctly in multiple locales.

Related terms
application, locale

Contrast with
localization

IP address

The unique node identifier on a TCP/IP network.

Related term
node

J2EE See Java Platform Enterprise Edition (Java EE).

J2SE See Java Platform Standard Edition (Java SE).

JAR See Java archive (.jar) file.

Java An object-oriented programming language used to develop and extend BIRT technology.

Related terms
Business Intelligence and Reporting Tools (BIRT) technology, object-oriented programming

Contrast with
JavaScript

Java 2 Enterprise Edition (J2EE)

See Java Platform Enterprise Edition (Java EE).

Java 2 Runtime Standard Edition (J2SE)

See Java Platform Standard Edition (Java SE).

Java archive (.jar) file

A compressed file format used to deploy Java applications.

Related terms
application, Java

Contrast with
web archive (.war) file

Java Database Connectivity (JDBC)

A standard protocol that Java uses to access databases in a platform-independent manner.

Related terms
bridge driver, database, Java, protocol

Contrast with
data element, schema

Java Development Kit (JDK)

A software development kit that defines the application programming interfaces (API) used to build Java applications. As well as software tools, the kit contains documentation and examples.

Related terms
application, application programming interface (API), Java

Contrast with
Java Platform Enterprise Edition (Java EE), Java Platform Standard Edition (Java SE), JavaServer Page (JSP)

Java Naming and Directory Interface (JNDI)

An application programming interface (API) that provides unified access to named components and directory services in an enterprise system.

Related terms
application programming interface (API), enterprise

Java Platform Enterprise Edition (Java EE)

A platform-independent development environment that includes application programming interfaces (API), such as Java Database Connectivity (JDBC), Remote Method Invocation (RMI), and web services. A programmer uses Java EE to develop a highly scalable, fault-tolerant, web-based application.

Related terms
application, application programming interface (API), Java Database Connectivity (JDBC)

Contrast with
Java Development Kit (JDK), Java Platform Standard Edition (Java SE), Java Virtual Machine (JVM)

Java Platform Standard Edition (Java SE)

A smaller-scale, platform-independent development environment defining the Java programming language and application programming interfaces (API) supporting interaction with file systems, networks, and graphical interfaces. A programmer uses Java SE to develop an application to run on a virtual machine.

Related terms
application, application programming interface (API), Java

Contrast with
Java Development Kit (JDK), Java Platform Enterprise Edition (Java EE), Java Virtual Machine (JVM)

Java Virtual Machine (JVM)

The Java SDK interpreter that converts Java bytecode into machine language for execution in a specified software and hardware configuration.

Related terms
Java, SDK (Software Development Kit)

JavaBean

A reusable, serializable, standards-based component that encapsulates application logic.

Related terms
application, encapsulation

Contrast with
Enterprise JavaBean (EJB)

JavaScript

An interpreted, platform-independent, scripting language used to embed additional processing in a web page or server. For example, BIRT uses JavaScript to support aggregate expressions and event handling.

Related terms
Business Intelligence and Reporting Tools (BIRT), event handler, web page, web server

Contrast with
aggregate function, Java

JavaServer Page (JSP)

A standard Java extension that supports the generation of dynamic web pages. A JavaServer Page combines HyperText Markup Language (HTML) and JSP tags in one document. A servlet container interprets a JSP tag as a call to a Java class. The servlet container compiles the Java classes to generate a web page.

Related terms
class, container, extension, HyperText Markup Language (HTML), Java, servlet, tag, web page

JDBC See Java Database Connectivity (JDBC).

JDK See Java Development Kit (JDK).

JNDI See Java Naming and Directory Interface (JNDI).

join A SQL (Structured Query Language) query operation that combines records from two tables and returns them in a result set based on the values in the join fields. Without additional qualification, join usually refers to the join in which field values are equal. For example, customer and order tables are joined on a common field such as customer ID. The result set contains combined customer and order records in which the customer IDs are equal.

Related terms
field, query, result set, SQL (Structured Query Language), table, value

Contrast with
inner join, join condition, outer join, SQL SELECT statement

join condition

A condition that specifies a match in the values of related fields in two tables. Typically, the values are equal. For example, if two tables have a field called customer ID, a join condition exists where the customer ID value in one table equals the customer ID value in the second table.

Related terms
field, join, table, value

joint data set

A data set that combines data from two or more data sets.

Related terms
data, data set

JSP See JavaServer Page (JSP).

JVM See Java Virtual Machine (JVM).

keyword

A reserved word that is recognized as part of a programming language.

label element

A report item that displays a short piece of static text in a report. Figure G-17 shows label elements used as column headings in a table header row.

Related terms
column, header, report item, row, table

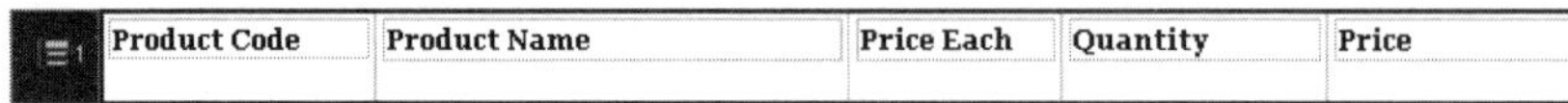

Product Code
Product Name
Price Each
Quantity
Price

Figure G-17 Label elements in a table header row

Contrast with
data element, text element

layout The designed appearance of a report. Designing a report entails arranging report items on a page so that a report user can analyze the information easily. A report displays information in a combination of charts, footers, headers, paragraphs, subreports, and tabular lists.

Related terms
chart, footer, header, report, report item, subreport

layout editor

A tool in a report designer in which a report developer arranges, formats, and sizes report items.

Related terms
design, format, report, report item

Contrast with
report editor

lazy load

The capability in a run-time environment to load a code segment to memory. By lazily loading a code segment, the run-time environment minimizes start-up time and conserves memory resources. For example, BIRT Report Engine builds a registry at startup that contains the list of available plug-ins, then loads a plug-in only if the processing requires it.

Related terms
Business Intelligence and Reporting Tools (BIRT) Report Engine, plug-in, run time

left outer join

See outer join.

library

1. A file used when creating or running a program. For example, Windows library files are dynamic link libraries. UNIX library files are shared libraries.

2. A collection of reusable and shareable report elements. A library can contain data sets, data sources, embedded images, JavaScript code, styles, and visual report items. A report developer uses a report designer to develop a library and to retrieve report elements from a library for use in a report design.

Related terms
Business Intelligence and Reporting Tools (BIRT) Report Designer, data set, data source, design, image, JavaScript, report element, report item, style, variable

Contrast with
file types

library (.rptlibrary) file

In BIRT Report Designer, an Extensible Markup Language (XML) file that contains reusable and shareable report elements. A report developer uses a report design tool to create a library file directly or from a report design (.rptdesign) file.

Related terms
Business Intelligence and Reporting Tools (BIRT) Report Designer, design, Extensible Markup Language (XML), library, report design (.rptdesign) file, report element

Contrast with
file types

link See hyperlink.

listener See event listener.

list element

A report item that iterates through the data rows in a data set. The list element contains and displays other report items in a variety of layouts.

Related terms
data row, data set, layout, report item

Contrast with
grid element, table element

listing report

A report that provides a simple view of data. Typically, a listing report displays a single line for each data row. Figure G-18 shows a listing report.

Customer List

Customer	Phone	Contact
ANG Resellers	(91) 745 6555	Alejandra Camino
AV Stores, Co.	(171) 555-1555	Rachel Ashworth
Alpha Cognac	61.77.6555	Annette Roulet

Figure G-18 Listing report

Related terms
data, data row, report

local variable

A variable that is available only at the current level in an application. A local variable stays in memory in the scope of an executing procedure until the procedure terminates. When the procedure finishes, the run-time system destroys the variable and returns the memory to the system.

Related terms
application, procedure, run time, scope, variable

locale A location and the currency format, date format, language, sorting sequence, time format, and other characteristics associated with that location. The location is not always identical to the country. There can be multiple languages and locales within one country. For example, China has two locales: Beijing and Hong Kong. Canada has two language-based locales: French and English.

Related term
format

Contrast with
localization

localization

The process of translating database content, printed documents, and software programs into another language. Report developers localize static text in a report so that the report displays text in another language that is appropriate to the locale configured on the user's machine.

Related terms
database, locale, report

Contrast with
internationalization

manifest

A text file in a Java archive (.jar) file that describes the contents of the archive.

Related term
Java archive (.jar) file

mashup

A web application that combines data and functionality from multiple sources into a single presentation. For example, the Google Maps® mashup combines maps and directions to assist a user in locating and traveling to a destination.

Related term
application, data

master page

A predefined layout that specifies a consistent appearance for all pages of a report. A master page typically includes standard headers and footers that display information such as a copyright statement, a date, or page numbers. The master page can contain report elements in the header and footer areas only, as shown in Figure G-19.

The master page's header and footer content appears on every page of the report in paginated formats, as shown in Figure G-20.

Related terms
footer, header, layout, report, report element

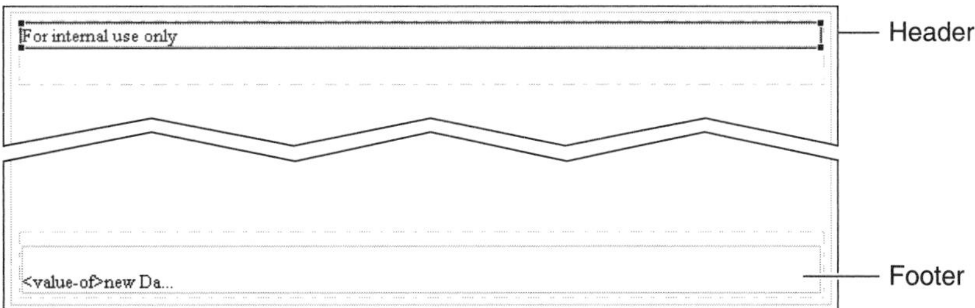

Figure G-19 Master page layout

Contrast with
template

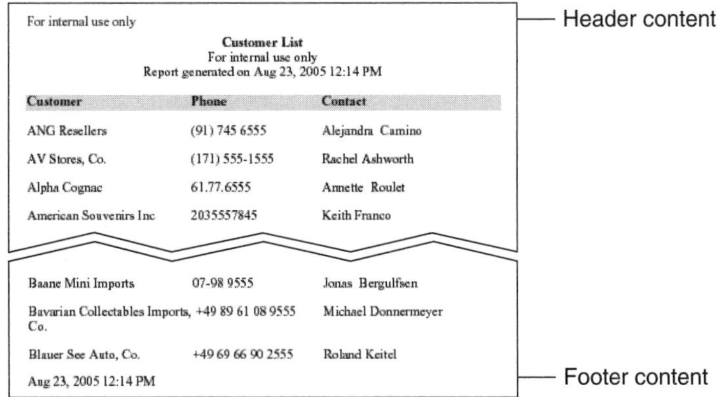

Figure G-20 Master page header and footer in report

measure

In a cube, aggregated values, such as average cost or total units of products.

Related terms
aggregate value, cube

Contrast with
dimension

member

A method or variable defined in a class. A member provides or uses information about the state of a single object.

Related terms
class, method, object, variable

Contrast with
global variable, instance variable, static variable

member variable

A declared variable within a class. The member variables for an object contain its data or state.

Related terms
class, data, declaration, object, variable

metadata

Information about the structure of data enabling a program to process information. For example, a relational database stores metadata that describes the data type, name, and size of objects in a database, such as tables and columns.

Related terms
column, data, data type, database, object, table

method

A routine that provides functionality to an object or a class.

Related terms
class, object

Contrast with
data, function

modal window

A window that retains focus until explicitly closed by the user. Typically, dialog boxes and message windows are modal. For example, an error message dialog box remains on the screen until the user responds.

Contrast with
modeless window

mode

An operational state of a system. Mode implies that there are at least two possible states. Typically, there are many modes for both hardware and software.

modeless window

A window that solicits input but permits users to continue using the current application without closing the modeless window, for example, an Eclipse view.

Related terms
application, Eclipse view

Contrast with
modal window

multidimensional data

Any set of records that you can break down or filter according to the contents of individual fields or dimensions, such as location, product, or time. This data organization supports presenting and analyzing complex relationships.

Related terms
data, dimension, field, filter

Contrast with
analytics

multithreaded application

An application that handles multiple simultaneous sessions and users.

Related term
application

Navigator

In BIRT Report Designer, an Eclipse view that shows all projects, reports, and associated files within each project. Each project is a directory in the file system. Use Navigator to manage report files, for example, deleting files, moving files from one project to another, or renaming files. Figure G-21 shows Navigator.

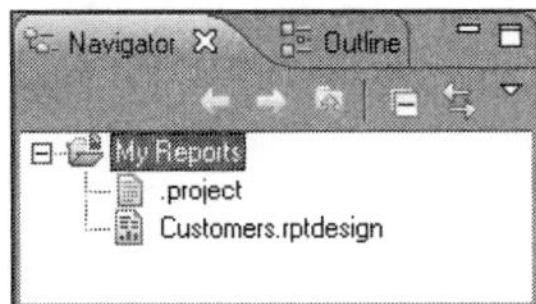

Figure G-21 Navigator

Related terms
Business Intelligence and Reporting Tools (BIRT) Report Designer, Eclipse project, Eclipse view, report

node A computer that is accessible on the internet.

Contrast with
domain name

null A value indicating that a variable or field contains no data.

Related terms
data, field, value, variable

number data type

A data type used to display numeric values. Report items that contain expressions or fields having a number data type display numeric values in the report document. The appearance of these values depends on the formats and locale settings specified by your computer and the report design.

Related terms
data type, design, expression, field, format, locale, report, report item, value

numeric expression

A numeric constant, a simple numeric variable, a scalar reference to a numeric array, a numeric-valued function reference, or a sequence of these items, separated by numeric operators. For example:

```
dataSetRow["PRICEEACH"] * dataSetRow["QUANTITYORDERED"]
```

Related terms
array, constant, function, operator, variable

Contrast with
Boolean expression

object An instance of a particular class, including its characteristics, such as instance variables and methods.

Related terms
class, instance variable, method, variable

object-oriented programming

A paradigm for writing applications using classes, not algorithms, as the fundamental building blocks. The design methodology uses four main concepts: abstraction, encapsulation, inheritance, and polymorphism.

Related terms
abstraction, application, class, encapsulation, inheritance, polymorphism

Contrast with
object

ODA See open data access (ODA).

online analytical processing (OLAP)

The process of analyzing, collecting, managing, and presenting multidimensional data.

Related terms
data, multidimensional data

Contrast with
analytics

online help

Information that appears on the computer screen to help the user understand an application.

Related term
application

open data access (ODA)

A technology that handles communication between a data source and an application. ODA provides interfaces for creating data drivers to establish connections, access metadata, and execute queries to retrieve data. ODA also provides interfaces to integrate query builder tools within an application designer tool. The Eclipse Data Tools Project plug-ins provide ODA to BIRT.

Related terms
application, Business Intelligence and Reporting Tools (BIRT), Connection, data, data source, Eclipse, interface, metadata, open data access (ODA) driver, plug-in, query

open data access (ODA) driver

An ODA driver communicates between a data source and an application. An ODA driver establishes a connection to a data source, accesses metadata about the data, and executes queries on the data source. In BIRT, ODA drivers are plug-in extensions to the Eclipse Data Tools Platform project.

Related terms
application, Business Intelligence and Reporting Tools (BIRT) technology, data, data source, driver, Eclipse, extension, metadata, open data access (ODA), plug-in, query

open database connectivity (ODBC)

A standard protocol used by software products as a database management system (DBMS) interface to connect applications and reports to databases.

Related terms
application, bridge driver, database, database management system (DBMS), interface, protocol, report

Contrast with
Connection, data source, Java Database Connectivity (JDBC)

open source

A software development methodology in which the community of programmers and users has complete access to the source code. For example, BIRT is an open-source project built on the Eclipse platform.

Related terms
Business Intelligence and Reporting Tools (BIRT), Eclipse platform

operator

A symbol or keyword that performs an operation on expressions.

Related terms
expression, keyword

outer join

A type of join that returns records from one table even when no matching values exist in the other table. The three types of outer join are left, right, and full outer join. A left outer join returns all records from the table on the left side of the join expression, even if no matching values exist in the table on the right side. A right outer join returns all records from the table on the right side of the join expression, even if no matching values exist in the table on the left side. For example, joining customers and orders tables on customerID with the customers table on the left side of the expression returns a result set that contains all customer records, including customers who have no orders. A full outer join is the union of the result sets of both left and right outer joins.

Related terms
join, result set, table, value

Contrast with
inner join

Outline An Eclipse view that shows all report elements in a report design, report library, or report template. Outline shows the report elements' containment hierarchy in a tree-structured diagram. Figure G-22 shows Outline.

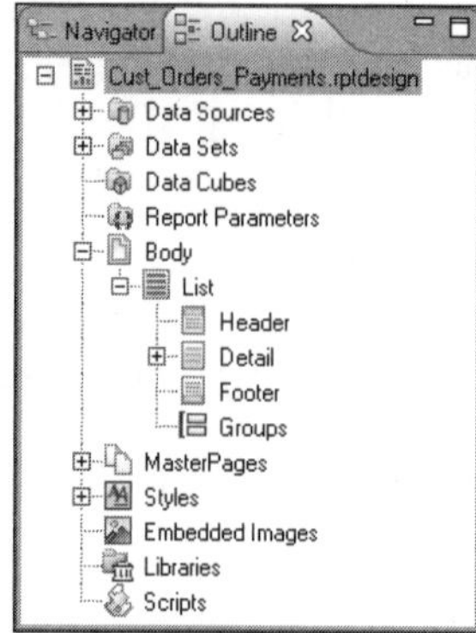

Figure G-22 Outline

Related terms
design, Eclipse view, hierarchy, library, report, report element, template

package

1 A set of functionally related Java classes organized in one directory.

2 A complete application, including all configuration files and programs.

Related terms
application, class, configuration file, Java

page An area in a window that arranges and displays related information. A window can contain several pages, each of which is accessed by a tab.

Related term
tab

Contrast with
JavaServer Page (JSP), master page, web page

Palette An Eclipse view that shows the report items used to display and organize data in a report. Figure G-23 shows Palette.

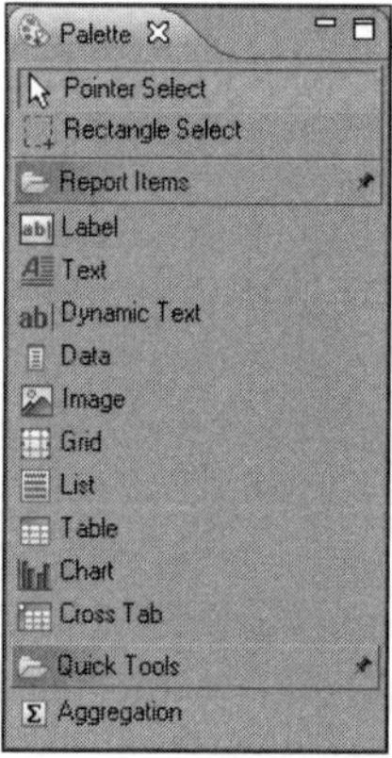

Figure G-23 Palette of report items

Related terms
data, Eclipse view, report, report item

parameter

1 A report element that provides input to the execution of the report. Parameters provide control over report data formatting, processing, and selection.

2 The definition of an argument to a procedure.

Related terms
argument, data, format, procedure, report, report element

Contrast with
cascading parameters, data set parameter, report parameter

parent class

See superclass.

password

An optional code that restricts user name access to a resource on a computer system.

pattern

A template or model for implementing a solution to a common problem in object-oriented programming or design. For example, the singleton design pattern restricts the instantiation of a class to only one object. The use of the singleton pattern prevents the proliferation of identical objects in a run-time environment and requires a programmer to manage access to the object in a multithreaded application.

Related terms
class, design, instantiation, multithreaded application, object, object-oriented programming, run time, template

PDF converter

A tool that converts a report to a PDF file.

Related terms
converter, report

perspective

See Eclipse perspective.

platform

The software and hardware environment in which a program runs. Linux, MacOS, Microsoft Windows, Solaris OS, and UNIX are examples of software systems that run on hardware processors made by vendors such as AMD, Apple, Hewlett-Packard, IBM, Intel, Motorola, and Sun.

Contrast with
Eclipse platform

plug-in 1 An extension used by the Eclipse development environment. At run time, Eclipse scans its plug-in subdirectory to discover any extensions to the platform. Eclipse places the information about each extension in a registry, using lazy load to access the extension.

2 A software program that extends the capabilities of a web browser. For example, a plug-in gives you the ability to play audio samples or video movies.

Related terms
Eclipse, extension, lazy load, run time

Contrast with
Eclipse Plug-in Development Environment (PDE)

plug-in fragment

A separately loaded plug-in that adds functionality to an existing plug-in, such as support for a new language in a localized application. The plug-in fragment manifest contains named values that associate the fragment with the existing plug-in.

Related terms
application, localization, manifest, plug-in, value

polymorphism

The ability to provide different implementations with a common interface, simplifying the communication among objects. For example, defining a unique print method for each kind of document in a system supports printing any document by sending the instruction to print without concern for how that method is actually carried out for a given document.

Related terms
interface, method, object

Contrast with
object-oriented programming

PostScript converter

A tool that converts a report to a PostScript (.ps) file.

Related terms
converter, report

PowerPoint converter

A tool that converts a report to a Microsoft PowerPoint (.ppt) file.

Related terms
converter, report

Contrast with
Excel converter, PDF converter, PostScript converter, Word converter, XML converter

previewer

A tool that supports displaying data or a report. A data previewer enables the report developer to review the values of columns returned by a query before designing the report layout. A report previewer enables the report developer to review and improve the report layout before delivery to the user.

Related terms
column, data, design, layout, query, report, value

Contrast with
viewer

procedure

A set of commands, input data, and statements that perform a specific set of operations. For example, methods are procedures.

Related terms
data, method, statement

process

A computer program that has no user interface. For example, the servlet that generates a BIRT report is a process.

Related terms
Business Intelligence and Reporting Tools (BIRT), interface, report, servlet

project See Eclipse project.

Properties

A grouped alphabetical list of all properties of report elements in a report design. Experienced report developers use this Eclipse view to modify any property of a report element. Figure G-24 shows Properties.

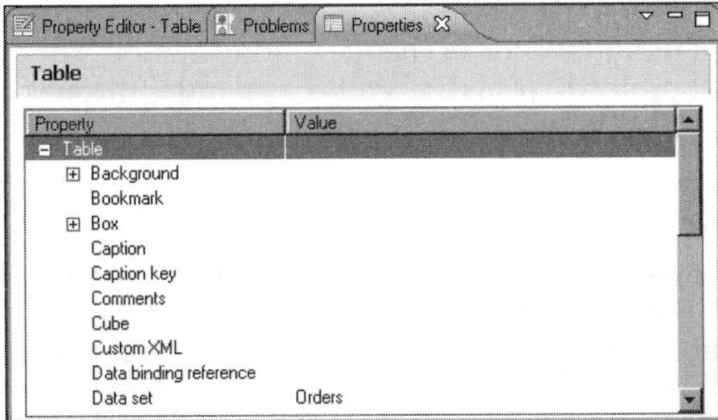

Figure G-24 Properties displaying a sample of table element properties

Related terms
design, Eclipse view, property, report, report element, table element

Contrast with
Property Editor

property

A characteristic of a report item that controls its appearance and behavior. For example, a report developer can specify a font size for a label element.

Related terms

font, label element, report item

Contrast with

method

Property Editor

An Eclipse view that displays sets of key properties of report elements in a report design. The report developer uses Property Editor to modify those properties. Figure G-25 shows Property Editor.

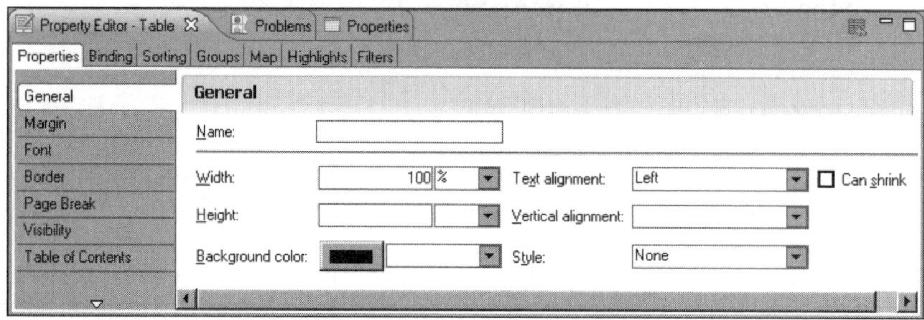

Figure G-25 Property Editor

Related terms

design, Eclipse view, property, report, report element

Contrast with

Properties

protocol

A communication standard for the exchange of information. For example, in TCP/IP, the internet protocol (IP) is the syntax and order through which messages are received and sent.

Related term

syntax

publish To copy files to a shared folder to make them available to report users and developers. BIRT Report Designer publishes libraries and resource files to the resources folder. Published templates reside in the templates folder.

Related terms

library, report, resource file, template

query A statement specifying the data rows to retrieve from a data source. For example, a query that retrieves data from a database typically is a SQL SELECT statement.

Related terms

data, data row, data source, database, SQL SELECT statement

query editor

A graphical tool used to write a statement that requests data from a data source.

Related terms
data, data source, statement

Contrast with
SQL SELECT statement

range A continuous set of values of any data type. For example, 1–31 is a numeric range.

Related terms
data type, value

regular expression

A JavaScript mechanism that matches patterns in text. The regular expression syntax can validate text data, find simple and complex strings of text within larger blocks of text, and substitute new text for old.

Related terms
data, expression, JavaScript, string, syntax

rendering extension

A BIRT extension that produces a report in a specific format. For example, BIRT provides rendering extensions for Adobe PDF, Adobe PostScript, HyperText Markup Language (HTML), Microsoft Excel, Microsoft PowerPoint, and Microsoft Word.

Related terms
Business Intelligence and Reporting Tools (BIRT), Business Intelligence and Reporting Tools (BIRT) extension, extension, format, HyperText Markup Language (HTML), report

report A category of documents that presents formatted and structured content from a data source, such as a database or text file.

Related terms
data source, database, format, structured content

report design (.rptdesign) file

An Extensible Markup Language (XML) file that contains the complete description of a report. The report design file describes the structure and organization of the report, the constituent report items, data sets, data sources, and Java and JavaScript event handler code. A report developer uses BIRT Report Designer to create the report design file and the BIRT Report Engine processes it to create a formatted report.

Related terms
Business Intelligence and Reporting Tools (BIRT) Report Designer, Business Intelligence and Reporting Tools (BIRT) Report Engine, data set, data source, design, event handler, Extensible Markup Language (XML), format, Java, JavaScript, report, report item

Contrast with
file types

report document (.rptdocument) file

A binary file that encapsulates the report item identifiers and values, and additional information, such as data rows, pagination, and table of contents.

Related terms
data row, report item, table of contents, value

Contrast with
file types

report editor

In BIRT Report Designer, the main window where a report developer designs and previews a report. The report editor supports opening multiple report designs. For each report design, the report editor displays these five pages: Extensible Markup Language (XML) source editor, layout editor, master page editor, previewer, and script editor.

Related terms
Business Intelligence and Reporting Tools (BIRT) Report Designer, design, Extensible Markup Language (XML), master page, layout editor, previewer, report, script editor

Contrast with
report design (.rptdesign) file

report element

A visual or non-visual component of a report design. A visual report element, such as a table or a label, is a report item. A non-visual report element, such as a report parameter or a data source, is a logical component.

Related terms
data source, design, element, label element, report, report item, report parameter, table element

report executable file

A file that contains instructions for generating a report document.

Related term
report

Contrast with
file types

report item

A report element that is a visual component of a report design. A report item displays content in the report output. For example, a data element displays data from a data set.

Related terms
data, data element, data set, design, report, report element

Contrast with
structured content

report item extension

A BIRT extension that implements a custom report item.

Related terms
Business Intelligence and Reporting Tools (BIRT) extension, report item

report library file

See library (.rptlibrary) file.

Report Object Model (ROM)

The abstract specification for BIRT technology. The ROM defines the visual and non-visual components of a report. The ROM specification is an Extensible Markup Language (XML) document. The complete ROM specification is at:

`http://www.eclipse.org/birt/ref`

Related terms
Business Intelligence and Reporting Tools (BIRT) technology, Extensible Markup Language (XML), report

Contrast with
Report Object Model definition file (rom.def), Report Object Model (ROM) element, Report Object Model (ROM) schema

Report Object Model definition file (rom.def)

The deployment file containing the Report Object Model (ROM) specification that BIRT technology uses to generate and validate a report design.

Related terms
Business Intelligence and Reporting Tools (BIRT) technology, design, report

Contrast with
Report Object Model (ROM), Report Object Model (ROM) element, Report Object Model (ROM) schema

Report Object Model (ROM) element

An Extensible Markup Language (XML) element in the Report Object Model (ROM) that describes a visual or non-visual component of a report. Visual elements include items appearing in a report such as a label, list, or table element. Non-visual elements include data sets, data sources, and report parameters.

Related terms
data set, data source, element, Extensible Markup Language (XML), label element, list element, report, report item, Report Object Model (ROM), report parameter, table element

Contrast with
report element, Report Object Model definition file (rom.def), Report Object Model (ROM) schema

Report Object Model (ROM) schema

The Extensible Markup Language (XML) schema defining the content, semantics, and structure of the components in the BIRT Report Object Model (ROM). The ROM schema is at:

`http://www.eclipse.org/birt/2005/design`

Related terms
Business Intelligence and Reporting Tools (BIRT), Extensible Markup Language (XML), Report Object Model (ROM), schema

Contrast with
Report Object Model definition file (rom.def), Report Object Model (ROM) element

report parameter

A report element that enables a user to provide a value as input to the execution of the report. Using a parameter to customize a report provides more focused information to meet specific needs. For example, parameters support selecting sales information by country and city.

Related terms
parameter, report, report element, value

Contrast with
cascading parameters, data set parameter

report template

See template.

report template (.rpttemplate) file

An Extensible Markup Language (XML) file that contains a reusable design providing a start position for developing a new report.

Related terms
design, Extensible Markup Language (XML), report

Contrast with
file types, library (.rptlibrary) file, report design (.rptdesign) file, report document (.rptdocument) file, template

report viewer servlet

A Java EE web application servlet that produces a report from a report design (.rptdesign) file or a report document (.rptdocument) file. When deployed to a Java EE application server, the report viewer servlet makes reports available for viewing over the web. The report viewer servlet is also an active component of the report previewer of BIRT Report Designer.

Related terms
application, Business Intelligence and Reporting Tools (BIRT) Report Designer, Java Platform Enterprise Edition (Java EE), previewer, report, report design (.rptdesign) file, report document (.rptdocument) file, servlet, web server

request

A message that an application sends to a component to perform an action.

Related term
application

reserved word

See keyword.

resource

An application component, such as a class, configuration file, image, library, or template.

Related terms
application, class, configuration file, image, library, template

Contrast with
resource file

resource file

A text file that contains the mapping from resource keys to string values for a particular locale. Resource files support producing a report having localized values for label and text elements.

Related terms
label element, locale, report, resource key, string, text element, value

Contrast with
localization, resource

resource key

A unique value that maps to a string in a resource file. For example, the resource key, greeting, can map to Hello, Bonjour, and Hola in the resource files for English, French, and Spanish, respectively.

Related terms
resource file, string, value

result set

Data rows from an external data source. For example, the data rows that are returned by a SQL SELECT statement performed on a relational database are a result set.

Related terms
data row, data source, database, SQL SELECT statement

Rich Client Platform (RCP)

See Eclipse Rich Client Platform (RCP).

right outer join

See outer join.

ROM See Report Object Model (ROM).

row

1 A record in a table.

2 A horizontal sequence of cells in a cross tab, grid element, or table element.

Related terms
cell, cross tab, grid element, table, table element

Contrast with
data row

row key

An expression used to collect data rows into row groups and subgroups in a cross-tab element.

Related terms
cross-tab element, data row, group, expression

Contrast with
column key

RPTDESIGN

See report design (.rptdesign) file.

RPTDOCUMENT

See report document (.rptdocument) file.

RPTLIBRARY

See library (.rptlibrary) file.

RPTTEMPLATE

See report template (.rpttemplate) file.

run

To execute a program, utility, or other machine function.

run time

The period of time in which a computer program executes. For example, a report executable generates a report during run time.

Related terms
report, report executable file

Contrast with
design time, view time

schema

1 A database schema specifies the structure of database components and the relationships among those components. The database components are items such as tables.

2 An Extensible Markup Language (XML) schema defines the structure of an XML document. An XML schema consists of element declarations and type definitions that describe a model for the information that a well-formed XML document must contain. The XML schema provides a

common vocabulary and grammar for XML documents that support exchanging data among applications.

Related terms
application, data, database, declaration, element, Extensible Markup Language (XML), object, table, well-formed XML

scope The parts of a program in which a symbol or object exists or is visible. The location of an item's declaration determines its scope. Scopes can be nested. A method introduces a new scope for its parameters and local variables. A class introduces a scope for its member variables, member functions, and nested classes. Code in a method in one scope has visibility to other symbols in that same scope and, with certain exceptions, to symbols in outer scopes.

Related terms
class, declaration, function, member, method, object, parameter, variable

script editor

In the report editor in BIRT Report Designer, the page where a report developer adds or modifies JavaScript for a report element.

Related terms
Business Intelligence and Reporting Tools (BIRT) Report Designer, JavaScript, page, report, report editor, report element

scripting language

See JavaScript.

SDK (Software Development Kit)

A collection of programming tools, utilities, compilers, debuggers, interpreters, and application programming interfaces (API) that a developer uses to build an application to run on a specified technology platform. For example, the Java SDK supports developers in building an application that users can download to run on any operating system. The Java Virtual Machine (JVM), the Java SDK interpreter, executes the application in the specified software and hardware configuration.

Related terms
application, application programming interface (API), Java, Java Virtual Machine (JVM), platform

section A horizontal band in a report design. A section uses a grid element, list element, or table element to contain data values, images, and text.

Related terms
data, design, grid element, image, list element, report, table element, value

select To highlight one or more items in a user interface, such as a dialog box or a layout editor. Figure G-26 shows selected items in a report design in the layout editor.

Related terms
data element, design, interface, layout editor, report

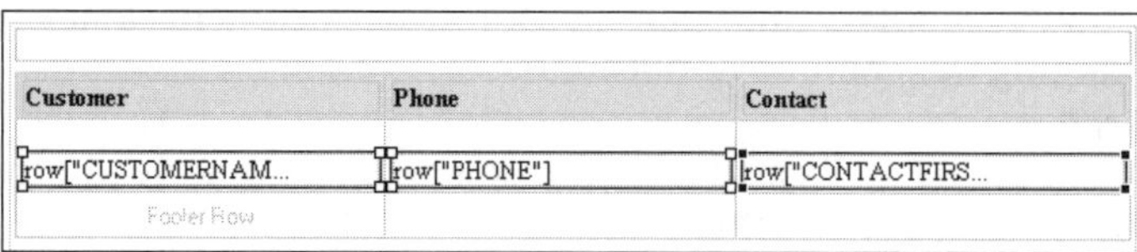

Figure G-26 Three selected data elements

SELECT

See SQL SELECT statement.

series A sequence of related values. In a chart, for example, a series is a set of related points. Figure G-27 shows a bar chart that displays a series of quarterly sales revenue figures over four years.

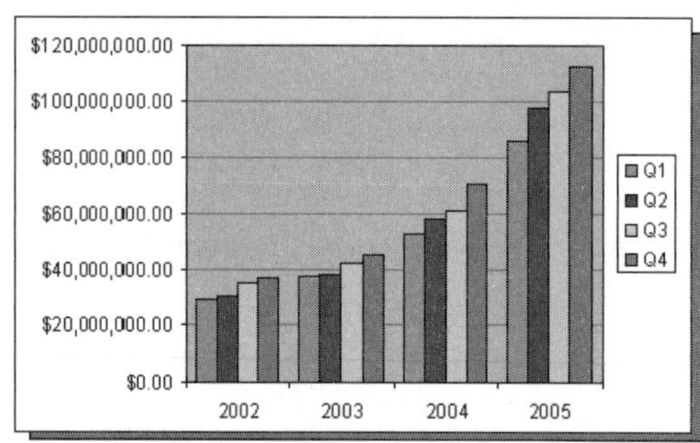

Figure G-27 Series in a chart

Related terms
chart, value

Contrast with
category

servlet A small Java application running on a web server that extends the server's functionality.

Related terms
application, Java, run, web server

Simple Object Access Protocol (SOAP)

A message-based protocol using Extensible Markup Language (XML). Use SOAP to access applications and their services on the web. SOAP employs XML syntax to send text commands across the internet using Hypertext Transfer Protocol (HTTP).

Related terms
application, Extensible Markup Language (XML), HyperText Transfer Protocol (HTTP), protocol, syntax

slot A construct that represents a set of ROM elements contained in another ROM element. For example, the body slot of the report design element can contain one or more of any type of report item. Figure G-28 shows a body slot.

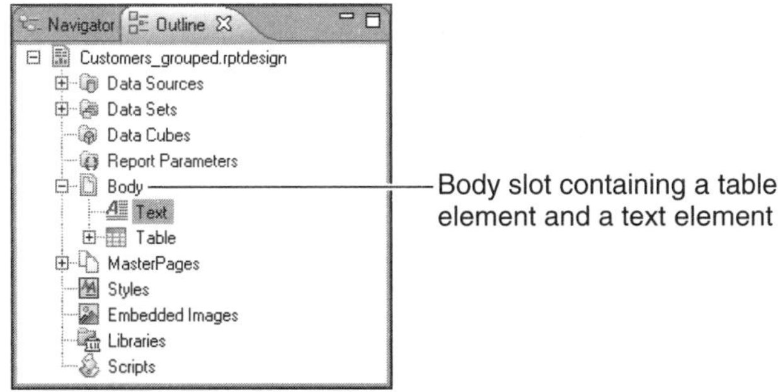

Figure G-28 Body slot

Related terms

design, report, report element, report item, Report Object Model (ROM) element

sort

To specify the order in which data is processed or displayed. For example, customer names can be sorted in alphabetical order.

Related term

data

Contrast with

sort key

sort key

An expression used to sort data. For example, if you sort data by country, the country field is a sort key. You can sort data using one or more sort keys.

Related terms

data, expression, field, sort

SQL (Structured Query Language)

A language used to access and process data in a relational database.

Related terms

data, database, query

Contrast with

SQL SELECT statement

SQL SELECT statement

A query statement in SQL (Structured Query Language) that provides instructions about the data to retrieve from a database. For example, the following SQL query accesses a database's customers table and retrieves the customer name and credit limit values where the credit limit is less than or equal to 100,000. The SQL query then sorts the values by customer name.

```
SELECT customers.customerName,
customers.creditLimit
FROM customers
WHERE customers.creditLimit <= 100000
ORDER BY customers.customerName
```

Related terms
data, database, query, report, sort, SQL (Structured Query Language), statement, table

statement

A syntactically complete unit in a programming language that expresses one action, declaration, or definition.

Related term
declaration

Contrast with
SQL SELECT statement

static variable

A variable shared by all instances of a class and its descendant classes. In Java, a static variable is known as a class variable. The compiler specifies the memory allocation for a static variable. The program receives the memory allocation for a static variable as the program loads.

Related terms
class, class variable, descendant class, Java, variable

string

An array of characters.

Related terms
array, character

String data type

A data type that consists of a sequence of contiguous characters including letters, numerals, punctuation marks, and spaces.

Related terms
character, data type, string

Contrast with
string expression

string expression

An expression that evaluates to a series of contiguous characters. Parts of the expression can include a function that returns a string, a string constant, a string literal, a string operator, or a string variable. For example, "abc"+"def" is a string expression that evaluates to "abcdef".

Related terms
character, constant, expression, function, operator, string, variable

Contrast with
String data type

structured content

A formatted document that displays information from one or more data sources.

Related terms
data source, format

Contrast with
report

Structured Query Language (SQL)

See SQL (Structured Query Language).

style A named set of formatting characteristics, such as alignment, borders, color, and font that report developers apply to a report item to control its appearance.

Related terms
font, format, report, report item

Contrast with
cascading style sheet (CSS)

style sheet

See cascading style sheet (CSS).

subclass

The immediate descendant class.

Related terms
class, descendant class

Contrast with
superclass

subreport

An item using data from a different data set or data source from other items in a report design. An outer report can contain multiple subreports, also called nested reports. In this case, the subreports typically use data values from the outer report to filter data rows for display. Alternatively, multiple independent subreports exist at the same level in the report design.

Related terms
data, data set, data source, design, report, value

superclass

The immediate ancestor class.

Related terms
ancestor class, class

Contrast with
descendant class, subclass

syntax The rules that govern the structure of a language.

tab The label above or below a page in a window that contains multiple pages. Figure G-29 shows tabs that access different Eclipse views in BIRT Report Designer.

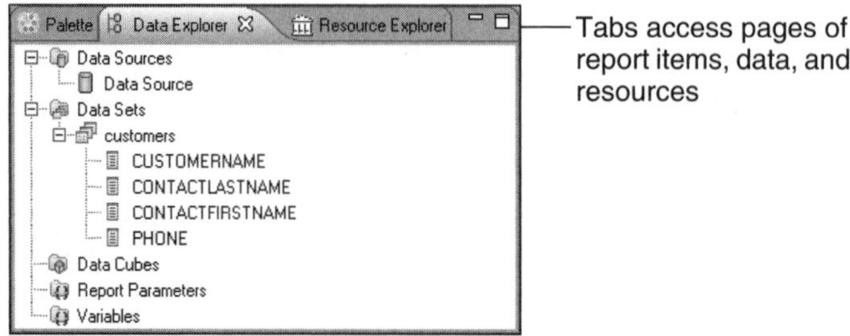

Figure G-29 Tabs in BIRT Report Designer

Related terms

Business Intelligence and Reporting Tools (BIRT) Report Designer, Eclipse view, page

Contrast with

label element

table A named set of columns in a relational database. Figure G-30 shows tables in the query editor in BIRT Report Designer.

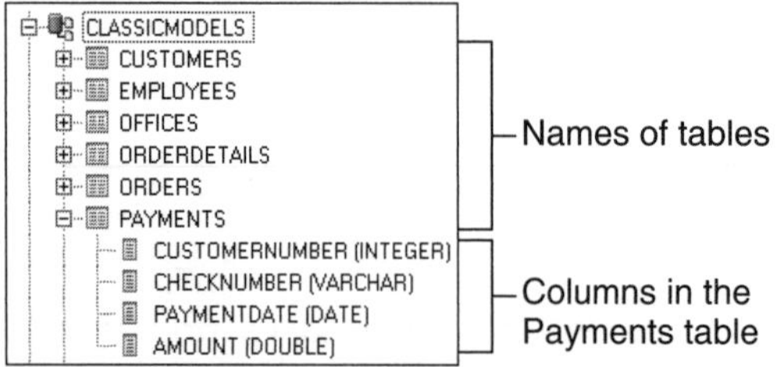

Figure G-30 Tables in the query editor

Related terms

Business Intelligence and Reporting Tools (BIRT) Report Designer, column, database, query editor

Contrast with

table element

table element

A report item that contains and displays data in a row and column layout. The table element iterates through the data rows in a data set. Figure G-31 shows a table element.

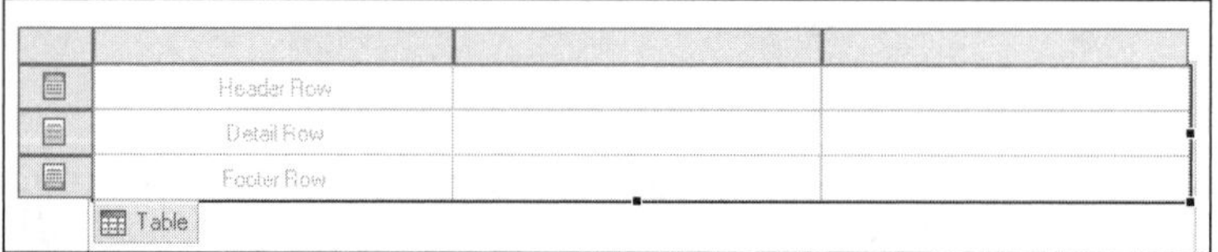

Figure G-31 Table element

Related terms

column, data, data row, data set, layout, report item, row

Contrast with
grid element, list element, table

table of contents

A hyperlinked outline of report contents.

Related terms
hyperlink, report

tag

An element in a markup language that identifies how to process a part of a document.

Related term
element

Contrast with
Extensible Markup Language (XML)

template

In BIRT Report Designer, a predefined structure for a report design. A report developer uses a report template to maintain a consistent style across a set of report designs and to streamline the report design process. A report template is a model for a complete report or a component of a report. BIRT Report Designer provides standard templates and supports custom templates.

In Figure G-32, New Report displays the available templates and Preview displays a representation of the report layout for the selected My First Report, a customer-listing report template.

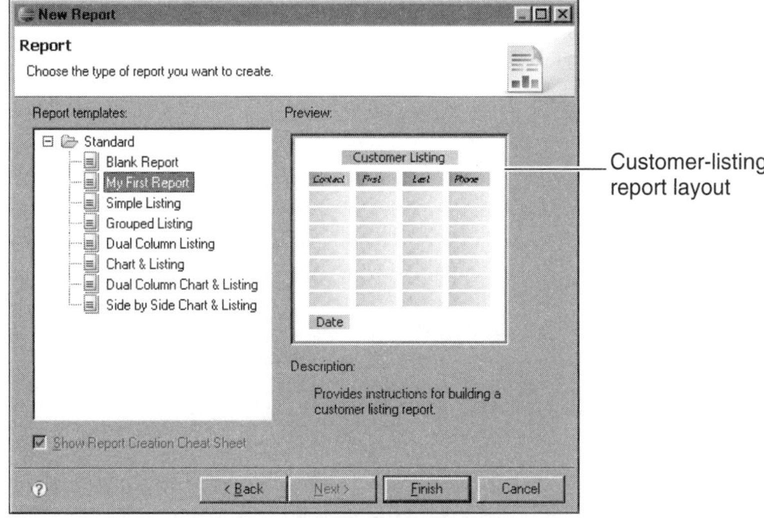

Figure G-32 Templates available for a new report design

Related terms
Business Intelligence and Reporting Tools (BIRT) Report Designer, design, layout, listing report, report, style

Contrast with
report template (.rpttemplate) file

text element

A report item that displays user-specified text. The text can span multiple lines and can contain HyperText Markup Language (HTML) formatting and dynamic values derived from data set fields or expressions.

Related terms
data set, expression, field, format, HyperText Markup Language (HTML), report item, value

Contrast with
data element, dynamic text element, label element

text file See flat file.

theme A set of related styles stored in a library (.rptlibrary) file. A theme provides a preferred appearance for the report items in a report design. A library file can store multiple themes. A report design can use styles from a single theme as well as styles defined in the report design itself.

Related terms
design, library (.rptlibrary) file, report, report item, style

Contrast with
cascading style sheet (CSS)

tick A marker that occurs at regular intervals along the *x*- or *y*-axis of a chart. Typically, the value of each tick appears on the axis.

Related terms
chart, value

Contrast with
tick interval

tick interval

The distance between ticks on an axis. Figure G-33 shows a tick interval in a chart.

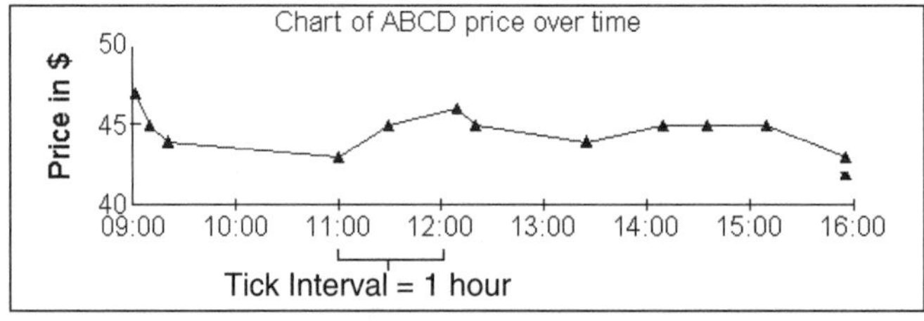

Figure G-33 Chart displaying multiple tick intervals

Related terms
chart, tick

Time data type

A Java data type used to represent time values in SQL (Structured Query Language) statements. The Time data type stores a time value as hour:minute:second.millisecond.

Related terms
data type, Java, statement, Structured Query Language (SQL), value

Contrast with
Date data type, Timestamp data type

Timestamp data type

A Java data type used to represent date-and-time values in SQL statements. The Timestamp data type stores a combined date and time (hour:minute:second.millisecond).

Related terms
data type, Java, statement, Structured Query Language (SQL), value

Contrast with
Date data type, Time data type

toolbar A user interface component that provides access to common tasks. Different toolbars are available for different kinds of tasks.

Related term
interface

translator

See converter.

type See data type.

Unicode

A living language standard managed by the Technical Committee of the Unicode Consortium. The current Unicode standard provides code points for more than 65,000 characters. Unicode encoding has no dependency on a platform or software program and thus provides a basis for software internationalization.

Related terms
code point, character, internationalization

Uniform Resource Locator (URL)

A character string that identifies the location and type of a piece of information that is accessible over the web. http:// is the indicator that an item is accessible over the web. The URL typically includes the domain name, type of organization, and a precise location within the directory structure where the item is located.

Related terms
character, domain name, HyperText Transfer Protocol (HTTP), string

Contrast with
Universal Resource Identifier (URI)

universal hyperlink

See hyperlink.

Universal Resource Identifier (URI)

A set of names and addresses in the form of short strings that identify resources on the web. Resources are items such as documents, downloadable files, and images.

Related term
image

Contrast with
Uniform Resource Locator (URL), string

URI See Universal Resource Identifier (URI).

URL See Uniform Resource Locator (URL).

value

1. The content of a constant, parameter, symbol, or variable.
2. A specific occurrence of an attribute. For example, blue is a possible value for an attribute color.

Related terms
attribute, constant, parameter, variable

Varchar data type

A data type used for string calculations. The Varchar data type stores a sequence of Unicode characters. The Varchar data type supports specifying a maximum character length for the string.

Related terms
character, data type, string, Unicode

variable

A named storage location for data that a program can modify. Each variable has a unique name that identifies it within its scope and contains a certain type of data.

Related terms
data, data type, scope

Contrast with
class variable, dynamic variable, field variable, global variable, instance variable, local variable, member variable, static variable

view A predefined query that retrieves data from one or more tables in a relational database. Unlike a table, a view does not store data. Users can use views to select, delete, insert, and update data. The database uses the definition of the view to determine the appropriate action on the underlying tables. For example, a database queries a view by combining the requested data from the underlying tables.

Related terms
data, database, query, table

Contrast with
Eclipse view, previewer

view time

The period of time in which a user examines a report.

Related term
report

Contrast with
design time, run time

viewer A tool that supports basic viewing tasks, such as navigating a report, using a table of contents, viewing parameter information, and exporting data.

Related terms
data, parameter, report, table of contents

Contrast with
previewer

web archive (.war) file

A file format used to bundle web applications.

Related terms
application, format

Contrast with
file types, Java archive (.jar) file

web page

A HyperText Markup Language (HTML) page containing tags that a web browser interprets and displays.

Related terms
HyperText Markup Language (HTML), tag

Contrast with
page

web server

A computer or a program that provides web services on the internet. A web server accepts requests based on the HyperText Transfer Protocol (HTTP). A web server also executes server-side scripts, such as Active Server Pages (ASP) and JavaServer Pages (JSP).

Related terms
HyperText Transfer Protocol (HTTP), JavaServer Page (JSP), request, web service

web service

A software system designed to support interoperable machine-to-machine interaction over a network. Web service refers to a client and server that communicate using Extensible Markup Language (XML) messages adhering to the Simple Object Access Protocol (SOAP) standard. A web service is invoked remotely using SOAP or Hypertext Transfer Protocol (HTTP)-GET and HTTP-POST protocols. The web service returns a response to the client in XML format. Any operating system that supports the SOAP protocol and XML can build and consume a web service.

Related terms
Extensible Markup Language (XML), HyperText Transfer Protocol (HTTP), protocol, Simple Object Access Protocol (SOAP)

Contrast with
request

well-formed XML

An Extensible Markup Language (XML) document that follows syntax rules established in the XML 1.0 recommendation. Well-formed means that a document must contain one or more elements and that the root element must contain all the other elements. Each element must nest inside any enclosing elements, following the syntax rules.

Related terms
element, Extensible Markup Language (XML), syntax

Word converter

A tool that converts a BIRT report to a Microsoft Word (.doc) file.

Related terms
Business Intelligence and Reporting Tools (BIRT), converter, report

workbench

See Eclipse Workbench.

workspace

See Eclipse workspace.

World Wide Web Consortium (W3C)

An international standards body that provides recommendations regarding web standards. The World Wide Web Consortium publishes several levels of documents, including notes, working drafts, proposed recommendations, and recommendations about web applications related to topics such as Extensible Markup Language (XML) and HyperText Markup Language (HTML).

Related terms
application, Extensible Markup Language (XML), HyperText Markup Language (HTML)

XML (Extensible Markup Language)

See Extensible Markup Language (XML).

XML converter

A tool that converts a report to an Extensible Markup Language (XML) file.

Related terms
converter, Extensible Markup Language (XML), report

XML element

See element.

XML PATH language (XPath)

XPath supports addressing an element or elements within an Extensible Markup Language (XML) document based on a path through the document hierarchy.

Related terms
element, Extensible Markup Language (XML)

XML schema

See schema.

XPath See XML PATH language (XPath).

Z-order The order in which a combination, multiple *y*-axis, or three-dimensional chart element displays the chart series. Series having a higher Z-order hide series having a lower Z-order. The example in Figure G-34 shows a bar series having a Z-order of 1 and area series having a Z-order of 0.

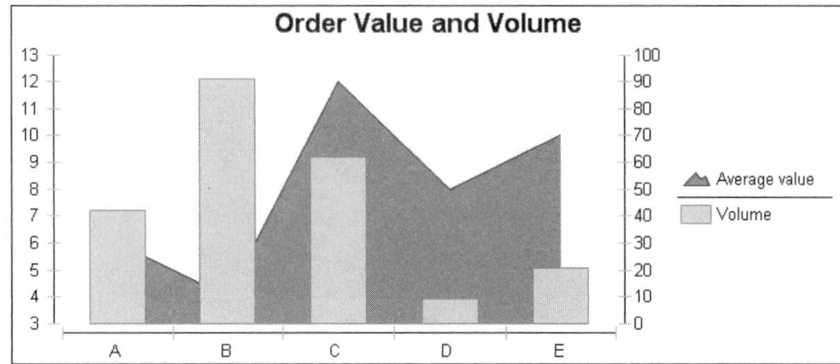

Figure G-34 Multiple *y*-axis chart having bar series in front of area series

Related terms
chart element, combination chart, series

Index

Symbols

A

B

C

E

F

G

H

J

K

L

M

P

Q

R

S

U

V

W

X

Y

Z